D

SOUTHWESTERN ARCHAEOLOGY

GARLAND REFERENCE LIBRARY
OF SOCIAL SCIENCE
(VOL. 69)

Contents   *vii*

PREFACE

Sometime in 1975, after many years of increasing dissatisfaction with the common practice of separating archaeology and ethnography in the usual area courses in anthropology, I decided to try to do something constructive about this by inaugurating a course which I called "Pueblo Culture History." Both aspects of cultural anthropology were to be taken up, with a systematic attempt to link them together in a meaningful story. The course has had some moderate success, though I am by no means entirely satisfied with it.

One of the main difficulties, which I encountered very soon after the beginning of the semester in which the course was first offered, was the lack of a bibliographical source for the archaeological materials. Ethnography was well covered by Murdock's compilation, but nothing comparable existed for archaeology. In the course of correspondence with professionals in the field, it seemed that no one was currently engaged in attempting to correct this situation, so I decided that I would compile a usable bibliography for my students, largely on the basis of my own fairly extensive library.

It soon became clear that with some help I might be able to extend the scope of the work sufficiently to make it useful to a larger public. It is still directed, in my thinking, primarily to students, but I hope that professionals will find it a handy compendium of citations which they are familiar with but cannot locate accurately. Scholars in other, related fields may also have occasion to consult it—at least so I hope. I hope also that it will not cause me to be regarded as a fool of an outsider who has rushed in where the insiders have feared to tread.

Assistance has been rendered by many individuals. Those who have helped with the library research are Carol Taghavi, Richard Hedgpeth, Sara Polk, and Donald Steinman, to all of whom I am grateful for conscientious work which I could not undertake myself. They in turn were assisted most courteously and ably by Mr. Jack Marquardt and his associates on the library staff of the Smithsonian Institution, and to them I now express my thanks directly.

Late in 1977, I sent out a form letter requesting the updating of their publication lists to 238 archaeologists in the field. To my immense gratification, 161 replied, many including highly encouraging remarks as to the desirability of my project. I am grateful to all of them, but particularly to the following, who included valuable information or advice beyond that which I had requested: J. Richard Ambler, Mark R. Barnes, Thomas Bowen, David M. Brugge, Kent C. Day, Florence Hawley Ellis, Gerald X. Fitzgerald, James N. Hill, Arthur J. Jelinek, Volney H. Jones, Marjorie F. Lambert, Alexander J. Lindsay, William A. Longacre, David B. Madsen, James McDonald, L. Mark Raab, Michael B. Schiffer, James Schoenwetter, Douglas D. Scott, Watson Smith, Donald R. Tuohy, William J. Wallace, John P. Wilson, Regge N. Wiseman, and Richard B. Woodbury.

By no means the least of my thanks go to Mark Leone, whose encouragement, advice, and good-natured needling have been in large part responsible for keeping me at work, and to Sandy Harpe for her highly professional typing of the manuscript.

Lastly, for their professional advice and encouragement, I feel a great debt of gratitude to Mr. Richard Newman and Mr. Karl Schick, of Garland Publishing, Inc., without whose help the work would very likely have never been brought to a conclusion.

Part I
The Bibliography

INTRODUCTION

The geographical area covered by this bibliography includes
all of the American Southwest as usually defined by anthropolo-
gists, with minor extensions rendered desirable by practicality.
Specifically, it covers all of the states of Utah, Arizona,
New Mexico, Chihuahua, and Sonora, plus western and southern
Colorado, trans-Pecos Texas, and the southeastern fringes of
Nevada and California. All periods of the archaeological record, from the earliest remains to the historical materials,
are included. An effort has been made to list all significant
works appearing before the end of 1977, and in this sense the
work is comprehensive, though not complete.

In general, the list is limited to published works, including all of the professional and respectable amateur journals,
series, and books. However, unpublished works in two categories
are systematically included. First, in the several cases where
the contracting agencies made lists available to me, I have
included reports with limited distribution of the types referred to as cultural resource management studies, archaeological clearance surveys, etc. Second, all dissertations available through University Microfilms International are listed.
Inconsistency has prevailed in a few cases, however, when I
have included unpublished titles of miscellaneous character.

Popular works by professional archaeologists are included,
unless of an extremely minor nature, but such pieces by other
authors are listed only if they seem possibly useful for teach-
ing, or are well illustrated, or are on areas or sites that
are not otherwise well covered. No systematic search has been
made for these.

Works concentrating on theoretical or methodological matters are included only if the theory or method discussed is
directly applied in some significant way to Southwestern materials or problems.

Reviews appearing in the American Anthropologist (cited as
AA) and American Antiquity (cited as AAq) are referred to under
the appropriate entries.

The general emphasis is on the archaeological aspects of
cultural anthropology, but a few works dealing mainly with
ethnographic materials have been included when they provide

the archaeologist with especially useful information. Items
dealing with the physical anthropology of the archaeological
populations have been included, as well as geological and environmental studies making direct reference to cultural matters,
but few such studies of a purely background nature will be
found.

It will no doubt be discovered that inconsistencies abound.
I admit that I have relied at times on a "feel" for what might
be useful, and this may well be unjustifiable, but if the work
proves to be of value to any serious student, I will feel
well rewarded.

ABARR, James

1959   Tenth century apartment house. New Mexico Magazine,
        37, no. 4:18-19, 51.

1960   Legendary Pecos - "village of 500 warriors." Des-
        ert Magazine, 23, no. 1:15-17.

1961   Apartment living 1000 years ago. New Mexico Maga-
        zine, 39, no. 4:14-17.

ABBOTT, Ellen (See under Kelley, J. Charles. Also listed as
Kelley, Ellen Abbott.)

ABEL, Leland J.

1955   Pottery types of the Southwest: Wares 5A, 10A, 10B,
        12A, San Juan Red Ware, Mesa Verde Gray, and White
        Ware, San Juan White Ware. Museum of Northern Ari-
        zona, Ceramic Series, 3B, 63 pp. (not numbered).
        Reviewed AAq 23:200 (Wheat).

ABEL, L.J., and VAN VALKENBURGH, Sallie

1961   The Tonto labyrinth. Kiva, 27, no. 1:29-31.

ACKERLY, Neal, and RIEGER, Ann

1976   An archaeological overview of southwest Pinal County,
        Arizona. Arizona State Museum, Archaeological Series,
        104, 70 pp.

ACKLEN, John C. (See under Gauthier, Rory.)

ADAM, David P. (See under Grebinger, Paul F.)

ADAMS, Ethan Charles

1974   Location strategy employed by prehistoric inhabi-
        tants of the Piedra district, Colorado. Southwestern
        Lore, 40, no. 1:13-26.

1975   Causes of prehistoric settlement systems in the
        lower Piedra district, Colorado. University of
        Colorado, dissertation, 232 pp.; University Micro-
        films International.

1976   Locations of some Navajo Refugee period sites in
        southwest Colorado. Awanyu, 4, no. 2:23-30.

ADAMS, Karen R. (See under Bohrer, Vorsila L.)

ADAMS, Nettie K. (See under Adams, William Y.)

ADAMS, Richard N.

1951   Half House: a pit house in Chaco Canyon, New Mex-
        ico. Papers of the Michigan Academy of Science,
        Arts, and Letters, 35:273-295.

ADAMS, William Y.

1957   A cache of prehistoric implements from northeastern
        Arizona. Plateau, 29, no. 3:49-55.

1959   Navajo and Anglo reconstruction of prehistoric sites
        in southeastern Utah. American Antiquity, 25:269-
        272.

1960   Ninety years of Glen Canyon archaeology, 1869-1959.
        Museum of Northern Arizona, Bulletin 33, 29 pp.
            Reviewed AA 64:894 (Woodbury), AAq 26:446 (Lister).

1966   An additional note on Long Fort and Long House.
        Plateau, 39, no. 2:88-89.

ADAMS, W.Y., and ADAMS, Nettie K.

1959   An inventory of prehistoric sites on the lower San
        Juan River, Utah. Museum of Northern Arizona, Bul-
        letin 31, 53 pp.
            Reviewed AAq 25:428 (Peckham).

ADAMS, W.Y., LINDSAY, Alexander J., Jr., and TURNER, Christy
    G., II

1961   Survey and excavations in lower Glen Canyon, 1952-
        1958. Museum of Northern Arizona, Bulletin 36, 62
        pp.
            Reviewed AA 64:894 (Woodbury), AAq 28:111 (Rinaldo).

ADDIS, Y.H.

1893   Pueblos at Casa Grande. American Antiquarian, 15:
        175-179.

ADOVASIO, James M. (See also under Fry, Gary F.; Marwitt, John P.)

1970   The origin, development and distribution of Western Archaic textiles. Tebiwa, 13, no. 2:1-40.

1974   Prehistoric North American basketry. Nevada State Museum, Anthropological Papers, 16, 148 pp.

1975   Fremont basketry. Tebiwa, 17, no. 2.

ADOVASIO, J.M., and FRY, Gary F.

1972   An equilibrium model for culture change in the Great Basin. *In* D.D. Fowler 1972, pp. 67-71.

1976   Prehistoric psychotropic drug use in northeastern Mexico and Trans-Pecos Texas. Economic Botany, 30: 94-96.

ADOVASIO, J.M., and GUNN, Joel

1975   Basketry and basketmakers at Antelope House. *In* Rock and Morris 1975, pp. 71-80.

1977   Style, basketry, and basketmakers. *In* The Individual in Prehistory, ed. James N. Hill and Joel Gunn. Academic Press, New York, pp. 137-153.

AFTON, Jean

1971   Cultural analysis of burial goods from certain Anasazi sites. Southwestern Lore, 37, no. 1:15-27.

AGENBROAD, Larry D. (See also under Haynes, C. Vance.)

1967   The distribution of fluted points in Arizona. Kiva, 32, no. 4:113-120.

1975   The alluvial geology of upper Grand Gulch, Utah: its relationship to Anasazi inhabitation of the Cedar Mesa area. *In* Canyonlands Guidebook, 1975 Field Conference, pp. 63-66. Four Corners Geological Society, Farmington, New Mexico.

1978   Cultural implications from the distributional analysis of a lithic site, San Pedro Valley, Arizona. *In* Grebinger 1978a, pp. 55-71.

AGOGINO, George A. (See also under East-Smith, Shirley; Haynes, C. Vance; Kunz, Michael; Rovner, Irving; Smith, Calvin B.; Smith, Shirley; Stevens, Dominique E.)

1952   The Santa Ana pre-ceramic site, a report on a cultural

          level in Sandoval County, New Mexico. Texas Journal
          of Science, 4:32-37.

1957a   The Gypsum Dune blowouts: Sandia-like points in the
          San Jose Valley. El Palacio, 64:115-118.

1957b   The significance of the parallel-flaked points at
          the San Jose sites. Texas Journal of Science, 9,
          no. 3:364-367.

1958   Recent archaeological developments involving pre-
          ceramic cultures in the middle Rio Grande. Syra-
          cuse University, dissertation, 188 pp.; University
          Microfilms International.

1960a   The Santa Ana pre-ceramic sites: an Archaic seed-
          gathering culture in Sandoval County, New Mexico.
          Southwestern Lore, 25, no. 4:17-21.

1960b   The San Jose sites: a Cochise-like manifestation in
          the middle Rio Grande. Southwestern Lore, 26, no.
          2:43-48.

1961a   Ancient seed gatherers - the Cochise complex. Sci-
          ence of Man, 1:84-88.

1961b   Possible Paleo-Indian skeletal material in the mid-
          dle Rio Grande. Science of Man, 1:123-125.

1961c   A survey of Paleo-Indian sites along the middle Rio
          Grande drainage. Plains Anthropologist, 6, no. 11:
          7-12.

1963   New radiocarbon date for the Folsom complex. Current
          Anthropology, 4, no. 1:113-114.

1965a   The Blackwater Draw site and the people of New Mex-
          ico; a thirty year perspective. Wyoming Archaeolo-
          gist, 8, no. 1:21-23.

1965b   The mammoth hunters of the Llano Estacado. Earth
          Science, 18, no. 5. Midwest Federation of Miner-
          alogical Societies.

1968a   Archaeological excavations at Blackwater Draw Local-
          ity No. 1, New Mexico, 1963-64. National Geographic
          Society Research Reports, 1968, pp. 1-7.

1968b   A brief history of Early Man in the western high
          plains. *In* Irwin-Williams 1968d, pp. 1-5.

1969   The Midland complex: is it valid? American Anthro-
          pologist, 71, no. 6:1117-1118.

AGOGINO, G.A., and FEINHANDLER, Sherwin

    1957   Amaranth seeds from a San Jose site in New Mexico.
            Texas Journal of Science, 9, no. 2:154-156.

AGOGINO, G.A., and FOLSOM, F.

    1975a   Fact and fiction on the Folsom discovery. Liberal
            Arts Review, 1, no. 2:23-34.

    1975b   New light on an old site: events leading up to the
            discovery of the Folsom type site. Anthropological
            Journal of Canada, 13, no. 3:2-5.

AGOGINO, G.A., and HESTER, Jim

    1953   The Santa Ana pre-ceramic sites. El Palacio, 60:
            131-140.

    1956   A re-evaluation of the San Jose non-ceramic cultures.
            El Palacio, 63:6-21.

    1958   Comments on the San Jose radiocarbon date. American
            Antiquity, 24:187-188.

AGOGINO, G.A., and HIBBEN, Frank C.
    1958   Central New Mexico Paleo-Indian cultures. American
            Antiquity, 23:422-425.

AGOGINO, G.A., and ROVNER, Irwin

    1964a   Paleo-Indian traditions: a current evaluation.
            Archaeology, 17:237-243.

    1964b   A typological re-evaluation of the Paleo-Indian
            cultures of the High Plains. New World Antiquity,
            11, nos. 9-10:98-106.

    1969   Preliminary report of a stratified post-Folsom se-
            quence at Blackwater Draw Locality No. 1. American
            Antiquity, 34:175-176.

AGOGINO, G.A., and others

    1973   The material culture from Billy the Kid Cave and
            the late cultural history of Blackwater Draw.
            Awanyu, 1:38-48.

    1976   Blackwater Draw Locality No. 1, south bank: report
            for the summer of 1974. Plains Anthropologist, 21:
            213-223.

AHLO, Hamilton

1975   Archaeological survey of the eastern area of TG&E
        138 KV line. Arizona State Museum, Archaeological
        Series, 89, 11 pp.

AIKENS, C. Melvin (See also under Fowler, Don D.)

1961   The prehistory of central and northern Utah. Utah
        Archaeology, 7, no. 3:3-15.

1963   Preliminary report on excavations in southwestern
        Utah, 1962. Utah Archaeology, 9, no. 1:6-10; no.
        2:2-7.

1965a   Excavations in southwest Utah. University of Utah,
        Anthropological Papers, 76, 164 pp.
        Reviewed AA 69:403 (Longacre), AAq 32:415 (Schroe-
        der).

1965b   Preliminary report on excavations at the Injun
        Creek site, Warren, Utah. Utah Archaeology, 11,
        no. 4:1-21.

1966a   Virgin-Kayenta cultural relationships. University
        of Utah, Anthropological Papers, 79, 66+19 pp.
        Reviewed AA 70:160 (Meighan).

1966b   Fremont-Promontory-Plains relationships. University
        of Utah, Anthropological Papers, 82, 110 pp.
        Reviewed AA 70:419 (Ezell), AAq 35:396 (DeBoer).

1966c   Plains relationships of the Fremont culture: a sum-
        mary statement of a hypothesis. Utah Archaeology,
        12, no. 4:3-12.

1967a   Excavations at Snake Rock Village and the Bear
        River No. 2 site. University of Utah, Anthropo-
        logical Papers, 87, 65 pp.
        Reviewed AA 71:559 (Leach), AAq 36:223 (Vivian).

1967b   Plains relationships of the Fremont culture: a
        hypothesis. American Antiquity, 32:198-209.

1970   Hogup Cave. University of Utah, Anthropological
        Papers, 93, 286 pp.
        Reviewed AAq 40:501 (Thomas).

1971   (ed.) Great Basin Anthropological Conference, 1970:
        selected papers. University of Oregon, Anthropo-
        logical Papers, 1, 184 pp.
        Reviewed AA 74:1508 (Browman).

1972   Fremont culture: restatement of some problems. Amer-
        ican Antiquity, 37:61-66.

1976   Cultural hiatus in the eastern Great Basin? Ameri-
        can Antiquity, 41:543-550.

The Bibliography   11

AIKENS, C.M., HARPER, Kimball T., and FRY, Gary F.

1967-   Hogup Mountain Cave: interim report. Utah
  68   Archaeology, 13, no. 3; 14, nos. 1-4:5-11.

ALBRITTON, Claude C. (See under Bryan, Kirk.)

ALDER, G.M. (See under Harper, Kimball T.)

ALDER, Thomas P.

1951   'Talking Dust' tells story of Indians. Chicago
        Natural History Museum Bulletin, 22, no. 10:5, 7.

1952   An ancient trade route of Indians traced. Chicago
        Natural History Museum Bulletin, 23, no. 9:6.

ALESSIO ROBLES, Carmen

1929   La region arqueológica de Casas Grandes de Chi-
        huahua. Imprenta Nuñez, Mexico, 46 pp.

ALEXANDER, Hartley Burr

1929   Field notes at Jemez. El Palacio, 27, no. 10:
        95-106.

ALEXANDER, Hubert G.

1935   The excavation of "Jemez Cave." El Palacio, 38,
        nos. 18-20:97-108.

ALEXANDER, H.G., and REITER, Paul

1935   Report on the excavation of Jemez Cave, New Mexico.
        University of New Mexico Bulletin, Monograph Series,
        vol. 1, no. 3, 67 pp.
        Reviewed AA 38:659 (Roberts).

ALEXANDER, Robert K.

1963   Crownpoint-North Highway salvage project. Labora-
        tory of Anthropology Notes, 16.

1966a   Archaeological and historical survey along New Mex-
        ico highways. Museum of New Mexico, Research Rec-
        ords, 2, 31 pp.

1966b   An archaeological survey of the 345KV transmission
        line from the Four Corners power plant to the Albu-
        querque substation. Laboratory of Anthropology
        Notes, 110.

1970   Archaeological investigations at Parida Cave, Val
        Verde County, Texas. Texas Archaeological Salvage
        Project, Papers, 19, 103 pp.
        Reviewed AA 74:959 (Beeson).

1974   The archaeology of Conejo Shelter: a study of cultur-
        al stability at an Archaic rockshelter site in south-
        western Texas. University of Texas, dissertation,
        355 pp.; University Microfilms International.

ALEXANDER, Wayne, and RUBY, Jay W.

1963   1962 excavations at Summit, Utah; a progress report.
        Nevada State Museum, Anthropological Papers, 9, pp.
        15-32.

ALGER, Norman T. (See under Minckley, W.L.)

ALLAN, William C. (See also under Broilo, Frank J.; Gauthier,
Rory; Stuart, David E.)

1972   The Red Rock project: a final report. Laboratory
        of Anthropology Notes, 81.

1974   Archaeological clearance survey: Manning Gas and
        Oil Company Apache no. 101 well site. University
        of New Mexico, contract report 101-103A (NPS).

1975a   Archaeological clearance survey: Rijan Oil Company
        well no. 18. University of New Mexico, contract
        report 101-103C (NPS).

1975b   Archaeological clearance survey: Northwest Pipeline
        Barbara Kay no. 2, first relocation. University of
        New Mexico, contract report 101-103D (NPS).

1975c   Archaeological clearance survey: Northwest Pipeline
        Barbara Kay no. 2, second relocation. University
        of New Mexico, contract report 101-103G (NPS).

1975d   Archaeological survey of a floodwater retarding
        structure in the Corrales watershed. University
        of New Mexico, contract report 101-103L (State
        Historic Preservation Office).

1975e   Archaeological clearance survey: Public Service
        Company of New Mexico, 46KV Tijeras Canyon Power-
        line. University of New Mexico, contract report
        101-103N (USFS).

1975f   Archaeological survey of a Southern Union Gas Com-
        pany pipeline in Tijeras Canyon, New Mexico. Uni-
        versity of New Mexico, contract report 101-103P
        (USFS).

1975g   TVA archaeological survey phase III: seven mineral
         exploration drillholes on the ABE Pena Ranch. Uni-
         versity of New Mexico, contract report 101-128 (TVA).

1975h   Archaeological clearance survey: 115KV powerline
         easement for Public Service Company of New Mexico.
         University of New Mexico, contract report 101-103R
         (USFS).

ALLAN, W.C., ESCHMAN, Peter, and STUART, David E.

1975   Archaeological clearance survey: K.B. Kennedy pipe-
         line, Chaves County, New Mexico. University of
         New Mexico, contract report 101-113 (BLM).

ALLAN, W.C., and others

1976   Archaeological survey of road construction rights-
         of-way: Block II - Navajo Indian irrigation project.
         University of New Mexico, contract reports 101-107,
         101-110 (NPS).

ALLEN, Jack (See under Haynes, C. Vance.)

ALLEN, Joseph W.

1966   An archaeological survey of the transmission line
         to Truth or Consequences and Hatch, New Mexico.
         Laboratory of Anthropology Notes, 37.

1967   Excavations at Twin Hills site, Santa Fe County,
         New Mexico. Laboratory of Anthropology Notes, 44.

1969   Archaeological salvage excavations along State Road
         32 near Apache Creek, New Mexico. Laboratory of
         Anthropology Notes, 51.

1970   Archaeological salvage investigations along State
         Road 44 near Zia Pueblo, New Mexico. Laboratory of
         Anthropology Notes, 52.

1972   The Mexican Wash Project: archaeological excavations
         along U.S. Highway 666 near Buffalo Springs, New
         Mexico. Laboratory of Anthropology Notes, 55.

1973a   The Tsogue Site: highway salvage excavations near
         Tesuque Pueblo, New Mexico. Laboratory of Anthro-
         pology Notes, 73.

1973b   The Pueblo Alamo project: archaeological salvage
         at the junction of U.S. 85 and U.S. 285, south of
         Santa Fe, New Mexico. Laboratory of Anthropology
         Notes, 86.

ALLEN, J.W., and KAYSER, David W.

1971   The Defiance project: archaeological salvage exca-
        vations along interstate Highway 40 near Manuelito,
        New Mexico. Laboratory of Anthropology Notes, 58.

ALLEN, J.W., and McNUTT, C.H.

1955   A pit house site near Santa Ana Pueblo, New Mexico.
        American Antiquity, 20:241-255.

ALLEN, Norton

1953   A Hohokam pottery bell. El Palacio, 60:16-19.

ALLIOT, Hector

1912   Fouilles de Tyuonyi, village préhistorique des Tewa,
        Nouveau-Mexique. Journal de la Société des Améri-
        canistes de Paris, 9, no. 1:111-116.

ALMADA, Francisco R.

1950   Bosquejo sobre las ruinas de Casas Grandes. Socie-
        dad chihuahuense de estudios históricos, Boletín,
        7:378-380.

ALPERS, Frank H.

1963   Surface surveys of prehistoric Ponil River sites.
        El Palacio, 70:35-42.

ALVES, Eileen E.

1930   Shelter caves of the El Paso district. Bulletin of
        the Texas Archaeological and Paleontological Society,
        2:64-68.

1931   Pottery of the El Paso region. Bulletin of the
        Texas Archaeological and Paleontological Society,
        3:57-59.

1932a   Perishable artifacts of the Hueco Caves. Bulletin
        of the West Texas Historical and Scientific Society,
        44, no. 4:20-23.

1932b   A small ruin in New Mexico. Bulletin of the Texas
        Archaeological and Paleontological Society, 4:40-43.

1933   A metate factory in New Mexico. Bulletin of the
        Texas Archaeological and Paleontological Society,
        5:66-68.

1934   Fetish stones from near El Paso. Bulletin of the

Texas Archaeological and Paleontological Society, 6:70-74.

AMBLER, J. Richard (See also under Berlin, G. Lennis; Lambert, Marjorie F.; Lindsay, Alexander J., Jr.; Lister, Robert H.)

1959   A preliminary note on 1959 excavations at the Coombs Site, Boulder, Utah. Utah Archaeology, 5, no. 3: 4-11.

1962   An archaeological survey of Casa Grande National Monument, Arizona. Kiva, 27, no. 4:10-23.

1966a   Caldwell Village and Fremont prehistory. University of Colorado, dissertation, 344 pp.; University Microfilms International.

1966b   Caldwell Village. University of Utah, Anthropological Papers, 84, 118 pp. Reviewed AA 71:559 (Leach), AAq 33:524 (Aikens).

1969   The temporal span of the Fremont. Southwestern Lore, 34, no. 4:107-117.

1977   The Anasazi: prehistoric people of the Four Corners region. Museum of Northern Arizona, Special Publication no. 13, 54 pp.

AMBLER, J.R., and OLSON, Alan P.

1977   Salvage archaeology in the Cow Springs area, 1960. Museum of Northern Arizona, Technical Series, 15, 57 pp.

AMBLER, J.R., LINDSAY, Alexander J., Jr., and STEIN, Mary Anne

1964   Survey and excavations on Cummings Mesa, Arizona and Utah, 1960-1961. Museum of Northern Arizona, Bulletin 39, 105 pp. Reviewed AA 67:582 (Rohn), AAq 31:587 (Lister).

AMSDEN, Charles A. (See also under Kidder, Alfred V.; Wyman, Leland C.)

1927a   Archaeology on horseback. Masterkey, 1, no. 2:5-9.

1927b   The Pecos conference. Masterkey, 1, no. 4:14-18.

1929   Kiva Sixteen. Masterkey, 3, no. 4:4-11.

1930a   The two Sessions Expeditions. Masterkey, 4, no. 1: 5-12.

1930b   What is clockwise? American Anthropologist, 32: 579-580.

1931   Man-hunting. Masterkey, 5, no. 2:37-47.

1932   Navajo origins. New Mexico Historical Review, 7:
        193-209.

1933a   Friendly volcanos. Masterkey, 7, no. 1:29-33.

1933b   Nothing new. Masterkey, 7:104-105.

1933c   The prehistoric Southwest. Masterkey, 7, no. 5:
        140-147.

1935   Shifting frontiers. Masterkey, 9, no. 5:164-165.

1936a   An analysis of Hohokam pottery design. Gila Pueblo,
        Medallion Papers, 23, 54 pp.

1936b   A prehistoric rubber ball. Masterkey, 10, no. 1:
        7-8.

1938-   The ancient Basketmakers. Masterkey, 12, no. 6:
  39   205-214; 13, no. 1:18-25; 13, no. 3:96-105; 13, no.
        5:125-131 (also as Southwest Museum, Leaflet no. 11,
        1939, 34 pp.).

1949   Prehistoric Southwesterners from Basketmaker to
        Pueblo. Southwest Museum, 163 pp.
        Reviewed AA 52:545 (Colton), AAq 16:273 (Taylor).

AMSDEN, Monroe

1928a   Archaeological reconnaissance in Sonora. Southwest
        Museum, Papers, 1, 51 pp.
        Reviewed AA 31:513 (Kroeber).

1928b   Thoughts on the future of Southwestern archaeology.
        Masterkey, 2, no. 1:5-9.

ANDERSON, Adrienne Barbara (See also under Anderson, Douglas.)

1975   "Least cost" strategy and limited activity site
        location, upper Dry Cimarron River Valley, north-
        eastern New Mexico. University of Colorado, dis-
        sertation, 249 pp.; University Microfilms Inter-
        national.

ANDERSON, Bruce A.

1970   A Basketmaker III burial from Archuleta County,
        Colorado. Southwestern Lore, 36, no. 2:34-40.

ANDERSON, Byron C.

1970   The Hohokam and their Axes. The Redskin, 5, no.
        1:18-21.

ANDERSON, David G. (See under Fitting, James E.)

ANDERSON, Douglas, and ANDERSON, Barbara

1976   Chaco Canyon. Southwest Parks and Monuments As-
       sociation, Popular Series no. 17, 50pp.

ANDERSON, Duane C.

1967   Stone balls of the Fremont culture: an interpre-
       tation. Southwestern Lore, 32, no. 4:79-81.

ANDERSON, Edgar (See also under Carter, George F.; Hurst,
Clarence T.)

1944   Two collections of prehistoric maize tassels from
       Utah. Annals of the Missouri Botanical Gardens,
       31:345-350.

ANDERSON, E., and BLANCHARD, F.D.

1942   Prehistoric maize from Canyon del Muerto. American
       Journal of Botany, 29, no. 10:832-835.

ANDERSON, Helen Ashley

1950   Tribesmen of Tuzigoot. Desert Magazine, 13:16-19.

ANDERSON, Howard

1958   New pueblo in Arizona brought to light. Bulletin
       of the Chicago Natural History Museum, 29, no. 9:5.

ANDERSON, Kathryn

1964   Dripping Rocks Cave Site. Southwestern Lore, 30,
       no. 2:26-35.

ANDERSON, Keith M. (See also under Sharrock, Floyd W.)

1962   Archaeological survey of Fish Springs National
       Wildlife Refuge. University of Utah, Miscellaneous
       Collected Papers no. 6, Anthropological Papers,
       60:109-126.
       Reviewed AA 67:1592 (Schwartz).

1963   Ceramic clues to Pueblo-Puebloid relationships.
       American Antiquity, 28:303-307.

1966   NA 3533: a second kiva for Betatakin. Plateau,
       39, no. 1:61-70.

1969a Archaeology on the Shonto Plateau, northeast Ari-
       zona. Southwestern Monuments Association, Technical

Series no. 7, 68 pp.
Reviewed AA 72:946 (Ambler).

1969b Ethnographic analogy and archaeological interpreta-
       tion. Science, 163, no. 3863:133-138.

1969c Tsegi phase technology. University of Washington,
       dissertation, 446 pp.; University Microfilms Inter-
       national.

1971   Excavations at Betatakin and Keet Seel. Kiva, 37,
       no. 1:1-29.

ANDERSON, Kevin (See under Pierson, Lloyd M.)

ANDERSON, Roger Y.

1955   Pollen analysis, a research tool for the study of
       cave deposits. American Antiquity, 21:84-85.

ANDREWS, Tracy J.

1975a Archaeological resources of the BLM Skull Valley
       Planning Unit. Arizona State Museum, Archaeological
       Series, 69, 28 pp.

1975b Archaeological resources of the BLM Harquvar,
       Aquarius, and Hualapai Planning Units. Arizona
       State Museum, Archaeological Series, 73, 47 pp.

ANNAND, Richard E.

1967   A description and analysis of surface collected
       pottery from the Collbran region, Colorado. South-
       western Lore, 33, no. 2:47-60.

ANNIS, Hazel I.

1959   The broken burial jar. Desert Magazine, 22:7-8.

ANTEVS, Ernst (See also under Haury, Emil W.; Martin, Paul
Sidney; Sayles, E.B.)

1935a The occurrence of flints and extinct animals in
       pluvial deposits near Clovis, New Mexico. Part 2.
       Age of the Clovis Lake clays. Proceedings of the
       Academy of Natural Sciences of Philadelphia, 87:
       304-312.

1935b The spread of aboriginal man in North America.
       Geographical Review, 25, no. 2:302-309.

1936   Dating records of Early Man in the Southwest. Amer-
       ican Naturalist, 70, no. 729:332-336.

1937a Climate and Early Man in North America. *In* Early
       Man, ed. G.G. MacCurdy, pp. 125-132. Academy of
       Natural Sciences of Philadelphia.

1937b Studies on the climate in relation to Early Man in
       the Southwest. Carnegie Institution of Washington,
       Year Book no. 36:335.

1938   Studies on the climate in relation to Early Man in
       the Southwest. Carnegie Institution of Washington,
       Year Book no. 37:348.

1948   Climate changes and pre-White man. University of
       Utah Bulletin, 38, no. 20:168-191.

1949   Geology of the Clovis sites. *In* Wormington 1949,
       pp. 185-190.

1953   Artifacts with mammoth remains, Naco, Arizona.
       II. Age of the Clovis Fluted points with the Naco
       mammoth. American Antiquity, 19:15-17.

1954   Climate of New Mexico during the last glacio-pluvial.
       Journal of Geology, 62:182-191.

1955   Geologic-climatic dating in the West. American
       Antiquity, 20, no. 4:317-335.

1959   Geological age of the Lehner mammoth site. American
       Antiquity, 25, no. 1:31-34.

1962   Late Quaternary climates in Arizona. American
       Antiquity, 28:193-198.

ANTIEAU, John M.

1976   An archaeological survey of portions of the Har-
       quahala Valley Flood Control Project, Maricopa
       County, Arizona. Arizona State University, Office
       of Cultural Resource Management, report no. 15, 31
       pp.

1977a An archaeological survey of selected portions of
       the Roosevelt Water Conservation District Flood-
       way, Pinal County, Arizona. Arizona State Uni-
       versity, Office of Cultural Resource Management,
       report no. 22, 31 pp.

1977b Investigations of archaeological sites along the
       500KV Tonto National Forest Boundary to Kyrene
       Transmission Line Route, Coronado Station Project,
       Pinal and Maricopa Counties, Arizona. Arizona
       State University, Office of Cultural Resource Man-
       agement, report no. 23, 96 pp.

1977c   An archaeological survey of Reach 6, Granite Reef
        Aqueduct, Central Arizona Project, Maricopa County,
        Arizona. Arizona State University, Office of Cul-
        tural Resource Management, report no. 27, 34 pp.

APPLEGARTH, Susan

1974   Survey of the Bayfield-Pagosa transmission line.
        Southwestern Lore, 40, nos. 3-4:99-102.

1976   Prehistoric utilization of the environment of the
        eastern slopes of the Guadalupe Mountains, south-
        eastern New Mexico. University of Wisconsin, dis-
        sertation, 326 pp.; University Microfilms Inter-
        national.

ARISS, Robert

1939   Distribution of smoking pipes in the Pueblo area.
        New Mexico Anthropologist, 3, nos. 3-4:53-57.

ARMELAGOS, George J. (See also under Carlson, Roy L.)

1968   Aikens' Fremont hypothesis and the use of skeletal
        material in archaeological interpretation. Ameri-
        can Antiquity, 33, no. 3:385-386.

ARMELAGOS, G.J., DEWEY, John R., and CARLQUIST, David A.

1968   Physical anthropology and the Uto-Aztecan problem.
        In Swanson 1968, pp. 131-147.

ARMS, B.C. (See under Martin, Paul Schultz.)

ARNOLD, Oren

1948   Winning a degree - the pick and shovel way. Des-
        ert Magazine, 11, no. 12:13-18.

ASCH, C.M.

1960   Post-Pueblo occupation at the Willow Creek ruin,
        Point of Pines. Kiva, 26, no. 2:31-42.

ASCHER, Robert

1962   Ethnography for archaeology: a case from the Seri
        Indians. Ethnology, 1:360-369.

ASCHER, R., and CLUNE, Francis J., Jr.

1960   Waterfall Cave, southern Chihuahua, Mexico. Ameri-
        can Antiquity, 26:270-274.

ASHTON, Sherley

1958   The earliest American Madonna? Masterkey, 32:104-
       106.

ATEN, L.E.

1972   Evaluation of the cultural resources of the North-
       gate Site, El Paso County, Texas. Texas Archaeo-
       logical Salvage Project, Research Report no. 5.

AVENI, Anthony F.

1975   (ed.) Archaeoastronomy in pre-Columbian America.
       University of Texas Press, 436 pp.
       Reviewed AA 79:497 (Eddy).

AVERITT, Beej, and AVERITT, Paul

1947   Mastodon of Moab. Desert Magazine, 10, no. 10:24-
       27.

AVERITT, Paul (See under Averitt, Beej.)

AYER, Mary Youngman

1936   The archaeological and faunal material from Williams
       Cave, Guadalupe Mountains, Texas. Proceedings of
       the Academy of Natural Sciences of Philadelphia,
       88:599-618.
       Reviewed AAq 4:291 (Eiseley).

AYRES, James E. (See also under Longacre, William A.)

1966   A Clovis Fluted point from the Kayenta, Arizona,
       area. Plateau, 38, no. 4:76-78.

1967   A prehistoric farm site near Cave Creek, Arizona.
       Kiva, 32, no. 3:106-111.

1970a Two Clovis Fluted points from southern Arizona.
       Kiva, 35, no. 3:121-124.

1970b An early historic burial from the village of Bac.
       Kiva, 36, no. 2:44-48.

1971   Proposed archaeological excavations in Conoco's
       Flor project area. Arizona State Museum, Archaeo-
       logical Series, 4, 5 pp.

BAERREIS, David A.

1948   Culture change in the Taos region, New Mexico.
       Central States Bulletin, 2, no. 3:14-15.

BAHR, Donald M.

1971   Who were the Hohokam? The evidence from Pima-
        Papago myths. Ethnohistory, 18, no. 3:245-266.

BAHTI, Mark

1970   A cache at Huerfano Butte. Kiva, 36, no. 2:17-22.

BAHTI, Thomas N.

1949   A Largo-Gallina pithouse and two surface structures.
        El Palacio, 56:52-59.

BAIN, James G.

1970   Rock art. El Palacio, 77, no. 1:1-12.

1973   Catron County rock art. El Palacio, 79, no. 2:
        39-47.

1976   Art on the rocks. El Palacio, 82, no. 2:9-11.

BAKER, Galen R.

1964   The archaeology of the Park Plateau in southeastern
        Colorado. Southwestern Lore, 30, no. 1:1-18.

BAKER, Gayla S.

1971   The Riverside site, Grant County, New Mexico. Case
        Western Reserve University, Southwestern New Mexico
        Research Reports, 5, 48 pp.

BAKER, Sherman

1941   The Devil's Highroad. Natural History, 49:4-11.

BAKER, William E., and CAMPBELL, T.N.

1960   Artifacts from pre-ceramic sites in northeastern
        and southern New Mexico. El Palacio, 67:78-86.

BAKKEGARD, B.M., and MORRIS, E.A.

1961   Seventh century flutes from Arizona. Ethnomusi-
        cology, 5, no. 3:184-186.

BALDWIN, Gordon C. (See also under Haury, Emil W.)

1935a   Dates from Kinishba Pueblo. Tree-Ring Bulletin, 1,
        no. 4:30.

1935b   Ring record of the great drought (1276-1299) in
        eastern Arizona. Tree-Ring Bulletin, 2:11-12.

1937   The pottery of Kinishba. Kiva, 3, no. 1:1-4.

1938a   An analysis of Basketmaker III sandals from north-
          eastern Arizona. American Anthropologist, 40, no.
          3:465-485.

1938b   Basket Maker and Pueblo sandals. Southwestern
          Lore, 4, no. 1:1-6.

1938c   A new pottery type from eastern Arizona. South-
          western Lore, 4, no. 2:21-26.

1938d   Excavations at Kinishba Pueblo, Arizona. American
          Antiquity, 4, no. 1:11-21.

1939a   A Basket Maker III sandal tablet. Southwestern
          Lore, 5, no. 3:48-52.

1939b   Dates from Kings Ruin. Tree-Ring Bulletin, 5, no.
          3:23-24.

1939c   Further notes on Basket Maker III sandals from
          northeastern Arizona. American Anthropologist, 41:
          223-244.

1939d   The material culture of Kinishba. American Antiquity,
          4:314-327.

1939e   Prehistoric textiles in the Southwest. Kiva, 4, no.
          4:15-18.

1940   Prehistoric Southwestern basketry. Kiva, 5, no. 7:
          25-28.

1941   Survey of Southwestern prehistory. Kiva, 6, no. 8:
          29-32.

1942a   Archaeological field work in the Boulder Dam area.
          Clearinghouse for Southwestern Museums, News-Letter,
          51:186-187.

1942b   Archaeology in southern Nevada. Kiva, 7, no. 4:
          13-16.

1943   Archaeological survey in northwestern Arizona.
          Clearinghouse for Southwestern Museums, News-Letter,
          67:236.

1944a   Mescal knives from southern Nevada. American
          Antiquity, 9:330-332.

1944b   An occurrence of Jeddito Black-on-yellow pottery
          in northwestern Arizona north of the Grand Canyon.
          Plateau, 17, no. 1:14-16.

1945   Notes on ceramic types in southern Nevada. Ameri-
          can Antiquity, 10, no. 4:389-390.

1946   Notes on Rampart Cave. Masterkey, 20, no. 3:94-96.

1947   An archaeological reconnaissance of the Yampa and
        Green Rivers. Kiva, 12, no. 3:31-36.

1948   Notes on Colorado River Basin archaeology. American
        Antiquity, 14, no. 2:128-129.

1949   Archaeological survey in southeastern Utah. South-
        western Journal of Anthropology, 5:393-404.

1950a   Archaeological survey of the Lake Mead area. *In*
        Reed and King 1950, pp. 41-49.

1950b   The pottery of the southern Paiute. American An-
        tiquity, 16:50-56.

1963   The ancient ones: basketmakers and cliff dwellers
        of the Southwest. Norton, New York.

1967   Archaeological survey of Whitmore Wash and Shivwits
        Plateau, northwestern Arizona. Utah Archaeology,
        13, no. 1:3-15.

BALDWIN, Stuart J.

1976   Archaeological salt at Mesa Verde and trade with
        areas to the north and west. Kiva, 42, no. 2:177-
        191.

BALL, Sidney H.

1941   The mining of gems and ornamental stones by American
        Indians. Anthropological Papers, no. 13, Bureau of
        American Ethnology, Bulletin 128, pp. 1-77.

BANCROFT, Hubert Howe

1875   The native races of the Pacific states: antiquities.
        Works of Hubert Howe Bancroft, vol. 4. D. Appleton
        & Co., New York.

BANDELIER, Adolph F.

1881   Historical introduction to studies among the seden-
        tary Indians of New Mexico. Papers of the Archaeo-
        logical Institute of America, American Series, 1,
        pt. 1:1-33.

1883a   Investigations in New Mexico in the spring and sum-
        mer of 1882. Archaeological Institute of America,
        Bulletin, 1, January, pp. 13-33.

1883b   A visit to the aboriginal ruins in the valley of
        the Rio Pecos. Papers of the Archaeological

Institute of America, American Series, 1, pt. 2:
37-133.

1884a   Investigations in New Mexico during the years 1883-
84. Fifth Annual Report of the Archaeological Institute of America, pp. 55-87.

1884b   Report of an archaeological tour in Mexico in 1881.
Papers of the Archaeological Institute of America,
American Series, vol. 2, 326 pp.

1885   An archaeological reconnaissance into Mexico.
Cupples and Hurd, Boston.

1890a   Final report of investigations among the Indians
of the southwestern United States, Part I.   Papers
of the Archaeological Institute of America, American Series, vol. 3, 323 pp.

1890b   Contributions to the history of the southwestern
portion of the United States.   Papers of the
Archaeological Institute of America, American Series,
vol. 5, 206 pp.

1890c   The ruins of Casas Grandes.   The Nation, 51, no.
1314:166-168, 185-187.

1892a   Final report of investigations among the Indians
of the southwestern United States, Part II.   Papers
of the Archaeological Institute of America, American
Series, vol. 4, 591 pp.

1892b   An outline of the documentary history of the Zuni
tribe.   Journal of American Ethnology and Archaeology, 3:1-115.

1910   Documentary history of the Rio Grande Pueblos of
New Mexico.   Papers of the School of American Archaeology, no. 13, 27 pp.

BANNISTER, Bryant (See also under Smiley, Terah L.)

1951   Tree-ring dates from the Gallina area, New Mexico.
Tree-Ring Bulletin, 17, no. 3:21-22.

1960   Southwestern dated ruins, VII.   Tree-Ring Bulletin,
23, nos. 1-4:19-21.

1962   The interpretation of tree-ring dates.   American
Antiquity, 27, no. 4:508-514.

1964   Tree-ring dating of the archaeological sites in the
Chaco Canyon region, New Mexico.   Southwestern Monuments Association, Technical Series, no. 6, pt. 2:

117-201.
Reviewed AA 69:100 (Ellis).

1966   Recent developments in New World dendrochronology.
        Proceedings of the 36th International Congress of
        Americanists, 1:121-125.

1969   Dendrochronology. *In* Science of Archaeology (rev.
        ed.), ed. D. Brothwell and E. Higgs, pp. 191-205.
        Thames and Hudson, London.

1973   The interpretation of tree-ring dates. *In* In Search
        of Man: readings in archaeology, ed. E.L. Green,
        pp. 159-164. Little, Brown & Co.

BANNISTER, B., and ROBINSON, William J.

1971   Tree-ring dates from Arizona U-W, Gila-Salt Rivers
        area. Laboratory of Tree-ring Research, University
        of Arizona, 47 pp.

1975   Tree-ring dating in archaeology. World Archaeology,
        7, no. 2:210-225.

BANNISTER, B., and SCOTT, Stuart D.

1964   Dendrochronology in Mexico. Proceedings of the
        35th International Congress of Americanists, pp.
        211-216.

BANNISTER, B., DEAN, Jeffrey S., and GELL, Elizabeth A.M.

1966   Tree-ring dates from Arizona E, Chinle-de Chelly-
        Red Rock area. Laboratory of Tree-ring Research,
        University of Arizona, 54 pp.

BANNISTER, B., DEAN, J.S., and ROBINSON, William J.

1968   Tree-ring dates from Arizona C-D, eastern Grand
        Canyon-Tsegi Canyon-Kayenta area. Laboratory of
        Tree-ring Research, University of Arizona, 78 pp.

1969   Tree-ring dates from Utah S-W, southern Utah area.
        Laboratory of Tree-ring Research, University of
        Arizona, 62 pp.

BANNISTER, B., GELL, Elizabeth A.M., and HANNAH, John W.

1966   Tree-ring dates from Arizona N-Q, Verde-Show Low-
        St. Johns area. Laboratory of Tree-ring Research,
        University of Arizona, 63 pp.

BANNISTER, B., HANNAH, John W., and ROBINSON, William J.

1966   Tree-ring dates from Arizona K, Puerco-Wide Ruin-
        Ganado area. Laboratory of Tree-ring Research,
        University of Arizona, 48 pp.

1970   Tree-ring dates from New Mexico M-N, S, Z, south-
        western New Mexico area. Laboratory of Tree-ring
        Research, University of Arizona, 69 pp.

BANNISTER, B., ROBINSON, W.J., and WARREN, Richard L.

1967   Tree-ring dates from Arizona J, Hopi Mesas area.
        Laboratory of Tree-ring Research, University of
        Arizona, 44 pp.

1970   Tree-ring dates from New Mexico A, G-H, Shiprock-
        Zuni-Mt. Taylor areas. Laboratory of Tree-ring
        Research, University of Arizona, 65 pp.

BARBER, EDWIN A.

1876a   Ancient art in northwestern Colorado. Bulletin of
        the United States Geological and Geographical Sur-
        vey of the Territories, 1876, 2:65-66.

1876b   The ancient pottery of Colorado, Utah, Arizona, and
        New Mexico. American Naturalist, 10:449-464.

1876c   Rock inscription of the "Ancient Pueblos" of Colo-
        rado, Utah, New Mexico, and Arizona. American
        Naturalist, 10, no. 12:716-725.

1876d   Bead ornaments employed by the ancient tribes of
        Utah and Arizona. Bulletin of the United States
        Geological and Geographical Survey of the Terri-
        tories, 2:67-69.

1877a   Stone implements and ornaments from the ruins of
        Colorado, Utah, and Arizona. American Naturalist,
        11:264-275.

1877b   On the ancient and modern Pueblo tribes of the
        Pacific slope of the United States. American Nat-
        uralist, 11:591-599.

1878   The ancient Pueblos, or the ruins of the valley of
        the Rio San Juan; parts 1, 2. American Naturalist,
        12:526-536, 606-614.

1881   Ancient ruins in Utah. American Antiquarian and
        Oriental Journal, 4, no. 1:78.

BARNES, Mark R.

1971   Majolica from excavations at San Xavier del Bac,
        1968-1969. Kiva, 37, no. 1:61-64.

1972   Majolica of the Santa Cruz Valley, Arizona. Pacific
        Coast Archaeological Society, Occasional Papers,
        2.

BARNES, Robert A.

1947   Clues to the fabulous seven cities of Cibola? Des-
        ert Magazine, 10, no. 5:22-25.

BARNETT, Franklin

1968   Birds on Rio Grande pottery. Albuquerque Archaeo-
        logical Society, 27 pp.

1969   Tonque Pueblo: a report of partial excavation of
        an ancient Pueblo IV Indian ruin in New Mexico.
        Albuquerque Archaeological Society, 237 pp.

1970   Matli Ranch ruins: a report of excavations of five
        small prehistoric Indian ruins of the Prescott
        culture in Arizona. Museum of Northern Arizona,
        Technical Series, no. 10, 90 pp.

1973a   Dictionary of prehistoric Indian artifacts of the
        American southwest. Northland Press, Flagstaff,
        130 pp.

1973b   Lonesome Valley ruin in Yavapai County, Arizona.
        Museum of Northern Arizona, Technical Series, no.
        13, 26 pp.

1973c   San Ysidro Pueblos: two prehistoric Pueblo IV
        Indian ruins in New Mexico. Albuquerque Archaeo-
        logical Society, 64 pp.

1974a   Excavation of main pueblo at Fitzmaurice Ruin:
        Prescott culture in Yavapai County, Arizona.
        Museum of Northern Arizona, Special Publication
        no. 10, 138 pp.

1974b   Sandstone Hill Pueblo ruin: Cibola culture in
        Catron County, New Mexico. Albuquerque Archaeo-
        logical Society, 59 pp.

1975   Excavation of a lower room at Fitzmaurice Ruin
        (NA4031). Yavapai College Press, Prescott.

BARRE, Susan

1970   Pottery types from five sites in southern Nevada.
        Nevada Archaeological Survey Reporter, 4, no. 2:
        11-15.

BARRERA, Bill, Jr.

1969a   A Desert Culture site near Two Guns, northern
        Arizona. Kiva, 34, nos. 2-3:103-108.

1969b   The Eztagito site, central Arizona. Kiva, 34,
        nos. 2-3:176-184.

BARRETT, Samuel A.

1923   A trip to Cave Hill, Arizona. Public Museum of
        the City of Milwaukee, Yearbook 2 (for 1922), pp.
        176-182.

1927   Reconnaissance of the Citadel group of Pueblo ruins
        in Arizona. Public Museum of the City of Milwaukee,
        Yearbook, 6 (for 1926), pp. 7-58.

BARTER, Eloise R. (See under Martin, Paul Sidney.)

BARTER, James T. (See also under Martin, Paul Sidney.)

1953   Archaeological 3-D applied by southwest expedition.
        Bulletin of the Chicago Natural History Museum, 24.
        no. 9:5-6.

BARTH, A.W.

1933   New notes on El Morro. Art and Archaeology, 34:
        146-156.

BARTLETT, John R.

1854   Personal narrative of explorations and incidents
        in Texas, New Mexico, California, Sonora, and Chi-
        huahua. 2 vols., D. Appleton & Co., New York.

BARTLETT, Katharine

1930a   Stone artifacts; San Francisco Mountain region.
        Museum of Northern Arizona, Museum Notes, 3, no.
        6:1-4.

1930b   Two female basketmakers from New Mexico and Ari-
        zona. El Palacio, 28:57-61.

1931   Prehistoric Pueblo foods. Museum of Northern Ari-
        zona, Museum Notes, 4, no. 4:1-4.

1932   A unique Pueblo II bird fetish. American Anthro-
        pologist, 34:315-319.

1933a   Life in Pueblo II (ca. 700-1000 A.D.). Museum of
        Northern Arizona, Museum Notes, 6, no. 3:13-18.

1933b   Pueblo milling stones of the Flagstaff region and
        their relation to others in the Southwest. Museum
        of Northern Arizona, Bulletin, 3, 32 pp.

1934   The material culture of Pueblo II in the San Fran-
        cisco Mountains, Arizona. Museum of Northern Ari-
        zona, Bulletin 7, 76 pp.
        Reviewed AA 38:661 (Roberts).

1935   Prehistoric mining in the Southwest. Museum of
        Northern Arizona, Museum Notes, 7, no. 10:41-44.

1936   The utilization of maize among the ancient Pueblos.
        In Brand 1936, pp. 29-34.

1939   A prehistoric "mine" of red argillite, resembling
        pipestone, near Del Rio, Arizona. Museum of North-
        ern Arizona, Museum Notes, 11, no. 12:75-78.

1942   Notes upon a primitive stone industry of the Little
        Colorado Valley. Plateau, 14, no. 3:37-41.

1943   A primitive stone industry of the Little Colorado
        Valley, Arizona. American Antiquity, 8, no. 3:
        266-268.

1946   Prehistoric use of onyx marble. Plateau, 19, no.
        1:13-14.

1953   Twenty-five years of anthropology. Plateau, 26,
        no. 1:38-60.

1977   A history of Hopi pottery. Plateau, 49, no. 3:2-13.

BASKIN, B.J. (See under Lynn, W.M.)

BASSHAM, Elbert

1971   Application of probability theory to recurring
        variables in some El Paso phase archaeological
        sites. Transactions of the 6th Regional Archaeo-
        logical Symposium on Southeastern New Mexico and
        Western Texas, pp. 83-90.

BASSO, Keith H., and OPLER, Morris E.

1971 (ed.) Apachean culture history and ethnology. University of Arizona, Anthropological Papers, 21, 168 pp.

BAUM, H.M.

1902 Pueblo and cliff dwellers of the Southwest. Records of the Past, 1:357-361.

1903 De Chelly, del Muerto, and Monument Canyons. Records of the Past, 2:163-173.

BAUMANN, Gustave

1939 Frijoles Canyon pictographs. Writers' Editions, Inc., Santa Fe, 37 pp.

BAUMHOFF, Martin A., and HEIZER, Robert F.

1965 Postglacial climates and archaeology in the Desert West. *In* The Quaternary of the United States, ed. H.E. Wright and D.G. Frey, pp. 697-708. Princeton University Press.

BAXTER, Frank C. (See under Colton, Harold S.)

BAXTER, Sylvester

1888 The old new world: an account of the explorations of the Hemenway southwestern archaeological expedition in 1887-88. Salem, Mass.

1889 Archaeological camping in Arizona. American Architect and Building News, 25, no. 10.

BEAL, John D.

1973 Tapeats Creek - a survey in the Grand Canyon. School of American Research, Exploration 1973, pp. 22-23.

1974 The excavation of a plaza. School of American Research, Exploration 1974, pp. 12-15.

1975a An archaeological survey of the #1 Marcelina well site, McKinley County, New Mexico. School of American Research, contract #12.

1975b An archaeological survey of the Conchas Dam area. School of American Research, contract #13.

1975c   An archaeological clearance survey of AFA 532-84,
        a natural gas pipeline serving the American Quazar
        Federal 24-No. 1 well site. School of American Re-
        search, contract #21.

1975d   An archaeological evaluation of a prehistoric oc-
        cupation site on Palma Mesa, Chaves County, New
        Mexico. School of American Research, contract #23.

1975e   A recommendation of archaeological clearance for
        the Marcelina #2, #3, #4 well sites in McKinley
        County, New Mexico. School of American Research,
        contract #25.

1975f   An archaeological clearance survey of 8 parcels of
        land in the Jackpile mining lease, Laguna Indian
        Reservation, Valencia County, New Mexico. School
        of American Research, contract #28.

1976a   An archaeological survey of four uranium test drill-
        ing sites, McKinley County, New Mexico. School of
        American Research, contract #35.

1976b   An archaeological survey of two sections of land
        in McKinley County, New Mexico. School of American
        Research, contract #38.

1976c   An archaeological survey of the volcanoes west of
        Albuquerque, New Mexico. School of American Research,
        contract #45.

1976d   Archaeological clearance recommendations for seven
        city parks within the city of Albuquerque, New Mex-
        ico. School of American Research, contract #45A.

1977a   Cultural resource evaluation in the Malpais Recrea-
        tion area. School of American Research, contract
        #41.

1977b   Preliminary report on testing evaluation activities
        in the El Malpais Recreation Area. School of Amer-
        ican Research, contract #41.

1977c   Cultural resource evaluation of two proposed elec-
        trical generating stations in McKinley County,
        New Mexico. School of American Research, contract
        #43.

1977d   Archaeological clearance survey in Cañada de las
        Vacas. School of American Research, contract #48.

1977e   A structured reconnaissance survey in San Lucas
        Canyon near San Mateo, New Mexico. School of Amer-
        ican Research, contract #69.

BEAL, J.D., and WHITMORE, Jane

1976a An archaeological survey of a portion of the Gamerco coal lease, McKinley County, New Mexico. School of American Research, contract #36.

1976b Archaeological survey of six natural gas pipelines for Gas Company of New Mexico. School of American Research, contract #39.

BEALS, Ralph L.

1942 Shell mounds and other sites in Sonora and northern Sinaloa. Society for American Archaeology, Notebook, 2:38-40.

1944a Northern Mexico and the Southwest. *In* El norte de México y el sur de Estados Unidos, Tercera Reunión de Mesa Redonda sobre Problemas Antropológicas de México y Centro América, pp. 191-198. Sociedad mexicana de antropología.

1944b Relations between Mesoamerica and the Southwest. *In* El norte de México y el sur de Estados Unidos, Tercera Reunión de Mesa Redonda sobre Problemas Antropológicas de México y Centro América, pp. 245-252. Sociedad mexicana de antropología.

BEALS, R.L., BRAINERD, G.W., and SMITH, Watson

1945 Archaeological studies in northeast Arizona. University of California, Publications in American Archaeology and Ethnology, 44, no. 1:1-236. Reviewed AA 48:253 (Colton).

BEAM, G.L.

1909 The prehistoric ruin of Tsankawi. National Geographic Magazine, 20, no. 9:807-822.

BEARDEN, Susan E. (See under Skinner, Elizabeth.)

BEARDSLEY, John

1975 Archaeological clearance survey: Ideal Basic Industries, Cement Division, 16 acre quarrying project. University of New Mexico, contract report 101-1030 (USFS).

BEATY, Janice J.

1964 Land rush to Wupatki. Desert Magazine, 27, no. 5: 26-27.

1966   The rise and fall of Wupatki. Pacific Discovery,
        19, no. 1:2-7.

BEAUBIEN, Paul

    1937   Excavations at Tumacacori, 1934. Southwestern Monu-
            ments Monthly Report, March, pp. 179-220. (Also
            as Special Report no. 15, 36 pp.)

BEAUVAIS, Lester

    1955   Primitive people of the Gunnison Basin. South-
            western Lore, 21, no. 3:29-34.

BECKETT, Patrick H.

    1973   Gardner Springs Site. Awanyu, 1, no. 2:45-47.

    1976   Seasonal utilization of the Mescalero Sands.
            Awanyu, 4, no. 4:23-33.

BECKWITH, Frank

    1927a   To the ancient hieroglyphs. Improvement Era, 30,
            no. 4:343-345.

    1927b   Rare Indian curios. Improvement Era, 30, no. 5:
            413-417.

    1927c   The persistency of a religious ceremonial. Im-
            provement Era, 30, no. 9:785-794.

    1927d   The high priest's vestments, used by the ancient
            cliff dwellers of Wayne County centuries ago. Im-
            provement Era, 30, no. 11:1028-1037.

    1927e   Why is the Indian taciturn? Improvement Era, 30,
            no. 12:1088-1092.

    1931a   Some interesting pictographs in Nine Mile Canyon,
            Utah. El Palacio, 31, no. 14:216-222.

    1931b   Indian rock pictures in Utah. El Palacio, 31, nos.
            22-23:361-368.

    1932   Serpent petroglyph in Nine Mile Canyon. El Palacio,
            33, nos. 15-16:147-149.

    1934a   Basketmaker sandals from near Moab, Utah. El Pa-
            lacio, 36:174-176.

    1934b   Group of petroglyphs near Moab, Utah. El Palacio,
            36:177-178.

    1935   Ancient Indian petroglyphs of Utah. El Palacio,
            38, nos. 6-8:33-40.

1940   Glyphs that tell the story of an ancient migration.
        Desert Magazine, 3, no. 10:4-7.

BECKWITH, Mary

1959   Life from the earth.   Desert Magazine, 22, no. 1:
        4-7.

BEESON, William J.

1957a   The stages of fill of room 10 at the Pollock site.
        Plateau, 29, no. 3:66-70.

1957b   A possible prehistoric shrine in eastern Arizona.
        Plateau, 30, no. 1:20-22.

1966   Archaeological survey near St. Johns, Arizona: a
        methodological study.   University of Arizona, dis-
        sertation, 318 pp.; University Microfilms Inter-
        national.

BEESON, W.J., and GOLDFRIED, Howard P.

1976   The Kahorsho site (NA 10, 937), Coconino National
        Forest, Arizona--an interim report.   United States
        Forest Service, Southwestern Region, Archaeological
        Report no. 12, 65 pp.

BEEZLEY, John (See under Ferguson, T.J.; Olsen, Stanley J.)

BEGOLE, Robert S.

1974   Archaeological phenomena in the California deserts:
        desert cairns and rock alignments.   Pacific Coast
        Archaeological Society Quarterly, 10, no. 2:51-69.

BENFER, Robert Alfred, Jr. (See also under Greer, John W.)

1968   An analysis of a prehistoric skeletal population,
        Casas Grandes, Chihuahua, Mexico.   University of
        Texas, dissertation, 172 pp.; University Microfilms
        International.

BENHAM, Blake L. (See also under Wasley, William W.)

1966   Excavation of La Plata phase pit houses near To-
        hatchi, New Mexico.   Laboratory of Anthropology
        Notes, 38.

BENNETT, Cynthia R.

1973   A note on the identification of pulled handles on
        Anasazi pottery.   Plateau, 45, no. 4:170-172.

BENNETT, Kenneth A.

1973   The Indians of Point of Pines, Arizona. University
        of Arizona, Anthropological Papers, 23, 75 pp.
        Reviewed AAq 40:500 (Turner).

1975   Skeletal remains from Mesa Verde National Park,
        Colorado. National Park Service, Publications in
        Archaeology, no. 7F, 43 pp.

BENNETT, M. Ann

1974   Basic ceramic analysis. Eastern New Mexico Uni-
        versity, Contributions in Anthropology, 6, no. 1.

BENNYHOFF, James A.

1958   The Desert West: a trial correlation of culture and
        chronology. *In* Current Views on Great Basin Ar-
        chaeology, pp. 98-112. University of California,
        Archaeological Survey Reports, 42.

BERGE, Dale L.

1968a   The Gila Bend stage station. Kiva, 33, no. 4:169-
        243.

1968b   Historical archaeology in the American Southwest.
        University of Arizona, dissertation, 463 pp.; Uni-
        versity Microfilms International.

BERGER, Alan J. (See under Wilson, John P.)

BERGER, R. (See under Heizer, Robert F.)

BERLIN, G. Lennis, AMBLER, J.R., HEVLY, R.H., and SCHABER, G.G.

1975   Archaeological field patterns revealed in north-
        central Arizona by aerial thermography. Proceed-
        ings of the American Society of Photogrammetry.

1977   Identification of a Sinagua agricultural field by
        aerial thermography, soil chemistry, pollen/plant
        analysis, and archaeology. American Antiquity, 42:
        588-600.

BERNHEIMER, Charles L.

1924   Rainbow Bridge. Doubleday, Page, & Co., 182 pp.

BERRY, Michael S. (See also under Madsen, David B.)

1972   The Evans Site. University of Utah, Dept. of
        Anthropology, Special Report.

BESSELS, Emil

    1876   The human remains found near the ancient ruins of southwestern Colorado and New Mexico. United States Geological and Geographical Survey of the Territories, Bulletin, 2, no. 1:47-64.

BICE, Richard A.

    1967   Site AS-1, Basketmaker campsite. El Palacio, 74, no. 4:44-45.

    1968   Tonque Pueblo: an exhibition prepared by the Albuquerque Archaeological Society at the Museum of Albuquerque. 15 pp., Albuquerque, N.M.

    1970   Basketmaker III-Pueblo I manifestations on the Rio Puerco of the East. Albuquerque Archaeological Society, Technical Note no. 1, 8 pp.

    1975   Prehispanic Pueblo pottery. Museum of Albuquerque and Albuquerque Archaeological Society, 20 pp.

BICE, R.A., and DAVIS, Phyllis

    1970   Progress report on Cochiti lithic sites. Laboratory of Anthropology Notes, 80D.

    1972   A report on the impact of Cochiti Dam on the archaeological resources of the Cochiti area, New Mexico. Laboratory of Anthropology Notes, 80E.

BICE, R.A., and SUNDT, William M.

    1968   An early Basketmaker campsite. Albuquerque Archaeological Society, 56 pp.
            Reviewed AAq 34:337 (Lindsay).

    1972   Prieta Vista: a small Pueblo III ruin in north-central New Mexico. Albuquerque Archaeological Society, 216 pp.

BICK, Edgar M. (See under Jarcho, Saul.)

BICKFORD, F.T.

    1890   Prehistoric cave-dwellings. Century Magazine, 40 (October):896-911.

BIELLA, Jan V., and CHAPMAN, Richard C.

    1977   Cochiti mitigation program. University of New Mexico, contract report 101-127B (NPS).

BIERBOWER, Susan

    1905   Among the cliff and cavate dwellings of New Mexico.
           Records of the Past, 4:227-233.

BILBO, Michael (See also under Sutherland, Kay.)

    1969   An El Paso polychrome olla from the Hueco Bolson.
           The Artifact, 7, no. 2:31-39.

    1972   The Castner Annex Range dam site, EPAS-10: prelim-
           inary report. The Artifact, 10, no. 2:59-81.

    1976   A high elevation survey of Castner Range, Fort
           Bliss, Texas. The Artifact, 14, no. 1:19-44.

BILLECK, William T. (See under DeBoer, Warren R.)

BILLINGS, J.S. (See under Matthews, Washington.)

BIRDSALL, W.R.

    1892   The cliff-dwellings of the canyons of the Mesa
           Verde. American Antiquarian, 14, no. 3:123-138.

BIRKBY, Walter H. (See also under Reiley, Daniel E.; Windmiller, Ric.)

    1970   Human skeletal material from Arizona J:6:1. Pla-
           teau, 43, no. 1:39-42.

    1971   Laboratory analysis of hair from hunting net A-22,
           415 in the collections of the Arizona State Museum.
           Kiva, 36, no. 3:53-54.

    1973a   Discontinuous morphological traits of the skull
           as population markers in the prehistoric Southwest.
           University of Arizona, dissertation, 126 pp.; Uni-
           versity Microfilms International.

    1973b   Human skeletal remains from the DoBell site. Kiva,
           39, no. 1:69-73.

BIRKEDAL, Terje Gjert

    1976   Basketmaker III residence units: a study of pre-
           historic social organization in the Mesa Verde ar-
           chaeological district. University of Colorado,
           dissertation, 563 pp.; University Microfilms Inter-
           national.

BLACK, Donald M. (See under Ferguson, C.W., Jr.)

BLACKBURN, Thomas (See under Ruby, Jay W.)

BLACKISTON, A.H.

1905a   Cliff-dwellings of northern Mexico. Records of the
        Past, 4:355-361.

1905b   Prehistoric ruins of northern Mexico. American
        Antiquarian, 27:65-69.

1906a   Cliff ruins of Cave Valley, northern Mexico. Rec-
        cords of the Past, 5:5-11.

1906b   Casas Grandian outposts. Records of the Past, 5:
        142-147.

1906c   Ruins on the Cerro de Montezuma. American Anthro-
        pologist, n.s., 8, no. 2:256-261.

1908   Ruins of the Tenaja and the Rio San Pedro. Records
        of the Past, 7:282-290.

1909   Recently discovered cliff-dwellings of the Sierras
        Madres. Records of the Past, 8:20-32.

BLAIR, William C. (See also under Enger, Walter D.)

1949   Additional data on crania from the Warren Mounds,
        Utah. American Antiquity, 14:224-225.

BLAKE, Leonard W. (See under Cutler, Hugh C.)

BLAKE, WILLIAM P.

1899   Aboriginal turquoise mining in Arizona and New
        Mexico. American Antiquarian, 21, no. 5:278-284.

1900   A prehistoric mountain village in Arizona. American
        Antiquarian, 22:191-192.

BLANCHARD, F.D. (See under Anderson, Edgar.)

BLEIBTREU, Hermann K. (See under Giles, Eugene.)

BLESSING, FRED

1935   A brief summary of the eight cultures of the South-
        west. Minnesota Archaeologist, 1, no. 5:1-4.

BLISS, Wesley L.

1936a   Cave exploration and exploitation. El Palacio, 40:
        60-62.

1936b   Problems of the Kuaua mural paintings. El Palacio,
        40, nos. 16-18:81-86.

1940   A chronological problem presented by Sandia Cave,
          N.M. American Antiquity, 5, no. 3:200-202.

1948a   Early and late lithic horizons in the Plains. Pro-
          ceedings of the 6th Plains Archaeology Conference,
          University of Utah, Anthropological Papers, 11:108-
          116.

1948b   Preservation of the Kuaua mural paintings. Amer-
          ican Antiquity, 13, no. 3:218-222.

1960   Impact of pipeline archaeology on Indian prehistory.
          Plateau, 33:10-13.

BLISS, W.L., and EZELL, Paul H.

1956   The Arizona section of the San Juan Pipeline. *In*
          Wendorf, Fox, and Lewis 1956, pp. 81-156.

BLOOM, Lansing B. (See also under Bradfield, Wesley.)

1921   The emergence of Chaco Canyon. Art and Archaeology,
          11:29-35.

1922   The West Jemez culture area. El Palacio, 12, no.
          2:18-25.

1923   The Jemez expedition of the School. Summer of 1922.
          El Palacio, 14, no. 2:14-20.

BLUHM, Elaine A. (See also under Martin, Paul Sidney; Rinaldo,
   John B.)

1957   The Sawmill Site, a Reserve Phase village, Pine
          Lawn Valley, western New Mexico. Fieldiana: Anthro-
          pology, 47, no. 1:1-86.
          Reviewed AA 60:783 (Thompson), AAq 23:202 (Wasley).

1960   Mogollon settlement patterns in Pine Lawn Valley,
          New Mexico. American Antiquity, 25, no. 4:538-546.

BLUMENSCHEIN, Helen G.

1956   Excavations in the Taos area, 1953-1955. El Palacio,
          63:53-56.

1958   Further excavations and surveys in the Taos area.
          El Palacio, 65:107-111.

1964   Report on Site 268. El Palacio, 70:48-49.

BLUMENTHAL, E.H., Jr. (See also under Reiter, Paul.)

1940   An introduction to Gallina archaeology. New Mex-
          ico Anthropologist, 4, no. 1:10-13.

BOEKELMAN, Henry J.

1936   Shell trumpet from Arizona. American Antiquity,
        2:27-31.

BOGAN, Samuel D.

1946   Let the Coyotes Howl. G.P. Putnam's Sons.

BOHRER, Vorsila L.

1962   Nature and interpretation of ethnobotanical mater-
        ials from Tonto National Monument, 1957. *In* Cay-
        wood, 1962, pp. 75-114.

1967   Plant resources in a human ecosystem in southern
        Arizona, 100 B.C.-1100 A.D. Bioscience 17:903.

1970   Ethnobotanical aspects of Snaketown, a Hohokam vil-
        lage in southern Arizona. American Antiquity, 35:
        413-430.

1971   Paleoecology of Snaketown. Kiva, 36, no. 3:11-19.

1972   Paleoecology of the Hay Hollow site, Arizona. Field-
        iana: Anthropology, 63, no. 1:1-30.

1973   Ethnobotany of Point of Pines Ruin, Arizona W: 10:
        50. Economic Botany, 27, no. 4:423-437.

1975   The role of seasonality in the annual harvest of
        native food plants in the Puerco Valley, northwest
        of Albuquerque, New Mexico. New Mexico Academy of
        Science, Bulletin, 15, no. 2:3 (abstract).

BOHRER, V.L., and ADAMS, Karen R.

1977   Ethnobotanical techniques and approaches at Salmon
        Ruin, New Mexico. Eastern New Mexico University,
        Contributions in Anthropology, 8, no. 1, 214 pp.

BOHRER, V.L., CUTLER, Hugh C., and SAUER, Jonathan D.

1969   Carbonized plant remains from two Hohokam sites,
        Arizona BB:13:41 and Arizona BB:13:50. Kiva, 35:
        1-10.

BOIES, L.C.

1928   Ruins of Verde Valley. Arizona Old and New, 1, no.
        2:6, 29-32.

BOOTHLY, H.E.

1888   Ancient canals in Nevada. American Antiquarian, 10,

no. 6:380-381.

BORHEGYI, Stephan F. de

1956   The excavation of Site 9 near Apache Creek, Catron
        County, New Mexico. *In* Wendorf 1956a, pp. 1-9.

BOTELHO, Eugene

1955   Pinto Basin points in Utah. American Antiquity,
        21, no. 2:185-186.

BOURKE, John G.

1890   Vesper hours of the stone age. American Anthro-
        pologist, o.s., 3:55-64.

BOWEN, Thomas G.

1965   A survey of archaeological sites near Guaymas,
        Sonora. Kiva, 31, no. 1:14-36.

1976a   Seri prehistory: the archaeology of the central
        coast of Sonora, Mexico. University of Arizona,
        Anthropological Papers, 27, 120 pp.

1976b   Esquema de la historia de la cultura Trincheras.
        In Braniff and Felger 1976, pp. 267-280.

BOWEN, William M.

1950   Gran Quivira, city of mystery. New Mexico Magazine,
        28, no. 5:20-21, 37-39.

BOYD, E.

1970   17th century Spanish medal found in Estancia Valley.
        El Palacio, 76, no. 3:16.

BOYD, Henrietta H. (Mrs. William F.)

1940   Saguache antelope traps. Southwestern Lore, 6, no.
        no. 2:28-34.

1942   Saguache archaeological problems. Southwestern Lore,
        8:20.

1949   Archaeological sites around Saguache. Southwestern
        Lore, 15, no. 2:40-43.

BOYD, William C. (See under Wyman, Leland C.)

BOYER, W.W., and ROBINSON, Peter

   1956   Obsidian artifacts of northwestern New Mexico and
            their correlation with source material. El Palacio,
            63:333-345.

BRADBURY, John (See under Wendorf, Fred.)

BRADFIELD, Wesley

   1921   Economic resources of Chaco Canyon. Art and Ar-
            chaeology, 11, nos. 1-2:36-38.

   1923a   Summary of work on Cameron Creek Site, Mimbres
            Section. El Palacio, 15, no. 4:53-54.

   1923b   Excavations on Cameron Creek. El Palacio, 15:60.

   1923c   Preliminary report on excavating at Cameron Creek
            Site. El Palacio, 15, no. 5:66-73.

   1925a   A day's work on the Mimbres. El Palacio, 19:170-
            172.

   1925b   Pit houses of Cameron Creek. El Palacio, 19, no.
            8:173-177.

   1927   Notes on Mimbres culture. El Palacio, 22, no. 26:
            550-559.

   1928a   Early Pueblo pot from Santa Fe. El Palacio, 24:
            78-79.

   1928b   Mimbres excavation in 1928. El Palacio, 25, nos.
            8-11:151-160.

   1929   Excavations in the Sacramentos. El Palacio, 27,
            nos. 1-7:3-6.

   1931   Cameron Creek Village, a site in the Mimbres area
            in Grant County, New Mexico. School of American
            Research, Monograph no. 1, 127 pp.

BRADFIELD, W., BLOOM, L.B., and CHAPMAN, K.M.

   1928   A preliminary survey of the archaeology of south-
            western New Mexico. El Palacio, 24, no. 6:99-112.

BRADFORD, James E. (See under James, Charles D., III.)

BRADLEY, Bruce (See also under Grebinger, Paul F.)

   1974   Preliminary report of excavations at Wallace Ruin,
            1969-1974. Southwestern Lore, 40, nos. 3-4:63-71.

BRADLEY, Zorro A.

1959   Three prehistoric farm structures at Wupatki National Monument. Plateau, 32, no. 1:12-22.

1960   The Whitmore-McIntyre dugout, Pipe Spring National Monument. Part I: history. Plateau, 33:40-45.

1961   The Whitmore-McIntyre dugout, Pipe Spring National Monument. Part II: excavation. Plateau, 33:69-82.

1971   Site BC 236, Chaco Canyon National Monument, New Mexico. National Park Service, Division of Archaeology, 127 pp.

1973   Canyon de Chelly: the story of its ruins and people. National Park Service, Washington, 57 pp.

BRAINERD, George W. (See also under Beals, Ralph L.)

1935   Preliminary report on site RB-MV 568. Rainbow Bridge-Monument Valley Expedition, Preliminary Bulletin no. 10, 4 pp.

1949   Human effigy vessels of Pueblo culture. Masterkey, 23:121-124.

BRANCATO, Melody J., and DODGE, William A.

1973   Archaeological survey of Indian Rt. 8, Point of Pines. Arizona State Museum, Archaeological Series, 28, 12 pp.

BRAND, Donald D. (See also under Sauer, Carl.)

1935a   The distribution of pottery types in northwest Mexico. American Anthropologist, 37:287-305.

1935b   Hawley's study of Chetro Ketl. El Palacio, 38, nos. 3-5:17-29.

1935c   Prehistoric trade in the southwest. New Mexico Business Review, 4:202-209.

1936   (ed.) Symposium on prehistoric agriculture. University of New Mexico Bulletin, Anthropological Series, 1, no. 5, 72 pp.
        Reviewed AA 39:537 (I.T. Kelly).

1937a   The bison nomads. New Mexico Magazine, 15, no. 3: 18-19, 37-38.

1937b   Southwestern trade in shell products. American Antiquity, 2:300-302.

1938   Aboriginal trade routes for sea shells in the South-
        west. Yearbook of the Association of Pacific Coast
        Geographers, 4:3-10.

1943   The Chihuahua culture area. New Mexico Anthropolo-
        gist, 6-7, no. 3:115-158.

1944   Archaeological relations between northern Mexico
        and the Southwest. *In* El Norte de México y el Sur
        de Estados Unidos, Tercera Reunión de Mesa Redonda
        sobre Problemas antropológicas de México y Centro
        América, pp. 199-202. Sociedad mexicana de antro-
        pología.

BRAND, D.D., and HARVEY, Fred E.

1939   (ed.) So Live the Works of Men. University of New
        Mexico Press, 366 pp.
        Reviewed AA 42:530 (Stirling), AAq 6:91 (Wissler).

BRAND, D.D., HAWLEY, Florence M., and HIBBEN, Frank C.

1937   Tseh So, a small house ruin, Chaco Canyon, New
        Mexico. University of New Mexico Bulletin, Anthro-
        pological Series, 2, no. 2, 174 pp.
        Reviewed AAq 4:80 (Baldwin).

BRANDES, Raymond S.

1957   An early ball court near Globe, Arizona. Kiva, 23,
        no. 1:10-11.

1960   Archaeological awareness of the Southwest as il-
        lustrated in literature to 1890. Arizona and the
        West, 2, no. 1:6-25.

BRANDT, John C., and others

1975   Possible rock art records of the Crab Nebula super-
        nova in the western United States. *In* Aveni 1975,
        pp. 45-58.

BRANHAM, Mary

1961   Ghost town, 1200 A.D. New Mexico Magazine, 39, no.
        8:9-11.

BRANIFF, Beatriz

1975   The West Mexican tradition and the southwestern
        United States. Kiva, 41, no. 2:215-222.

1978   Preliminary interpretations regarding the role of
        the San Miguel River, Sonora, Mexico. *In* Riley
        and Hedrick 1978, pp. 67-82.

BRANIFF, B., and FELGER, Richard S.

1976   (ed.) Sonora: antropología del desierto. Instituto
        Nacional de Antropología e Historia, Colección
        Científica, 27.

BREAZEALE, James F.

1937   Possible effects of soil puddling upon migration
        of primitive people. Southwest Monuments, Monthly
        Report, Supplement, November, pp. 389-390.

BREAZEALE, John M.

1925   An Arizona Cliff Dweller's shawl. Art and Archae-
        ology, 20, no. 2:85-88.

BREED, William J. (See under Schreiber, John P.)

BREMER, Michael (See under Teague, Lynn S.)

BRETERNITZ, Cory D. (See under Breternitz, David A.; Harrill,
    Bruce G.)

BRETERNITZ, David A.   (See also under Miller, William C.; White,
    Adrian S.)

1957a   Additional stone tool types from Concho. Plateau,
        29, no. 4:78-80.

1957b   A brief archaeological survey of the lower Gila
        River. Kiva, 22, nos. 2-3:1-13.

1957c   Heltagito rockshelter (NA 6380). Plateau, 30, no.
        1:1-16.

1957d   Highway salvage archaeology by the Museum of North-
        ern Arizona, 1956-57. Kiva, 23, no. 2:8-17.

1957e   1956 excavations near Flagstaff, Part I. Plateau,
        30, no. 1:22-30.

1957f   1956 excavations near Flagstaff, Part II. Plateau,
        30, no. 2:43-54.

1958   The Calkins Ranch Site, NA 2385: preliminary report.
        Plateau, 31, no. 1:19-20.

1959a   Basketmaker III clay figurine from Flagstaff region.

El Palacio, 66, no. 5:175.

1959b   Excavations at Nantack Village, Point of Pines,
        Arizona. University of Arizona, Anthropological
        Papers, 1, 77 pp.
        Reviewed AA 62:914 (Martin), AAq 26:297 (Rinaldo).

1959c   Excavations at two Cinder Park Phase sites. Plateau,
        31, no. 3:66-72.

1960a   Excavations at three sites in the Verde Valley,
        Arizona. Museum of Northern Arizona, Bulletin 34,
        29 pp.
        Reviewed AA 64:894 (Woodbury), AAq 28:251 (John-
        son).

1960b   Orme Ranch Cave, NA 6656. Plateau, 33:25-39.

1963a   The archaeological interpretation of tree-ring
        specimens for dating Southwestern ceramic styles.
        University of Arizona, dissertation, 526 pp.; Uni-
        versity Microfilms International.

1963b   Excavation of some pre-Sunset eruption pit-houses
        near Flagstaff, Arizona. Plateau, 35, no. 4:135-
        143.

1964   Limonite crystal beads in the Southwest: a query.
        American Antiquity, 30:215.

1966   An appraisal of tree-ring dated pottery in the
        Southwest. University of Arizona, Anthropological
        Papers, 10, 128 pp.
        Reviewed AA 70:819 (Dittert), AAq 33:403 (Gell).

1967a   Ceremonial structures at Double Wall Ruin, site NA
        4207, Navajo Canyon. Plateau, 40, no. 1:22-27.

1967b   The eruption(s) of Sunset Crater: dating and effects.
        Plateau, 40, no. 2:72-76.

1969   Archaeological investigations in Turkey Cave (NA
        2520), Navajo National Monument, 1963. Museum
        of Northern Arizona, Technical Series, 8, 26 pp.

1970   (ed.) Archaeological investigations in Dinosaur
        National Monument, Colorado-Utah, 1964-1965. Uni-
        versity of Colorado Studies, Series in Anthropology,
        17, 167 pp.

1973   Tree-ring dated Basketmaker III and Pueblo I sites
        in Mesa Verde National Park. National Park Service,
        Midwest Archaeological Center (Lincoln), 16 pp.

1975   Mesa Verde Research Center, 1975. Southwestern
        Lore, 41, no. 4:17-21.

BRETERNITZ, D.A., and BRETERNITZ, Cory D.

1973   Inventory of cliff dwellings, Johnson Canyon drain-
        age, Ute Mountain Indian Reservation, 1972. Bureau
        of Indian Affairs, Albuquerque Area Office, 282 pp.

BRETERNITZ, D.A., and NORDBY, Larry V.

1972   Site MV 1824-71, a Basketmaker III pithouse and
        cist on Wetherill Mesa. *In* Archaeological Salvage
        Excavations, Wetherill Mesa, Mesa Verde National
        Park, 1971. National Park Service, Midwest Region
        (Omaha), 42 pp.

BRETERNITZ, D.A., and SCHLEY, Robert A.

1962   Excavations at the New Leba 17 site near Cameron,
        Arizona. Plateau, 35:60-68.

BRETERNITZ, D.A., GIFFORD, James C., and OLSON, Alan P.

1957   Point of Pines phase sequence and utility pottery
        type revisions. American Antiquity, 22:412-416.

BRETERNITZ, D.A., NORDBY, L.V., and NICKENS, Paul R.

1974   Activities of the University of Colorado Mesa Verde
        Archaeological Research Center for 1974. South-
        western Lore, 40:15-22.

BRETERNITZ, D.A., ROHN, Arthur H., and MORRIS, Elizabeth A.

1974   Prehistoric ceramics of the Mesa Verde region.
        Museum of Northern Arizona, Ceramic Series, 5,
        70 pp.

BREW, Alan P. (See also under Flinn, Lynn.)

1962a   The excavation of LA 6481, the Question Mark Site.
        Laboratory of Anthropology Notes, 117D.

1962b   The excavation of LA 6485, the Terrace Site. Labor-
        atory of Anthropology Notes, 117E.

BREW, John Otis (See also under Montgomery, Ross Gordon.)

1935   Digging in southern Utah. Harvard Alumni Bulletin,
        December 20, pp. 404-410.

1937   The first two seasons at Awatovi. American Antiquity, 3, no. 2:122-137.

1939a   Peabody Museum excavations in Arizona. Harvard Alumni Bulletin, 41, no. 27:870-875.

1939b   Preliminary report of the Peabody Museum Awatovi Expedition of 1937. American Antiquity, 5:103-114.

1940   Mexican influence upon the Indian cultures of the southwestern United States in the sixteenth and seventeenth centuries. *In* The Maya and Their Neighbors, ed. C.L. Hay et al., pp. 314-348.

1941   Preliminary report of the Peabody Museum Awatovi Expedition of 1939. Plateau, 13, no. 3:37-48.

1944   On the Pueblo IV and on the Katchina-Tlaloc relations. *In* El Norte de México y el Sur de Estados Unidos, Tercera Reunión de Mesa Redonda sobre Problemas antropológicos de México y Centro América, pp. 241-245. Sociedad mexicana de antropología.

1946   Archaeology of Alkali Ridge, southeastern Utah. Papers of the Peabody Museum of American Archaeology and Ethnology, vol. 21, 345 pp. Reviewed AAq 15:64 (Haury).

BREW, J.O., and DANSON, E.B.

1948   The 1947 reconnaissance and the proposed Upper Gila Expedition of the Peabody Museum of Harvard University. El Palacio, 55, no. 7:211-222.

BREW, J.O., and HACK, John T.

1939   Prehistoric use of coal by Indians of northern Arizona. Plateau, 12, no. 1:8-14.

BREW, Susan A. (See also under Ciolek-Torrello, Richard; Doelle, William H.)

1975   Archaeological assessment of Cañada del Oro. Arizona State Museum, Archaeological Series, 87, 40 pp.

1976   Cañada del Oro sewer and treatment plant survey: final report. Arizona State Museum, Archaeological Series, 96, 25 pp.

BREWER, James W., Jr. (See also under Reed, Erik K.)

1936   An interesting room at Wupatki. Southwestern Monuments Monthly Report, Supplement, May, pp. 401-402.

1946   Anasazi Boghan of Navajo National Monument. Arizona
        Highways, 22 (July):15-16.

BREWER, J.W., and BREWER, Sally

1935   Wupatki petroglyphs. Southwestern Monuments Monthly
        Report, August, pp. 129-132.

1941   A trip to Navajo National Monument. Arizona High-
        ways, 17, no. 7:14-17, 36-37.

BREWER, Jay P.

1936   Prehistory of the Southwest. Minnesota Archaeolo-
        gist, 2, no. 9:1-5.

BREWER, Sally (See under Brewer, James W., Jr.)

BRICE, Chuck L., and PHILLIPS, John B.

1967   A report on the White Rock Cave Site. The Artifact,
        5, no. 3:1-11.

BRITT, Claude, Jr.

1970a   Flint saws from New Mexico. The Redskin, 5, no.
        1:22-23.

1970b   The Lehner Clovis Site. The Redskin, 5, no. 2:
        46-47.

1970c   A Casas Grandes cache pot. The Redskin, 5, no.
        3:74-77.

1971a   A fish effigy cache pot. The Redskin, 6, no. 1:
        10-11.

1971b   Padilla points: a New Mexico type. The Redskin, 6,
        no. 2:52-54.

1971c   Canyon de Chelly and the Anasazi. The Redskin, 6,
        no. 3:96-99.

1973a   Excavations at Antelope House ruin. The Redskin,
        8, no. 1:30-37.

1973b   Pre-Columbian copper bells. The Redskin, 8, no.
        3:94-95.

1973c   An old Navajo trail with associated petroglyph
        trail markers, Canyon de Chelly, Arizona. Plateau,
        46, no. 1:6-11.

1975   Early Navajo astronomical pictographs in Canyon de
        Chelly, northeastern Arizona, U.S.A. *In* Aveni 1975,
        pp. 89-107.

BRODY, J.J. (See also under Ellis, Florence H.; Vytlacil,
Natalie.)

1969   The kiva murals of Pottery Mound. Proceedings of
        the 38th International Congress of Americanists,
        2:101-110.

1977a   Mimbres art rediscovered. School of American Re-
        search, Exploration 1977, pp. 3-7.

1977b   Mimbres painted pottery: art without artists. Uni-
        versity of New Mexico Press, Southwest Indian Arts
        Series, 1, 253 pp.

1978   Mimbres painting and the Northern Frontier. *In*
        Riley and Hedrick 1978, pp. 11-21.

BRODY, J.J., and COLBERG, Anne

1966   A Spanish American homestead near Placitas, New
        Mexico. El Palacio, 73, no. 2:11-20.

BROILO, Frank J.

1971   The Glencoe Project: archaeological salvage in-
        vestigations along U.S. Highway 70 near Ruidoso,
        New Mexico. Laboratory of Anthropology Notes, 68.

1973   Archaeological salvage excavations at three sites
        on the Western Coal Company Fruitland lease, San
        Juan County, New Mexico. Laboratory of Anthro-
        pology Notes, 72.

1974a   Archaeological salvage excavations at three sites
        on the Western Coal Company Fruitland lease, San
        Juan County, New Mexico, 1972. Laboratory of
        Anthropology Notes, 89.

1974b   Archaeological excavations at three sites on the
        Western Coal Company Fruitland lease, San Juan
        County, New Mexico. Awanyu, 2, no. 3:13-35.

BROILO, F.J., and ALLAN, William C.

1973   An archaeological salvage excavation of a Basket
        Maker III site near Naschitti, New Mexico. Labora-
        tory of Anthropology Notes, 82.

1975   Excavation at LA 10943. Awanyu, 3, no. 1:37-45.

BROILO, F.J., and REHER, Charles A.

1977   Research and mitigation considerations in the re-
       gional contract survey. *In* Schiffer and Gumerman
       1977.

BROMS, Robert S.D., and MORIARTY, James R., III

1967   The antiquity and inferred use of stone spheroids
       in Southwestern archaeology. Masterkey, 41, no.
       3:98-112.

BRON, R.T.

1884   Ancient remains in White River Canyon. Annual Re-
       port of the Smithsonian Institution for 1882, pp.
       681-682.

BRONITSKY, Gordon

1975   Jemez and Tiguex: a test of an ethnological infer-
       ence. *In* Frisbie 1975a, pp. 22-46.

1977   An ecological model of trade: prehistoric economic
       change in the northern Rio Grande region of New
       Mexico. University of Arizona, dissertation, 372
       pp.; University Microfilms International.

BROOK, Richard A., DAVIDSON, Howard M., SIMMONS, Alan H., and
STEIN, Pat H.

1977   Archaeological studies of the Liberty to Gila Bend
       230 KV transmission system. Museum of Northern Ari-
       zona, Research Papers, 5, 54 pp.

BROOK, Vernon Ralph (See also under Quimby, Byron.)

1964   The Jornada branch of the Mogollon: the Hueco
       phase. The Artifact, 2, no. 4:5-7.

1965a Cultural traits of the El Paso phase of the Mogol-
       lon. Transactions of the 1st Regional Archaeologi-
       cal Symposium on Southeastern New Mexico and West-
       ern Texas, pp. 18-22.

1965b Surveys and salvage: Southern Pacific jet fuel
       pipeline survey. The Artifact, 3, no. 1:2-5.

1965c Altar piece. The Artifact, 3, no. 2:4-5.

1966a Cruciform artifacts from the vicinity of El Paso,
       Texas. American Antiquity, 31:574-575.

1966b   They didn't barter to fill the larder. The Arti-
         fact, 4, no. 3:1-15.

1966c   The McGregor Site (32:106:16:4; E.P.A.S. 4). The
         Artifact, 4, no. 4:1-22.

1967a   Adobe steps of the El Paso phase. The Artifact, 5,
         no. 1:37-58.

1967b   The Sarge site: an El Paso phase ruin. The Arti-
         fact, 5, no. 2:45-48.

1968a   A Scottsbluff point from the vicinity of El Paso.
         The Artifact, 6, no. 1:17-20.

1968b   A Folsom and other related points found near El
         Paso. The Artifact, 6, no. 3:11-15.

1970   Four archaeo-magnetic dates from the Hot Wells Site
         (EPAS-3). The Artifact, 8, no. 1:1-16.

1971   Some hypotheses about prehistoric settlement in
         the Tularosahueco Bolson between A.D. 1250-1350.
         Transactions of the 6th Regional Archaeological
         Symposium on Southeastern New Mexico and Western
         Texas, pp. 63-82.

1972   The Temporal point: a new diagnostic type. Trans-
         actions of the 7th Regional Archaeological Symposi-
         um for Southeastern New Mexico and Western Texas,
         pp. 83-88.

1975a   Development of prehistoric house types in the Jor-
         nada Branch. Awanyu, 3, no. 4:16-31.

1975b   Some aberrant forms of the Jornada Branch. Pottery
         Southwest, 2, no. 4:2-5.

1977   Hand metates? Awanyu, 5, no. 3:17-35.

BROOK, V.R., and GREEN, John W.

1967   The New Mexico rock art survey. The Artifact, 5,
         no. 3:25-40.

BROOK, V.R., and others

n.d.   The Sabina Mountain Site. El Paso Archaeological
         Society, Special Report no. 7.

BROOKS, Danny, and VIVIAN, R. Gwinn

1975   Archaeological investigation of the Queen Creek
         Floodway Project. Arizona State Museum, Archae-
         ological Series, 66, 91 pp.

BROOKS, Prudence

  1973   An analysis of painted pottery designs of the Casas
          Grandes culture. Awanyu, 1, no. 2:11-33.

BROOKS, Richard H.

  1965   The feasibility of micro-analysis in Southwestern
          archaeological sites. *In* Osborne 1965a, pp. 182-
          185.

  1967   A comparative analysis of bone from Locality 2,
          Tule Springs, Nevada. *In* Wormington and Ellis 1967,
          pp. 403-411.

  1971   Lithic traditions in northwestern Mexico, Paleo-
          Indian to Chalchihuites. University of Colorado,
          dissertation, 203 pp.; University Microfilms Inter-
          national.

BROSTER, John, and GAUTHIER, Rory

  1976   Archaeological clearance survey: Mountain Bell
          underground cable right-of-way. University of New
          Mexico, contract report 101-103T (BIA).

BROTT, C.W. (See under Davis, Emma Lou.)

BROWN, A.L.

  1929   Additional Indian ruins of Clear Creek region.
          Grand Canyon Nature Notes, 3, no. 7:1.

BROWN, Barnum

  1936   The Folsom culture: an occurrence of prehistoric
          man with extinct animals near Folsom, New Mexico.
          Report of the 16th International Geological Con-
          gress, 2:813.

BROWN, Donald H.

  1967   The distribution of sound instruments in the pre-
          historic southwestern United States. Ethnomusi-
          cology, 11:71-90.

  1971   Ethnomusicology and the prehistoric Southwest.
          Ethnomusicology, 15:363-378.

BROWN, F. Martin

  1937a   America's Yesterday. J.B. Lippincott Co., 319 pp.

  1937b   The prehistoric ruins of Castle Park. Southwestern

Lore, 3, no. 2:22-28.

1953   Radiocarbon dates from the Southwest and its pe-
        riphery. Clearinghouse for Southwestern Museums,
        Newsletter, 157:573-577.

BROWN, H.

1899   Stone squares in Arizona. American Antiquarian,
        21:184.

BROWN, James A., and FREEMAN, L.G., Jr.

1964   A Univac analysis of sherd frequencies from the
        Carter Ranch Pueblo, eastern Arizona. American
        Antiquity, 30:162-167.

BROWN, Jeffrey L.

1967   An experiment in problem-oriented highway salvage
        archaeology. Kiva, 33, no. 2:60-66.

1969   A supplement to "A high status burial from Grass-
        hopper Ruin, Arizona." Kiva, 35, no. 2:87-90.

1973   The origin and nature of Salado: evidence from the
        Safford Valley, Arizona. University of Arizona,
        dissertation, 176 pp.; University Microfilms Inter-
        national.

1974   Pueblo Viejo Salado sites and their relationship
        to Western Pueblo culture. The Artifact, 12, no.
        2:1-53.

BROWN, J.L., and GREBINGER, Paul

1969   A lower terrace compound at San Cayetano del Tuma-
        cacori. Kiva, 34, nos. 2-3:185-198.

BROWN, Joy

1975   Preliminary report on the 1975 excavations at site
        5MT3 near Yellow Jacket, Colorado. Southwestern
        Lore, 41, no. 4:47-50.

BROWN, O.H.

1928   Skeleton Cave. Arizona, Old and New, 1, no. 1:7,
        22-24; no. 2:9, 16-18; no. 3:9, 31-32.

BROWN, Patricia Eyring

1976a   An archaeological survey of the Reach 10 realignment of the Granite Reef Aqueduct, Central Arizona Project. Arizona State University, Office of Cultural Resource Management, report no. 8, 19 pp.

1976b   An archaeological survey of the floodwater detention basin, Granite Reef Aqueduct, Reach 5A, Central Arizona Project, Yuma and Maricopa Counties, Arizona. Arizona State University, Office of Cultural Resource Management, report no. 9, 13 pp.

1976c   An archaeological clearance survey of a borrow area associated with the Granite Reef Aqueduct, Central Arizona Project, Maricopa County, Arizona. Arizona State University, Office of Cultural Resource Management, report no. 10, 5 pp.

1976d   Archaeological investigations within a borrow area associated with the Granite Reef Aqueduct, Central Arizona Project, Maricopa County, Arizona. Arizona State University, Office of Cultural Resource Management, report no. 11, 9 pp.

1976e   Archaeological investigations within a floodwater detention basin, Reach 5A, Granite Reef Aqueduct, Central Arizona Project, Yuma and Maricopa Counties, Arizona. Arizona State University, Office of Cultural Resource Management, report no. 12, 11 pp.

1976f   Investigations of archaeological sites along Reach 10 realignment, Granite Reef Aqueduct, Central Arizona Project, Maricopa County, Arizona. Arizona State University, Office of Cultural Resource Management, report no. 13, 63 pp.

1976g   An archaeological survey of the Vaiva Vo/Kohatk Road, Papago Indian Reservation, Southern Arizona. Arizona State University, Office of Cultural Resource Management, report no. 14, 32 pp.

1977a   An archaeological survey of the Reach 9 realignment, Granite Reef Aqueduct, Central Arizona Project, Maricopa County, Arizona. Arizona State University, Office of Cultural Resource Management, report no. 17, 29 pp.

1977b   Investigations of archaeological sites along Reach 9 realignment, Granite Reef Aqueduct, Central Arizona Project, Maricopa County, Arizona. Arizona State University, Office of Cultural Resource Management, report no. 26, 96 pp.

BROWN, P.E., and WEAVER, Donald E., Jr.

1975   Archaeological investigations for the evaluation of alternative sludge disposal for the Yuma Desalting Plant. Arizona State University, Office of Cultural Resource Management, report no. 7, 8 pp.

BRUDER, J. Simon

1975a   Hecla IV: an archaeological survey in the northeastern Papagueria, Arizona. Arizona State University, Office of Cultural Resource Management, report no. 6, 16 pp.

1975b   Historic Papago archaeology. *In* Goodyear 1975, pp. 271-337.

BRUGGE, David M. (See also under Peckham, Stewart L.)

1955   A kiva bell from Bandelier National Monument, New Mexico. American Antiquity, 21:83-84.

1963a   Navajo pottery and ethnohistory. Navajoland Publications, Series 2. Window Rock.

1963b   A Sonoran grooved-stone tool. Katunob, 4, no. 1:11.

1965   Charred maize and "nubbins." Plateau, 38, no. 2: 49-51.

1967   Revised dates for Navajo hogans near Canyon de Chelly. American Antiquity, 32:396-398.

1968   Pueblo influence on Navajo architecture. El Palacio, 75, no. 3:14-20.

1976a   An early Anasazi burial from Ganada, Arizona. Southwestern Lore, 42, nos. 1-2:39-43.

1976b   The horse in Navajo rock art at Chaco Canyon. Awanyu, 4, no. 4:34-46.

1977   The Ye'i or Holy People in Navajo rock art. Awanyu, 5, no. 3:8-16.

BRUIER, Frederick L.

1976   New clues to stone tool function: plant and animal residues. American Antiquity, 41:478-484.

BRUNNER, H.L.

1891   Aboriginal rock mortars near El Paso, Texas. American Anthropologist, o.s., 4:385-386.

BRYAN, Alan L.

1965   Paleo-American prehistory. Idaho State University
        Museum, Occasional Papers, 16.

1972   Summary of the archaeology of Smith Creek and
        Council Hall Caves, White Pine County, Nevada, 1971.
        Nevada Archaeological Survey Reporter, 6, no. 1:6-7.

BRYAN, Bruce

1927a   The Galaz Ruin in the Mimbres Valley. El Palacio,
        23, no. 12:323-337.

1927b   The Mimbres Expedition. Masterkey, 1, no. 4:19-30.

1931a   Excavation of the Galaz Ruin, Mimbres Valley, N.M.
        Masterkey, 4, no. 6:179-189; no. 7:221-226.

1931b   Excavation of the Galaz Ruin, New Mexico. Art and
        Archaeology, 32, nos. 1-2:35-42.

1933a   Archaeology of the Dragoons. El Palacio, 35, nos.
        1-2:1-6.

1933b   Some observations of the prehistoric pottery of
        the Dragoons. El Palacio, 35, nos. 11-12:97-112.

1933c   Unearthing early America. American Magazine of Art,
        26, no. 5:243-246.

1961a   Initial report on Galaz sherds. Masterkey, 35, no.
        1:13-18.

1961b   An Anasazi human effigy from Arizona. Masterkey,
        35, no. 2:56-59.

1962   An unusual Mimbres bowl. Masterkey, 36, no. 1:
        29-32.

1963   A Hohokam "Venus." Masterkey, 37, no. 3:85.

1968   Tule Springs Site re-evaluated. Masterkey, 42,
        no. 3:112.

BRYAN, Frank

1938   A review of the geology of the Clovis finds reported
        by Howard and Cotter. American Antiquity, 4:113-
        130.

BRYAN, Kirk (See also under Hibben, Frank C.)

1926   Recent deposits of Chaco Canyon, New Mexico, in
        relation to the life of prehistoric peoples of
        Pueblo Bonito. Journal of the Washington Academy
        of Science, 16:75-76 (abstract).

1937   Geology of the Folsom deposits in New Mexico and
        Colorado. *In* Early Man, ed. G.G. MacCurdy, pp.
        139-152. Academy of Natural Sciences, Philadelphia.

1938   Prehistoric quarries and implements of pre-Amer-
        indian aspect in New Mexico. Science, 87:343-346.

1939   Stone cultures near Cerro Pedernal and their geo-
        logical antiquity. Bulletin of the Texas Archae-
        ological and Paleontological Society, 11:9-46.

1941   Pre-Columbian agriculture in the Southwest, as con-
        ditioned by periods of alluviation. Annals of the
        Association of American Geographers, 31:219-242.

1950   Flint quarries - the sources of tools and, at the
        same time, the factories of the American Indian.
        Papers of the Peabody Museum of American Archae-
        ology and Ethnology, 17, no. 3, 40 pp.

1954   The geology of Chaco Canyon, New Mexico, in rela-
        tion to the life and remains of the prehistoric
        peoples of Pueblo Bonito. Smithsonian Miscellaneous
        Collections, 122, no. 7, 65 pp.
        Reviewed AA 57:372 (Danson), AAq 21:324 (Stearns).

BRYAN, K., and ALBRITTON, Claude C.

1942   Wind-polished rocks in the Trans-Pecos region,
        Texas and New Mexico. Bulletin of the Geological
        Society of America, 53:1403-1416.

BRYAN, K., and BUTLER, Arthur P., Jr.

1940   Artifacts made of the glassy andesite of San
        Antonio Mountain, Rio Arriba County, New Mexico.
        University of New Mexico Bulletin, Anthropological
        Series, 3, no. 4:26-31.

BRYAN, K., and COLBERT, Edwin H.

1950   The geology and fossil vertebrates of Ventana Cave.
        In Haury 1950b, pp. 75-148.

BRYAN, K., and McCANN, F.T.

1943   Sand dunes and alluvium near Grants, New Mexico.
        American Antiquity, 8, no. 3:281-290.

BRYAN, K., and TOULOUSE, Joseph H., Jr.

1943   The San Jose non-ceramic culture and its relation
        to a Puebloan culture in New Mexico. American
        Antiquity, 8, no. 3:269-280.

BRYAN, W.A.

1929   The recent bone-cavern find at Bishop's Cap, New
        Mexico. Science, 70:39-41.

BRYANT, Vaughan M., Jr. (See also under Shafer, Harry J.;
    Story, Dee Ann; Williams-Dean, Glenna.)

1974   Prehistoric diet in southwest Texas: the coprolite
        evidence. American Antiquity, 39:407-420.

BUCHENBERG, A.E.

1941   Preliminary report on ruin stabilization, South-
        western National Monuments. National Park Service,
        Southwestern Monuments, Special Report no. 29, 6 pp.

BUCKLES, William G.

1968   Archaeology in Colorado; historic tribes. South-
        western Lore, 34, no. 3:53-67.

1971   The Uncompahgre complex: historic Ute archaeology
        and prehistoric archaeology on the Uncompahgre
        Plateau in west central Colorado. University of
        Colorado, dissertation, 1582 pp.; University Micro-
        films International.

BUEHLER, W.C.

1927   Mummy from petrified forest. El Palacio, 23:619.

BUETTNER-JANUSCH, John

1954   Human skeletal material from Deadman Cave, Utah.
        University of Utah, Anthropological Papers, 19,
        9 pp.

BULLARD, William Rotch, Jr. (See also under Cassidy, Francis E.)

1962   The Cerro Colorado site and pit house architecture
        in the southwestern United States prior to A.D. 900.
        Papers of the Peabody Museum of Archaeology and
        Ethnology, 44, no. 2, 205 pp.
            Reviewed AA 65:1186 (Daifuku, AAq 29:249 (Long-
        acre).

BULLEN, Adelaide K.

1947   Archaeological theory and anthropological fact.
        American Antiquity, 13:128-134.

BULLEN, A.K., and BULLEN, Ripley P.

1942   A Pueblo cave site at Tres Piedras, New Mexico.
        American Antiquity, 8:57-64.

BULLEN, Ripley P. (See also under Bullen, Adelaide K.)

1944   Corn goddesses or phalli? American Antiquity, 9,
        no. 4:448-449.

BURGH, Robert F. (See also under Morris, Earl H.)

1932a   Diseases among prehistoric Pueblo peoples. Mesa
        Verde Notes, 3, no. 2:27-28.

1932b   Archaeological methods. Mesa Verde Notes, 3:33-36.

1933   Cliff dweller burial customs. Mesa Verde Notes, 4,
        no. 2:5-7.

1934   The Far View group of ruins. Mesa Verde Notes, 5,
        no. 2:32-36.

1937   Mesa Verde coiled basketry. Mesa Verde Notes, 7,
        no. 2:7-14.

1950   A Fremont Basket Maker house in Dinosaur National
        Monument. Tree-Ring Bulletin, 16, no. 3:19-20.

1959   Ceramic profiles in the western mound at Awatovi,
        northeastern Arizona. American Antiquity, 25:184-
        202.

1960   Potsherds and forest fires in the Pueblo country.
        Plateau, 33:54-56.

BURGH, R.F., and SCOGGIN, Charles

1948   The archaeology of Castle Park. University of
        Colorado Studies, Series in Anthropology, 2, 118
        pp.

BURNET, R.M.P.

1937   Early Man and extinct fauna of the Carlsbad region.
        New Mexico Anthropologist, 2, no. 2:44-45.

1938a   Exploring a new cave...in the Guadalupe Mountains
        of New Mexico. Natural History, 41:374-383.

1938b   The recent skeletal find near Portales. El Palacio,
        44, nos. 10-12:80-84.

BURNS, Peter E.

    1972   The Heron ruin, Grant County, New Mexico. Case
              Western Reserve University, Southwestern New Mexico
              Research Reports, 7, 55 pp.

BURR, R.T.

    1880   Ruins in White River Canyon, Arizona. Annual Re-
              port of the Smithsonian Institution for 1879, pp.
              333-334.

BURROUGHS, Carroll A.

    1959   Searching for cliff dwellers' secrets. National
              Geographic Magazine, 116:618-625.

BURSEY, Joseph A.

    1936   Off the beaten path. New Mexico Magazine, 14, no.
              5:11-13, 38-41.

BURT, W.H.

    1961   A fauna from an Indian site near Redington, Arizona.
              Journal of Mammalogy, 42:115-116.

BURTON, Susan S. (See also under Weaver, Donald E., Jr.)

    1975a   An archaeological reconnaissance survey of the
              Harquahala Valley Flood Control Project. Arizona
              State University, Office of Cultural Resource Man-
              agement, report no. 2, 14 pp.

    1975b   An archaeological overview of the proposed Gila
              Floodway, Maricopa County, Arizona. Arizona State
              University, Office of Cultural Resource Management,
              report no. 5, 25 pp.

    1976   A regional archaeological overview of the Phoenix
              metropolitan area, Maricopa County, Arizona. Ari-
              zona State University, Office of Cultural Resource
              Management, report no. 16, 40 pp.

BUSCH, C.D., RAAB, L. Mark, and BUSCH, R.C.

    1976   Q=A·V: prehistoric water canals in southern Arizona.
              American Antiquity, 41:531-534.

BUSCH, R.C. (See under Busch, C.D.)

BUSHNELL, Geoffrey H.S.

1955   Some Pueblo IV pottery types from Kechipauan, New
        Mexico, U.S.A. Proceedings of the 31st Internation-
        al Congress of Americanists, 2:657-665.

BUSSEY, Stanley D. (See also under Hammack, Laurens C.)

1963   The Llaves site: salvage excavations at LA 5859.
        Laboratory of Anthropology Notes, 23.

1965a   Highway salvage excavations near Aneth, Utah.
        Laboratory of Anthropology Notes, 31.

1965b   The Llaves pipeline salvage project: preliminary
        report. Laboratory of Anthropology Notes, 32.

1966   The Mesita-Laguna highway salvage project: excava-
        tions at LA 8679. Laboratory of Anthropology Notes,
        39.

1972   Late Mogollon manifestations in the Mimbres branch,
        southwestern New Mexico. University of Oregon,
        dissertation, 327 pp.; University Microfilms Inter-
        national.

1975   The archaeology of Lee Village: a preliminary report.
        Center of Anthropological Study (Las Cruces), Mono-
        graph no. 2, 73 pp.

BUTCHER, Devereux

1955   Exploring our prehistoric Indian ruins. National
        Parks Association, Washington.

BUTLER, Arthur P., Jr. (See under Bryan, Kirk.)

BUTLER, Barbara Helen

1971   The people of Casas Grandes: cranial and dental
        morphology through time. Southern Methodist Uni-
        versity, dissertation, 208 pp.; University Micro-
        films International.

BYERS, Douglas S.

1935   An ancient cave town in Arizona. Harvard Alumni
        Bulletin, 37:1070-1075.

BYERS, D.S., and MORSS, Noel

1957   Unfired clay objects from Waterfall Ruin, north-
        eastern Arizona. American Antiquity, 23:81-83.

BYERS, William (See under Martin, Paul Schultz.)

CADY, Jean, and REITER, Paul

    1937   The new Pecos room exhibits. El Palacio, 42:76-80.

CALAMIA, Bob

    1964   Artifacts found in Gila Forest. The Artifact, 2, no. 4:9.

    1965   The corner tang implements. The Artifact, 3, no. 1:6-10.

CALLEN, Eric O., and MARTIN, Paul S.

    1969   Plant remains in some coprolites from Utah. American Antiquity, 34:329-331.

CALVIN, Ross

    1942   Cliff homes of the Gila. New Mexico Magazine, 20, no. 4:16-17, 29-30.

CAMARA-HERNANDEZ, J. (See under Mangelsdorf, Paul C.)

CAMPBELL, John Martin, and ELLIS, Florence H.

    1952   The Atrisco sites: Cochise manifestations in the middle Rio Grande Valley. American Antiquity, 17: 211-221.

CAMPBELL, Robert G.

    1963   Test excavation of Medina rock shelter, Chacuaco Creek Canyon. Southwestern Lore, 29, no. 3:53-60.

    1968   Dating prehistoric rock art of southeastern Colorado. Florida Anthropologist, 21, no. 1:1-7 (also in Southwestern Lore, 35, no. 1:1-10, 1969).

    1969   Prehistoric Panhandle culture on the Chaquaqua Plateau, southeast Colorado. University of Colorado, dissertation, 606 pp.; University Microfilms International.

CAMPBELL, Thomas N. (See also under Baker, William E.; Kelley, J. Charles.)

    1958·   Origin of the mescal bean cult. American Anthropologist, 60:156-160.

CANOUTS, Valetta (See also under Grady, Mark A.; Stewart, Yvonne G.)

    1977   Problem domains in the Santa Rosa Wash project,

Arizona. *In* Schiffer and Gumerman 1977.

CANOUTS, V., and PHILLIPS, David A.

1974   An archaeological survey of the APS Cholla-Saguaro
       345KV transmission line proposed route. Arizona
       State Museum, Archaeological Series, 43, 31 pp.

CANOUTS, V., FRITZ, Gordon L., and HARD, Robert J.

1975   Archaeological survey of APS Cholla-Saguaro pro-
       posed route: Antelope Peak-Superior. Arizona State
       Museum, Archaeological Series, 81, 38 pp.

CANOUTS, V., GERMESHAUSEN, Edward, and LARKIN, Robert

1972   Archaeological survey of the Santa Rosa Wash proj-
       ect. Arizona State Museum, Archaeological Series,
       18, 149 pp.

CANOUTS, V., and others

1975   Archaeological survey of the Orme Reservoir. Ari-
       zona State Museum, Archaeological Series, 92, 409
       pp.

CAPITAN, Louis

1928   Comparison de céramique des Pueblos avec les céra-
       miques eneolithiques du vieux monde. Proceedings
       of the 22nd International Congress of Americanists,
       1:467-469.

CARAVEO, Carlos, and SCHALK, Randall

1977   Archaeological survey of two lineal tracts on Kerr-
       McGee and BLM lands in Rio Puerco drainage. Uni-
       versity of New Mexico, contract report 195-2J (BLM).

CAREY, (Mrs.) C.E.

1926   Archaeological tour, School of American Research,
       August 1926. El Palacio, 21:173-194.

CAREY, Henry A.

1931   An analysis of the northwestern Chihuahua culture.
       American Anthropologist, 33:325-374.

1955   The ancient Indian culture centering in the Casas
       Grandes Valley, northwestern Chihuahua, Mexico.
       American Philosophical Society, Year Book, 1954,
       pp. 313-316.

1956   The Casas Grandes culture, Chihuahua, Mexico. American Philosophical Society, Year Book, 1955, pp. 314-316.

CARLETON, James Henry

1855   Excursions to the ruins of Abo, Quarra, and Gran Quivira, in New Mexico. Annual Report of the Smithsonian Institution for 1854, pp. 296-316 (reprinted 1965, Stagecoach Press, Santa Fe, 61 pp.)

CARLQUIST, David A. (See under Armelagos, George J.)

CARLSON, Raymond

1951   (ed.) A journey into many yesterdays ago. Arizona Highways, 27, no. 5, 44 pp.

CARLSON, Roy L.

1963   Basket Maker III sites near Durango, Colorado. University of Colorado Studies, Series in Anthropology, no. 8, 56 pp.
        Reviewed AA 66:707 (Gunnerson), AAq 30:231 (Lipe).

1964   Two Rosa Phase pit houses. Southwestern Lore, 29, no. 4:69-76.

1965   Eighteenth century Navajo fortresses of the Gobernador district. University of Colorado Studies, Series in Anthropology, no. 10, 116 pp.
        Reviewed AA 69:402 (Ducey), AAq 31:754 (Wilmeth).

1966   Twin Angels Pueblo. American Antiquity, 31:676-682.

1970   White Mountain Redware: a pottery tradition of east-central Arizona and western New Mexico. University of Arizona, Anthropological Papers, 19, 122 pp.
        Reviewed AAq 37:458 (W. Smith).

CARLSON, R.L., and ARMELAGOS, George J.

1965   Cradleboard hoods, not corsets. Science, 194: 204-205.

CARR, Harry

1929   Archaeologists delve into secrets of forgotten race. Masterkey, 2, no. 7:21-31.

CARROLL, Charles (See also under Cattle, Dorothy; Grigg, Paul.)

1976a   Archaeological survey of the Todilto Exploration

and Development Company's Warnock lease. University
of New Mexico, contract report 101-103V (NPS).

1976b   Archaeological survey of ten Anaconda Company proposed exploratory drill sites. University of New
Mexico, contract report 101-103W (NPS).

CARROLL, C., HOOTEN, Jean, and STUART, David

1976   Anaconda P-15, P-17 Jackpile Mines. University of
New Mexico, contract report 101-155 (BIA).

1977   Anaconda Laguna lease #4, Jackpile-Paguate. University of New Mexico, contract report 101-154 (BIA).

CARROLL, C., MARSHALL, Michael P., and STUART, David

1976   Archaeological survey of Public Service Company of
New Mexico right-of-way, Four Corners to Ambrosia
Lake 345 KV transmission line. University of New
Mexico, contract report 101-147 (NPS).

CARTER, Diana B.

1932   Potsherds and their significance. El Palacio, 32,
nos. 7-8:89-101.

CARTER, George F.

1945   Plant geography and culture history in the American
Southwest. Viking Fund Publications in Anthro-
pology, 5, 140 pp.
Reviewed AA 49:272 (Stanislawski), AAq 11:262
(Jones), 266 (Roberts).

1964   Stone circles in the deserts. Anthropological
Journal of Canada, 2, no. 3:2-6.

1966   On pebble tools and their relatives in North America. Anthropological Journal of Canada, 4, no. 4:
10-19.

CARTER, G.F., and ANDERSON, Edgar

1945   A preliminary survey of maize in the southwestern
United States. Annals of the Missouri Botanical
Gardens, 32:297-322.

CARTER, Oscar C.S.

1906   The plateau country of the Southwest and La Mesa
Encantada. Journal of the Franklin Institute
(Philadelphia), June, pp. 451-467.

CARTLEDGE, Thomas R.

1976   Prehistory in Vosberg Valley, central Arizona. *In* Doyel and Haury 1976, pp. 95-104.

1977   Human ecology and changing patterns of co-residence in the Vosberg locality, Tonto National Forest, central Arizona. United States Forest Service, Southwestern Region, Cultural Resources Report no. 17, 197 pp.

CARTLEDGE, T.R., and WEAVER, Donald E., Jr.

1974   An archaeological reconnaissance survey of the Buckhorn-Mesa Flood Control Project. Arizona State University, Office of Cultural Resource Management, report no. 1, 8 pp.

CASEBIER, Dennis (See under King, Chester.)

CASEY, T. Allen

1937   Rheumatic Cliff Dwellers. Mesa Verde Notes, 7, no. 2:1-4.

CASSELL, Richard L.

1945   Prehistoric remains in southern Nevada. Natural History, 54:433.

CASSELLS, E. Steve

1972   A test concerning artificial cranial deformation and status from the Grasshopper site, east-central Arizona. Kiva, 37, no. 2:84-92.

CASSIDY, Donnelly D. (See under Fontana, Bernard L.)

CASSIDY, Francis E., and BULLARD, William R., Jr.

1956   The New Mexico section of the San Juan pipeline. *In* Wendorf, Fox, and Lewis 1956, pp. 4-80.

CATE, Caroline

1970   An introduction to prehistoric southwestern Indian jewelry. The Artifact, 8, no. 2:17-31.

CATTANACH, George S., Jr.

1956   Two Pueblo sites on Trunk 3-C, near Farmington, New Mexico. *In* Wendorf, Fox, and Lewis 1956, pp. 198-204.

1966   A San Pedro Stage site near Fairbank, Arizona.
        Kiva, 32, no. 1:1-24.

1972   Wetherill Mesa excavations, Long House, Mesa Verde
        National Park. National Park Service, Wetherill
        Project, Contribution 51, 2 vols.

CATTLE, Dorothy, CARROLL, Charles, and STUART, David E.

1977   Ethnographic and ethnohistorical investigation of
        eight historic Laguna archaeological sites within
        the Anaconda Company's P-15/P-17 and Dames & Moore
        acreages: the Jackpile Mine, Paguate, New Mexico.
        University of New Mexico, contract report 185-6
        (BIA).

CAUSEY, Christopher S.

1975   An archaeological clearance survey of AFA 532-84, a
        natural gas pipeline serving the American Quazar
        Federal 24-No. 1 well site and AFA 532-106, a natur-
        al gas pipeline serving the Samedan Amoco Federal
        No. 1 well site. School of American Research, con-
        tract #26.

1976a   An archaeological clearance survey of a natural
        gas pipeline serving the G.W. Duffield Storage
        Facility. School of American Research, contract
        #31.

1976b   An archaeological survey of the G.W. Duffield Stor-
        age Facility. School of American Research, contract
        #33.

CAUSEY, C.S., and WHITMORE, Jane

1975   Archaeological clearance survey of two gathering
        lines near Carlsbad, New Mexico, Yates Stonewall
        "EP" right of way and Amax loop line. School of
        American Research, contract #30.

CAYWOOD, Louis R. (See also under Fast, John E.; Spicer, Ed-
    ward H.)

1934   Mesa Verde sandals. Mesa Verde Notes, 5, no. 2:
        19-23.

1935   Tuzigoot - the excavation and repair of a ruin on
        the Verde River near Clarkdale, Arizona. South-
        western Monuments Monthly Report, Supplement, May,
        pp. 248-254.

1937   Tumacacori. Southwestern Monuments Monthly Report,
        August, pp. 157-158.

1942   A plea for dating European materials in Southwestern
        sites. Clearinghouse for Southwestern Museums,
        Newsletter, 4:189-190.

1946a   Save our ruins. Kiva, 11:27-32.

1946b   Walnut Canyon. Arizona Highways, 22, no. 7:27.

1950   Hispanic pottery as a guide in historical studies.
        In Reed and King 1950, pp. 77-97.

1962   (ed.) Archaeological studies at Tonto National Monu-
        ment, Arizona. Southwestern Monuments Association,
        Technical Series, 2, 176 pp.
        Reviewed AA 65:978 (Shutler), AAq 29:528 (Smith).

1966   Excavations at Rainbow House, Bandelier National
        Monument, New Mexico. National Park Service, South-
        west Archaeology Center, Globe.

1972   The restored mission of Nuestra Señora de Guadalupe
        de Zuni, Zuni, New Mexico. St. Michael's Press,
        St. Michael's, Ariz., 101 pp.

CAYWOOD, L.R., and SPICER, Edward H.

1935a   Tuzigoot: the excavation and repair of a ruin on
        the Verde River near Clarkdale, Arizona. National
        Park Service, Field Division of Education, Berkeley,
        119 pp.
        Reviewed AA 39:538 (Stallings).

1935b   Tuzigoot, Arizona's new Pueblo. Arizona Highways,
        11, no. 4:3-5, 27.

CHAMBERLIN, R.V.

1946-   Man and nature in early Utah. Proceedings of the
47   Utah Academy of Science, 24:3-22.

CHANDLER, Susan M. (see under Euler, Robert C.)

CHAPIN, Frederick Hastings

1890   Cliff-dwellings of the Mancos canyon. American
        Antiquarian, 12, no. 4:193-210.

1892   The land of the cliff dwellers. W.B. Clarke & Co.,
        Boston, 188 pp.
        Reviewed AA o.s. 6:100 (Hodge).

CHAPMAN, A.

1916   Among the ruins of Mesa Verde. Out West, 44:153-
        160.

CHAPMAN, Kenneth M. (See also under Bradfield, Wesley.)

1916   Graphic art of the Cave Dwellers. El Palacio, 3,
        no. 2:37-41.

1917   The cave pictographs of the Rito de los Frijoles,
        N.M. El Palacio, 4, no. 1:29-31 (also as Papers
        of the School of American Archaeology, 37, 6 pp.)

1921   What the potsherds tell. Art and Archaeology, 11,
        nos. 1-2:39-44.

1922   Life forms in Pueblo pottery decoration. Art and
        Archaeology, 13, no. 3:120-122.

1923   Casas Grandes pottery. Art and Archaeology, 16:
        25-34.

1926   An archaeological site in the Jornada del Muerto,
        New Mexico. El Palacio, 20, no. 6:118-122.

1927a   Post-Spanish Pueblo pottery. El Palacio, 22:469-
        482.

1927b   Stone wall construction in ancient pueblos and
        cliff dwellings. El Palacio, 23, no. 19:478-485.

1927c   A feather symbol of the ancient Pueblos. El Palacio,
        23, no. 21:526-540.

1930   Ceremonial lightning stones of the upper Rio Grande
        Pueblos. Museum of Northern Arizona, Museum Notes,
        2, no. 11:4.

1938a   Pajaritan pictography: the cave pictographs of the
        Rito de los Frijoles. *In* Hewett 1938c, pp. 139-148.

1938b   Pueblo Indian pottery of the post-Spanish period.
        Laboratory of Anthropology, General Series Bulletin
        4, 14 pp.

1961   New light upon a rare Southwestern pottery type.
        El Palacio, 68:214-217.

1966   Three ceremonial objects. El Palacio, 73, no. 3:
        31.

CHAPMAN, K.M., and ELLIS, Bruce T.

1951   The line-break, problem child of Pueblo pottery.
        El Palacio, 58:251-289.

CHAPMAN, Richard C. (See also under Biella, Jan V.)

    1967   Toadlena highway salvage: final report. Laboratory
            of Anthropology Notes, 102.

    1974   Archaeological survey of a Mobil Oil Company pipe-
            line. University of New Mexico, contract report
            101-101 (BIA).

CHAPMAN, Richard M.

    1973   Lithic analysis techniques. *In* Human Systems Re-
            search 1973.

CHAPPELL, Clifford C. (See under Hayes, Alden C.)

CHARD, Chester S.

    1940   Distribution and significance of ball courts in the
            Southwest. Papers of the Excavators' Club, 1, no.
            2, 18 pp.
            Reviewed AA 45:132 (Haury), AAq 7:419 (McGregor).

CHATFIELD, Jennifer

    1953   Sculptured quartz frog from the Southwest. Brooklyn
            Museum Bulletin, 14, no. 2:1-9.

CHATIN, Janet (See under Renaud, Etienne B.)

CHEEK, Annetta Lyman

    1974   The evidence for acculturation in artifacts: Indians
            and non-Indians at San Xavier del Bac, Arizona.
            University of Arizona, dissertation, 293 pp.; Uni-
            versity Microfilms International.

CHELF, Carl (See also under Davenport, J. Walker.)

    1945   Boat-shaped objects from Val Verde and Bosque
            Counties, Texas. Bulletin of the Texas Archae-
            ological and Paleontological Society, 16:91-97.

CHENHALL, Robert G.

    1967a   The importance of archaeological field records.
            Arizona Archaeologist, 1:11-24.

    1967b   The Silo site. Arizona Archaeologist, 2:1-56.

    1972   Random sampling in an archaeological survey. Ari-
            zona State University, dissertation, 341 pp.; Uni-
            versity Microfilms International.

1975   A rationale for archaeological sampling. *In* Sampling in Archaeology, ed. James W. Mueller, pp. 3-25. University of Arizona Press.

CHITTENDEN, N.G.

1903   Prehistoric rock paintings, etchings, and pictographs in California, Arizona, and New Mexico. Overland Monthly, 42:107-110.

CHRISTENSEN, Ross T.

1949   On the prehistory of Utah Valley. Proceedings of the Utah Academy of Science, Arts and Letters, 25: 101-111.

1960   Some views on archaeology and its role at Brigham Young University. Brigham Young University Archaeological Society, Miscellaneous Papers, 19, 23 pp.

CHRISTENSEN, R.T., and LEIGH, Maxine

1950   Exploring Utah's prehistoric past. Brigham Young University Archaeological Society, Bulletin, 1:1-6.

CIOLEK-TORRELLO, Richard, and BREW, Susan A.

1976   Archaeological test excavation at the San Xavier Bicentennial Plaza site. Arizona State Museum, Archaeological Series, 102, 56 pp.

CIOLEK-TORRELLO, R., and REID, J.J.

1975   Change in household size at Grasshopper. Kiva, 40: 39-47.

CLARK, Arthur B.

1968   Vegetation on archaeological sites compared with non-site locations at Walnut Canyon, Flagstaff, Arizona. Plateau, 40: no. 3:77-90.

CLARK, Darell F.

1967   A net from Chihuahua, Mexico. Kiva, 32, no. 4:121-127.

CLARK, Geoffrey A.

1967   A cache of Papago miniature pottery from Kitt Peak, south-central Arizona. Kiva, 32, no. 4:128-142.

1969   A preliminary analysis of burial clusters at the

Grasshopper site, east central Arizona. Kiva, 35, no. 2:57-86.

CLARK, Robin B.

1972   Westwing-El Sol and El Sol-Agua Fria transmission line study area: phase II. Arizona State Museum, Archaeological Series, 14, 9 pp.

CLARKE, Eleanor P.

1935   Designs on the prehistoric pottery of Arizona. University of Arizona Social Science Bulletin no. 9, 77 pp.

CLARKE, J.C.

1928   Primitive child burials near Flagstaff. El Palacio, 24:206-207.

CLARKE, Locke

1972   Social implications on Black Mesa: shifting functions of the kiva. Student Anthropologist (Prescott, Ariz.), 4, no. 2:6-24.

CLARKE, Steven K.

1974   A method for the estimation of prehistoric Pueblo populations. Kiva, 39, nos. 3-4:283-287.

CLEMEN, Robert T.

1976   Aspects of prehistoric social organization on Black Mesa. In Gumerman and Euler 1976, pp. 113-135.

CLEMENTS, Lydia

1954   A preliminary study of some Pleistocene cultures of the California desert. Masterkey, 28, no. 5: 177-185.

CLENDENEN, Nancy W. (See under Vivian, R. Gwinn.)

CLEVELAND, David (See also under Fawcett, William B.)

CLEVELAND, D.A., and MASSE, W. Bruce

1973   Archaeological survey of Indian Bend Wash. Arizona State Museum, Archaeological Series, 29, 11 pp.

CLEWLOW, C. William, Jr. (See under Donnan, Christopher B.;
Heizer, Robert F.; Pastron, A.G.)

CLONTS, John B.

1974a   Hickiwan Site and PIR route. Arizona State Museum,
Archaeological Series, 40, 5 pp.

1974b   Survey of 15 acres of land 9 miles east of Chandler,
Arizona. Arizona State Museum, Archaeological Series, 41, 6 pp.

CLUNE, Dorris

1960   Textiles and matting from Waterfall Cave, Chihuahua.
American Antiquity, 26:274-277.

CLUNE, Francis J., Jr. (See under Ascher, Robert.)

COALE, George L.

1963   A study of Shoshonean pottery. Tebiwa, 6, no. 2:
1-11.

COBEAN, Robert H. (See under Wiseman, Regge N.)

COCHRAN, Clarion (See under Williamson, Ray A.)

CODY, Bertha P.

1942   Simply strung on a single strand. Masterkey, 16,
no. 5:175-176.

COE, Carol N., and FULLER, Steven L.

1975   Archaeological resources of the Little Colorado and
Apache-Navajo Planning Units (BLM). Arizona State
Museum, Archaeological Series, 82, 49 pp.

COFFIN, Edwin F.

1929   Bee Cave Canyon shelter, Brewster County, Texas.
Museum of the American Indian, Indian Notes, 6, no.
4:407-411.

1932   Archaeological exploration of a rock shelter in
Brewster County, Texas. Museum of the American
Indian, Indian Notes and Monographs, no. 48, 72 pp.

COLBERG-SIGLEO, Anne (See also under Brody, J.J.)

1975   Turquoise mine and artifact correlation for Snaketown Site, Arizona. Science, 189, no. 4201:459-460.

COLBERT, Edwin H. (See also under Bryan, Kirk.)

1973   Further evidence concerning the presence of horse
        at Ventana Cave. Kiva, 39, no. 1:25-33.

COLLIER, Donald (See under Martin, Paul Sidney.)

COLLINS, Michael B.

1969a   Test excavations in Amistad International Reservoir,
        fall, 1967. Texas Archaeological Salvage Project,
        Papers, 16, 103 pp.

1969b   What is the significance of the Southwestern ceram-
        ics found on the Llano Estacado? Transactions of
        the Fifth Regional Archaeological Symposium for
        Southeastern New Mexico and Western Texas.

1971   A review of Llano Estacado archaeology and ethno-
        history. Plains Anthropologist, 16:85-104.

COLLINS, M.B., and HESTER, Thomas Roy.

1968   A wooden mortar and pestle from Val Verde County,
        Texas. Bulletin of the Texas Archaeological Society,
        39:1-8.

COLLINS, Susan Margaret

1975   Prehistoric Rio Grande settlement patterns and the
        inference of demographic change. University of
        Colorado, dissertation, 379 pp.; University Micro-
        films International.

COLTON, Harold Sellers (See also under Colton, Mary-Russell F.;
    Hargrave, Lyndon L.)

1918   The geography of certain ruins near the San Fran-
        cisco Mountains, Arizona. Bulletin of the Geo-
        graphical Society of Philadelphia, 16, no. 2:37-60.

1920   Did the so-called cliff dwellers of central Arizona
        also build "hogans"? American Anthropologist, 22,
        no. 3:298-301.

1927   Some notes on the "Elden Pueblo." Science, 65:141-
        142.

1928a   Archaeological survey in northern Arizona. El
        Palacio, 25:200-201.

1928b   The geographical distribution of potsherds in the
        San Francisco Mountains of Arizona. Proceedings
        of the 20th International Congress of Americanists,
        2, pt. 1:119-121.

1929   Walnut Canyon. Museum of Northern Arizona, Museum
        Notes, 2, no. 3:1-6.

1930a   Arizona Pueblo buried under lava. El Palacio, 29:
        181.

1930b   The Citadel. Museum of Northern Arizona, Museum
        Notes, 2, no. 8:1-4.

1931   The archaeological survey of the Museum of Northern
        Arizona. Museum of Northern Arizona, Museum Notes,
        4, no. 1:1-3.

1932a   Sunset Crater: the effect of a volcanic eruption on
        an ancient Pueblo people. Geographical Review, 22,
        no. 4:582-590.

1932b   A survey of prehistoric sites in the region of
        Flagstaff, Arizona. Bureau of American Ethnology,
        Bulletin 104, 69 pp.

1932c   Walnut Canyon National Monument. Museum of Northern
        Arizona, Museum Notes, 4, no. 11:1-6.

1933a   Pueblo II in the San Francisco Mountains, Arizona.
        Museum of Northern Arizona, Bulletin 4, pp. 3-14.

1933b   Wupatki, the Tall House. Museum of Northern Ari-
        zona, Museum Notes, 5, no. 11:61-64.

1933c   The earliest dated dwelling in the United States.
        Science, 77:240.

1934a   Archaeological report on excavation at Wupatki.
        Southwestern Monuments Monthly Report, February,
        pp. 2-5.

1934b   Archaeological report on Wupatki. Southwestern
        Monuments Monthly Report, March, pp. 16-19.

1935a   Discovery of a large oval "bowl" at Flagstaff.
        Science, 82, no. 2132:9.

1935b   Stages in northern Arizona prehistory. Museum of
        Northern Arizona, Museum Notes, 8, no. 1:1-7.

1936a   Hopi coal mines. Museum of Northern Arizona, Museum
        Notes, 8, no. 12:59-61.

1936b   The rise and fall of the prehistoric population of
        northern Arizona. Science, 84, no. 2181:337-343.

1938a   Economic geography of the Winona Phase. Southwest-
        ern Lore, 3, no. 4:64-66.

1938b   Names of the four culture roots in the Southwest.
        Science, 87, no. 2268:551-552.

1938c   The basic culture of the early pottery making people
         who lived about the San Francisco Mountains, Arizona.
         New Mexico Anthropologist, 2, nos. 4-5:82.

1939a   An archaeological survey of northwestern Arizona
         including the descriptions of fifteen new pottery
         types. Museum of Northern Arizona, Bulletin 16,
         29 pp.

1939b   The date of Three Turkey House. Tree-Ring Bulletin,
         5, no. 4:26.

1939c   Prehistoric culture units and their relationships
         in northern Arizona. Museum of Northern Arizona,
         Bulletin 17, 76 pp.
            Reviewed AAq 6:189 (Reed), 366 (Steward).

1939d   The reducing atmosphere and oxidizing atmosphere
         in prehistoric Southwestern ceramics. American
         Antiquity, 4, no. 3:224-231.

1939e   Three Turkey House. Plateau, 12, no. 2:26-31.

1939f   Primitive pottery firing methods. Museum of North-
         ern Arizona, Museum Notes, 11, no. 1.

1939g   Find Indian buried under 400 arrows. Science News
         Letter, 36, no. 12:184.

1940a   Notes on a pottery type called Lino Gray. American
         Antiquity, 5:338.

1940b   Tracing the lost mines of the padres. Plateau, 13,
         no. 2:17-22.

1940c   Ball court notes. Plateau, 13, no. 1:5; no. 2:22.

1941a   Black Mesa Black-on-white. American Antiquity, 7:
         164-165.

1941b   Prehistoric trade in the Southwest. Scientific
         Monthly, 52:308-319.

1941c   Winona and Ridge Ruin, Part II: notes on the tech-
         nology and taxonomy of the pottery. Museum of
         Northern Arizona, Bulletin 19, 75 pp.
            Reviewed AA 43:654 (Rinaldo and Martin).

1942   Archaeology and the reconstruction of history.
         American Antiquity, 8, no. 1:33-40.

1943a   The principle of analogous pottery-types. American
         Anthropologist, 43:316-320.

1943b   Reconstruction of Anasazi history. Proceedings of
         the American Philosophical Society, 86, no. 2:264-
         269.

1944   Troy Town on the Hopi Mesas. Scientific Monthly, 58, no. 2:129-134.

1945a   Another unfired sherd from Black Dog Cave, Logan-ville Gray. Plateau, 17, no. 4:69-70.

1945b   The Patayan problem in the Colorado River Valley. Southwestern Journal of Anthropology, 1, no. 1: 114-121.

1945c   A revision of the date of the eruption of Sunset Crater. Southwestern Journal of Anthropology, 1, no. 3:345-355.

1945d   Sunset Crater. Plateau, 18:7-14.

1946a   "Fools' names like fools' faces..." Plateau, 19, no. 1:1-8.

1946b   The Sinagua: a summary of the archaeology of the region of Flagstaff, Arizona. Museum of Northern Arizona, Bulletin 22, 328 pp. Reviewed AAq 13:258 (Reed).

1947   A revised date for Sunset Crater. Geographical Review, 37, no. 1:144.

1948   Indian life - past and present. *In* The Inverted Mountains: canyons of the West, ed., Roderick Peattie, pp. 111-128. Vanguard Press.

1949   The prehistoric population of the Flagstaff area. Plateau, 22, no. 2:21-25.

1952a   Kendrick Spring: a prehistoric walk-in well. Plateau, 25, no. 1:19-20.

1952b   Pottery types of the Arizona Strip and adjacent areas in Utah and Nevada. Museum of Northern Arizona, Ceramic Series, 1, 98 pp. Reviewed AAq 21:327 (Meighan).

1953a   Field methods in archaeology: prepared for archaeological expeditions of the Museum of Northern Arizona. Museum of Northern Arizona, Technical Series, 1, 30 pp.

1953b   Potsherds: an introduction to the study of prehistoric Southwestern ceramics and their use in historic reconstruction. Museum of Northern Arizona, Bulletin 25, 86 pp. Reviewed AA 57:162 (Rowe), AAq 20:187 (Brainerd).

1955a   Check list of Southwestern pottery types. Museum of Northern Arizona, Ceramic Series, 2, 43 pp. Reviewed AAq 21:327 (Meighan).

1955b   Pottery types of the Southwest: Wares 8A, 8B, 9A,
          9B, Tusayan Gray, and White Ware, Little Colorado
          Gray, and White Ware. Museum of Northern Arizona,
          Ceramic Series, 3[A], 98 pp. (not numbered).
          Reviewed AAq 23:200 (Wheat).

1956   Pottery types of the Southwest: Wares 5A, 5B, 6A,
          6B, 7A, 7B, 7C, San Juan Red Ware, Tsegi Orange
          Ware, Homolovi Orange Ware, Winslow Orange Ware,
          Awatovi Yellow Ware, Jeddito Yellow Ware, Sicho-
          movi Red Ware. Museum of Northern Arizona, Ceramic
          Series, 3C, 148 pp. (not numbered).
          Reviewed AAq 25:619 (McGregor).

1957   Stonemans Lake. Plateau, 29:56-58.

1958   The Hubbell trading post at Ganado. Plateau, 30:
          85-88.

1960   Black Sand: prehistory in northern Arizona. Uni-
          versity of New Mexico Press, 132 pp.
          Reviewed AA 64:443 (Schwartz), AAq 27:256 (Rinaldo).

1961   Reminiscences in Southwest archaeology: IV. Kiva,
          26, no. 3:1-7.

1965a   Experiments in raising corn in the Sunset Crater
          ashfall area east of Flagstaff, Arizona. Plateau,
          37, no. 3:77-79.

1965b   Long Fort, who built it? Plateau 38, no. 2:33-35.

1965c   Check list of Southwestern pottery types. Museum
          of Northern Arizona, Ceramic Series, 2, revised,
          55 pp.

1968   Frontiers of the Sinagua. *In* Schroeder 1968a, pp.
          9-16.

1970   The aboriginal Southwestern Indian dog. American
          Antiquity, 35:153-159.

COLTON, H.S., and BAXTER, Frank C.

1932   Days in the Painted Desert and the San Francisco
          Mountains: a guide. Museum of Northern Arizona,
          Bulletin, 2 (2nd ed.), 113 pp.

COLTON, H.S., and HARGRAVE, Lyndon L.

1935   Naming pottery types and rules of priority. Science,
          82, no. 2153:462-463.

1937   Handbook of northern Arizona pottery wares. Museum

of Northern Arizona, Bulletin 11, 267 pp.
Reviewed AA 40:489 (Reiter), AAq 5:261 (Matson
and Ford).

COLTON, H.S., HARGRAVE, L.L., and HUBERT, Virgil

1940   Handbook of northern Arizona pottery wares. Supplement no. 1 - colored plates of San Juan Red Ware
and Tsegi Orange Ware. Museum of Northern Arizona,
12 plates.

COLTON, H.S., EULER, R., DOBYNS, H., and SCHROEDER, A.H.

1958   Pottery types of the Southwest: Wares 14, 15, 16,
17, 18, Alameda Brown Ware, Tizon Brown Ware, Lower
Colorado Buff Ware, Prescott Gray Ware, San Francisco Mt. Gray Ware. Museum of Northern Arizona,
Ceramic Series, 3D, 164 pp. (not numbered).

COLTON, Mary-Russell F., and COLTON, Harold S.

1918   The little-known small house ruins in the Coconino
forest. Memoirs of the American Anthropological
Association, 5, no. 4:101-126.

1931   Petroglyphs, the record of a great adventure. American Anthropologist, 33:32-37.

COMPTON, Carl B.

1956   An introductory survey of bird-form vessels. Bulletin of the Texas Archaeological Society, 27.

1957   More cruciforms and some problematical objects.
Bulletin of the Texas Archaeological Society, 28:
127-134.

CONKLING, Roscoe P.

1932   Conkling Cavern: the discoveries in the bone cave
at Bishop's Cap, New Mexico. Bulletin of the West
Texas Historical and Scientific Society, 44, no. 4:
7-19.

CONNOLLY, Charlene, and ECKERT, Nan

1969   The archaeological significance of the desert tor-
toise. Nevada State Museum, Anthropological Papers,
14:80-93.

CONNOLLY, Florence M. (See also under Tanner, Clara Lee.)

1940   Two pottery types from east-central Arizona: a

revised and a new description. Southwestern Lore, 5, no. 4:77-78.

CONNOR, Sydney

1943   Excavations at Kinnikinnick, Arizona. American Antiquity, 8:376-379.

CONRAD, Carl M. (See under Haury, Emil W.)

CONTRERAS, Eduardo

1970   Restauraciones en Casas Grandes, 1969-70. Instituto Nacional de Antropología e Historia, Boletin, 40:4-11.

COOK, Edwin A.

1961   A new Mogollon structure. Kiva, 26, no. 3:24-32.

COOK, Harold J.

1927   New geological and paleontological evidence bearing on the antiquity of mankind in America. Natural History, 27, no. 3:240-247.

1928   Glacial-age man in New Mexico. Scientific American, 139, no. 1:38-40.

COOLEY, Harold E.

1938   Mimbres "modernists." New Mexico Magazine, 16, no. 12:20-21, 40-41.

COOLEY, Maurice E. (See also under Turner, Christy G., II.)

1959   Ancient cave deposit near Thoreau, New Mexico. Plateau, 31:89.

COON, John Henry

1948   The Three Turkey House, an ancient settlement in a remote section of Arizona. Natural History, 42:382.

COPE, E.D.

1875   Report on the remains of population observed on and near the Eocene plateau of northwestern New Mexico. Report of the Geographical Explorations and Surveys West of the 100th Meridian, pp. 166-173.

CORBETT, John M.

1962   Aztec Ruins National Monument, New Mexico. National
        Park Service, Historical Handbook Series, 36, 66 pp.

CORDELL, Linda S.

1975a   Predicting site abandonment at Wetherill Mesa. Kiva,
        40, no. 3:189-202.

1975b   The 1974 excavation of Tijeras Pueblo, Cibola Na-
        tional Forest, New Mexico. United States Forest
        Service, Southwestern Region, Archeological Report
        5, 82 pp.

1977   Late Anasazi farming and hunting strategies: one
        example of a problem in congruence. American An-
        tiquity, 42:449-461.

CORLEY, John A.

1965   Proposed eastern extension of the Jornada branch of
        the Mogollon culture. Transactions of the 1st Re-
        gional Archaeological Symposium on Southeastern
        New Mexico and Western Texas, pp. 30-36.

CORNELIUS, Olive Frazier

1938   Basket maker sandals (?). Southwestern Lore, 3,
        no. 4:74-78.

CORNELIUS, T.H. (See under Flora, I.F.)

CORNWALL, Claude C.

1936   Restoration of an ancient pueblo, Kinishba. Indians
        At Work, 4, no. 9:34-37.

CORRUCCINI, Robert S.

1972   The biological relationships of some prehistoric
        and historic Pueblo populations. American Journal
        of Physical Anthropology, 37, no. 3:373-388.

COSGROVE, Cornelius Burton (See also under Cosgrove, Harriet S.;
    Kidder, Alfred V.)

1923   Two kivas at Treasure Hill. El Palacio, 15, no. 2:
        18-21.

1929   The Basket makers and their artifacts. Harvard
        Alumni Bulletin, Feb. 28, pp. 624-627.

1947   Caves of the Upper Gila and Hueco areas in New Mexico

and Texas. Papers of the Peabody Museum of American
Archaeology and Ethnology, 24, no. 2, 181 pp.
Reviewed AAq 14:236 (Lehmer).

1948   Hueco Mt. caves. National Speleogical Society, no.
10:79-84.

COSGROVE, C.B., and COSGROVE, H.S.

1965   The Cosgrove report; a preliminary survey of the
El Paso Pueblo district. El Paso Archaeological
Society, Special Report no. 3, 23 pp.

COSGROVE, C.B., Jr., and FELTS, W.E.

1927a   How we found the Casa Grande graveyards. Masterkey,
1, no. 1:15-19.

1927b   At work on the Mimbres. Masterkey, 1, no. 3:21-24.

COSGROVE, Harriet S. (See also under Cosgrove, Cornelius B.;
Kidder, Alfred V.)

COSGROVE, H.S., and COSGROVE, C.B.

1932   The Swarts Ruin, a typical Mimbres site in southwestern New Mexico. Papers of the Peabody Museum
of American Archaeology and Ethnology, 15, no. 1,
178 pp.

COSNER, Aaron J.

1960   A Salado spinning stick. Kiva, 26, no. 1:16-18.

COTTER, John L.

1937   The occurrence of flints and extinct animals in
pluvial deposits near Clovis, New Mexico, Part IV.
Proceedings of the Academy of Natural Sciences of
Philadelphia, 89:2-16.
Reviewed AAq 4:291 (Eiseley).

1938   The occurrence of flints and extinct animals in
pluvial deposits near Clovis, New Mexico, Part VI.
Proceedings of the Academy of Natural Sciences of
Philadelphia, 90:113-117.

1941   Tuzigoot National Monument. Arizona Highways, 17,
no. 11:20-23, 39.

1954   Indications of a Paleo-Indian co-tradition for North
America. American Antiquity, 20:64-67.

COUNT, E.W.

1930   A Grand Canyon cliff-ruin. Grand Canyon Nature
        Notes, 4, no. 5:31.

COWAN, J.L.

1910   Prehistoric apartment houses of the Southwest.
        Overland Monthly, 44:340-346.

COWGILL, George

1957   Early agriculture in the American Southwest. Anthro-
        pology Tomorrow, 5, no. 2:139-150.

CRABTREE, Don E.

1973   Experiments in replicating Hohokam points. Tebiwa,
        16, no. 1:10-45.

CRAMPTON, C. Gregory

1960   Historical sites in Glen Canyon, mouth of San Juan
        River to Lees Ferry. University of Utah, Anthro-
        pological Papers, 46, 146 pp.
        Reviewed AA 64:688 (Koehler).

1962   Historical sites in Glen Canyon, mouth of Hansen
        Creek to mouth of San Juan River. University of
        Utah, Anthropological Papers, 61, 128 pp.
        Reviewed AAq 29:529 (Schroeder).

1964a   The San Juan Canyon historical sites. University
        of Utah, Anthropological Papers, 70, 92 pp.

1964b   Historical sites in Cataract and Narrow Canyons,
        and in Glen Canyon to California Bar. University
        of Utah, Anthropological Papers, 72, 122 pp.

CRANE, H.R.

1955   Antiquity of the Sandia culture: carbon-14 measure-
        ments. Science, 122:689-690.

CRESSMAN, Luther S.

1951   Western prehistory in the light of carbon 14 dat-
        ing. Southwestern Journal of Anthropology, 7:289-
        313.

CRIM, J.J., Jr. (See under McConnell, Robert B.)

CRIMMINS, Martin L.

1925   Petroglyphs of the Jumanos. El Palacio, 19:44.

1926   Petroglyphs, pictographs, and the diffusion of prim-
        itive culture. Art and Archaeology, 21:297-298.

1929   An archaeological survey of the El Paso district.
        Bulletin of the Texas Archaeological and Paleonto-
        logical Society, 1:36-42.

1930   Some Indian illustrations, prehistoric and historic.
        Bulletin of the Texas Archaeological and Paleonto-
        logical Society, 2:69-75.

1931   The pictographs at the Hueco Tanks. Bulletin of
        the Texas Archaeological and Paleontological Society,
        3:24-30.

1932   The Aztec influence on the primitive culture of the
        Southwest. Bulletin of the Texas Archaeological
        and Paleontological Society, 4:32-39.

CROSS, John L.

1960   The artifacts of Camp Maple Dell, Payson Canyon,
        Utah County, Utah. Utah Archaeology, 6, no. 2:11-15.

1962   Report of an Indian skull find. Utah Archaeology,
        8, no. 1:14-19.

1963   Unusual petroglyph find in Utah. Utah Archaeology,
        9, no. 1:1.

1969   "Manitou stones." Utah Archaeology, 15, no. 3:10-14.

CROSS, R.T.

1954   Arizona's Cliff Dwellings. Plateau, 27, no. 2:18-20.

CROUSE, Hubert Y.

1954   A Folsom point from the Uintah Basin, Utah. Master-
        key, 28, no. 2:50-51.

CRUMRINE, N. Ross

1974   God's Daughter-in-Law, the Old Man, and the Olla:
        an archaeological challenge. Kiva, 39, nos. 3-4:
        277-281.

CUMMINGS, Byron

1910   The ancient inhabitants of the San Juan Valley.
        Bulletin of the University of Utah, vol. III, no. 3,
        pt. 2, 45 pp.

1915a   Kivas of the San Juan drainage. American Anthro-
        pologist, 17, no. 2:272-282.

1915b   The textile fabrics of the Cliff Dwellers. National
        Association of Cotton Manufacturers, Boston.

1920   The National Monuments of Arizona. Art and Archae-
        ology, 10:27-36.

1927a   Ancient canals of the Casa Grande. Progressive
        Arizona, 3, no. 5:9-10.

1927b   Pithouse people in Arizona. El Palacio, 23:602-603.

1928   Cochise of yesterday. Arizona, Old and New, 1, no.
        4:9-10, 26-28.

1930   Turkey Hill ruin. Museum of Northern Arizona,
        Museum Notes, 2, no. 11:6.

1935a   The archaeology of the Southwest. Kiva, 1, no. 1:
        1-2.

1935b   Prehistoric pottery of the Southwest. Kiva, 1, no.
        2:1-8.

1936   Shall Arizona save and preserve her heritage? Kiva,
        2:5-8.

1938   Kinishba - the Brown House. Kiva, 4, no. 1:1-4.

1939   Early days in Utah. *In* Brand and Harvey 1939, pp.
        117-120.

1940   Kinishba, a prehistoric pueblo of the Great Pueblo
        Period. Hohokam Museum Association and University
        of Arizona, 128 pp.
        Reviewed AA 43:653 (Martin).

1941   Segazlin Mesa ruins. Kiva, 7, no. 1:1-4.

1945   Some unusual kivas near Navajo Mountain. Kiva, 10,
        no. 4:30-36.

1953   First inhabitants of Arizona and the Southwest.
        Cummings Publication Council, Tucson, 251 pp.

CUMMINGS, Ellen (See under Roubicek, Dennis.)

CUMMINGS, Malcolm B.

1936   Mountain sheep effigies. American Antiquity, 2:
        130-132.

CUMMINGS, Thomas S. (See under Fenenga, Franklin.)

CUMMINS, Gary T. (See under Hammack, Nancy S.)

CURREY, D.R. (See under Madsen, David B.)

CUSHING, Frank Hamilton

   1886   A study of Pueblo pottery as illustrative of Zuni
          culture growth. Fourth Annual Report of the Bureau
          of American Ethnology, pp. 467-521.

   1888   Ancient cities in Arizona. American Antiquarian,
          10:325-326.

   1890   Preliminary notes on the origin, working hypothesis
          and primary researches of the Hemenway Southwestern
          Archaeological Expedition. 7th International Con-
          gress of Americanists, Compte-rendu, pp. 151-194.

CUTLER, Hugh C. (See also under Bohrer, Vorsila L.; Martin,
   Paul Sidney.)

   1951   The oldest corn in the world. Bulletin of the Chi-
          cago Natural History Museum, 22, no. 2:4-5.

   1960   Cultivated plant remains from Waterfall Cave, Chi-
          huahua. American Antiquity, 26:277-279.

   1966   Corn, cucurbits, and cotton from Glen Canyon. Uni-
          versity of Utah, Anthropological Papers, 80, 126 pp.

CUTLER, H.C., and BLAKE, Leonard W.

   1970   Plants from Arizona J:6:1. Plateau, 43, no. 1:42-44.

CUTLER, H.C., and KAPLAN, Lawrence

   1956   Some plant remains from Montezuma Castle and nearby
          caves. Plateau, 28, no. 4:98-100.

CUTLER, H.C., and MEYER, Winton

   1965   Corn and cucurbits from Wetherill Mesa. *In* Osborne
          1965a, pp. 136-152.

CUTLER, H.C., and WHITAKER, T.W.

   1961   History and distribution of the cultivated cucurbits
          in the Americas. American Antiquity, 26:469-485.

DAIFUKU, Hiroshi

   1952   A new conceptual scheme for prehistoric cultures in
          the southwestern United States. American Anthropolo-
          gist, 54, no. 2:191-200.

1961   Jeddito 264: a report on the excavation of a Basket-
        maker III-Pueblo I site in northeastern Arizona.
        Papers of the Peabody Museum of Archaeology and
        Ethnology, 33, no. 1, 86 pp.
        Reviewed AA 64:671 (Woodbury), AAq 27:604 (Olson).

DALLEY, Gardiner F. (See under Marwitt, John P.)

DANFELSER, M.A. (See under Green, Roger C.)

DANIEL, D. Scott (See under Sims, Jack R., Jr.)

DANIELS, Helen Sloan (See also under Flora, I.F.)

1940   (ed.) The Durango Public Library Museum project.
        3 vols., Durango, Colorado.
        Reviewed AAq 7:85 (Amsden).

DANIELS, M.

1916a   Mesa Verde and Casa Grande National Parks. American
        Forestry, 22:139-145.

1916b   Ancient cliff dwellings of the Mesa Verde. American
        Institute of Architects Journal, 4:384-388.

DANSON, Edward Bridge (See also under Brew, John Otis; Pilles,
    Peter J., Jr.)

1950   Preliminary report of the Peabody Museum Upper
        Gila Expedition, Reconnaissance Division, 1949. El
        Palacio, 57:383-391.

1954   University of Arizona archaeological fieldwork,
        1952-1953. Southwestern Lore, 19, no. 4:12.

1957   An archaeological survey of west central New Mex-
        ico and east central Arizona. Papers of the Peabody
        Museum of American Archaeology and Ethnology, 44,
        no. 1, 133 pp.
        Reviewed AA 60:606 (Reed), AAq 23:448 (Rinaldo).

1958   The Glen Canyon project. Plateau, 30, no. 3:75-78.

1961   Early Man points from the vicinity of Sanders, Ari-
        zona. Plateau, 34:67-68.

1967   A boned porcupine tail from Sedona, Arizona. Pla-
        teau, 40, no. 2:59-60.

DANSON, E.B., and MALDE, Harold E.

1950   Casa Malpais, a fortified Pueblo site at Springerville,

Arizona. Plateau, 22, no. 4:61-67.

DANSON, E.B., and WALLACE, Roberts M.

1956   A petrographic study of Gila Polychrome. American
       Antiquity, 22:180-183.

DAUGHERTY, Richard D.

1962   The Intermontane Western Tradition. American An-
       tiquity, 28:144-150.

DAVENPORT, J. Walker

1938a Archaeological exploration of Eagle Cave, Langtry,
       Texas. Witte Memorial Museum, Bulletin 4, 32 pp.

1938b Big Bend Basket Makers. National Archaeological
       News, 1:22-23.

DAVENPORT, J.W., and CHELF, Carl

1941   Painted pebbles from the lower Pecos and Big Bend
       regions of Texas. Witte Memorial Museum, Bulletin
       5, 23 pp.

DAVIDSON, Howard M. (See under Brook, Richard A.; James,
    Charles P., III.)

DAVIN, Eric, and DOLPHIN, Gabrielle

1973   Petroglyphs of Wupatki. Southwestern Lore, 39, no.
       1:1-8.

DAVIS, E.C.

1932   Pueblo excavation near Houck, Arizona. El Palacio,
       33:128-129.

1941   Work at San Jon camp site. El Palacio, 48:164.

DAVIS, Emma Lou

1964   Anasazi mobility and Mesa Verde migrations. Uni-
       versity of California (Los Angeles), dissertation,
       378 pp.; University Microfilms International.

1965   Small pressures and cultural drift as explanations
       for abandonment of the San Juan area, New Mexico
       and Arizona. American Antiquity, 30:353-355.

DAVIS, E.L., and WINKLER, James H.

1959   A late Mesa Verde site in the Rio Puerco Valley.

El Palacio, 66, no. 3:92-100.

1975   Ceremonial rooms as kiva alternatives: SOC-45 and
        SDV-3. *In* Frisbie 1975a, pp. 47-59.

DAVIS, E.L., and WINSLOW, Sylvia

1965   Giant ground figures of the prehistoric deserts.
        Proceedings of the American Philosophical Society,
        109, no. 8:8-21.

DAVIS, E.L., BROTT, C.W., and WEIDE, D.L.

1968   The Western lithic co-tradition.   San Diego Museum
        Papers, no. 6, 97 pp.
        Reviewed AA 73:417 (Tuohy).

DAVIS, E.L., TRUE, Delbert, and STERUD, Gene

1965   Notes on two sites in eastern California: unusual
        finds. University of California Archaeological
        Survey, Annual Report 7:323-332.

DAVIS, E. Mott (See under Jelks, Edward B.)

DAVIS, Gordon

1975   Archaeological conservation at Salmon Ruin, New
        Mexico. The Artifact, 13, no. 3:15-37.

DAVIS, Irvine

1959   Linguistic clues to northern Rio Grande prehistory.
        El Palacio, 66, no. 3:73-84.

DAVIS, James T.

1959   Further notes on clay human figurines in the western
        United States. University of California Archaeo-
        logical Survey, Report no. 48:16-31.

1960   An appraisal of certain speculations on prehistoric
        Puebloan subsistence. Southwestern Journal of
        Anthropology, 16:15-21.

DAVIS, Jan

1968   A postulated typical dwelling at Hot Well (site
        EPAS 3). The Artifact, 6, no. 2:17-24.

DAVIS, John V. (See also under Everitt, Cindi.)

1975   A Paleo-Indian projectile point from Hueco Firing

Range. The Artifact, 13, no. 1:26-29.

DAVIS, J.V., and TONESS, Kay S.

1974   A rock art inventory at Hueco Tanks State Park,
        Texas. El Paso Archaeological Society, Special
        Report no. 12, 114 pp.

DAVIS, Leslie B.

1967   A stone head from near Casas Grandes Viejo, Chihua-
        hua, Mexico. The Artifact, 5, no. 1:33-35.

1968   Recent excavations at Hot Well site. Transactions
        of the 3rd Regional Archaeological Symposium on
        Southeastern New Mexico and Western Texas, pp. 23-32.

1969   Bishop Cap Cave. Transactions of the 5th Regional
        Archaeological Symposium on Southeastern New Mexico
        and Western Texas, pp. 35-43.

DAVIS, Natalie Y., and GOSS, Robert C.

1977   Cocospera: lonely sentinel of resurrection. El
        Palacio, 83, no. 2:24-43.

DAVIS, Phyllis (See under Bice, Richard A.)

DAVIS, Watson

1931   Investigation of cliff dwelling on Arizona-New
        Mexico line. Science Service, Research Announcement
        no. 52, 2 pp.

1932   Oldest house in United States. El Palacio, 33:182-
        184.

DAVIS, William (See under Graham, John A.)

DAWSON, Jerry (See also under Judge, W. James.)

DAWSON, J., and JUDGE, W.J.

1969   Paleo-Indian sites and topography in the middle
        Rio Grande Valley of New Mexico. Plains Anthro-
        pologist, 14:149-163.

DAWSON, J., and STANFORD, Dennis

1975   The Linger site: a re-investigation. Southwestern
        Lore, 41, no. 4:11-16.

DAY, Kent C. (See also under Sharrock, Floyd W.)

1961   Archaeological survey and testing in Moqui Canyon and Castle Wash, 1961. Utah Archaeology, 7, no. 4: 12-14.

1962   Preliminary report of the Flaming Gorge survey. Utah Archaeology, 8, no. 4:3-7.

1964   Thorne Cave, northeastern Utah: archaeology. American Antiquity, 30:50-59.

1965   Archaeological survey of the Uintah Basin, northeastern Utah. University of Utah, Dept. of Anthropology.

1966a   Preliminary report on excavations at Gunlock Flats, southwestern Utah. Utah Archaeology, 12, no. 2:2-9.

1966b   Excavations at Gunlock Flats, southwestern Utah. University of Utah, Miscellaneous Collected Papers, 11, Anthropological Papers, 83:1-48.

DAY, K.C., and DIBBLE, David S.

1963   Archeological survey of the Flaming Gorge Reservoir area, Wyoming-Utah. University of Utah, Anthropological Papers, 65, 90 pp.

DEAN, Jeffrey S. (See also under Bannister, Bryant; Lindsay, Alexander J., Jr.; Plog, Fred T.; Robinson, William J.)

1969a   Chronological analysis of Tsegi Phase sites in northeastern Arizona. University of Arizona, Laboratory of Tree-Ring Research, Papers, no. 3, 207 pp.
        Reviewed AA 73:935 (Fritz).

1969b   Dendrochronology and archaeological analysis: a possible Ute example from southwestern Colorado. Southwestern Lore, 35, no. 3:29-41.

1970   Aspects of Tsegi Phase social organization: a trial reconstruction. *In* Longacre 1970b, pp. 140-174.

1975   Tree-ring dates from Colorado W: Durango area. Laboratory of Tree-Ring Research, University of Arizona.

1978   An evaluation of the initial SARG research design. *In* Euler and Gumerman 1978, pp. 103-117.

DEAN, J.S., and ROBINSON, William J.

1977   Dendroclimatic variability in the American Southwest,

A.D. 680 to 1970. National Technical Information
Service, PB-266 340/9ST, 150 pp.

DEAN, J.S., LINDSAY, Alexander J., Jr., and ROBINSON, William J.

1978   Prehistoric settlement in Long House Valley, north-
        eastern Arizona. *In* Euler and Gumerman 1978, pp.
        25-44.

DeATLEY, Suzanne P. (See under Lightfoot, Kent G.)

DeBLOOIS, Evan I.

1975   The Elk Ridge archaeological project: a test of
        random sampling in archeological surveying. United
        States Forest Service, Intermountain Region, Archae-
        ological Report no. 2.

DeBLOOIS, E.I., and GREEN, Dee F.

1978   SARG Research on the Elk Ridge project, Manti-Lasal.
        National Forest, Utah. *In* Euler and Gumerman 1978,
        pp. 13-23.

DeBOER, Warren R.

1976   Archaeological explorations in northern Arizona -
        NA10754: a Sinagua settlement of the Rio de Flag
        Phase. Queens College Publications in Anthropology,
        1, 69 pp.

DeBOER, W.R., and BILLECK, William T.

1976   Notes on the archaeology of NA 11553, Flagstaff,
        Arizona. Queens College Laboratory of Archaeology,
        Reports of Investigations.

DEBOWSKI, Sharon S., and FRITZ, Gordon L.

1974   Middle Gila Planning Unit - BLM. Arizona State
        Museum, Archaeological Series, 46, 38 pp.

DEBOWSKI, S.S., and others

1976   Archaeological survey of the Buttes Reservoir.
        Arizona State Museum, Archaeological Series, 93,
        Vols. 1-2, 245+289 pp.

DECHERT, Peter

1971   1971 excavations at Arroyo Hondo. School of Amer-
        ican Research, Exploration 1971, pp. 4-9.

DEGARMO, Glen Dean

  1975   Coyote Creek site 01: a methodological study of a
          prehistoric Pueblo population. University of Cali-
          fornia (Los Angeles), dissertation, 454 pp.; Uni-
          versity Microfilms International.

DE HARPORT, David L.

  1951   An archaeological survey of Canyon de Chelly: pre-
          liminary report of the field sessions of 1948, 1949,
          and 1950. El Palacio, 58:35-48.

  1953   An archaeological survey of Canyon de Chelly: pre-
          liminary report for the 1951 field season. El Pa-
          lacio, 60:20-25.

DeHOFF, Sue

  1977   Medicine Man Cave excavation. Awanyu, 5, no. 1:11-26..

DEKORNE, James B.

  1970   How to photograph rock art. El Palacio, 77, no. 1:
          14-24.

DENNINGER, Henri Stearns

  1938   Syphilis of Pueblo skull before 1350. Archives of
          Pathology, 26:724-727.

DENNISON, James T.

  1933   Scratches under the surface of the Mesa Verde.
          Mesa Verde Notes, 4, no. 2:12-13.

DERING, J. Phil, and SHAFER, Harry J.

  1976   Analysis of matrix samples from a Crockett County
          shelter: a test for seasonality. Bulletin of the
          Texas Archaeological Society, 47:209-229.

DeSAUSSURE, Raymond (See under Farmer, Malcolm F.; Schwartz,
  Douglas W.)

DEWEY, John R. (See under Armelagos, George J.)

DIBBLE, Charles E. (See also under Malouf, Carling.)

  1942   Recent archaeological investigation of the Great
          Salt Lake region of Utah. Proceedings of the 27th
          International Congress of Americanists, 1:207-208.

DIBBLE, David S. (See also under Day, Kent C.; Sharrock, Floyd W.)

1965   Bonfire Shelter, a stratified bison kill site in the Amistad Reservoir area, Val Verde County, Texas. Texas Archaeological Salvage Project, Miscellaneous Papers, 5, 127 pp.

1970   On the significance of additional radiocarbon dates from Bonfire Shelter, Texas: part I. Plains Anthropologist, 15, no. 50:251-254.

1975   Archaeological investigations at Bonfire Shelter, Texas. Washington State University, dissertation, 207 pp.; University Microfilms International.

DIBBLE, D.S., and LORRAIN, Dessamae

1968   Bonfire Shelter: a stratified bison kill site, Val Verde County, Texas. Texas Memorial Museum, Miscellaneous Papers, 1, 138 pp. Reviewed AA 70:1023 (Warnica), AAq 34:90 (Forbis).

DIBBLE, D.S., and PREWITT, Elton

1967   Survey and test excavations at Amistad Reservoir, 1964-1965. Texas Archaeological Salvage Project, Survey Report no. 3.

DICK, Herbert W. (See also under Hibben, Frank C.; Hurt, Wesley R., Jr.; Lister, Robert H.; Mangelsdorf, Paul C.; Smith, Landon D.; Wolfman, Daniel.)

1943   Alluvial sites of central New Mexico. New Mexico Anthropologist, 6-7, no. 1:19-22.

1946   Piedra depressions. American Antiquity, 11, no. 4: 257.

1949   Report of archaeological research in the Yampa and Green River canyons, Dinosaur National Monument, Colorado. 1949. Plains Archaeological Conference, Newsletter, 2, no. 4:7-8.

1952   Evidences of Early Man in Bat Cave and on the Plains of San Augustin, New Mexico. Proceedings of the 29th International Congress of Americanists, 3: 158-163.

1953a   The Hodges Site. I. Two rock shelters near Tucumcari, New Mexico. Bureau of American Ethnology, Bulletin 154, pp. 267-284.

1953b The status of Colorado archaeology, with a biblio-
graphic guide. Southwestern Lore, 18, no. 4:53-77.

1954a The Bat Cave pod corn complex: a note on its distribution and archaeological significance. El
Palacio, 61, no. 5:138-144.

1954b Projectile points from Bat Cave, New Mexico. Bulletin of the Oklahoma Anthropological Society, 2:
9-10.

1954c Trinidad State Junior College archaeological field
work, 1952-1953. Southwestern Lore, 19, no. 4:4-5.

1965a Bat Cave. School of American Research, Monograph
no. 27, 114 pp.
Reviewed AA 69:254 (Swanson), AAq 32:123 (Jennings).

1965b Picuris Pueblo excavations: a project of the Inter-
agency Archaeological and Paleontological Salvage
Program. Clearinghouse for Federal Scientific
and Technical Information, PB-177 047, 240 pp.

1968 Six historic pottery types from Spanish sites in
New Mexico. *In* Schroeder 1968a, pp. 77-94.

1976 Archaeological excavations in the Llaves area, Santa
Fe National Forest, New Mexico, 1972-74: Part I -
architecture. United States Forest Service, Southwestern Region, Archaeological Report no. 13, 112 pp.

DICKEY, Beth L. (See under Dittert, Alfred E., Jr.; Eddy, Frank
W.)

DICKEY, Roland

1957 The potters of the Mimbres Valley. New Mexico
Quarterly, 27, nos. 1-2:45-51.

DICKSON, D. Bruce

1972 Arroyo Hondo's place in a regional system. School
of American Research, Exploration 1972, pp. 8-9,
23-24.

1973 Settlement pattern stability and change in the
Pueblo cultures of the middle northern Rio Grande
area, New Mexico. University of Arizona, dissertation, 217 pp.; University Microfilms International.

1975 Settlement pattern stability and change in the middle northern Rio Grande region, New Mexico: a test

of some hypotheses. American Antiquity, 40:159-171.

DIETRICH, Margretta S.

1936 Their culture survives. New Mexico Magazine, 14, no. 2:22-23, 45-46.

DIETZ, W.H.

1936 A few Mimbres bowls. Central Texas Archaeological Society, Bulletin 2:61-64.

DI PESO, Charles C.

1949 Preliminary report of a Babocomari Indian village. Kiva, 14, nos. 1-4:10-14.

1950 Painted stone slabs of Point of Pines, Arizona. American Antiquity, 16:57-65.

1951a The Babocomari Village site on the Babocomari River, southeastern Arizona. Amerind Foundation, no. 5, 248 pp.
Reviewed AAq 17:267 (Danson).

1951b A ball court located on the San Pedro River in southeastern Arizona. American Antiquity, 16:257-260.

1953a Clovis Fluted points from southeastern Arizona. American Antiquity, 19:82-85.

1953b The Sobaipuri Indians of the upper San Pedro River Valley, southeastern Arizona. Amerind Foundation, no. 6, 285 pp.
Reviewed AA 56:319 (Schroeder), AAq 21:430 (Wheat).

1955 Two Cerro Guamas Clovis Fluted points from Sonora, Mexico. Kiva, 21, nos. 1-2:13-15.

1956 The Upper Pima of San Cayetano del Tumacacori. Amerind Foundation, no. 7, 589 pp.
Reviewed AA 59:1124 (Hinton), AAq 23:316 (Reed).

1957 A tubular stone pipe (?) from Sonora. American Antiquity, 22:288-290.

1958a The Reeve Ruin of southeastern Arizona. Amerind Foundation, no. 8, 189 pp.
Reviewed AAq 25:139 (Danson).

1958b Western Pueblo intrusion into the San Pedro Valley. Kiva, 23, no. 4:12-16.

1959   El enfoque arqueo-histórico. *In* Esplendor del Mé-
        xico antiguo, 2:671-686. Centro de Investigaciones
        Antropológicas de México.

1960   Recent excavations at Casas Grandes (Chihuahua).
        Katunob, 1, no. 4:47-48.

1963   Cultural development in northern Mexico. Smith-
        sonian Miscellaneous Collections, 146, no. 1:1-16.

1965   The Clovis Fluted point from the Timmy site, north-
        west Chihuahua, Mexico. Kiva, 31, no. 2:83-87.

1966   Archaeology and ethnohistory of the northern Sierra.
        In Ekholm and Willey 1966, pp. 3-25.

1968a   Casas Grandes, a fallen trading center of the Gran
        Chichimeca. Masterkey, 42, no. 1:20-37.

1968b   Casas Grandes and the Gran Chichimeca. El Palacio,
        75, no. 4:45-61.

1968c   The correlation question in general archaeological
        perspective for northern Mesoamerica and beyond.
        Proceedings of the 37th International Congress of
        Americanists, 3:23-37.

1969   Eleventh Southwestern Ceramic Seminar: Casas Grandes
        pottery types. Amerind Foundation, Dragoon.

1971a   Casas Grandes water control system. Cochise Quarter-
        ly, 1:7-11.

1971b   Use and abuse of Southwestern rivers: the Pueblo
        dweller. *In* Hydrology and water resources in Ari-
        zona and the Southwest; Proceedings of the 1971
        meetings of the American Water Resources Associa-
        tion, Arizona Section, and the Arizona Academy of
        Science, Hydrology Section, 1:381-396.

1973   Three dimensional records in the Spanish and Mexi-
        can periods. El Palacio, 78, no. 4:2-13.

1976a   Art as a key to prehistory in the Southwest. El
        Palacio, 82, no. 1:2-8.

1976b   Gila Polychrome in the Casas Grandes region. *In*
        Doyel and Haury 1976, pp. 57-63.

1977   Casas Grandes effigy vessels. American Indian Art
        Magazine, 2, no. 4.

DI PESO, C.C., RINALDO, John B., and FENNER, Gloria J.

1974   Casas Grandes: a fallen trading center of the Gran
        Chichimeca. Amerind Foundation, no. 9, 8 vols.
        Reviewed AA 78:469 (Euler).

DITTERT, Alfred E., Jr. (See also under Eddy, Frank W.; Goodyear, Albert C., III; Ruppé, Reynold J.; Schoenwetter, James;
Stubbs, Stanley A.; Zaslow, Bert.)

1957   Salvage excavations at Blackwater No. 1 locality,
        near Portales, New Mexico. *In* Peckham 1957a, pp.
        1-9.

1958a   Navajo Project Studies, I. Preliminary archae-
        ological investigations in the Navajo Project area
        of northwestern New Mexico. Museum of New Mexico,
        Papers in Anthropology, 1, 26 pp.

1958b   Salvage archaeology and the Navajo Project: a prog-
        ress report. El Palacio, 65:61-72.

1958c   Recent developments in Navajo Project salvage ar-
        chaeology. El Palacio, 65:201-211.

1959   Culture change in the Cebolleta Mesa region, central
        western New Mexico. University of Arizona, disserta-
        tion, 620 pp.; University Microfilms International.

1962a   An aerial survey of the Public Service Company of
        New Mexico 230 KV transmission line, northwestern
        New Mexico. Laboratory of Anthropology Notes, 3.

1962b   A proposal for salvage archaeology research at the
        Cochiti and Galisteo Dam projects. Laboratory of
        Anthropology Notes, 4.

1967   (comp.) New Mexico historic sites; a survey pre-
        pared by the staff of the Museum of New Mexico.
        Phase I. State resources development plan. New
        Mexico State Planning Office, Santa Fe, 82 pp.

1968a   Minerals and rocks at archaeological sites: some
        interpretations from central western New Mexico.
        Arizona Archaeologist, 3.

1968b   Some factors affecting Southwestern populations
        during the period A.D. 900-1540. *In* Irwin-Williams
        1968a, pp. 14-16.

1972   They came from the south. Arizona Highways, 48:
        34-39.

1976   (assembler) An archaeological survey in the Gila
        River Basin, New River and Phoenix City Streams,
        Arizona Project Area. U.S. Army Corps of Engineers,
        Los Angeles District.

DITTERT, A.E., and EDDY, Frank W.

1963   (ed.) Pueblo period sites in the Piedra River

section, Navajo Reservoir district. Museum of New
Mexico, Papers in Anthropology, 10, 120 pp.
Reviewed AA 66:707 (Suhm), AAq 30:357 (Sharrock).

DITTERT, A.E., and RUPPÉ, Reynold J., Jr.

1951   The archaeology of Cebolleta Mesa: a preliminary
        report. El Palacio, 58:116-129.

1952   The development of scientific investigation of the
        Cebolleta Mesa area, central western New Mexico.
        Kiva, 18, nos. 1-2:13-17.

DITTERT, A.E., and WENDORF, Fred

1963   Procedural manual for archaeological research proj-
        ects of the Museum of New Mexico. Museum of New
        Mexico, Papers in Anthropology, 12, 70 pp.
        Reviewed AA 66:1440 (Gunnerson).

DITTERT, A.E., EDDY, F.W., and DICKEY, Beth L.

1963   Evidences of early ceramic phases in the Navajo
        Reservoir district. El Palacio, 70, nos. 1-2:
        5-12.

DITTERT, A.E., FISH, P., and SIMONIS, D.

1969   A cultural inventory of the proposed Granite Reef
        and Salt-Gila aqueducts, Agua Fria River to Gila
        River, Arizona. Arizona State University, Anthro-
        pological Research Papers, 1, 26 pp.

DITTERT, A.E., HESTER, James J., and EDDY, Frank W.

1961   An archaeological survey of the Navajo Reservoir
        district, northwestern New Mexico. School of
        American Research, Monograph no. 23, 277 pp.

DIXON, Keith A.

1956a   Archaeological objectives and artifact sorting
        techniques: a re-examination of the Snaketown
        sequence. Western Anthropology, no. 3, 33 pp.

1956b   Hidden House, a cliff ruin in Sycamore Canyon,
        central Arizona. Museum of Northern Arizona, Bul-
        letin 29, 90 pp.
        Reviewed AA 60:783 (Thompson), AAq 23:202 (Schroe-
        der).

1958   The mystery of a prehistoric baby blanket. Masterkey,

32, no. 6:186-188.

1959   An unusual jar-bowl vessel from eastern Arizona.
       Masterkey, 33, no. 1:26-28.

1963   The interamerican diffusion of a cooking technique:
       the culinary shoe-pot. American Anthropologist, 65:
       593-619.

1964a The acceptance and persistence of ring vessels and
       stirrup spout-handles in the Southwest. American
       Antiquity, 29:455-460.

1964b Culinary shoe-pots: the interamerican diffusion of
       a cooking technique. Proceedings of the 35th Inter-
       national Congress of Americanists, 1:579-586.

1965   A petroglyph-decorated metate from the Bradshaw
       Mountains, Arizona. Kiva, 31, no. 1:54-56.

1976   Shoe-pots, patojos, and the principle of whimsy.
       American Antiquity, 41:386-391.

DOBERENZ, A.R. (See under Haynes, C. Vance.)

DOBYNS, Henry F. (See also under Colton, Harold S.; Euler,
Robert C.)

1959   A Mohave potter's experiment, Parker Black-on-red.
       Kiva, 24, no. 4:24.

1974   Prehistoric Indian occupation within the eastern
       area of the Yuman complex: a study in applied
       archaeology. American Indian Ethnohistory, Huala-
       pai Indians I, 3 vols., Garland Publishing, Inc.,
       713 pp.

DOCKSTADER, Frederick J.

1961   A figurine cache from Kino Bay, Sonora. *In* Essays
       in Pre-Columbian Art and Archaeology, ed. S.K.
       Lothrop, pp. 182-191. Harvard University Press.

DODGE, William A. (See under Brancato, Melody J.)

DODGEN, Dulce N. (See under Vivian, R. Gwinn.)

DOELLE, William H.

1975a Prehistoric resource exploitation within the CONOCO
       Florence Project. Arizona State Museum, Archae-
       ological Series, 62, 102 pp.

1975b   Archaeological resources of the BLM Geronimo Plan-
         ning Unit. Arizona State Museum, Archaeological
         Series, 71, 28 pp.

1975c   Archaeological resources of the BLM Greenbelt Plan-
         ning Unit. Arizona State Museum, Archaeological
         Series, 72, 26 pp.

1976a   Management plan: Santa Cruz Riverpark. Arizona
         State Museum, Archaeological Series, 91, 26 pp.

1976b   Four petroglyph sites - Gila River Indian Reserva-
         tion. Arizona State Museum, Archaeological Series,
         95, 24 pp.

1976c   Desert resources and Hohokam subsistence: the CONOCO
         Florence Project. Arizona State Museum, Archaeo-
         logical Series, 103, 286 pp.

1978   Hohokam use of nonriverine resources. *In* Grebinger
         1978a, pp. 245-274.

DOELLE, W.H., and BREW, Susan A.

1976   An archaeological survey of proposed housing loca-
         tions in Sells and Vaya Chin, Papago Indian Reserva-
         tion, Arizona. Arizona State Museum, Archaeological
         Series, 107, 27 pp.

DOELLE, W.H., and FRITZ, Gordon L.

1975   Archaeological resources of BLM Planning Unit 18.
         Arizona State Museum, Archaeological Series, 76,
         13 pp.

DOELLE, W.H., and HEWITT, James

1974   Preliminary report on archaeological resources
         within the CONOCO Florence Project. Arizona State
         Museum, Archaeological Series, 56, 15 pp.

DOLPHIN, Gabrielle (See under Davin, Eric.)

DONALDSON, Bruce R.

1975   An archaeological sample of the White Mountain Plan-
         ning Unit, Apache-Sitgreaves National Forest, Ari-
         zona. United States Forest Service, Southwestern
         Region, Archaeological Report no. 6, 36 pp.

1977   Lessons from the White Mountain Planning Unit: a
         small-sample survey design for large areas. U.S.
         Forest Service, Southwestern Region, Archaeological

Report no. 16:35-50.

DONDELINGER, Norman W. (See also under Tatum, Robert M.)

DONDELINGER, N.W., and TATUM, Robert M.

1942   Preliminary survey of sites in Las Animas County,
        Colorado. Southwestern Lore, 8, no. 1:2-6.

1944   Stone images in southern Colorado. American An-
        tiquity, 10:59-64.

DONNAN, Christopher B., and CLEWLOW, C. William, Jr.

1977   Ethnoarchaeology. University of California (Los
        Angeles), Institute of Archaeology, Monographs,
        no. 4, 181 pp.

DONNELLY, Maurice (See under Stewart, Guy R.)

DOTY, Roy

1977   An analysis of lithic remains from the Mt. Taylor
        district, Cibola National Forest, New Mexico. U.S.
        Forest Service, Southwestern Region, Miscellaneous
        Paper no. 7, Archaeological Report no. 15:53-59.

DOUGLAS, Charles L. (See under Erdman, James A.; Word, James H.)

DOUGLAS, Frederick H. (See also under Jeançon, Jean Allard.)

1939   Types of Southwestern coiled basketry. Denver Art
        Museum, Dept. of Indian Art, Leaflet 88, pp. 150-
        152.

1940a   Main types of Pueblo cotton textiles. Denver Art
        Museum, Dept. of Indian Art, Leaflets 92-93, pp.
        166-172.

1940b   Southwestern twined, wicker, and plaited basketry.
        Denver Art Museum, Dept. of Indian Art, Leaflets
        99-100, pp. 194-199.

DOUGLAS, F.H., and RAYNOLDS, F.R.

1941   Pottery design terminology - final report on ques-
        tionnaires. Clearinghouse for Southwest Museums,
        Newsletter, 35:120-124.

DOUGLASS, Andrew E.

1901   Montezuma's Well and the Soda Spring, Arizona.

Land of Sunshine, 14 (April):290-299.

1921   Dating our prehistoric ruins. Natural History, 21, no. 1:27-30.

1929   The secret of the Southwest solved by talkative tree rings. National Geographic Magazine, 56:736-770.

1930   Chronology of the Southwest. El Palacio, 28:24-25.

1931   Tree growth and chronology of Pueblo prehistory. *In* Source Book in Anthropology (rev. ed.), ed. A.L. Kroeber and T.T. Waterman, Harcourt Brace & Co., pp. 177-187.

1934-   Accuracy in dating. Tree-Ring Bulletin, 1:10-11,
35   19-21.

1935   Dating Pueblo Bonito and other ruins of the Southwest. National Geographic Society, Pueblo Bonito Series, Contributed Technical Papers, 1, 74 pp. Reviewed AAq 1:248 (Haury).

1935-   Estimated ring chronology. Tree-Ring Bulletin,
40   1:27; 2:6, 13-16, 24; 3:16; 4:8; 5:8, 18-20; 6:39.

1936   The central Pueblo chronology. Tree-Ring Bulletin, 2, no. 4:29-34.

1937a   Tree rings and chronology. University of Arizona Bulletin, 8, no. 4, 36 pp.

1937b   Typical tree-ring record from Chaco Canyon, 700-800 A.D., CK 31. Tree-Ring Bulletin, 3, no. 3:20-23.

1938   Southwestern dated ruins: V. Tree-Ring Bulletin, 5, no. 2:10-13.

1941   Age of Forestdale Ruin excavated in 1939. Tree-Ring Bulletin, 8, no. 1:7-8.

1942   Checking the date of Bluff Ruin, Forestdale: a study in technique. Tree-Ring Bulletin, 9, no. 2:2-7.

1944   Tabulation of dates for Bluff Ruin, Forestdale, Arizona. Tree-Ring Bulletin, 11, no. 2:10-16.

1947a   Photographic tree-ring chronologies and the Flagstaff sequence. Tree-Ring Bulletin, 14:10-16.

1947b   Precision of ring dating in tree-ring chronologies. University of Arizona Bulletin, 17, no. 3:1-21.

1949   Note on the early Durango collections. Tree-Ring Bulletin, 15:24.

DOUGLASS, William Boone

    1917a The land of the small house people. El Palacio,
            4, no. 2:3-23.

    1917b Notes on the shrines of the Tewa and other Pueblo
            Indians of New Mexico. Proceedings of the 19th
            International Congress of Americanists, pp. 344-
            378.

    1917c The shrines of the small house people. El Palacio,
            4, no. 3:19-29.

DOVE, Christopher

    1967   Locality 4 (Cl247), Tule Springs, Nevada. *In*
           Wormington and Ellis 1967, pp. 367-369.

DOVE, Donald E.

    1970   A site survey along the lower Agua Fria River, Ari-
           zona. Arizona Archaeologist, 5:1-36.

DOWNS, James T.

    1959   Further notes on clay human figurines in the western
           United States. University of California, Archae-
           ological Survey Reports, 48:16-31.

DOYEL, David E.

    1972   Archaeological survey of the Clifton-Vail section,
           San Juan-Vail transmission line. Arizona State
           Museum, Archaeological Series, 15, 50 pp.

    1974a Excavations in the Escalante Ruin group, southern
            Arizona. Arizona State Museum, Archaeological
            Series, 37, 342 pp.

    1974b The Miami Wash project: a preliminary report on
            excavations in Hohokam and Salado sites near Miami,
            central Arizona. Arizona Highway Salvage, Prelim-
            inary Report no. 11.

    1976a Revised phase system for the Globe-Miami and Tonto
            Basin areas, central Arizona. Kiva, 41, nos. 3-4:
            241-266.

    1976b Salado cultural development in the Tonto Basin and
            Globe-Miami areas, central Arizona. *In* Doyel and
            Haury 1976, pp. 5-16.

    1976c Classic Period Hohokam in the Gila River Basin,
            Arizona. *In* Doyel and Haury 1976, pp. 27-37.

1976d   Reply to Raab's "A prehistoric cactus camp in Papa-
         gueria." Journal of the Arizona Academy of Science,
         11, no. 1:42-43.

1977   Excavations in the middle Santa Cruz River Valley,
         southeastern Arizona. Arizona State Museum, Contri-
         butions to Highway Salvage Archaeology in Arizona,
         44, 193 pp.

DOYEL, D.E., and HAURY, Emil W.

1976   (ed.) The 1976 Salado Conference. Kiva, 42, no. 1:
         1-134.

DOZIER, Edward P.

1958   Ethnological clues for the sources of Rio Grande
         Pueblo population. In Migrations in New World
         Culture History, ed. R.H. Thompson, pp. 21-32.
         University of Arizona, Social Science Bulletin no.
         27.

1965   Southwestern social units and archaeology. Ameri-
         can Antiquity, 31:38-47.

DRAKE, Robert J.

1954a   Sonora building foundations. El Palacio, 61:344-
         346.

1954b   Study of Arizona Pleistocene and Recent mollusks:
         a tool for local geochronological research. El
         Palacio, 61:355-367.

DREGNE, Harold C. (See under Eddy, Frank W.)

DREW, Linda G.

1972   (ed.) Tree-ring chronologies of western America,
         Vol. II: Arizona, New Mexico, Texas. Laboratory
         of Tree-Ring Research, Chronology Series, 1.

1974   (ed.) Tree-ring chronologies of western America,
         Vol. IV: Colorado, Utah, Nebraska and South Dakota.
         Laboratory of Tree-Ring Research, Chronology Series,
         1.

DUFF, U. Francis

1897   The prehistoric ruins of the Rio Tularosa. Journal
         of the American Geographical Society, 29:261-270.

1902a   The prehistoric ruins of the Southwest. Records

of the Past, 1:66-75.

1902b   The ruins of the Mimbres Valley. American Anti-
         quarian, 24:397-400.

1904   Some exploded theories concerning Southwestern ar-
         cheology. American Anthropologist, n.s., 6, no.
         2:303-306.

DUFFEN, William A.

1937a   Some notes on a summer's work near Bonita, Arizona.
         Kiva, 2, no. 4:13-16.

1937b   Tonto ruins stabilization, May 27 to June 30, 1937.
         Southwestern Monuments Monthly Report, Supplement,
         July, pp. 43-54 (reprinted in Caywood 1962, pp. 69-
         73).

DUFFIELD, Lathel F. (See under Nunley, John P.)

DUFFIELD, M.S.

1904   Aboriginal remains in Nevada and Utah. American
         Anthropologist, n.s., 6, no. 1:148-150.

DURHAM, Dorothy

1955   Petroglyphs at Mesa de los Padillas. El Palacio,
         62:3-17.

DUTTON, Bertha P. (See also under Hewett, Edgar Lee.)

1936   Report on Leyit Kin. Southwestern Monuments Monthly
         Report, November, pp. 309-319.

1938a   The Jemez Mountain region. El Palacio, 44, nos.
         19-21:133-143.

1938b   Leyit Kin, a small house ruin, Chaco Canyon, New
         Mexico. University of New Mexico Bulletin, Mono-
         graph Series, 1, no. 6, 101 pp.

1947   Girl Scout archaeological expedition. El Palacio,
         54, no. 8:191-194.

1948a   The magic circle. New Mexico Magazine, 26, no. 3:
         11-13, 41-45.

1948b   Senior Scout Mobile Camp of 1948. El Palacio, 55,
         no. 8:252-256.

1949   Senior Girl Scout archaeological camps of 1949.
         El Palacio, 56, no. 9:278-285.

1950   Archaeological mobile camps, senior Girl Scouts,
        1950. El Palacio, 57:366-371.

1951   The diggers complete their fifth season of Girl
        Scout archaeological mobile camps. El Palacio, 58,
        no. 11:354-370.

1952a   Highlights of the Jemez region. El Palacio, 59,
        no. 5:131-158 (also as Papers of the School of Amer-
        ican Research, 46, 32 pp.).

1952b   Senior Girl Scout-Museum archaeological program of
        1952. El Palacio, 59, no. 11:342-352.

1953   Galisteo Basin again scene of archaeological re-
        search. El Palacio, 60:339-351.

1955   Report on Senior Girl Scout archaeological mobile
        camp. Southwestern Lore, 21, no. 3:35-41.

1962   Let's explore! Indian villages past and present.
        Museum of New Mexico Press, 56 pp.

1963   Sun Father's Way: the kiva murals of Kuaua. Uni-
        versity of New Mexico Press, 237 pp.
        Reviewed AA 66:1212 (Woodbury), AAq 30:358 (Lange).

1964a   Las Madres in the light of Anasazi migrations.
        American Antiquity, 29:449-454.

1964b   Mesoamerican culture traits which appear in the
        American Southwest. Proceedings of the 35th Inter-
        national Congress of Americanists, 1:481-492.

1964c   An archaeological survey of the proposed Galisteo
        dam and reservoir. Laboratory of Anthropology Notes,
        24.

1966a   Pots pose problems. El Palacio, 73, no. 1:5-15.

1966b   Prehistoric migrations into the Galisteo Basin,
        New Mexico. Proceedings of the 36th International
        Congress of Americanists, 1:287-299.

1970   Anthropological interpretation of prehistoric cere-
        monial Indian art in the American Southwest. Pro-
        ceedings of the 7th International Congress of Anthro-
        pological and Ethnological Sciences, 11:36-40.

EAGLETON, N. Ethie

1955   An historic Indian cache in Pecos County. Bulletin
        of the Texas Archaeological Society, 26:200-217.

EAST-SMITH, Shirley (Also listed as Smith, Shirley.)

EAST-SMITH, S., and AGOGINO, G.A.

  1966   A statistical analysis of fluted and Plano points
         from Blackwater Draw, New Mexico. Plains Anthro-
         pologist, 11, no. 31.

EATON, Theodore H., Jr.

  1937   Prehistoric man in the Navajo country. National
         Youth Administration, Bulletin, Project 6677-Y,
         43 pp.

EBERT, James I. (See under Judge, W. James; Lyons, Thomas R.)

ECK, L.J. (See under Raun, Gerald G.)

ECKERT, Nan (See under Connolly, Charlene.)

EDDY, Frank W. (See also under Dittert, Alfred E., Jr.; Schoenwetter, James.)

  1962   An interim report to the National Park Service on
         the Navajo project. Laboratory of Anthropology
         Notes, 5.

  1964   Metates and manos: the basic corn grinding tools
         of the Southwest. Museum of New Mexico, Popular
         Series Pamphlet no. 1, 10 pp.

  1966   Prehistory in the Navajo Reservoir district, north-
         western New Mexico. Museum of New Mexico, Papers
         in Anthropology, 15, pts. I-II, 631 pp.
           Reviewed AA 70:420 (Ellis).

  1972   Culture ecology and the prehistory of the Navajo
         Reservoir district. Southwestern Lore, 38, nos.
         1-2:1-75.

  1974   Population dislocation in the Navaho Reservoir dis-
         trict, New Mexico and Colorado. American Antiquity,
         39:75-84.

  1975   A settlement model for reconstructing prehistoric
         social organization at Chimney Rock Mesa, southern
         Colorado. *In* Frisbie 1975a, pp. 60-79.

  1977   Archaeological investigations at Chimney Rock Mesa:
         1970-72. Colorado Archaeological Society, Memoirs,
         no. 1.

EDDY, F.W., and DICKEY, Beth L.

  1961   Excavations at Los Pinos Phase sites in the Navajo

Reservoir district. Museum of New Mexico, Papers in Anthropology, 4, 106 pp. Reviewed AAq 28:404 (Danson).

EDDY, F.W., and DREGNE, Harold C.

1964   Soil tests on alluvial and archaeological deposits, Navajo Reservoir district. El Palacio, 71, no. 4: 5-21.

EDDY, F.W., HESTER, James J., and DITTERT, Alfred

1963   Pueblo period sites in the Piedra River district. Museum of New Mexico, Papers in Anthropology, 10, 122 pp.

EDMONDS, Kermit M., and VIVIAN, R. Gwinn

1968   Report of inspection of Camp Willow Springs, April 1868. Plateau, 41, no. 1:14-26.

EFFLAND, Richard (See also under Plog, Fred T.)

1978   Applications of computer graphic techniques to SARG data. *In* Euler and Gumerman 1978, pp. 149-167.

EKHOLM, Gordon F.

1939   Results of an archaeological survey of Sonora and northern Sinaloa. Revista Mexicana de Estudios Antropológicos, 3:7-10.

1940   The archaeology of northern and western Mexico. *In* The Maya and Their Neighbors, ed. C.L. Hay et al., pp. 320-330.

1947   Recent archaeological work in Sonora and northern Sinaloa. Proceedings of the 27th International Congress of Americanists, pp. 69-73.

1953   Exploración arqueológica en Sonora y la parte norte de Sinaloa. Yan; ciencias antropológicas, 1:34-36.

EKHOLM, G.F., and WILLEY, Gordon R.

1966   (ed.) Archaeological frontiers and external connections. Handbook of Middle American Indians, ed. R. Wauchope, vol. 4, 367 pp. University of Texas Press.

ELISHA, M.J.

1968   The present status of Basketmaker II and III sites in Colorado. Southwestern Lore, 34, no. 2:33-47.

ELLIS, Bruce T. (See also under Chapman, Kenneth M.; Stubbs, Stanley A.)

    1953   Vessel-lip decoration as a possible guide to Southwestern group movements and contacts. Southwestern Journal of Anthropology, 9:436-457.

    1955   A possible chain mail fragment from Pottery Mound. El Palacio, 62:181-184.

    1957   Crossbow boltheads from historic Pueblo sites. El Palacio, 64, nos. 7-8:209-214.

    1976   Santa Fe's seventeenth century plaza, parish church, and convent reconsidered. *In* Schroeder 1976, pp. 183-198.

ELLIS, D. (See under Wormington, H. Marie.)

ELLIS, Florence H. (See also under Campbell, John Martin. Also listed as Hawley, Florence M., and Senter, Florence Hawley.)

    1951   Pueblo social organization and Southwestern archaeology. American Antiquity, 17:148-151.

    1952   Jemez kiva magic and its relation to features of prehistoric kivas. Southwestern Journal of Anthropology, 8:147-163.

    1964a   Archaeological history of Nambé Pueblo, 14th century to the present. American Antiquity, 30:34-42.

    1964b   Comment on Jett's "Pueblo Indian migrations." American Antiquity, 30:213-215.

    1966a   The immediate history of Zia Pueblo as derived from excavation in refuse deposits. American Antiquity, 31:806-811.

    1966b   Pueblo boundaries and their markers. Plateau, 38:97-106.

    1966c   On distinguishing Laguna from Acoma Polychrome. El Palacio, 73, no. 3:37-39.

    1967a   Use and significance of the tcamahia. El Palacio, 74, no. 1:35-43.

    1967b   Where did the Pueblo people come from? El Palacio, 74, no. 3:35-43.

    1968a   An interpretation of prehistoric death customs in terms of modern Southwestern parallels. *In* Schroeder 1968a, pp. 57-76.

1968b What Utaztecan ethnology suggests of Utaztecan pre-
       history. *In* Swanson 1968, pp. 53-105.

1974a An anthropological study of the Navajo Indians.
       American Indian Ethnohistory, Navajo Indians I.
       Garland Publishing, Inc., 580 pp.

1974b Anthropological data pertaining to the Taos land
       claim. American Indian Ethnohistory, Pueblo Indians
       I. Garland Publishing, Inc., pp. 29-150.

1974c Archaeologic and ethnologic data: Acoma-Laguna
       land claims. American Indian Ethnohistory, Pueblo
       Indians II. Garland Publishing, Inc., 326 pp.

1974d Anthropology of Laguna Pueblo land claims. American
       Indian Ethnohistory, Pueblo Indians III. Garland
       Publishing, Inc., pp. 9-120.

1974e The Hopi: their history and use of land. American
       Indian Ethnohistory, Hopi Indians. Garland Publish-
       ing, Inc., 403 pp.

1975a A thousand years of the Pueblo sun-moon-star calendar.
       In Aveni 1975, pp. 59-87.

1975b A pantheon of kachinas. New Mexico Magazine, 53,
       no. 3:13-28.

1975c Highways to the past. New Mexico Magazine, 53, no.
       5:18-25.

1975d Life in the Tesuque Valley and elsewhere in the
       Santa Fe area during the Pueblo II stage of develop-
       ment. Awanyu, 3, no. 2:27-49.

1976   Datable ritual components proclaiming Mexican in-
       fluence in the upper Rio Grande of New Mexico. *In*
       Schroeder 1976, pp. 85-108.

n.d.   What happened to the people of the Jornada Branch?
       El Paso Archaeological Society, Special Report no.
       9 (MS).

ELLIS, F.H., and BRODY, J.J.

1964   Ceramic stratigraphy and tribal history at Taos
       Pueblo. American Antiquity, 29:316-327.

ELLIS, F.H., and HAMMACK, Laurens

1965   Shrine of ancient warriors. New Mexico Magazine,
       43, no. 9:6-8, 32.

1968   The inner sanctum of Feather Cave, a Mogollon Sun

and Earth shrine linking Mexico and the Southwest. American Antiquity, 33:25-44.

EL-NAJJAR, Mahmoud Yosef (See also under Morris, Donald H.)

1974   People of Canyon de Chelly: a study of their biology and culture. Arizona State University, dissertation, 231 pp.; University Microfilms International.

EL-NAJJAR, M.Y., MORRIS, Don P., TURNER, Christy G., II, and RYAN, Dennis J.

1975   An unusual pathology with high incidence among the ancient cliff-dwellers of Canyon de Chelly. Plateau, 48, nos. 1-2:13-22.

ELSTON, Robert

1967   Notes on stone discs, site 26LC15. Nevada Archaeological Survey, Reporter, 1, no. 4:11-13.

ELY, Albert Grim (See also under Luhrs, Dorothy L.)

1935   The excavation and repair of Quarai Mission. El Palacio, 39:133-144.

1939   Field work at Pecos. El Palacio, 46, no. 6:124-126.

EL-ZUR, Arieh

1965   Soil, water and man in the desert habitat of the Hohokam culture: an experimental study in environmental anthropology. University of Arizona, dissertation, 451 pp.; University Microfilms International.

EMORY, William H.

1848   Notes of a military reconnaissance from Fort Leavenworth, in Missouri, to San Diego, in California, etc. 30th Congress, 1st session, Senate, executive document no. 41.

EMSLIE, Steven D.

1975   Petrographic analysis of Mesa Verde lithics. Journal of the Colorado-Wyoming Academy of Science, 7:2.

ENGER, Walter D.

1942   Archaeology of Black Rock 3 Cave, Utah. University of Utah, Anthropological Papers, 7, 21 pp.

ENGER, W.D., and BLAIR, W.C.

1947   Crania from the Warren mounds and their possible
        significance to Northern Periphery archaeology.
        American Antiquity, 13, no. 2:142-146.

ENGLERT, Edwin, Jr. (See under Moore, John G.)

ENLOE, James G.

1974   Archaeological survey of Northwest Pipeline wells
        Barbara Kay No. 1 and Judy Lee No. 1. University
        of New Mexico, contract report 101-100.

1976   Archaeological clearance survey: Public Service
        Company WW to Northbulk right-of-way. University
        of New Mexico, contract report 101-103U (BLM).

ENLOE, J.G., SMITH, Andrew T., and PECKHAM, Stewart L.

1974   An archaeological survey of the San Juan-to-Ojo
        345 KV transmission line, northwestern New Mexico.
        Laboratory of Anthropology Notes, 105.

ENLOE, J.G., and others

1973   An archaeological inventory and evaluation of some
        prehistoric and historic sites in the upper San
        Juan drainage, New Mexico. Laboratory of Anthro-
        pology Notes, 119.

EPSTEIN, Alice (See under Fenton, Carroll Lane.)

EPSTEIN, Jeremiah F.

1960   Burins from Texas. American Antiquity, 26, no. 1:
        93-97.

1963a   The burin-faceted projectile point. American An-
        tiquity, 29, no. 2:187-201.

1963b   Centipede and Damp Caves: excavations in Val Verde
        County, Texas, 1958. Bulletin of the Texas Ar-
        chaeological Society, 33:1-129.

1968   An archaeological view of Uto-Aztekan time perspec-
        tive. *In* Swanson 1968, pp. 106-130.

ERDMAN, James A., DOUGLAS, Charles L., and MARR, John W.

1969   Environment of Mesa Verde, Colorado. National Park
        Service, Archaeological Research Series, no. 7-B,
        72 pp.
        Reviewed AA 72:1548 (Martin), AAq 36:122 (Hevly).

ESCHMAN, Peter (See under Allan, William C.; Stuart, David E.)

ETHERTON, Bill

> 1937   Artifacts among the sand dunes. Southwestern Lore,
>   3, no. 2:21-22.

EULER, Robert C. (See also under Colton, Harold S.; Gumerman,
George J.; Karlstrom, Thor N.V.; Kunitz, Stephen J.; McNutt,
Charles H.; Sweeney, Catherine L.)

> 1954a An unusual masonry wall in a Kayenta Anasazi cliff
>   site. American Antiquity, 19:393-394.
>
> 1954b A salt specimen from the lower Virgin River: another
>   chemical analysis. Plateau, 27, no. 2:7-8.
>
> 1956   A large clay figurine from Prescott, Arizona. Kiva,
>   22, no. 1:4-7.
>
> 1957   A Cohonina burial. Plateau, 29, no. 3:59-62.
>
> 1958   Walapai culture-history. University of New Mexico,
>   dissertation, 396 pp.; University Microfilms Inter-
>   national.
>
> 1959a Pottery of southern California Yumans compared with
>   Tizon Brown Ware of Arizona. University of Cali-
>   fornia at Los Angeles, Archaeological Survey, Annual
>   Report for 1958-59, pp. 41-44.
>
> 1959b A prehistoric cache of cotton seeds from the Hopi
>   country. Plateau, 32, no. 1:23.
>
> 1961   A Basketmaker III pithouse in the Hopi country.
>   Southwestern Lore, 27, no. 3:46-47.
>
> 1963   Archaeological problems in western and northwestern
>   Arizona, 1962. Plateau, 35, no. 3:78-85.
>
> 1964a An archaeological survey of the south rim of Walnut
>   Canyon National Monument, Arizona. Arizona State
>   College (Flagstaff), Anthropological Papers, 1, 15
>   pp.
>
> 1964b Southern Paiute archaeology. American Antiquity,
>   29:379-381.
>
> 1966   Willow figurines from Arizona. Natural History,
>   75, no. 3:62-67.
>
> 1967   The canyon dwellers. American West, 4, no. 2:22-
>   27, 67-71.
>
> 1968   "Hit-and-run" archaeology: a rejoinder to Jett.
>   American Antiquity, 33, no. 4:509-511.

1969   The archeology of the Canyon country. *In* John Wes-
        ley Powell and the anthropology of the canyon coun-
        try, by D.D. Fowler, R.C. Euler, and C.S. Fowler,
        pp. 8-20. Geological Survey, Professional Paper 670.

1971   A prehistoric Pueblo pottery cache in Grand Canyon.
        Plateau, 43, no. 4:176-184.

1973a   Attributes of prehistoric Pueblo settlement patterns
        on Black Mesa, Arizona. Proceedings of the 40th
        International Congress of Americanists, pp. 77-81.

1973b   Exploring the past on Black Mesa. American West,
        10, no. 5.

1974   Future archaeological research in Grand Canyon.
        Plateau, 46, no. 4:139-148.

1975   The Pai: cultural conservatives in environmental
        diversity. *In* Frisbie 1975a, pp. 80-87.

EULER, R.C., and CHANDLER, Susan M.

1978   Aspects of prehistoric settlement patterns in Grand
        Canyon. *In* Euler and Gumerman 1978, pp. 73-85.

EULER, R.C., and DOBYNS, Henry F.

1962   Excavations west of Prescott, Arizona. Plateau, 34,
        no. 3:69-84.

EULER, R.C., and GUMERMAN, George J.

1974   A résumé of the archaeology of northern Arizona.
        In The geology of northern Arizona with notes on
        archaeology and paleoclimate, ed. T.N.V. Karlstrom.
        27th Annual Meeting, Rocky Mountain Section, Geo-
        logical Society of America.

1978   (ed.) Investigations of the Southwestern Anthro-
        pological Research Group: an experiment in archae-
        ological cooperation. Museum of Northern Arizona,
        Bulletin 50, 186 pp.

EULER, R.C., and JONES, Volney H.

1956   Hermetic sealing as a technique of food preserva-
        tion among the Indians of the American Southwest.
        Proceedings of the American Philosophical Society,
        100, no. 1:87-99.

EULER, R.C., and OLSON, Alan P.

1965   Split-twig figurines from northern Arizona: new

radiocarbon dates. Science, 148:368-369.

EULER, R.C., and TAYLOR, Walter W.

1966   Additional archaeological data from upper Grand
        Canyon: Nankoweap to Unkar revisited. Plateau, 39,
        no. 1:26-45.

EVANS, Cecelia, and SOWERS, Ted, Jr.

1939   First survey on upper Puerco-Jemez pottery. South-
        western Lore, 5, no. 1:9-14.

EVANS, Glen L. (See also under Sellards, E.H.)

1951   Prehistoric wells in eastern New Mexico. American
        Antiquity, 17:1-9.

EVANS, Harold

1961   Archaic manifestations in the Southwest and Texas.
        Iowa Archaeological Society, Northwest Chapter,
        Newsletter, 9, no. 6:5-6.

EVENSTAD, Martin O.

1936   More about Tumacacori alcoves. Southwestern Monu-
        ments Monthly Report, November, pp. 360-361.

EVERIT, R.S.

1924   Arizona ruins. Science, 60:455.

EVERITT, Cindi

1973   Black-on-white Mimbres pottery: a bibliography.
        The Artifact, 11, no. 4:69-88.

1975   Paleo-Indian bison kill sites in North America.
        The Artifact, 13, no. 3:39-49.

EVERITT, C., and DAVIS, John V.

1974   The Cruz Tarin paleo site. Awanyu, 2, no. 4:17-31.

EWING, George H. (See under Kayser, David W.)

EZELL, Paul H. (See also under Bliss, Wesley L.)

1937   Shell work of the prehistoric Southwest. Kiva, 3,
        no. 3:9-12.

1954   An archaeological survey of northwestern Papagueria.
        Kiva, 19, nos. 2-4:1-26.

1955   The archaeological delineation of a cultural bound-
        ary in Papagueria. American Antiquity, 20:367-374.

1963   Is there a Hohokam-Pima culture continuum? American
        Antiquity, 29, no. 1:61-66.

EZELL, P.H., and OLSON, Alan P.

1955   An artifact of human bone from eastern Arizona.
        Plateau, 27, no. 3:8-10.

FARMER, Malcolm F.

1935   The Mohave trade route. Masterkey, 9:155-157.

1942   Navaho archaeology of upper Blanco and Largo Can-
        yons, northern New Mexico. American Antiquity, 8:
        65-79.

1947   Upper Largo Navaho - 1700-1775. Kiva, 12, no. 2:15-
        24.

1954   Awatovi mural decorations. Plateau, 27, no. 2:21-
        24.

1955a   Awatovi bows. Plateau, 28, no. 1:8-10.

1955b   The identification of Ho-vi-itci-tu-qua Pueblo.
        Plateau, 28, no. 2:44-45.

1957a   Mr. Gladwin and the Athapascans: a review. David-
        son Journal of Anthropology, 3:31-36.

1957b   A suggested typology of defensive systems of the
        Southwest. Southwestern Journal of Anthropology,
        13:249-266.

1960   A note on the distribution of the metate and muller.
        Tebiwa, 3:31-38.

FARMER, M.F., and DeSAUSSURE, R.

1955   Split-twig animal figurines. Plateau, 27, no. 4:
        13-23.

FAST, John E., and CAYWOOD, Louis R.

1936   Life figures on Hohokam pottery. Southwestern
        Monuments Special Report, 2, March, pp. 187-190.

FAWCETT, William B., and CLEVELAND, David

1973   Archaeological resources: Parker Division, Colo-
        rado River. Arizona State Museum, Archaeological
        Series, 33, 47 pp.

FAY, George E.

1953   The archaeological cultures of the southern half of
        Sonora, Mexico. Year Book of the American Philo-
        sophical Society, pp. 266-269.

1954   A classic Folsom point from Clovis-Portales, New
        Mexico. El Palacio, 61:310-312.

1955a   A preliminary report of an archaeological survey
        in southern Sonora, Mexico, in 1953. Transactions
        of the Kansas Academy of Science, 58, no. 4:566-
        587.

1955b   Prepottery lithic complex from Sonora, Mexico. Sci-
        ence, 121, no. 3152:777-778.

1956a   Another cruciform artifact from Sonora. American
        Antiquity, 21:410-411.

1956b   Peralta complex, a Sonoran variant of the Cochise
        culture. Science, 124:1029.

1956c   A Seri fertility figurine from Bahia Kino, Sonora.
        Kiva, 21, nos. 3-4:11-12.

1957a   Peralta complex, a Sonoran variant of the Cochise
        culture. New World Antiquity, 4, no. 3:41-44.

1957b   A prepottery, lithic complex from Sonora, Mexico.
        Man, 57, no. 118:98-99.

1958a   A note on field work in Sonora, Mexico. El Palacio,
        65, no. 3:111-112.

1958b   The Peralta complex: a Sonoran variant of the Co-
        chise culture. Proceedings of the 32nd International
        Congress of Americanists, pp. 491-493.

1958c   A hematite iron deposit in Sonora, Mexico. South-
        western Lore, 24:5-6.

1959   Peralta complex, a Sonoran variant of the Cochise
        culture: new data, 1958. El Palacio, 66:21-24.

1961   A shell circle at Puerto Kino, Sonora. Man, 61,
        art. 53:56.

1963   Archaeological remains from Sonora. Masterkey, 37,
        no. 3:98-101.

1967a   An archaeological study of the Peralta complex in
        Sonora, Mexico. Colorado State College (Greeley),
        Museum of Anthropology, Occasional Publications in
        Anthropology, Archaeology Series, 1, 145 pp.

1967b   El complejo arqueológico de "Peralta" en Sonora.
        Revista Mexicana de Estudios Antropológicos, 21:
        7-15.

1968   A preliminary archaeological survey of Guaymas,
        Sonora, Mexico, Part I. Colorado State College
        (Greeley), Museum of Anthropology, Occasional
        Publications in Anthropology, Archaeological Series,
        no. 3, 152+175 pp.

FEINHANDLER, Sherwin (See under Agogino, George A.)

FELGER, Richard S. (See also under Braniff, Beatriz; Henrickson, James.)

1976   Investigación ecológica en Sonora y localidades
        adyacentes en Sinaloa: una perspectiva. In Braniff
        and Felger 1976, pp. 21-62.

FELTS, W.E. (See under Cosgrove, C.B., Jr.)

FENENGA, Franklin

1956   Excavations on Trunk O. In Wendorf, Fox, and Lewis
        1956, pp. 204-207.

FENENGA, F., and CUMMINGS, Thomas S.

1956   The eastern section of the Permian-San Juan Project.
        In Wendorf, Fox, and Lewis 1956, pp. 216-255.

FENENGA, F., and WENDORF, Fred

1956   Excavations at the Ignacio, Colorado, field camp:
        site LA 2605. In Wendorf, Fox, and Lewis 1956, pp.
        207-214.

FENENGA, F., and WHEAT, Joe Ben

1940   An atlatl from the Baylor Rock Shelter, Culberson
        County, Texas. American Antiquity, 5:221-223.

FENNER, Gloria J. (See under Di Peso, Charles C.)

FENTON, Carroll Lane, and EPSTEIN, Alice

1960   Cliff Dwellers of Walnut Canyon. John Day, New
        York, 63 pp.

FERDON, Edwin N., Jr. (See also under Peckham, Stewart L.;
Reed, Erik K.; Wendorf, Fred.)

1946   An excavation of Hermit's Cave, New Mexico. School

of American Research, Monograph no. 10, 29 pp.

1952   Treasure hunt at Abo and Quarai. El Palacio, 59:
        288-290.

1954   A surface jacal site in the Chaco Basin. El Palacio,
        61:35-42.

1955   A trial survey of Mexican-Southwestern architectural
        parallels. School of American Research, Monograph
        no. 21, 36 pp.
        Reviewed AAq 22:317 (Lister).

1967   The Hohokam "ball court": an alternate view of its
        function. Kiva, 33, no. 1:1-14.

FERDON, E.N., and REED, Erik K.

1950   A pit-house site near Belen, New Mexico. El Palacio,
        57:40-41.

FERG, Alan

1977a   Archaeological survey of the Westwing to Deer Val-
        ley Transmission Line, Maricopa County. Arizona
        State Museum, Archaeological Series, 111, 36 pp.

1977b   The Poor Canyon scatter: a Cochise site near Red-
        ington, Arizona. Arizona State Museum, Archae-
        ological Series, 114, 45 pp.

FERG, A., and VOGLER, Larry

1976   An archaeological survey of Route PIR 21: Kom Vo to
        Papago Farms. Arizona State Museum, Archaeological
        Series, 110, 31 pp.

FERGUSON, C.W., Jr.

1949   Additional dates for Nine Mile Canyon, northeastern
        Utah. Tree-Ring Bulletin, 16, no. 2:10-11.

1959   Growth rings in woody shrubs as potential aids in
        archaeological interpretation. Kiva, 25, no. 2:
        24-30.

FERGUSON, C.W., and BLACK, Donald M.

1952   Tree-ring chronologies on the north rim of the
        Grand Canyon. Tree-Ring Bulletin, 19, no. 2:12-18.

FERGUSON, Marjorie (Also listed as Lambert, Marjorie F., and
    Tichy, Marjorie Ferguson.)

1933   Preliminary report on Tecolote ruin. El Palacio,

34:196-198.

FERGUSON, T.J., and BEEZLEY, John

1974   Archaeological resources in the San Manuel-Red Rock
        area. Arizona State Museum, Archaeological Series,
        42, 31 pp.

FERRY, Philip

1953   Scaffold House. Arizona Highways, 29, no. 6:8-11.

FEWKES, Jesse Walter

1891   Reconnaissance of ruins in or near the Zuni Reserva-
        tion. Journal of American Ethnology and Archaeology,
        1:93-133.
        Reviewed AA o.s. 4:289 (Hodge).

1892a   A few Tusayan pictographs. American Anthropologist,
        o.s. 5, no. 1:9-26.

1892b   A report on the present condition of a ruin in Ari-
        zona called Casa Grande. Journal of American Eth-
        nology and Archaeology, 2:176-193.

1893   A-wa-to-bi; an archaeological verification of a
        Tusayan legend. American Anthropologist, o.s. 6,
        no. 4:363-376.

1895a   Another find in Arizona. American Antiquarian, 17:
        362.

1895b   Catalogue of the Hemenway Collection in the historico-
        American exposition of Madrid. Report of the United
        States Commission to the Madrid Exposition, 1892,
        pp. 279-326.

1896a   The prehistoric culture of Tusayan. American Anthro-
        pologist, o.s. 9, no. 5:151-173.

1896b   Preliminary account of an expedition to the cliff
        villages of the Red Rock country, and the Tusayan
        ruins of Sikyatki and Awatobi, Arizona, in 1895.
        Annual Report of the Smithsonian Institution for
        1895, pp. 557-588.

1896c   Southern extension of prehistoric Tusayan. American
        Anthropologist, o.s. 9, no. 7:253.

1896d   Two ruins recently discovered in the Red Rock coun-
        try, Arizona. American Anthropologist, o.s. 9, no.
        8:263-283.

1896e   Pacific coast shells from prehistoric Tusayan
        Pueblos. American Anthropologist, o.s. 9, no. 11:
        359-367.

1896f   Studies of Tusayan archaeology. Internationales
        Archiv für Ethnographie, 9:204-205.

1897   Tusayan totemic signatures. American Anthropologist,
        o.s. 10:1-11.

1898a   Archaeological expedition to Arizona in 1895. Seven-
        teenth Annual Report of the Bureau of American Eth-
        nology, pt. 2:519-744.
            Reviewed AA n.s. 3:353 (Chamberlain).

1898b   The feather symbol in ancient Hopi designs. Ameri-
        can Anthropologist, o.s. 11, no. 1:1-14.

1898c   An ancient human effigy vase from Arizona. Ameri-
        can Anthropologist, o.s. 11, no. 6:165-170.

1898d   Preliminary account of an expedition to the pueblo
        ruins near Winslow, Arizona, in 1896. Annual Re-
        port of the Smithsonian Institution for 1896, pp.
        517-539.

1898e   Preliminary account of archaeological field work in
        Arizona in 1897. Annual Report of the Smithsonian
        Institution for 1897, pp. 601-623.

1900   Pueblo ruins near Flagstaff, Arizona: a preliminary
        notice. American Anthropologist, n.s. 2, no. 3:
        422-450.

1902a   The Pueblo settlements near El Paso, Texas. Ameri-
        can Anthropologist, n.s., 4:57-75.

1902b   The ruined pueblo in New Mexico discovered by Vargas
        in 1692. Bulletin of the American Geographical
        Society, 34, no. 3:217-222.

1904a   A cluster of Arizona ruins which should be preserved.
        Records of the Past, 3, pt. 1:3-10.

1904b   Two summers' work in Pueblo ruins. Twenty-second
        Annual Report of the Bureau of American Ethnology,
        pt. 1:3-195.

1906a   The sun's influence on the form of Hopi pueblos.
        American Anthropologist, n.s., 8:88-100.

1906b   Hopi ceremonial frames from Canyon de Chelly, Ari-
        zona. American Anthropologist, n.s. 8, no. 4:664-
        670.

1907a Excavations at Casa Grande, Arizona, in 1906-07.
       Smithsonian Miscellaneous Collections, 50 (quarterly
       issue, 4, pt. 3):289-329.

1907b A fictitious ruin in Gila Valley, Arizona. Ameri-
       can Anthropologist, n.s., 9:510-512.

1908a Report on the excavation and repair of the Spruce
       Tree House, Mesa Verde National Park, Colorado.
       Annual Report of the Dept. of the Interior for
       1908, 1:490-505.

1908b Ventilators in ceremonial rooms of prehistoric
       cliff-dwellings. American Anthropologist, n.s.
       10, no. 3:387-398.

1909a Ancient Zuni pottery. Putnam Anniversary Volume,
       New York, pp. 43-82.

1909b Antiquities of the Mesa Verde National Park: Spruce-
       tree House. Bureau of American Ethnology, Bulletin
       41, 57 pp.

1909c Prehistoric ruins of the Gila Valley. Smithsonian
       Miscellaneous Collections, 52 (quarterly issue, 5,
       pt. 4):403-436.

1910a Cremation in cliff-dwellings. Records of the Past,
       9, pt. 3:154-156.

1910b A new type of Southwestern ruin. Records of the
       Past, 9, pt. 6:291-297.

1910c Note on the occurrence of adobes in cliff-dwellings.
       American Anthropologist, 12:434-436.

1910d Report on the excavation and repair of Cliff Palace,
       Mesa Verde National Park, Colorado, in 1909. Re-
       port of the Dept. of the Interior for 1909, 1:483-
       503.

1911a Preliminary report on a visit to the Navaho National
       Monument, Arizona. Bureau of American Ethnology,
       Bulletin 50, 35 pp.

1911b Antiquities of the Mesa Verde National Park: Cliff
       Palace. Bureau of American Ethnology, Bulletin 51,
       82 pp.

1912a Casa Grande, Arizona. Twenty-eighth Annual Report
       of the Bureau of American Ethnology, pp. 25-179.

1912b Antiquities of the upper Verde River and Walnut
       Creek Valleys, Arizona. Twenty-eighth Annual Re-
       port of the Bureau of American Ethnology, pp. 181-
       220.

1912c   Western neighbors of the prehistoric Pueblo. Jour-
        nal of the Washington Academy of Science, 2, no. 5:
        137-139.

1914   Archaeology of the lower Mimbres Valley, New Mexico.
        Smithsonian Miscellaneous Collections, 63, no. 10,
        53 pp.

1915a   The origin of the unit type of Pueblo architecture.
        Journal of the Washington Academy of Sciences, 5:
        543-552.

1915b   Prehistoric remains in New Mexico. Smithsonian
        Miscellaneous Collections, 65, no. 6:62-72.

1916a   Animal figures on prehistoric pottery from Mimbres
        Valley, New Mexico. American Anthropologist, 18,
        no. 4:535-545.

1916b   The cliff-ruins in Fewkes Canyon, Mesa Verde Nation-
        al Park, Colorado. Holmes Anniversary Volume, Wash-
        ington, pp. 96-117.

1916c   Excavation and repair of Sun Temple, Mesa Verde
        National Park. Department of the Interior, 32 pp.

1916d   Prehistoric remains in Arizona, New Mexico and
        Colorado. Smithsonian Miscellaneous Collections,
        66, no. 3:82-98.

1916e   The relation of Sun Temple, a new type of ruin late-
        ly excavated in the Mesa Verde National Park, to
        prehistoric "towers." Journal of the Washington
        Academy of Sciences, 6, no. 8:212-221.

1916f   A Sun Temple in the Mesa Verde National Park. Art
        and Archaeology, 3, no. 6:341-346.

1916g   Excavations in the Mesa Verde Park. Old Santa Fe,
        3:161-165.

1916h   Uncovering a prehistoric dwelling in southwestern
        Colorado. Scientific American, 115, no. 7:156.

1917a   Far View House - a pure type of pueblo ruin. Art
        and Archaeology, 6:133-141.

1917b   The Mesa Verde types of pueblos. Proceedings of the
        National Academy of Science, 3:497-501.

1917c   A prehistoric Mesa Verde pueblo and its people.
        Annual Report of the Smithsonian Institution for
        1916, pp. 461-488.

1917d   Prehistoric remains in New Mexico, Colorado, and

Utah. Smithsonian Miscellaneous Collections, 66, no. 17:76-92.

1917e Archaeological investigations in New Mexico, Colorado, and Utah. Smithsonian Miscellaneous Collections, 68, no. 1, 38 pp.

1917f Types of prehistoric Southwestern architecture. Proceedings of the American Antiquarian Society, 27, pt. 1:67-80.

1917g The first pueblo ruin in Colorado mentioned in Spanish documents. Science, 46, no. 1185:255.

1917h The pueblo culture and its relationships. Pan-American Scientific Congress, 2nd session, Proceedings, Section I: Anthropology, 1:410-416.

1917i A prehistoric stone mortar from southern Arizona. Journal of the Washington Academy of Sciences, 7: 459-463.

1918a Prehistoric ruins in southwestern Colorado and southeastern Utah. Smithsonian Miscellaneous Collections, 68, no. 12:108-133.

1918b Prehistoric towers and castles of the Southwest. Art and Archaeology, 7, no. 9:353-366.

1918c A unique form of prehistoric pottery. Journal of the Washington Academy of Sciences, 8, no. 18:598-601.

1919a Archaeological field-work in southwestern Colorado and Utah in 1918. Smithsonian Miscellaneous Collections, 70, no. 2:68-80.

1919b Designs on prehistoric Hopi pottery. Thirty-third Annual Report of the Bureau of American Ethnology, pp. 207-284.

1919c Prehistoric villages, castles, and towers of southwestern Colorado. Bureau of American Ethnology, Bulletin 70, 79 pp.

1920a Ancient remains in Colorado; the Mesa Verde National Park, landmark of a lost race. Scientific American, 122:598, 606-610.

1920b Field-work on the Mesa Verde National Park, Colorado. Smithsonian Miscellaneous Collections, 72, no. 1: 47-64.

1920c The genesis of the cliff dwellings. Journal of the Washington Academy of Sciences, 10:334-335.

1920d   Square Tower House. Southern Workman, 49:309-314.

1921a   Field-work on the Mesa Verde National Park. Smith-
        sonian Miscellaneous Collections, 72, no. 6:75-94.

1921b   New Fire House, a ruin lately excavated in the Mesa
        Verde. Art and Archaeology, 10, nos. 1-2:44-46.

1921c   Two types of Southwestern cliff houses. Annual
        Report of the Smithsonian Institution for 1919,
        pp. 421-426.

1921d   Excavating cliff dwellings in Mesa Verde. Scientific
        American, 123:9-13.

1921e   The Fire Temple of the cliff dwellers. American
        Anthropologist, 23:501-503.

1922a   Archaeological field-work on the Mesa Verde National
        Park. Smithsonian Miscellaneous Collections, 72,
        no. 15:64-83.

1922b   Architectural types of Mesa Verde. Annual Report
        of the Smithsonian Institution for 1920, pp. 58-61.

1923a   Archaeological field-work on the Mesa Verde National
        Park, Colorado. Smithsonian Miscellaneous Collec-
        tions, 74, no. 5:89-115.

1923b   Designs on prehistoric pottery from the Mimbres
        Valley, New Mexico. Smithsonian Miscellaneous Col-
        lections, 74, no. 6, 47 pp.

1923c   Designs on prehistoric pottery from the Mimbres
        Valley. El Palacio, 15:9-13.

1923d   The Hovenweep National Monument. American Anthro-
        pologist, 25, no. 2:145-155 (also Annual Report of
        the Smithsonian Institution for 1923, pp. 465-480).

1923e   Additional designs on prehistoric Mimbres pottery.
        Smithsonian Miscellaneous Collections, 76, no. 8,
        46 pp.

1924   Archaeological field-work in New Mexico. Smithson-
        ian Miscellaneous Collections, 76, no. 10:82-88.

1926a   An archaeological collection from Young's Canyon,
        near Flagstaff, Arizona. Smithsonian Miscellaneous
        Collections, 77, no. 10, 15 pp.

1926b   Archaeological studies of the Wupatki National Monu-
        ment. Smithsonian Miscellaneous Collections, 78,
        no. 1:96-105.

1926c   The chronology of the Mesa Verde. American Journal

of Archaeology, 2nd ser., 30, no. 3:270-282.

1926d   Elden Pueblo. Science, 64, no. 1664:508.

1927   Archaeological field work in Arizona, field season
        of 1926. Smithsonian Miscellaneous Collections, 78,
        no. 7:207-232.

FIERO, Donald C. (See under Kayser, David W.)

FIGGINS, Jesse Dade

1927   The antiquity of man in America. Natural History,
        27, no. 3:229-239.

FINDLOW, Frank J.

1975   Investigations into the determinants of settlement
        placement in Pimeria Alta. University of California
        (Los Angeles), dissertation, 192 pp.; University
        Microfilms International.

FINDLOW, F.J., and others

1975   A new obsidian hydration rate for certain obsidians
        in the American Southwest. American Antiquity, 40:
        344-348.

FINK, Colin G., and POLUSHKIN, E.P.

1946   Metallographic examination of the San Gabriel bell
        fragment. New Mexico Historical Review, 21:145-148.

FISH, Paul R. (See also under Dittert, Alfred E., Jr.)

1971   The Lake Pleasant project: a preliminary report on
        the excavation of the Beardsley Canal site. Arizona
        State Museum.

1974   Prehistoric land use in the Perkinsville Valley.
        Arizona Archaeologist, 8:1-36.

FISH, P.R., and FISH, Suzanne K.

1977   Verde Valley archaeology: review and prospective.
        Museum of Northern Arizona, Research Papers, 8, 72
        pp.

FISH, P.R., KITCHEN, Suzanne, and McWILLIAMS, Kenneth

1971   A slab-covered burial from the Perkinsville Valley,
        Arizona. Plateau, 43, no. 3:138-144.

FISH, Suzanne K. (See under Fish, Paul R. Also listed as Kitchen, Suzanne.)

FISHER, Howard J. (See under Williamson, Ray A.)

FISHER, Reginald G. (See also under Hewett, Edgar Lee; Reiter, Paul.)

 1930 Archaeological survey of the Pueblo plateau. University of New Mexico Bulletin, Archaeological Series, 1, no. 1, 22 pp.

 1931 Second report of the archaeological survey of the Pueblo plateau. Santa Fe sub-quadrangle A. University of New Mexico Bulletin, Survey Series, 1, no 1.

 1933 Engineering in Southwestern excavation and research. El Palacio, 34:116-119.

 1934a The Chaco Canyon in 1934. El Palacio, 37:117-131.

 1934b Some geographic factors that influenced the ancient populations of the Chaco Canyon, New Mexico. University of New Mexico Bulletin, Archaeological Series, 3, no. 1, 24 pp.

 1935 The relation of North American prehistory to post-glacial climatic fluctuations. University of New Mexico Bulletin, Monograph Series, 1, no. 2, 91 pp. Reviewed AA 39:334 (Cressman), AAq 2:237 (Richardson).

 1937 The Jeddito project of Peabody Museum. El Palacio, 43:97-101.

FITTING, James E. (See also under Lekson, Stephen.)

 1963 Thickness and fluting of Paleo-Indian projectile points. American Antiquity, 29, no. 1:105-106.

 1970 Preliminary notes on some southwestern New Mexico lithic industries. Kiva, 36, no. 1:15-21.

 1971a The Burris ranch site, Dona Ana County, New Mexico. Case Western Reserve University, Southwestern New Mexico Research Reports, 1, 50 pp.

 1971b Excavations at MC110, Grant County, New Mexico. Case Western Reserve University, Southwestern New Mexico Research Reports, 2, 33 pp.

 1971c The Hermanas ruin, Luna County, New Mexico. Case Western Reserve University, Southwestern New Mexico

Research Reports, 3, 44 pp.

1972a   Chipped stone from the 1967 Mimbres area survey,
         Pts. I-II. Case Western Reserve University, South-
         western New Mexico Research Reports, 8, 2 vols.,
         132 pp.

1972b   Preliminary notes on Cliff Valley settlement pat-
         terns. The Artifact, 10, no. 4:15-30.

1973a   An early Mogollon community: a preliminary report
         on the Winn Canyon site. The Artifact, 11, nos.
         1-2, 94 pp.

1973b   Four archaeological sites in the Big Burro Mountains
         of New Mexico. Center of Anthropological Study (Las
         Cruces), Monograph no. 1, 50 pp.

FITTING, J.E., and PRICE, Theron D.

1968   Two late Paleo-Indian sites in southwestern New
         Mexico. Kiva, 34, no. 1:1-8.

FITTING, J.E., and STONE, Lyle M.

1969   Distance and utility in the distribution of raw
         materials in the Cedar Mountains of New Mexico.
         Kiva, 34, no. 4:207-212.

FITTING, J.E., KLINGER, Timothy, and ANDERSON, David G.

1972   Archaeological survey and excavations in Dark Thund-
         er Canyon. Case Western Reserve University, South-
         western New Mexico Research Reports, 9, 70 pp.

FITTING, J.E., ROSS, James L., and GRAY, B. Thomas

1971   Preliminary report on the 1971 Intersession exca-
         vations at the Saige-McFarland site (MC146). Case
         Western Reserve University, Southwestern New Mexico
         Research Reports, 4, 57 pp.

FITZGERALD, Gerald X.

1973   (ed.) The Mimbres report. The Artifact, 11, no.
         4, 88 pp.

FITZPATRICK, George

1946   Stone Age apartment house. New Mexico Magazine,
         24, no. 10:11-13, 33, 35.

FITZWATER, Robert

    1967   Localities 3 and 4A (Cl-246, Cl-259), Tule Springs,
            Nevada. *In* Wormington and Ellis 1967, pp. 353-364.

FLAIM, Francis R., and WARBURTON, Austen D.

    1961   Additional figurines from Rasmussen Cave. Masterkey,
            35, no. 1:19-24.

FLETCHER, Henry T.

    1930   Notes on the ethnobotany of Bee Cave Canyon. West
            Texas Historical and Scientific Society, Publica-
            tions, no. 3:37-44.

    1931   Some types of archaeological sites in Trans-Pecos
            Texas. Bulletin of the Texas Archaeological and
            Paleontological Society, 3:7-17.

FLIEDNER, D.

    1975   Pre-Spanish pueblos in New Mexico. Annals of the
            Association of American Geographers, 65:363-377.

FLINN, Lynn, TURNER, Christy G., II, and BREW, Alan

    1976   Additional evidence for cannibalism in the South-
            west: the case of LA 4528. American Antiquity, 41:
            308-318.

FLORA, I.F. (See also under Haury, Emil W.)

FLORA, I.F., DANIELS, H.S., and CORNELIUS, T.H.

    1940-   Sherds and Points. 2 vols, reprinted from Durango
    41   News, Durango, Colorado.

FOLSOM, F. (See under Agogino, George A.)

FONNER, Robert L. (See under Jones, Volney H.)

FONTANA, Bernard L. (See also under Smith, Watson.)

    1965a   On the meaning of historic sites archaeology. Amer-
            ican Antiquity, 31:61-65.

    1965b   The tale of a nail: on the ethnological interpreta-
            tion of historic artifacts. Florida Anthropologist,
            18, no. 3:85-102.

    1968a   Bottles and history: the case of Magdalena de Kino,
            Sonora. Historical Archaeology, 2:45-55.

1968b A British lead seal from northern New Spain. Post-
       medieval Archaeology, 2:166-168.

1968c "President pipes" from Arizona. The Chesopiean,
       6, no. 6:160-161.

FONTANA, B.L., and GREENLEAF, J. Cameron

1962   Johnny Ward's Ranch: a study in historic archae-
       ology. Kiva, 28, nos. 1-2:1-115.
       Reviewed AA 65:1188 (G.H. Smith).

FONTANA, B.L., GREENLEAF, J.C., and CASSIDY, Donnelly D.

1959   A fortified Arizona mountain. Kiva, 25, no. 2:41-53.

FONTANA, B.L., and others

1962   Papago Indian pottery. University of Washington
       Press.

FORBES, Jack D.

1961   Pueblo pottery in the San Fernando Valley. Master-
       key, 35, no. 1:36-38.

FORD, Richard I.

1975   Re-excavation of Jemez Cave, New Mexico. Awanyu,
       3, no. 3:13-27.

FORD, R.I., SCHROEDER, Albert H., and PECKHAM, Stewart L.

1972   Three perspectives on Puebloan prehistory. *In* New
       Perspectives on the Pueblos, ed. A. Ortiz, Univer-
       sity of New Mexico Press, pp. 19-39.

FOSBERG, Stephen (See also under Grigg, Paul.)

1977   Archaeological survey of five mine site locations
       of United Nuclear, Dalton Pass, New Mexico. Uni-
       versity of New Mexico, contract report 185-2G (NPS).

FOSSNOCK, Annette

1935   Pictographs and murals in the Southwest. El Palacio,
       39, nos. 16-18:81-90.

FOSTER, Gene

1952   A brief archaeological survey of Glen Canyon. Pla-
       teau, 25, no. 2:21-26.

    1954   Petrographic art in Glen Canyon. Plateau, 27, no.
            1:6-18.

FOSTER, John W.
    1975   Shell middens, paleoecology, and prehistory: the
            case from Estero Morua, Sonora, Mexico. Kiva, 41,
            no. 2:185-194.

FOWKE, Gerard
    1896   Stone art. Thirteenth Annual Report of the Bureau
            of American Ethnology, pp. 47-178.

FOWLER, Catherine S.
    1970   Great Basin anthropology - a bibliography. Uni-
            versity of Nevada, Desert Research Institute, Pub-
            lications in the Social Sciences, 5, 418 pp.

FOWLER, Don D. (See also under Wheeler, S.M.)
    1958   Archaeological survey in Glen Canyon: a preliminary
            report of 1958 work. Utah Archaeology, 4, no. 4:
            14-16.

    1959   Glen Canyon Main Stem survey. *In* Jennings and others
            1959, pt. II, pp. 473-539.

    1961   1960 archaeological survey and testing in the Glen
            Canyon region. Utah Archaeology, 7, no. 1:18-24.

    1963   1961 excavations, Harris Wash, Utah. University of
            Utah, Anthropological Papers, 64, 116 pp.

    1968a   Archaeological survey in eastern Nevada, 1966.
            Desert Research Institute, Social Sciences and
            Humanities Publication no. 2, 60 pp.

    1968b   The archaeology of Newark Cave, White Pine County,
            Nevada. Desert Research Institute, Social Sciences
            and Humanities Publication no. 3, 39 pp.

    1972   (ed.) Great Basin cultural ecology: a symposium.
            University of Nevada, Desert Research Institute,
            Publications in the Social Sciences, 8, 160 pp.
                Reviewed AA 77:677 (Bettinger), AAq 40:375 (Swan-
            son).

    1973   Dated split-twig figurine from Etna Cave, Nevada.
            Plateau, 46, no. 2:54-63.

FOWLER, D.D., and AIKENS, C. Melvin

1962   A preliminary report of 1961 excavations in Harris
        Wash and on the Kaiparowits Plateau. Utah Archae-
        ology, 8, no. 1:5-13.

1963   1961 excavations, Kaiparowits Plateau, Utah. Uni-
        versity of Utah, Anthropological Papers, 66, 100 pp.

FOWLER, D.D., and LISTER, Florence C.

1959   The Glen Canyon archaeological survey, Part III.
        University of Utah, Anthropological Papers, 39, 98
        pp.

FOWLER, D.D., MADSEN, David B., and HATTORI, Eugene M.

1973   Prehistory of southeastern Nevada. University of
        Nevada, Desert Research Institute, Publications in
        the Social Sciences, 6, 145 pp.

FOX, Nancy (See also under Wendorf, Fred.)

1975   Potsui'i Incised cylindrical vessels. *In* Frisbie
        1975a, pp. 88-97.

FRANK, LARRY (See under Harlow, Francis H.)

FRANKE, Paul R.

1931   Talkative tree rings may reveal mesa's secrets.
        Mesa Verde Notes, 2:9-11.

1932   Incised pottery designs on building blocks of Mesa
        Verde masonry. Mesa Verde Notes, 3, no. 3:29-32.

1933   New dates from Mesa Verde ruins. Mesa Verde Notes,
        4, no. 1:19-20.

1934a   Sun symbol markings. Mesa Verde Notes, 5, no. 1:
        7-12.

1934b   A unique pot from Mesa Verde. Mesa Verde Notes, 5,
        no. 2:38-40.

1935a   Mesa Verde's place in the Southwest story. South-
        western Lore, 1, no. 3:11-16.

1935b   Premeditated discovery. Mesa Verde Notes, 6, no.
        1:6-10.

FRANKE, P.R., and WATSON, Don

1936   An experimental corn field in Mesa Verde National

Park. *In* Brand 1936, pp. 35-41.

FRANKLIN, Hayward H., and MASSE, W. Bruce

1976   The San Pedro Salado: a case of prehistoric migra-
        tion. *In* Doyel and Haury 1976, pp. 47-55.

FRAPS, Clara Lee (Also listed as Tanner, Clara Lee.)

1935   Tanque Verde ruins. Kiva, 1, no. 4:1-4.

FREEMAN, Leslie G., Jr. (See also under Brown, James A.; Martin,
Paul Sidney.)

1962   Statistical analysis of painted pottery types from
        Upper Little Colorado drainage. *In* Martin, Rinaldo,
        and others 1962, pp. 87-104.

FREIDAY, Dean

1951   Bulldozers vs. trowels. Natural History, 60:248-
        253, 288.

FRISBIE, Theodore R. (See also under Galinat, Walton C.)

1971   An archaeo-ethnological interpretation of maize
        deity symbols in the Greater Southwest. Southern
        Illinois University, dissertation, 288 pp.; Univer-
        sity Microfilms International.

1973   Field report: the Newton Site, Catron County, New
        Mexico. Awanyu, 1, no. 4:31-36.

1975a   (ed.) Collected papers in honor of Florence Hawley
        Ellis. Archaeological Society of New Mexico, Papers,
        no. 2, 489 pp.
             Reviewed AA 78:933 (Morris).

1975b   *Hishi* as money in the Puebloan Southwest. *In* Fris-
        bie 1975a, pp. 120-142.

1975c   On the validity of Tamaya Red. Pottery Southwest,
        2, no. 1:4.

1975d   Query: typological variations of San Marcial Black-
        on-white. Pottery Southwest, 2, no. 1:4.

1977a   Ceramic Typology Forum. Pottery Southwest, Special
        Issue, January.

1978   High status burials in the Greater Southwest: an
        interpretative synthesis. *In* Riley and Hedrick
        1978, pp. 202-227.

FRITTS, Harold

 1965   Tree-ring evidence for climatic changes in western
        North America. Monthly Weather Review, 93, no. 7:
        421-443.

FRITZ, Gordon L. (See also under Canouts, Valetta; Debowski,
        Sharon S.; Doelle, William H.; Kinkade, Gay M.)

 1966   North Gate site two. The Artifact, 4, no. 2:3-4.

 1968   Five pottery vessels from near Casas Grandes, Chi-
        huahua. The Artifact, 6, no. 2:25-32.

 1969   Investigations at the Rancho El Espia site, north-
        western Chihuahua. Transactions of the 5th Region-
        al Archaeological Symposium on Southeastern New Mex-
        ico and Western Texas, pp. 51-63.

 1973   Archaeological resources in the Tucson Basin. Ari-
        zona State Museum, Archaeological Series, 35, 25
        pp.

 1974   Archaeological survey for Tucson sewage project.
        Arizona State Museum, Archaeological Series, 36,
        36 pp.

 1975   Archaeological resources of the Kofa and Little
        Horn Planning Units (BLM). Arizona State Museum,
        Archaeological Series, 84, 21 pp.

FRITZ, G.L., and GRADY, Mark

 1974   Tucson sewage project appendix: Santa Cruz River
        section. Arizona State Museum, Archaeological
        Series, 38, 12 pp.

FRITZ, G.L., and others

 1974   Cultural and environmental overviews of 16 BLM
        Planning Units. Arizona State Museum, Archaeologi-
        cal Series, 57, 55 pp.

FRITZ, John (See under Martin, Paul Sidney.)

FRITZ, W.C.

 1941   A Texas Sandia point. Bulletin of the Texas Ar-
        chaeological and Paleontological Society, 13:168-
        173.

FRIZELL, John (See under Stein, John R.)

FRY, Gary F. (See also under Adovasio, James M.; Aikens, C.
Melvin; Marwitt, John P.; Moore, John G.)

1970   Prehistoric human ecology in Utah: based on the
        analysis of coprolites. University of Utah, dis-
        sertation, 142 pp.; University Microfilms Inter-
        national.

1976   Prehistoric diet and disease in the Desert West of
        North America. *In* Prehistoric Cultural Adaptations
        in Western North America, ed. David L. Bowman. Al-
        dine Publishing Co.

FRY, G.F., and ADOVASIO, J.M.

1970   Population differentiation in Hogup and Danger Caves,
        two Archaic sites in the eastern Great Basin. Ne-
        vada State Museum, Anthropological Papers, 15, pp.
        207-215.

1976   Human adaptation during the Altithermal in the east-
        ern Great Basin. *In* Holocene Environmental Change
        in the Great Basin, ed. Robert Elston, Nevada Ar-
        chaeological Survey, Research Paper no. 6, pp. 68-
        73.

FRY, G.F., and HALL, H.J.

1975   Human coprolites from Antelope House: preliminary
        analysis. *In* Rock and Morris 1975, pp. 87-96.

FRY, G.F., and MOORE, John G.

1969   Enterobius vermicularis: 10,000-year-old human in-
        fection. Science, 166:1620.

FULLBRIGHT, H.J. (See under Snow, David H.)

FULLER, Steven L. (See also under Coe, Carol N.; Rogge, A.E.)

1974a   The archaeological resources of the BLM Silver Bell
        Planning Unit. Arizona State Museum, Archaeological
        Series, 58, 25 pp.

1974b   The archaeological resources of the BLM Ajo Plan-
        ning Unit. Arizona State Museum, Archaeological
        Series, 59, 20 pp.

1975a   Archaeological resources of the BLM Rainbow-Stan-
        field Planning Units. Arizona State Museum, Archae-
        ological Series, 63, 29 pp.

1975b   Archaeological resources of the Black Mountains and

the Cerbat Mountains BLM Planning Units. Arizona
State Museum, Archaeological Series, 70, 40 pp.

FULLER, S.L., and others

1976   Orme alternatives: archaeological resources of
        Roosevelt Dam and Horseshoe Reservoir. Arizona
        State Museum, Archaeological Series, 98, vols. 1-2,
        320+127 pp.

FULTON, William Shirley

1934-   Archaeological notes on Texas Canyon, Arizona.
38   Museum of the American Indian, Contributions, 12,
        nos. 1-3, 23+23+22 pp.

1941   A ceremonial cave in the Winchester Mountains,
        Arizona. Amerind Foundation, no. 2, 35 pp.

FULTON, W.S., and TUTHILL, Carr

1940   An archaeological site near Gleeson, Arizona.
        Amerind Foundation, no. 1, 66 pp.
        Reviewed AA 44:701 (Haury).

GABEL, Norman E.

1950   The skeletal remains of Ventana Cave. *In* Haury
        1950b, pp. 473-520.

GAILLARD, D.D.

1896   A gigantic earthwork in New Mexico. American
        Anthropologist, o.s. 9, no. 9:311-313.

GAINES, Sylvia W. (See also under Plog, Fred. T.; Schoenwetter,
James.)

1978   Computer application of SARG data: an evaluation.
        In Euler and Gumerman 1978, pp. 119-138.

GALINAT, Walton C., and GUNNERSON, James H.

1963   Spread of eight-rowed maize from the prehistoric
        Southwest. Harvard University Botanical Museum,
        Leaflets, 20, no. 5:117-160.

1969   Fremont Maize. *In* J.H. Gunnerson, 1969b, pp. 198-
        206.

GALINAT, W.C., and RUPPÉ, R.J.

1961   Further archaeological evidence on the effects of

teosinte introgression in the evolution of modern
maize. Harvard University Botanical Museum, Leaflets, 19, no. 8:163-181.

GALINAT, W.C., MANGELSDORF, P.C., and PIERSON, L.

1956   Estimates of teosinte introgression in archaeological
maize. Harvard University Botanical Museum, Leaflets, 17:101-124.

GALINAT, W.C., REINHART, Theodore R., and FRISBIE, Theodore R.

1970   Early eight-rowed maize from the middle Rio Grande
Valley, New Mexico. Harvard University Botanical
Museum, Leaflets, 22, no. 9:313-331.

GALLENKAMP, Charles B.

1950   The mystery of New Mexico's lost cities. New
Mexico Magazine, 28, no. 6:13-15, 41-42.

1953   New Mexico's vanished tower dwellers. Natural
History, 62, no. 7:312-319.

1954   Mystery of the vanished Gallinas. Desert Magazine,
17, no. 2:16-19.

1955   Where ancients wrote in stone. Desert Magazine, 18,
no. 5:6-18.

GAMACHE, Glen L. (See under Kunz, Michael.)

GANNETT, Henry

1880   Prehistoric ruins in southern Colorado. Popular
Science Monthly, 16:666-673.

GARDNER, Fletcher, and MARTIN, George C.

1933   A new type of atlatl from a cave shelter on the
Rio Grande near Shumla, Val Verde County, Texas.
Witte Memorial Museum, Bulletin no. 2, 18 pp.

GARDNER, W.A.

1940   Place of the gods: Canyon de Chelly.' Natural History, 45 (January):40-43.

GARRETT, C.K. (See under Plog, Fred T.)

GASSER, ROBERT E.

1976   Hohokam subsistence: a 2,000 year continuum in the

indigenous exploitation of the Lower Sonoran Desert. U.S. Forest Service, Southwestern Region, Archaeological Report, 11, 64 pp.

GAUMER, Alfred Elliott

1937   Basketmaker caves in Desolation Canyon, Green River, Utah. Masterkey, 11, no. 5:160-165.

1939   A Fremont River culture cradle. Masterkey, 13, no. 4:139-140.

GAUTHIER, Rory (See also under Broster, John; Grigg, Paul.)

1977   Archaeological survey of three tracts in the Manzano Mountains for KNME-TV. University of New Mexico, contract report 185-2C.

GAUTHIER, R., and ACKLEN, John C.

1977a   Archaeological survey in Rio Puerco Valley (East): Public Service Company of New Mexico Marquez line. University of New Mexico, contract report 185-2 (BLM).

1977b   Archaeological survey of the proposed Gallegos power line in the Gallegos Wash area. University of New Mexico, contract report 185-2B (BLM).

GAUTHIER, R., and LENT, Stephen C.

1978   Archaeological survey of Conoco's Bernable road modification and improvement. University of New Mexico, contract report 185-18 (BLM, NPS, BIA).

GAUTHIER, R., and MASHBURN, C.H.R.

1977   Archaeological survey of Public Service Company's 345 KV San Ildefonso powerline. University of New Mexico, contract report 185-2H (BIA).

GAUTHIER, R., and STEIN, John R.

1976   GASCO survey: 100 mile pipeline from Star Lake to Gallup, New Mexico. University of New Mexico, contract report 101-141 (State Historic Preservation Office, BLM, NPS, BIA).

GAUTHIER, R., ACKLEN, J.C., and STEIN, John R.

1977   Archaeological survey of Anaconda Company's Bluewater Mill tailing pond expansion, New Mexico. University of New Mexico, contract report 101-170 (State

Historic Preservation Office).

GAUTHIER, R., STUART, David E., and ALLAN, William

1976   Archaeological survey of Wesco 8.8 mile Burnham
        access road. University of New Mexico, contract
        report 101-132 (NPS).

GAVAN, J.A.

1940   Physical anthropology of Besh-ba-gowah. Kiva, 6,
        no. 3:9-12.

GEBHARD, David A.

1957   Pictographs in the Sierra Blanca Mountains. El
        Palacio, 64:215-221.

1958   Hidden Lake pictographs. El Palacio, 65, no. 4:
        146-149.

1960   Prehistoric paintings of the Diablo region of west-
        ern Texas: a preliminary report. Roswell Museum and
        Art Center, Publications in Art and Sciences, 3, 102
        pp.
        Reviewed AAq 26:445 (Cain).

1962   Prehistoric rock drawings at Painted Grotto, New
        Mexico. El Palacio, 69:218-223.

GEBHARD, P.H.

1943   The excavation of an archaeological site on the
        Purgatoire River, southeastern Colorado. Papers
        of the Excavators' Club, 2, no. 2, 29 pp.

GEHLBACH, F.R., and MILLER, R.R.

1961   Fishes from archaeological sites in northern New
        Mexico. Southwestern Naturalist, 6, no. 1.

GELL, Elizabeth Ann Morris (See also under Bannister, Bryant.
    Also listed as Morris, Elizabeth Ann.)

1967   A pine gum thimble from Point of Pines. Kiva, 33,
        no. 2:80-81.

GERALD, Rex E. (See also under Wright, Barton A.)

1954   1954 archaeological expedition into northwestern
        Chihuahua: a preliminary report. Philadelphia
        Anthropological Society, Bulletin, 8, no. 1:3-4.

The Bibliography *143*

1958   Two wickiups on the San Carlos Indian Reservation, Arizona. Kiva, 23, no. 3:5-11.

1968a   The Mimbres Indians. El Paso Centennial Museum, 9 pp.

1968b   Spanish presidios of the late eighteenth century in northern New Spain. Museum of New Mexico, Research Records, 7, 60 pp.

1976   A conceptual framework for evaluating Salado and Salado-related material in the El Paso area. *In* Doyel and Haury 1976, pp. 65-70.

GERMANN, Frank E.E.

1926   Ceramic pigments of the Indians of the Southwest. Science, 63, no. 1636:480-482.

GERMESHAUSEN, Edward (See under Canouts, Valetta.)

GETTY, Harry T.

1933   Pursuing the elusive tree ring. Mesa Verde Notes, 4, no. 2:14-16.

1935a   New dates from Mesa Verde. Tree-Ring Bulletin, 1, no. 3:21-23.

1935b   New dates for Spruce Tree House, Mesa Verde. Tree-Ring Bulletin, 1, no. 4:28-29.

1936   Prehistoric man in the Southwest. Grand Canyon Natural History Association, Natural History Bulletin 7, 19 pp.

GIBSON, Gordon D.

1947   On Gladwin's method of correlation in tree-ring analysis. American Anthropologist, 49:337-340.

GIFFORD, Carol A. (See under Haury, Emil W.)

GIFFORD, D.S., and GIFFORD, E.W.

1949   The Cochise culture *Olivella*. American Antiquity, 15:163.

GIFFORD, Edward Winslow (See also under Gifford, D.S.; Schenck, W. Egbert.)

1928   Pottery making in the Southwest. University of California Publications in American Archaeology and Ethnology, 23, no. 8:353-373.

1946   Archaeology in the Punta Peñasco region, Sonora.
       American Antiquity, 11:215-221.

1949   Early central California and Anasazi shell artifact
       types. American Antiquity, 15:156-157.

GIFFORD, James C. (See also under Breternitz, David A.; Wheat,
Joe Ben.)

1953   (ed.) A guide to the description of pottery types
       in the Southwest. University of Arizona, Dept. of
       Anthropology, 16 pp.

GIFFORD, J.C., and SMITH, Watson

1978   Gray corrugated pottery from Awatovi and other
       Jeddito sites in northeastern Arizona. Peabody
       Museum of Archaeology and Ethnology, Papers, 69,
       155 pp.

GILBERT, Elizabeth X.

1961   A pithouse village on the San Juan River, N.M.
       Southwestern Lore, 27, no. 1:9-16.

GILBERT, Hope

1942   Pecos ruin. New Mexico Magazine, 20:12-13, 33-34.

GILES, Eugene, and BLEIBTREU, Hermann K.

1961   Cranial evidence in archaeological reconstruction:
       a trial of multivariate techniques for the South-
       west. American Anthropologist, 63:48-61.

GILLIN, John

1938a Archaeological investigations in Nine Mile Canyon,
       Utah. University of Utah Bulletin, 28, no. 11
       (reprinted as Anthropological Papers, 21, 45 pp.,
       1955).
          Reviewed AA 42:140 (Roberts), AAq 5:75 (Steward).

1938b A method of notation for the description and com-
       parison of Southwestern pottery sherds by formula.
       American Antiquity, 4, no. 1:22-29.

1940   A barbed bone projectile point from Utah. American
       Antiquity, 6:170-171.

1941   Archaeological investigations in central Utah.

Papers of the Peabody Museum of American Archaeology and Ethnology, 17, no. 2, 50 pp.

GILMAN, Patricia A. (See also under Kinkade, Gay M.)

1976   Walnut Canyon National Monument: an archaeological overview. National Park Service, Western Archaeological Center, Publications in Anthropology, no. 4, 84 pp.

GILMAN, P.A., and RICHARDS, Barry

1975   Archaeological survey in Arivaipa Canyon Primitive Area. Arizona State Museum, Archaeological Series, 77, 35 pp.

GILMAN, P.A., and SHERMAN, Peter

1975   Archaeological survey of the Graham-Curtis Project. Arizona State Museum, Archaeological Series, 65, 28 pp.

GILMORE, Melvin R.

1937   An interesting vegetal artifact from the Pecos region of Texas. Anthropological Papers, 1, no. 5, University of Texas Bulletin 3734:21-26.

GIVENS, R. Dale (See under Luebben, Ralph A.)

GLADWIN, Harold S. (See also under Gladwin, Winifred.)

1928   Excavations at Casa Grande, Arizona, Feb. 12-May 1, 1927. Southwest Museum Papers, 2, 30 pp. Reviewed AA 31:513 (Kroeber).

1930   An outline of Southwestern prehistory. Arizona Historical Review, 3:77-87.

1933   Aboriginal man in Arizona and his forerunners. Grand Canyon Nature Notes, 7:97-107.

1934   The archaeology of the Southwest and its relation to the cultures of Texas. Bulletin of the Texas Archaeological and Paleontological Society, 6: 19-37.

1936   Methodology in the Southwest. American Antiquity, 1:256-259.

1937a   Excavations at Snaketown, II. Comparisons and theories. Gila Pueblo, Medallion Papers, 26, 167 pp.

Reviewed AA 41:139 (Vaillant), AAq 5:180 (Weckler).

1937b The significance of early cultures in Texas and
       southeastern Arizona. *In* Early Man, ed. G.G. Mac-
       Curdy, Academy of Natural Sciences of Philadelphia,
       pp. 133-138.

1940a Methods and instruments for use in measuring tree-
       rings. Gila Pueblo, Medallion Papers, 27, 13 pp.

1940b Tree-ring analysis. Methods of correlation. Gila
       Pueblo, Medallion Papers, 28, 63 pp.
       Reviewed AA 48:433 (Antevs).

1942   Excavations at Snaketown, III. Revisions. Gila
       Pueblo, Medallion Papers, 30, 19 pp.
       Reviewed AA 45:466 (Hall).

1943   A review and analysis of the Flagstaff culture.
       Gila Pueblo, Medallion Papers, 31, 97 pp.

1944   Tree-ring analysis. Problems of dating, I. The
       Medicine Valley sites. Gila Pueblo, Medallion
       Papers, 32, 45 pp.
       Reviewed AA 48:436 (Antevs).

1945   The Chaco Branch: excavations at White Mound and
       in the Red Mesa Valley. Gila Pueblo, Medallion
       Papers, 33, 159 pp.

1946   Tree ring analysis. Problems of dating, II. The
       Tusayan Ruin. Gila Pueblo, Medallion Papers, 36,
       21 pp.
       Reviewed AAq 13:259 (Bell).

1947   Tree ring analysis. Tree rings and droughts. Gila
       Pueblo, Medallion Papers, 37, 36 pp.

1948   Excavations at Snaketown, IV. Reviews and conclu-
       sions. Gila Pueblo, Medallion Papers, 38, 267 pp.
       Reviewed AA 52:415 (Lehmer), AAq 16:172 (Wood-
       ward).

1957   A history of the ancient Southwest. Bond, Wheel-
       right Co., Portland, 383 pp.
       Reviewed AA 59:926 (Martin and Rinaldo), AAq 23:
       314 (Burgh).

GLADWIN, H.S., HAURY, Emil W., SAYLES, E.B., and GLADWIN, Nora

1937   Excavations at Snaketown, I. Material culture.
       Gila Pueblo, Medallion Papers, 25, 305 pp.
       Reviewed AA 41:139 (Vaillant), AAq 5:176 (Martin),
       31:884 (Ruppé).

GLADWIN, Nora (See under Gladwin, Harold S.)

GLADWIN, Winifred, and GLADWIN, Harold S.

1928a   A method for designation of ruins in the Southwest.
         Gila Pueblo, Medallion Papers, 1, 11 pp.
         Reviewed AA 32:692 (I. Kelly).

1928b   The use of potsherds in an archaeological survey
         of the Southwest. Gila Pueblo, Medallion Papers,
         2, 14 pp.
         Reviewed AA 32:692 (I. Kelly).

1929   The Red-on-Buff Culture of the Gila Basin. Gila
         Pueblo, Medallion Papers, 3, 72 pp.
         Reviewed AA 32:692 (I. Kelly).

1930a   The Red-on-Buff Culture of the Papagueria. Gila
         Pueblo, Medallion Papers, 4, pp. 73-134.
         Reviewed AA 32:692 (I. Kelly).

1930b   The western range of the Red-on-Buff Culture. Gila
         Pueblo, Medallion Papers, 5, pp. 135-162.

1930c   An archaeological survey of the Verde Valley. Gila
         Pueblo, Medallion Papers, 6, pp. 163-201.

1930d   A method for designation of Southwestern pottery
         types. Gila Pueblo, Medallion Papers, 7, 5 pp.

1930e   Some Southwestern pottery types, Series I. Gila
         Pueblo, Medallion Papers, 8.

1931   Some Southwestern pottery types, Series II. Gila
         Pueblo, Medallion Papers, 10.

1933   Some Southwestern pottery types, Series III. Gila
         Pueblo, Medallion Papers, 13, 31 pp.

1934   A method for designation of cultures and their
         variations. Gila Pueblo, Medallion Papers, 15, 30
         pp.

1935   The eastern range of the Red-on-Buff Culture. Gila
         Pueblo, Medallion Papers, 16, pp. 203-287.

GLASSOW, Michael A.

1972a   Changes in the adaptations of Southwestern Basket-
         makers: a systems perspective. *In* Contemporary
         Archaeology, ed. M.P. Leone, Southern Illinois
         University Press, pp. 289-302.

1972b   The evolution of early agricultural facilities
         systems in the northern Southwest. University of

California (Los Angeles), dissertation, 281 pp.;
University Microfilms International.

GLAZIER, Ellen (See under Morris, Richard.)

GLOCK, Waldo S.

   1934   The language of tree rings. Scientific Monthly, 38.

   1937   Principles and methods of tree-ring analysis. Car-
          negie Institution of Washington, Publication no.
          486, 100 pp.
          Reviewed AA 40:320 (Stallings).

GLUBOCK, Shirley (See under Tamarin, Alfred.)

GODDARD, Pliny Earle

   1928a Deserted cities of the cliffs. Natural History,
          28:407-412.

   1928b Pottery of the Southwestern Indians. American
          Museum of Natural History, Guide Leaflet, 30 pp.

GODDARD, Sarah

   1933   Excavations at Tunque. El Palacio, 34, no. 25-26:
          193-196.

GOLDFRIED, Howard P. (See under Beeson, William J.)

GOODING, John D. (See also under Schaafsma, Curtis.)

   1974   The highway salvage program in Colorado. South-
          western Lore, 40, nos. 3-4:7-11.

GOODYEAR, Albert C., III

   1975   Hecla II and III: an interpretive study of archae-
          ological remains from the Lakeshore Project, Papago
          Reservation, south central Arizona. Arizona State
          University, Anthropological Research Papers, 9, 401
          pp.
          Reviewed AAq 42:141 (Gumerman).

   1977a The historical and ecological position of proto-
          historic sites in the Slate Mountains, south central
          Arizona. *In* Research Strategies in Historical Archae-
          ology, ed. Stanley South, Academic Press, pp. 203-
          239.

   1977b Regional model building in the contract framework:

the Hecla projects of southern Arizona. *In* Schiffer and Gumerman 1977.

GOODYEAR, A.C., and DITTERT, A.E., Jr.

1973   Hecla I: a preliminary report on the archaeological investigations at the Lakeshore Project, Papago Reservation, south central Arizona. Arizona State University, Anthropological Research Papers, 4, 81 pp.

GORDON, G.H.

1935   A visit to the Gila cliff ruins. Southwestern Monuments Monthly Report, March, pp. 160-161.

GOREE, Patricia, LARKIN, Robert, and MEAD, James

1972   Cholla-Saguaro transmission line study: Phase I. Arizona State Museum, Archaeological Series, 13, 43 pp.

GORMAN, Frederick J.

1969   The Clovis hunters: an alternative view of their environment and ecology. Kiva, 35:91-102.

1972   The Clovis hunters: an alternate view of their environment and ecology. *In* Contemporary Archaeology, ed. M.P. Leone, Southern Illinois University Press, pp. 206-221.

1976   An information-theoretic approach to the system dynamics of a prehistoric culture in east-central Arizona. University of Arizona, dissertation, 289 pp.; University Microfilms International.

1978   Inventory operations research in Southwestern prehistory: an example from east central Arizona. *In* Grebinger 1978a, pp. 165-194.

GOSS, James A.

1964   Cultural development in the Great Basin. Utah Archaeology, 10, no. 2:4-13; no. 3:4-13; no. 4: 4-12.

GOSS, Robert C. (See under Davis, Natalie Y.)

GOULD, Lois

1929   A grooved club and other artifacts from a cave 70

miles northeast of El Paso, Texas. Proceedings of
the Oklahoma Academy of Sciences, n. s. 9, no. 456:
155-159.

GOULD, Richard A.

1977   (ed.) Explorations in ethnoarchaeology. Univer-
        sity of New Mexico Press.

GOWIN, K.L. (See under Harris, R.K.)

GRADY, Mark A. (See also under Fritz, Gordon L.)

1972a   Archaeological survey of Agua Fria-Grand Terminal
        transmission route. Arizona State Museum, Ar-
        chaeological Series, 10, 4 pp.

1972b   Westwing-El Sol and El Sol-Agua Fria transmission
        line study area: Phase III. Arizona State Museum,
        Archaeological Series, 17, 14 pp.

1973   Archaeological survey of the ASARCO Project area.
        Arizona State Museum, Archaeological Series, 31,
        6 pp.

1974   Archaeological sites within the Copper Cities mine
        area: a preliminary report. Arizona State Museum,
        Archaeological Series, 55, 24 pp.

1975   Tucson sewage project: SW interceptor realignment.
        Arizona State Museum, Archaeological Series, 80,
        8 pp.

1976   Aboriginal agrarian adaptation to the Sonoran Des-
        ert: a regional synthesis and research design. Uni-
        versity of Arizona, dissertation, 277 pp.; Univer-
        sity Microfilms International.

1977a   Significance evaluation and the Orme reservoir proj-
        ect. *In* Schiffer and Gumerman 1977.

1977b   Mitigation recommendations for the Orme reservoir
        project. *In* Schiffer and Gumerman 1977.

GRADY, M.A., CANOUTS, Valetta, and PHILLIPS, David

1974   An archaeological survey of the Buttes Reservoir -
        Phase I (preliminary report). Arizona State Mu-
        seum, Archaeological Series, 50, 65 pp.

GRADY, M.A., and others

1973   Archaeological survey of the Salt-Gila aqueduct.

Arizona State Museum, Archaeological Series, 23, 98 pp.

GRAHAM, C.C. (See under McLoyd, Charles.)

GRAHAM, John A., and DAVIS, William

1958   Appraisal of the archaeological resources of Diablo Reservoir, Val Verde County, Texas. Report by the Archaeological Salvage Program Field Office, Austin, to the National Park Service.

GRAHAM, Samuel A.

1965   Entomology: an aid in archaeological studies. *In* Osborne 1965a, pp. 167-174.

GRANGE, Roger, Jr. (See under Martin, Paul Sidney.)

GRANT, Campbell

1978   Canyon de Chelly: its people and rock art. University of Arizona Press, 279 pp.

GRATER, Russel K.

1954   Prehistoric trading post. Arizona Highways, 30, no. 10:34-39.

GRATZ, Kathleen E.

1977   Archaeological excavations along Route Z4 near Zuni, New Mexico. Museum of Northern Arizona, Research Papers, 7, 112 pp.

GRAVES, Michael W. (See under Longacre, William A.)

GRAY, B. Thomas (See under Fitting, James E.)

GRAYBILL, Donald A.

1973   Prehistoric settlement pattern analysis in the Mimbres region, New Mexico. University of Arizona, dissertation, 272 pp.; University Microfilms International.

1975   Mimbres-Mogollon adaptations in the Gila National Forest, Mimbres District, New Mexico. United States Forest Service, Southwestern Region, Archaeological Report no. 9, 199 pp.

GREBINGER, Paul F. (See also under Brown, Jeffrey L.)

1971a   The Potrero Creek site: activity structure. Kiva, 37, no. 1:30-52.

1971b   Hohokam cultural development in the middle Santa Cruz Valley, Arizona. University of Arizona, dissertation, 257 pp.; University Microfilms International.

1973   Prehistoric social organization in Chaco Canyon, New Mexico: an alternative reconstruction. Kiva, 39, no. 1:3-23.

1976   Salado - perspectives from the middle Santa Cruz Valley. *In* Doyel and Haury 1976, pp. 39-46.

1978a   (ed.) Discovering past behavior: experiments in the archaeology of the American Southwest. Gordon and Breach, New York, 279 pp.

1978b   Prehistoric social organization in Chaco Canyon, New Mexico: an evolutionary perspective. *In* Grebinger 1978a, pp. 73-100.

GREBINGER, P.F., and ADAM, David P.

1974   Hard times?: Classic Period Hohokam cultural development in the Tucson Basin, Arizona. World Archaeology, 6, no. 2:226-241.

1978   Santa Cruz Valley Hohokam: cultural development in the Classic Period. *In* Grebinger 1978a, pp. 215-244.

GREBINGER, P.F., and BRADLEY, Bruce

1969   Excavations at a prehistoric camp site on the Mogollon Rim, east central Arizona. Kiva, 34, nos. 2-3:109-123.

GREEN, C.H.

1891   Catalogue of a unique collection of Cliff Dweller relics: taken from the lately discovered ruins of southwestern Colorado and adjacent parts of Utah, New Mexico, and Arizona. Privately printed, Chicago, 35 pp.

GREEN, Dee F. (See also under DeBloois, Evan I.; Plog, Fred T.)

1961   Archaeological investigations at the G.M. Hinckley Farm site, Utah County, Utah, 1956-1960. Brigham

Young University Press, 90 pp.

1964   The Hinckley figurines as indicators of the position of Utah Valley in the Sevier culture. American Antiquity, 30:74-80.

1969   Testing Matheny Alcove, southeastern Utah. Utah Archaeology, 15, no. 3:6-9.

1971   The Elk Ridge archaeological project, Manti-La Sal National Forest: summary of the 1971 field season. U.S. Forest Service, Intermountain Region, Archaeological Report.

1974   Random model testing of archaeological site locations in Allen and South Cottonwood Canyons, southeastern Utah. Kiva, 39, nos. 3-4:289-299.

1975   Lithic sites of the La Sal Mountains, southeastern Utah. United States Forest Service, Intermountain Region, Archaeological Report no. 3.

1977a   Surface artifacts from site 08-7, Apache-Sitgreaves National Forest, Arizona. U.S. Forest Service, Southwestern Region, Miscellaneous Paper no. 3, Archaeological Report no. 15:27-31.

1977b   Surface artifacts from two sites on the Sedona Ranger District, Coconino National Forest, Arizona. U.S. Forest Service, Southwestern Region, Miscellaneous Paper no. 5, Archaeological Report no. 15: 38-45.

1977c   (ed.) Introduction to three papers on AZ U:12:2 (ASU). U.S. Forest Service, Southwestern Region, Archaeological Report no. 15:89-91.

GREEN, D.F., and LUNT, Michael J.

1977   Locating archaeological sites using an infrared thermal line scanner. U.S. Forest Service, Southwestern Region, Miscellaneous Paper no. 6, Archaeological Report no. 15:46-52.

GREEN, D.F., and WYLIE, Henry G.

1977   Surface materials from site 06-122, Coconino National Forest, Arizona. U.S. Forest Service, Southwestern Region, Miscellaneous Paper no. 4, Archaeological Report no. 15:32-37.

GREEN, Earl

1955   Excavations near Gran Quivira, New Mexico. Bulletin

of the Texas Archaeological Society, 26:182-185.

GREEN, Elizabeth H.

1954   Survey of Pine River drainage area, southwestern
        Colorado, 1952-1953. Southwestern Lore, 19, no.
        4:5-7.

GREEN, Ernestene L.

1976   Valdez Phase occupation near Taos, New Mexico.
        Fort Burgwin Research Center, no. 10, 88 pp.

GREEN, F. Earl

1962   Additional notes on prehistoric wells at the Clovis
        site. American Antiquity, 28:230-234.

1963   The Clovis blades: an important addition to the
        Llano Complex. American Antiquity, 29:145-165.

GREEN, Frank O. (See under Green, L.M.)

GREEN, John W. (See also under Brook, Vernon R.)

1965   A recurring symbol engraved on arrow shaft smoothers
        from the Tularosa Basin. The Artifact, 3, no. 3:4-5.

1966   A preliminary survey of the Atlatl pictograph site
        in the Sierra de Kilo, Chihuahua, Mexico. Transac-
        tions of the Southeastern New Mexico and Western
        Texas Regional Archaeological Symposium, Special
        Bulletin no. 1, pp. 9-23.

1967a   Fusselman Canyon petroglyph site; EPAS-44. The
        Artifact, 5, no. 1:1-19.

1967b   Rock art of the El Paso Southwest: reinvestigation
        of the Fusselman Canyon petroglyph site. The Arti-
        fact, 5, no. 2:35-44.

1967c   White Rock Cave pictograph site; EPAS-49. The Arti-
        fact, 5, no. 3:13-23.

1968a   A human effigy axe. The Artifact, 6, no. 3:8-10.

1968b   A preliminary report on the salvage of an El Paso
        phase house ruin, EPAS-53. Transactions of the
        4th Regional Archaeological Symposium on South-
        eastern New Mexico and Western Texas, pp. 73-77.

1969b   Preliminary report on site EPAS-60: an El Paso
        house ruin. Transactions of the 5th Regional
        Archaeological Symposium on Southeastern New Mexico

and Western Texas, pp. 1-12.

1969b Sitting Bull Falls pictograph site. The Artifact, 7, no. 2:7-13.

1971 Progress report on the excavation of site EPAS-49 and a preliminary report on the excavation of shelter one, White Rock Cave. Transactions of the 6th Regional Archaeological Symposium on Southeastern New Mexico and Western Texas, pp. 101-110.

GREEN, Judith Strupp

1971 Archaeological Chihuahuan textiles and modern Tarahumara weaving. Ethnos, 36, nos. 1-4:115-130.

GREEN, L.M., and GREEN, Frank O.

1974 Notes on archaeology of Allen Ranch rock shelters. The Artifact, 12, no. 1:1-26.

GREEN, Roger C.

1956a Excavations near Mayhill, New Mexico. *In* Wendorf 1956a, pp. 10-16.

1956b A pit house of the Gallina Phase. American Antiquity, 22:188-193.

1962 The Hormigas site of the Largo-Gallina Phase. El Palacio, 69:142-157.

1964 The Carricito community. El Palacio, 71:27-40.

GREEN, R.C., DANFELSER, M.A., and VIVIAN, G.

1958 Interpretation of Bg 91; a specialized Largo-Gallina surface structure. El Palacio, 65:41-60.

GREENLEAF, J. Cameron (See also under Fontana, Bernard L.)

1975a Excavations at Punta de Agua in the Santa Cruz River Basin, southeastern Arizona. University of Arizona, Anthropological Papers, 26, 122 pp.

1975b The fortified hill site near Gila Bend, Arizona. Kiva, 40, no. 4:213-282.

GREENLEAF, J.C., and VIVIAN, R. Gwinn

1971 Preliminary archaeological tests on the Queen Creek Floodway project. Arizona State Museum, Archaeological Series, 6, 15 pp.

GREENLEAF, Richard E.

1967   Atrisco and Las Ciruelas, 1722-1769. New Mexico
        Historical Review, 42, no. 1:5-25.

GREENWOOD, N.H., and WHITE, C.W.

1970   Mogollon ritual: a spacial configuration of a non-
        village pattern. Archaeology, 23, no. 4:298-301.

GREER, John W.

1965a   A burin from western Bernalillo County, New Mexico.
        Southwestern Lore, 30, no. 4:79-80.

1965b   A typology of midden circles and mescal pits.
        Southwestern Lore, 31, no. 3:41-55.

1966a   Results of archaeological excavation at the Castle
        Canyon site, Val Verde County, Texas. Southwestern
        Lore, 32, no. 1:10-18.

1966b   The Louden site (CO-1), Las Animas County, Colorado.
        Southwestern Lore, 32, no. 3:57-65.

1967a   Midden circles versus mescal pits. American An-
        tiquity, 32:108-109.

1967b   Notes on excavated ring midden sites, 1963-1968.
        Bulletin of the Texas Archaeological Society, 38:
        39-46.

1968a   Excavations at a midden circle site in El Paso
        County, Texas. Bulletin of the Texas Archaeological
        Society, 39:111-131.

1968b   Some unusual artifacts from Val Verde County, Texas.
        Texas Journal of Science, 20, no. 2:183-192.

1969   Micro-eccentrics from the Four Corners region of
        the Southwest. Kiva, 34, no. 4:251-257.

1975   On sotol, seasonality, and ring middens. Texas
        Archaeology, 19, no. 4:5-9.

1976a   Fauna in Val Verde County, Texas, Castle Canyon
        site. The Artifact, 14, no. 1:9-18.

1976b   Some thoughts on faunal procurement: considerations
        for southwest Texas. The Artifact, 14, no. 3:1-20.

1976c   A late Archaic burial from southwestern Texas.
        Plains Anthropologist, 21, no. 73:181-186.

1976d   Notes on bison in Val Verde County, Texas. Plains
        Anthropologist, 21, no. 73:237-239.

GREER, J.W., and BENFER, Robert A.

1964   Langtry Creek burial cave, Val Verde County, Texas.
        Bulletin of the Texas Archaeological Society, 33:
        229-251.

GREGORY, David A.

1975a   Defining variability in prehistoric settlement mor-
        phology. *In* Martin and others 1975, pp. 40-46.

1975b   Fort Bowie archaeological pre-stabilization studies.
        Arizona State Museum, Archaeological Series, 88,
        56 pp.

GREISER, T.W. (See under O'Laughlin, Thomas C.)

GREMINGER, Henry C. (See also under Sciscenti, James V.)

1961   (ed.) Papers from a training program in salvage
        archaeology. Museum of New Mexico, Papers in
        Anthropology, 3, 67 pp.

GRIEDER, Terence

1965   Report on a study of the pictographs in Satan Can-
        yon, Val Verde County, Texas. Texas Archaeological
        Salvage Project, Miscellaneous Papers, 2, 15 pp.

1966   Periods in Pecos style pictographs. American An-
        tiquity, 31:710-720.

GRIFFIN, P. Bion

1967   A high status burial from Grasshopper Ruin, Arizona.
        Kiva, 33, no. 2:37-53.

1969   Late Mogollon readaptation in east-central Arizona.
        University of Arizona, dissertation, 198 pp.; Uni-
        versity Microfilms International.

GRIFFITH, James S. (See under Shutler, Richard, Jr.)

GRIFFITHS, Thomas M. (See under Howard, William A.)

GRIGG, Paul

1974   Mountain Bell project - excavation LA 6546. Labora-
        tory of Anthropology Notes, 99A.

GRIGG, P., and CARROLL, Charles

1976   Puerco channelization project - archaeological

survey. University of New Mexico, contract report
101-103Z (U.S. Army Corps of Engineers).

GRIGG, P., and STEIN, John R.

1977   Archaeological clearance survey for proposed mining
        exploration in the Borrego Pass region, New Mexico.
        University of New Mexico, contract report 185-2E
        (State Archaeologist).

GRIGG, P., FOSBERG, Stephen, and GAUTHIER, Rory

1977   Archaeological survey of Anaconda Company's Oak
        Canyon tract in the Jackpile Mine, Paguate, New
        Mexico. University of New Mexico, contract report
        185-2D (BIA).

GRIGG, P., STEIN, J.R., and STUART, David E.

1976   Archaeological survey of six housing sites on the
        Laguna Indian Reservation. University of New Mex-
        ico, contract report 101-103Y (BIA).

GRITZNER, Charles F.

1966   Hohokam culture origin: a geographical interpreta-
        tion. Journal of the Arizona Academy of Sciences,
        4, no. 2:134 (abstract).

1969   Hohokam culture origin: the possibility of diffusion
        from coastal Peru and Ecuador. NEARA Newsletter,
        4:69-72.

GROGITSKY, Norman

1961   Cochise (Paleo-Indian) manifestation in the Rio
        Grande Valley. Totem Pole, 44, no. 2:2.

GROSS, Hugo

1957   Age of the Sandia culture. Science, 126:305-306.

GROSSCUP, Gordon L.

1962   Excavations in the Hill Creek area, Grand County,
        Utah. Utah Archaeology, 8, no. 3:3-7.

GUERNSEY, Samuel James (See also under Kidder, Alfred V.;
    Nusbaum, Jesse L.)

1931   Explorations in northeastern Arizona. Papers of
        the Peabody Museum of American Archaeology and

Ethnology, 12, no. 1, 123 pp.

GUERNSEY, S.J., and KIDDER, A.V.

1921   Basket-maker caves of northeastern Arizona. Papers
        of the Peabody Museum of American Archaeology and
        Ethnology, 8, no. 2, 121 pp.

GUMERMAN, George J. (See also under Euler, Robert C.; Karlstrom,
Thor N.V.; Schaber, Gerald G.; Schiffer, Michael B.)

1966a   A Folsom point from the area of Mishongovi, Arizona.
        Plateau, 38, no. 4:79-80.

1966b   Two Basket Maker II pithouse villages in eastern
        Arizona: a preliminary report. Plateau, 39, no. 2:
        80-87.

1969   The archaeology of the Hopi Buttes district, Ari-
        zona. University of Arizona, dissertation, 460 pp.;
        University Microfilms International.

1970   Black Mesa: survey and excavation in northeastern
        Arizona, 1968. Prescott College, Studies in Anthro-
        pology, 2, 127 pp.
        Reviewed AAq 38:251 (Judge).

1971   (ed.) The distribution of prehistoric population
        aggregates. Prescott College, Anthropological Re-
        ports, 1, 164 pp.
        Reviewed AA 79:181 (Thomas).

1972   (ed.) Proceedings of the Second Annual Meeting of
        the Southwestern Anthropological Research Group.
        Prescott College, Anthropological Reports, 3.

1973   A rural-urban continuum for the prehistoric Pueblo
        Southwest: Black Mesa and Chaco Canyon. Proceedings
        of the 40th International Congress of Americanists.

1975   Alternative cultural models for demographic change:
        Southwestern examples. *In* Swedlund 1975, pp. 104-
        115.

1978   Regional variation in the Southwest and the question
        of Mesoamerican relationships. *In* Riley and Hedrick
        1978, pp. 22-33.

GUMERMAN, G.J., and EULER, Robert C.

1976   (ed.) Papers on the archaeology of Black Mesa,
        Arizona. Southern Illinois University Press, 186
        pp.
        Reviewed AA 79:969 (Morris).

GUMERMAN, G.J., and JOHNSON, R.R.

  1971   Prehistoric human population distribution in a
         biological transition zone. *In* Gumerman 1971, pp.
         83-102.

GUMERMAN, G.J., and OLSON, Alan P.

  1968   Prehistory in the Puerco Valley, eastern Arizona.
         Plateau, 40, no. 4:113-127.

GUMERMAN, G.J., and SKINNER, S. Alan

  1968   A synthesis of the prehistory of the central Little
         Colorado Valley, Arizona. American Antiquity, 33:
         185-199.

GUMERMAN, G.J., and WEED, Carol S.

  1976   The question of Salado in the Agua Fria and New
         River drainages of central Arizona. *In* Doyel and
         Haury 1976, pp. 105-112.

GUMERMAN, G.J., WEED, C.S., and HANSON, J.A.

  1976   Adaptive strategies in a biological and cultural
         transition zone: the central Arizona ecotone proj-
         ect - an interim report. Southern Illinois Univer-
         sity, University Museum Studies, Research Records,
         6.

GUMERMAN, G.J., WESTFALL, Deborah, and WEED, Carol S.

  1972   Archaeological investigations on Black Mesa, the
         1969-1970 seasons. Prescott College, Studies in
         Anthropology, 4, 250 pp.
            Reviewed AA 77:689 (Breternitz), AAq 40:499 (Hill).

GUNCKEL, Lewis W. (See also under Moorehead, Warren King.)

  1893   Pictographs and rock paintings of the Southwest.
         American Antiquarian, 15, no. 4:223.

  1897   Ruins and picture writings in the canyons of the
         McElmo and Hovenweep. American Antiquarian, 19:
         223-226.

GUNN, Joel D. (See also under Adovasio, James M.)

  1974   The Hogup system: a causal analysis of prehistoric
         envirotechnological interaction in the desert west.

University of Pittsburgh, dissertation, 219 pp.; University Microfilms International.

1975 An envirotechnological system for Hogup Cave. American Antiquity, 40:3-21.

GUNNERSON, Dolores A. (See also under Gunnerson, James H.)

1956 The southern Athabascans: their arrival in the Southwest. El Palacio, 63:346-365.

GUNNERSON, James H. (See also under Galinat, Walton C.)

1955a University of Utah's archaeological field work. Utah Archaeology, 1, no. 3:3-4.

1955b Archaeological evidence of hunting magic. Utah Archaeology, 1, no. 3:5-8.

1956a A fluted point site in Utah. American Antiquity, 21, no. 4:412-414.

1956b Fremont ceramics. University of Utah, Anthropological Papers, 26, pp. 54-62.

1956c Plains-Promontory relationships. American Antiquity, 22:69-72.

1956d Utah statewide survey activities - 1955. Utah Archaeology, 2, no. 1:4-12 (also 15, no. 2:13-19, 1969).

1956e Petrographs. Utah Archaeology, 2, no. 2:11-15.

1956f 1956 archaeological activities of the University of Utah. Utah Archaeology, 2, no. 3:4-14.

1957a An archeological survey of the Fremont area. University of Utah, Anthropological Papers, 28, 160 pp. Reviewed AA 60:980 (Meighan), AAq 24:327 (Burgh).

1957b Prehistoric figurines from Castle Valley. Archaeology, 10, no. 2:137-140.

1957c Preliminary report of 1957 work at Snake Rock. Utah Archaeology, 3, no. 4:7-12.

1957d Uinta Basin archaeology. *In* Guidebook to the geology of Uinta Basin, ed. Otto G. Seal, Intermountain Association of Petroleum Geologists, Eighth Annual Field Conference.

1958a Pottery in archeological interpretation. Utah Archaeology, 4, no. 2:3-6.

1958b Archaeological survey of the Kaiparowits Plateau -

a preliminary report. Utah Archaeology, 4, no. 3: 9-20.

1959a Archaeological survey in the Dead Horse Point area. Utah Archaeology, 5, no. 2:4-9.

1959b Archaeological survey of the Kaiparowits Plateau. *In* Jennings and others 1959, pt. II, pp. 317-469.

1959c An enigmatic unfired clay disk. El Palacio, 66, no. 3:107-108.

1959d Archaeological survey in northeastern New Mexico. El Palacio, 66, no. 5:145-154.

1959e 1957 excavations, Glen Canyon area. University of Utah, Anthropological Papers, 43, 163 pp. Reviewed AA 64:203 (Briggs), AAq 28:112 (Dittert).

1959f The Utah statewide archaeological survey: its background and first ten years. Utah Archaeology, 5, no. 4:3-16.

1960a Archaeological survey in the Hammond Canyon area, southeastern Utah. University of Utah, Dept. of Anthropology, Special Report to the U.S. Forest Service, 36 pp.

1960b The Fremont culture: internal dimensions and external relationships. American Antiquity, 25:373-380.

1960c An introduction to Plains Apache archaeology - the Dismal River Aspect. Bureau of American Ethnology, Anthropological Papers, no. 58, Bulletin 173, pp. 131-260. Reviewed AA 63:867 (Secoy), AAq 27:130 (Holder).

1962a Three wooden shovels from Nine Mile Canyon. University of Utah, Miscellaneous Collected Papers, no. 1, Anthropological Papers, 60:1-8. Reviewed AA 67:1592 (Schwartz).

1962b Archaeological survey in the Hammond Canyon area, southeastern Utah. University of Utah, Miscellaneous Collected Papers, no. 2, Anthropological Papers, 60:9-44. Reviewed AA 67:1592 (Schwartz).

1962c Highway salvage archaeology: St. George, Utah. University of Utah, Miscellaneous Collected Papers, no. 3, Anthropological Papers, 60:45-65. Reviewed AA 67:1592 (Schwartz).

1962d Unusual artifacts from Castle Valley, central Utah.

University of Utah, Miscellaneous Collected Papers, no. 4, Anthropological Papers, 60:67-91. Reviewed AA 67:1592 (Schwartz).

1962e   Plateau Shoshonean prehistory: a suggested reconstruction. American Antiquity, 28:41-45.

1968   Plains Apache archaeology: a review. Plains Anthropologist, 13:167-189.

1969a   Apache archaeology in northeastern New Mexico. American Antiquity, 34:23-39.

1969b   The Fremont culture, a study in culture dynamics on the northern Anasazi frontier. Peabody Museum of Archaeology and Ethnology, Papers, 59, no. 2, 221 pp. Reviewed AA 72:447 (Aikens), AAq 35:396 (De Boer).

GUNNERSON, J.H., and GUNNERSON, Dolores A.

1970   Evidence of Apaches at Pecos. El Palacio, 76, no. 3:1-6.

1971   Apachean culture: a study in unity and diversity. *In* Basso and Opler 1971, pp. 7-27.

GUSINDE, Martin

1948   Cliff-dwellings of St. Michaels in Arizona. Proceedings of the 26th International Congress of Americanists, 1:145-152.

GUTHE, Alfred K.

1949   A preliminary report on excavations in southwestern Colorado. American Antiquity, 15:144-154.

GUTHE, Carl E.

1917   The Pueblo ruin at Rowe, N.M. El Palacio, 4, no. 4:33-39.

1927   A method of ceramic description. Papers of the Michigan Academy of Science, Arts, and Letters, 8:23-29.

HAAS, Jonathan

1971   The Ushklish ruin: a preliminary report on excavations of a Colonial Hohokam site in the Tonto Basin, central Arizona. Arizona State Museum, Arizona Highway Salvage Preliminary Report.

HABERLAND, Wolfgang

    1966   Bat Cave - Anmerkungen und methodische Gedanken zu
             Herbert W. Dicks Untersuchung. Tribus, Neue Folge,
             15:149-159.

HACK, John T. (See also under Brew, John Otis.)

    1942a   The changing physical environment of the Hopi
             Indians of Arizona. Papers of the Peabody Museum
             of American Archaeology and Ethnology, 35, no. 1,
             85 pp.
               Reviewed AA 45:129 (Colton).

    1942b   Prehistoric coal mining in the Jeddito Valley,
             Arizona. Papers of the Peabody Museum of American
             Archaeology and Ethnology, 35, no. 2, 24 pp.

HADDON, Alfred C.

    1914   Relics of a lost culture in Arizona. Nature, 93,
             no. 2335:570.

HADLOCK, Harry L.

    1962   Surface surveys of lithic sites on the Gallegos
             Wash. El Palacio, 69:174-184.

HAEKEL, Josef

    1953   Zum Problem der Korrelation prähistorischer und
             rezenter Kulturen. Wiener völkerkundliche Mitteil-
             ungen, 1, no. 2:63-76.

HAGEMAN, Warren C.

    1961   Artifacts from a site in Box Elder County, Utah.
             Utah Archaeology, 7, no. 4:1-5.

HAGENSTAD, Brett

    1969   A glance at the history and archaeology of the
             lower Verde River. Arizona Archaeologist, 4, pp.
             24-32.

HAGIE, C.E.

    1932   Previously unknown Pueblo Indian territory. Art
             and Archaeology, 33:161.

HALASI, Judith A. (See under Huse, Hannah.)

HALES, Henry

1893   Prehistoric New Mexican pottery. Annual Report of
        the Smithsonian Institution for 1892, pp. 535-554.

HALL, Ansel Franklin

1934   General report on the Rainbow Bridge-Monument Val-
        ley Expedition of 1933. Preliminary Bulletin, no.
        1, University of California Press, 32 pp.

1935   The romance of modern exploration. Scientific
        Monthly, 41:272-274.

HALL, Edward T., Jr.

1935   Report on archaeological survey of Main Tsegi, from
        mouth of Betatakin Wash to two miles north of Peach
        Orchard Spring. Rainbow Bridge-Monument Valley Ex-
        pedition, Preliminary Bulletin no. 9, 8 pp.

1942   Archaeological survey of Walhalla Glades. Museum
        of Northern Arizona, Bulletin 20, 32 pp.

1944a   Early stockaded settlements in the Governador, New
        Mexico. Columbia University, Studies in Archae-
        ology and Ethnology, 2, pt. 1, 96 pp.
        Reviewed AAq 11:129 (Reiter).

1944b   Recent clues to Athapaskan prehistory in the South-
        west. American Anthropologist, 46, no. 1:98-105.

1950   Ceramic traits and the nature of culture contacts
        between Anasazi and Mogollon. *In* Reed and King
        1950, pp. 63-75.

1951   Southwestern dated ruins, VI. Tree-Ring Bulletin,
        17, no. 4:26-28.

HALL, Gordon

1973   Infant burial: Fresnal Shelter. *In* Human Systems
        Research 1973, pp. 386-395.

HALL, H.J. (See under Fry, Gary F.)

HALL, Sharlot M.

1895   The cliff-dwellings of the lower Verde Valley,
        northern Arizona. The Archaeologist, 3, no. 5:
        119-122.

1898   Prehistoric fancy-work. Land of Sunshine, 8 (April):
        221-223.

HALL, Thelma Bonney

1947   "Awatovi." Arizona Highways, 23:12-15.

HALLISY, Stephen J. (See under Lister, Robert H.; McLellan,
    George E.)

HALLOCK, Charles

1910   The caves and ruins of Arizona and Colorado. Amer-
        ican Antiquarian, 32:133-136.

HALSETH, Odd S.

1926   Fieldwork at Gran Quivira, 1926. El Palacio, 21:
        223-226.

1928   Archaeology and the public. Arizona, Old and New,
        1, no. 3:5-6, 26-28.

1931   The civic side of archaeology. Masterkey, 5, no.
        1:8-12.

1932a   Investigation of a prehistoric farming community
        in the Superstition Mountains, Arizona. Science
        Service Research Announcements, no. 104.

1932b   Prehistoric irrigation in central Arizona. Master-
        key, 5, no. 6:165-178.

1933   Archaeology in the making. Masterkey, 7, no. 2:37-
        40.

1934   Archaeology as a municipal enterprise. Masterkey,
        8, no. 4:101-108.

1936   Prehistoric irrigation in the Salt River Valley.
        In Brand 1936, pp. 42-47.

1941   (ed.) Hohokam pottery designs. Kelley and Baum-
        gartner, Phoenix, 4 pp., 52 pls.
        Reviewed AAq 7:418 (Douglas).

1947a   Arizona's 1500 years of irrigation history. Rec-
        lamation Era, 33, no. 12:251-254.

1947b   Random notes on the 1947 Chaco Conference. El
        Palacio, 54, no. 9:218-220.

HALSETH, O.S., and HUDDELSON, Sam

1926   Work at Gran Quivira. El Palacio, 21:217-218.

HAMILTON, Alice L.

1974   Carnero Creek pictographs, La Garita, Colorado. Southwestern Lore, 40, nos. 3-4:75-82.

HAMMACK, Laurens C. (See also under Ellis, Florence H.)

1961   Missile range archaeology. Laboratory of Anthropology Notes, 2.

1962a   Excavations at two cairn sites near San Antonio, New Mexico. Laboratory of Anthropology Notes, 6.

1962b   Highway salvage excavations near Lordsburg, New Mexico. Laboratory of Anthropology Notes, 7.

1962c   LA 5599: a pit house village near Rincon, New Mexico. Laboratory of Anthropology Notes, 8.

1963a   The Las Cruces dam sites: lithic sites near Las Cruces. Laboratory of Anthropology Notes, 17.

1963b   LA 5539 - The Tohatchi School site. Laboratory of Anthropology Notes, 18.

1964a   Archaeology of the New Mexico section of the American Telephone and Telegraph communications cable. Laboratory of Anthropology Notes, 25.

1964b   LA 9152 - Aneth, Utah. Laboratory of Anthropology Notes, 26.

1964c   The McCune highway salvage project. Laboratory of Anthropology Notes, 27.

1964d   The Tohatchi road salvage project: 1963-64. Laboratory of Anthropology Notes, 28.

1965a   Archaeology of the Ute Dam and Reservoir, northeastern New Mexico. Museum of New Mexico, Papers in Anthropology, 14, 69 pp.
       Reviewed AA 70:163 (Krieger), AAq 32:123 (Gunnerson.)

1965b   The Lagunitas highway salvage project. Laboratory of Anthropology Notes, 33.

1965c   The Mangus highway salvage project. Laboratory of Anthropology Notes, 34.

1966a   Diablo highway salvage archaeology. Laboratory of Anthropology Notes, 41.

1966b   The Tunnard site: a fourteenth century ruin near Albuquerque, New Mexico. Museum of New Mexico, Research Records, no. 3, 29 pp.

1969a   Highway salvage archaeology in the Forestdale Val-
        ley, Arizona. Kiva, 34, nos. 2-3:58-89.

1969b   Highway salvage excavations in the upper Tonto Basin,
        Arizona. Kiva, 34, nos. 2-3:132-175.

1969c   A preliminary report of the excavations at Las
        Colinas. Kiva, 35, no. 1:11-28.

1971   The Peppersauce Wash project: a preliminary report
        on the salvage excavation of four archaeological
        sites in the San Pedro Valley, southeastern Arizona.
        Arizona Highway Salvage Preliminary Report.

1973   Arizona highway salvage archaeology - 1974. Kiva,
        39, no. 2:97-103.

1974   Effigy vessels in the prehistoric Southwest. Ari-
        zona Highways, 50 (February):33-35.

HAMMACK, L.C., BUSSEY, Stanley D., and ICE, Ronald

1966   The Cliff highway salvage project. Laboratory of
        Anthropology Notes, 40.

HAMMACK, Nancy S., and CUMMINS, Gary T.

1975   Archaeological survey: Cyprus-Bagdad pipeline route.
        Arizona State Museum, Archaeological Series, 90, 59
        pp.

HAMMERSEN, Martha M.

1972   (comp.) The prehistoric Mogollon culture and its
        regional aspects in the El Paso area. The Artifact,
        10, no. 1, 57 pp.

HAMMOND, Philip C., and MARWITT, John P.

1970   An archaeometric survey of Anasazi Indian village
        historical site, Boulder, Utah. Southwestern Lore,
        36, no. 2:24-31.

HANNA, Phil T.

1926   The Lost City of Nevada. Touring Topics, 8, no.
        6:16-19.

HANNAH, John W. (See under Bannister, Bryant; Robinson, William
J.)

HANSEN, George H.

1934   Utah skull cap. American Anthropologist, 36:431-433.

HANSEN, G.H., and STOKES, William L.

1941   An ancient cave in American Fork Canyon. Proceed-
        ings of the Utah Academy of Sciences, Arts and Let-
        ters, 18:27-37.

HANSON, John A. (See also under Gumerman, George J.)

1975   Stress response in cultural systems: a prehistoric
        example from east-central Arizona. *In* Martin and
        others 1975, pp. 92-102.

HANSON, J.A., and SCHIFFER, Michael B.

1975   The Joint site - a preliminary report. *In* Martin
        and others 1975, pp. 47-91.

HANTMAN, Jeff (See also under Plog, Fred T.)

1977   An archaeological survey of the Chevelon Juniper
        Push, Apache-Sitgreaves National Forest, Chevelon
        Ranger District, Coconino County, Arizona. Arizona
        State University, Office of Cultural Resource Man-
        agement, Report no. 29, 15 pp.

HARBOUR, Jerry

1956   Preliminary geology of the Lucy site. El Palacio,
        63:50-52.

HARCUM, C.G.

1923   Indian pottery from the Casas Grandes region, Chi-
        huahua, Mexico. Bulletin of the Royal Ontario
        Museum, 2:4-11.

HARD, Robert J. (See under Canouts, Valetta.)

HARDACRE, G.C.

1878   The Cliff Dwellers. Science Monthly (London), 17:
        266-276.

HARGRAVE, Lyndon Lane (See also under Colton, Harold S.; Haury,
    Emil W.; Lockett, H. Claiborne.)

1929   Elden Pueblo. Museum of Northern Arizona, Museum
        Notes, 2, no. 5:1-3.

1930   Prehistoric earth lodges of the San Francisco
        Mountains. Museum of Northern Arizona, Museum
        Notes, 3, no. 5:1-4.

1931a   First Mesa. Museum of Northern Arizona, Museum
        Notes, 3, no. 8:1-6.

1931b   The Museum of Northern Arizona archaeological ex-
        pedition, 1931. Museum of Northern Arizona, Museum
        Notes, 4, no. 5:1-4.

1931c   The influence of economic geography upon the rise
        and fall of the Pueblo culture in Arizona. Museum
        of Northern Arizona, Museum Notes, 4, no. 6:1-3.

1932a   Guide to forty pottery types from the Hopi country
        and the San Francisco Mountains, Arizona. Museum
        of Northern Arizona, Bulletin 1, 48 pp.

1932b   The Museum of Northern Arizona archaeological ex-
        pedition, 1932. Museum of Northern Arizona, Museum
        Notes, 5, no. 5:25-28.

1933a   Pueblo II houses of the San Francisco Mountains,
        Arizona. Museum of Northern Arizona, Bulletin 4,
        pp. 15-75.

1933b   A review of archaeological activities in the San
        Francisco Mountain region, Arizona. Museum of
        Northern Arizona, Museum Notes, 5, no. 7:33-35.

1933c   The Museum of Northern Arizona archaeological ex-
        pedition, 1933: Wupatki National Monument. Museum
        of Northern Arizona, Museum Notes, 6, no. 5:23-26.

1933d   Archaeological report on excavation at Wupatki.
        Southwestern Monuments Monthly Report, October,
        pp. 19-21.

1934a   A note on Poncho Ruin, Utah. American Anthropolo-
        gist, 36, no. 3:490.

1934b   The Tsegi country. Museum of Northern Arizona,
        Museum Notes, 6, no. 11:51-54.

1934c   A recently discovered Basket Maker burial cave in
        the Tsegi. Museum of Northern Arizona, Museum
        Notes, 7, no. 4:13.

1935a   Archaeological investigations in the Tsegi Canyons
        of northeastern Arizona in 1934. Museum of Northern
        Arizona, Museum Notes, 7, no. 7:25-28.

1935b   Concerning the names of Southwestern pottery types.
        Southwestern Lore, 1, no. 3:17-23.

1935c   Jeddito Valley and the first pueblo towns in Arizona
        to be visited by Europeans. Museum of Northern Ari-
        zona, Museum Notes, 8, no. 4:17-32.

1935d   Report on archaeological reconnaissance in the Rain-
         bow Plateau area of northern Arizona and southern
         Utah. University of California Press, 56 pp.
         Reviewed AA 40:307 (Roberts).

1936a   Notes on a red ware from Bluff, Utah. Southwestern
         Lore, 2, no. 2:29-34.

1936b   The field collector of beam material. Tree-Ring
         Bulletin, 2, no. 3:22-24.

1937a   A new sub-culture in Arizona. Southwestern Lore,
         3, no. 2:54-57.

1937b   Sikyatki: were the inhabitants Hopi? Museum of
         Northern Arizona, Museum Notes, 9, no. 12:63-66.

1938   Results of a study of the Cohonina branch of the
         Patayan culture in 1938. Museum of Northern Arizona,
         Museum Notes, 11, no. 6:43-50.

1939   Bird bones from abandoned Indian dwellings in Ari-
         zona and Utah. Condor, 41, no. 5:206-210.

1962   Ceramics of the Prewitt district, New Mexico. Labor-
         atory of Anthropology Notes, 117F.

1965a   Archaeological bird bones from Chapin Mesa, Mesa
         Verde National Park. *In* Osborne 1965a, pp. 156-160.

1965b   Turkey bones from Wetherill Mesa. *In* Osborne 1965a,
         pp. 161-166.

1970a   Feathers from Sand Dune Cave: a Basketmaker cave
         near Navajo Mountain, Utah. Museum of Northern
         Arizona, Technical Series, 9, 52 pp.

1970b   Mexican macaws: comparative osteology and survey
         of remains from the Southwest. University of Ari-
         zona, Anthropological Papers, 20, 67 pp.

1974   Type determinants in Southwestern ceramics and some
         of their implications. Plateau, 46, no. 3:76-95.

HARGRAVE, L.L., and COLTON, Harold S.

1935   What do potsherds tell us? Museum of Northern Ari-
         zona, Museum Notes, 7, no. 12:49-51.

HARGRAVE, L.L., and SMITH, Watson

1936   A method for determining the texture of pottery.
         American Antiquity, 2, no. 1:32-36.

HARLAN, Mark, and MANIRE, Larry

    1975   Computerized data analysis at Antelope House. *In*
            Rock and Morris 1975, pp. 113-122.

HARLAN, Thomas (See under Nichols, Robert F.)

HARLOW, Francis H.

    1965a   Recent finds of Pajaritan pottery. El Palacio, 72,
            no. 2:27-33.

    1965b   Tewa Indian ceremonial pottery. El Palacio, 72,
            no. 4:13-23.

    1967   Historic Pueblo Indian pottery. Museum of New Mex-
            ico, Popular Handbook no. 6, 50 pp.

    1973   Matte-paint pottery of the Tewa, Keres, and Zuni
            Pueblos. Museum of New Mexico Press, 270 pp.

HARLOW, F.H., and FRANK, Larry

    1974   Historic pottery of the Pueblo Indians, 1600-1880.
            New York Graphic Society.

HARNER, Michael J.

    1953   Gravel pictographs of the Lower Colorado River
            region. University of California Archaeological
            Survey, Report no. 20, pp. 1-32.

    1956   Thermo-facts vs. artifacts: an experimental study
            of the Malpais industry. University of California,
            Archaeological Survey Reports, 33:39-43.

    1957   Potsherds and the tentative dating of the San
            Gorgonio-Big Maria Trail. University of California,
            Archaeological Survey Reports, 37:35-39.

    1958   Lowland Patayan phases in the Lower Colorado River
            Valley and Colorado Desert. University of Cali-
            fornia Archaeological Survey, Report no. 42, pp.
            93-97.

HARNONCOURT, Rene d'

    1940   Murals 30 layers deep found in Indian ruins. Sci-
            ence News Letter, 38, no. 9:132-133.

HARPER, Kimball T. (See also under Aikens, C. Melvin.)

HARPER, K.T., and ALDER, G.M.

 1972   Paleoclimatic inferences concerning the last 10,000
        years from a resampling of Danger Cave, Utah. Des-
        ert Research Institute, Publications in the Social
        Sciences, 8, pp. 13-23.

HARRILL, Bruce G. (See also under Robinson, William J.)

 1967   Prehistoric burials near Young, Arizona. Kiva, 33,
        no. 2:54-59.

 1968   A small prehistoric rock shelter in northwestern
        Arizona. Plateau, 40, no. 4:157-165.

 1972   Archaeological salvage in a prehistoric campsite,
        Petrified Forest National Park. Plateau, 44, no.
        4:163-175.

 1973   The DoBell site: archaeological salvage near the
        Petrified Forest. Kiva, 39, no. 1:35-67.

HARRILL, B.G., and BRETERNITZ, Cory D.

 1976   Chronology and cultural activity in Johnson Canyon
        cliff dwellings: interpretations from tree-ring
        data. Journal of Field Archaeology, 3:375-390.

HARRINGTON, Edna L.

 1930   Camp "Se-We-Mu." Masterkey, 3, no. 8:12-14.

 1933   More kachina pictographs in Nevada. Masterkey, 7,
        no. 2:48-50.

HARRINGTON, E.R.

 1939   Digging for turquoise in America's first mines.
        New Mexico Magazine, 17, no. 7:12-13, 45-46.

HARRINGTON, John Peabody

 1916a The ethnogeography of the Tewa Indians. Twenty-
        ninth Annual Report of the Bureau of American Eth-
        nology, pp. 29-636.
        Reviewed AA 20:450 (Kroeber).

 1916b House-builders of the desert. Art and Archaeology,
        4, no. 6:299-306.

 1940   Southern peripheral Athapaskawan origins, divisions,
        and migrations. Smithsonian Miscellaneous Collec-
        tions, 100:503-532.
        Reviewed AAq 7:336 (Voegelin).

HARRINGTON, Mark Raymond

1925a   Pueblo sites near St. Thomas, Nevada. Museum of
         the American Indian, Indian Notes, 2, no. 1:74-76.

1925b   Archaeological researches in Nevada. Museum of the
         American Indian, Indian Notes, 2, no. 2:125-127.

1925c   Ancient salt mine near St. Thomas, Nevada. Museum
         of the American Indian, Indian Notes, 2, no. 3:227-
         231.

1925d   The "Lost City" of Nevada. Scientific American,
         133:14-16.

1926a   Ancient salt mines of the Indians. Scientific Amer-
         ican, 135:116-117.

1926b   Western extension of early Pueblo culture. Museum
         of the American Indian, Indian Notes, 3:69-73 (also
         in El Palacio, 20:227-231).

1926c   Primitive Pueblo ruins in northwestern Arizona.
         Museum of the American Indian, Indian Notes, 3,
         no. 3:172-177.

1926d   Another ancient salt mine in Nevada. Museum of
         the American Indian, Indian Notes, 3, no. 4:221-232.

1926e   A pre-Pueblo site on Colorado River. Museum of the
         American Indian, Indian Notes, 3, no. 4:274-284.

1927a   An unusual hafted flint implement from Nevada.
         Museum of the American Indian, Indian Notes, 4, no.
         1:88-91.

1927b   A hafted stone hammer from Nevada. Museum of the
         American Indian, Indian Notes, 4, no. 2:127-131.

1927c   On the trail of the first Pueblos. Outlook, 145,
         no. 10:305-309.

1927d   A primitive Pueblo city in Nevada. American Anthro-
         pologist, 29:262-277.

1928a   Sandal Cave, a new "book" of Southwestern prehistory.
         Masterkey, 2, no. 2:4-10.

1928b   Tracing the Pueblo boundary in Nevada. Museum of
         the American Indian, Indian Notes, 5, no. 2:235-240.

1928c   A new archaeological field in Texas. Museum of the
         American Indian, Indian Notes, 5, no. 3:307-316.

1929a   Ruins and legends of Zuni land. Masterkey, 3, no.
         1:5-16.

1929b   Dead men tell tales. Masterkey, 3, no. 1:29-30.

1929c   The mystery pit. Masterkey, 3, no. 2:28-30.

1930a   The Gypsum Cave murder case: a detective story in
         the making. Masterkey, 4, no. 2:37-42.

1930b   Paiute Cave. In Harrington, Hayden, and Schellbach
         1930, pp. 106-126.

1930c   A goblin bone-hunter. Masterkey, 4, no. 2:61-62.

1930d   Early Pueblo settlements in Nevada. El Palacio,
         28:25-27.

1931   Lights and shadows in Gypsum Cave: the final phases.
         Masterkey, 4, no. 8:232-235.

1932a   Relics of an abandoned colony. Masterkey, 6, no.
         4:115-116.

1932b   More cave-hunting. Masterkey, 6, no. 4:119-121.

1932c   The Kachina rockshelter in Nevada. Masterkey, 6,
         no. 5:149-151.

1933a   Gypsum Cave, Nevada. Southwest Museum Papers, 8,
         197 pp.
         Reviewed AAq 1:239 (Sayles).

1933b   Rescuing more ancient treasures. Masterkey, 7,
         no. 4:100-104.

1934a   A camel hunter's camp in Nevada. Masterkey, 8, no.
         1:22-24.

1934b   American horses and ancient man in Nevada. Master-
         key, 8, no. 6:165-169.

1934c   The meaning of Gypsum Cave. Bulletin of the Texas
         Archaeological and Paleontological Society, 6:58-
         69.

1934d   Boulder Dam site to be explored. El Palacio, 36:
         13-14.

1935   Progress in Nevada. Masterkey, 9:189-190.

1936   A new ground-sloth den. Masterkey, 10:225-227.

1937a   Ancient Nevada Pueblo cotton. Masterkey, 11, no.
         1:5-7.

1937b   Ancient tribes of the Boulder Dam country. South-
         west Museum Leaflets, 9, 28 pp.

1937c   Excavation of Pueblo Grande de Nevada. Bulletin

of the Texas Archaeological and Paleontological
Society, 9:130-145.

1937d A stratified camp site near Boulder Dam. Masterkey,
       11, no. 3:86-89.

1937e Some early pit-dwellings in Nevada. Masterkey, 11,
       no. 4:122-124.

1937f Recent archaeological work in Nevada (U.S.A.).
       Boletin bibliográfico de antropología americana,
       1:43-45.

1939   Some rare Casas Grandes specimens. Masterkey, 13:
       205-206.

1940   Man and beast in Gypsum Cave. Desert Magazine, 3,
       no. 6:3-5, 34.

1941a Copper figurines from Arizona. Masterkey, 15, no.
       1:8-9.

1941b Our oldest bone implement. Masterkey, 15, no. 6:
       232-233.

1941c Ancient hunters of the Nevada desert. Desert Maga-
       zine, 4, no. 4:4-6.

1942a A rare mescal knife. Masterkey, 16, no. 2:67-68.

1942b New facts on old rubber. Masterkey, 16:122.

1942c Black Dog Cave. Masterkey, 16, no. 5:173-174.

1944a Prehistoric dots and dashes. Masterkey, 18, no.
       6:196.

1944b An old wooden image. Masterkey, 18:117.

1945a Nevada excursion. Masterkey, 19, no. 5:160-161.

1945b Nevada's salt cave mystery. Desert Magazine, 8,
       no. 4:9-11.

1945c Adventure with a mummy. Desert Magazine, 9, no.
       2:17-18.

1949   An Archaic axe. Masterkey, 23:176.

1951   The magic of carbon 14. Masterkey, 25, no. 1:25-
       26.

1952   Effigy axe. Masterkey, 26, no. 2:66.

1953a Southern Nevada pit-dwellings. Masterkey, 27, no.
       4:136-142.

1953b Early Pueblo houses in southern Nevada. Masterkey,

27, no. 6:203-209.

1954 The oldest camp-fires. Masterkey, 28, no. 6:233-234.

1955a Man's oldest date in America. Natural History, 64, no. 10:512-517, 554-555.

1955b A new Tule Springs expedition. Masterkey, 29, no. 4:112-114.

1956 The latest from Tule Springs. Masterkey, 30, no. 4:108-109.

1962- Reminiscences of an archeologist, I-VII. Masterkey,
65 36, no. 4:138-142; 37, no. 2:66-71; no. 3:114-118; 38, no. 1:26-34; no. 3:106-110.

HARRINGTON, M.R., and SIMPSON, Ruth DeEtte

1961 Tule Springs, Nevada: with other evidences of Pleistocene man in North America. Southwest Museum Papers, 18, 146 pp. Reviewed AAq 28:105 (Jennings).

HARRINGTON, M.R., HAYDEN, I., and SCHELLBACH, L.

1930 Archaeological explorations in southern Nevada. Southwest Museum Papers, 4, 126 pp.

HARRIS, Arthur H.

1963 Vertebrate remains and past environmental reconstruction in the Navajo Reservoir district. Museum of New Mexico, Papers in Anthropology, 11, 68 pp. Reviewed AAq 30:359 (Olsen).

1970 Past climate of the Navajo Reservoir district. American Antiquity, 35, no. 3:374-377.

HARRIS, A.H., SCHOENWETTER, James, and WARREN, A.H.

1967 An archaeological survey of the Chuska Valley and the Chaco Plateau, New Mexico. Part I. Natural science studies. Museum of New Mexico, Research Records, 4, 144 pp.

HARRIS, Hugh H.

1906 Pajarito ruins: their accessibility. Records of the Past, 5:291-295.

1907 Unusual and unknown points in Pajarito Park, New Mexico. American Journal of Archaeology, 2nd ser., 11:42-46.

HARRIS, R.K., and GOWIN, K.L.

1941   A report on an Indian burial blanket from Val Verde
        County, Texas. Dallas Archaeological Society, Rec-
        ord, 2, no. 6:27-29.

HARTMAN, Dana

1975   Preliminary assessment of mass burials in the South-
        west. American Journal of Physical Anthropology,
        42:305-306 (abstract).

1976a   A chronicle in wood and stone: an archaeologist
        views the Wupatki-Sunset Crater region. Plateau,
        49, no. 2:22-32.

1976b   Tuzigoot, an archaeological overview. Museum of
        Northern Arizona, Research Papers, 4, 80 pp.

HARTMAN, D., and WOLF, Arthur H.

1977   Wupatki: an archaeological assessment. Museum of
        Northern Arizona, Research Papers, 6, 74 pp.

HARTMAN, Gayle H. (See under Roubicek, Dennis; Vivian, R.
  Gwinn.)

HARVEY, Fred E. (See under Brand, Donald D.)

HARVEY, James Rose

1938   Turquoise among the Indians and a Colorado tur-
        quoise mine. Colorado Magazine, 15:186-192.

HASKELL, J. Loring

1970   The Paria Plateau survey. Lambda Alpha Journal
        of Man (Wichita), 2, no. 1:31-73.

1975   The Navajo in the eighteenth century: an investiga-
        tion involving anthropological archaeology in the
        San Juan Basin, northwestern New Mexico. Washing-
        ton State University, dissertation, 206 pp.; Uni-
        versity Microfilms International.

HASSE, Georges

1936   Une coupe en lave du Mexique. Société royale
        belge d'anthropologie et de préhistoire, Bulletin,
        51:283-284.

HASSEL, Carol (See under Hassel, Francis K.)

HASSEL, Francis K. (See also under Pendergast, David M.)

1960   Archaeological notes on the northeastern margin of
        Great Salt Lake. Utah Archaeology, 6, no. 3:10-15.

1964   Surface material from a site in Weber County. Utah
        Archaeology, 10, no. 3:1-3.

1967   A handled olla from the Injun Creek site (42-Wb-34).
        Utah Archaeology, 13, no. 2:8-10.

HASSEL, F.K., and HASSEL, Carol

1961   42-Bo-79 - an open site near Plain City, Utah. Utah
        Archaeology, 7, no. 2:5-13.

HASTINGS, Homer F. (See also under Schroeder, Albert H.)

1946   Montezuma Castle. Arizona Highways, 22, no. 7:36-
        37.

HASTINGS, Russell

1934a   Report of excavations at Casa Grande. Southwest
        Monuments Monthly Report, Supplement, March, pp.
        A-C.

1934b   Second preliminary report on excavations at Casa
        Grande, 1934. Southwestern Monuments Monthly Re-
        port, January, pp. 46-48.

HATTAN, Joseph M.

1893   Ruins of Quivira: the city of temples. The Archae-
        ologist, 1:105-107.

HATTORI, Eugene M. (See under Fowler, Don D.)

HAURY, Emil W. (See also under Doyel, David E.; Gladwin, Harold
S.; Kelly, Isabel T.)

1930   A sequence of decorated redware from the Silver
        Creek drainage. Museum of Northern Arizona, Museum
        Notes, 2, no. 11:4.

1931a   Kivas of the Tusayan Ruin, Grand Canyon, Arizona.
        Gila Pueblo, Medallion Papers, 9, 26 pp.

1931b   Minute beads from prehistoric pueblos. American
        Anthropologist, 33, no. 1:80-87.

1932a   The age of lead glaze decorated pottery in the
        Southwest. American Anthropologist, 34, no. 3:
        418-425.

1932b   Roosevelt:9:6, a Hohokam site of the Colonial Period.
        Gila Pueblo, Medallion Papers, 11, 134 pp.

1934   The Canyon Creek Ruin and the cliff dwellings of
        the Sierra Ancha. Gila Pueblo, Medallion Papers,
        14, 173 pp.

1935a   Dates from Gila Pueblo. Tree-Ring Bulletin, 2, no.
        1:3-5.

1935b   Tree rings - the archaeologist's time-piece. Amer-
        ican Antiquity, 1, no. 2:98-108.

1936a   A glimpse of the prehistoric Southwest. Indians At
        Work, 4, no. 9:15-22.

1936b   The Snaketown Canal. *In* Brand 1936, pp. 48-50.

1936c   Some Southwestern pottery types, series IV. Gila
        Pueblo, Medallion Papers, 19, 49 pp.
            Reviewed AA 39:145 (Shepard).

1936d   The Mogollon culture of southwestern New Mexico.
        Gila Pueblo, Medallion Papers, 20, 146 pp.
            Reviewed AA 39:145 (Shepard), AAq 2:233 (Martin).

1936e   Vandal Cave. Kiva, 1, no. 6:1-4.

1937   A pre-Spanish rubber ball from Arizona. American
        Antiquity, 2, no. 4:282-288.

1938a   Legged vessels from the Southwest. American Antiq-
        uity, 3:264-265.

1938b   Southwestern dated ruins, II. Tree-Ring Bulletin,
        4, no. 3:3-4.

1940a   Excavations at Forestdale. Kiva, 6, no. 2:5-8.

1940b   Excavations in the Forestdale Valley, east-central
        Arizona. University of Arizona, Social Science
        Bulletin 12, 147 pp.
            Reviewed AA 44:485 (Morris), AAq 9:247 (Hall).

1940c   New tree-ring dates from the Forestdale Valley,
        east-central Arizona. Tree-Ring Bulletin, 7, no.
        2:14-16.

1941   Excavation of a pre-Spanish village site on Forest-
        dale Creek in the Fort Apache Indian Reservation,
        Arizona. American Philosophical Society, Yearbook,
        1940, pp. 186-188.

1942a   Recent field work by the Arizona State Museum. Kiva,
        7, nos. 5-6:17-24.

1942b   Some implications of the Bluff Ruin dates. Tree-Ring Bulletin, 9, no. 2:7-8.

1942c   Excavations of pre-Spanish village sites on Forestdale Creek in the Fort Apache Indian Reservation, Arizona. American Philosophical Society, Yearbook, 1941, pp. 222-225.

1943a   The stratigraphy of Ventana Cave, Arizona. American Antiquity, 8, no. 3:218-223.

1943b   A possible Cochise-Mogollon-Hohokam sequence. Proceedings of the American Philosophical Society, 86, no. 2:260-263.

1944a   Mexico and the southwestern United States. *In* El Norte de México y el Sur de Estados Unidos, Tercera Reunión de Mesa Redonda sobre Problemas antropológicas de México y Centro América, Sociedad mexicana de antropología, pp. 203-205.

1944b   Tree-rings continue to tell their story. Kiva, 9, no. 2:10-14.

1945a   The archaeological survey on the San Carlos Indian Reservation. Kiva, 11, no. 1:5-9.

1945b   Arizona's ancient irrigation builders. Natural History, 54, no. 7:300-310, 335.

1945c   Dating Early Man in the Southwest. Arizona Quarterly, 1, no. 4:5-13.

1945d   The excavation of Los Muertos and neighboring ruins in the Salt River Valley, southern Arizona. Papers of the Peabody Museum of American Archaeology and Ethnology, 24, no. 1, 223 pp.
        Reviewed AA 48:255 (Colton), AAq 11:127 (McGregor).

1945e   Painted Cave, northeastern Arizona. Amerind Foundation, no. 3, 87 pp.

1945f   The problem of contacts between the southwestern United States and Mexico. Southwestern Journal of Anthropology, 1, no. 1:55-74.

1946   Summer activities at Point of Pines. Kiva, 12, no. 1:3-5.

1947   A large pre-Columbian copper bell from the Southwest. American Antiquity, 13:80-82.

1949   The 1948 Southwestern Archaeological Conference. American Antiquity, 14:254-256.

1950a A sequence of great kivas in the Forestdale Valley,
       Arizona. *In* Reed and King 1950, pp. 29-39.

1950b The stratigraphy and archaeology of Ventana Cave,
       Arizona. University of New Mexico Press, 599 pp.
       Reviewed AA 53:557 (Kidder), AAq 17:152 (Kelley).

1952a Exploring the corridors of time. Kiva, 17, nos.
       3-4:1-28.

1952b The Naco mammoth. Kiva, 18, nos. 3-4:1-19.

1955a Archaeological stratigraphy. *In* Geochronology, ed.
       T.L. Smiley, University of Arizona Physical Science
       Bulletin 2, pp. 126-134.

1955b A mammoth hunt in Arizona. Archaeology, 8, no. 1:
       51-55.

1956a The Lehner mammoth site. Kiva, 21, nos. 3-4:23-24.

1956b Speculations on prehistoric settlement patterns in
       the Southwest. *In* Willey 1956, pp. 3-10.

1957   An alluvial site on the San Carlos Indian Reserva-
       tion, Arizona. American Antiquity, 23:2-27.

1958a Evidence at Point of Pines for a prehistoric migra-
       tion from northern Arizona. *In* Migrations in New
       World culture history, ed. R.H. Thompson, University
       of Arizona, Social Science Bulletin, 27, pp. 1-8.

1958b Post-Pleistocene human occupation of the Southwest.
       In Climate and Man in the Southwest, ed. T.L. Smiley,
       University of Arizona Bulletin, 28, no. 4:69-75.

1958c Two fossil elephant kill sites in the American
       Southwest. Proceedings of the 32nd International
       Congress of Americanists, pp. 433-440.

1960a Association of fossil fauna and artifacts of the
       Sulphur Springs Stage, Cochise culture. American
       Antiquity, 25, no. 4:609-610.

1960b The people and their past. *In* Arizona: its People
       and Resources, ed. J.C. Cross, E.H. Shaw, and K.
       Scheifele, University of Arizona Press, pp. 2-72.

1960c The Arizona Antiquities Act of 1960. Kiva, 26, no.
       1:19-24.

1962a The Greater American Southwest. *In* Courses toward
       Urban Life, ed. R.J. Braidwood and G.R. Willey,
       Viking Fund Publications in Anthropology, 32, pp.
       106-131.

1962b HH-39: recollections of a dramatic moment in Southwestern archaeology. Tree-Ring Bulletin, 24, nos.
3-4:11-14.

1965 Snaketown: 1964-1965. Kiva, 31, no. 1:1-13.

1967 The Hohokam, first masters of the American desert.
National Geographic Magazine, 131:670-695.

1976a The Hohokam, desert farmers and craftsmen: excavations at Snaketown, 1964-1965. University of Arizona Press, 412 pp.
Reviewed AA 79:729 (McGregor).

1976b Salado: the view from Point of Pines. *In* Doyel and
Haury 1976, pp. 81-84.

HAURY, E.W., and CONRAD, Carl M.

1938 The comparison of fiber properties of Arizona cliff-
dweller and Hopi cotton. American Antiquity, 3, no.
3:224-227.

HAURY, E.W., and FLORA, I.F.

1937 Basket-Maker III dates from the vicinity of Durango,
Colorado. Tree-Ring Bulletin, 4, no. 1:7-8.

HAURY, E.W., and GIFFORD, Carol A.

1959 A thirteenth century "strongbox." Kiva, 24, no.
4:1-11.

HAURY, E.W., and HARGRAVE, Lyndon L.

1931 Recently dated Pueblo ruins in Arizona. Smithsonian Miscellaneous Collections, 82, no. 11, 120 pp.

HAURY, E.W., and SAYLES, E.B.

1947 An early pit house village of the Mogollon culture,
Forestdale Valley, Arizona. University of Arizona,
Social Science Bulletin 16, 93 pp.
Reviewed AAq 15:66 (Rinaldo).

HAURY, E.W., ANTEVS, Ernst, and LANCE, J.F.

1953 Artifacts with mammoth remains, Naco, Arizona.
American Antiquity, 19:1-24.

HAURY, E.W., BALDWIN, Gordon C., and NUSBAUM, Jesse L.

1950 Prehistory of man. *In* A Survey of the Recreational

              Resources of the Colorado River Basin, National
              Park Service, Washington, pp. 79-101.

HAURY, E.W., SAYLES, E.B., and WASLEY, William W.
    1959   The Lehner mammoth site, southeastern Arizona.
            American Antiquity, 25, no. 1:2-30.

HAWLEY, Florence M. (See also under Brand, Donald D. Also
    listed as Ellis, Florence H., and Senter, Florence Hawley.)
    1929   Prehistoric pottery pigments in the Southwest.
            American Anthropologist, 31, no. 4:731-754.

    1930a   Chemical examination of prehistoric smudged wares.
            American Anthropologist, 32:500-502.

    1930b   Prehistoric pottery and culture relations in the
            Middle Gila. American Anthropologist, 32:522-536.

    1931   Chemistry in prehistoric American arts. Journal of
            Chemical Education, 8:35-42.

    1932a   The Bead Mountain pueblos of southern Arizona.
            Art and Archaeology, 33, no. 5:226-236.

    1932b   Oldest tree ring record of ancient Pueblos. El
            Palacio, 32:108-110.

    1932c   Reply to Herman F.C. ten Kate's criticism of "Pre-
            historic pottery and culture relations in the Middle
            Gila." American Anthropologist, 34:548-550.

    1933   Tree ring chronology in Chaco Canyon. El Palacio,
            34:204-205.

    1934   The significance of the dated prehistory of Chetro
            Ketl, Chaco Canyon, New Mexico. University of New
            Mexico Bulletin, Monograph Series, 1, no. 1, 80 pp.
            Reviewed AA 38:494 (Schenck), AAq 1:331 (Cole).

    1936a   Field manual of prehistoric Southwestern pottery
            types. University of New Mexico Bulletin, Anthro-
            pological Series, 1, no. 4, 122 pp.
            Reviewed AA 43:286 (Haury).

    1936b   The missing rings: no mystery story. New Mexico
            Quarterly, 6:277-285.

    1937a   Kokopelli, of the prehistoric southwestern Pueblo
            pantheon. American Anthropologist, 39:644-646.

    1937b   Reversed stratigraphy. American Antiquity, 2:297-
            299.

1937c   Ancient New Mexicans.   New Mexico Magazine, 15, no. 7:22-23, 42-44.

1938a   Classification of black pottery pigments and paint areas.   University of New Mexico Bulletin, Anthropological Series, 2, no. 4:3-14. Reviewed AAq 4:367 (Shepard).

1938b   The family tree of Chaco Canyon masonry.   American Antiquity, 3:247-255.

1939a   Mummy dusters; New Mexico style.   New Mexico Magazine, 17, no. 3:20-21, 34-37.

1939b   New applications of tree ring analysis.   In Brand and Harvey 1939, pp. 177-186.

1940   Squash-blossom headdress in Basketmaker III.   American Antiquity, 6:167.

1950a   Big kivas, little kivas, and moiety houses in historical reconstruction.   Southwestern Journal of Anthropology, 6:286-302.

1950b   Field manual of prehistoric Southwestern pottery types.   (2nd ed.)   University of New Mexico Bulletin, Anthropological Series, 1, no. 4, 126 pp.

HAWLEY, Fred G.

1938   The chemical analysis of prehistoric Southwestern glaze-paint, with components.   University of New Mexico Bulletin, Anthropological Series, 2, no. 4: 15-27. Reviewed AAq 4:367 (Shepard).

1947   The use of lead mineral by the Hohokam in cremation ceremonials.   Southwestern Journal of Anthropology, 3:69-77.

1953   The manufacture of copper bells found in Southwestern sites.   Southwestern Journal of Anthropology, 9:99-111.

HAYDEN, Irwin (See also under Harrington, Mark Raymond.)

1929a   An archaeologist afield.   Masterkey, 2, no. 8:16-20.

1929b   It could not happen: but it did, at Mesa House.   Masterkey, 3, no. 5:22-25.

1930a   The last stand of the Nevada Pueblos.   Scientific American, 142, February, pp. 132-134.

1930b   Mesa House. *In* Harrington, Hayden, and Schellbach
        1930, pp. 26-92.

HAYDEN, Julian D. (See also under Stacy, V.K. Pheriba.)

1942   Plaster mixing bowls. American Antiquity, 7, no.
        4:405-407.

1945   Salt erosion. American Antiquity, 10:373-378.

1956   Notes on the archaeology of the central coast of
        Sonora, Mexico. Kiva, 21, nos. 3-4:19-23.

1957   Excavations, 1940, at University Indian Ruin.
        Southwest Monuments Association, Technical Series,
        5, 234 pp.
        Reviewed AAq 25:140 (Di Peso).

1965   Fragile-pattern areas. American Antiquity, 31:272-
        276.

1967   A summary prehistory and history of the Sierra
        Pinacate, Sonora. American Antiquity, 32:335-344.

1969   Gyratory crushers of the Sierra Pinacate, Sonora.
        American Antiquity, 34:154-161.

1970   Of Hohokam origins and other matters. American
        Antiquity, 35:87-93.

1972   Hohokam petroglyphs of the Sierra Pinacate, Sonora,
        and the Hohokam shell expeditions. Kiva, 37, no.
        2:74-83.

1976a   Pre-Altithermal archaeology in the Sierra Pinacate,
        Sonora, Mexico. American Antiquity, 41:274-289.

1976b   Resumen de la arqueología del distrito do los rios
        Sonoita y Altar. *In* Sonora: Antropología del De-
        sierto. Primera reunión de antropología e historia
        del noroeste, Centro regional del Noroeste, Co-
        lección Científica, diversa, pp. 261-265.

1976c   La arqueología de la Sierra del Pinacate, Sonora,
        Mexico. *In* Sonora: Antropología del Desierto.
        Primera reunión de antropología e historia del
        Noroeste, Centro regional del Noroeste, Colección
        Científica, diversa, pp. 281-304.

HAYES, Alden C. (See also under Osborne, Douglas.)

1964   The archaeological survey of Wetherill Mesa, Mesa
        Verde National Park, Colorado. National Park Ser-
        vice, Archaeological Research Series, 7-A, 157 pp.
        Reviewed AA 69:101 (Ellis), AAq 33:402 (Dittert).

1965   An early occupied cave: site 1205. *In* Osborne 1965a,
        pp. 5-13.

1968   The missing convento of San Isidro. El Palacio, 75,
        no. 4.

1969   The Wetherill Mesa project. Naturalist, 20, no.
        2:18-25.

1974   The four churches of Pecos. University of New Mex-
        ico Press, 77 pp.

1976   A cache of gardening tools: Chaco Canyon. *In*
        Schroeder 1976, pp. 73-84.

HAYES, A.C., and CHAPPELL, Clifford C.

1962   A copper bell from southwest Colorado. Plateau,
        35:53-56.

HAYES, A.C., and LANCASTER, James A.

1962   Site 1060, a Basket Maker III pithouse on Chapin
        Mesa, Mesa Verde National Park. Tree-Ring Bulletin,
        24, nos. 1-2:14-16 (reprinted in Lister 1968b).

1975   Badger House community, Mesa Verde National Park.
        National Park Service, Archaeological Research
        Series, 7-E, 205 pp.

HAYES, A.C., and OSBORNE, Douglas

1961   Fixing site locations by radiodirection finder at
        Mesa Verde. American Antiquity, 27, no. 1:110-112.

HAYES, A.C., and WINDES, Thomas C.

1975   An Anasazi shrine in Chaco Canyon. *In* Frisbie
        1975a, pp. 143-156.

HAYES, Charles F.

1955   Prelude to excavation - reflections on an archae-
        ological survey in Utah. Museum Service, 32:54-55.

HAYNES, C. Vance (See also under Hemmings, E. Thomas; Irwin-
Williams, Cynthia; Mehringer, Peter J.)

1955   Evidence of Early Man in Torrance County, New Mex-
        ico. Bulletin of the Texas Archaeological Society,
        26:144-164.

1962   Radiocarbon dating of Sandia Cave, New Mexico.
        National Geographic Society Research Reports, 1961-

1962, pp. 121-122.

1964   Fluted projectile points: their age and dispersion. Science, 145, no. 3639:1408-1413.

1965   Carbon-14 dates and Early Man in the New World. Clearinghouse for Federal Scientific and Technical Information, PB-174 115, 30 pp.

1966a Elephant-hunting in North America. Scientific American, 214, no. 6:104-112.

1966b Geochronology of Late Quaternary alluvium. University of Arizona, Geochronology Laboratories, Interim Research Reports, 10.

1967   Quaternary geology of the Tule Springs area, Clark County, Nevada. *In* Wormington and Ellis 1967, pp. 15-104.

1968   Geochronology of Late Quaternary alluvium. INQUA VII International Congress, Proceedings, 8, University of Utah Press, pp. 591-631.

1969   The earliest Americans. Science, 166, no. 3906: 709-715.

HAYNES, C.V., and AGENBROAD, Larry D.

1975   *Bison bison* remains at Murray Springs, Arizona. Kiva, 40, no. 4:309-313.

HAYNES, C.V., and AGOGINO, George A.

1966   Prehistoric springs and geochronology of the Clovis site, New Mexico. American Antiquity, 31:812-821.

HAYNES, C.V., and HEMMINGS, E.T.

1968   Mammoth-bone shaft wrench from Murray Springs, Arizona. Science, 159:186-187.

HAYNES, C.V., and IRWIN-WILLIAMS, Cynthia

1970   Climatic change and early population dynamics in the southwestern United States. Quaternary Research, 1, no. 1:59-71.

HAYNES, C.V., DOBERENZ, A.R., and ALLEN, Jack

1966   Geological and geochemical evidence concerning the antiquity of bone tools from Tule Springs, site 2, Clark County, Nevada. American Antiquity, 31, no. 4:517-521.

HEALD, Weldon F.

    1952   Cliff home of the ancients. Desert Magazine, 15,
            no. 10:18-21.

HEDGES, Ken

    1973a   Hakataya figurines from southern California. Pa-
            cific Coast Archaeological Society, Quarterly, 9,
            no. 3:1-40.

    1973b   Rock art in Southern California. Pacific Coast
            Archaeological Society, Quarterly, 9, no. 4:1-28.

HEDRICK, Basil C. (See also under Riley, Carroll L.)

HEDRICK, B.C., KELLEY, J. Charles, and RILEY, Carroll L.

    1971   (ed.) The north Mexican frontier: readings in
            archaeology, ethnohistory, and ethnography. South-
            ern Illinois University Press, 288 pp.

    1973   (ed.) The Classic Southwest: readings in archae-
            ology, ethnohistory, and ethnology. Southern Illi-
            nois University Press, 193 pp.
            Reviewed AA 77:459 (Dittert).

    1974   (ed.) The Mesoamerican Southwest: readings in
            archaeology, ethnohistory, and ethnology. South-
            ern Illinois University Press, 208 pp.
            Reviewed AA 79:499 (Di Peso).

HEDRICK, John A.

    1968   Plateau Station area survey. The Artifact, 6, no.
            1:1-16.

    1971   Tigua potters and pottery at Ysleta del Sur, Texas.
            The Artifact, 9, no. 2:1-18.

    1975   Archaeology of Plateau Site, Culberson County. The
            Artifact, 13, no. 4:45-82.

HEDRICK, Mrs. John A.

    1967   Escondida survey. The Artifact, 5, no. 2:19-24.

HEGLAR, Rodger

    1974   The prehistoric population of Cochiti Pueblo and
            selected inter-population biological comparisons.
            University of Michigan, dissertation, 193 pp.;
            University Microfilms International.

HEINDL, L.A.

1955   "Clean fill" at Point of Pines, Arizona. Kiva, 20,
        no. 4:1-8.

HEISTER, A.L.

1894   Pueblo graves. The Archaeologist, 2, no. 5:153-
        154.

HEIZER, Robert F. (See also under Baumhoff, Martin A.; Hester,
    Thomas Roy.)

1941   Aboriginal trade between the Southwest and Cali-
        fornia. Masterkey, 15, no. 5:185-188.

1942   Ancient grooved clubs and modern rabbit-sticks.
        American Antiquity, 8:41-56.

1946   The occurrence and significance of Southwestern
        grooved axes in California. American Antiquity,
        11, no. 3:187-193.

1951   The sickle in aboriginal western North America.
        American Antiquity, 16, no. 3:247-252.

1970   A mescal knife from near Overton, Moapa Valley,
        southern Nevada. University of California Archae-
        ological Research Facility, Contributions, 7:28-38.

HEIZER, R.F., and BERGER, R.

1970   Radiocarbon age of the Gypsum culture. University
        of California Archaeological Research Facility,
        Contributions, 7:13-18.

HEIZER, R.F., and CLEWLOW, C.W., Jr.

1973   Prehistoric rock art of California. 2 vols. Bal-
        lena Press, Ramona, California.

HEMMINGS, E. Thomas (See also under Haynes, C. Vance.)

1967   Cruciform and related artifacts of Mexico and the
        southwestern United States. Kiva, 32, no. 4:150-
        169.

1969   Salvage excavations in a buried Hohokam site near
        Tucson, Arizona. Kiva, 34, nos. 2-3:199-205.

1970   Early Man in the San Pedro Valley, Arizona. Uni-
        versity of Arizona, dissertation, 393 pp.; Univer-
        sity Microfilms International.

HEMMINGS, E.T., and HAYNES, C. Vance, Jr.

1969   The Escapule mammoth and associated projectile
        points, San Pedro Valley, Arizona. Journal of the
        Arizona Academy of Science, 5, no. 3:184-188.

HENDERSON, Junius (See also under Hewett, Edgar Lee.)

1927   The prehistoric peoples of Colorado. *In* Colorado:
        short studies of its past and present, University
        of Colorado Press, pp. 1-22.

HENDERSON, Mark

1976   An archaeological inventory of Brantley Reservoir,
        New Mexico. Southern Methodist University, Contri-
        butions in Anthropology, no. 18.

HENDERSON, Palmer

1893   Cliff-dwellers' houses. American Antiquarian, 15:
        170-172.

HENDERSON, Randall

1940   Watering place on the Devil's Highway. Desert
        Magazine, 3, no. 6:7-10, 34.

1946   Glyph hunters in the Indian country. Desert Maga-
        zine, 10, no. 1:11-16.

1949   19 days on Utah trails. Desert Magazine, 12, no.
        2:5-11; 13, no. 1:19-25.

1953   Field day in Muggins Hills. Desert Magazine, 16,
        no. 6:15-19.

1957a   We camped in the Land of the Standing Rocks. Desert
        Magazine, 20, no. 10:5-10.

1957b   Giant desert figures have been restored. Desert
        Magazine, 20, no. 11:5-8.

1958   Canyon boat ride in Utah. Desert Magazine, 21, no.
        12:21-25.

HENDRICKS, Lawrence J. (See under Hurst, Clarence T.)

HENDRON, J.W.

1937   The stabilization of the restored Talus House, El
        Rito de los Frijoles, Bandelier National Monument,
        New Mexico. Southwestern Monuments Monthly Report,
        Supplement, December, pp. 478-485.

1938a   The stabilization of the kiva in the Great Cere-
        monial Cave, El Rito de los Frijoles, Bandelier
        National Monument, New Mexico. Southwestern Monu-
        ments Monthly Report, Supplement, January, pp. 70-74.

1938b   Archaeological report on the stabilization of Ty-
        uonyi, El Rito de los Frijoles, Bandelier National
        Monument, New Mexico. Southwestern Monuments
        Monthly Report, Supplement, February, pp. 176-181.

1940   Prehistory of El Rito de los Frijoles, Bandelier
        National Monument. Southwestern Monuments Associa-
        tion, Technical Series, 1, 69 pp.
        Reviewed AAq 7:195 (McGregor).

1946a   Atomic man in the haunts of the ancient cave man.
        Desert Magazine, 9, no. 12:5-9.

1946b   Frijoles: a hidden valley in the New World (ed.
        Dorothy Thomas). Rydal Press, Santa Fe, 91 pp.

1947   The happy pueblo. New Mexico Magazine, 25, no. 7:
        14, 43, 45.

HENDRY, Thomas P.

1943   Excavation of burial at Van's ruin, western New
        Mexico. Totem Pole, 11, no. 1:1.

HENLEY, Ruth W.

1929   Catching archaeology alive. Masterkey, 2, no. 8:
        23-27.

HENRICKSON, James, and FELGER, Richard S.

1973   Microanalysis and identification of a basket frag-
        ment from Sonora, Mexico. Kiva, 38, nos. 3-4:173-
        177.

HEROLD, Joyce L.

1961   Prehistoric settlement and physical environment in
        the Mesa Verde area. University of Utah, Anthro-
        pological Papers, 53, 226 pp.
        Reviewed AA 65:414 (Woodbury).

HEROLD, Laurance C. (See also under Luebben, Ralph A.)

1965   Trincheras and physical environment along the Rio
        Gavilan, Chihuahua, Mexico. University of Denver,
        Publications in Geography, Technical Papers, no.
        65-1.

1968   An archaeological-geographical survey of the Rio
        Grande de Ranchos. *In* Papers on Taos Archaeology,
        Fort Burgwin Research Center, no. 7, pp. 9-42.
        Reviewed AA 71:1208 (Leone), AAq 35:233 (Gunnerson).

HERSKOVITZ, Robert M.

1974   The Superstition freeway project: a preliminary
        report on the salvage excavation of a dual com-
        ponent Hohokam site in Tempe, Arizona. Arizona
        State Museum.

1978   Fort Bowie National Historic Site, Arizona: identi-
        fication and analysis of material culture. Uni-
        versity of Arizona, Anthropological Papers, 31,
        176 pp.

HESTER, James J. (See also under Agogino, George A.; Eddy,
    Frank W.)

1962a   Early Navajo migrations and acculturation in the
        Southwest. Museum of New Mexico, Papers in Anthro-
        pology, 6, 131 pp.
        Reviewed AAq 30:112 (Lange).

1962b   A Folsom lithic complex from the Elida site, Roose-
        velt County, N.M. El Palacio, 69:92-113.

1966   Origins of the Clovis culture. Proceedings of the
        36th International Congress of Americanists, pp.
        129-142.

1970   Ecology of the North American Paleo-Indian. Bio-
        science, 20, no. 4:213-217.

1972   Blackwater Locality No. 1: a stratified Early Man
        site in eastern New Mexico. Fort Burgwin Research
        Center, no. 8, 262 pp.

1974   Archaeology in Colorado. Southwestern Lore, 40,
        nos. 3-4:1-5.

HESTER, J.J., and SHINER, J.L.

1963   Studies at Navajo Period sites in the Navajo Reser-
        voir district. Museum of New Mexico, Papers in
        Anthropology, 9, 77 pp.
        Reviewed AAq 31:126 (Ruppé).

HESTER, Joseph A., Jr. (See under Macgowan, Kenneth.)

HESTER, Thomas Roy (See also under Collins, Michael B.; Hill, T.C.)

1971   An additional note on Texas atlatl spurs.   Master-
        key, 45, no. 2:72-73.

1973   Chronological ordering of Great Basin prehistory.
        University of California Archaeological Research
        Facility, Contribution no. 17.

1974   On fluted points and south Texas archaeology.
        Texas Archaeology, 18, no. 2:11-14.

HESTER, T.R., and HEIZER, Robert F.

1973   Review and discussion of Great Basin projectile
        points: forms and chronology.   University of Cali-
        fornia Archaeological Research Facility.

HESTER, T.R., and HILL, T.C., Jr.

1969   Mogollon ceramics from southern Texas.   The Arti-
        fact, 7, no. 3:11-15.

HESTON, James W.

1961   Some archaeological evidence of the distribution
        of cotton in the American Southwest.   University
        of Oklahoma, Papers in Anthropology, 3, no. 1:35-43.

HEVLY, Richard H. (See also under Berlin, G. Lennis; Hill,
James N.)

1964   Paleoecology of Laguna Salada.   *In* Martin, Rinaldo,
        Longacre, and others 1964, pp. 171-187.

1970   Botanical studies of sealed storage jar cached near
        Grand Falls, Arizona.   Plateau, 42, no. 4:150-156.

HEWETT, Edgar Lee

1904a   Studies on the extinct pueblo of Pecos.   American
        Anthropologist, n.s. 6, no. 4:426-439.

1904b   Archaeology of Pajarito Park, New Mexico.   American
        Anthropologist, n.s. 6, no. 5:629-659.

1905a   A general view of the archaeology of the Pueblo
        region.   Annual Report of the Smithsonian Insti-
        tution for 1904, pp. 583-605.

1905b   Historic and prehistoric ruins of the Southwest
        and their preservation.   Department of the Interior,
        19 pp.

1905c   Prehistoric irrigation in the Navajo desert.   Records of the Past, 4, pt. 11:322-329.

1905d   The so-called "oldest house" in Santa Fe, New Mexico.   American Anthropologist, n.s. 7:576.

1906   Antiquities of the Jemez Plateau, New Mexico.   Bureau of American Ethnology, Bulletin 32, 55 pp.

1908   Les communautés anciennes dans le désert américain.   Librairie Kundig, Geneva, 107 pp.

1909a   Archaeology of the Rio Grande Valley.   Out West, 31, no. 2:692-719 (same as 1909b).

1909b   The excavations at Puye, New Mexico, in 1907.   Archaeological Institute of America, School of American Archaeology, Papers, no. 4, 29 pp. (same as 1909a).

1909c   The excavations at Tyuonyi, New Mexico, in 1908.   American Anthropologist, n.s. 11, no. 3:434-455 (also as Papers of the School of American Archaeology, no. 5).

1909d   The excavations at El Rito de los Frijoles in 1909.   American Anthropologist, n.s. 11, no. 4:651-673 (also as Papers of the School of American Archaeology, no. 10).

1909e   The Pajaritan culture.   American Journal of Archaeology, 2nd ser., 13, no. 3:334-344 (also as Papers of the School of American Archaeology, no. 3).

1916   The proposed "National park of the cliff cities."   Old Santa Fe, 3:150-160 (also as Papers of the School of American Archaeology, 34).

1920a   Antiquities of Colorado.   Art and Archaeology, 10: 39-43.

1920b   The cliff maiden.   El Palacio, 8, nos. 5-6:109.

1921a   The Chaco Canyon and its ancient monuments.   Art and Archaeology, 11, nos. 1-2:3-28.

1921b   The excavation of Chetro Ketl, Chaco Canyon, 1920.   Art and Archaeology, 11, nos. 1-2:45-62.

1922   The Chaco Canyon in 1921.   Art and Archaeology, 14, no. 3:115-131.

1923   Anahuac and Aztlan; retracing the legendary footsteps of the Aztecs.   Art and Archaeology, 16:35-50.

1926a   The archaeology of the Southwest. El Palacio, 20,
         no. 4:78-82, 92-93.

1926b   How old is Pueblo culture? El Palacio, 21:116-118.

1928   Pueblo ruins at Agua Fria. El Palacio, 24:483.

1929   Chaco Canyon past and present. El Palacio, 26:313-
         315.

1930   Ancient life in the American Southwest. Bobbs-
         Merrill Co., Indianapolis, 392 pp.

1932a   The Chaco Canyon in 1932. Art and Archaeology, 33:
         147-158.

1932b   New dates from Chaco Canyon. El Palacio, 32:185-
         186.

1932c   Excavations at Chetro Ketl. El Palacio, 33:13-20.

1934   The excavation of Chetro Ketl, Chaco Canyon, 1932-
         33. Art and Archaeology, 35, no. 2:50-58, 68.

1936a   Archaeological resources of New Mexico. El Palacio,
         40:133-139.

1936b   The Chaco Canyon and its monuments. University of
         New Mexico Press, 234 pp.

1938a   The frescoes of Kuaua. El Palacio, 45, nos. 6-8:
         21-28.

1938b   Pre-Hispanic frescoes in the Rio Grande Valley.
         School of American Research, Papers, n.s., no. 27,
         14 pp.

1938c   Pajarito Plateau and its ancient people. Univer-
         sity of New Mexico Press, 191 pp.
         Reviewed AAq 6:188 (Spicer).

1938d   Hispanic monuments. El Palacio, 45:53-67.

1940   Coronado Monument and museum. El Palacio, 47, no.
         8:172-181.

HEWETT, E.L., and DUTTON, Bertha P.

1953   Pajarito Plateau and its ancient people. (2nd ed.)
         University of New Mexico Press, 174 pp.
         Reviewed AAq 21:194 (Euler).

HEWETT, E.L., and FISHER, Reginald G.

1943   Mission monuments of New Mexico. University of
         New Mexico Press, 269 pp.
         Reviewed AAq 12:280 (Hurt).

HEWETT, E.L., HENDERSON, Junius, and ROBBINS, Wilfred William

1913   The physiography of the Rio Grande Valley, New
Mexico, in relation to Pueblo culture. Bureau of
American Ethnology, Bulletin 54, 76 pp.

HEWITT, James (See under Doelle, William H.)

HIBBEN, Frank C. (See also under Agogino, George A.; Brand,
Donald D.)

1936   The excavation of a pre-biscuit ware ruin in the
Chama Valley. El Palacio, 41, nos. 8-10:48-53.

1937a   Association of man with Pleistocene mammals in the
Sandia Mountains, New Mexico. American Antiquity,
2, no. 4:260-263.

1937b   Excavation of the Riana Ruin and Chama Valley Survey. University of New Mexico Bulletin, Anthropological Series, 2, no. 1, 60 pp.
Reviewed AA 39:679 (Mera).

1938a   A cache of wooden bows from the Mogollon Mountains.
American Antiquity, 4:36-38.

1938b   The Gallina Phase. American Antiquity, 4, no. 2:
131-136.

1940   Sandia Man. Scientific American, 163, no. 1:14-16.

1941a   Excavation of the Sandia Cave, New Mexico. American
Philosophical Society, Yearbook for 1940, pp. 190-
191.

1941b   Sandia Cave. American Antiquity, 6:266.

1942   Pleistocene stratification in the Sandia Cave, New
Mexico. Proceedings of the 8th American Scientific
Congress, 2:45-48.

1943   Discoveries in Sandia Cave and early horizons in
the Southwest. Proceedings of the American Philosophical Society, 86:247-254.

1946   The first thirty-eight Sandia points. American
Antiquity, 11, no. 4:257-258.

1948a   Association of man with Pleistocene mammals in
Sandia Mountains. American Antiquity, 12:260-263.

1948b   The Gallina architectural forms. American Antiquity, 13, no. 1:32-36.

1949   The pottery of the Gallina complex. American

Antiquity, 14, no. 3:194-202.

1951a   Murder in the Gallina country. Southwestern Review, 36, no. 2:90-96.

1951b   Sites of the Paleo-Indian in the middle Rio Grande Valley. American Antiquity, 17:41-46.

1951c   A survey of the sites of the Paleo-Indian in the middle Rio Grande Valley, New Mexico. Texas Journal of Science, 3:362-367.

1953   Early Man in New Mexico. Archaeology, 6, no. 3:184.

1955a   Excavations at Pottery Mound, New Mexico. American Antiquity, 21:179-180.

1955b   Specimens from Sandia Cave and their possible significance. Science, 122:688-689.

1959   Excavations of a site of the Sandia culture near Lucy, New Mexico. American Philosophical Society, Yearbook for 1958, pp. 376-379.

1960   Prehispanic paintings at Pottery Mound. Archaeology, 13, no. 4:267-274.

1966   A possible pyramidal structure and other Mexican influences at Pottery Mound, New Mexico. American Antiquity, 31:522-529.

1967   Mexican features of mural paintings at Pottery Mound. Archaeology, 20:84-87.

1975   Kiva art of the Anasazi at Pottery Mound. KC Publications, Las Vegas, 145 pp.
        Reviewed AA 79:730 (Longacre).

HIBBEN, F.C., and BRYAN, Kirk

1941   Evidences of early occupation in Sandia Cave, New Mexico, and other sites in the Sandia-Manzano region. Smithsonian Miscellaneous Collections, 99, no. 23, 64 pp.
        Reviewed AAq 7:415 (Eiseley).

HIBBEN, F.C., and DICK, Herbert W.

1944   A Basketmaker III site in Canyon Largo, New Mexico. American Antiquity, 9:381-385.

HIBBEN, F.C., and others

1954   University of New Mexico archaeological field-work, 1952-1953. Southwestern Lore, 19, no. 4:9-10.

HILL, Gertrude

    1942   On bone daggers. Society for American Archaeology, Notebook, 2:38.

HILL, James N. (See also under Martin, Paul Sidney; Plog, Fred T.)

    1966   A prehistoric community in eastern Arizona. Southwestern Journal of Anthropology, 22:9-30.

    1968   Broken K Pueblo: patterns of form and function. *In* New Perspectives in Archaeology, ed. S.R. and L.R. Binford, Aldine Publishing Co., pp. 103-142.

    1970a   Broken K Pueblo: prehistoric social organization in the American Southwest. University of Arizona, Anthropological Papers, 18, 149 pp. Reviewed AA 77:460 (Morris), AAq 38:249 (Muller).

    1970b   Prehistoric social organization in the American Southwest: theory and method. *In* Longacre 1970b, pp. 11-58.

    1971   Research propositions for consideration, Southwestern Anthropological Research Group. *In* Gumerman 1971, pp. 55-61.

    1977a   (ed.) Explanation of prehistoric change. University of New Mexico Press.

    1977b   Individual variability in ceramics and the study of prehistoric social organization. *In* The Individual in Pre-history, ed. James N. Hill and Joel Gunn, Academic Press.

HILL, J.N., and HEVLY, Richard H.

    1968   Pollen at Broken K Pueblo: some new interpretations. American Antiquity, 33:200-210.

HILL, Mack (See also under Toness, Kay.)

    1971   Preliminary report of an El Paso Brown Ware site, El Paso County, Texas. Transactions of the Sixth Regional Archaeological Symposium on Southeastern New Mexico and Western Texas, pp. 91-100.

HILL, T.C., Jr. (See also under Hester, Thomas Roy.)

HILL, T.C., HOUSE, J.W., and HESTER, Thomas Roy

    n.d.   Notes on incised and grooved stones from southern and western Texas. Bulletin of the Lower Plains

Archaeological Society, no. 3:1-10.

HILLMAN, E.D.

1930   Ancient rock carvings from southern California.
        El Palacio, 29:175-180.

HILTON, Grace

1918   The castles of the Chama. El Palacio, 5, no. 4:
        51-55.

HILTON, John W.

1940   Salt caves of the ancients. Desert Magazine, 3,
        no. 12:11-14.

1941   "Desert Roses" in Arizona. Desert Magazine, 4, no.
        7:19-22.

HINTON, Thomas B.

1955   A survey of archaeological sites in the Altar Val-
        ley, Sonora. Kiva, 21, nos. 1-2:1-12.

HITCHCOCK, Robert K. (See under Judge, W. James; Lyons, Thomas
R.)

HOBLER, Audrey E. (See under Hobler, Philip N.)

HOBLER, Philip M. (See also under Lindsay, Alexander J., Jr.)

1974   The late survival of pithouse architecture in the
        Kayenta Anasazi area. Southwestern Lore, 40, no.
        2:1-44.

HOBLER, P.M., and HOBLER, Audrey E.

1967   Navajo racing circles. Plateau, 40, no. 2:45-50.

HODGE, Frederick Webb

1893   Prehistoric irrigation in Arizona. American Anthro-
        pologist, o.s. 6, no. 3:323-330.

1895a   Aboriginal use of adobes. The Archaeologist, 3:
        265-266.

1895b   The first discovered city of Cibola. American
        Anthropologist, o.s. 8, no. 2:142-152.

1897a   The Enchanted Mesa. National Geographic Magazine,
        8, no. 10:273-284.

1897b   The verification of a tradition. American Anthro-
         pologist, o.s. 10, no. 9:299-302.

1904   Hopi pottery fired with coal. American Anthropolo-
         gist, n.s. 6, no. 4:581-582.

1907-   (ed.) Handbook of American Indians north of Mexico.
10   Bureau of American Ethnology, Bulletin 30, 2 vols.
         971+1221 pp.
         Reviewed AA n.s. 9:403 (Wissler).

1914   Archaeological explorations in western New Mexico.
         Smithsonian Miscellaneous Collections, 63, no. 8:
         53-58.

1918a   Excavations at Hawikuh. El Palacio, 5, no. 11:180-
         184.

1918b   Excavations at Hawikuh, New Mexico. Smithsonian
         Miscellaneous Collections, 68, no. 12:61-72.

1918c   Excavations at the Zuni Pueblo of Hawikuh in 1917.
         Art and Archaeology, 7, no. 9:367-379.

1920a   The age of the Zuni Pueblo of Kechipauan. Museum
         of the American Indian, Indian Notes and Monographs,
         3, no. 2:41-60.

1920b   Hawikuh bonework. Museum of the American Indian,
         Indian Notes and Monographs, 3, no. 3:61-151.
         Reviewed AA 23:363 (Kidder).

1921   Turquois work of Hawikuh, New Mexico. Museum of
         the American Indian, Leaflets, no. 2, 30 pp.

1922   Recent excavations at Hawikuh. El Palacio, 12,
         no. 1:2-11.

1923   Circular kivas near Hawikuh, New Mexico. Museum of
         the American Indian, Contributions, 7, no. 1, 37 pp.

1924a   Pottery of Hawikuh. Museum of the American Indian,
         Indian Notes, 1:8-15.

1924b   Excavations at Kechipauan, New Mexico. Museum of
         the American Indian, Indian Notes, 1, no. 1:35-36.

1924c   Snake-pens at Hawikuh, New Mexico. Museum of the
         American Indian, Indian Notes, 1:111-119.

1924d   How a Pueblo potter treated a broken handle. Mu-
         seum of the American Indian, Indian Notes, 1:235-
         236.

1926   The six cities of Cibola. New Mexico Historical
         Review, 1, no. 4:478-488.

1928   How old is southwestern Indian silverwork? El
       Palacio, 25:224-232.

1935   Coral among early Southwestern Indians. Masterkey,
       9, no. 5:157-159.

1936   Bezoars. Masterkey, 10, no. 5:190-191.

1937a "Dig your cellar." Masterkey, 11, no. 1:20-21.

1937b History of Hawikuh, New Mexico: one of the so-called
       cities of Cibola. Southwest Museum, Publications
       of the Frederick Webb Hodge Anniversary Publication
       Fund, 1, 155 pp.
       Reviewed AA 40:147 (Hammond), AAq 3:286 (Judd).

1939   A square kiva at Hawikuh. *In* Brand and Harvey
       1939, pp. 195-214.

1942   A prehistoric Hitler? Masterkey, 16, no. 6:220-221.

1943   Coral among early Southwestern Indians. Masterkey,
       17, no. 3:99-102.

1950   Those small pottery discs. Masterkey, 24, no. 5:
       171-172.

1952   Turkeys at Hawikuh, New Mexico. Masterkey, 26, no.
       1:13-14.

HOEBEL, E. Adamson

1953   Underground kiva passages. American Antiquity, 19:
       76.

HOFFMAN, Charles M.

1977a An archaeological survey of the proposed Ehrenberg
       Pump Station Transmission Line Routes, West Coast-
       Mid Continent Pipeline, Yuma County, Arizona. Ari-
       zona State University, Office of Cultural Resource
       Management, Report no. 19, 17 pp.

1977b An archaeological survey of the proposed Livingston
       Pump Station Transmission Line Routes, West Coast-
       Mid Continent Pipeline, Yuma County, Arizona. Ari-
       zona State University, Office of Cultural Resource
       Management, Report no. 20, 13 pp.

1977c An archaeological survey of the proposed Casa Grande
       Pump Station Transmission Line Routes, West Coast-
       Mid Continent Pipeline, Pinal County, Arizona. Ari-
       zona State University, Office of Cultural Resource
       Management, Report no. 21, 10 pp.

HOFFMAN, E.L.

1920   Why the Cliff Dwellers vanished. Scientific Ameri-
        can, 123:630, 641-642.

HOFFMAN, W.J.

1880   Notice of an interesting Pueblo weapon. Journal
        of the Anthropological Institute, 9:464-465.

1883   Remarks on the antiquities of New Mexico and Ari-
        zona. Proceedings of the Davenport Academy of
        Natural Sciences, 3:108-127.

HOLBROOK, Sally J., and MACKEY, James C.

1976   Prehistoric environmental change in northern New
        Mexico: evidence from a Gallina Phase archaeological
        site. Kiva, 41, nos. 3-4:309-317.

HOLDEN, Jane (Also listed as Kelley, Jane Holden.)

1952   The Bonnell site. Bulletin of the Texas Archaeo-
        logical and Paleontological Society, 23:78-132.

1955a   A preliminary report on Arrowhead Ruin. El Palacio,
        62:102-119.

1955b   Preliminary report on the Bloom Mound, Chaves
        County, New Mexico. Bulletin of the Texas Archae-
        ological Society, 26:165-181.

HOLDEN, W.C.

1930   The Canadian Valley expedition of March, 1930.
        Bulletin of the Texas Archaeological and Paleonto-
        logical Society, 2:21-32.

1931   Texas Tech archaeological expedition, summer 1930.
        Bulletin of the Texas Archaeological and Paleonto-
        logical Society, 3:43-52.

1932   Excavations at Tecolote during summer of 1931.
        Bulletin of the Texas Archaeological and Paleonto-
        logical Society, 4:25-28.

1937   Excavation of Murrah Cave. Bulletin of the Texas
        Archaeological and Paleontological Society, 9:48-
        73.
            Reviewed AAq 4:177 (Sayles).

1938   Blue Mountain rock shelter. Bulletin of the Texas
        Archaeological and Paleontological Society, 10:208-
        221.

1941   McKenzie Cave and adjacent sites in Pecos County.
        Bulletin of the Texas Archaeological and Paleonto-
        logical Society, 13:46-57.

HOLIDAY, William G.

1974   Archaeological investigations in the Cave Creek
        drainage, Tonto National Forest, Arizona. U.S.
        Forest Service, Southwestern Region, Archaeological
        Report, 1, 72 pp.

HOLIEN, Thomas

1975   Pseudo-cloisonné in the Southwest and Mesoamerica.
        In Frisbie 1975a, pp. 157-177.

HOLLIMAN, Rhodes B.

1967   Engraved basalt stones from the Great Salt Desert,
        Utah. Southwestern Lore, 32, no. 4:86-87.

1969   Further studies on incised stones from the Great
        Salt Desert, Utah. Southwestern Lore, 35, no. 2:
        23-25.

HOLMES, William H.

1876   A notice of the ancient ruins of southwestern
        Colorado, examined during the summer of 1875.
        Bulletin of the United States Geological and Geo-
        graphical Survey of the Territories, 2, no. 1:3-24.

1878   Report on the ancient ruins of southwestern Colo-
        rado, examined during the summers of 1875 and 1876.
        Tenth Annual Report of the United States Geological
        and Geographical Survey of the Territories, 1876,
        pp. 383-408.

1883   Art in shell of the ancient Americans. Second
        Annual Report of the Bureau of American Ethnology,
        pp. 179-305.

1884   Prehistoric textile fabrics of the United States,
        derived from impressions on pottery. Third Annual
        Report of the Bureau of American Ethnology, pp. 393-
        425.

1886   Pottery of the ancient Pueblos. Fourth Annual
        Report of the Bureau of American Ethnology, pp.
        257-360.

1905   Notes on the antiquities of Jemez Valley, New Mex-
        ico. American Anthropologist, n.s. 7, no. 2:198-212.

1919   Handbook of aboriginal American antiquities, Part I:
        Introductory; the lithic industries. Bureau of
        American Ethnology, Bulletin 60, 380 pp.
        Reviewed AA 22:75 (MacCurdy).

1920   Description of Yucca House. Art and Archaeology,
        10:42.

HOLMQUIST, A.C.

1923   The prehistoric Southwest. El Palacio, 15:35-39.

HOLSCHLAG, Stephanie Lynn

1975   Pot Creek Pueblo and the question of prehistoric
        Northern Tiwa household configuration. Washington
        State University, dissertation, 158 pp.; University
        Microfilms International.

HOLSINGER, S.J.

1933   Report on the Chaco Canyon 1901. El Palacio, 34:
        128-135.

HOLTERMAN, Jack

1959   The mission of San Miguel de Oraibi. Plateau, 32,
        no. 2:39-47.

HOLZKAMPER, Frank M.

1956   Artifacts from Estero Tastiota, Sonora, Mexico.
        Kiva, 21, nos. 3-4:12-19.

HONEA, Kenneth H.

1964   A late Archaic horizon site near Folsom, New Mex-
        ico (LA 8120). Laboratory of Anthropology Notes,
        29.

1965a   Early Man projectile points in the Southwest. Mu-
        seum of New Mexico, Popular Series Pamphlet no. 4,
        23 pp.

1965b   Evolution in lithic traditions of the Southwest.
        El Palacio, 72, no. 4:32-36.

1965c   A morphology of scrapers and their methods of pro-
        duction. Southwestern Lore, 31, no. 2:25-40.

1965d   The bipolar flaking technique in Texas and New
        Mexico. Texas Archaeological Society, Bulletin,
        36:259-267.

1965e   The Caballo highway salvage project.   Laboratory of
        Anthropology Notes, 35.

1966   A proposed revision of Rio Grande glaze paint pot-
        tery.   Eighth Southwestern Ceramic Seminar, Museum
        of New Mexico.

1967   Revised sequence of Rio Grande glaze pottery.   Texas
        Tech Archaeological Survey Bulletin.

1969   The Rio Grande complex and the northern Plains.
        Plains Anthropologist, 14:57-70.

1973   The technology of eastern Puebloan pottery on the
        Llano Estacado.   Plains Anthropologist, 18:73-88.

HOOTON, Earnest A.

1930   The Indians of Pecos Pueblo: a study of their skel-
        etal remains.   Phillips Academy, Papers of the South-
        west Expedition, 4, 391 pp.
        Reviewed AA 34:142 (G. Woodbury).

HOOTON, Jean (See under Carroll, Charles.)

HOOVER, J.W.

1935   House and village types of the Southwest as condi-
        tioned by aridity.   Scientific Monthly, 40.

1941   Cerros de trincheras of the Arizona Papagueria.
        Geographical Review, 31, no. 2:228-239.

HOPKINS, Nicholas A.

1965   Great Basin prehistory and Uto-Aztecan.   American
        Antiquity, 31:48-60.

HORNE, Sam W.

1937   A Mimbres cremation burial and an effigy pot.
        Central Texas Archaeologist, 3:49-51.

1942   Rare type Mimbres pottery decoration.   Central
        Texas Archaeological Society, News Letter, 3:25-27.

HOUCK, Ed

1966   Lost treasure of the Hohokam.   Desert Magazine, 29,
        no. 11:22-24.

HOUGH, Walter

1898   Environmental interrelations in Arizona.   American

Anthropologist, o.s. 11:133-155.

1902   Ancient peoples of the Petrified Forest of Arizona. Harper's Magazine, 105 (November):897-901.

1903   Archaeological field-work in northeastern Arizona: the Museum-Gates expedition of 1901. Annual Report of the United States National Museum for 1901, pp. 279-358.

1906   Pueblo environment. Proceedings of the 55th Meeting of the American Association for the Advancement of Science, pp. 447-454.

1907   Antiquities of the Upper Gila and Salt River Valleys in Arizona and New Mexico. Bureau of American Ethnology, Bulletin 35, 96 pp.

1914   Culture of the ancient pueblos of the upper Gila River region, New Mexico and Arizona. United States National Museum, Bulletin 87, 139 pp.

1917   Archaeological investigations in New Mexico. Smithsonian Miscellaneous Collections, 66, no. 17, pp. 99-103.

1918   Ancient pit dwellings in New Mexico. Smithsonian Miscellaneous Collections, 68, no. 12:72-74.

1919a   Archaeological exploration in Arizona. Smithsonian Miscellaneous Collections, 70, no. 2:90-93.

1919b   Exploration of a pit house village at Luna, New Mexico. Proceedings of the United States National Museum, 55:409-431.

1920a   Archaeological excavations in Arizona. Smithsonian Miscellaneous Collections, 72, no. 1:64-66.

1920b   The cliff dweller housekeeper. American Indian Magazine, 7:7-10.

1923a   Casas Grandes pottery in the National Museum. Art and Archaeology, 16:34.

1923b   Pit dwellings and square kivas of the upper San Francisco River. El Palacio, 15, no. 1:3-9.

1927a   Explorations in a great sacred cave in eastern Arizona. Art and Archaeology, 28:117-125.

1927b   A new type of stone knife. American Anthropologist, 29:296-298.

1928   The lead glaze decorated pottery of the Pueblo region. American Anthropologist, 30, no. 2:243-249.

1930a   Ancient Pueblo subsistence. Proceedings of the
        Twenty-third International Congress of Americanists,
        pp. 67-69.

1930b   Exploration of ruins in the White Mountain Apache
        Indian Reservation, Arizona. Proceedings of the
        United States National Museum, 78, art. 13, 20 pp.

1932a   A cache of Basket Maker baskets from New Mexico.
        Proceedings of the United States National Museum,
        81, art. 10, 3 pp.

1932b   Decorative designs on Elden Pueblo pottery, Flag-
        staff, Arizona. Proceedings of the United States
        National Museum, 81, art. 7, 11 pp.

HOUSE, J.W. (See under Hill, T.C.)

HOUSER, Nicholas P.

1969   The Tigua settlement of Ysleta del Sur. Kiva, 36,
        no. 2:23-39.

HOWARD, Agnes McClain

1954   Cruciform artifacts of the Sierra Occidental. Amer-
        ican Antiquity, 20:174-175.

HOWARD, Edgar B.

1930a   Archaeological research in the Guadalupe Mountains.
        University of Pennsylvania Museum Journal, 21, nos.
        3-4:189-202.

1930b   The New Mexico-Texas excavations. University of
        Pennsylvania Museum, Bulletin, 2:46-49.

1931   Field work in the Southwest. University of Penn-
        sylvania Museum, Bulletin, 3, no. 1:11-14.

1932a   Caves along the slopes of the Guadalupe Mountains.
        Bulletin of the Texas Archaeological and Paleonto-
        logical Society, 4:7-19.

1932b   Prehistoric finds in New Mexico. University of
        Pennsylvania Museum, Bulletin, 4, no. 1:25-26.

1933a   Association of artifacts with mammoths and bison
        in eastern New Mexico. Science, 78:524.

1933b   Folsom points and glacial man. University of Penn-
        sylvania Museum, Bulletin, 4:79-83.

1933c   Excavations in New Mexico. University of Pennsyl-
        vania Museum, Bulletin, 4:126-131.

1934   Grooved spearpoints. Pennsylvania Archaeologist, 3, no. 6:11-15.

1935a   Early human remains in the Southwest. Report of the 16th International Geological Congress, 2:3-5.

1935b   Evidence of Early Man in North America. University of Pennsylvania Museum Journal, 24:61-175. Reviewed AA 39:139 (Hawley), AAq 1:237 (Nelson).

1935c   Occurrence of flints and extinct animals in pluvial deposits near Clovis, New Mexico. Part I. Introduction. Proceedings of Academy of Natural Sciences of Philadelphia, 87:299-303.

1936a   The association of a human culture with an extinct fauna in New Mexico. American Naturalist, 70, no. 729:314-323.

1936b   An outline of the problem of man's antiquity in North America. American Anthropologist, 38:394-413.

1936c   Archaeological blundering. American Antiquity, 2: 37-38.

1937   The emergence of a general Folsom pattern. Philadelphia Anthropological Society, Publications, 1, pp. 111-115.

1943   Folsom and Yuma problems. Proceedings of the American Philosophical Society, 86:255-259.

HOWARD, Hildegarde, and MILLER, Alden H.

1933   Bird remains from cave deposits in New Mexico. Condor, 35:15-18.

HOWARD, Richard M.

1959   Comments on the Indians' water supply at Gran Quivira National Monument. El Palacio, 66:85-91.

1960   Tabira - identification and historical sketch. El Palacio, 67, no. 2:68-71.

1968   The Mesa Verde Museum. Mesa Verde Association, KC Publications, Flagstaff.

1975   The Mesa Verde mug. American Indian Art, 1, no. 1: 20-25.

HOWARD, William A., and GRIFFITHS, Thomas M.

1966   Trinchera distribution in the Sierra Madre Occidental,

Mexico. University of Denver, Publications in Geography, Technical Papers, no. 66-1.

HOWARTH, Fred

1929   Finds in Folsom Cave. El Palacio, 26:116.

HOWE, Sherman

1947   My story of the Aztec ruins. Times Hustler Press, Farmington, 40 pp.

HOWELL, David H.

1940   Pipestone and red shale artifacts. American Antiquity, 6:45-62.

HOWELLS, William White

1932   The skeletal material [Swarts Ruin]. *In* Cosgrove and Cosgrove 1932, pp. 115-170.

HRANICKY, William Jack

1972   Village-city sequences, the American Southwest. The Chesopiean (Norfolk, Virginia), 10, no. 5:145-161.

HRDLIČKA, Aleš

1931   Catalogue of human crania in the United States National Museum collections. Proceedings of the United States National Museum, 78, art. 2, no. 2845, 95 pp.

HUBBARD, Samuel

1927   Discoveries relating to prehistoric man by the Doheny Scientific Expedition in the Hava Supai Canyon, northern Arizona. Sunset Press, San Francisco, 38 pp.

HUBERT, Virgil (See under Colton, Harold S.)

HUCKELL, Bruce B. (See also under Windmiller, Ric.)

1972   A fragmentary Clovis point from southwestern New Mexico. Kiva, 37, no. 2:114-116.

1973a   The Gold Gulch site: a specialized Cochise site near Bowie, Arizona. Kiva, 39, no. 2:105-129.

1973b   The Hardt Creek site. Kiva, 39, no. 2:171-197.

1973c Lake Pleasant II: a preliminary report on the second
       excavation at the Beardsley Canal site, a Pioneer
       and Colonial Hohokam site on the lower Agua Fria
       River, central Arizona. Arizona State Museum.

1978   The Oxbow Hill-Payson project: archaeological exca-
       vations south of Payson, Arizona. Arizona State
       Museum, Contributions to Highway Salvage Archae-
       ology in Arizona, 48, 131 pp.

HUDDELSON, Sam (See under Halseth, Odd S.)

HUDGENS, Bruce
1975   The archaeology of Exhausted Cave: a study in pre-
       historic cultural ecology on the Coconino National
       Forest, Arizona. United States Forest Service,
       Southwestern Region, Archaeological Report no. 8,
       95 pp.

HUDSON, Dee T.
1972a Anasazi measurement systems at Chaco Canyon, New
       Mexico. Kiva, 38, no. 1:27-42.

1972b A meteorite discovery with archaeological importance
       from the Camp Verde area, central Arizona. Plateau,
       45, no. 1:41-43.

HUDSON, W.R., Jr. (See under Lynn, W.M.)

HUFFMAN, J.W.
1925   Turquoise mosaics from Casa Grande. Art and Archae-
       ology, 20:82-84.

HUGHES, Jack T.
1955   Anthropomorphic mat from New Mexico. American
       Antiquity, 20:412-413.

HUGHES, T.B.
1954   Ceremonial and possibly ceremonial structures of
       the Mogollon area. El Palacio, 61:211-233.

HULL, Clinton R.
1953   Boat trip in Mohave Canyon. Desert Magazine, 16,
       no. 2:11-15.

HULL, Deborah A., and SCOTT, Douglas D.

1978   A bibliography of the archaeology of southwestern
        Colorado: Archuleta, Dolores, La Plata, and Monte-
        zuma Counties. Bureau of Land Management (Colorado),
        Cultural Resources Series, 5, 88 pp.

HUMAN SYSTEMS RESEARCH

1973   Technical manual; 1973. Survey of the Tularosa
        Basin. Albuquerque, 495 pp.

HUNT, Alice P.

1953   Archaeological survey of the La Sal Mountain area,
        Utah. University of Utah, Anthropological Papers,
        14, 248 pp.
        Reviewed AA 57:1330 (Fenenga).

1956   Archaeology of southeastern Utah. *In* Geology and
        Economic Deposits of East Central Utah, Intermoun-
        tain Association of Petroleum Geologists, 1956
        Field Conference, pp. 13-18.

1960   A sketch of Utah prehistory. Utah Archaeology, 6,
        no. 1:4-14.

HUNT, A.P., and TANNER, Dallas

1960   Early Man sites near Moab, Utah. American Antiq-
        uity, 26:110-117.

HUNT, Charles B.

1954   Desert varnish. Science, 120:183-184.

1959   Dating of mining camps with tin cans and bottles.
        Geotimes, 3, no. 8:8-10, 34.

HUNT, John D. (See under Keller, Gordon N.)

HUNTER, Russell Vernon

1955   Remarkable burial remains exhibited at Roswell Mu-
        seum. El Palacio, 62:58-59.

HUNTINGTON, C. Frank (See under Lipe, William D.)

HUNTINGTON, Ellsworth

1912   The physical environment of the Southwest in pre-
        Columbian days. Records of the Past, 11, no. 3:
        128-141.

1914   The climatic factor as illustrated in arid America.
         Carnegie Institution of Washington, Publication no.
         192, 341 pp.

HUNTINGTON, W.D.

1953   Discovery of prehistoric ruins in Colorado, 1854.
         Colorado Magazine, 30:275-280.

HURLBETT, Robert E.

1977   Environmental constraint and settlement predicta-
         bility, northwestern Colorado. Bureau of Land
         Management (Colorado), Cultural Resources Series,
         3, 90 pp.

HURST, Blanche H.

1957   A comparative study of the peripheral excavations
         of C.T. Hurst. Southwestern Lore, 23, no. 2:15-31.

HURST, Clarence Thomas

1933   Some interesting models of Southwestern sites. El
         Palacio, 35:81-86.

1936   Some interesting Mimbres bowls. El Palacio, 40,
         nos. 7-9:37-41.

1937   Early Man in Colorado. El Palacio, 43, nos. 22-26:
         137-139.

1937-   The Gunnison Collection, VI-VIII. Southwestern
  38   Lore, 3, no. 3:48-52; 4, no. 1:14-17; 4, no. 3:
         54-57.

1939   A Ute shelter in Saguache County, Colorado. South-
         western Lore, 5, no. 3:57-66.

1940a   Geometric designs on Mimbres bowls (The Gunnison
         Collection, IX). American Antiquity, 6:107-114.

1940b   Preliminary work in Tabeguache Cave - 1939. South-
         western Lore, 6, no. 1:4-18.

1941a   The second season in Tabeguache Cave. Southwestern
         Lore, 7, no. 1:4-19.

1941b   A Folsom location in the San Luis Valley, Colorado.
         Southwestern Lore, 7, no. 2:31-34.

1942a   Completion of work in Tabeguache Cave. Southwestern
         Lore, 8, no. 1:7-16.

1942b   The Gunnison Collection, X. Southwestern Lore, 8,

no. 3:36-40.

1943a   A Folsom site in a mountain valley of Colorado.
        American Antiquity, 8:250-253.

1943b   Preliminary work in Tabeguache Cave II. South-
        western Lore, 9, no. 1:10-16.

1944a   1943 excavation in Cave II, Tabeguache Canyon, Mont-
        rose County, Colorado. Southwestern Lore, 10, no.
        1:2-14.

1944b   The Gunnison Collection, XI. Southwestern Lore,
        10, no. 3:43-44.

1945a   Completion of excavation of Tabeguache Cave II.
        Southwestern Lore, 11, no. 1:8-12.

1945b   Surface collecting on Tabeguache Creek. American
        Antiquity, 11:105-108.

1945-   Colorado's old-timers. Southwestern Lore, 10:45-
46   56; 11:18-29, 31-42, 44-59; 12:19-30.

1946a   Colorado's old timers. Colorado Archaeological
        Society, Gunnison, 64 pp.

1946b   The 1945 Tabeguache expedition. Southwestern Lore,
        12, no. 1:7-16.

1946c   Pueblo finds in western Colorado. Southwestern
        Lore, 12, no. 1.

1947a   Eight years in the Tabeguache and Dolores country
        of Colorado. Southwestern Journal of Anthropology,
        3:367-370.

1947b   Excavation of Dolores Cave - 1946. Southwestern
        Lore, 13, no. 1:8-17.

1947c   The prehistory of western Colorado. Southwestern
        Lore, 13, no. 2.

1947d   The Gunnison Collection, XII. Southwestern Lore,
        13, no. 3:45-49.

1948a   The Cottonwood Expedition, 1947 - a cave and a
        Pueblo site. Southwestern Lore, 14, no. 1:4-19.

1948b   Preliminary excavations at Cottonwood Cave and
        Pueblo, Montrose County, Colorado. Yearbook of
        the American Philosophical Society, 1947, pp. 197-
        200.

HURST, C.T., and ANDERSON, Edgar

1949   A corn cache from western Colorado. American Antiq-
         uity, 14:161-167.

HURST, C.T., and HENDRICKS, Lawrence J.

1952   Some unusual petroglyphs near Sapinero, Colorado.
         Southwestern Lore, 18, no. 1:14-18.

HURST, C.T., and LOTRICH, V.F.

1932   An unusual mug from Yellow Jacket Canyon. El Pa-
         lacio, 33, nos. 21-22:195-198.

1933a   Another unusual bowl from Yellow Jacket Canyon.
         El Palacio, 34, nos. 15-16:111-115.

1933b   The "Square-Mug House" of the Mesa Verde culture.
         Journal of the Colorado-Wyoming Academy of Science,
         1, no. 5:70-71.

1935   A Colorado burial of the proto-Mesa Verde culture.
         El Palacio, 38, nos. 24-26:133-143.

1935-   The Gunnison Collection, I-V. Southwestern Lore,
36   1, no. 2:14-16; 1, no. 3:6-11; 2, no. 1:8-11; 2,
         no. 2:26-28; 2, no. 3:62-63.

HURT, Amy P.

1948   Exploring ancient caves. New Mexico Magazine, 26,
         no. 5:12-13, 45-48.

HURT, Wesley R., Jr.

1939   A method for cataloguing pictographs. New Mexico
         Anthropologist, 3:40-44.

1940   Ruins that defy time. New Mexico Magazine, 18,
         no. 9:16, 43-44.

1942a   Folsom and Yuma points from the Estancia Valley,
         New Mexico. American Antiquity, 7:400-402.

1942b   Eighteenth century Navaho hogans from Canyon de
         Chelly National Monument. American Antiquity, 8:
         89-104.

1947   Development of architecture, Canyon de Chelly.
         American Antiquity, 12:270-272.

1952   A comparative study of the preceramic occupations
         of North America. University of Michigan, disserta-
         tion, 605 pp.; University Microfilms International.

1953   A comparative study of the preceramic occupations
        of North America. American Antiquity, 18:204-222.

HURT, W.R., and DICK, Herbert W.

1946   Spanish American pottery from New Mexico. El Pala-
        cio, 53, no. 10:280-288; no. 11:307-312.

HURT, W.R., and McKNIGHT, Daniel

1949   Archaeology of the San Augustin Plains, a prelim-
        inary report. American Antiquity, 14:172-194.

HUSCHER, Betty H., and HUSCHER, Harold A.

1940a   Conventionalized bear-track petroglyphs of the
        Uncompahgre Plateau. Southwestern Lore, 6, no.
        2:25-28.

1940b   Potsherds from a piñon tree! Masterkey, 14, no. 4:
        137-142.

1940c   Archaeological frauds from southern Colorado. Amer-
        ican Antiquity, 6:173.

1942a   Athapaskan migration via the intermontane region.
        American Antiquity, 8, no. 1:80-88.

1942b   Continuation of archaeological survey of southern
        and western Colorado. American Philosophical Soci-
        ety, Yearbook, 1941, pp. 226-229.

1943   The hogan builders of Colorado. Southwestern Lore,
        9, no. 2:1-92.
        Reviewed AAq 11:62 (Tatum).

HUSCHER, Harold A. (See also under Huscher, Betty H.)

1939   Influence of the drainage pattern of the Uncompahgre
        Plateau on the movements of primitive peoples.
        Southwestern Lore, 5, no. 2:22-41.

HUSE, Hannah

1976   Identification of the individual in archaeology:
        a case-study from the prehistoric Hopi site of
        Kawaika-a. University of Colorado, dissertation,
        487 pp.; University Microfilms International.

HUSE, H., NOISAT, Bradley A., and HALASI, Judith A.

1978   The Bisti-Star Lake project: a sample survey of
        cultural resources in northwestern New Mexico.

Bureau of Land Management (Albuquerque).

HUSTED, Wilfred M.

1964   Pueblo pottery from northern Colorado. Southwestern
       Lore, 30, no. 2:21-25.

HUSTED, W.M., and MALLORY, Oscar L.

1967   The Fremont culture: its derivation and ultimate
       fate. Plains Anthropologist, 12, no. 36:222-232.

HUTTON, James D.

1976   Cache from edge of a dry lake at McGregor Range.
       The Artifact, 14, no. 3:21-27.

HYMAN, Charles A.

1962   Artifacts from Utah and the Southwest. Ohio Ar-
       chaeologist, 12, nos. 3-4:72-74.

ICE, Ronald J. (See also under Hammack, Laurens C.)

1968   West Fork ruin: a stratified site near Gila Cliff
       Dwellings Monument, New Mexico. Laboratory of
       Anthropology Notes, 48.

INGERSOLL, Ernest

1928   Ruins in southwestern Colorado. Museum of the
       American Indian, Indian Notes, 5, no. 2:183-206.

INGMANSON, J. Earl

1969   The cultural sequence at the Mesa Verde. Natural-
       ist, 20, no. 2:1-12.

INSALL, Shirley

1957   Ancient city on the Ruidoso. New Mexico Magazine,
       35, no. 1:20-21, 49.

IRELAND, Stephen K.

1971   The Upper Purgatoire complex - a re-appraisal.
       Southwestern Lore, 37, no. 2:37-51.

IRWIN, Henry T.

1964   Possible eastern connections for the San Jose-Pinto
       Basin complex. American Antiquity, 29:496-497.

IRWIN-WILLIAMS, Cynthia (See also under Haynes, C. Vance.)

1967   Picosa: the elementary Southwestern culture. Amer-
        ican Antiquity, 32:441-457.

1968a   (ed.) Contributions to Southwestern prehistory.
        Eastern New Mexico University, Contributions in
        Anthropology, 1, no. 1, 23 pp.

1968b   Configurations of preceramic development in the
        southwestern United States. *In* Irwin-Williams
        1968a, pp. 1-9.

1968c   The reconstruction of Archaic culture history in
        the southwestern United States. *In* Archaic Pre-
        history in the Western United States, ed. C. Irwin-
        Williams, Eastern New Mexico University, Contri-
        butions in Anthropology, 1, no. 3:19-23.

1968d   (ed.) Early Man in western North America. Eastern
        New Mexico University, Contributions in Anthropology,
        1, no. 4, 87 pp.

1968e   Archaic culture history in the southwestern United
        States. *In* Irwin-Williams 1968d, pp. 48-54.

1972a   Prehistoric cultural and linguistic patterns in
        the Southwest since 5000 B.C. Eastern New Mexico
        University, Contributions in Anthropology, Miscel-
        laneous Publication no. 2.

1972b   (ed.) The structure of Chacoan society in the
        northern Southwest: investigations at the Salmon
        site, 1972. Eastern New Mexico University, Contri-
        butions in Anthropology, 4, no. 3, 144 pp.

1973a   The Oshara tradition: origins of Anasazi culture.
        Eastern New Mexico University, Contributions in
        Anthropology, 5, no. 1, 21 pp.

1973b   The seasonal strategy. Proceedings of the 40th
        International Congress of Americanists.

1977   A network approach to the analysis of prehistoric
        trade. *In* Exchange Systems in Prehistory, ed. J.
        Ericson and T. Earle.

IRWIN-WILLIAMS, C., and HAYNES, C.V.

1970   Climatic change and early population dynamics in
        the southwestern United States. Quaternary Research,
        1:59-71.

IRWIN-WILLIAMS, C., and TOMPKINS, S.

1968   Excavations at En Medio Shelter, New Mexico. East-
        ern New Mexico University, Contributions in Anthro-
        pology, 1, no. 2, 44 pp.

ISHAM, Dana

1973   Zuni archaeological survey and training program.
        Arizona State Museum, Archaeological Series, 32,
        61 pp.

IVANCOVICH, Jane H.

1956   49 south. Kiva, 21, nos. 3-4:25-26.

IVES, Ronald L.

1936   A trinchera near Quitovaquita, Sonora. American
        Anthropologist, 38:257-259.

1941a   A cultural hiatus in the Rocky Mountain region.
        Southwestern Lore, 7:42-46.

1941b   The origin of the Sonoyta townsite, Sonora, Mexico.
        American Antiquity, 7:20-28.

1942   Early human occupation of the Colorado headwaters
        region, an archaeological reconnaissance. Geo-
        graphical Review, 32:448-462.

1946a   Ancient trails in the Dugway area, Utah. Masterkey,
        20, no. 4:113-124.

1946b   Manje's description of Casa Grande, 1697. Master-
        key, 20, no. 5:148-151.

1963a   The bell of San Marcelo. Kiva, 29, no. 1:14-22.

1963b   The problem of the Sonoran littoral cultures. Kiva,
        28, no. 3:28-32.

1971   An archaeologically sterile area in northern Sonora.
        Kiva, 36, no. 3:1-10.

JACK, Robert N.

1971   The source of obsidian artifacts in northern Ari-
        zona. Plateau, 43, no. 3:103-114.

JACKSON, Alvin T. (See also under Pearce, James E.)

1936   A "perpetual fire" site. Bulletin of the Texas
        Archaeological and Paleontological Society, 8:
        134-172.

1937   Exploration of certain sites in Culberson County,
        Texas. Bulletin of the Texas Archaeological and
        Paleontological Society, 9:146-192.
        Reviewed AAq 4:177 (Sayles).

1938   Picture-writing of Texas Indians. University of
        Texas, Anthropological Papers, 2, 490 pp.
        Reviewed AA 41:313 (Knowles), AAq 5:356 (Renaud).

1940   Tubular pipes and other tubes in Texas. Bulletin
        of the Texas Archaeological and Paleontological
        Society, 12:99-137.

1948   Picture-writing of Texas Indians. National Speleo-
        logical Society, no. 10:85-88.

JACKSON, Betty

1935   Hidden door at Montezuma Castle. Southwestern
        Monuments Monthly Report, December, pp. 464-465.

JACKSON, Earl

1935   The kiva and its function. Southwestern Monuments
        Monthly Report, November, pp. 357-363.

1937   Rio Grande glazes. Southwestern Monuments Monthly
        Report, August, pp. 156-157.

1939a   Archaeological notes from Montezuma Castle. South-
        western Monuments Monthly Reports, Supplement, June,
        pp. 455-458.

1939b   Ruins stabilization at Montezuma Castle. South-
        western Monuments Monthly Report, December, pp. 473-
        475.

1941   Stabilization of Montezuma Castle National Monument.
        National Park Service Southwestern Monuments Office,
        Coolidge.

1946   Tumacacori. Arizona Highways, 22, no. 7:4-5.

1951   Tumacacori's yesterdays. Southwestern Monuments
        Association, Popular Series, no. 6 (revised 1973),
        96 pp.

JACKSON, E., and VAN VALKENBURGH, Sallie P.

1954   Montezuma Castle archaeology. Part I. Excavations.
        Southwestern Monuments Association, Technical Se-
        ries, 3, pt. 1, 86 pp.
        Reviewed AA 58:392 (Bluhm), AAq 21:325 (Shaeffer).

JACKSON, William H.

1875   Ancient ruins in southwestern Colorado. United
        States Geological and Geographical Survey of the
        Territories, Bulletin, 2nd series, 1:17-38.

1876a   Ancient ruins in southwestern Colorado. Eighth
        Annual Report of the United States Geological and
        Geographical Survey of the Territories, 1874, pp.
        367-381.

1876b   A notice of the ancient ruins in Arizona and Utah
        lying about the Rio San Juan. United States Geo-
        logical and Geographical Survey of the Territories,
        Bulletin, 2, no. 1:25-46.

1876c   Ancient ruins in southwestern Colorado. American
        Naturalist, 10:31-37, 161-165.

1878   Report on the ancient ruins examined in 1875 and
        1877. Tenth Annual Report of the United States
        Geological and Geographical Survey of the Terri-
        tories, 1876, pp. 411-450.

1924   First official visit to the cliff dwellings. Colo-
        rado Magazine, 1, no. 4:151-159.

JAMES, Charles D., III

1977a   Historic Navajo studies in northeastern Arizona.
        Museum of Northern Arizona, Research Papers, 1,
        128 pp.

1977b   The Mule Shoe Bend site: a study of a Cohonina
        lithic quarry and plant processing area. Museum
        of Northern Arizona, Research Papers, 9, 45 pp.

JAMES, C.D., and BRADFORD, James E.

1974   Four wooden figurines from the western portion of
        the Navajo Reservation. Plateau, 47, no. 2:70-76.

JAMES, C.D., and DAVIDSON, Howard M.

1976   Style changes of the horse motif in Navajo rock
        art: a preliminary analysis. American Indian Rock
        Art (El Paso Archaeological Society), 2:26-46.

JAMES, C.D., and LINDSAY, Alexander J., Jr.

1973   Ethnoarchaeological research at Canyon del Muerto,
        Arizona: a Navajo example. Ethnohistory, 20, no.
        4:361-374.

JAMES, George Wharton

  1900   Discovery of cliff dwellings in the Southwest.
         Scientific American, 82 (January):40-41.

JAMESON, Sydney J.S.

  1958   Archaeological notes on Stansbury Island. Univer-
         sity of Utah, Anthropological Papers, 34, 52 pp.
         Reviewed AAq 25:137 (Grosscup).

JANES, Mrs. S.M.

  1930   Seven trips to Mount Livermore. West Texas Histor-
         ical and Scientific Society, Publications, 3:8-9.

JARCHO, Saul

  1964   Lead in the bones of prehistoric lead-glaze potters.
         American Antiquity, 30, no. 1:94-96.

JARCHO, S., SIMON, Norman, and BICK, Edgar M.

  1963   A fused hip from Wupatki. Plateau, 35, no. 3:69-74.

JEANÇON, Jean Allard

  1911   Explorations in Chama Basin, New Mexico. Records
         of the Past, 9, pt. 2:92-108.

  1912   Ruins of Pesedeuinge. Records of the Past, 11,
         pt. 1:28-37.

  1919   Preliminary report of the excavations at Po Shu
         Ouinge, near Abiquiu. El Palacio, 7, no. 4:66-69.

  1921   Archaeological explorations in New Mexico. Smith-
         sonian Miscellaneous Collections, 72, no. 6:120-125.

  1922a Archaeological research in the northeastern San
         Juan Basin of Colorado during the summer of 1921.
         State Historical and Natural History Society of
         Colorado and University of Denver, 31 pp.

  1922b Two seasons work in Colorado. Bulletin of the
         Colorado State Historical and Natural History
         Society, 1.

  1923a Excavations in the Chama Valley, New Mexico. Bu-
         reau of American Ethnology, Bulletin 81, 80 pp.

  1923b Summer plans for the section of archaeology and
         ethnology. Bulletin of the Colorado State Histor-
         ical and Natural History Society, 1, no. 4:71-73.

1923c   Ruins in Moffat County. Bulletin of the Colorado
         State Historical and Natural History Society, 1,
         no. 4:75-76.

1924   Pottery of the Pagosa-Piedra region. Colorado
         Magazine, 1:213-224, 260-276, 301-307.

1925   Primitive Coloradoans. Colorado Magazine, 2, no.
         1:35-40.

1926a   A petroglyph on La Sal Creek, Utah. Colorado Maga-
         zine, 3, no. 2, pl. IIIb, c.

1926b   Pictographs of Colorado. Colorado Magazine, 3, no.
         2:33-45.

1926c   A rectangular ceremonial room. Colorado Magazine,
         3, no. 4:133-137.

1927   Antiquities of Moffat County, Colorado. Colorado
         Magazine, 4:18-27.

1929a   Archaeological investigations in the Taos Valley,
         New Mexico, during 1920. Smithsonian Miscellaneous
         Collections, 81, no. 12, 29 pp.

1929b   The Dulce ruin. El Palacio, 27, nos. 13-18:161-174.

JEANÇON, J.A., and DOUGLAS, F.H.

1930a   Periods of Pueblo culture and history. Denver Art
         Museum, Dept. of Indian Art, Leaflet no. 11, 4 pp.
         (2nd ed., 1942).

1930b   The Pueblo Golden Age. Denver Art Museum, Dept. of
         of Indian Art, Leaflet no. 14, 4 pp.

JEANÇON, J.A., and ROBERTS, F.H.H., Jr.

1923-   Further archaeological research in the northeastern
24   San Juan Basin of Colorado during the summer of
         1922. Colorado Magazine, 1:10-36, 65-70, 108-118,
         163-173, 213-224, 260-276, 301-307.

JELINEK, Arthur J.

1952   Pottery of the Rio Bonito area of Lincoln County,
         New Mexico. Bulletin of the Texas Archaeological
         and Paleontological Society, 23:147-167.

1958   Archaeological materials from the middle Pecos
         River Valley, New Mexico. Papers of the Michigan
         Academy of Science, Arts and Letters, 43:159-168.

1960   An archaeological survey of the middle Pecos River
       Valley and the adjacent Llano Estacado. University
       of Michigan, dissertation, 295 pp.; University
       Microfilms International.

1961   Mimbres warfare? Kiva, 27, no. 2:28-30.

1966a Correlation of archaeological and palynological
       data. Science, 152, no. 3728:1507-1509.

1966b Some distinctive flakes and flake tools from the
       Llano Estacado. Papers of the Michigan Academy
       of Science, Arts and Letters, 51:399-405.

1967   A prehistoric sequence in the middle Pecos Valley,
       New Mexico. University of Michigan Museum of Anthro-
       pology, Anthropological Papers, 31, 175 pp.

JELKS, Edward B. (See also under Nunley, John P.; Suhm, Dee
Ann.)

JELKS, E.B., DAVIS, E. Mott, and STURGIS, Henry F.

1960   (ed.) A review of Texas archaeology, Part I. Bul-
       letin of the Texas Archaeological Society, 29 (for
       1958), 254 pp.
         Reviewed AA 63:442 (Krieger), AAq 27:130 (Ste-
       phenson).

JENKS, Albert E.

1928   The Mimbres Valley Expedition. Bulletin of the
       Minneapolis Institute of Arts, 17, no. 31:154-159.

1931   The significance of mended bowls in Mimbres cul-
       ture. El Palacio, 31, nos. 10-11:153-172.

1932a Architectural plans of geometric art on Mimbres
       bowls. El Palacio, 33, no. 3-6:21-64.

1932b Geometric designs on Mimbres bowls. Art and Ar-
       chaeology, 33, no. 3.

JENNINGS, Calvin H. (See also under Lindsay, Alexander J., Jr.)

1968a Highway salvage excavations in Medicine Valley,
       north-central Arizona. Plateau, 41, no. 2:43-60.

1968b The Paleo-Indian and Archaic stages in western
       Colorado. Southwestern Lore, 34, no. 1:11-20.

1971   Early prehistory of the Coconino Plateau, north-
       western Arizona. University of Colorado, disserta-
       tion, 538 pp.; University Microfilms International.

JENNINGS, Jesse D.

1940   A variation of Southwestern Pueblo culture. Laboratory of Anthropology, Technical Series, Bulletin 10, 11 pp.

1953   Danger Cave: a progress summary. El Palacio, 60: 179-213.

1956a   (ed.) The American Southwest: a problem in cultural isolation. *In* Seminars in Archaeology: 1955, ed. R. Wauchope, Society for American Archaeology, Memoirs, 11, pp. 59-127. Reviewed AA 59:924 (Siegel), AAq 23:186 (Spicer).

1956b   Early Man in the west. Utah Archaeology, 2, no. 4: 2-5.

1956c   Radiocarbon dates from Danger Cave, Utah. Utah Archaeology, 2, no. 2:3-4.

1957a   Danger Cave. Society for American Archaeology, Memoirs, 14, 328 pp. (also as University of Utah, Anthropological Papers, 27). Reviewed AA 60:979 (Heizer), AAq 24:206 (Meighan).

1957b   Upper Colorado River Basin archaeological salvage project: summer 1957. Utah Archaeology, 3, no. 3: 7-9.

1960   Early Man in Utah. Utah Historical Quarterly, 28, no. 1:2-27.

1964   The Desert West. *In* Jennings and Norbeck 1964, pp. 149-174. Reviewed AAq 30:503 (Meighan).

1966a   Early Man in the Desert West. Quaternaria, 8:81-89.

1966b   Glen Canyon: a summary. University of Utah, Anthropological Papers, 81, 84 pp. Reviewed AA 70:162 (Meighan).

1968   Prehistory of North America. McGraw-Hill Book Co.

1969   Radiocarbon dates from Danger Cave, Utah. Utah Archaeology, 15, no. 3:17-21.

1974   Prehistory of North America. (2nd ed.) McGraw-Hill Book Co., 436 pp. Reviewed AA 78:467 (Browman).

JENNINGS, J.D., and NORBECK, Edward

1955   Great Basin prehistory: a review. American Antiquity, 21, no. 1:1-11.

1964   (ed.) Prehistoric man in the New World. University
        of Chicago Press, 633 pp.
        Reviewed AA 67:157 (Ford).

JENNINGS, J.D., and SHARROCK, Floyd W.

1965   The Glen Canyon: a multi-discipline project.   Utah
        Historical Quarterly, 33, no. 1:35-50.

JENNINGS, J.D., and others

1959   The Glen Canyon archaeological survey, Parts I-II.
        University of Utah, Anthropological Papers, 39,
        707 pp.
        Reviewed AA 62:725 (Schwartz), AAq 26:135 (Wheat).

JERNIGAN, E. Wesley

1978   Jewelry of the prehistoric Southwest. University
        of New Mexico Press, Southwest Indian Arts Series,
        2, 240 pp.

JETER, Marvin D.

1977   Archaeology in Copper Basin, Yavapai County, Ari-
        zona: model building for the prehistory of the
        Prescott region. Arizona State University, Anthro-
        pological Research Papers, 11, 434 pp.

JETT, Stephen C.

1964   Pueblo Indian migrations: an evaluation of the
        possible physical and cultural determinants. Amer-
        ican Antiquity, 29:281-300.

1965a   Comment on Davis' hypothesis of Pueblo Indian migra-
        tions. American Antiquity, 30:276-277.

1965b   Reply to Ellis' "Comment" on "Pueblo Indian migra-
        tions." American Antiquity, 31:116-118.

1965c   Red Rock country. Plateau, 37, no. 3:80-84.

1968   Grand Canyon dams, split-twig figurines, and "hit-
        and-run" archaeology. American Antiquity, 33:341-
        351.

1969   "Hit-and-run" archaeology: a reply to Euler. Amer-
        ican Antiquity, 34:85-87.

1973   Testimony of the sacredness of Rainbow Natural
        Bridge to Puebloans, Navajos, and Paiutes. Plateau,
        45, no. 4:133-142.

JOHNSON, Alfred E. (See also under Wasley, William W.)

1961   A ball court at Point of Pines, Arizona. American
        Antiquity, 26:563-567.

1963a   An appraisal of the archaeological resources of five
        regional parks in Maricopa County, Arizona. Arizona
        State Museum.

1963b   The Trincheras culture of northern Sonora. Ameri-
        can Antiquity, 29:174-186.

1964   Archaeological excavations in Hohokam sites of
        southern Arizona. American Antiquity, 30:145-161.

1965   The development of Western Pueblo culture. Univer-
        sity of Arizona, dissertation, 124 pp.; University
        Microfilms International.

1966   Archaeology of Sonora, Mexico. In Ekholm and Wil-
        ley 1966, pp. 26-37.

JOHNSON, A.E., and THOMPSON, Raymond H.

1963a   The Ringo Site, southeastern Arizona. American
        Antiquity, 28:465-481.

1963b   Artifact descriptions and proveniences for the
        Ringo site, southeastern Arizona. Archives of
        Archaeology, no. 22, 48 pp. (2 microcards).
        Reviewed AA 67:583 (Ascher).

JOHNSON, A.E., and WASLEY, William W.

1961   Pottery and artifact provenience data from sites
        in the Painted Rocks Reservoir, western Arizona.
        Archives of Archaeology, no. 18, 62 pp. (microcards).

1966   Archaeological excavations near Bylas, Arizona.
        Kiva, 31, no. 4:205-253.

JOHNSON, Ann Stofer

1958   Similarities in Hohokam and Chalchihuites artifacts.
        American Antiquity, 24:126-130.

1971   Finger-loops and cruciform objects. American An-
        tiquity, 36:188-194.

JOHNSON, Chester R., Jr.

1961   A note on the excavation of Yunque, San Gabriel.
        El Palacio, 68:121-124.

1962a   An archaeological survey of the Shiprock-Cortez

230 KV powerline. Laboratory of Anthropology Notes, 9.

1962b   Excavation of the Thoreau site, LA 6372. Laboratory of Anthropology Notes, 10.

1962c   The Twin Lakes site, LA 2507. El Palacio, 69:158-173.

1963   Tohalina Bikitsiel: a Pueblo ruin at Toadlena, New Mexico. El Palacio, 70, no. 4:21-32.

JOHNSON, Frederick

1957   Radiocarbon dates from Sandia Cave: correction. Science, 125:234-235.

JOHNSON, Leonard G. (See also under Martin, Paul Sidney.)

1947   Some ancient "DP's" of New Mexico. Chicago Natural History Museum Bulletin, 18, no. 9:1, 8.

JOHNSON, LeRoy, Jr.

1961   The Devil's Mouth site: a river terrace midden, Diablo Reservoir, Texas. Bulletin of the Texas Archaeological Society, 30:253-285.

1963   Pollen analysis of two archaeological sites at Amistad Reservoir, Texas. Texas Journal of Science, 15, no. 2:225-230.

1964   The Devil's Mouth site: a stratified campsite at Amistad Reservoir, Val Verde County, Texas. University of Texas, Archaeological Series, 6, 115 pp. Reviewed AAq 30:224 (Wyckoff).

1967   Toward a statistical overview of the Archaic cultures of central and southwestern Texas. Texas Memorial Museum, Bulletin 12, 110 pp. Reviewed AA 71:1210 (Hammatt).

JOHNSON, R.R. (See under Gumerman, George J.)

JOHNSTON, Bernice

1964   A newly discovered turquoise mine of prehistory, Mohave County, Arizona. Kiva, 29:76-83.

JOHNSTON, Francis J., and JOHNSTON, Patricia H.

1957   An Indian trail complex of the central Colorado Desert: a preliminary survey. University of California, Archaeological Survey Reports, 37:22-39.

JOHNSTON, Patricia H. (See under Johnston, Francis J.)

JONES, Carl Hugh

    1958   A Puebloid site in Utah Valley. Utah Archaeology, 4, no. 2:7-13.

    1961   An archaeological survey of Utah County, Utah. Brigham Young University, 92 pp. Reviewed AAq 28:115 (Green).

JONES, David J.

    1935   Progress of the excavation at Kinishba. Kiva, 1, no. 3:1-4.

    1942   Red ruins in the black cinder. Arizona Highways, 18, no. 11:16-21, 40.

    1946   Wupatki. Arizona Highways, 22, no. 7:28-29.

JONES, (Mrs.) E.

    1893   Prehistoric ruins in New Mexico. American Antiquarian, 15:150-151.

JONES, Stan

    1965   The mystery of the Hohokams. Desert Magazine, 28, no. 11:24-26.

JONES, Volney H. (See also under Euler, Robert C.; Morris, Elizabeth Ann; Steen, Charlie R.)

    1936   A summary of data on aboriginal cotton in the Southwest. *In* Brand 1936, pp. 51-64.

    1938   An ancient food plant of the Southwest and Plateau regions. El Palacio, 44, nos. 5-6:41-53.

    1944   Was tobacco smoked in the Pueblo region in pre-Spanish times? American Antiquity, 9:451-456.

    1952   Material from the Hemenway Archaeological Expedition (1887-1888) as a factor in establishing the American origin of the garden bean. *In* Indian Tribes of Aboriginal America, ed. Sol Tax, Selected Papers of the 29th International Congress of Americanists, pp. 177-184.

    1965   Seeds from an early Pueblo pit house near Albuquerque. El Palacio, 72, no. 2:24-26.

JONES, V.H., and FONNER, Robert L.

1954   Plant materials from sites in the Durango and La
        Plata areas, Colorado. *In* Morris and Burgh 1954,
        pp. 93-115.

JONES, V.H., and MORRIS, Elizabeth Ann

1960   A seventh-century record of tobacco utilization in
        Arizona. El Palacio, 67:115-117.

JONES, W. Paul, and TURNER, Christy G., II

1976   A burial from Hubbell Trading Post National Historic
        Site, northeast Arizona. Southwestern Lore, 42,
        nos. 1-2:44-46.

JONES, William K.

1963   Pueblo pottery of the Southwest. University of
        Oklahoma, Papers in Anthropology, 4, no. 1:37-44.

JORDE, L.B.

1977   Precipitation cycles and cultural buffering in the
        prehistoric Southwest. *In* For Theory Building in
        Archaeology, ed. Lewis R. Binford, Academic Press,
        pp. 385-396.

JORGENSEN, Julia

1976   A room use analysis of Table Rock Pueblo, Arizona.
        Journal of Anthropological Research, 31:149-161.

JUDD, Neil Merton

  1916a Archaeological reconnaissance in western Utah.
         Smithsonian Miscellaneous Collections, 66, no. 3:
         64-71.

  1916b The use of adobe in prehistoric dwellings of the
         Southwest. Holmes Anniversary Volume, Washington,
         pp. 241-252.

  1917a Archaeological reconnaissance in western Utah.
         Smithsonian Miscellaneous Collections, 66, no. 17:
         103-108.

  1917b Evidence of circular kivas in western Utah ruins.
         American Anthropologist, 19, no. 1:34-40.

  1917c Notes on certain prehistoric habitations in western
         Utah. Proceedings of the 19th International Con-
         gress of Americanists, pp. 119-124.

1918   Archaeological work in Arizona and Utah. Smithsonian Miscellaneous Collections, 68, no. 12:74-83.

1919a   Archaeological reconnaissance of northwestern Arizona. Smithsonian Miscellaneous Collections, 70, no. 2:93-97.

1919b   Archaeological investigations at Paragonah, Utah. Smithsonian Miscellaneous Collections, 70, no. 3, 22 pp.

1920   Archaeological investigations in Utah and Arizona. Smithsonian Miscellaneous Collections, 72, no. 1: 66-69.

1921   Archaeological investigations in Utah, Arizona, and New Mexico. Smithsonian Miscellaneous Collections, 72, no. 6:96-102.

1922a   Archaeological investigations at Pueblo Bonito, New Mexico. Smithsonian Miscellaneous Collections, 72, no. 15:106-117.

1922b   The Pueblo Bonito expedition of the National Geographic Society. National Geographic Magazine, 41, no. 3:322-331.

1923a   Archaeological investigations at Pueblo Bonito, New Mexico. Smithsonian Miscellaneous Collections, 74, no. 5:134-143.

1923b   Pueblo Bonito, the ancient. National Geographic Magazine, 44:99-108.

1924a   Archaeological investigations at Pueblo Bonito. Smithsonian Miscellaneous Collections, 76, no. 10:71-77.

1924b   Explorations in San Juan County, Utah. Smithsonian Miscellaneous Collections, 76, no. 12:77-82.

1924c   Two Chaco Canyon pit houses. Annual Report of the Smithsonian Institution for 1922, pp. 399-413.

1924d   Beyond clay hills. National Geographic Magazine, 45, no. 3:275-302.

1924e   Chaco Canyon pit houses. El Palacio, 17:286-288.

1924f   Report on illegal excavations in Southwestern ruins. American Anthropologist, 26:428-432.

1925a   Archaeological investigations at Pueblo Bonito, New Mexico. Smithsonian Miscellaneous Collections, 77, no. 2:83-91.

1925b   Everyday life in Pueblo Bonito. National Geographic
        Magazine, 48, no. 3:227-262.

1926a   Archaeological investigations at Pueblo Bonito and
        Pueblo del Arroyo, 1925. Smithsonian Miscellaneous
        Collections, 78, no. 1:80-88.

1926b   Archaeological observations north of the Rio Colo-
        rado. Bureau of American Ethnology, Bulletin 82,
        171 pp.

1927a   Archaeological investigations in Chaco Canyon, New
        Mexico. Smithsonian Miscellaneous Collections, 78,
        no. 7:158-168.

1927b   The architectural evolution of Pueblo Bonito. Pro-
        ceedings of the National Academy of Science, 13, no.
        7:561-563 (also in El Palacio, 22:466-467).

1928   Prehistoric Pueblo Bonito, New Mexico. Explorations
        and Field-Work of the Smithsonian Institution in
        1927, pp. 144-148.

1930a   Dating our prehistoric Pueblo ruins. Explorations
        and Field-Work of the Smithsonian Institution in
        1929, pp. 167-176.

1930b   Arizona sacrifices her prehistoric canals. Explora-
        tions and Field-Work of the Smithsonian Institution
        in 1929, pp. 177-182.

1930c   The excavation and repair of Betatakin. Proceedings
        of the United States National Museum, 77, art. 5,
        77 pp.

1930d   Pueblo Bonito and its architectural development.
        Proceedings of the 23rd International Congress of
        Americanists, pp. 70-73.

1931   Arizona's prehistoric canals from the air. Explor-
        ations and Field-Work of the Smithsonian Institution
        in 1930, pp. 157-166.

1932   Hunting baskets in Arizona. Explorations and Field-
        Work of the Smithsonian Institution in 1931, pp.
        125-132.

1940   Progress in the Southwest. Smithsonian Miscellaneous
        Collections, 100:417-444.
           Reviewed AAq 7:334 (Hibben).

1950a   A mistreated Pueblo figurine. Kiva, 16, no. 3:6-7.

1950b   Pioneering in Southwestern archaeology. *In* Reed
        and King 1950, pp. 11-27.

1952   A Pueblo III war club from southeastern Utah. Mas-
        terkey, 26, no. 2:60-62.

1954   The material culture of Pueblo Bonito. Smithsonian
        Miscellaneous Collections, 124, 398 pp.
        Reviewed AA 58:200 (Di Peso), AAq 21:322 (Vivian).

1959a   The braced-up cliff at Pueblo Bonito. Annual Re-
        port of the Smithsonian Institution for 1958, pp.
        501-511.

1959b   Pueblo del Arroyo, Chaco Canyon, New Mexico. Smith-
        sonian Miscellaneous Collections, 138, no. 1, 222 pp.

1960   Reminiscences in Southwest archaeology: II. Kiva,
        26, no. 1:1-6.

1962   1910 in El Rito de los Frijoles. El Palacio, 69,
        no. 3:139-141.

1964   The architecture of Pueblo Bonito. Smithsonian
        Miscellaneous Collections, 147, no. 1, 349 pp.
        Reviewed AA 67:581 (Schroeder), AAq 31:129 (Martin).

1967   The passing of a small Pueblo III ruin. Plateau,
        39:131-133.

1968   Men met along the trail: adventures in archaeology.
        University of Oklahoma Press, 162 pp.
        Reviewed AA 71:1207 (Lister), AAq 35:391 (Smith).

1970   Basketmaker artifacts from Moki Canyon, Utah. Pla-
        teau, 43, no. 1:16-20.

JUDGE, W. James (See also under Dawson, Jerry.)

1970   Systems analysis and the Folsom-Midland question.
        Southwestern Journal of Anthropology 26:40-51.

1971   An interpretive framework for understanding site
        location. *In* Gumerman 1971, pp. 38-44.

1973a   Paleo-Indian occupation of the central Rio Grande
        Valley in New Mexico. University of New Mexico
        Press, 361 pp.
        Reviewed AA 77:156 (Morris).

1973b   The University of New Mexico 1973 season field
        session in archaeology. Awanyu, 1, no. 4:19-21,
        47.

1974   The excavation of Tijeras Pueblo 1971-73: prelim-
        inary report. United States Forest Service, South-
        western Region, Archeological Report 3, 56 pp.

1978   Synthesis and comparison of project results. *In*
        Euler and Gumerman, 1978, pp. 95-101.

JUDGE, W.J., and DAWSON, Jerry

1972   Paleo-Indian settlement technology in New Mexico.
        Science, 176:1210-1216.

JUDGE, W.J., EBERT, James I., and HITCHCOCK, Robert K.

1975   Sampling in regional archaeological survey. *In*
        Sampling in Archaeology, ed. James W. Mueller,
        University of Arizona Press, pp. 82-123.

JUDSON, Sheldon

1953a   Geology of the San Jon site, eastern New Mexico.
        Smithsonian Miscellaneous Collections, 121, no. 1,
        70 pp.

1953b   The Hodges site, II. Geology of the Hodges site,
        Quay County, New Mexico. Bureau of American Eth-
        nology, Bulletin 154, pp. 285-302.

JULIAN, Hurst R.

1933   Chaco Canyon cavities report. Southwestern Monu-
        ments Monthly Report, September, Supplement, pp.
        A-K.

KABOTIE, Fred

1949   Designs from the ancient Mimbreños with a Hopi
        interpretation. Grabhorn Press, San Francisco,
        83 pp.

KAEMLEIN, Wilma R.

1963   A prehistoric twined-woven bag from the Trigo
        Mountains, Arizona. Kiva, 28, no. 3:1-13.

1967   An inventory of Southwestern American Indian speci-
        mens in European museums. Arizona State Museum,
        229 pp.

1971   Large hunting nets in the collections of the Ari-
        zona State Museum. Kiva, 36, no. 3:20-52.

KANE, Margaret H. (See under Lister, Robert H.)

KAPLAN, Lawrence (See also under Cutler, Hugh C.)

1956   The cultivated beans of the prehistoric Southwest.

Annals of the Missouri Botanical Gardens, 43:189-251.

1963   Archeoethnobotany of Cordova Cave, New Mexico. Economic Botany, 17:350-359.

1965   Beans of Wetherill Mesa. *In* Osborne 1965a, pp. 153-155.

KARLSTROM, Thor N.V., GUMERMAN, George J., and EULER, Robert C.

1974   Paleoenvironmental and cultural changes in the Black Mesa region, northeastern Arizona. *In* The Geology of Northern Arizona with Notes on Archaeology and Paleoclimate, ed. T.N.V. Karlstrom, 27th Annual Meeting, Rocky Mountain Section, Geological Society of America, pp. 768-792.

1976   Paleoenvironmental and cultural correlates in the Black Mesa region. *In* Gumerman and Euler 1976, pp. 149-161.

KASPER, Jan C.

1977   Animal resource utilization at Colorado Paradox Valley site. Southwestern Lore, 43, no. 1:1-17.

KATE, H.F.C. ten

1887   Sur quelques objets indiens trouvés près de Guaymas (Mexique). Revue d'Ethnographie, 6:234-238.

1892   Somatological observations on Indians of the Southwest. Journal of American Ethnology and Archaeology, 3:117-144.

1931   Prehistoric pottery and culture relations in the middle Gila. American Anthropologist, 33:268-270.

KAYSER, David W. (See also under Allen, Joseph W.; Valcarce, Joseph P.)

1969   Screwtail Cave. Kiva, 34, nos. 2-3:124-131.

1971   An archaeological survey of Mobil Oil Corporation uranium lease areas on the Laguna Indian Reservation, Valencia County, New Mexico. Laboratory of Anthropology Notes, 59.

1972a   Armijo Springs project: archaeological salvage in the Harris Creek Valley area of the Gallo Mountains. Laboratory of Anthropology Notes, 56.

1972b   Whiskey Creek project: archaeological highway salvage along State Highway 32 in Apache Creek Valley,

Catron County, New Mexico. Laboratory of Anthropology Notes, 57.

1972c   Gallita Springs project: archaeological exploration and salvage in the Gallo Mountains, Apache National Forest, Catron County, New Mexico. Laboratory of Anthropology Notes, 69.

1973   Castle Rock project: archaeological salvage along State Highway 32 in Agua Fria and Largo Creek Canyons, Catron County, New Mexico. Laboratory of Anthropology Notes, 71.

1975   The mesa top Mogollon: a report on the excavations at Gallita Springs, Gallo Mountains, Gila National Forest, Catron County, New Mexico. Laboratory of Anthropoloy Notes, 113.

KAYSER, D.W., and EWING, George H.

1971   (ed.) Salvage archaeology in the Galisteo dam and reservoir area, New Mexico. Laboratory of Anthropology Notes, 101.

KAYSER, D.W., and FIERO, Donald C.

1970   Pipeline salvage near Willcox, Arizona. Kiva, 35, no. 3:131-137.

KAYSER, Joyce

1965   Phantoms in the pinyon: an investigation of Ute-Pueblo contacts. *In* Osborne 1965a, pp. 82-91.

KEAN, William L.

1965   Marine mollusks and aboriginal trade in the Southwest. Plateau, 38, no. 1:17-31.

KEANE, Edward G. (See under Sharrock, Floyd W.)

KEECH, R.A.

1933a   The saline Pueblo strongholds. El Palacio, 34:1-13.

1933b   To Chaco Canyon (by way of Laguna, Enchanted Mesa, and Acoma). El Palacio, 35:161-181.

1934   Pueblo dwelling architecture. El Palacio, 36:49-53.

KELLAHIN, Jason W.

1973   Cicuye: the ruins of Pecos Pueblo. School of

American Research, Exploration 1973, pp. 24-27.

1976   The three forts of Fort Union. School of American
        Research, Exploration 1976, pp. 11-15.

KELLAR, James H.

1955   The atlatl in North America. Indiana Historical
        Society, Prehistory Research Series, 3, no. 3:275-
        352.
        Reviewed AAq 22:86 (Johnson).

KELLER, Donald R., and WILSON, Suzanne M.

1976   New light on the Tolchaco problem. Kiva, 41, nos.
        3-4:225-239.

KELLER, Gordon N., and HUNT, John D.

1967   Lithic materials from Escalante Valley, Utah. Uni-
        versity of Utah, Miscellaneous Collected Papers,
        no. 17, Anthropological Papers, 89, pp. 51-59.
        Reviewed AAq 36:227 (Ambler).

KELLER, Marvin

1976   Impressions of a foot effigy: a reorientation to
        ceremonial objects. Kiva, 42, no. 2:203-207.

KELLEY, Ellen Abbott (See under Kelley, John Charles. Also
    listed as Abbott, Ellen.)

KELLEY, James E.

1974   Bighorn Sheep at Grasshopper Ruin: precautions in
        analysis. Kiva, 40, nos. 1-2:71-79.

1975   Zooarchaeological analysis at Antelope House: be-
        havioral inferences from distribution data. *In*
        Rock and Morris 1975, pp. 81-85.

KELLEY, Jane Holden (Also listed as Holden, Jane.)

1964   Comments on the archaeology of the Llano Estacado.
        Bulletin of the Texas Archaeological Society, 35:
        1-17.

KELLEY, John Charles (See also under Hedrick, Basil C.; Smith,
    Victor J.)

1933   Report on the archaeological field work in the
        Madera Valley area. West Texas Historical and

Scientific Society Publications, 5:53-59.

1937   The route of Antonio de Espejo down the Pecos River
        and across the Texas Trans-Pecos region in 1583: its
        relation to West Texas archaeology. West Texas His-
        torical and Scientific Society, Publications, 7, pp.
        7-25.

1939   Archaeological notes on the excavation of a pit-
        house near Presidio, Texas. El Palacio, 46, no.
        10:221-234.

1940   Recent field work in the Texas Big Bend: (1) Pre-
        sidio. Texas Archaeological News, 2:1-4.

1948   Arrow or dart shaft tools and problematical incised
        stones from central and western Texas. El Palacio,
        55, no. 3:73-85.

1949   Archaeological notes on two excavated house struc-
        tures in western Texas. Bulletin of the Texas Ar-
        chaeological and Paleontological Society, 20:89-114.

1950   Atlatls, bows and arrows pictographs, and the Pecos
        River Focus. American Antiquity, 16:71-74.

1951   A Bravo Valley aspect component of the lower Rio
        Conchos Valley, Chihuahua, Mexico. American Antiq-
        uity, 17:114-119.

1952   Factors involved in the abandonment of certain pe-
        ripheral southwestern settlements. American Anthro-
        pologist, 54:356-387.

1953   Reconnaissance and excavation in Durango and south-
        ern Chihuahua, Mexico. Year Book of the American
        Philosophical Society, pp. 172-176.

1956   Settlement patterns in north-central Mexico. *In*
        Willey 1956, pp. 128-139.

1957   The Livermore Focus: a clarification. El Palacio,
        64:44-52.

1959   The Desert cultures and the Balcones Phase: Archaic
        manifestations in the Southwest and Texas. American
        Antiquity, 24:276-288.

1960   North Mexico and the correlation of Mesoamerican and
        Southwestern cultural sequences. Selected Papers
        of the 5th International Congress of Anthropological
        and Ethnological Sciences, ed. A.F.C. Wallace, pp.
        566-573.

1966   Mesoamerica and the southwestern United States.
        In Ekholm and Willey 1966, pp. 95-110.

KELLEY, J.C., and ABBOTT, Ellen

1966   The cultural sequence on the north central frontier
        of Mesoamerica. Proceedings of the 36th Interna-
        tional Congress of Americanists, 1:325-344.

KELLEY, J.C., and CAMPBELL, Thomas N.

1942   What are the burnt rock mounds of Texas? American
        Antiquity, 7:319-322.

KELLEY, J.C., and KELLEY, Ellen Abbott

1975   An alternative hypothesis for the explanation of
        Anasazi culture history. *In* Frisbie 1975a, pp.
        178-223.

KELLEY, J.C., CAMPBELL, T.N., and LEHMER, Donald J.

1940   The association of archaeological materials with
        geological deposits in the Big Bend region of Texas.
        West Texas Historical and Scientific Society Publi-
        cations, 10:9-173.
        Reviewed AAq 8:302 (Setzler).

KELLNER, Larry

1959   Tonto national monument. Arizona Highways, 35,
        no. 1:6-11.

KELLY, Charles

1942   Playground in the Utah wilderness. Desert Maga-
        zine, 5, no. 10:25-28.

1943a   We climbed to the Moki ruin. Desert Magazine, 6,
        no. 3:5-8.

1943b   Ancient antelope run. Desert Magazine, 6, no. 5:
        7-9.

1943c   We found a gallery of Indian etchings. Desert
        Magazine, 6, no. 11:18-19.

1945   Petroglyphs of the Capitol Reef National Monument.
        Fruita, Utah.

1950   Murals painted by ancient tribesmen. Desert Maga-
        zine, 13, no. 8:11-12.

KELLY, Isabel T.

1944   West Mexico and the Hohokam. *In* El Norte de Méx-
        ico y el Sur de Estados Unidos, Tercera Reunión
        de Mesa Redonda sobre Problemas Antropológicas de
        México y Centro América, pp. 206-222. Sociedad
        Mexicana de Antropología.

KELLY, I.T., OFFICER, James E., and HAURY, Emil W.

1978   The Hodges Ruin: a Hohokam community in the Tucson
        basin. University of Arizona, Anthropological
        Papers, 30, 152 pp.

KELLY, Marjorie (See under Martin, Paul Sidney.)

KELLY, Roger E. (See also under Wilson, John P.)

1966   Split-twig figurines from Sycamore Canyon, central
        Arizona. Plateau, 38, no. 3:65-67.

1968   Fourteen prehistoric sites in Nankoweap Canyon,
        Grand Canyon National Park. Arizona Archaeologist,
        3.

1969a   Salvage excavations at six Sinagua sites. Plateau,
        41, no. 3:112-133.

1969b   An archaeological survey in the Payson Basin, cen-
        tral Arizona. Plateau, 42, no. 2:46-65.

1970a   Elden Pueblo: an archaeological account. Plateau,
        42, no. 3:79-91.

1970b   Obsidian debitage from Elden Pueblo, north central
        Arizona: a trial study. Arizona Archaeologist, 5,
        pp. 37-46.

1971   Diminishing returns: twelfth and thirteenth cen-
        tury Sinagua environmental adaptation in north
        central Arizona. University of Arizona, disserta-
        tion, 161 pp.; University Microfilms International.

KELLY, R.E., and WARD, Albert E.

1972   Lessons from the Zeyouma Trading Post near Flag-
        staff, Arizona. Historical Archaeology, 6:65-76.

KELLY, Thomas C.

1963   Archaeological investigations at Roark Cave, Brew-
        ster County, Texas. Bulletin of the Texas Archae-
        ological Society, 33:191-227.

KELLY, T.C., and SMITH, Harvey P.

1963   An investigation of archaeological sites in Reagan Canyon, Brewster County, Texas. Bulletin of the Texas Archaeological Society, 33:167-190.

KELLY, William S.

1936   University Ruin. Kiva, 1, no. 8:1-4.

KELSO, Gerald Kay

1976   Absolute pollen frequencies applied to the interpretation of human activities in northern Arizona. University of Arizona, dissertation, 201 pp.; University Microfilms International.

KEMRER, Meade

1974   The dynamics of western Navajo settlement, A.D. 1750-1900: an archaeological and dendrochronological analysis. University of Arizona, dissertation, 222 pp.; University Microfilms International.

1978   Maximizing the interpretive potential of archaeological tree-ring dates. *In* Grebinger 1978a, pp. 29-53.

KEMRER, Sandra, and others

1972   Archaeological survey of the Granite Reef aqueduct. Arizona State Museum, Archaeological Series, 12, 129 pp.

KENDRICK, Grace

1967   Bottle fragments betray age of historical sites. El Palacio, 74, no. 2:19-24.

KENT, Arthur

1947   New Pueblo excavations. Arizona Highways, 23, no. 6:22-25.

KENT, Kate Peck (See also under Wade, William D.)

1941   Notes on the weaving of prehistoric Pueblo textiles. Plateau, 14, no. 1:1-11.

1944   A method for studying color in prehistoric Pueblo cotton fabrics. Clearing-House for Southwestern Museums, News-Letter, 1:252-254.

1945   A comparison of prehistoric and modern Pueblo weav-
        ing. Kiva, 10, no. 2:14-20.

1954   Montezuma Castle archaeology, Part 2: Textiles.
        Southwest Monuments Association, Technical Series,
        3, pt. 2, 102 pp.
        Reviewed AA 58:392 (Bluhm), AAq 21:326 (Dixon).

1957   The cultivation and weaving of cotton in the pre-
        historic southwestern United States. Transactions
        of the American Philosophical Society, 47, pt. 3,
        pp. 457-732.
        Reviewed AAq 24:205 (Burgh).

1962   An analysis and interpretation of the cotton tex-
        tiles from Tonto National Monument, 1958. *In* Cay-
        wood 1962, pp. 115-159.

1966   Archaeological clues to early historic Navajo and
        Pueblo weaving. Plateau, 39, no. 1:46-60.

KESSLER, Evelyn Seinfeld

1970   Mesoamerican contacts in the American Southwest
        and Southeast. Columbia University, dissertation,
        300 pp.; University Microfilms International.

KEUR, Dorothy Louise

1941   Big Bead Mesa: an archaeological study of Navajo
        acculturation, 1745-1812. Memoirs of the Society
        for American Archaeology, 1, 90 pp.
        Reviewed AA 44:488 (Wyman).

1944   A chapter in Navaho-Pueblo relations. American
        Antiquity, 10:75-86.

KHALIL, Carole L. (See under LeBlanc, Steven A.)

KIDDER, Alfred Vincent (See also under Guernsey, Samuel J.;
    Kidder, Madeleine A.; Morley, Sylvanus G.; Nusbaum, Jesse L.)

1910   Explorations in southeastern Utah in 1908. Amer-
        ican Journal of Archaeology, 2nd ser., 14:337-359.

1913   Some undescribed ruins of the historic period from
        the upper San Juan, New Mexico. American Journal
        of Archaeology, 2:89-90.

1915   Pottery of the Pajarito Plateau and of some adja-
        cent regions in New Mexico. Memoirs of the American
        Anthropological Association, 2, pt. 6, pp. 407-462.

1916a   Archaeological explorations at Pecos, New Mexico.
         Proceedings of the National Academy of Sciences,
         2:119-123.

1916b   The pottery of the Casas Grandes district, Chihua-
         hua. Holmes Anniversary Volume, Washington, pp.
         253-268.

1916c   The pueblo of Pecos. Archaeological Institute of
         America, Papers of the School of American Archae-
         ology, 33 (also El Palacio, 3, no. 3:43-49).

1917a   The condition of the main Pecos ruin. El Palacio,
         4, no. 1:19-21.

1917b   A design-sequence from New Mexico. Proceedings
         of the National Academy of Sciences, 3:369-370.

1917c   The old north pueblo of Pecos. Archaeological
         Institute of America, Papers of the School of Amer-
         ican Archaeology, 38 (also El Palacio, 4, no. 1:
         13-17).

1917d   Prehistoric cultures of the San Juan drainage.
         Proceedings of the 19th International Congress of
         Americanists, pp. 108-113.

1920   Ruins of the historic period in the upper San Juan
         Valley, New Mexico. American Anthropologist, 22,
         no. 4:322-329.

1921   Excavations at Pecos in 1920. El Palacio, 10, nos.
         1-2:2-4, 13-16.

1922   Excavations at Pecos, 1922. El Palacio, 13, no. 9:
         107-109.

1923   Basket Maker caves in the Mesa Verde. El Palacio,
         15, no. 10:164-165.

1924   An introduction to the study of Southwestern archae-
         ology, with a preliminary account of the excava-
         tions at Pecos. Phillips Academy, Papers of the
         Southwestern Expedition, 1, 151 pp.
             Reviewed AA 27:461 (Goddard).

1925a   The Academy's archaeological work in the Southwest.
         Phillips Bulletin, 19, no. 2:15-20.

1925b   Pecos excavations in 1924. Archaeological Insti-
         tute of America, Papers of the School of American
         Research, new ser., 11 (also El Palacio, 18, nos.
         10-11:217-223).

1926a   The excavations at Pecos. Archaeological Institute

of America, Papers of the School of American Research, new ser., 14 (also El Palacio, 20, no. 1:
2-32).

1926b Early Pecos ruins on the Forked Lightning Ranch.
Archaeological Institute of America, Papers of the
School of American Research, new ser., 16 (also El
Palacio, 21, no. 10:274-283).

1926c A sandal from northeastern Arizona. American Anthropologist, 28:618-632.

1927a Early Man in America. Masterkey, 1, no. 5:5-13.

1927b Southwestern archaeological conference. Science,
66, no. 1716:489-491.

1927c The museum's expeditions to Canyon de Chelly and
Canyon del Muerto, Arizona. Natural History, 27:
203-209.

1928a A pipe of unique form from Pecos, New Mexico.
Museum of the American Indian, Indian Notes, 5:
293-295.

1928b Recent researches in the science of Man. I. North
America. Masterkey, 2, no. 4:5-23.

1932   The artifacts of Pecos. Phillips Academy, Papers
of the Southwestern Expedition, 6, 314 pp.

1936a The archaeology of peripheral regions. Southwestern Lore, 2, no. 3:46-48.

1936b Speculations on New World prehistory. *In* Essays
in Anthropology in Honor of Alfred Louis Kroeber,
ed. R.H. Lowie, University of California Press, pp.
143-151.

1938   Arrowheads or dart points. American Antiquity, 4,
no. 2:156-157.

1939   Notes on the archaeology of the Babicora district,
Chihuahua. *In* Brand and Harvey 1939, pp. 221-230.

1951a Pecos Pueblo. El Palacio, 58:82-89.

1951b Whistles from Arizona. American Antiquity, 16:256.

1957   European knife handles at Pecos - a correction.
American Antiquity, 22:297-298.

1958   Pecos, New Mexico: archaeological notes. Phillips
Academy, Papers of the Robert S. Peabody Foundation,
5, 360 pp.
    Reviewed AA 61:711 (Reed), AAq 25:281 (Haury).

1960   Reminiscences in Southwest archaeology - 1. Kiva, 25:1-32.

KIDDER, A.V., and AMSDEN, Charles A.

1931   The pottery of Pecos. Vol. I: the dull-paint wares. Phillips Academy, Papers of the Southwestern Expedition, 5, 166 pp.

KIDDER, A.V., and GUERNSEY, Samuel J.

1919   Archaeological explorations in northeastern Arizona. Bureau of American Ethnology, Bulletin 65, 228 pp.

1921   Peabody Museum Arizona Expedition, 1920. Proceedings of the National Academy of Sciences, 7:69-71.

KIDDER, A.V., and ROUSE, Irving

1962   An introduction to the study of Southwestern archaeology. Revised edition, with a summary of Southwestern archaeology today. Yale University Press, 377 pp.

KIDDER, A.V., and SHEPARD, Anna O.

1936   The pottery of Pecos. Vol. II: the glaze-paint, culinary and other wares. Phillips Academy, Papers of the Southwestern Expedition, 7, 636 pp. Reviewed AAq 2:322 (Guthe), 325 (Matson).

KIDDER, A.V., COSGROVE, Harriet S., and COSGROVE, Cornelius B.

1949   The Pendleton Ruin, Hidalgo County, New Mexico. Carnegie Institution of Washington, Contributions to American Anthropology and History, 10, no. 50: 109-152.
        Reviewed AAq 17:156 (Carey).

KIDDER, Madeleine A., and KIDDER, Alfred Vincent

1917   Notes on the pottery of Pecos. American Anthropologist, 19, no. 3:325-360.

KING, Chester, CASEBIER, Dennis, and others

1976   Background to historic and prehistoric resources of the east Mojave Desert region. Bureau of Land Management, Department of the Interior.

KING, Dale S. (See also under Reed, Erik K.)

 1946 A story of the Tonto ruins. Arizona Highways, 22, no. 7:12-13.

 1949 Nalakihu: excavations at a Pueblo III site on Wupatki National Monument, Arizona. Museum of Northern Arizona, Bulletin 23, 183 pp. Reviewed AAq 17:66 (Wendorf).

KING, Mary Alice

 1973 Petroglyphs at Cooks Peak. Awanyu, 1, no. 4:37-42.

KING, Mary Elizabeth, and TRAYLOR, Idris R.

 1974 (ed.) Art and environment in native America. Texas Tech University, Special Publication no. 7, 169 pp. Reviewed AA 79:496 (Fritz).

KING, Thomas Gordon

 1893 An exploration of the region occupied by the Cliff Dwellers. The Archaeologist, 1, no. 6:101-105.

KINKADE, Gay M.

 1975 Foote Wash/No Name Wash Project. Arizona State Museum, Archaeological Series, 67, 26 pp.

 1976 Cultural resource management program: BLM Safford District. Arizona State Museum, Archaeological Series, 100, 45 pp.

KINKADE, G.M., and GILMAN, Patricia A.

 1974 Survey of the APS Cholla to Saguaro transmission line proposed route. Arizona State Museum, Archaeological Series, 54, 32 pp.

KINKADE, G.M., FRITZ, Gordon L., and others

 1975 Tucson Sewage Project: studies at two archaeological sites. Arizona State Museum, Archaeological Series, 64, 68 pp.

KIRCHHOFF, Paul

 1954 Gatherers and farmers in the Greater Southwest: a problem in classification. American Anthropologist, 56:529-550.

KIRK, Ruth F.

1939   Glimpses of the ancients. Desert Magazine, 2, no.
        5:3-6.

1941   Architecture of the ancients. New Mexico Maga-
        zine, 19, no. 5:14-15, 33-35.

KIRKLAND, Forrest

1937   A study of Indian pictures in Texas. Bulletin of
        the Texas Archaeological and Paleontological So-
        ciety, 9:89-119.

1938   A description of Texas pictographs. Bulletin of
        the Texas Archaeological and Paleontological So-
        ciety, 10:11-40.

1939   Indian pictures in the dry shelters of Val Verde
        County, Texas. Bulletin of the Texas Archaeologi-
        cal and Paleontological Society, 11:47-76.

1940   Pictographs of Indian masks at Hueco Tanks. Bul-
        letin of the Texas Archaeological and Paleonto-
        logical Society, 12:9-30.

1942   Historic material from Fielder Canyon Cave. Bul-
        letin of the Texas Archaeological and Paleonto-
        logical Society, 14:61-71.

KIRKLAND, F., and NEWCOMB, W.W., Jr.

1966   The rock art of Texas Indians. University of Texas
        Press, 240 pp.
        Reviewed AAq 33:262 (Heizer).

KIRKPATRICK, David T.

1976   Archaeological investigations in the Cimarron
        district, northeastern New Mexico: 1929-1975.
        Awanyu, 4, no. 3:6-15.

KITCHEN, Suzanne (See under Fish, Paul R. Also listed as
    Fish, Suzanne K.)

KLAENHAMMER, Anita M.

1975   Public Service Company San Juan to Ojo transmission
        line project: archaeological exploration and sal-
        vage at LA 11836, Rio Arriba County, New Mexico.
        Laboratory of Anthropology Notes, 111A.

KLEINER, Sally (See under Terrel, James.)

KLINCK, Richard E.

1960   Casa Grande. Arizona Highways, 36, no. 1:1-3.

KLINGER, Timothy (See also under Fitting, James E.; Lekson, Stephen.)

KLINGER, T., and LEKSON, Stephen

1973   A bead cache from Saige-McFarland, a Mimbres site in southwestern New Mexico. The Artifact, 11, no. 4:66-68.

KLUCKHOHN, Clyde

1927   To the foot of the rainbow. Century Co., New York, 242 pp.

1932   Beyond the rainbow. Christopher Publishing House, Boston, 271 pp.

KLUCKHOHN, C., and REITER, Paul

1939   (ed.) Preliminary report on the 1937 excavations, Bc 50-51, Chaco Canyon, New Mexico. University of New Mexico Bulletin, Anthropological Series, 3, no. 2, 190 pp.
        Reviewed AAq 6:192 (McGregor).

KNIPE, Dorothy A.

1942   A date from Chaco Yuma West, southern Arizona. Tree-Ring Bulletin, 8:24.

KNOX, Lloyd

1953   Arizona excavations prove man hunted prehistoric mammoth. Ohio Archaeologist, 3, no. 4:13-21.

KOERNER, Betty

1966   A yucca bag from the Mimbres. The Artifact, 4, no. 2:5-8.

KONITZKY, Gustav A.

1955a   Die Indianer der Mesa Verde. Kosmos, 51, no. 2: 65-69.

1955b   In den Tuffklippen von Bandelier. Kosmos, 51, no. 5:208-213.

1959   Ruinen in der Wüste; die Indianer von Wupatki. Kosmos, 55, no. 3:105-110.

1967   Versunkene Städte der Indianer: die Pueblo-Ruinen
        im Chaco Canyon in Neu-Mexico. Kosmos, 63, no. 9:
        379-386.

KOWTA, Makoto (See under Mulroy, Mary E.)

KRIEGER, Alex D. (See also under Suhm, Dee Ann.)

1953   New World culture history: Anglo-America. *In*
        Anthropology Today: an Encyclopedia Inventory,
        ed. A.L. Kroeber, University of Chicago Press,
        pp. 238-264.

1962   The earliest cultures in the western United States.
        American Antiquity, 28, no. 2:138-143.

1964   Early Man in the New World. *In* Jennings and Nor-
        beck 1964, pp. 23-81.
        Reviewed AAq 30:500 (Bell).

KROEBER, Alfred Louis

1916a   Zuni culture sequences. Proceedings of the Nation-
        al Academy of Sciences, 2:42-45.

1916b   Zuni potsherds. American Museum of Natural His-
        tory, Anthropological Papers, 18, pt. 1, pp. 1-37.

KRONE, Milton F.

1974   Little Peaks site report. The Artifact, 12, no.
        3:9-25.

1975   Report on Folsom points found in El Paso area.
        The Artifact, 13, no. 4:1-19.

1976a   Ahumada point. The Artifact, 14, no. 2:41-43.

1976b   Clovis point from El Paso area. The Artifact, 14,
        no. 2:44-48.

KUNITZ, Stephen J.

1970   Disease and death among the Anasazi. El Palacio,
        76, no. 3:17-22.

KUNITZ, S.J., and EULER, Robert C.

1972   Aspects of Southwestern paleoepidemiology. Pres-
        cott College, Anthropological Reports, no. 2, 55
        pp.

KUNZ, Michael

1969   The cultural implications of the archaeology of

Billy the Kid Cave. Transactions of the 5th Regional Archaeological Symposium on Southeastern New Mexico and Western Texas, pp. 13-23.

KUNZ, M., GAMACHE, Glen L., and AGOGINO, George A.

1973   The material culture from Billy the Kid Cave and the late cultural history of Blackwater Draw. Awanyu, 1, no. 3:38-48.

LaCAZE, S.C.

1965   Site survey. The Artifact, 3, no. 2:2-3.

LaFARGE, Christopher

1945   Mesa Verde. Vail Ballew Press, Binghamton.

LAGUNA, Frederica de

1942   The Bryn Mawr dig at Cinder Park, Arizona. Plateau, 14, no. 4:53-56.

LAMBERT, Marjorie F. (Also listed as Ferguson, Marjorie, and Tichy, Marjorie Ferguson.)

1952   Oldest armor in United States discovered at San Gabriel del Yunque. El Palacio, 59:83-87.

1953   The oldest armor found in the United States, the San Gabriel del Yunque helmet. Archaeology, 6, no. 2:108-110.

1953- Cities before Columbus: prehistoric town planning
54   in the Puebloan Southwest. Landscape, 3, no. 2: 12-15.

1954   Paa-ko: archaeological chronicle of an Indian village in north central New Mexico. School of American Research, Monograph no. 19, pts. I-V, 183 pp. Reviewed AAq 22:203 (Ruppé).

1955   Early Man in the Southwest exhibit installed in the Palace of the Governors. El Palacio, 62:290-293.

1956a Rare Glaze I-yellow potsherd from San Cristóbal. El Palacio, 63:35.

1956b A prehistoric stone elbow pipe from the Taos area. El Palacio, 63:67-68.

1956c Some clay and stone figurines from the Mogollon-Mimbres area, Luna County, New Mexico. El Palacio,

63:259-283.

1957a   Mogollon-Mimbres exhibition opened in Palace of the Governors. El Palacio, 64:29-40.

1957b   A rare stone humpbacked figurine from Pecos Pueblo, New Mexico. El Palacio, 64:93-108.

1958   A pottery bell from northwestern New Mexico. American Antiquity, 24:184-185.

1966a   Pueblo Indian pottery: materials, tools, and techniques. Museum of New Mexico, Popular Series Pamphlet, 5, 24 pp.

1966b   A unique Kokopelli jar. El Palacio, 73, no. 2:21-25.

1967a   A Kokopelli effigy pitcher from northwestern New Mexico. American Antiquity, 32:398-401.

1967b   A unique prehistoric Anasazi pipe. El Palacio, 74, no. 4:41-42.

1967c   Excavations at Twin Hills site, Santa Fe County, New Mexico. Laboratory of Anthropology Notes, 45.

LAMBERT, M.F., and AMBLER, J. Richard

1965   A survey and excavation of caves in Hidalgo County, New Mexico. School of American Research, Monograph no. 25, 107 pp.
        Reviewed AAq 31:586 (Jennings).

LANCASTER, James A. (See also under Hayes, Alden C.)

LANCASTER, J.A., and PINKLEY, Jean M.

1954   Excavation at site 16 of three Pueblo II mesa-top ruins. *In* Lancaster, Pinkley, Van Cleave, and Watson 1954, pp. 23-86.

LANCASTER, J.A., and VAN CLEAVE, Philip F.

1954   The excavation of Sun Point Pueblo. *In* Lancaster, Pinkley, Van Cleave, and Watson 1954, pp. 87-111.

LANCASTER, J.A., and WATSON, Don W.

1943   Excavation of Mesa Verde pit houses. American Antiquity, 9, no. 2:190-198.

1954   Excavation of two late Basketmaker III pithouses. *In* Lancaster, Pinkley, Van Cleave, and Watson 1954,

pp. 7-22.

LANCASTER, J.A., PINKLEY, J.M., VAN CLEAVE, Philip F., and
    WATSON, Don

    1954   Archaeological excavations in Mesa Verde National
           Park, Colorado, 1950. National Park Service, Ar-
           chaeological Research Series, 2, 118 pp.
           Reviewed AA 58:202 (Judd), AAq 22:85 (O'Bryan).

LANCE, John F. (See also under Haury, Emil W.)

    1959   Faunal remains from the Lehner mammoth site. Amer-
           ican Antiquity, 25:35-39.

LANG, Richard W. (See also under Schwartz, Douglas W.)

    1976   An archaeological survey of certain lands adjacent
           to the Galisteo Dam, New Mexico. School of Ameri-
           can Research, contract #32.

    1977a Archaeological survey of the upper San Cristobal
           Arroyo drainage, Galisteo Basin, Santa Fe County,
           New Mexico. School of American Research, contract
           #37.

    1977b An archaeological survey of certain state lands
           within the drainages of Arroyo de la Vega de los
           Tanos and Arroyo Tonque, Sandoval County, New Mex-
           ico. School of American Research, contract #54.

    1977c An archaeological survey of the Galisteo Dam boun-
           dary line, Santa Fe County, New Mexico. School of
           American Research, contract #58.

    1977d An archaeological survey of the southern margin
           of San Mateo Mesa, McKinley County, New Mexico.
           School of American Research, contract #62.

LANG, Walter B.

    1937   Sun symbol markings. Journal of the Washington
           Academy of Sciences, 27, no. 4:137-143.

LANGE, Arthur L. (See under Schwartz, Douglas W.)

LANGE, Charles H.

    1940   A brief summary of a cranial series from north
           central New Mexico. New Mexico Anthropologist,
           4, no. 1:13-17.

    1944   Tiponi, or corn goddess symbols. American Antiquity,

9:446-448.

1950   Notes on the use of turkeys by Pueblo Indians.   El
       Palacio, 57, no. 7:204-209.

1953   A reappraisal of evidences of Plains influences
       among the Rio Grande Pueblos.   Southwestern Journal
       of Anthropology, 9:212-230.

1956   The Evans site and the archaeology of the Gallina
       region, New Mexico.   El Palacio, 63:72-92.

1968   (assembler) The Cochiti Dam archaeological salvage
       project, Part I: report on the 1963 season.   Museum
       of New Mexico, Research Records, 6, 330 pp.
       Reviewed AA 72:183 (Johnson), AAq 35:231 (Luebben).

1978   The Spanish-Mexican presence in the Cochiti-Bande-
       lier area, New Mexico.   *In* Riley and Hedrick 1978,
       pp. 34-52.

LANGE, C.H., and RILEY, Carroll L.

1966   The southwestern journals of Adolph F. Bandelier,
       Vol. 1, 1880-1882.   University of New Mexico Press,
       480 pp.

1970   The southwestern journals of Adolph F. Bandelier,
       Vol. 2, 1883-1884.   University of New Mexico Press,
       546 pp.

LANGE, C.H., RILEY, C.L., and LANGE, Elizabeth M.

1975   The southwestern journals of Adolph F. Bandelier,
       Vol. 3, 1885-1888.   University of New Mexico Press,
       680 pp.

LANGE, Elizabeth M. (See under Lange, Charles H.)

LARK, W.B. (See under Shiner, Joel L.)

LARKIN, Robert (See under Canouts, Valetta; Goree, Patricia.)

LARSON, Stephen M.

1972   The Tumamoc Hill site near Tucson, Arizona.   Kiva,
       38, no. 2:95-101.

LARUE, Gerald A.

1964   A curious parallel in pottery.   Masterkey, 38, no.
       3:111-114.

LATHRAP, Donald W.

1956   (ed.) An archaeological classification of culture
        contact situations. *In* Seminars in Archaeology:
        1955, ed. R. Wauchope, Society for American Archae-
        ology, Memoirs, no. 11, pp. 1-30.
        Reviewed AA 59:924 (Siegel), AAq 23:186 (Spicer).

LAUGHLIN, Minnabell (See under Weaver, Donald E., Jr.)

LAURITZEN, Jonreed

1948   Children of the yellow twilight. Arizona Highways,
        24, no. 8:12-21.

LAVINE-LISCHKA, Leslie

1975   Lithic analysis and cultural inferences from the
        Miami Wash project. University of Arizona, disserta-
        tion, 97 pp.; University Microfilms International.

1976   The use of lithic technology and the inference of
        cultural behavior patterns. Newsletter of Lithic
        Technology, 5:11-17.

LAYBOURNE, E.B.

1932   The probable stature of the Cliff Dwellers. Mesa
        Verde Notes, 3:17-19.

LEACH, Larry L.

1966   The archaeology of Boundary Village. University
        of Utah, Miscellaneous Collected Papers, no. 13,
        Anthropological Papers, 83, pp. 85-129.

1967   Archaeological investigations of Deluge Shelter,
        Dinosaur National Monument. Clearinghouse for
        Federal Scientific and Technical Information, pub-
        lication PB 176 960, 109 pp.

1970   Archaeological investigations at Deluge Shelter in
        Dinosaur National Monument. University of Colorado,
        dissertation, 389 pp.; University Microfilms Inter-
        national.

LeBLANC, Steven A.

1974   New Mexico research. Institute of Archaeology,
        University of California at Los Angeles, Newsletter,
        no. 4.

1975a   Micro-seriation: a method for fine chronologic dif-
        ferentiation. American Antiquity, 40:22-38.

1975b   Mimbres Archaeological Center: preliminary report
         of the first season of excavation, 1974. Institute
         of Archaeology, University of California at Los
         Angeles, Occasional Paper no. 1, 21 pp.

1976a   Temporal and ceramic relationships between some
         late PIII sites in the Zuni area. Plateau, 48, nos.
         3-4:75-83.

1976b   Mimbres Archaeological Center: preliminary report
         of the second season of excavations, 1975. Journal
         of New World Archaeology, 1, no. 6, 23 pp.

1977   The 1976 field season of the Mimbres Foundation in
         southwestern New Mexico. Journal of New World Ar-
         chaeology, 2, no. 2, 24 pp.

1978   Settlement patterns in the El Morro Valley, New
         Mexico. *In* Euler and Gumerman 1978, pp. 45-51.

LeBLANC, S.A., and KHALIL, Carole L.

1976   Flare-rimmed bowls: a subtype of Mimbres Classic
         Black-on-white. Kiva, 41, nos. 3-4:289-298.

LeBLANC, S.A., and NELSON, Ben

1976   The Salado in southwestern New Mexico. *In* Doyel
         and Haury 1976, pp. 71-79.

LEE, J.C.

1873   Ancient ruin in Arizona. Annual report of the
         Smithsonian Institution for 1872, p. 412.

LEE, Thomas A., Jr. (See also under Olson, Alan P.)

1962   The Beale's Saddle site: a nonconformity? Plateau,
         34:113-128.

LEH, Leonard L.

1936   Prehistoric Pueblo ruins in Range Creek Canyon,
         Utah. University of Colorado Studies, 23, no. 2:
         159-168.

1937   New explorations in archaeology. University of
         Colorado, Bulletin, 37, no. 15.

1938   Some surprises at the Wilson ruins in San Juan
         County, Utah. Southwestern Lore, 3, no. 4:66-73.

1939   Further studies at the Wilson ruins. Southwestern
         Lore, 4, no. 4:68-72.

1940   A prehistoric population center in the Southwest.
        Southwestern Lore, 6, no. 2:21-25.

1942   A preliminary account of the Monument ruins in San
        Juan County, Utah. University of Colorado Studies,
        Series in the Social Sciences, 1, no. 3:261-295.

LEHMER, Donald J. (See also under Kelley, J. Charles; Wendorf,
Fred.)

1948   The Jornada Branch of the Mogollon. University of
        Arizona, Social Science Bulletin 17, 99 pp.
        Reviewed AAq 15:67 (Smith).

1949   Archaeological survey of Sonora, Mexico. Chicago
        Natural History Museum Bulletin, 20, no. 12:4-5.

1960   A review of Trans-Pecos Texas archaeology. In
        Jelks, Davis, and Sturgis 1960, pp. 109-144.

LEIGH, Maxine (See under Christensen, Ross T.)

LEKSON, Stephen (See also under Klinger, Timothy.)

LEKSON, S., and KLINGER, Timothy

1973a   A Mimbres stone effigy vessel. The Artifact, 11,
        no. 4:5-8.

1973b   Villareal II: preliminary notes on an Animas Phase
        site in southwestern New Mexico. Awanyu, 1, no.
        2:33-38.

LEKSON, S., ROSS, James L., and FITTING, James E.

1971   The Stailey Cave collection. Case Western Reserve
        University, Southwestern New Mexico Research Re-
        ports, 6, 42 pp.

LENSINK, Stephen C.

1976a   An archaeological survey of the West Coast, Mid-
        Continent Pipeline project. Arizona State Museum,
        Archaeological Series, 105, 28 pp.

1976b   An archaeological survey of the Diablo Village
        Estates housing development, Tucson, Arizona. Ari-
        zona State Museum, Archaeological Series, 106, 20
        pp.

1976c   An assessment of the probable impact on cultural
        resources of a 230 KV transmission line between
        the Westwing and Deer Valley substations, Maricopa

County. Arizona State Museum, Archaeological Series, 108, 18 pp.

LENT, Stephen C. (See also under Gauthier, Rory; Schalk, Randall.)

LENT, S.C., and SCHALK, Randall

1977   Archaeological survey of 13.5 mile powerline right-of-way on Santa Clara Pueblo lands and BLM lands. University of New Mexico, contract report 185-19 (BLM).

LEONE, Mark P.

1968a   Economic autonomy and social distance: archaeological evidence. University of Arizona, dissertation, 171 pp.; University Microfilms International.

1968b   Neolithic economic autonomy and social distance. Science, 162:1150-1151.

1973   Archeology as the science of technology: Mormon town plans and fences. *In* Research and Theory in Current Archeology, ed. Charles Redman, John Wiley and Sons, pp. 125-150.

LEOPOLD, E.B. (See under Wendorf, Fred.)

LEOPOLD, L.B. (see under Wendorf, Fred.)

LESLIE, Robert H.

1965   The Merchant site (a Mogollon site). Transactions of the 1st Regional Archaeological Symposium on Southeastern New Mexico and Western Texas, pp. 23-29.

1968   The Monument Spring site LCAS no. D16, Lea County, New Mexico. Transactions of the 4th Regional Archaeological Symposium on Southeastern New Mexico and Western Texas, pp. 79-83.

LeVINESS, W. Thetford

1959   Pottery mound murals. New Mexico Magazine, 37, no. 3:22-23, 52.

1960a   The "dig" at Casas Grandes. Desert Magazine, 23, no. 12:12-13.

1960b   Unearthing history at Casas Grandes. Americas, 12, no. 7:8-13.

1961 Open air archaeology: the story of the Chicago Natural History Museum's field camp near Vernon, Arizona. Desert Magazine, 24, no. 5:42-43.

LEWIS, Mel

1966 The Anasazi trail. Desert Magazine, 29, no. 5:23-27.

LEWIS, Orian L. (See under Wendorf, Fred.)

LEWIS, Rhoda

1950 Digging the Cedro site. Brigham Young University Archaeological Society, Bulletin, 1:7-12.

LEWIS, Thomas H.

1950 Some artifacts from the Tularosa Basin of New Mexico. El Palacio, 57:198-203.

LIGHTFOOT, Kent G., and DeATLEY, Suzanne P.

1977 An archaeological survey of the Left Hand Draw and Pinedale timber sales, Apache-Sitgreaves National Forest, Pinedale Ranger District, Apache County, Arizona. Arizona State University, Office of Cultural Resource Management, Report no. 28, 31 pp.

LINCOLN, Edward P.

1962 Mammalian fauna from Wupatki ruin. Plateau, 34, no. 4:129-134.

LINDIG, Wolfgang H.

1964a Einige Bemerkungen zur Feldbau der prä-historischen Pueblo-Indianer (Anasazi) des Mesa-Verde-Gebietes (Südwest-Colorado). Baessler-Archiv, 12 (37), heft 2:311-315.

1964b Wildbeuter- und Pflanzerkulturen des nordamerikanischen Südwestens: Versuch einer Kulturgenetischen Gliederung. *In* Festschrift für Ad. E. Jensen, ed. Haberland, Eike, et al., 1:331-352.

1964c Zum gegenwürtigen Stand des Hohokam-Problems. Ethnos, 29, nos. 1-2:49-57.

1965 Hakataya und Patayan: eine Untersuchung zur Vorgeschichte des nordamerikanischen Südwestens, insbesondere des unteren Coloradotales. Zeitschrift für Ethnologie, 90, heft 2:219-246.

1966   Zum Frühkeramikum des nordamerikanischen Südwestens.
        Mitteilungen zur Kulturkunde, 1:117-127.

LINDSAY, Alexander J., Jr. (See also under Adams, William Y.;
    Ambler, J. Richard; Dean, Jeffrey S.; James, Charles D., III;
    Lipe, William D.)

1961a   The Beaver Creek agricultural community on the San
        Juan River, Utah. American Antiquity, 27, no. 2:
        174-187.

1961b   Saving prehistoric sites in the Southwest. Archae-
        ology, 14, no. 4:245-249.

1969   The Tsegi phase of the Kayenta cultural tradition
        in northeastern Arizona. University of Arizona,
        dissertation, 479 pp.; University Microfilms Inter-
        national.

LINDSAY, A.J., and AMBLER, J. Richard

1963   Recent contributions and research problems in
        Kayenta Anasazi prehistory. Plateau, 35:86-92.

LINDSAY, A.J., and DEAN, Jeffrey S.

1971   Changing patterns of human settlement in the Long
        House valley, northeastern Arizona. *In* Gumerman
        1971, pp. 111-125.

LINDSAY, A.J., and JENNINGS, Calvin H.

1968   (ed.) Salado Redware conference - Ninth Southwest-
        ern Ceramic Seminar. Museum of Northern Arizona,
        Ceramic Series, 4, 18 pp.

LINDSAY, A.J., AMBLER, J.R., STEIN, M.A., and HOBLER, P.M.

1968   Survey and excavations north and east of Navajo
        Mountain, Utah, 1959-1962. Museum of Northern
        Arizona, Bulletin 45, 400 pp.
            Reviewed AA 72:1549 (Irwin-Williams), AAq 38:243
        (Lipe).

LINDSAY, La Mar W. (See under Madsen, David B.)

LINNÉ, Sigvald

1946   Prehistoric and modern Hopi pottery. Ethnos, 2:
        89-98.

LINSKEY, Patricia K.

   1975   Cochise and Mogollon hunting patterns in west-central
           New Mexico. *In* Frisbie 1975a, pp. 246-271.

LINTON, Ralph

   1941   Some recent developments in Southwestern archaeology.
           Transactions of the New York Academy of Sciences,
           series 2, 4:66-69.

   1944a   North American cooking pots. American Antiquity,
           9, no. 4:369-380.

   1944b   Nomad raids and fortified pueblos. American Antiq-
           uity, 10:28-32.

LIPE, William D. (See also under Matson, Richard G.; Smith,
   Watson.)

   1958   Archaeological excavations in Glen Canyon: a pre-
           liminary report of 1958 work. Utah Archaeology,
           4, no. 4:4-13.

   1960   1958 excavations, Glen Canyon area. University of
           Utah, Anthropological Papers, 44, 241 pp.
           Reviewed AA 64:203 (Briggs), AAq 28:112 (Dittert).

   1964   A conservation model for American archaeology. Kiva,
           39, nos. 3-4:213-245.

   1967   Anasazi culture and its relationship to the environ-
           ment in the Red Rock Plateau region, southeastern
           Utah. Yale University, dissertation, 522 pp.;
           University Microfilms International.

   1970   Anasazi communities in the Red Rock Plateau, south-
           eastern Utah. *In* Longacre 1970b, pp. 84-139.

LIPE, W.D., and HUNTINGTON, C. Frank

   1969   Centrographic indices: some methods for analyzing
           complex areal distributions in archaeology. Kiva,
           35, no. 1:29-54.

LIPE, W.D., and LINDSAY, Alexander J., Jr.

   1974   Proceedings of the 1974 Cultural Resource Manage-
           ment Conference. Museum of Northern Arizona, Tech-
           nical Series, 14, 248 pp.

LIPE, W.D., and MATSON, Richard G.

   1971   Human settlement and resources in the Cedar Mesa

area, southeastern Utah. *In* Gumerman 1971, pp. 125-152.

1975   Archaeology and alluvium in the Grand Gulch-Cedar Mesa area, southeastern Utah. *In* Four Corners Geological Society Guidebook, 8th Field Conference, Farmington, pp. 103-110.

LIPE, W.D., and others

1960   1959 excavations, Glen Canyon area. University of Utah, Anthropological Papers, 49, 274 pp. Reviewed AAq 28:114 (McGregor).

1975   Lake Pagahrit, southeastern Utah. *In* Four Corners Geological Society Guidebook, 8th Field Conference, Farmington, pp. 67-71.

LISCHKA, Joseph J.

1975   Broken K revisited: a short discussion of factor analysis. American Antiquity, 40:220-227.

LISCHKA, Leslie

1969   A possible noncultural bias in lithic debris. American Antiquity, 34, no. 4:483-485.

LISTER, Florence C. (See also under Fowler, Don D.; Lister, Robert H.)

1964   Kaiparowits Plateau and Glen Canyon prehistory: an interpretation based on ceramics. University of Utah, Anthropological Papers, 71, 100 pp. Reviewed AA 69:403 (Longacre), AAq 32:414 (Smith).

LISTER, F.C., and LISTER, Robert H.

1966   Chihuahua: storehouse of storms. University of New Mexico Press, 360 pp.

1968   Earl Morris and Southwestern archaeology. University of New Mexico Press, 222 pp. Reviewed AA 71:157 (Fontana), AAq 34:91 (Judd).

1976   Distribution of Mexican maiolica along the northern borderlands. *In* Schroeder 1976, pp. 113-140.

LISTER, Robert H. (See also under Lister, Florence C.; Mangelsdorf, Paul C.; Wormington, H. Marie.)

1939   A report on the excavations made at Agua Zarca and La Morita in Chihuahua. Research, 3:42-54.

1940a   Arrows recovered from Long House ruin, Bandelier
        National Monument. Southwestern Monuments Monthly
        Report, January, pp. 64-66.

1940b   Otowi artifacts. Southwestern Monuments Monthly
        Report, October, pp. 272-277.

1946   Survey of archaeological remains in northwestern
        Chihuahua. Southwestern Journal of Anthropology,
        2:433-453.

1948   Notes on the archaeology of the Watrous Valley,
        New Mexico. El Palacio, 55:35-41.

1951a   Excavations at Hell's Midden, Dinosaur National
        Monument. University of Colorado Studies, Series
        in Anthropology, 3, 49 pp.
        Reviewed AAq 18:83 (Rudy).

1951b   Two projectile point types from Dinosaur National
        Monument, Colorado. Southwestern Lore, 17, no. 1:
        19-20.

1953a   The stemmed indented base point, a possible horizon
        marker. American Antiquity, 18:264-265.

1953b   Excavations in Cave Valley, Chihuahua, Mexico: a
        preliminary note. American Antiquity, 19:166-169.

1954   University of Colorado archaeological fieldwork,
        1952-1953. Southwestern Lore, 19, no. 4:3-4.

1957   Salvage archaeology in the Southwest. Southwestern
        Lore, 23:34-35.

1958a   Archaeological excavations in the northern Sierra
        Madre Occidental, Chihuahua and Sonora, Mexico.
        University of Colorado Studies, Series in Anthro-
        pology, 7, 121 pp.
        Reviewed AA 61:337 (A.E. Johnson), AAq 24:443
        (Kelley).

1958b   The Glen Canyon survey in 1957. University of Utah,
        Anthropological Papers, 30, 52 pp.
        Reviewed AA 60:980 (Meighan), AAq 24:212 (Wasley).

1958c   A preliminary note on excavations at the Coombs site,
        Boulder, Utah. Utah Archaeology, 4, no. 3:4-8.

1959a   The Glen Canyon right bank survey. *In* Jennings and
        others 1959, pt. 1, pp. 27-161.

1959b   The Waterpocket Fold: a distributional problem. *In*
        Jennings and others 1959, pt. 1, pp. 285-316.

1960a   Plugging the cultural gap. Desert Magazine, 23, no. 12:8-11.

1960b   History of archaeological fieldwork in northwestern Mexico. El Palacio, 67:118-124.

1961   Twenty-five years of archaeology in the Greater Southwest. American Antiquity, 27, no. 1:39-45.

1962   Archaeological survey of the Blue Mesa Reservoir, Colorado. Southwestern Lore, 28, no. 3:41-45.

1965   Contributions to Mesa Verde archaeology: II, site 875, Mesa Verde National Park, Colorado. University of Colorado Studies, Series in Anthropology, 11, 112 pp. Reviewed AA 69:101 (Ellis), AAq 32:122 (Brew).

1966   Contributions to Mesa Verde archaeology: III, site 866, and the cultural sequence at four villages in the Far View group, Mesa Verde National Park, Colorado. University of Colorado Studies, Series in Anthropology, 12, 117 pp.

1967   Contributions to Mesa Verde archaeology: IV, site 1086, an isolated, above-ground kiva in Mesa Verde National Park, Colorado. University of Colorado Studies, Series in Anthropology, 13, 25 pp.

1968a   Archaeology for layman and scientist at Mesa Verde. Science, 160:489-496.

1968b   (ed.) Contributions to Mesa Verde archaeology: V, emergency archaeology in Mesa Verde National Park, Colorado, 1948-1966. University of Colorado Studies, Series in Anthropology, 15, 108 pp.

1969a   Environment and man in Mesa Verde. Naturalist, 20, no. 2:31-37.

1969b   University of Colorado Archaeological Research Center. Naturalist, 20, no. 2:38-45.

1978   Mesoamerican influences at Chaco Canyon, New Mexico. *In* Riley and Hedrick 1978, pp. 233-241.

LISTER, R.H., and DICK, Herbert W.

1952   Archaeology of the Glade Park area: a progress report. Southwestern Lore, 17, no. 4:69-92.

LISTER, R.H., and LISTER, Florence C.

1964   Contributions to Mesa Verde archaeology: I, site

499, Mesa Verde National Park, Colorado. University of Colorado Studies, Series in Anthropology, 9, 91 pp.
Reviewed AA 67:1590 (Rohn), AAq 31:280 (Sharrock).

1969   The Earl H. Morris Memorial pottery collection. University of Colorado Studies, Series in Anthropology, 16, 94 pp.

LISTER, R.H., and SANBURG, Monte

1963   Artifacts from the Hauser site, Montrose, Colorado. Southwestern Lore, 28, no. 4:61-72.

LISTER, R.H., AMBLER, J. Richard, and LISTER, Florence C.

1959-   The Coombs site. University of Utah, Anthropological Papers, 41, pts. I-III, 126+300+144 pp.
61   Reviewed AA 65:415 (R.B. Woodbury), AAq 25:620 (Euler), 28:251 (Green).

LISTER, R.H., HALLISY, Stephen J., KANE, Margaret H., and McLELLAN, George E.

1970   Site 5LP11, a Pueblo I site near Ignacio, Colorado. Southwestern Lore, 35, no. 4:57-67.

LLOYD, Carl (See also under Martin, Paul Sidney.)

1938   Expedition to Southwest finds another prehistoric village. Field Museum News, 9, no. 10:1.

LOBO, Frank

1965   A year in the Verde Valley. Pacific Coast Archaeological Society, Quarterly, 1, no. 2:9-13.

LOCKETT, H. Claiborne

1934   Northern Arizona's first farmers. Museum of Northern Arizona, Museum Notes, 7, no. 4:14-16.

LOCKETT, H.C., and HARGRAVE, Lyndon L.

1953   Woodchuck Cave: a Basketmaker II site in Tsegi Canyon, Arizona. Museum of Northern Arizona, Bulletin 26, 33 pp.
Reviewed AAq 20:183 (Rinaldo).

LOEW, Oscar

1875   Report on the ruins of New Mexico. Annual Report

of the Geographical Explorations and Surveys West
of the 100th Meridian, pp. 174-178.

LOFGREN, Laurel (See under Turner, Christy G., II.)

LOHR, Edison P.

1948   Winter dig in Yampa Canyon. Desert Magazine, 11,
        no. 6:9-12.

LONG, Paul V., Jr.

1960   I. Archaeology of Curtain Cliff site. Plateau,
        33:17-18.

1966   Archaeological excavations in lower Glen Canyon,
        Utah, 1959-1960. Museum of Northern Arizona, Bul-
        letin 42, 80 pp.
        Reviewed AA 70:162 (Meighan), AAq 33:401 (Lipe).

LONGACRE, William A. (See also under Martin, Paul Sidney; Thompson, Raymond H.)

1962   Archaeological reconnaissance in eastern Arizona.
        In Martin, Rinaldo, and others 1962, pp. 148-167.

1964a   Archaeology as anthropology: a case study. Science,
        144:1454-1455.

1964b   A synthesis of upper Little Colorado prehistory,
        eastern Arizona. *In* Martin, Rinaldo, Longacre, and
        others 1964, pp. 201-215.

1966   Changing patterns of social integration: a prehis-
        toric example from the American Southwest. Amer-
        ican Anthropologist, 68:94-102.

1968   Some aspects of prehistoric society in east-central
        Arizona. *In* New Perspectives in Archaeology, ed.
        S.R. and L.R. Binford, Aldine Publishing Co., pp.
        89-102.

1970a   Archaeology as anthropology: a case study. Uni-
        versity of Arizona, Anthropological Papers, 17,
        57 pp.
        Reviewed AA 73:1391 (Brew), AAq 38:117 (Stanis-
        lawski).

1970b   (ed.) Reconstructing prehistoric Pueblo societies.
        School of American Research, Advanced Seminar Series,
        247 pp.
        Reviewed AA 74:133 (Ellis).

1973   Current directions in Southwestern archaeology.
        Annual Review of Anthropology, ed. B.J. Siegel,
        2:201-219.

1974   Models of cultural process; testing hypotheses:
        suggestions from Southwestern archaeology. *In*
        Reconstructing Complex Societies - an Archaeological
        Colloquium, ed. C. Moore, American Schools of Oriental
        Research, Cambridge, pp. 29-40.

1975   Population dynamics at the Grasshopper Pueblo, Ari-
        zona. *In* Swedlund 1975, pp. 71-74.

1976   Population dynamics at the Grasshopper Pueblo, Ari-
        zona. *In* Zubrow 1976, pp. 169-184.

LONGACRE, W.A., and AYRES, James E.

1968   Archaeological lessons from an Apache wickiup. *In*
        New Perspectives in Archaeology, ed. S.R. and L.R.
        Binford, Aldine Publishing Co., pp. 151-159.

LONGACRE, W.A., and GRAVES, Michael W.

1976   Probability sampling applied to an early multi-
        component surface site in east-central Arizona.
        Kiva, 41, nos. 3-4:277-287.

LONGACRE, W.A., and REID, J. Jefferson

1971   Research strategy for locational analysis: an out-
        line. *In* Gumerman 1971, pp. 103-110.

1974   The University of Arizona archaeological field
        school at Grasshopper: eleven years of multi-disci-
        plinary research and teaching. Kiva, 40, nos. 1-2:
        3-38.

LOOSE, Ann A.

1974   Archaeological excavations near Arroyo Hondo, Car-
        son National Forest, New Mexico. United States
        Forest Service, Southwestern Region, Archaeological
        Report no. 4, 47 pp.

LORRAIN, Dessamae (See also under Dibble, David S.)

1968a   Archaeological investigations in northwestern Crock-
        ett County, Texas, 1966-1967. State Building Com-
        mission Archaeological Program, Report no. 12, 71
        pp.

1968b   Excavation at Red Bluff shelter (Sotol site) X41CX8,
         Crockett County, Texas. Transactions of the 4th
         Regional Archaeological Symposium on Southeastern
         New Mexico and Western Texas, pp. 18-39.

LOTRICH, Victor F. (See also under Hurst, Clarence T.)

1938   Pendants from the San Francisco River, New Mexico.
         Colorado Magazine, 16, no. 1:28-30.

1939   Shortened-barb type arrowhead. Colorado Magazine,
         16, no. 6:210-212.

LOVE, Marian F.

1975   A survey of the distribution of T-shaped doorways
         in the Greater Southwest. *In* Frisbie 1975a, pp.
         296-311.

LUCAS, Ken

1972   A preview at Mesa Verde's Mug House. Popular Ar-
         chaeology, 1, no. 3:4-9.

LUEBBEN, Ralph A.

1953   Leaf Water site. *In* Wendorf 1953b, pp. 9-33.

1968   Site TA 32: a deep pit house and surface manifesta-
         tion in north-central New Mexico. *In* Papers on
         Taos Archaeology, Fort Burgwin Research Center, 7:
         43-57.
             Reviewed AA 71:1208 (Leone), AAq 35:233 (Gunner-
         son).

LUEBBEN, R.A., HEROLD, Laurence, and ROHN, Arthur

1960   An unusual Pueblo III ruin, Mesa Verde, Colorado.
         American Antiquity, 26:11-20.

LUEBBEN, R.A., ROHN, Arthur, and GIVENS, R. Dale

1962   A partially subterranean Pueblo III structure. El
         Palacio, 69:225-239.

LUHRS, Dorothy L.

1937a   (ed.) Hogan Number - Chaco Archaeological Station.
         El Palacio, 43:71-90.

1937b   Observations on the Rio Puerco of the East. El
         Palacio, 42:126-134.

268

The Bibliography

LUHRS, D.L., and ELY, Albert G.

    1939   Burial customs at Kuaua. El Palacio, 46, no. 2:
            27-32.

LUMHOLTZ, Carl

    1891a   Explorations in the Sierra Madre. Scribner's Month-
            ly Magazine (November):532-548.

    1891b   Report of explorations in northern Mexico. Bulletin
            of the American Geographical Society, 23, no. 3:
            386-402.

    1894   The American cave-dwellers. Bulletin of the Amer-
            ican Geographical Society, 26, no. 3:299-325.

    1902   Unknown Mexico. 2 vols., Charles Scribner's Sons,
            New York.
            Reviewed AA n.s. 5:345 (McGee).

    1912   New Trails in Mexico. Scribner, New York, 411 pp.

LUMMIS, Charles F.

    1896a   The cave city of the Tyuonyi. Land of Sunshine,
            5:11-20.

    1896b   The city of the cliff. Land of Sunshine, 5:184-190.

    1897   "Montezuma's Castle." Land of Sunshine, 6:70-72.

    1901   The Cliff-Dweller expedition. Land of Sunshine, 14,
            no. 3:220-222.

    1907   The Swallow's-Nest people. Out West, 26:485-514.

LUMMIS, C.F., and VOGT, Evon Z.

    1926   Inscription Rock. El Palacio, 21:232-237.

LUNDQUIST, Karen

    1963   A Verde Valley dig. Masterkey, 37, no. 1:18-21.

LUNT, Michael J. (See under Green, Dee F.)

LUTES, Eugene

    1959   A marginal prehistoric culture of northeastern New
            Mexico. El Palacio, 66, no. 2:59-68.

LYNN, W.M.

    1976   Archaeological testing at the Northeast Sewage

Treatment Plant, El Paso County, Texas. Texas Historical Commission, Archaeological Survey Report 15.

LYNN, W.M., BASKIN, B.J., and HUDSON, W.R., Jr.

1975   A preliminary archaeological reconnaissance of selected public free school lands in El Paso County, Texas. Texas Historical Commission, Archaeological Survey Report 13.

LYON, Marcus Ward, Jr.

1906   Mammal remains from two prehistoric village sites in New Mexico and Arizona. Proceedings of the United States National Museum, 31:647-649.

LYONS, Ray D.

1974   Old Agency fortified site, preliminary report. Southwestern Lore, 40, nos. 3-4:57-62.

LYONS, Thomas R.

1969   A study of the Paleo-Indian and Desert Culture complexes of the Estancia Valley area, New Mexico. University of New Mexico, dissertation, 448 pp.; University Microfilms International.

1976   (ed.) Remote sensing experiments in cultural resources studies: non-destructive methods of archaeological exploration, survey, and analysis. Reports of the Chaco Center, 1, National Park Service and University of New Mexico.

LYONS, T.R., and HITCHCOCK, Robert K.

1977   (ed.) Aerial remote sensing techniques in archaeology. Reports of the Chaco Center, 2, National Park Service and University of New Mexico.

LYONS, T.R., and SWITZER, Ronald R.

1975   Archaeological excavations at Tillery Springs, Estancia, New Mexico. *In* Frisbie 1975a, pp. 312-337.

LYONS, T.R., EBERT, James I., and HITCHCOCK, Robert K.

1976   Archaeological analysis of imagery of Chaco Canyon region, New Mexico. *In* ERTS-1, A New Window on Our Planet, ed. R.S. Williams, Jr., and W.D. Carter, United States Geological Survey, Professional Paper 929, pp. 304-306.

LYONS, T.R., POULS, Basil G., and HITCHCOCK, Robert K.

1972   The Kin Bineola irrigation study: an experiment in
the use of aerial remote sensing techniques in archaeology. Proceedings of the Third Annual Conference on Remote Sensing in Arid Lands, Office of
Arid Lands Studies, University of Arizona, pp. 266-
283.

LYTLE-WEBB, Jamie

1978   Pollen analysis in Southwestern archaeology. *In*
Grebinger 1978a, pp. 13-28.

MacCLARY, J.S.

1927   The first American farmers. Art and Archaeology,
24:83-88.

1929   El Morro, the desert register. Art and Archaeology,
28:167-169.

1935   Ancient American "mystery" stories. Southwestern
Lore, 1, no. 2:8-12.

MACGOWAN, Kenneth

1950   Early Man in the New World. Macmillan Co., New
York, 260 pp.
      Reviewed AA 53:262 (Strong), AAq 17:61 (Krieger).

MACGOWAN, K., and HESTER, Joseph A., Jr.

1962   Early Man in the New World. American Museum of
Natural History and Doubleday & Co., 333 pp.
      Reviewed AAq 28:569 (Hester).

MacHARG, J.B.

1926   The lions of Cochiti. El Palacio, 20:99-104.

MACKEY, James C. (See under Holbrook, Sally J.)

MACOMB, J.N.

1876   Report of the exploring expedition from Santa Fe,
New Mexico, to the junction of the Grand and Green
Rivers of the West in 1859. Government Printing
Office.

MADSEN, David B. (See also under Fowler, Don D.; Marwitt,
John P.)

1975a   Dating Paiute-Shoshoni expansion in the Great Basin.

American Antiquity, 40:82-86.

1975b   Three Fremont sites in Emery County, Utah. Division of State History (Utah), Antiquities Section, Selected Papers, 1, no. 1:1-28.

1976   Bulldozer Dune (42SL46). Division of State History (Utah), Antiquities Section, Selected Papers, 2, no. 6:59-66.

MADSEN, D.B., and BERRY, Michael S.

1975   A reassessment of northeastern Great Basin prehistory. American Antiquity, 40:391-405.

MADSEN, D.B., and LINDSAY, La Mar W.

1977   Backhoe Village. Division of State History (Utah), Antiquities Section, Selected Papers, 4, no. 12.

MADSEN, D.B., CURREY, D.R., and MADSEN, J.H.

1976   Man, mammoth, and lake fluctuations in Utah. Division of State History (Utah), Antiquities Section, Selected Papers, 2, no. 5:43-58.

MADSEN, J.H. (See under Madsen, David B.)

MADSEN, Rex E.

1977   Prehistoric ceramics of the Fremont. Museum of Northern Arizona, Ceramic Series, 6, 40 pp.

MAGERS, Pamela C.

1975   The cotton industry at Antelope House. *In* Rock and Morris 1975, pp. 39-48.

1976   Navajo settlement in Canyon del Muerto. University of Arizona, dissertation, 230 pp.; University Microfilms International.

MAGOFFIN, Ralph V.D.

1929   Excavations in New Mexico. El Palacio, 26, nos. 9-12:163-172.

1930   A thousand miles of American archaeology. El Palacio, 28:61-71.

MAHER, Thomas M.

1966   Mesa Verde, the prehistoric cliff dwellers and the

effect of the supernova of 1054 A.D. Tri-State
Printing Co., Cincinnati.

MALCOLM, Roy L.

1939   Archaeological remains, supposedly Navaho, from
        Chaco Canyon, New Mexico. American Antiquity, 5:
        4-20.

MALDE, Harold E. (See also under Danson, Edward B.)

1964   Environment and man in arid America. Science, 145,
        no. 3628:123-129.

MALDE, H.E., and SCHICK, Asher P.

1964   Thorne Cave, northeastern Utah: geology. American
        Antiquity, 30:60-73.

MALLERY, Garrick

1886   Pictographs of the North American Indians: a pre-
        liminary paper. Fourth Annual Report of the Bureau
        of American Ethnology, pp. 4-256.

1893   Picture-writing of the American Indians. Tenth
        Annual Report of the Bureau of American Ethnology,
        pp. 3-807.

MALLORY, Oscar L. (See under Husted, Wilfred M.)

MALOUF, Carling

1939   Prehistoric exchange in Utah. University of Utah,
        Anthropological Papers, 1, 8 pp.

1940   Prehistoric exchange in the northern periphery of
        the Southwest. American Antiquity, 6:115-122.

1941   Notes on the archaeology of the Barrier Canyon re-
        gion, Utah. Masterkey, 15, no. 4:150-153.

1944   Thoughts on Utah archaeology. American Antiquity,
        9:319-328.

1946   The Deep Creek region, the northwestern frontier
        of the Pueblo culture. American Antiquity, 12:117-
        121.

MALOUF, C., DIBBLE, Charles E., and SMITH, Elmer R.

1940   The archaeology of the Deep Creek region, Utah.
        University of Utah, Anthropological Papers, 5, 27
        pp.

MANGELSDORF, Paul C. (See also under Galinat, Walton C.)

1958   Archaeological evidence on the evolution of maize
        in northwestern Mexico. *In* Lister, R.H., 1958a,
        pp. 96-109.

MANGELSDORF, P.C., and LISTER, Robert H.

1956   Archaeological evidence on the evolution of maize
        in northwestern Mexico. Harvard University Botan-
        ical Museum, Leaflets, 17, no. 6:151-178.

MANGELSDORF, P.C., and SMITH, C.E., Jr.

1949   New archaeological evidence on evolution in maize.
        Harvard University Botanical Museum, Leaflets, 13,
        no. 8.

MANGELSDORF, P.C., DICK, Herbert, W., and CAMARA-HERNANDEZ, J.

1967   Bat Cave revisited. Harvard University Botanical
        Museum, Leaflets, 22, no. 1:1-37.

MANIRE, Larry (See under Harlan, Mark.)

MANNING, William C.

1875   Ancient pueblos of New Mexico and Arizona. Harper's
        New Monthly Magazine, 51:327-333.

MARKLEY, Max C.

1941   Distribution of Pueblo pottery in southeastern New
        Mexico. Minnesota Archaeologist, 7, no. 2:87-95.

MARMON, Lee H., and PEARL, George Clayton

1958   A fortified site near Ojo del Padre: Big Bead Mesa
        revisited. El Palacio, 65:136-142.

MARQUARDT, William H.

1974   A temporal perspective on late prehistoric societies
        in the eastern Cibola area: factor analytic approach-
        es to short-term chronological investigation. Wash-
        ington University, dissertation, 293 pp.; University
        Microfilms International.

MARQUART, Cynthia

1968   Basic data on early sites in Colorado and adjacent
        regions. Southwestern Lore, 34, no. 1:21-30.

MARQUINA, Ignacio

    1944   Los monumentos de México y los del suroeste y
            sureste de Estados Unidos. Tercera Reunión de
            Mesa Redonda sobre problemas antropológicos de
            México y Centro América, Sociedad mexicana de Antro-
            pología, pp. 252-255.

MARR, John W. (See under Erdman, James A.)

MARRIOTT, Alice

    1952   Indians of the Four Corners: a book about the Ana-
            sazi Indians and their modern descendants.   Thomas
            Y. Crowell Co., New York, 229 pp.

MARRS, Otis

    1953   Some Mimbres pottery finds.   Central Texas Archae-
            ologist, 6:88-101.

MARSHALL, Michael P. (See also under Carroll, Charles.)

    1973   Background information on the Jornada culture area.
            In Human Systems Research 1973, pp. 49-119.

MARTIN, George Castor (See also under Gardner, Fletcher.)

    1933   The Big Bend Basket Maker.   Southwest Texas Archae-
            ological Society, Big Bend Basket Maker Papers, no.
            1, Witte Memorial Museum, Bulletin 1, 14 pp.

    1934   Archaeological exploration of the Shumla Caves.
            Southwest Texas Archaeological Society, Big Bend
            Basket Maker Papers, no. 3, Witte Memorial Museum,
            Bulletin 3, 94 pp.

    1935   Report on four Shumla Cave packets.   Bulletin of
            the Texas Archaeological and Paleontological Soci-
            ety, 7:115-117.

MARTIN, G.C, and WOOLFORD, Samuel

    1932   Painted pebbles of the Texas Big Bend.   Bulletin
            of the Texas Archaeological and Paleontological
            Society, 4:20-24.

MARTIN, H.T. (See also under Williston, S.W.)

    1909   Further notes on the Pueblo ruins of Scott County.
            Kansas University Science Bulletin, 5, no. 2:11-22.

MARTIN, Paul Schultz (See also under Callen, Eric O.; Mehringer, Peter J.)

1963a   Early Man in Arizona: the pollen evidence. American Antiquity, 29, no. 1:67-73.

1963b   The last 10,000 years: a fossil pollen record of the American Southwest. University of Arizona Press, 87 pp.

1967   Prehistoric overkill. *In* Pleistocene Extinctions: the Search for a Cause, ed. P.S. Martin and H.E. Wright, Jr., Yale University Press, pp. 75-120.

MARTIN, P.S., and BYERS, William

1965   Pollen and archaeology at Wetherill Mesa. *In* Osborne 1965a, pp. 122-135.

MARTIN, P.S., and MEHRINGER, Peter J., Jr.

1965   Pleistocene pollen analysis and biogeography of the Southwest. *In* The Quarternary of the United States, ed. H.E. Wright, Jr., and David G. Frey, Princeton University Press, pp. 433-451.

MARTIN, P.S., and SCHOENWETTER, James

1960   Arizona's oldest cornfield. Science, 132:33-34.

MARTIN, P.S., and SHARROCK, Floyd W.

1964   Pollen analysis of prehistoric human feces: a new approach to ethnobotany. American Antiquity, 30, no. 2:168-180.

MARTIN, P.S., SCHOENWETTER, J., and ARMS, B.C.

1961   Southwestern palynology and prehistory: the last 10,000 years. University of Arizona, Program in Geochronology, Contribution no. 50.

MARTIN, Paul Sidney

1927   The Pecos Conference on Southwest Archaeology. Colorado Magazine, 4, no. 5:180-182.

1929a   The 1928 archaeological expedition of the State Historical and Natural History Society of Colorado. Colorado Magazine, 6, no. 1:1-35.

1929b   Tower and kiva in one. El Palacio, 26:323-325.

1930a   Archaeological expedition to the Southwest.   Field
        Museum News, 1, no. 11:3.

1930b   Kiva revealed on Lowry ruin.   Field Museum News, 1,
        no. 19:1.

1930c   The 1929 archaeological expedition of the State His-
        torical Society of Colorado.   Colorado Magazine, 7,
        no. 1:1-40.

1931a   Expedition to the Southwest returns with collections.
        Field Museum News, 2, no. 11:3.

1931b   Recent archaeological excavations in southwestern
        Colorado.   Pan American Magazine, 44, no. 3:228-236.

1933   Archaeology of North America.   Field Museum of Natur-
        al History, 122 pp.
           Reviewed AA 37:498 (McKern).

1934   The bow-drill in North America.   American Anthro-
        pologist, 36:94-97.

1938a   Ancient Colorado village and temple uncovered.
        Field Museum News, 9, no. 9:3.

1938b   Expedition to Southwest ends successful season.
        Field Museum News, 9, no. 11:3.

1941   Expedition discovers new prehistoric house type.
        Field Museum News, 12, no. 11:4-5.

1942   Recent Mogollon discoveries.   Scientific Monthly,
        54:385-389.

1943   The SU site: excavations at a Mogollon village,
        western New Mexico, second season, 1941.   Field Mu-
        seum of Natural History, Anthropological Series,
        32, no. 2, pp. 99-271.
           Reviewed AA 48:251 (Haury & Sayles), AAq 9:361
        (Reed).

1946   Nature imposed rationing on the Mogollon Indians.
        Chicago Natural History Museum Bulletin, 17, nos.
        9-10:1-2.

1947   Delving into unwritten history of the Southwest.
        Chicago Natural History Museum Bulletin, 18, no.
        11:1-2.

1950a   Resurrecting a prehistoric Indian village.   Chicago
        Natural History Museum Bulletin, 21, no. 2:4-5.

1950b   Mummies, sandals, snares from Mogollons' cave.
        Chicago Natural History Museum Bulletin, 21, no.
        11:6-7.

1951a   Expedition finds victim of sacrifice in cliff house.
         Chicago Natural History Museum Bulletin, 22, no. 11:
         3-4.

1951b   The peoples of Pine Lawn Valley. Scientific American,
         185, no. 1:46-51.

1952   With pick and shovel in Pine Lawn Valley. Archae-
         ology, 5:14-21.

1953a   Further discoveries in Pine Lawn Valley. Archae-
         ology, 6:217-220.

1953b   Southwest expedition digs at a mystery. Chicago
         Natural History Museum Bulletin, 24, no. 6:3-4.

1954a   Chicago Natural History Museum archaeological field-
         work, 1953. Southwestern Lore, 19, no. 4:11-12.

1954b   The Mogollon culture in western New Mexico. South-
         western Lore, 20, no. 1:1-4.

1955   "D.P.'s" of 14th century in our Southwest. Bulletin
         of the Chicago Natural History Museum, 26, no. 11:
         6-7.

1957a   History of an ancient people unfolds in Arizona.
         Bulletin of the Chicago Natural History Museum, 28,
         no. 11:3-4.

1957b   Recent archaeological work in Arizona of the Chicago
         Natural History Museum. Kiva, 23, no. 2:19-20.

1958   Cultural crossroads of the Southwest. Bulletin of
         the Chicago Natural History Museum, 29, no. 11:3, 5.

1959a   Digging into History: a brief account of fifteen
         years of archaeological work in New Mexico. Chicago
         Natural History Museum, Popular Series, Anthropology,
         no. 38, 157 pp.
            Reviewed AA 62:727 (McKusick), AAq 25:282 (Wor-
         mington).

1959b   Katchina cult traced back to A.D. 1250. Bulletin
         of the Chicago Natural History Museum, 30, no. 9:
         7-8.

1959c   Mystery of handwriting on the wall in Southwest.
         Bulletin of the Chicago Natural History Museum, 30,
         no. 11:6-7, 11.

1961   A human effigy of stone from a great kiva near
         Springerville, Arizona. Kiva, 26, no. 4:1-5.

1962   Archaeological investigations in east-central Arizona.

Science, 139:825-827.

1966   Putting together the pieces. Field Museum of Natur-
       al History, Bulletin, 37, no. 6:6-7.

1967   Hay Hollow site. Field Museum of Natural History,
       Bulletin, 38, no. 5:6-10.

1968   Lowry Pueblo, then and now. Field Museum of Natural
       History, Bulletin, 39, no. 4.

1974   Early development in Mogollon research. *In* Archae-
       ological Researches in Retrospect, ed. G.R. Willey,
       Winthrop Publishers, Inc., pp. 3-29.

MARTIN, P.S., and BARTER, James T.

1954   Great Kiva, two pueblos uncovered on Southwest dig.
       Bulletin of the Chicago Natural History Museum, 25,
       no. 10:4-5.

MARTIN, P.S., and FRITZ, John

1966   Prehistoric social change in east central Arizona.
       Field Museum of Natural History, Bulletin, 36.

MARTIN, P.S., and JOHNSON, Leonard G.

1948   Peace from 4000 B.C. to A.D. 1000 in Indian Utopia.
       Chicago Natural History Museum Bulletin, 19, no.
       11:3, 5.

MARTIN, P.S., and PLOG, Fred

1973   The archaeology of Arizona: a study of the South-
       west region. Natural History Press, 422 pp.
       Reviewed AAq 41:243 (Washburn).

MARTIN, P.S., and RINALDO, John B.

1939   Modified Basket-Maker sites, Ackmen-Lowry area,
       southwestern Colorado, 1938. Field Museum of Nat-
       ural History, Anthropological Series, 23, no. 3,
       pp. 305-499.
       Reviewed AA 43:455 (Baldwin), AAq 6:378 (Morris).

1947   The SU site: excavations at a Mogollon village,
       western New Mexico, 3rd season, 1946. Field Mu-
       seum of Natural History, Anthropological Series,
       32, no. 3, pp. 273-382.
       Reviewed AAq 14:137 (Hurt).

1950a Turkey Foot Ridge site, a Mogollon village, Pine

Lawn Valley, western New Mexico. Fieldiana: Anthropology, 38, no. 2, pp. 235-396.
Reviewed AA 54:88 (Brainerd).

1950b Sites of the Reserve Phase, Pine Lawn Valley, western New Mexico. Fieldiana: Anthropology, 38, no. 3, pp. 401-577.

1951 The Southwestern co-tradition. Southwestern Journal of Anthropology, 7, no. 3:215-229.

1960a Excavations in the upper Little Colorado drainage, eastern Arizona. Fieldiana: Anthropology, 51, no. 1, pp. 1-127.
Reviewed AA 62:1106 (R.B. Woodbury), AAq 26:446 (Sayles).

1960b Table Rock Pueblo, Arizona. Fieldiana: Anthropology, 51, no. 2, pp. 129-298.
Reviewed AA 63:871 (Jennings), AAq 27:129 (Wheat).

MARTIN, P.S., and WILLIS, Elizabeth S.

1940 Anasazi painted pottery in Field Museum of Natural History. Field Museum of Natural History, Anthropology, Memoirs, 5, 284 pp.
Reviewed AA 44:305 (Hall), AAq 7:197 (Colton).

MARTIN, P.S., HILL, J.N., and LONGACRE, W.A.

1966 Documentation for chapters in the prehistory of eastern Arizona, III. Archives of Archaeology, 27, 351 pp. (microcards).

MARTIN, P.S., LLOYD, Carl, and SPOEHR, Alexander

1938 Archaeological work in the Ackmen-Lowry area, southwestern Colorado, 1937. Field Museum of Natural History, Anthropological Series, 23, no. 2, pp. 217-304.
Reviewed AA 41:484 (Brew), AAq 6:378 (Morris).

MARTIN, P.S., LONGACRE, William, and HILL, James N.

1967 Chapters in the prehistory of eastern Arizona, III. Fieldiana: Anthropology, 57, 178 pp.
Reviewed AA 71:351 (Sciscenti), AAq 34:94 (Beeson).

MARTIN, P.S., QUIMBY, George I., and COLLIER, Donald

1947 Indians before Columbus. University of Chicago Press, 582 pp.
Reviewed AA 51:309 (Guthe), AAq 13:184 (Strong).

MARTIN, P.S., RINALDO, J.B., and ANTEVS, Ernst

   1949   Cochise and Mogollon sites, Pine Lawn Valley, west-
           ern New Mexico. Fieldiana: Anthropology, 38, no.
           1, pp. 1-232.
           Reviewed AA 52:419 (Rouse), AAq 17:154 (Lehmer).

MARTIN, P.S., RINALDO, J.B., and BARTER, Eloise R.

   1957   Late Mogollon communities: four sites of the Tula-
           rosa Phase, western New Mexico. Fieldiana: Anthro-
           pology, 49, no. 1, pp. 1-144.
           Reviewed AA 60:197 (Haury), AAq 24:93 (Smith).

MARTIN, P.S., RINALDO, J.B., and BLUHM, Elaine

   1954   Caves of the Reserve area. Fieldiana: Anthropology,
           42, 227 pp.
           Reviewed AA 57:1092 (Roberts), AAq 21:90 (Wheat).

MARTIN, P.S., RINALDO, J.B., and KELLY, Marjorie

   1940   The SU site: excavations at a Mogollon village,
           western New Mexico, 1939. Field Museum of Natural
           History, Anthropological Series, 32, no. 1, pp. 1-97.
           Reviewed AA 44:703 (McGregor), AAq 7:192 (Nesbitt).

MARTIN, P.S., RINALDO, J.B., and LONGACRE, William A.

   1960   Documentation for some late Mogollon sites in the
           upper Little Colorado drainage, eastern Arizona.
           Archives of Archaeology, 6, 199 pp. (3 microcards).

   1961   Mineral Creek site and Hooper Ranch Pueblo, eastern
           Arizona. Fieldiana: Anthropology, 52, 181 pp.
           Reviewed AA 64:441 (R.B. Woodbury), AAq 27:605
           (Gell).

   1964   Documentation for chapters in the prehistory of
           eastern Arizona, II. Archives of Archaeology, 24,
           365 pp. (7 microcards).

MARTIN, P.S., ROYS, Lawrence, and VON BONIN, Gerhardt

   1936   Lowry Ruin in southwestern Colorado. Field Museum
           of Natural History, Anthropological Series, 23, no.
           1, pp. 1-216.
           Reviewed AA 39:328 (Hawley), AAq 3:288 (Haury).

MARTIN, P.S., RINALDO, J.B., BLUHM, E., and CUTLER, Hugh C.

   1956   Higgins Flat Pueblo, western New Mexico. Fieldiana:

Anthropology, 45, 218 pp.
Reviewed AA 59:374 (Schroeder), AAq 23:201 (Danson).

MARTIN, P.S., RINALDO, J.B., LONGACRE, W.A., and FREEMAN, Leslie G., Jr.

1961 Documentation for prehistoric investigations in the upper Little Colorado drainage, eastern Arizona. Archives of Archaeology, 13, 139 pp. (3 microcards).

MARTIN, P.S., RINALDO, J.B., BLUHM, E., CUTLER, H.C., and GRANGE, Roger, Jr.

1952 Mogollon cultural continuity and change: the stratigraphic analysis of Tularosa and Cordova Caves. Fieldiana: Anthropology, 40, 528 pp. Reviewed AA 55:594 (Wendorf), AAq 19:298 (Kidder).

MARTIN, P.S., and others

1975 Chapters in the prehistory of eastern Arizona, IV. Fieldiana: Anthropology, 65, 174 pp.

MARTIN, P.S., RINALDO, J.B., and others

1961 Chapters in the prehistory of eastern Arizona, I. Fieldiana: Anthropology, 53, 244 pp. Reviewed AA 66:193 (Wendorf), AAq 29:530 (Di Peso).

MARTIN, P.S., RINALDO, J.B., LONGACRE, W.A., and others

1964 Chapters in the prehistory of eastern Arizona, II. Fieldiana: Anthropology, 55, 261 pp. Reviewed AA 68:1565 (Olson).

MARTINEZ DEL RIO, Pablo

1944 El panorama prehistorico. Tercera Reunión de Mesa Redonda sobre problemas antropológicos de México y Centro América, pp. 157-162. Sociedad mexicana de Antropología.

MARWITT, John P. (See also under Hammond, Philip C.; Sharrock, Floyd W.)

1967 Preliminary survey of the Manti-La Sal National Forest. University of Utah, Miscellaneous Collected Papers, no. 16, Anthropological Papers, 89:33-49. Reviewed AAq 36:227 (Ambler).

1968 Pharo Village. University of Utah, Anthropological Papers, 91, 84 pp. Reviewed AAq 36:224 (Lipe).

MARWITT, J.P., and FRY, Gary F.

    1973   Radiocarbon dates from Utah. Southwestern Lore, 38,
            no. 4:1-9.

MARWITT, J.P., FRY, G.F., and ADOVASIO, J.M.

    1971   Sandwich Shelter. *In* Aikens 1971, pp. 27-36.

MARWITT, J.P., MADSEN, David B., DALLEY, Gardiner F., and ADO-
VASIO, James

    1970   Median Village and Fremont culture regional varia-
            tion. University of Utah, Anthropological Papers,
            95, 193 pp.
            Reviewed AA 77:129 (Sharrock).

MASHBURN, C.H.R. (See under Gauthier, Rory.)

MASLAND, Frank E.

    1962   The land of the Anasazi. Explorers' Journal, 40,
            no. 3:14-30.

MASON, Edith Hart

    1948   The Cave of the Flutists. Masterkey, 22, no. 1:
            6-9.

MASON, J. Alden

    1928   Some unusual spear throwers of ancient America.
            University of Pennsylvania Museum Journal, 19, no.
            3:290-323.

    1930   The Texas expedition. University of Pennsylvania
            Museum Journal, 20:318-339.

    1936   Notes on the archaeology of southwestern Texas.
            Bulletin of the Texas Archaeological and Paleonto-
            logical Society, 8:192-195.

MASON, Otis T.

    1897   The cliff-dweller's sandal, a study in comparative
            technology. Popular Science Monthly, 50:676-679.

    1904   Aboriginal American basketry. Report of the United
            States National Museum for 1902, pp. 171-548.
            Reviewed AA n.s. 6:710 (Goddard).

MASSE, W. Bruce (See also under Cleveland, David A.; Franklin, Hayward H.)

1976   The Hohokam expressway project: a study of prehistoric irrigation in the Salt River Valley, Arizona. Arizona State Museum, Contributions to Highway Salvage Archaeology in Arizona, 43, 88 pp.

MATHENY, Ray T.

1971   Possible approach to population distribution studies in southeastern Utah. *In* Gumerman 1971, pp. 152-164.

MATHEWS, Tom W. (See under Vivian, R. Gordon.)

MATSON, Richard G. (See also under Lipe, William D.)

1971   Adaptation and environment in the Cerbat Mountains, Arizona. University of California (Davis), dissertation, 333 pp.; University Microfilms International.

1974   The determination of archaeological structure: an example from the Cerbat Mountains, Arizona. Plateau, 47, no. 1:26-40.

MATSON, R.G., and LIPE, W.D.

1975   Regional sampling: a case study of Cedar Mesa, Utah. *In* Sampling in Archaeology, ed. J.W. Mueller, University of Arizona Press, pp. 124-143.

1978   Settlement patterns on Cedar Mesa: boom and bust on the northern periphery. *In* Euler and Gumerman 1978, pp. 1-12.

MATTHEWS, Washington

1894   Explorations in the Salado Valley. The Archaeologist, 2, no. 12:351-366.

1899   The cities of the dead. Land of Sunshine, 12:213+.

MATHEWS, W., WORMAN, J.L., and BILLINGS, J.S.

1893   The human bones of the Hemenway collection in the United States Army Medical Museum at Washington. Memoirs of the National Academy of Sciences, 6: 139-286.
      Reviewed AA o.s. 8:86 (Baker).

MAULE, Stuart H.

1963   Corn growing at Wupatki. Plateau, 36, no. 1:29-32.

MAXON, James C.

1961   A pit complex in the Aztec Ruin. Southwestern Lore,
        27, no. 3:33-36.

MAYER, Dorothy

1976   Some comments on an astronomical petroglyph panel
        in Capitol Reef National Park reported and described
        by Klaus F. Wellmann. Southwestern Lore, 42, nos.
        1-2:14-20.

MAYNARD, C.C.

1911   Hieroglyphics near Benjamin, Utah.   Improvement
        Era, 14, no. 6:582-590.

MAYRO, Linda L., WHITTLESEY, Stephanie M., and REID, J. Jef-
    ferson

1976   Observations on the Salado presence at Grasshopper
        Pueblo. *In* Doyel and Haury 1976, pp. 85-94.

McALLISTER, M.E.

1977   Description and analysis of the polychrome pottery
        excavated from Superior, Arizona, AZ U:12:2 (ASU),
        Tonto National Forest. U.S. Forest Service, South-
        western Region, Miscellaneous Paper no. 11, Archae-
        ological Report no. 15:110-136.

McALLISTER, S.L.

1977   An analysis of the ground stone tools recovered
        from sites AZ U:12:2 (ASU) through AZ U:12:7 (ASU),
        Tonto National Forest, Arizona. U.S. Forest Service,
        Southwestern Region, Miscellaneous Paper no. 10,
        Archaeological Report no. 15:82-109.

McCABE, Helen M.

1973   The settlement system of five prehistoric Pueblo
        sites of the Upper Purgatoire complex. Southwest-
        ern Lore, 39, no. 3:12-29.

McCABE, Robert A.

1955   The prehistoric engineer-farmers of Chihuahua.

Transactions of the Wisconsin Academy of Science,
Arts and Letters, 44:75-85.

McCANN, Franklin T. (See also under Bryan, Kirk.)

1940   A new source for agate artifacts in central New
        Mexico. Science, 92:259.

McCLELLAN, Carole

1976   Archaeological survey of Vail-Bicknell transmission
        line. Arizona State Museum, Archaeological Series,
        97, 23 pp.

McCLELLAN, C., and VOGLER, Lawrence E.

1977   An archaeological assessment of Luke Air Force
        Range located in southwestern Arizona. Arizona
        State Museum, Archaeological Series, 113, 143 pp.

McCLUNEY, Eugene B.

1961   The Hatchet site: a preliminary report. Southwest-
        ern Lore, 26, no. 4:70-72.

1962   A new name and revised description for a Mogollon
        pottery type from southern New Mexico. Southwestern
        Lore, 27, no. 4:49-55.

1965   Clanton Draw and Box Canyon: an interim report on
        two prehistoric sites in Hidalgo County, New Mexico.
        School of American Research, Monographs, no. 26,
        55 pp.
        Reviewed AAq 31:752 (McGregor).

1968   A Mimbres shrine at the West Baker site. Archae-
        ology, 21, no. 3:196-205.

1973   Bobcat Cave: a contribution to the ethnohistory of
        the Spanish borderlands. Texas Christian University,
        dissertation, 340 pp.; University Microfilms Inter-
        national.

McCONNELL, Robert B., and CRIM, J.J., Jr.

1941   Buried hearths and pottery in alluvium of the Finlay
        Mountains, Texas. Field and Laboratory (Dallas);
        Contributions from the Science Departments, 9:48-52.

McDONALD, James A.

1976   An archaeological assessment of Canyon de Chelly
        National Monument. National Park Service, Western

Archaeological Center, Publications in Anthropology, 5, 156 pp.

McDONALD, J.A., and others

1974 Archaeological survey of the T.G. & E. El Sol-Vail transmission line. Arizona State Museum, Archaeological Series, 53, 152 pp.

McFARLAND, Elizabeth Fleming

1967· Forever frontier; the Gila cliff dwellings. University of New Mexico, Publications Office, 62 pp.

McGIMSEY, Charles R., III

1951 Peabody Museum Upper Gila Expedition - Pueblo Division preliminary report, 1950 season. El Palacio, 58:299-312.

McGREGOR, John C.

1930 Tree ring dating. Museum of Northern Arizona, Museum Notes, 3, no. 4:1-4.

1931 Prehistoric cotton fabrics of Arizona. Museum of Northern Arizona, Museum Notes, 4, no. 2:1-4.

1932 Additional prehistoric dates from Arizona. Museum of Northern Arizona, Museum Notes, 5, no. 3:13-16.

1934 Dates from the Tsegi. Tree-Ring Bulletin, 1, no. 1:6-8.

1935 Additional houses beneath the ash from Sunset Crater. Museum of Northern Arizona, Museum Notes, 8, no. 5: 25-28.

1936a Additional dates from Tsegi. Tree-Ring Bulletin, 2, no. 4:37.

1936b Ball courts in northern Arizona? Museum of Northern Arizona, Museum Notes, 8, no. 11:55-58.

1936c Culture of sites which were occupied shortly before the eruption of Sunset Crater. Museum of Northern Arizona, Bulletin 9, 52 pp.

1936d Dates from Tsegi and Nalakihu. Tree-Ring Bulletin, 3, no. 2:15-16.

1936e Dating the eruption of Sunset Crater, Arizona. American Antiquity, 2, no. 1:15-26.

1936f The time factor in archaeology. Southwestern Lore,

2, no. 2:39-40.

1937a A small island of culture near Flagstaff, Arizona. Southwestern Lore, 3, no. 2:28-32.

1937b Winona Village: a prehistoric site showing Hohokam influence in the Flagstaff area. Museum of Northern Arizona, Museum Notes, 9, no. 7:39-42.

1937c Winona Village, a XIIth century settlement with a ball court near Flagstaff, Arizona. Museum of Northern Arizona, Bulletin 12, 53 pp.

1938a How some important northern Arizona pottery types were dated. Museum of Northern Arizona, Bulletin 13, 19 pp.

1938b Some Southwestern dated ruins: III. Tree-Ring Bulletin, 4, no. 4:6.

1939 Archaeological problems. Southwestern Lore, 5, no. 3:52-56.

1941a Southwestern Archaeology. John Wiley and Sons, New York, 403 pp.
       Reviewed AAq 8:191 (Brew).

1941b Winona and Ridge Ruin, Part I: architecture and material culture. Museum of Northern Arizona, Bulletin 18, 313 pp.
       Reviewed AA 43:654 (Rinaldo and Martin), AAq 8: 188 (Roberts).

1942a Dates from Wupatki Pueblo. Tree-Ring Bulletin, 8, no. 3:18-21.

1942b Dates from Kinnikinnick Pueblo. Tree-Ring Bulletin, 8, no. 3:21-23.

1943 Burial of an early American magician. Proceedings of the American Philosophical Society, 86, no. 2: 270-298.

1945a Nose plugs from northern Arizona. American Antiquity, 10:303-307.

1945b An unfired sherd from Black Dog Cave. Plateau, 17, no. 4:68-69.

1947 Archaeology and social change. Transactions of the Illinois State Academy of Science, 40:9-24.

1948 A clay sandal last from Utah. Plateau, 21, no. 2: 24-28.

1950a Excavation of Cohonina sites, 1949. Plateau, 22,

no. 4:68-74.

1950b   Weighted traits and traditions. *In* Reed and King
        1950, pp. 291-298.

1951   The Cohonina culture of northwestern Arizona. Uni-
        versity of Illinois Press, 158 pp.
        Reviewed AAq 18:79 (Schroeder).

1955   A Sinagua kiva. Plateau, 27, no. 3:11-17.

1956   The 1955 Pollock site excavation. Plateau, 28, no.
        3:49-54.

1958   The Pershing site. Plateau, 31, no. 2:33-36.

1961   The Pershing site in northern Arizona. Plateau,
        34:23-27.

1965   Southwestern Archaeology. (2nd ed.) University
        of Illinois Press, 511 pp.
        Reviewed AA 68:813 (Woodbury), AAq 31:883 (Rouse).

1967   The Cohonina culture of Mount Floyd, Arizona. Uni-
        versity of Kentucky, Studies in Anthropology, no. 5,
        145 pp.
        Reviewed AA 70:635 (Euler), AAq 33:268 (Kelly).

McGREGOR, J.C., and WETHERILL, Milton A.

1939   Winona Village, 1938 (a report of progress). Mu-
        seum of Northern Arizona, Museum Notes, 11, no. 7:
        51-54.

McGUIRE, Randall H.

1977   The Copper Canyon-McGuireville project: archaeologi-
        cal investigations in the middle Verde Valley, Ari-
        zona. Arizona State Museum, Contributions to High-
        way Salvage Archaeology in Arizona, 45, 143 pp.

McKEE, Barbara H.

1933   A large cliff dwelling. Grand Canyon Nature Notes,
        8, no. 7:198-201.

McKEE, Edwin D.

1945   Oak Creek Canyon. Plateau, 18, no. 2:25-32.

McKEE, Thomas M.

1935   Experiences in Mesa Verde. Southwestern Lore, 1,
        no. 2:17-22.

McKERN, William C.

1978   Western Colorado petroglyphs (ed. by Douglas D. Scott). Bureau of Land Management (Colorado), Cultural Resources Series, no. 8, 112 pp.

McKNIGHT, Daniel (See under Hurt, Wesley R., Jr.)

McKUSICK, Marshall

1961   Puebloid cultures in Iron County; progress report. Utah Archaeology, 7, no. 2:19-24.

McLELLAN, George Edwin (See also under Lister, Robert H.)

1969   The origin, development, and typology of Anasazi kivas and great kivas. University of Colorado, dissertation, 205 pp.; University Microfilms International.

McLELLAN, G.E., and HALLISY, Stephen J.

1970   Salvage excavation of site 5MTUMR1268 in Mancos Canyon, Ute Mountain Indian Reservation, Colorado. Southwestern Lore, 35, no. 4:68-75.

McLOYD, Charles, and GRAHAM, C.C.

1894   Catalogue and description of a very large collection of prehistoric relics, obtained in the cliff houses and caves of southeastern Utah. Durango, Colorado, 42 pp.
        Reviewed in The Archaeologist, 2:184.

McNITT, Frank

1957   Richard Wetherill: Anasazi. University of New Mexico Press, 370 pp.
        Reviewed AAq 24:94 (Gillmor).

McNUTT, Charles H. (See also under Allen, Joseph W.)

1969   Early Puebloan occupations at Tesuque By-pass and in the upper Rio Grande Valley. University of Michigan Museum of Anthropology, Anthropological Papers, 40, 133 pp.
        Reviewed AAq 36:225 (Glassow).

1975   Wing-walls and weeping eyes. *In* Frisbie 1975a, pp. 360-370.

McNUTT, C.H., and EULER, Robert C.

    1966   The Red Butte lithic sites near Grand Canyon, Ari-
            zona. American Antiquity, 31:410-419.

McPHERSON, Gale (See also under Zier, Christian J.)

    1975   White Mountain Redware from NA11,527 and NA11,530.
            Pottery Southwest, 2, no. 3:4-5.

McWHIRT, Jean

    1939   Esther. Mesa Verde Notes, 9, no. 1:1-5.

McWILLIAMS, Kenneth Richard (See also under Fish, Paul R.)

    1974   Gran Quivira Pueblo and biological distance in the
            United States Southwest. Arizona State University,
            dissertation, 282 pp.; University Microfilms Inter-
            national.

MEAD, George R.

    1968   Rock art north of the Mexican-American border: an
            annotated bibliography. Colorado State College
            (Greeley), Museum of Anthropology, Occasional Publi-
            cations in Anthropology, Archaeology Series, 5, 67
            pp.

MEAD, James (See under Goree, Patricia.)

MEARNS, Edgar A.

    1890   Ancient dwellings of the Rio Verde Valley. Popular
            Science Monthly, 37:745-763.

MEHRINGER, Peter J., Jr. (See also under Martin, Paul Schultz.)

    1967   Pollen analysis and the alluvial chronology. Kiva,
            32, no. 3:96-101.

MEHRINGER, P.J., and HAYNES, C. Vance, Jr.

    1965   The pollen evidence for the environment of Early
            Man and extinct mammals at the Lehner mammoth site,
            southeastern Arizona. American Antiquity, 31, no.
            1:17-23.

MEHRINGER, P.J., MARTIN, P.S., and HAYNES, C.V., Jr.

    1967   Murray Springs, a mid-postglacial pollen record
            from southern Arizona. American Journal of Science,

265:786-797.

MEIGHAN, Clement W.

1955   Excavation at Paragonah, Utah. Utah Archaeology,
        1, no. 3:4.

1959a   A new method for the seriation of archaeological
        collections. American Antiquity, 25:203-211.

1959b   Varieties of prehistoric cultures in the Great
        Basin region. Masterkey, 33, no. 2:46-59.

1960   Prehistoric copper objects from western Mexico.
        Science, 131, no. 3412:1534.

1966   Prehistoric New World farmers: the Paragonah site.
        In Archaeology: An Introduction, Chap. 9, Chandler
        Publishing Co., pp. 157-167.

MEIGHAN, C.W., and others

1956   Archaeological excavations in Iron County, Utah.
        University of Utah, Anthropological Papers, 25, 132
        pp.
            Reviewed AA 59:744 (Schroeder), AAq 23:206
        (Schwartz).

MERA, Harry P. (See also under Scholes, France V.)

1930   An archaeological survey of New Mexico. Museum of
        Northern Arizona, Museum Notes, 2, no. 11:5-6.

1931   Chupadero Black-on-white. Laboratory of Anthro-
        pology, Technical Series Bulletin 1, 4 pp.

1932   Wares ancestral to Tewa Polychrome. Laboratory of
        Anthropology, Technical Series Bulletin 4, 12 pp.

1933a   Mescal pits - a misnomer. Science, 77, no. 1989:
        168-169.

1933b   A proposed revision of the Rio Grande glazed paint
        sequence. Laboratory of Anthropology, Technical
        Series Bulletin 5, 12 pp.

1934a   A survey of the Biscuit Ware area in northern New
        Mexico. Laboratory of Anthropology, Technical
        Series Bulletin 6, 21 pp.

1934b   Observations on the archaeology of the Petrified
        Forest National Monument. Laboratory of Anthro-
        pology, Technical Series Bulletin 7, 24 pp.

1935   Ceramic clues to the prehistory of north central

New Mexico. Laboratory of Anthropology, Technical
Series Bulletin 8, 43 pp.

1938a   The "Rain Bird": a study in Pueblo design. Labora-
         tory of Anthropology, Memoirs, 2, 113 pp.
         Reviewed AAq 5:355 (Nesbitt).

1938b   Reconnaissance and excavation in southeastern New
         Mexico. Memoirs of the American Anthropological
         Association, 51, 70 pp.

1938c   Some aspects of the Largo cultural phase, northern
         New Mexico. American Antiquity, 3, no. 3:236-243.

1939   Style trends of Pueblo pottery in the Rio Grande
         and Little Colorado cultural areas from the six-
         teenth to the nineteenth century. Laboratory of
         Anthropology, Memoirs, 3, 164 pp.
         Reviewed AA 43:285 (Haury).

1940a   An approach to the identity of the Jumano Pueblos
         in the Saline-Medano district through archaeological
         evidence. *In* Scholes and Mera 1940.

1940b   Population changes in the Rio Grande glaze-paint
         area. Laboratory of Anthropology, Technical Series
         Bulletin 9, 41 pp.
         Reviewed AA 44:304 (Hall), AAq 6:368 (White).

1942   The present status of archaeological investigation
         in the Southwest. Southwestern Lore, 8:18-19 (ab-
         stract).

1943   An outline of ceramic developments in southern and
         southeastern New Mexico. Laboratory of Anthropology,
         Technical Series Bulletin 11, 20 pp.

1944   Jaritas rock shelter, northeastern New Mexico.
         American Antiquity, 9:295-301.

1945   Negative painting on Southwest pottery. South-
         western Journal of Anthropology 1:161-166.

MERA, H.P., and STALLINGS, W.S., Jr.

1931   Lincoln Black-on-red. Laboratory of Anthropology,
         Technical Series Bulletin 2, 2 pp.

MERBS, Charles F.

1967   Cremated human remains from Point of Pines, Arizona:
         a new approach. American Antiquity, 32:498-506.

MERRIAM, J.C.

1930   Critical elements in study of Early Man in south-
        western United States. Science, 72:405.

MESSINGER, Norman

1965   Methods used for identification of feather remains
        from Wetherill Mesa. American Antiquity, 31, no. 2:
        206-215.

METCALF, George

1970   Some wooden scraper handles from the Great Plains
        and the Southwest. Plains Anthropologist, 15:46-
        53.

MEYER, Winton (See under Cutler, Hugh C.)

MICHELS, Joseph W.

1964   The Snow Creek rock shelter site (Riv-210). Uni-
        versity of California at Los Angeles, Annual Report
        of the Archaeological Survey, 1963/64, pp. 85-135.

MIDVALE, Frank

1965   Prehistoric irrigation of the Casa Grande ruins
        area. Kiva, 30, no. 3:82-86.

1968   Prehistoric irrigation in the Salt River Valley,
        Arizona. Kiva, 34, no. 1:28-32.

1970   Prehistoric "canal-irrigation" in the Buckeye Val-
        ley and Gila Bend areas in western Maricopa County,
        Arizona. *In* Pecos Conference Water Control Symposi-
        um, Santa Fe, pp. 29-32.

1974   Prehistoric ruins and irrigation in the eastern
        Buckeye Valley. Arizona Archaeologist, 8, pp. 37-
        39.

MILES, James S. (See also under Osborne, Douglas.)

1975   Orthopedic problems of the Wetherill Mesa popula-
        tions. National Park Service, Publications in Ar-
        chaeology, 7G, 52 pp.

MILFORD, Stanley J.

1940   A San Juan burial. El Palacio, 47, no. 11:233-242.

MILLER, Alden H. (See also under Howard, Hildegarde.)

1932   Bird remains from Indian dwellings in Arizona. Condor, 34, no. 3:138-139.

MILLER, Carl F., Jr.

1934   Report on dates on the Allantown, Arizona, ruins. Tree-Ring Bulletin, 1, no. 2:15-16.

1935   Additional dates from Allantown. Tree-Ring Bulletin, 1, no. 4:31.

MILLER, J.D.

1897   The Montezuma Castle repair expedition. Antiquarian, 1:225-228.

MILLER, Jay

1975   Kokopelli. *In* Frisbie 1975a, pp. 371-380.

MILLER, John L.

1942   Dates from Fort Grant Pueblo. Tree-Ring Bulletin, 8:24.

MILLER, John P. (See also under Wendorf, Fred.)

MILLER, J.P., and WENDORF, Fred

1958   Alluvial chronology of the Tesuque Valley, New Mexico. Journal of Geology, 66, no. 2:177-194.

MILLER, K.K.

1967   A case for food production. Nevada Archaeological Survey, Reporter, 1, no. 2:10-11.

MILLER, Robert R. (See also under Gehlbach, F.R.)

1955   Fish remains from archaeological sites in the lower Colorado River Basin, Arizona. Papers of the Michigan Academy of Science, Arts and Letters, 40:125-136.

MILLER, William C. (See also under Turner, Christy G., II.)

1955   Two possible astronomical pictographs found in northern Arizona. Plateau, 27, no. 4:6-13.

1963   Arizona pictograph find - records in rock of a 1054 A.D. star explosion. Desert Magazine, 26, no.

1:28-30.

MILLER, W.C., and BRETERNITZ, David A.

1958a   1957 Navajo Canyon survey - preliminary report.
         Plateau, 30, no. 3:72-74.

1958b   1958 Navajo Canyon survey - preliminary report.
         Plateau 31, no. 1:3-7.

MILLS, Jack P., and MILLS, Vera M.

1957   The Webb site: a report on an archaeological sal-
         vage operation. El Paso, 72 pp.

1966   The Glass Ranch Site: a pre-historic village in
         southeastern Arizona. El Paso Archaeological
         Society, Special Report no. 4, 25 pp.

1969a   The Kuykendall Site: a pre-historic Salado village
         in southeastern Arizona. El Paso Archaeological
         Society, Special Report no. 6, 168 pp.

1969b   Burned house; an additional excavation at the Kuy-
         kendall Site. The Artifact, 7, no. 3:21-32.

1970   Carved stone head and other material from a storage
         room at the Dinwiddie Site. The Artifact, 8, no.
         2:11-13.

1971   The Slaughter Ranch Site: a prehistoric village
         near the Mexican border in southeastern Arizona.
         The Artifact, 9, no. 3:23-52.

1972a   The Dinwiddie Site: a prehistoric Salado ruin on
         Duck Creek, western New Mexico. The Artifact, 10,
         no. 2:1-50.

1972b   The Pitts Site. The Artifact, 10, no. 4:31-53.

MILLS, Vera M. (See also under Mills, Jack P.)

1966   A brief sketch of the Salado culture. The Arti-
         fact, 4, no. 3:16-17.

MINCKLEY, W.L., and ALGER, Norman T.

1968   Fish remains from an archaeological site along the
         Verde River, Yavapai County, Arizona. Plateau, 40,
         no. 3:91-97.

MINDELEFF, Cosmos

1895   Cliff ruins of Canyon de Chelly, Arizona. American
         Anthropologist, o.s. 8, no. 2:153-174.

1896a   Aboriginal remains in Verde Valley, Arizona. Thir-
        teenth Annual Report of the Bureau of American Eth-
        nology, pp. 179-261.

1896b   Casa Grande ruin. Thirteenth Annual Report of the
        Bureau of American Ethnology, pp. 289-319.

1897a   The repair of Casa Grande ruin, Arizona, in 1891.
        Fifteenth Annual Report of the Bureau of American
        Ethnology, pp. 315-349.

1897b   The cliff ruins of Canyon de Chelly, Arizona. Six-
        teenth Annual Report of the Bureau of American Eth-
        nology, pp. 73-198.

1898a   Origin of the cliff dwellings. Bulletin of the
        American Geographical Society, 30, no. 2:111-123.

1898b   Aboriginal architecture in the United States. Bul-
        letin of the American Geographical Society, 30, no.
        5:414-427.

1900   Localization of Tusayan clans. Nineteenth Annual
        Report of the Bureau of American Ethnology, pp.
        635-653.

1901   A cliff dwelling park in Colorado. Scientific
        American, 81:297-298.

MINDELEFF, Victor

1891   A study of Pueblo architecture: Tusayan and Cibola.
        Eighth Annual Report of the Bureau of American Eth-
        nology, pp. 3-228.

MINNIS, Paul E., and PLOG, Stephen E.

1976   A study of the site specific distribution of *Agave
        parryi* in east central Arizona. Kiva, 41, nos. 3-4:
        299-308.

MITALSKY, Frank

1931   Ancient ceremonial caves of central Arizona. Ari-
        zona Historical Review, 3 (January):99-105; 4 (April):
        69-94.

MOHR, Albert (See also under Sample, L.L.)

1951   The hunting crook: its use and distribution in the
        Southwest. Masterkey, 25, no. 5:145-154.

MOHR, A., and SAMPLE, L.L.

  1959   San Jose sites in southeastern Utah. El Palacio,
          66:109-119.

  1972   Archaeological excavations at site no. LA 102, Rio
          Arriba County, New Mexico - 1972. Laboratory of
          Anthropology Notes, 83.

MONTANDON, G.

  1923   Gravures et peintures rupestres des indiens du
          Cataract Canyon (Arizona). L'Anthropologie, 33:347-
          355.

MONTGOMERY, Arthur

  1963   The source of the fibrolite axes. El Palacio, 70,
          nos. 1-2:34-48.

MONTGOMERY, Charles M.

  1964   Rock Lake Indian shelter. El Palacio, 71, no. 3:
          5-14.

MONTGOMERY, Henry

  1894   Prehistoric man in Utah. The Archaeologist, 2:225-
          234, 298-306, 335-342.

MONTGOMERY, John

  1976   A review of the archaeology of the Pecos River Val-
          ley, New Mexico. Journal of the Texas Tech Anthro-
          pological Society, 1:1-28.

MONTGOMERY, Ross Gordon

  1940   Archaeological pot hunting. Masterkey, 14:28-29.

MONTGOMERY, R.G., SMITH, Watson, and BREW, J.O.

  1949   Franciscan Awatovi. Papers of the Peabody Museum
          of American Archaeology and Ethnology, 36, 362 pp.
          Reviewed AA 53:107 (Kubler).

MOODIE, R.L.

  1930   The ancient life of Yuma County, Arizona. Scien-
          tific Monthly, 31:401-407.

MOOMAW, Jack C.

1957   Aborigines of the Colorado highlands. Southwestern
        Lore, 23, no. 3:35-37.

MOONEY, James

1893   Recent archaeological find in Arizona. American
        Anthropologist, o.s., 6:283-284.

MOORE, Mrs. Glen E.

1947   Twelve Room House ruin. Bulletin of the Texas Ar-
        chaeological and Paleontological Society, 18:94-114.

MOORE, Mrs. G.E., and WHEAT, Mrs. Joe Ben

1951   An archaeological cache from the Hueco Basin, Texas.
        Bulletin of the Texas Archaeological and Paleonto-
        logical Society, 22:144-163.

MOORE, John G. (See also under Fry, Gary F.)

MOORE, J.G., FRY, Gary F., and ENGLERT, Edwin, Jr.

1969   Thorny-headed worm infection in North American pre-
        historic man. Science, 163:1324-1325.

MOORE, J.G., and others

1974   Human fluke infection in Glen Canyon at AD 1250.
        American Journal of Physical Anthropology, 41:115-
        117.

MOORE, W. Robert

1955   Escalante: Utah's river of arches. National Geo-
        graphic Magazine, 108, no. 3:399-425.

MOOREHEAD, Warren King

1892a   The great McLoyd collection. Illustrated American,
        12:23-26.

1892b   The ruins of southern Utah. American Antiquarian,
        14:324-327.

1892c   The great ruins of upper McElmo Creek. Illustrated
        American, 10.

1898   Some objects from the Salado Valley, Arizona. Amer-
        ican Archaeologist, 2, no. 8:207-210.

1902a   The field diary of an archaeological collector.

Andover, Massachusetts, 71 pp.

1902b   Stone effigies from the Southwest. Records of the
        Past, 1:246-250.

1906   A narrative of explorations in New Mexico, Arizona,
        Indiana, etc. Phillips Academy, Bulletin of the
        Dept. of Archaeology, 3, pp. 33-53, 89-107.

1908   Ruins at Aztec and on the Rio La Plata, New Mexico.
        American Anthropologist, n.s. 10, no. 2:255-263.

1910   The stone age in North America. 2 vols., Houghton
        Mifflin, Boston.
        Reviewed AA 13:153 (Bushnell).

1931   Archaeology of the Arkansas River Valley. Phillips
        Academy, Dept. of Archaeology, 204 pp.

1934   A forgotten tree ring record. Science, 80:16-17.

MOOREHEAD, W.K., and GUNCKEL, L.W.

1892   In search of a lost race. Illustrated American, 10,
        no. 116; 11, nos. 119, 121, 122, 124-130.

MORGAN, Alfred

1877   On the cliff-houses and antiquities of southwestern
        Colorado and New Mexico. Proceedings of the 66th
        Session of the Literary and Philosophical Society
        of Liverpool, no. 31, pp. 343-356.

MORGAN, James R.

1977   Were Chaco's great kivas ancient computers of as-
        tronomy? El Palacio, 83, no. 1:28-41.

MORGAN, Lewis H.

1880a   On the ruins of a stone pueblo on the Animas River
        in New Mexico. Reports of the Peabody Museum, 2:
        536-556.

1880b   A study of the houses of the American aborigines.
        Archaeological Institute of America, Annual Report,
        1:27-60.

1881   Houses and house-life of the American aborigines.
        Contributions to North American Ethnology, vol. 4,
        281 pp.

MORGAN, William Fellowes

1879   Description of a cliff-house on the Mancos River
        of Colorado, with a ground plan. Proceedings of
        the American Association for the Advancement of
        Science, 27:300-306.

MORIARTY, James Robert, III (See also under Broms, Robert S.D.)

1968   The environmental variations of the Yuman culture
        area of southern California. Anthropological Jour-
        nal of Canada, 6, no. 2:2-20; no. 3:9-23.

MORLEY, Sylvanus G.

1908   The excavation of the Cannonball ruins in south-
        western Colorado. American Anthropologist, n.s.
        10, no. 4:596-610.

1910   The South House, Puyé. Southwest Society, Bulletin
        6, 15 pp. (also as Papers of the School of American
        Research, no. 7).

MORLEY, S.G., and KIDDER, A.V.

1917   The archaeology of McElmo Canyon, Colorado. El
        Palacio, 4, no. 4:41-70.

MORRIS, Ann Axtell

1933   Digging in the Southwest. Doubleday, Doran & Co.,
        301 pp.

MORRIS, Donald H.

1969a   A 9th century Salado (?) kiva at Walnut Creek, Ari-
        zona. Plateau, 42, no. 1:1-10.

1969b   Red Mountain: an early Pioneer Period Hohokam site
        in the Salt River Valley of central Arizona. Amer-
        ican Antiquity, 34:40-53.

1970   Walnut Creek Village: a ninth-century Hohokam-
        Anasazi settlement in the mountains of central
        Arizona. American Antiquity, 35:49-61.

MORRIS, D.H., and EL-NAJJAR, Mahmoud

1971   An unusual Classic Period burial from Las Colinas,
        Salt River Valley, central Arizona. Kiva, 36, no.
        4:31-35.

MORRIS, Don P. (See also under El-Najjar, Mahmoud Yosef; Rock, James Taylor.)

1975   Architectural development and masonry style at Antelope House. *In* Rock and Morris 1975, pp. 33-38.

MORRIS, Earl H.

1915   The excavation of a ruin near Aztec, San Juan County, New Mexico. American Anthropologist, 17, no. 4:666-684.

1917a   Discoveries at the Aztec Ruin. American Museum Journal, 17, no. 3:169-179.

1917b   Explorations in New Mexico. American Museum Journal, 17, no. 7:461-471.

1917c   The place of coiled ware in Southwestern pottery. American Anthropologist, 19, no. 1:24-29.

1918   Further discoveries at the Aztec Ruin. American Museum Journal, 18, no. 7:603-610 (also in El Palacio, 6:17-23, 26).

1919a   The Aztec Ruin. American Museum of Natural History, Anthropological Papers, 26, pt. 1, pp. 1-108. Reviewed AA 21:194 (Kroeber).

1919b   Preliminary account of the antiquities of the region between the Mancos and La Plata Rivers in southwestern Colorado. Thirty-third Annual Report of the Bureau of American Ethnology, pp. 155-206. Reviewed AA 22:285 (Kidder and Guernsey), 383 (Kroeber).

1921a   Chronology of the San Juan area. Proceedings of the National Academy of Sciences, 7:18-22.

1921b   The house of the great kiva at the Aztec Ruin. American Museum of Natural History, Anthroplogical Papers, 26, pt. 2, pp. 109-138.

1922   An unexplored area of the Southwest. Natural History, 22, no. 6:498-515.

1924a   Burials in the Aztec Ruin. American Museum of Natural History, Anthropological Papers, 26, pt. 3, pp. 139-225.

1924b   The Aztec Ruin annex. American Museum of Natural History, Anthropological Papers, 26, pt. 4, pp. 227-257.

1925a   Exploring in the Canyon of Death.   National Geo-
         graphic Magazine, 48, no. 3:263-300.

1925b   Repair of Mummy Cave tower in the Canyon del Muerto,
         Arizona.   Smithsonian Miscellaneous Collections, 77,
         no. 2:108-112.

1927   The beginnings of pottery making in the San Juan
         area, unfired prototypes, and the wares of the
         earliest ceramic period.   American Museum of Natur-
         al History, Anthropological Papers, 28, pt. 2, pp.
         125-198.

1928a   Notes on excavations in the Aztec Ruin.   American
         Museum of Natural History, Anthropological Papers,
         26, pt. 5, pp. 259-420.

1928b   An aboriginal salt mine at Camp Verde, Arizona.
         American Museum of Natural History, Anthropological
         Papers, 30, pt. 3, pp. 75-97.

1928c   Burials in Canyon del Muerto.   El Palacio, 24:223.

1929a   Early Pueblos.   El Palacio, 27:279-281.

1929b   Golden Age of the Pueblos.   El Palacio, 27:282-283.

1934   Speaker Chief's House.   Mesa Verde Notes, 5, no.
         1:4-6.

1936   Archaeological background of dates in early Arizona
         chronology.   Tree-Ring Bulletin, 2, no. 4:34-36.

1938   Mummy Cave.   Natural History, 42:127-138.

1939   Archaeological studies in the La Plata district,
         southwestern Colorado and northwestern New Mexico.
         Carnegie Institution of Washington, Publication
         no. 519, 298 pp.
            Reviewed AA 43:451 (Roberts), AAq 7:198 (Brew).

1941   Prayer sticks in walls of Mummy Cave tower, Canyon
         del Muerto.   American Antiquity, 6:227-230.

1944a   Adobe bricks in a pre-Spanish wall near Aztec, New
         Mexico.   American Antiquity, 9:434-438.

1944b   Anasazi sandals.   Clearing-House for Southwestern
         Museums, News Letter, 68:239-242.

1947   Experiences in Southwestern archaeology.   South-
         western Lore, 8, no. 2.

1948   The tomb of the weaver.   Natural History, 57, no.
         2:66-71, 91.

1949   Basketmaker II dwellings near Durango, Colorado.
        Tree-Ring Bulletin, 15, no. 4:33-34.

1951   Basketmaker III human figurines from northeastern
        Arizona. American Antiquity, 17:33-40.

1952   Note on the Durango dates. Tree-Ring Bulletin,
        18, no. 4:36.

MORRIS, E.H., and BURGH, Robert F.

1941   Anasazi basketry, Basketmaker II through Pueblo III:
        a study based on specimens from the San Juan River
        country. Carnegie Institution of Washington, Pub-
        lication no. 533, 66 pp.
        Reviewed AA 46:387 (Weltfish), AAq 8:187 (Brew).

1954   Basketmaker II sites near Durango, Colorado. Car-
        negie Institution of Washington, Publication no. 604,
        135 pp.
        Reviewed AA 57:1331 (Lister), AAq 21:89 (Rinaldo).

MORRIS, E.H., and NELSON, N.C.

1917   The ruins at Aztec. El Palacio, 4: no. 3:43-69.

MORRIS, Elizabeth Ann (See also under Bakkegard, B.M.; Breternitz, David A.; Jones, Volney H. Also listed as Gell, Elizabeth Ann Morris.)

1958   A possible early projectile point from the Prayer
        Rock district, Arizona. Southwestern Lore, 24, no.
        1:1-5.

1959a   Basketmaker caves in the Prayer Rock district,
        northeastern Arizona. University of Arizona, dis-
        sertation, 808 pp., University Microfilms Inter-
        national.

1959b   Basketmaker flutes from the Prayer Rock district,
        Arizona. American Antiquity, 24:406-411.

1959c   A Pueblo I site near Bennett's Peak, northwestern
        New Mexico. El Palacio, 66, no. 5:169-175.

MORRIS, E.A., and JONES, Volney H.

1960   Seventh century evidence for the use of tobacco
        in northern Arizona. Proceedings of the 34th Inter-
        national Congress of Americanists, pp. 306-309.

MORRIS, Nancy T. (See under Turner, Christy G., II.)

MORRIS, Richard, GLAZIER, Ellen, and THALLON, Robert

    1937   Archaeological report of the Canyon of Lodore-Yampa
            River reconnaissance of 1936. Trail and Timberline,
            no. 219.

MORRISON, Charles Randall

    1975   A historical multiple burial at Fort Union, New
            Mexico: an exercise in forensic archaeology. *In*
            Frisbie 1975a, pp. 381-406.

MORROW, Herbert C.

    1973   Footprint of the Mimbres. The Artifact, 11, no.
            4:90.

MORSS, Noel (See also under Byers, Douglas S.)

    1927   Archaeological explorations on the middle Chinlee,
            1925. Memoirs of the American Anthropological As-
            sociation, 34, 41 pp.

    1931a   Notes on the archaeology of the Kaibito and Rainbow
            Plateaus in Arizona. Papers of the Peabody Museum
            of American Archaeology and Ethnology, 12, no. 2,
            18 pp.

    1931b   The ancient culture of the Fremont River in Utah.
            Papers of the Peabody Museum of American Archae-
            ology and Ethnology, 12, no. 3, 81 pp.

    1954   Clay figurines of the American Southwest. Papers
            of the Peabody Museum of American Archaeology and
            Ethnology, 49, no. 1, 74 pp.
            Reviewed AA 57:895 (Meighan), AAq 21:194 (Heizer).

MOSELEY, M. Edward

    1966   The discovery and definition of Basketmaker: 1890
            to 1941. Masterkey, 40, no. 4:140-154.

MOSER, Edward, and WHITE, Richard S., Jr.

    1968   Seri clay figurines. Kiva, 33, no. 3:133-154.

MOTT, Dorothy Challis

    1935   Some unusual textiles of the prehistoric Southwest.
            Kiva, 1, no. 1:3.

    1936   Progress of the excavation at Kinishba. Kiva, 2,
            no. 1:1-4.

1937   Prehistoric burials. Kiva, 2 , no. 6:19-24.

1940   Prehistoric textiles. Kiva, 5, no. 4:13-16.

MUELLER, James W.

1974   The use of sampling in archaeological survey. Society for American Archaeology, Memoirs, 28, 91 pp.

MUENCH, David, and PIKE, Donald G.

1974   Anasazi: ancient people of the rock. American West Publishing Co., Palo Alto.

MUENCH, Josef (See under Muench, Joyce Rockwood.)

MUENCH, Joyce Rockwood

1942   On the trail of Keetseel. Desert Magazine, 5, no. 10:11-14.

1943   "They lived up there." Desert Magazine, 7, no. 3: 16-21.

1961   The people of the Green Table - Mesa Verde National Park. Arizona Highways, 37, no. 9:8-13.

MUENCH, J.R., and MUENCH, Josef

1944   Cities in the sun. Natural History, 53:214-223.

1946a   Kinishba. Arizona Highways, 22, no. 4:32-37.

1946b   Kinishba - the brown house of long ago. Natural History, 55:114-119.

MULLOY, William T. (See under Reiter, Paul.)

MULROY, Mary E., and KOWTA, Makoto

1964   An archaeological survey of Capitol Reef National Monument. University of Utah, Special Report (National Park Service), 31 pp.

MURBARGER, Nell

1947   Proud city of the Pecos. New Mexico Magazine, 25, no. 1:23, 41, 43, 45.

1948   Arizona's first land rush. Natural History, 62, no. 1:37-41.

1949   City of the Crooked Water. Natural History, 58: 234-239.

1950   Montezuma's pink castle. Natural History, 59:38-
        42.

1951   Golden treasure of Tule Canyon. Desert Magazine,
        14, no. 14:4-9.

1953   City of the cavemen. Natural History, 63, no. 3:
        124-129.

MURRAY, Laura

1936   Kinishbah. Indians At Work, 3, no. 17:36-38.

MUSEO REGIONAL DE SONORA

1971   La Pintada. Imprenta Universitaria, Universidad
        de Sonora, Hermosillo.

MYERS, Richard D.

1967   The Folsom point from the Rising site, southeast
        Arizona. Kiva, 32, no. 3:102-105.

MYERS, Thomas P.

1976   Fluted points from the Sulphur Springs Valley,
        Cochise County, Arizona. Kiva, 42, no. 2:209-213.

NADAILLAC, J.F.A. du P., Marquis de

1896   Les cliff dwellers, une monographie. Revue des
        Questions scientifiques (Louvain), Octobre, 66 pp.

NANCE, C. Roger

1972   Cultural evidence for the Altithermal in Texas and
        Mexico. Southwestern Journal of Anthropology, 28,
        no. 2:169-192.

NAYLOR, Thomas

1969   The extinct Suma of northern Chihuahua. The Arti-
        fact, 7, no. 4:1-14.

NEAL, Arminta (See under Wormington, H. Marie.)

NEELY, James A.

1974   The prehistoric Lunt and Stove Canyon sites, Point
        of Pines. University of Arizona, dissertation,
        1140 pp.; University Microfilms International.

NEELY, J.A., and OLSON, Alan P.

1977   Archaeological reconnaissance of Monument Valley in northeastern Arizona. Museum of Northern Arizona, Research Papers, 3, 94 pp.

NEFF, J.M. (See under Reid, J. Jefferson.)

NELSON, Ben (See under LeBlanc, Steven A.)

NELSON, E.W.

1884   Explorations in southern Arizona. Annual Report of the Smithsonian Institution for 1884, pp. 20-24.

NELSON, Ethelyn G.

1917   Camp life in New Mexico. El Palacio, 4, no. 4:19-32.

NELSON, Nels C. (See also under Morris, Earl H.)

1913   Ruins of prehistoric New Mexico. American Museum Journal, 13, no. 2:63-81.

1914   Pueblo ruins of the Galisteo Basin, New Mexico. American Museum of Natural History, Anthropological Papers, 15, pt. 1, pp. 1-124.

1915   Ancient cities of New Mexico. American Museum Journal, 15, no. 8:389-394.

1916a Chronology of the Tano ruins, New Mexico. American Anthropologist, 18, no. 2:159-180.

1916b New Mexico field work in 1915. El Palacio, 3, no. 2:43-52.

1917a Archaeology of the Tano district, New Mexico. Proceedings of the 19th International Congress of Americanists, pp. 114-118.

1917b Excavation of the Aztec Ruin. American Museum Journal, 17, no. 2:85-99.

1919a The archaeology of the Southwest: a preliminary report. Proceedings of the National Academy of Sciences, 5:114-120 (also in El Palacio, 8:175-179, 1920).

1919b The Southwest problem. El Palacio, 6, no. 9:132-135.

1919c Archaeology of the Tano district, New Mexico. El

Palacio, 7, nos. 9-12:177-183.

1920   Notes on Pueblo Bonito. *In* Pepper 1920, pp. 381-
         390.

NELSON, Paula R.

1964   North American man's oldest home? Chicago Natural
         History Museum Bulletin, 35, no. 11:2-4.

NESBITT, Paul H.

1931   The ancient Mimbreños: based on investigations at
         the Mattocks ruin, Mimbres Valley, New Mexico.
         Beloit College, Logan Museum, Bulletin 4, 105 pp.
         Reviewed AA 33:636 (Sauer).

1932   Black-on-white pottery from the Mimbres Valley,
         New Mexico. Wisconsin Archaeologist, 11:82-90.

1937   A stone carving in bas-relief from the Upper Gila
         area. American Antiquity, 2:264-266.

1938   Starkweather ruin, a Mogollon-Pueblo site in the
         Upper Gila area of New Mexico, and affiliative
         aspects of the Mogollon culture. Beloit College,
         Logan Museum, Bulletin 6, 143 pp.
         Reviewed AA 41:314 (Kidder), AAq 5:352 (Colton).

NEUMANN, Georg K.

1940   Mogollon skeletal material from the Peñasco Valley,
         New Mexico. Laboratory of Anthropology, Technical
         Series Bulletin 10, pp. 13-20.

NEWBERRY, J.S.

1876   Report of the exploring expedition from Santa Fe,
         New Mexico, to the junction of the Grand and Green
         Rivers of the Great Colorado of the west, in 1859.
         United States Engineering Dept.

NEWCOMB, W.W., Jr. (See also under Kirkland, Forrest.)

1976   Pecos River pictographs: the development of an art
         form. *In* Cultural Change and Continuity: Essays
         in Honor of James Bennett Griffin, ed. Charles E.
         Cleland, Academic Press.

NEWELL, F.H.

1898   Mesa Verde. National Geographic Magazine, 9:431-
         434.

NEWHALL, Nancy

1952   Canyon de Chelly National Monument. Arizona High-
        ways, 28, no. 6:18-27.

NICHOLS, Robert F. (See also under Osborne, Douglas.)

1962   Dates from the site 1060 pithouse, Mesa Verde Na-
        tional Park. Tree-Ring Bulletin, 24, nos. 1-2:12-
        14.

1965   A large hewn plank from Mesa Verde, Colorado. *In*
        Osborne 1965a, pp. 51-56.

NICHOLS, R.F., and HARLAN, Thomas

1967   Archaeological tree-ring dates from Wetherill Mesa.
        Tree-Ring Bulletin, 28, nos. 1-4:13-40.

NICHOLS, R.F., and SMITH, David G.

1965   Evidence of prehistoric cultivation of Douglas-fir
        trees at Mesa Verde. *In* Osborne 1965a, pp. 57-64.

NICKENS, Paul R. (See also under Breternitz, David A.)

1975a   Osteological analysis of five human burials from
        Mesa Verde National Park, Colorado. Southwestern
        Lore, 41, no. 3:13-26.

1975b   Prehistoric cannibalism in the Mancos Canyon, south-
        western Colorado. Kiva, 40, no. 4:283-293.

1975c   The Johnson-Lion Canyon project: environmental ar-
        chaeology in southwestern Colorado. Journal of the
        Colorado-Wyoming Academy of Science, 7, no. 6:1
        (abstract).

1976   Paleoepidemiology of Mesa Verde Anasazi populations:
        lines of increased density. Journal of the Colorado-
        Wyoming Academy of Science, 8, no. 1:4-5 (abstract).

NIEHUIS, Charles C.

1946   Superstition ruins. Arizona Highways, 22:30-35.

NININGER, H.H.

1938   Meteorite collecting among ancient Americans. Amer-
        ican Antiquity, 4:39-40.

NOBLE, Catherine

1946   The valley of long ago. Arizona Highways, 22, no.

3:26-29.

NOBLE, David Grant

1973   Arroyo Hondo - the elements of research. School of
        American Research, Exploration 1973, pp. 2-8.

1975   Art and artifacts at Arroyo Hondo. School of Amer-
        ican Research, Exploration 1975, pp. 28-30.

1976   A view of the Anasazi. School of American Research,
        Exploration 1976, pp. 18-21.

NOGUERA, Eduardo

1926   Ruinas arqueológicas de Casas Grandes, Chihuahua.
        Secretaría de Educación Pública, Publicaciones,
        vol. 11, no. 14, 23 pp.

1930   Ruinas arqueológicas del norte de México: Casas
        Grandes (Chihuahua), La Quemada, Chalchihuites
        (Zacatecas). Secretaría de Educación Pública, 107
        pp.

1938   Casas Grandes. In Estado actual de los principales
        edificios arqueológicos de México, Dirección de
        arqueología, pp. 9-13.

1958   Reconocimiento arqueológico en Sonora. Instituto
        Nacional de Antropología e Historia, Dirección de
        Monumentos pre-Hispanicos, Informes, no. 10, 29 pp.

NOISAT, Bradley A. (See under Huse, Hannah.)

NOLAND, Melissa

1977   Abiquiu's roots: villagers unearth their past. El
        Palacio, 83, no. 4:31-34.

NORBECK, Edward (See under Jennings, Jesse D.)

NORDBY, Larry V. (See under Breternitz, David A.)

NORDENSKIÖLD, Gustav

1893   The cliff-dwellers of the Mesa Verde. Translated
        by D. Lloyd Morgan, Stockholm, 304 pp. (reprinted
        1973, introduction by Watson Smith, AMS Press,
        174 pp.)

NORTHNAGEL, E.W.

1959   The trail to Tsankawi. New Mexico Magazine, 37,

no. 6:19, 52-53, 57.

NOVELLI, Cona

1968   Two polychrome vessels depicting the god Quetzal-
        coatl. The Artifact, 6, no. 3:1-6.

NUNLEY, John P.

1971   Sociocultural units of the southwestern Texas Ar-
        chaic: an analytic approach. Southern Methodist
        University, dissertation, 408 pp.; University
        Microfilms International.

NUNLEY, J.P., DUFFIELD, Lathel F., and JELKS, Edward B.

1965   Excavations at Amistad Reservoir, 1962 season.
        Texas Archaeological Salvage Project, Miscellaneous
        Papers, no. 3, 129 pp.

NUSBAUM, Deric (Also listed as O'Bryan, Deric.)

1928   Ancient rattle found by Deric Nusbaum.   El Palacio,
        24:277-278.

NUSBAUM, Jesse L. (See also under Haury, Emil W.)

1911   The excavation and repair of Balcony House, Mesa
        Verde National Park. American Journal of Archae-
        ology, Second Series, 15:75 (abstract).

1928   Bird fetish from Mesa Verde. El Palacio, 25:29.

NUSBAUM, J.L., KIDDER, A.V., and GUERNSEY, S.J.

1922   A Basket-Maker Cave in Kane County, Utah; with notes
        on the artifacts. Museum of the American Indian,
        Indian Notes and Monographs, no. 29, 153 pp.

NYMEYER, Robert Bert

1941   Cave men of the Cornudas. New Mexico Magazine,
        19, no. 1:22-23, 41.

O'BRYAN, Deric (Also listed as Nusbaum, Deric.)

1948   Remarks on tree-ring analysis techniques in the
        Southwest. American Anthropologist, 50:708-714.

1949   Methods of felling trees and tree-ring dating in
        the Southwest. American Antiquity, 15:155-156.

1950   Excavations in Mesa Verde National Park, 1947-1948.

Gila Pueblo, Medallion Papers, 39, 144 pp.
Reviewed AAq 17:72 (Morris).

1952   The abandonment of the northern pueblos in the thir-
        teenth century. *In* The Indian Tribes of Aboriginal
        America: Selected Papers of the 29th International
        Congress of Americanists, ed. S. Tax, pp. 153-157.

1967   Climate and tree rings in the Mesa Verde. National
        Parks Magazine, 41, no. 235:17-19.

ODESCALCHI, Irma, Princess

1931   Bei den Pueblos in Neu-Mexiko. Atlantis: Länder,
        Völker, Reisen, 3:152-157.

OETTEKING, Bruno

1927   Pathologic plagiocephaly in a Nevada skull. Mu-
        seum of the American Indian, Indian Notes, 4, no.
        3:201-209.

1930   The skeleton from Mesa House. Southwest Museum
        Papers, 5, 48 pp.

OFFICER, James E. (See under Kelly, Isabel T.)

O'LAUGHLIN, Thomas C.

1965   La Cueva. The Artifact, 3, no. 2:5-11.

1966   The atlatl and fending stick; two ancient weapons.
        The Artifact, 4, no. 1:2-4.

1977   Excavations at the Sandy Bone site, Dona Ana County,
        New Mexico. Awanyu, 5, no. 2:11-42.

O'LAUGHLIN, T.C., and GREISER, T.W.

1973   Preliminary field report on the findings and re-
        sults of the cultural and historical resources of
        the spillway area of the Range Dam lying within
        the Northgate National Registry Site in El Paso,
        Texas. El Paso Centennial Museum.

OLDENDORPH, O.F.

1962   Keet Seel: journey into the human history of the
        American Southwest. National Parks Magazine, 36
        (January):8-10.

1964   Three Turkey House: Navajo archaeological site near
        Canyon de Chelly National Monument. National Parks
        Magazine, 38 (August):8-9.

OLDFIELD, Frank (See also under Schoenwetter, James.)

1964   Late Quarternary environments and Early Man on the southern High Plains. Antiquity, 38, no. 151:226-229.

OLSEN, John W. (See under Olsen, Stanley J.)

OLSEN, Stanley J. (See also under Wilson, John P.)

1964   Mammal remains from archaeological sites: Part I - southeastern and southwestern United States. Papers of the Peabody Museum of Archaeology and Ethnology, 56, no. 1, 162 pp. Reviewed AA 67:1066 (Flannery).

1967   The importance of fragmentary vertebrate remains in archaeological collections. Southwestern Lore, 32, no. 4:82-84.

1968a   Canid remains from Grasshopper Ruin. Kiva, 34, no. 1:33-40.

1968b   Fish, amphibian, and reptile remains from archaeological sites. Part I: southeastern and southwestern United States. Papers of the Peabody Museum of Archaeology and Ethnology, 56, no. 2, 137 pp. Reviewed AA 71:775 (Wing), AAq 36:122 (Douglas).

1972   The small Indian dogs of Black Mesa, Arizona. Plateau, 45, no. 2:47-54.

1974   An occurrence of the Desert Bighorn at a Hohokam site. Plateau, 47, no. 2:77-80.

OLSEN, S.J., and BEEZLEY, John

1975   Domestic food animals from Hubbell Trading Post. Kiva, 41, no. 2:201-206.

OLSEN, S.J., and OLSEN, John W.

1970   A preliminary report on the fish and herpetofauna of Grasshopper Ruin. Kiva, 36, no. 2:40-43.

OLSEN, S.J., and WILSON, John P.

1976   Faunal remains from Fort Sumner, New Mexico. Awanyu, 4, no. 3:16-32.

OLSON, Alan P. (See also under Ambler, J. Richard; Breternitz, David A.; Euler, Robert C.; Ezell, Paul H.; Gumerman, George J.; Neely, James A.)

1959   An evaluation of the phase concept in Southwestern archaeology: as applied to the eleventh and twelfth century occupations at Point of Pines, east central Arizona. University of Arizona, dissertation, 641 pp.; University Microfilms International.

1960   The Dry Prong site, east central Arizona. American Antiquity, 26:185-204.

1962   A history of the phase concept in the Southwest. American Antiquity, 27:457-472.

1963   Some archaeological problems of central and northeastern Arizona. Plateau, 35, no. 3:93-106.

1964a The 1959-1960 Transwestern Pipeline, Window Rock to Flagstaff. Archives of Archaeology, 25, 101 pp. (2 microcards).

1964b An unfinished Clovis point from Houck, Arizona. Plateau, 36, no. 4:123-124.

1966a A mass secondary burial from northern Arizona. American Antiquity, 31:822-826.

1966b Split-twig figurines from NA 5607, northern Arizona. Plateau, 38, no. 3:55-64.

1971   Archaeology of the Arizona Public Service Company 345KV line. Museum of Northern Arizona, Bulletin 46, 71 pp.

OLSON, A.P., and LEE, Thomas A., Jr.

1964   NA 7696, a stratified site in Three Turkey Canyon, northeastern Arizona. Plateau, 36, no. 3:73-82.

OLSON, A.P., and WASLEY, William W.

1956   An archaeological traverse survey in west-central New Mexico. *In* Wendorf, Fox, and Lewis 1956, pp. 256-390.

OLSON, Byron L.

1973   Archaeological survey near Imperial Dam and the Gila Gravity Main Canal. Arizona State Museum, Archaeological Series, 19, 3 pp.

OLSON, Wendy C.

  1955   Prehistoric jewelry shop unearthed. Chicago Natural
         History Museum Bulletin, 26, no. 9:5.

O'NEALE, Lila M.

  1948   Textiles of pre-Columbian Chihuahua. Carnegie
         Institution of Washington, Contributions to Amer-
         ican Anthropology and History, 9, no. 45:95-161.
         Reviewed AAq 16:83 (Jones).

OPLER, Marvin K.

  1939   Southern Ute pottery types. Masterkey, 13, no. 5:
         161-163.

OPLER, Morris E. (See also under Basso, Keith H.)

  1971   Pots, Apache, and the Dismal River culture aspect.
         In Basso and Opler 1971, pp. 29-33.

OPPELT, Norman T.

  1976   Southwestern pottery: an annotated bibliography
         and list of types and wares. University of North-
         ern Colorado, Museum of Anthropology, Occasional
         Publications in Anthropology, Archaeology Series,
         7, Parts I-II, 179 pp.

ORCHARD, William C.

  1925   Fine-line decoration of ancient Southwestern pot-
         tery, Museum of the American Indian, Indian Notes,
         2, no. 1:24-31.

ORELLANA T., Rafael

  1953   Petroglifos y pinturas rupestres de Sonora. Yan;
         ciencias antropológicas, 1:29-33.

ORLINS, Robert I. (See under Williams, Pete A.)

OSBORNE, Douglas (See also under Hayes, Alden C.)

  1941   Archaeological reconnaissance in western Utah and
         Nevada, 1939. Masterkey, 15, no. 5:189-195.

  1958   Western American prehistory - an hypothesis. Amer-
         ican Antiquity, 24:47-52.

  1964   Solving the riddles of Wetherill Mesa. National
         Geographic Magazine, 125:155-195.

1965a   (assembler)   Contributions of the Wetherill Mesa
        archaeological project. Memoirs of the Society for
        American Archaeology, 19, 230 pp.

1965b   Chipping remains as an indication of cultural change
        at Wetherill Mesa. *In* Osborne 1965a, pp. 30-44.

1976   Slow exodus from Mesa Verde. Natural History, 85,
        no. 1:38-45.

OSBORNE, D., and HAYES, Alden

1938   Some archaeological notes from southern Hidalgo
        County, New Mexico. New Mexico Anthropologist,
        3, no. 2:21-23.

OSBORNE, D., and MILES, James S.

1966   Diseases encountered at Mesa Verde, Colorado. *In*
        Human Paleopathology, ed. Saul Jarcho, New Haven,
        pp. 85-97.

OSBORNE, D., and NICHOLS, Robert F.

1967   Introduction. The dendrochronology of the Wether-
        ill Mesa archaeological project. Tree-Ring Bul-
        letin, 28:1-6.

OSBURN, Dodd N.

1941   Petroglyph and pictograph site in the Finlay Moun-
        tains. Field and Laboratory (Dallas), 9, no. 1:
        30-35.

OTTAWAY, Lucretia Vickery

1975   Some architectural features characteristic of the
        Taos, New Mexico area: early manifestations at TA-
        26. *In* Frisbie 1975a, pp. 407-436.

OWEN, Roger C.

1956   Some clay figurines and Seri dolls from coastal
        Sonora, Mexico. Kiva, 21, nos. 3-4:1-10.

1957   Paddle and anvil appearance of some Sonoran pottery.
        American Antiquity, 22:291.

PAGE, Robert G., Jr.

1970   Primitive warfare in the Prescott area. Arizona
        Archaeologist, 5, pp. 47-56.

PAILES, Richard Allen

1973   An archaeological reconnaissance of southern Sonora
        and reconsideration of the Rio Sonora culture. South-
        ern Illinois University, dissertation, 581 pp.; Uni-
        versity Microfilms International.

1976   Relaciones culturales prehistóricas en el noreste
        de Sonora. *In* Braniff and Felger 1976, pp. 213-
        228.

1978   The Rio Sonora culture in prehistoric trade systems.
        In Riley and Hedrick 1978, pp. 134-143.

PALMER, Edward

1876   Exploration of a mound in Utah. American Naturalist,
        10:410-414.

1877   A review of published statements regarding the
        mounds at Payson, Utah, with an account of their
        structure and origins. Proceedings of the Daven-
        port Academy of Natural Science, 2:167-171.

1880   Cave dwellings in Utah. Eleventh Annual Report
        of the Peabody Museum of American Archaeology and
        Ethnology, 2:269-272.

PALMER, F.M.

1905   Exploration in Arizona, a land of mystery. Out
        West, 23, no. 6:525-538.

1906   Reports on researches conducted by the Southwest
        Society of the Archaeological Institute of America.
        American Journal of Archaeology, 2nd ser., 10:21-40.

1907   The first Arizona expedition. Archaeological Insti-
        tute of America, Southwest Society, Bulletin no.
        3:40-48.

PALMER, Paul E., Jr.

1973   Introduction: the Mimbres branch of the Mogollon.
        The Artifact, 11, no. 4:1-4.

PALMER, S.L., Jr.

1940   Montezuma Castle in 1896. Southwestern Monuments
        Monthly Report, Supplement (January), pp. 62-64.

PARK, C.F.

1929   Government cave. Museum of Northern Arizona, Museum

Notes, 2, no. 6:1-3.

PARKS, Marion

1927   The old house of the chief: a layman's introduction
        to the work of the Southwest Museum expedition at
        Casa Grande. Masterkey, 1, no. 1:5-13.

PARMALEE, Paul W.

1967   Food animals utilized by the garrison stationed at
        Fort Fillmore, New Mexico, 1851-1862. El Palacio,
        74, no. 2:43-45.

PARSONS, Elsie Clews

1906   The Mesa Verde National Park. American Antiquarian,
        28:256-266.

1921   Cliff dwellers of the Mesa Verde. Travel, 14:5-14.

1940a   A pre-Spanish record of Hopi ceremonies. American
        Anthropologist, 42, no. 3:541-542.

1940b   Relations between ethnology and archaeology in the
        Southwest. American Antiquity, 5:214-220.

PARSONS, Francis B.

1955   A small Mimbres ruin near Silver City, New Mexico.
        El Palacio, 62:283-289.

1956   Stronghold of ancient tribes. New Mexico Magazine,
        34:28-29, 57.

1960   Unusual stone head from Chihuahua. El Palacio, 67,
        no. 2:66-67.

PARSONS, Mark L.

1965a   1963 test excavations at Fate Bell Shelter, Amistad
        Reservoir, Val Verde County, Texas. Texas Archae-
        ological Salvage Project, Miscellaneous Papers,
        4, 77 pp.

1965b   Painted and engraved pebbles. Texas Archaeological
        Salvage Project, Papers, 7:146-159.

PASTRON, A.G., and CLEWLOW, C.W., Jr.

1975   An obsidian cache cave in Chihuahua. Masterkey,
        49, no. 2:60-64.

PATRICK, H.R.

1903   The ancient canal systems and pueblos of the Salt
        River Valley, Arizona. Phoenix Free Museum, Bul-
        letin 1, 12 pp.

PATTERSON, J.L.

1936a   The sacred sword of Rahiroa.   New Mexico Magazine,
        14, no. 3:16-17, 37.

1936b   Exploring antiquity.   New Mexico Magazine, 14, no.
        7:26-27, 52.

1937   The temple of Rinconado.   Southwestern Lore, 2, no.
        4:80-83.

PATTERSON, J.T.

1936   The corner-tang flint artifacts of Texas.   Uni-
        versity of Texas, Anthropological Papers, 1, no. 4,
        54 pp.
        Reviewed AAq 2:241 (Ray).

1937   Supplementary notes on the corner-tang artifact.
        University of Texas, Anthropological Papers, 1, no.
        5:30-37.

PAVESIC, Max G.

1966   A note on the distribution of Promontory pegs.
        Tebiwa, 9, no. 1:40-44.

PEABODY, Charles

1909   A reconnaissance trip in western Texas.   American
        Anthropologist, n.s. 11:202-216.

1917   A prehistoric wind-instrument from Pecos, New
        Mexico.   American Anthropologist, 19, no. 1:30-33.

PEARCE, James E.

1932   The present status of Texas archaeology.   Bulletin
        of the Texas Archaeological and Paleontological
        Society, 4:44-54.

PEARCE, J.E., and JACKSON, Alvin T.

1933   A prehistoric rock shelter in Val Verde County,
        Texas.   University of Texas, Anthropological Papers,
        1, no. 3, 143 pp.
        Reviewed AA 37:676 (Roberts).

PEARL, George Clayton (See under Marmon, Lee H.)

PEARSALL, Al

    1939   Evidences of Pueblo culture in San Luis Valley.
            Southwestern Lore, 5, no. 1:7-9.

PECK, Fred R.

    1956   Note on a burial on the upper Verde River. Plateau,
            29, no. 2:46-47.

PECK, Stuart L.

    1953   Some pottery from the Sand Hills, Imperial County,
            California. Archaeological Survey Association of
            Southern California, Papers, 1, 14 pp.

    1955   The diffusion of pottery in the Southwest. Master-
            key, 29:130.

    1957   Playa artifacts from sites near Tule Springs. Mas-
            terkey, 31, no. 4:116-120.

PECKHAM, Stewart L. (See also under Enloe, James G.; Ford,
    Richard I.; Stein, John R.)

    1954a   A Pueblo III site at Farmington, New Mexico. *In*
            Wendorf 1954a, pp. 29-40.

    1954b   A Pueblo I site near San Felipe Pueblo, New Mexico.
            In Wendorf 1954a, pp. 41-51.

    1957a   (ed.) Highway salvage archaeology, Vol. 3. New
            Mexico State Highway Dept. and Museum of New Mex-
            ico, 101 pp.

    1957b   The Switchback Site: a stratified ruin near Reserve,
            New Mexico. *In* Peckham 1957a, pp. 10-38.

    1957c   Three pithouse sites near Albuquerque, New Mexico.
            In Peckham 1957a, pp. 39-70.

    1958a   Hillside Pueblo: early masonry architecture in the
            Reserve area, New Mexico. El Palacio, 65:81-94.

    1958b   Salvage archaeology in New Mexico 1957-58: a partial
            report. El Palacio, 65, no. 5:161-168.

    1962   Archaeological salvage excavations on Interstate 40
            near McCartys, New Mexico. Laboratory of Anthro-
            pology Notes, 11.

    1963a   (ed.) Highway salvage archaeology, Vol. 4. New
            Mexico State Highway Dept. and Museum of New Mexico,

122 pp.
Reviewed AA 66:194 (Martin), AAq 29:396 (Shaeffer).

1963b The Luna Junction site, an early pit house in the Pine Lawn Valley, New Mexico. *In* Peckham 1963a, pp. 41-55.

1963c The Red Willow site, a bi-walled kiva near Tohatchi, New Mexico. *In* Peckham 1963a, pp. 56-72.

1963d A Basket Maker III site near Tohatchi, New Mexico. *In* Peckham 1963a, pp. 73-82.

1963e Excavations at LA3560 and LA3562. *In* Peckham 1963a, pp. 83-91.

1963f Two Rosa Phase sites near Dulce, New Mexico. *In* Peckham 1963a, pp. 92-115.

1965 Prehistoric weapons in the Southwest. Museum of New Mexico, Popular Series Pamphlet no. 3, 26 pp.

1966 Archaeological salvage excavations in the vicinity of the proposed Cochiti dam: 1965 season. Laboratory of Anthropology Notes, 42.

1967a Archaeological salvage excavations along Interstate 40 near Laguna Pueblo, New Mexico. Laboratory of Anthropology Notes, 47.

1967b A preceramic house in New Mexico. Archaeology, 20, no. 3:222-223.

1968 The transitional period. *In* Irwin-Williams 1968a, pp. 10-13.

PECKHAM, S.L., and BRUGGE, David M.

1976 Taylor Draw: a Mogollon-Anasazi hybrid? *In* Schroeder 1976, pp. 37-72.

PECKHAM, S.L., and REED, Erik K.

1963 Three sites near Ranchos de Taos, New Mexico. *In* Peckham 1963a, pp. 1-28.

PECKHAM, S.L., and WELLS, Susan L.

1967 An inventory of archaeological sites at and in the vicinities of Bandelier National Monument and the Cochiti dam and reservoir, New Mexico. Laboratory of Anthropology Notes, 80F.

PECKHAM, S.L., WENDORF, Fred, and FERDON, Edwin N., Jr.

1956   Excavations near Apache Creek, New Mexico. *In*
        Wendorf 1956a, pp. 17-86.

PEET, Stephen D.

1888   Ruins of ancient cities in New Mexico. American
        Antiquarian, 10:255-256.

1890   The cliff-dwellers and their works. American An-
        tiquarian, 12, no. 2:85-104.

1895   The discovery of the Pueblos. American Antiquarian,
        17:339-354.

1896a   History and architecture of the Tusayans. American
        Antiquarian, 18, no. 1:1-21.

1896b   Early American explorations among the Pueblos.
        American Antiquarian, 18:228-245.

1896c   A study of the high cliff-dwellings and cave-towns.
        American Antiquarian, 18:285-302.

1896d   Ancient and modern Pueblos compared. American
        Antiquarian, 18:333-345.

1897a   Relative age of the Pueblos and cliff-dwellings.
        American Antiquarian, 19, no. 2:100-111.

1897b   The kivas and their history. American Antiquarian,
        19:171-176.

1898a   The Cliff Palace and its surroundings. American
        Antiquarian, 20, no. 1:19-36.

1898b   Cliff fortresses. American Antiquarian, 20, no.
        2:81-100.

1898c   Spanish and American explorations. American An-
        tiquarian, 20:143-164.

1898d   Caves and cliff-dwellings compared. American An-
        tiquarian, 20, no. 4:193-210.

1898e   The religious life and works of the cliff dwellers.
        American Antiquarian, 20, no. 5:275-298.

1898f   Great houses and fortresses. American Antiquarian,
        20:315-338.

1899a   The Cliff Dwellers and Pueblos. Chicago, American
        Antiquarian, 398 pp.

1899b   The social and domestic life of the cliff-dwellers.
        American Antiquarian, 21:17-40.

1899c   Relics of the cliff-dwellers. American Antiquarian,
        21:99-122.

1899d   Agriculture among the Pueblos and cliff-dwellers.
        American Antiquarian, 21:209-232.

1899e   The beginnings of pueblo architecture. American
        Antiquarian, 21:317-328.

1899f   The cliff dwellers and the wild tribes. American
        Antiquarian, 21, no. 6:349-368.

1900   The great plateau and its inhabitants. American
        Antiquarian, 22, no. 1:1-16.

PENDERGAST, David M.

1961a   Excavations at the Bear River site, Box Elder County,
        Utah. Utah Archaeology, 7, no. 2:14-18.

1961b   USAS-UCRBASP joint excavation in the Plainfield
        Reservoir. Utah Archaeology, 7, no. 3:15-21.

1962a   Archaeological resources of Fish Springs National
        Wildlife Refuge: preliminary report. University
        of Utah, Miscellaneous Collected Papers, no. 5,
        Anthropological Papers, 60:93-107.
        Reviewed AA 67:1592 (Schwartz).

1962b   The Frei site, Santa Clara, Utah. University of
        Utah, Miscellaneous Collected Papers, no. 7,
        Anthropological Papers, 60:127-163.
        Reviewed AA 67:1592 (Schwartz).

PENDERGAST, D.M., and HASSEL, Francis K.

1962   A burial from an open site in Willard Reservoir,
        Box Elder County. Utah Archaeology, 8, no. 1:22-24.

PENDLETON, LaVerna

1952   The Gallina Phase of northern New Mexico. *In*
        Indian Tribes of Aboriginal America: Selected
        Papers of the 29th International Congress of Amer-
        icanists, ed. S. Tax, pp. 145-152.

PEPPER, Choral

1963   The unsolved mystery of the Southwest. Desert
        Magazine, 26, no. 11:22-27.

1966   Needles' second mystic maze. Desert Magazine,
        29, no. 10:26-29.

PEPPER, George H.

1899   Ceremonial deposits found in an ancient Pueblo
        estufa in northern New Mexico. Monumental Records,
        1, no. 1:1-6.
        Reviewed AA n.s. 2:169 (Hodge).

1902   The ancient Basket Makers of southeastern Utah.
        American Museum Journal, 2, no. 4, Supplement,
        Guide Leaflet no. 6, 26 pp.

1905a   Ceremonial objects and ornaments from Pueblo Bonito,
        New Mexico. American Anthropologist, n.s. 7, no.
        2:183-197.

1905b   The throwing-stick of a prehistoric people of the
        Southwest. Proceedings of the 13th International
        Congress of Americanists, pp. 107-130.

1906   Human effigy vases from Chaco Canyon, New Mexico.
        Boas Anniversary Volume, New York, pp. 320-334.

1909   The exploration of a burial room in Pueblo Bonito,
        New Mexico. Putnam Anniversary Volume, New York,
        pp. 196-252.

1920   Pueblo Bonito. American Museum of Natural History,
        Anthropological Papers, 27, 398 pp.

1924   A strange type of pottery from Utah. Museum of
        the American Indian, Indian Notes, 1, no. 4:167-184.

PERKINS, R.F.

1967a   Engraved stones of southern Nevada. Nevada Archae-
        ological Survey, Reporter, 1, no. 7:11-13.

1967b   Clovis-like points in southern Nevada. Nevada
        Archaeological Survey, Reporter, 1, no. 9:9-11.

1968   Folsom and Sandia points from Clark County. Nevada
        Archaeological Survey, Reporter, 2, no. 4:4-5.

PETERSON, Alfred

1935a   El Morro petroglyph interpretation. Southwestern
        Monuments Monthly Report, September, p. 232.

1935b   Specimens from the Pueblo area collected by the
        First Beam Expedition, 1933. Tree-Ring Bulletin,
        1, no. 3:23-24.

1937   Further data on First Beam Expedition specimens,
        1923. Tree-Ring Bulletin, 3:23-24.

1939   Third report on Hopi specimens; collections of
        Second Beam Expedition, 1928. Tree-Ring Bulletin,
        6:6-8.

PETERSON, H. Merrill

1963   History and pre-history of Bear Lake Indians.
        Utah Archaeology, 9, no. 4:2-12.

1964   Indian cache uncovered. Utah Archaeology, 10, no.
        4:2-3.

PETERSON, Harold L.

1952   The helmet found at San Gabriel del Yunque, New
        Mexico. El Palacio, 59:283-287.

PFINGSTEN, Clark C. (See under Wiseman, Regge N.)

PHELPS, Alan L.

1964   Cultural analyzation of pre-historic Indian sites
        of northern Chihuahua, Mexico. El Paso Archae-
        ological Society, Special Report no. 2, 11 pp.

1966a   A burial at the McGregor site. The Artifact, 4,
        no. 2:2.

1966b   Cruciform - an unusual artifact of the El Paso
        Southwest. El Paso Archaeological Society, Special
        Report no. 5, 45 pp.

1967   Six stone balls - a cache. The Artifact, 5, no.
        1:21-31.

1968a   An incised stone pendant and a Soto projectile
        point from northwest Chihuahua. The Artifact, 6,
        no. 3:16-22.

1968b   A recovery of purslane seeds in an archaeological
        context. The Artifact, 6, no. 4:1-9.

PHILLIPS, David A. (See under Canouts, Valetta; Grady, Mark A.)

PHILLIPS, John B. (See under Brice, Chuck L.)

PHILLIPS, Philip (See under Willey, Gordon R.)

PIERSON, Lloyd M. (See also under Galinat, Walton C.)

1956   The archaeology of Richards Caves, Arizona. Pla-
        teau, 28, no. 4:91-97.

1957   A brief archaeological reconnaissance of White
        Canyon, southeastern Utah. El Palacio, 64:222-230.

1958   An undercut storage pit near Moab, Utah. Utah Ar-
        chaeology, 4, no. 1:4-6.

1959   The Winneman Ranch site, central Arizona. El Pa-
        lacio, 66, no. 4:128-139.

1960   Ute tipi poles. Utah Archaeology, 6, no. 4:10-12.

1962a   Archaeological resources of the Needles-Salt Creek
        area, Utah. Utah Archaeology, 8, no. 2:1-3.

1962b   Excavations at the Lower Ruin and Annex, Tonto
        National Monument, 1952. *In* Caywood 1962, pp. 33-
        69.

PIERSON, L.M., and ANDERSON, Kevin

1975   Another split-twig figurine from Moab, Utah. Pla-
        teau, 48, nos. 1-2:43-45.

PIKE, Donald G. (See under Muench, David.)

PILLES, Peter J., Jr.

1969   Habitation and field houses near Winona and Angell,
        Arizona. Kiva, 34, nos. 2-3:90-102.

1975   Petroglyphs of the Little Colorado River Valley.
        In American Indian Rock Art: Papers Presented at
        the 1974 Rock Art Symposium, ed. Shari T. Grove,
        San Juan County Museum Association, Farmington.

1976   Sinagua and Salado similarities as seen from the
        Verde Valley. *In* Doyel and Haury 1976, pp. 113-124.

PILLES, P.J., and DANSON, Edward B.

1974   The prehistoric pottery of Arizona. Arizona High-
        ways, 50, February, pp. 2-5, 10-15, 43-45.

PILLSBURY, Dorothy L.

1954   Bulldozers followed the archaeologists. Desert
        Magazine, 17, no. 1:13-16.

PINKLEY, Edna T. (See also under Pinkley, Frank H.)

1926   Casa Grande: the greatest valley pueblo of Arizona.
        Arizona Archaeological and Historical Society, Tuc-
        son, 23 pp.

1928   The Casa Grande as a national monument. Masterkey,
        1:26-28.

PINKLEY, Frank H. (See also under Tovrea, J.H.)

1927   Beam dating at Wupatki and Walnut Canyon. South-
        western Monuments Monthly Report, November.

1928   Montezuma's Castle. Phoenix, 24 pp.

1930   Tumacacori National Monument. Phoenix, 23 pp.

1935   Seventeen years ago. Southwestern Monuments
        Monthly Reports, Nov.-Dec., pp. 383-389, 455-459.

1936a   Northeast building. Southwestern Monuments Monthly
        Report, Supplement, March, pp. 233-235.

1936b   "Throne" room in the "Clan House" at the Casa Grande
        National Monument. Southwestern Monuments Monthly
        Report, March, pp. 235-236.

1936c   Repair and restoration of Tumacacori, 1921. South-
        western Monuments Monthly Report, October, pp. 261-
        287.

PINKLEY, F.H., and PINKLEY, Edna Townsley

1931   The Casa Grande National Monument in Arizona. 27
        pp.

PINKLEY, F.H., and others

1938   The sage of Threatening Rock. Southwestern Monu-
        ments Monthly Report, April, pp. 347-379.

PINKLEY, Jean M. (See also under Lancaster, James A.)

1965   The Pueblos and the turkey: who domesticated whom?
        In Osborne 1965a, pp. 70-72.

PINKLEY, Nancy M.

1931   Ten sixty-six to thirteen hundred. Mesa Verde
        Notes, 2, no. 2:1-19.

PLOG, Fred T. (See also under Martin, Paul Sidney.)

1971a   Chevelon archaeological research project, 1971.
        University of California at Los Angeles, Archae-
        ological Survey, Annual Report, 13:1-24.

1971b   Some operational considerations. *In* Gumerman 1971,
        pp. 45-54.

1974a Settlement patterns and social history. *In* Frontiers in Anthropology, ed. Murray Leaf, pp. 68-91.

1974b The study of prehistoric change. Academic Press, New York, 199 pp.

1975 Demographic studies in Southwestern prehistory. *In* Swedlund 1975, pp. 94-103.

1978 An analysis of variability in site locations in the Chevelon drainage, Arizona. *In* Euler and Gumerman 1978, pp. 53-71.

PLOG, F.T., and GARRETT, C.K.

1972 Explaining variability in prehistoric Southwestern water control systems. *In* Contemporary Archaeology, ed. M.P. Leone, Southern Illinois University Press, pp. 280-288.

PLOG, F.T, and HILL, James N.

1971 Explaining variability in the distribution of sites. *In* Gumerman 1971, pp. 7-36.

PLOG, F.T., and WOOD, Jon Scott

1977 The research potential of multiple-use studies. U.S. Forest Service, Southwestern Region, Archaeological Report, no. 16:51-57.

PLOG, F.T., EFFLAND, R., and GREEN, Dee F.

1978 Inferences using the SARG data bank. *In* Euler and Gumerman 1978, pp. 139-148.

PLOG, F.T., HANTMAN, Jeff, and WOOD, Jon Scott

1977 An archaeological survey of the Watts timber sale, Apache-Sitgreaves National Forest, Alpine Ranger District, Apache County, Arizona. Arizona State University, Office of Cultural Resource Management, Report no. 33, 24 pp.

PLOG, F.T., HILL, J.N., and READ, Dwight W.

1976 (eds.) Chevelon Archaeological Research Project. University of California at Los Angeles, Institute of Archaeology, Monograph II, 167 pp.

PLOG, F.T., EFFLAND, Richard, DEAN, Jeffrey S., and GAINES, Sylvia W.

1978   SARG: future research directions. *In* Euler and Gumerman 1978, pp. 177-186.

PLOG, Stephen E. (See also under Minnis, Paul E.)

1976   The inference of prehistoric social organization from ceramic design variability. Michigan Discussions in Anthropology I, pp. 1-47.

PLOWDEN, William W., Jr.

1958   Spanish and Mexican Majolica found in New Mexico. El Palacio, 65, no. 6:212-219.

POGUE, Joseph E.

1912   The aboriginal use of turquois in North America. American Anthropologist, 14:437-466.

1915   The turquois: a study of its history, mineralogy, geology, ethnology, archaeology, mythology, folklore, and technology. Memoirs of the National Academy of Sciences, 12, pt. 2, memoir 3, 162 pp. Reviewed AA 18:585 (Laufer).

POLK, Ann S. (See under Walker, Noel P., Jr.)

POLUSHKIN, E.P. (See under Fink, Colin G.)

POMEROY, John Anthony

1959   Hohokam etched shell. Kiva, 24, no. 4:12-21.

1974   A study of black-on-white painted pottery in the Tonto Basin, Arizona. Southwestern Lore, 39, no. 4:1-34.

POND, Gordon G.

1966   A painted kiva near Winslow, Arizona. American Antiquity, 31:555-558.

POOLER, Lolita H.

1940   Alameda Pueblo ruins. El Palacio, 47, no. 4:84-88.

POTEET, Sybil

1938   The occurrence and distribution of beveled knives. Bulletin of the Texas Archaeological and Paleontological Society, 10:245-262.

POULS, Basil G. (See under Lyons, Thomas R.)

POWERS, Margaret A.

1975a   Archaeological investigations at AZ 0:1:4 (ASM).
        Arizona State Museum, Archaeological Series, 75,
        31 pp.

1975b   Archaeological survey of WST right-of-way, Sitgreaves
        National Forest. Arizona State Museum, Archaeologi-
        cal Series, 79, 46 pp.

PRENTICE, Royal A.

1934   Were the makers of Chupadero pottery the Jumanos
        tribe of Indians? El Palacio, 37, nos. 5-6:33-39.

1951   Pictograph story of Koñate. El Palacio, 58, no.
        3:91-96.

PREWITT, Elton R. (See also under Dibble, David S.)

1966   A preliminary report on the Devil's Rockshelter
        site, Val Verde County, Texas. Texas Journal of
        Science, 18, no. 2:206-224.

1970   The Pedra del Diablo Site, Val Verde County, Texas,
        and notes on some Trans-Pecos Texas archaeological
        material in the Smithsonian Institution, Washington,
        D.C. Texas Historical Survey Committee, Archaeologi-
        cal Report, 18, pp. 1-52.

PRICE, Theron D. (See under Fitting, James E.)

PRICE, V. Armstrong

1944   The Clovis Site; regional physiography and geology.
        American Antiquity, 9:401-407.

PRINCE, L.B.

1904   The' stone lions of Cochiti. Records of the Past,
        3:151-160.

PRUDDEN, T. Mitchell

1896   A summer among cliff dwellings. Harper's Magazine,
        93:545-561.

1897   An elder brother to the cliff-dweller. Harper's
        Monthly Magazine, 95 (June):56-63.

1903   The prehistoric ruins of the San Juan watershed in

Utah, Arizona, Colorado, and New Mexico. American Anthropologist, n.s. 5, no. 2:224-288.

1907   On the Great American Plateau. New York, G.P. Putnam's Sons, 243 pp.

1914   The circular kivas of small ruins in the San Juan watershed. American Anthropologist, 16, no. 1:33-58.

1918   A further study of prehistoric small house ruins in the San Juan watershed. Memoirs of the American Anthropological Association, 5, no. 1:1-50.

PUTNAM, Frederick W., and others

1879   Reports upon archaeological and ethnological collections from the vicinity of Santa Barbara, Cal., and from ruined pueblos in Arizona and New Mexico, and certain interior tribes. Report of the United States Geographical Surveys West of the 100th Meridian, Archaeology, 7:315-485.

QUIMBY, Byron

1964   Artifacts from Elephant Butte area. The Artifact, 2, no. 4:8.

QUIMBY, B., and BROOK, V.R.

1967   A Folsom site near El Paso, Texas. The Artifact, 5, no. 4:31-47.

QUIMBY, George I. (See under Martin, Paul Sidney.)

QUINN, Kathleen, and RONEY, John

1973   Archaeological resources of the San Simon and Vulture Units of the Bureau of Land Management. Arizona State Museum, Archaeological Series, 34, 56 pp.

RAAB, L. Mark (See also under Busch, C.D.)

1973a   AZ AA:5:2: a prehistoric cactus camp in Papagueria. Journal of the Arizona Academy of Science, 8:116-118.

1973b   Research design for investigation of archaeological resources in Santa Rosa Wash: Phase I. Arizona State Museum, Archaeological Series, 26, 95 pp.

1975   A prehistoric water reservoir from Santa Rosa Wash,

southern Arizona. Kiva, 40, no. 4:295-307.

1976   The structure of prehistoric community organization
        at Santa Rosa Wash, southern Arizona. Arizona
        State University, dissertation, 377 pp.; University
        Microfilms International.

1977   The Santa Rosa Wash project: notes on archaeological
        research design under contract. *In* Schiffer and
        Gumerman 1977.

RAAB, L.M., and others

1974   Archaeological investigations for the Santa Rosa
        Wash Project - Phase I, preliminary report. Ari-
        zona State Museum, Archaeological Series, 60, 430
        pp.

RANSOM, Jay Ellis

1953   Gem stones in the Bradshaws. Desert Magazine, 16,
        no. 10:7-21.

1965   The Kinishba Pueblo ruins. Natural History, 74,
        no. 5:58-60, 62.

RAUN, Gerald G., and ECK, L.J.

1967   Vertebrate remains from four archaeological sites
        in the Amistad Reservoir area, Val Verde County,
        Texas. Texas Journal of Science, 19:138-150.

RAY, Cyrus N.

1940   Painted pebbles. Central Texas Archaeological
        Society, News Letter, 3:12-13.

RAY, Louis L.

1939   Distribution of artifacts made from chalcedony of
        Cerro Pedernal, New Mexico. Science, 90:372.

RAY, Terry

1955   Mountain village - 1200 A.D. New Mexico Magazine,
        33, no. 9:20, 45.

RAYNOLDS, F.R. (See under Douglas, Frederick H.)

RAYNOR, T.E.

1955   The mystery of the Mogollon migration. New Mexico
        Magazine, 33, no. 2:14-15, 37.

READ, Dwight W. (See under Plog, Fred T.)

READ, W.H.A.

1883   Description of ancient Aztec town in New Mexico.
        American Antiquarian, 5:65-70.

REAGAN, Albert B.

1917a   The story of Jemez and Zia. El Palacio, 4, no. 2:
        24-72.

1917b   The Deep Creek Indians. El Palacio, 4, no. 3:31-
        42.

1919   The ancient ruins in lower and middle Pine River
        Valley, Colorado. El Palacio, 7, nos. 9-12:170-
        176.

1920   Who made the Kayenta National Monument ruins?
        American Anthropologist, 22:387-388.

1922   Additional notes on the Jemez-Zia region. El
        Palacio, 12, no. 9:120-121.

1927a   Ancient cotton of the Southwest. Southern Workman,
        56, no. 9:426-429.

1927b   Archaeological notes on Pine River Valley, Colorado,
        and the Kayenta-Tuba region, Arizona. Transactions
        of the Kansas Academy of Science, 30:244-331, 394-
        429.

1927c   Records of the past in Arizona. El Palacio, 22:
        533-536.

1928a   Continued archaeological studies in the Navajo
        country, Arizona. Transactions of the Kansas
        Academy of Science, 31:142-279.

1928b   Some notes on the archaeology of the Navajo country.
        El Palacio, 24, no. 18:335-346.

1928c   Further notes on the archaeology of the Navajo
        country. El Palacio, 25, no. 1:3-26.

1928d   The small house ruins of the slab-house and black-
        on-white pottery series in the Cornfields-Hopi
        volcanic buttes' field, in the Navajo country, Ari-
        zona. El Palacio, 25, nos. 3-5:59-76.

1928e   The small house and semi-pueblo ruins of the painted
        (and shiny painted) ware series in the Cornfields-
        Hopi volcanic buttes' field, in the Navajo country,
        Arizona. El Palacio, 25, nos. 14-17:232-250.

1930a Ancient cities of northeastern Arizona. Wisconsin Archaeologist, 9:188-195.

1930b Archaeological notes on the Fort Apache region, Arizona. Transactions of the Kansas Academy of Science, 33:111-131.

1931a Archaeological notes on the Brush Creek region, northeastern Utah. Wisconsin Archaeologist, 10, no. 4:132-138.

1931b Early house builders of the Brush Creek region in northeastern Utah. American Anthropologist, 33: 660-661.

1931c The pictographs of Ashley and Dry Fork Valleys in northeastern Utah. Transactions of the Kansas Academy of Science, 34:168-216.

1931d Ruins and pictographs in Nine Mile Canyon, Utah. Transactions of the Illinois Academy of Science, 24, no. 2:369-370.

1931e Some notes on the ancient earth-lodge peoples of the Willard stage of Pueblo culture in the Uintah Basin, Utah. El Palacio, 30:236-241.

1931f Some archaeological notes on Nine Mile Canyon, Utah. El Palacio, 31, no. 4:45-71.

1931g Additional archaeological notes on Ashley and Dry Fork Canyons in northeastern Utah. El Palacio, 31: 122-131.

1931h Some archaeological notes on Hill Canyon in northeastern Utah. El Palacio, 31, no. 15:223-244.

1931i Collections of ancient artifacts from the Ashley-Dry Fork district of the Uintah Basin, etc. El Palacio, 31, no. 26:407-413.

1931j Rock drawings in Utah. Discoveries, 2, no. 3:6.

1932a Archaeological finds in the Uintah Basin in Utah. Wisconsin Archaeologist, 11:162-171.

1932b Finds in the Uintah Basin in Utah in 1931. American Anthropologist, 34, no. 3:505.

1932c The ancient agriculturalists of Brush Creek Valley, in northeastern Utah. Frontier, 12, no. 2:174-176.

1932d Some notes on picture writing north of Mexico. Wagner Institute of Science, 7:38-54.

1933a   Anciently inhabited caves of the Vernal district
        with some additional notes on Nine Mile Canyon,
        northeastern Utah. Transactions of the Kansas
        Academy of Science, 36:41-70.

1933b   Archaeological finds in northeastern Utah. Pro-
        ceedings of the Iowa Academy of Science, 40:131-132.

1933c   The Basket Makers and the people of the ancient
        culture of the Fremont River in Utah. Northwest
        Science, 7, no. 3, 4 pp.

1933d   Some notes on the snake pictographs of Nine Mile
        Canyon, Utah. American Anthropologist, 35:550-551.

1933e   Summary of archaeological finds in the Uintah Basin,
        Utah, to date. Proceedings of the Utah Academy of
        Science, Arts and Letters, 10:3-12.

1933f   Caves of the Vernal district of northeastern Utah.
        Proceedings of the Utah Academy of Science, Arts
        and Letters, 10:13-18.

1933g   Evidence of migration in ancient Pueblo times.
        American Anthropologist, 35:206-207.

1933h   Indian pictures in Ashley and Dry Fork Valleys, in
        northeastern Utah. Art and Archaeology, 34, no. 3:
        201-205, 210.

1934a   Additional archaeological notes on the Uintah Basin
        in northeastern Utah. Transactions of the Kansas
        Academy of Science, 37:39-54.

1934b   Some ancient Indian granaries. Proceedings of the
        Utah Academy of Science, Arts and Letters, 11:39-40.

1934c   Evidence of a possible migration in the very dawn-
        ing period of Pueblo culture. Primitive Man, 7:
        12-14.

1935a   Archaeological notes on the Brush Creek region in
        northeastern Utah. Wisconsin Archaeologist, 15,
        no. 1:23-24.

1935b   Archaeological report of field work done in Utah
        in 1934-35. Proceedings of the Utah Academy of
        Science, Arts and Letters, 12:50-88.

1935c   Petroglyphs show that the ancients of the Southwest
        wore masks. American Anthropologist, 37:707-708.

1935d   Some notes on an ancient culture of the Provo-Salt
        Lake region. Northwest Science, 9, no. 2:13-15.

1935e   Two rock pictures and their probable connection
         with the "Pied Piper" myth of the Indians. Colorado
         Magazine, 12, no. 2:55-59.

REAVES, Roy W., III

1969   The Casa Grande calendar holes: fact or fable?
         Arizona Archaeologist, 4:1-20.

1975   A case for limited problem-oriented research. *In*
         Frisbie 1975a, pp. 437-453.

REED, Allen C.

1952   Arrow fever. Arizona Highways, 28, no. 3:8-13.

1954   Point of Pines, Arizona Highways, 30, no. 1:18-27.

REED, Erik K. (See also under Ferdon, Edwin N., Jr.; Peckham,
Stewart L.; Scheans, Daniel J.; Wendorf, Fred.)

1937   Historic Site Survey: Section B, the prehistoric
         Indian cultures. Southwest Monuments Monthly Re-
         port, February, pp. 135-140.

1938   Archaeology of the Mimbres Valley, New Mexico.
         Central Texas Archaeologist, no. 4:9-20.

1939   Preliminary study of pottery from room 7, Wupatki
         Pueblo. Southwest Monuments Monthly Report, March,
         pp. 209-237.

1940   People of the petrified forest. National Park
         Service, Region III Quarterly, 2, no. 1:22-25.

1942   Implications of the Mogollon concept. American
         Antiquity, 8:27-32.

1943a   The problem of protohistoric Picuries. El Palacio,
         50, no. 3:65-68.

1943b   The Southern Tewa Pueblos in the historic period.
         El Palacio, 50, no. 11:254-264; no. 12:276-288.

1944a   The abandonment of the San Juan region. El Palacio,
         51, no. 4:61-74.

1944b   Archaeological work in Mancos Canyon, Colorado.
         American Antiquity, 10:48-58.

1944c   The place of Citadel Polychrome in San Juan Orange-
         ware. Southwestern Lore, 9, no. 4:5-7.

1944d   Late Redware intrusives in the Mesa Verde Focus.
         Southwestern Lore, 9, no. 4:7-9.

1944e   Pottery types of the Manuelito district. American
        Antiquity, 10:161-172.

1946a   Canyon de Chelly. Arizona Highways, 22, no. 7:32-
        33.

1946b   The distinctive features and distribution of the
        San Juan Anasazi culture. Southwestern Journal
        of Anthropology, 2, no. 3:295-305.

1947a   The 1947 Chaco Conference. El Palacio, 54, no. 9:
        217-218.

1947b   Flood damage to Chetro Ketl. El Palacio, 54:238-
        240.

1948a   Fractional burials, trophy skulls, and cannibalism.
        National Park Service, Region 3, Anthropological
        Notes, no. 79.

1948b   The Western Pueblo archaeological complex. El
        Palacio, 55:9-15.

1948c   The dating of early Mogollon horizons. El Palacio,
        55:382-386.

1949a   The possible origins of San Juan Orangeware. Nation-
        al Park Service, Region 3, Anthropological Interpre-
        tation Circular no. 2, pp. 5-7.

1949b   The significance of skull deformation in the South-
        west. El Palacio, 56:106-119.

1949c   Sources of upper Rio Grande Pueblo culture and pop-
        ulation. El Palacio, 56, no. 6:163-184.

1950a   Eastern-central Arizona archaeology in relation to
        the western Pueblos. Southwestern Journal of Anthro-
        pology, 6, no. 2:120-138.

1950b   Minerals and mining in the pre-Spanish Southwest.
        El Palacio, 57, no. 10:308-310.

1950c   Population shifts in the pre-Spanish Southwest.
        Bulletin of the Texas Archaeological and Paleonto-
        logical Society, 21:90-96.

1951a   Cultural areas of the pre-Spanish Southwest. New
        Mexico Quarterly Review, 21, no. 4:428-439.

1951b   Turkeys in Southwestern archaeology. El Palacio,
        58:195-205.

1951c   Types of stone axes in the Southwest. Southwestern
        Lore, 17, no. 3:45-51.

1954a   Test excavations at San Marcos Pueblo.   El Palacio,
        61:323-343.

1954b   Transition to history in the Pueblo Southwest.
        American Anthropologist, 56, no. 4:592-603.

1955a   Painted pottery and Zuni history. Southwestern
        Journal of Anthropology, 11:178-193.

1955b   Trends in Southwestern archaeology. In New Inter-
        pretations of Aboriginal American Culture History,
        ed. B.J. Meggers and C. Evans, Anthropological
        Society of Washington, pp. 46-58.

1955c   Bison beyond the Pecos. Texas Journal of Science,
        7, no. 2:130-135.

1956   Types of village-plan layouts in the Southwest.
        In Willey 1956, pp. 11-17.

1957   Human skeletal remains from some highway salvage
        excavations in New Mexico. In Peckham 1957a, pp.
        85-97.

1958   Excavations in Mancos Canyon, Colorado. University
        of Utah, Anthropological Papers, 35, 221 pp.
        Reviewed AAq 25:138 (Wheat).

1962a   Human skeletal material from site 59, Chaco Canyon
        National Monument. El Palacio, 69:240-247.

1962b   Pine trees, pollen, and recent climatic history of
        the Southwest. National Park Service, Region 3
        Research Abstracts, no. 292.

1962c   Cultural continuity from pre-Spanish archaeological
        groups to modern Indian tribes in the southwestern
        United States. Proceedings of the 34th International
        Congress of Americanists, pp. 298-300.

1963a   The beginnings of physical anthropology in the
        Southwest. Journal of the Arizona Academy of Sci-
        ence, 2:130-132.

1963b   Drought in the Southwest. National Park Service,
        Region 3 Research Abstracts, no. 296.

1963c   An early Gallina burial from the Jicarilla country
        (LA6163). El Palacio, 70, no. 3:24-35.

1963d   Tepehuan and Hohokam. National Park Service, Region
        3 Research Abstracts, no. 302.

1963e   The period known as Pueblo I. National Park Service,
        Region 3 Research Abstracts, no. 304.

1964   The Greater Southwest. *In* Jennings and Norbeck
        1964, pp. 175-191.
        Reviewed AAq 30:503 (Meighan).

1965   Human skeletal material from site 34, Mesa Verde
        National Park. El Palacio, 72, no. 3:31-45.

REED, E.K., and BREWER, J.W., Jr.

1937   Excavation of room 7, Wupatki. Southwest Monuments
        Special Report no. 13, January, pp. 41-63.

REED, E.K., and FERDON, Edwin N., Jr.

1950   A pit house site near Belen, New Mexico. El Pala-
        cio, 57, no. 2:40-42.

REED, E.K., and KING, Dale S.

1950   (ed.) For the Dean: essays in anthropology in
        honor of Byron Cummings. Hohokam Museums Associ-
        ation and Southwest Monuments Association, 307 pp.
        Reviewed AAq 16:360 (Smith).

REEDER, Grant M.

1965   Pictographs from Parrish Canyon, Davis County.
        Utah Archaeology, 11, no. 3:5-8.

1967   Split twig animal miniatures in the southwestern
        United States. Utah Archaeology 13:12-16.

REHER, Charles A. (See also under Broilo, Frank J.)

1975   Archaeological clearance survey of 16 Anaconda
        Company proposed exploration well sites. Univer-
        sity of New Mexico, contract report 101-103J (NPS).

1977   (ed.) Settlement and subsistence along the lower
        Chaco River: the CGP survey. University of New
        Mexico Press, 614 pp.

REID, J. Jefferson (See also under Longacre, William A.; Mayro,
Linda L.)

1975   Comments on environment and behavior at Antelope
        House. *In* Rock and Morris 1975, pp. 127-132.

1978   Response to stress at Grasshopper Pueblo, Arizona.
        In Grebinger 1978a, pp. 195-213.

REID, J.J., SCHIFFER, M.B., and NEFF, J.M.

1975   Archaeological considerations of intrasite sampling.

In Sampling in Archaeology, ed. J.W. Mueller, University of Arizona Press, pp. 209-224.

REILEY, Daniel E., and BIRKBY, Walter H.

1975   Two Kayenta Pueblo III cradle burials from upper Glen Canyon, Utah. Plateau, 48, nos. 1-2:23-30.

REILLY, P.T.

1966a   The Juno Ruin. Masterkey, 40, no. 1:16-22.

1966b   The sites at Vasey's Paradise. Masterkey, 40, no. 4:126-139.

1969   Was fire once part of the figurine ritual? Masterkey, 43:34-36.

1973   The Refuge Cave. Masterkey, 47, no. 2:46-54.

REINHARD, Karl (See under Vivian, R. Gwinn.)

REINHART, Theodore R. (See also under Galinat, Walton C.)

1967a   The Alameda Phase: an early Basketmaker III culture in the middle Rio Grande Valley, New Mexico. Southwestern Lore, 33, no. 1:24-32.

1967b   The Rio Rancho Phase: a preliminary report on early Basketmaker culture in the middle Rio Grande Valley, New Mexico. American Antiquity, 32:458-470.

1968   Late Archaic cultures of the middle Rio Grande Valley, New Mexico: a study of the process of culture change. University of New Mexico, dissertation, 406 pp.; University Microfilms International.

1971a   The background of a research project. School of American Research, Exploration 1971, pp. 10-15.

1971b   A revised working bibliography of northern Rio Grande prehistory, New Mexico. College of William and Mary and School of American Research, 21 pp.

REINMAN, Fred M. (See under True, D.L.)

REITER, Paul (See also under Alexander, Hubert G.; Cady, Jean; Kluckhohn, Clyde; Vivian, R. Gordon.)

1930   Cave investigated. El Palacio, 29:269-272.

1931   Preliminary examination of a ruin in the Rio Puerco Valley, New Mexico. El Palacio, 31, no. 26:414-416.

1938   The Jemez Pueblo of Unshagi, New Mexico; with notes
        on the earlier excavations at "Amoxiumqua" and
        Giusewa. University of New Mexico Bulletin, Mono-
        graph Series, 1, nos. 4-5, 211 pp.
        Reviewed AA 41:316 (Kidder), AAq 6:93 (Baldwin).

REITER, P., and FISHER, Reginald G.

1931   Airplane used in archaeological survey of Pueblo
        Plateau. El Palacio, 30:215-217, 224-225.

REITER, P., MULLOY, William T., and BLUMENTHAL, E.H., Jr.

1940   Preliminary report of the Jemez excavation at Nani-
        shagi, New Mexico. University of New Mexico Bul-
        letin, Anthropological Series, 3, no. 3, 39 pp.
        Reviewed AAq 6:296 (Fenenga).

REITER, Winifred

1933   An unknown city of ancient America. Illustrated
        London News, December 2, pp. 892-894.

RENAUD, Etienne B.

1925a   Figurines indiennes préhistoriques du Sud-ouest
        américain. Impr. Veuve P. Berthier, Dijon, 6 pp.

1925b   Notes sur la céramique indienne du Sud-ouest des
        Etats-Unis. Journal de la Société des Américanistes
        de Paris, n.s. 17:85-99, 101-117.

1925c   Propulseurs et sagaies préhistoriques des indiens
        "basket makers." Bulletin de la Société Préhisto-
        rique Française, 22:297-312.

1926a   Flutes indiennes préhistoriques du Sud-ouest améri-
        cain. Société Préhistorique Française, Bulletin,
        23:168-178.

1926b   Statuettes indiennes préhistoriques de l'Arizona.
        Impr. Veuve P. Berthier, Dijon, 2 pp.

1926c   Uncovering the first Americans. Forum, 75:109-113.
        (also El Palacio, 20:242-250).

1926d   Undeformed prehistoric skulls from the Southwest.
        Science, 64, no. 1661:430-432.

1927   Undeformed prehistoric Indian skulls from La Plata
        (Colorado) and Canyon del Muerto (Arizona). Uni-
        versity of Colorado Studies, 16:5-36.

1928a   Chronologie et évolution de la culture indienne du

Sud-ouest américain. Bulletin de la Société des
Américanistes de Belgique, 1:55-65.

1928b   Les origines de la céramique indienne du Sud-ouest
        américain. Revue Scientifique (Paris), 11 août, 11
        pp.

1929a   Evolution of population and dwelling in the Indian
        Southwest. El Palacio, 26, no. 5:75-88.

1929b   A mound builder cousin of the basket maker. El
        Palacio, 27:131-135.

1929c   Archaeological research in northeastern New Mexico
        and western Oklahoma. El Palacio, 27:276-279.

1929d   Expedition archeologique dans le Sud-ouest améri-
        cain. Journal de la Société des Américanistes de
        Paris, 21:429-431.

1930a   Les plus anciennes cultures préhistoriques du Sud-
        ouest américain. L'Anthropologie, 40:233-258.

1930b   Prehistoric cultures of the Cimarron Valley, north-
        eastern New Mexico and western Oklahoma. Proceed-
        ings of the Colorado Scientific Society, 12, no. 5:
        113-150.

1930c   A summary of the prehistoric cultures of the Cimar-
        ron Valley. El Palacio, 28:123-129.

1931a   Indian petroglyphs of southeastern Colorado. Colo-
        rado Magazine, 8:18-23.

1931b   Prehistoric flaked points from Colorado and neighbor-
        ing districts. Proceedings of the Colorado Museum
        of Natural History, 10:1-21.

1932   Yuma and Folsom artifacts (new material). Proceed-
        ings of the Colorado Museum of Natural History, 11,
        no. 2:5-18.

1934a   The first thousand Yuma-Folsom artifacts. University
        of Denver, Archaeological Series, 1, 12 pp.

1934b   Prehistoric female figurines from Arizona. El
        Palacio, 36:3-11.

1935   Arrowhead types of Colorado. Southwestern Lore, 1,
        no. 1:4-6.

1936a   Pictographs and petroglyphs of the High Western
        Plains. University of Denver, Archaeological Sur-
        vey of the High Western Plains, 8th report, 47 pp.
        Reviewed AA 39:330 (Steward).

1936b   Racial mixture of Mesa Verde Indians. Southwestern
         Lore, 1, no. 4:3-5.

1937a   The archaeological survey of the High Western Plains;
         ninth report, northeastern New Mexico. University
         of Denver, 69 pp.

1937b   Pictographs and petroglyphs of Colorado. Southwest-
         ern Lore, 2, no. 3:57-60; no. 4:74-79; 3, no. 1:12-
         19; no. 2:35-40; no. 3:45-48.

1938a   Petroglyphs of north central New Mexico. Univer-
         sity of Denver, Archaeological Survey Series, Re-
         port no. 11, 58 pp.

1938b   Petroglyphes serpentiformes indiens du Nouveau-
         Mexique. Revue Anthropologique, 48, no. 12:271-283.

1938c   The snake among the petroglyphs from north-central
         New Mexico. Southwestern Lore, 4, no. 3:42-47.

1939a   The Clactonian flake technique in the western states.
         Bulletin of the Texas Archaeological and Paleonto-
         logical Society, 11:129-138.

1939b   Indian petroglyphs from the western Plains. *In*
         Brand and Harvey 1939, pp. 295-310.

1940   The Clactonian flaking technique in Colorado, Wy-
         oming, and New Mexico. Southwestern Lore, 5, no.
         4:69-72.

1941   Western and Southwestern Indian skulls. University
         of Denver, Anthropological Series, 1, 94 pp.

1942a   Indian stone enclosures of Colorado and New Mexico.
         University of Denver, Archaeological Series, 2,
         48 pp.
         Reviewed AAq 8:404 (B.H. Huscher).

1942b   Reconnaissance work in the upper Rio Grande Valley,
         Colorado and New Mexico. University of Denver,
         Archaeological Series, 3, 35 pp.

1942c   The Rio Grande points. Southwestern Lore, 8, no.
         3:33-36.

1943a   Pre-history of the San Luis Valley. Colorado Maga-
         zine, 20:51-55.

1943b   Vertical compound sites. Southwestern Lore, 9, no.
         1:6-10.

1944a   Boulder and fence sites. Southwestern Lore, 9, no.
         4:2-5.

1944b   The upper Rio Grande culture. Southwestern Lore,
        10, no. 3:35-37.

1946   Archaeology of the upper Rio Grande Basin in south-
        ern Colorado and northern New Mexico. University
        of Denver, Archaeological Series, 6, 44 pp.
        Reviewed AAq 12:130 (Dick).

1947   Archaeology of the High Western Plains: seventeen
        years of archaeological research. University of
        Denver, 135 pp.
        Reviewed AAq 13:263 (Spaulding).

1948   Kokopelli: a study in Pueblo mythology. Southwest-
        ern Lore, 14, no. 2:25-40.

1953   Some anthropomorphic petroglyphs and pictographs.
        El Palacio, 60, no. 8:283-296.

RENAUD, E.B., and CHATIN, Janet

1943   Archaeological sites of the Cuchara drainage, south-
        ern Colorado. University of Denver, Archaeological
        Series, 4, 62 pp.

RENK, Thomas B.

1972   Archaeological survey of Buckskin Mountain Project
        area. Arizona State Museum, Archaeological Series,
        9, 9 pp.

RENSCH, Hero Eugene

1934   Chronology for Tumacacori National Monument. Na-
        tional Park Service, Field Division of Education,
        Berkeley, 37 pp.

RESSLER, John Q. (See under Woodbury, Richard B.)

RETZIUS, G.

1893   Human remains from the Cliff Dwellers of the Mesa
        Verde. Norstedt i Soner, Stockholm.

REYMAN, Jonathan E.

1976   Astronomy, architecture, and adaptation at Pueblo
        Bonito. Science, 193:957-962.

1978   *Pochteca* burials at Anasazi sites? *In* Riley and
        Hedrick 1978, pp. 242-259.

REYNOLDS, William E.

1974a   Excavations of AZ U:9:45 - Indian Bend Wash Project.
         Arizona State Museum, Archaeological Series, 45,
         7 pp.

1974b   Arizona U:5:13: a short term limited activity site.
         Arizona State Museum, Archaeological Series, 52,
         16 pp.

1975   Use of roof beams for defining social groups: an
         application of cluster analysis. Newsletter of
         Computer Archaeology, 10, no. 4:1-18.

REYNOLDS, W.E., and others

1974a   Archaeological investigations at Jackrabbit Mine
         - preliminary report. Arizona State Museum, Ar-
         chaeological Series, 39, 118 pp.

1974b   Archaeological investigations at Arizona U:9:45
         (ASM). Arizona State Museum, Archaeological Series,
         61, 78 pp.

RICE, Glen Eugene

1975   A systemic explanation of a change in Mogollon
         settlement patterns. University of Washington,
         dissertation, 310 pp.; University Microfilms Inter-
         national.

RICE, G.E., and SIMONIS, Don E.

1977   An archaeological survey of a portion of the Queen
         Creek Delta, Pinal County, Arizona. Arizona State
         University, Office of Cultural Resource Management,
         Report no. 31, 34 pp.

RICHARDS, Barry (See under Gilman, Patricia A.)

RICHARDS, Horace Gardiner

1936   Mollusks associated with Early Man in the Southwest.
         American Naturalist, 70:369-371.

RICHARDSON, Toney

1948   Trail to Inscription House. Desert Magazine, 11,
         no. 7:14-16.

RICHERT, Roland Von S.

1964   Excavation of a portion of the East Ruin, Aztec

Ruins National Monument, New Mexico. Southwest
Monuments Association, Technical Series, 4, 40 pp.
Reviewed AA 67:162 (Gell), AAq 31:280 (Ellis).

RICHERT, R.V.S., and VIVIAN, R. Gordon

1974   Ruins stabilization in the southwestern United
        States, National Park Service, Publications in
        Archaeology, 10, 158 pp.

RIEGER, Ann (See under Ackerly, Neal.)

RIFE, D.W.

1931   Primitive man's diet in the Mesa Verde area. Mesa
        Verde Notes, 2, no. 2:17-18.

RIGBY, Elizabeth

1960   Exploring ancient Honanki Palatki. Desert Magazine,
        23, no. 2:28-29.

RIGGS, Aaron D., Jr.

1967   Excavation of a buried midden, site 41CX11 in
        Crockett County, Texas. Bulletin of the Texas
        Archaeological Society, 38:76-82.

1968a   A Crockett County shelter (41CX10). Transactions
        of the Third Regional Archaeological Symposium for
        Southeastern New Mexico and Western Texas, pp. 41-
        50.

1968b   A preliminary report on a Crockett County, Texas,
        shelter: 41CX12. Transactions of the Fourth Region-
        al Archaeological Symposium for Southeastern New
        Mexico and Western Texas, pp. 2-18.

1969a   Rattlesnake Shelter: 41CX29. Bulletin of the Texas
        Archaeological Society, 40:107-117.

1969b   Yellowhouse crossing mesa petroglyphs. Transactions
        of the 5th Regional Archaeological Symposium on
        Southeastern New Mexico and Western Texas, pp. 25-
        33.

1974   Nan's Shelter: 41CX109. Transactions of the Ninth
        Regional Archaeological Symposium for Southeastern
        New Mexico and Western Texas, pp. 25-38.

RILEY, Carroll L. (See also under Hedrick, Basil C.; Lange, Charles H.)

1950   "Defensive" structures in the Hovenweep Monument. El Palacio, 57:339-344.

1951   Early Spanish reports of the Galisteo Basin. El Palacio, 58, no. 8:237-243.

1952   San Juan Anasazi and the Galisteo Basin. El Palacio, 59:77-82.

1954a   A skeletal series from Chaco Canyon. El Palacio, 61, no. 5:156-158.

1954b   A survey of Navaho archaeology. University of Colorado Studies, Series in Anthropology, 4:45-60.

1963   Adolph F. Bandelier as archaeologist. Kiva, 29, no. 1:23-27.

1975   The road to Hawikuh: trade and trade routes to Cibola-Zuni during late prehistoric and early historic times. Kiva, 41, no. 2:137-159.

1978   Pecos and trade. In Riley and Hedrick 1978, pp. 53-64.

RILEY, C.L., and HEDRICK, Basil C.

1978   (ed.) Across the Chichimec Sea: papers in honor of J. Charles Kelley. Southern Illinois University Press, 318 pp.

RILEY, Robert A.

1973   Rock art at La Bajada Mesa. Awanyu, 1, no. 1:21-44.

RINALDO, John B. (See also under Di Peso, Charles C.; Martin, Paul Sidney.)

1935   An archaeological reconnaissance of the San Juan and Colorado Rivers. Rainbow Bridge-Monument Valley Expedition Preliminary Bulletin, Archaeological Series, no. 5.

1941   Conjectures on the independent development of the Mogollon culture. American Antiquity, 7:5-19.

1947   How prehistoric Pueblo Indians of Southwest lived. Chicago Natural History Museum, Bulletin, 18, no. 8:1-2.

1948   Life of the Cochise, earliest Indians of the southwestern United States areas. Bulletin of the Chicago

Natural History Museum, 19, no. 5:7.

1950 An analysis of culture change in the Ackmen-Lowry area. Fieldiana: Anthropology, 36, no. 5, pp. 93-106. Reviewed AA 54:88 (Brainerd).

1952 On Daifuku's new conceptual scheme for the prehistoric Southwest. American Anthropologist, 54:580-586.

1959 Foote Canyon Pueblo, eastern Arizona. Fieldiana: Anthropology, 49, no. 2, pp. 147-298. Reviewed AA 61:1140 (Schwartz), AAq 25:427 (Dutton).

1964 Notes on the origins of historic Zuni culture. Kiva, 29, no. 4:86-98.

RINALDO, J.B., and BLUHM, Elaine A.

1956 Late Mogollon pottery types of the Reserve area. Fieldiana: Anthropology, 36, no. 7, pp. 149-187. Reviewed AAq 22:316 (Breternitz).

RIPLEY, Don

1961 Hovenweep - the deserted valley. Utah Archaeology, 7, no. 1:15-17.

RIPLEY, D., and SIMPSON, Ruth

1961 The deserted valley and a visit to Hovenweep National Monument. Masterkey, 35, no. 2:60-68.

RIPPETEAU, Bruce E.

1972 The need-achievement test applied to the Hohokam. American Antiquity, 37:504-513.

RIVET, Paul

1929 Expédition dans l'Arizona. Journal de la Société des Américanistes de Paris, n.s. 21:428.

RIXEY, Raymond, and VOLL, Charles B.

1962 Archaeological materials from Walnut Canyon cliff dwellings. Plateau, 34:85-96.

ROBBINS, Wilfred William (See under Hewett, Edgar Lee.)

The Bibliography   349

ROBERTS, Frank H.H., Jr. (See also under Jeançon, Jean Allard.)

1922   Report on the work of the 1922 season in the Piedra
        Parada archaeological field. University of Denver
        Bulletin, 23, no. 9, 12 pp.

1925   Report on archaeological reconnaissance in south-
        western Colorado in the summer of 1923. Colorado
        Magazine, 2, no. 2:3-80.

1927a   Recent finds in Chaco Canyon. El Palacio, 23:485-
        487.

1927b   Folsom find. El Palacio, 23:510-512.

1928   A late Basket Maker village of the Southwest. Ex-
        plorations and Field Work of the Smithsonian Insti-
        tution in 1927, pp. 165-172.

1929a   Recent archaeological developments in the vicinity
        of El Paso, Texas. Smithsonian Miscellaneous Col-
        lections, 81, no. 7, 14 pp.

1929b   Shabik'eshchee Village, a late Basket Maker site
        in the Chaco Canyon, New Mexico. Bureau of Ameri-
        can Ethnology, Bulletin 92, 164 pp.
        Reviewed AA 33:121 (Kidder).

1929c   Certain early Pueblo villages in southwestern Colo-
        rado. Explorations and Field-work of the Smithson-
        ian Institution in 1928, pp. 161-168.

1930a   Early Pueblo ruins in the Piedra district, south-
        western Colorado. Bureau of American Ethnology,
        Bulletin 96, 190 pp.
        Reviewed AA 33:121 (Kidder).

1930b   Two ancient Indian cultures in eastern Arizona.
        Explorations and Field-work of the Smithsonian
        Institution in 1929, pp. 187-194.

1931   The ruins at Kiatuthlanna, eastern Arizona. Bureau
        of American Ethnology, Bulletin 100, 195 pp.
        Reviewed AA 38:116 (Haury).

1932a   An important archaeological site in eastern Arizona.
        Explorations and Field-work of the Smithsonian Insti-
        tution in 1931, pp. 141-150.

1932b   The Village of the Great Kivas on the Zuni Reserva-
        tion, New Mexico. Bureau of American Ethnology,
        Bulletin 111, 197 pp.

1933   Some early Pueblo remains in eastern Arizona.

Explorations and Field-work of the Smithsonian
Institution in 1932, pp. 65-68.

1934   An Arizona village of a thousand years ago. Explor-
       ations and Field-work of the Smithsonian Institution
       in 1933, pp. 41-43.

1935   A survey of Southwestern Archaeology. American
       Anthropologist, 37, no. 1:1-35 (reprinted with re-
       visions in Annual Report of the Smithsonian Insti-
       tution for 1935, pp. 507-533).
       Reviewed AAq 1:73 (Guthe).

1936   Problems in American archaeology. Southwestern
       Lore, 1, no. 4:8-11.

1937a New World man. American Antiquity, 2:172-177.

1937b Archaeology in the Southwest. American Antiquity,
       3, no. 1:3-33.

1938   Chaco Canyon masonry. American Antiquity, 4:60-61.

1939a Archaeological remains in the Whitewater district,
       eastern Arizona. Part I: house types. Bureau of
       American Ethnology, Bulletin 121, 276 pp.

1939b The development of a unit-type dwelling. *In* Brand
       and Harvey 1939, pp. 311-323.

1940a Archaeological remains in the Whitewater district,
       eastern Arizona. Part II: artifacts and burials.
       Bureau of American Ethnology, Bulletin 126, 170 pp.

1940b Developments in the problem of the North American
       Paleo-Indian. Smithsonian Miscellaneous Collections,
       100:51-116.
       Reviewed AAq 7:327 (Hibben).

1940c Pre-pottery horizon of the Anasazi and Mexico. *In*
       The Maya and Their Neighbors, ed. C.L. Hay et al.,
       pp. 331-340.

1942   Archaeological and geological investigations in the
       San Jon district, eastern New Mexico. Smithsonian
       Miscellaneous Collections, 103, no. 4, 30 pp.
       Reviewed AAq 8:311 (Wormington).

1943   Evidence for a Paleo-Indian in the New World. Acta
       Americana, 1, no. 2:171-201.

1944   Etna Cave, Nevada. Scientific Monthly, 59, no. 2:
       153-158.

1945   The New World Paleo-Indian. Annual Report of the

Smithsonian Institution for 1944, pp. 403-433.

1946   Prehistoric peoples of Colorado. Colorado Magazine, 23, no. 4:145-156; no. 5:215-230.

ROBINSON, Peter (See under Boyer, W.W.)

ROBINSON, William J. (See also under Bannister, Bryant; Dean, Jeffrey S.)

1958   A new type of ceremonial pottery killing at Point of Pines. Kiva, 23, no. 3:12-14.

1963   Excavations at San Xavier del Bac, 1958. Kiva, 29, no. 2:35-57.

1968   Tree-ring materials as a basis for cultural interpretations. University of Arizona, dissertation, 123 pp.; University Microfilms International.

1976a   Tree-ring dating and archaeology in the American Southwest. Tree-Ring Bulletin, 36:9-20.

1976b   Mission Guevavi: excavations in the Convento. Kiva, 42, no. 2:135-175.

ROBINSON, W.J., and DEAN, J.S.

1969   Tree-ring evidence for climatic changes in the prehistoric Southwest from A.D. 1000 to 1200. Laboratory of Tree-Ring Research, University of Arizona, Annual Report to the National Park Service.

ROBINSON, W.J., and HARRILL, Bruce G.

1974   Tree-ring dates from Colorado V: Mesa Verde area. Laboratory of Tree-Ring Research, University of Arizona.

ROBINSON, W.J., and SPRAGUE, Roderick

1965   Disposal of the dead at Point of Pines, Arizona. American Antiquity, 30:442-453.

ROBINSON, W.J., and WARREN, R.L.

1971   Tree-ring dates from New Mexico C-D: Northern Rio Grande area. Laboratory of Tree-Ring Research, University of Arizona, 55 pp.

ROBINSON, W.J., HANNAH, John W., and HARRILL, Bruce G.

1972   Tree-ring dates from New Mexico I, O, U: Central

Rio Grande area. Laboratory of Tree-Ring Research, University of Arizona, 96 pp.

ROBINSON, W.J., HARRILL, B.G., and WARREN, Richard L.

1973   Tree-ring dates from New Mexico J-K, P, V: Santa Fe-Pecos-Lincoln area. Laboratory of Tree-Ring Research, University of Arizona, 70 pp.

1974   Tree-ring dates from New Mexico. B: Chaco-Gobernador area. Laboratory of Tree-Ring Research, University of Arizona, 114 pp.

1975   Tree-ring dates from Arizona H-I: Flagstaff area. Laboratory of Tree-Ring Research, University of Arizona.

ROBLES ORTIZ, Manuel, and TAYLOR, Francisco Manzo

1972   Clovis fluted points from Sonora, Mexico. Kiva, 37, no. 4:199-206.

ROCK, James Taylor

1974   The use of social models in archaeological interpretation. Kiva, 40, nos. 1-2:81-91.

1975   Antelope House methodology. *In* Rock and Morris 1975, pp. 23-31.

ROCK, J.T., and MORRIS, Don P.

1975   (ed.) Environment and behavior at Antelope House. Kiva, 41, no. 1:3-132.

RODECK, Hugo G.

1932   Arthropod designs on prehistoric Mimbres pottery. Annals of the Entomological Society of America, 24:688-693.

RODGERS, James B. (See also under Weaver, Donald E., Jr.)

1974   An archaeological survey of the Cave Buttes Dam alternative site and reservoir, Arizona. Arizona State University, Anthropological Research Papers, 8, 92 pp.

1975a An archaeological reconnaissance survey of the Roosevelt Water Conservation District Floodway Project, Maricopa County, Arizona. Arizona State University, Office of Cultural Resource Management, Report no. 3, 11 pp.

1975b   Archaeological investigations at AZ U:10:51 (ASU),
        Maricopa County, Arizona. Arizona State University,
        Office of Cultural Resource Management, Report no.
        4, 30 pp.

1976   An archaeological investigation of Buckeye Hills
        East, Maricopa County, Arizona. Arizona State
        University, Anthropological Research Papers, 10,
        116 pp.

1977   Archaeological investigations of the Granite Reef
        aqueduct, Cave Creek archaeological district, Ari-
        zona. Arizona State University, Anthropological
        Research Papers, 12, 185 pp.

ROGERS, Malcolm J.

1928a   A question of scumming. Arizona Old and New, 1,
        no. 2:5, 18, 21-22.

1928b   Remarks on the archaeology of the Gila River drain-
        age. Arizona Museum Journal, 1, no. 1.

1936   Yuman pottery making. San Diego Museum Papers,
        no. 2, 44 pp.
        Reviewed AA 39:144 (Gifford).

1939   Early lithic industries of the lower basin of the
        Colorado River and adjacent desert areas. San Di-
        ego Museum Papers, no. 3, 75 pp.
        Reviewed AA 43:453 (Strong).

1941   Aboriginal culture relations between southern Cali-
        fornia and the Southwest. San Diego Museum Bulletin,
        5, no. 3:1-6.

1945   An outline of Yuman prehistory. Southwestern Jour-
        nal of Anthropology, 1, no. 2:167-198.

1958   San Dieguito implements from the terraces of the
        Rincon-Pantano and Rillito drainage system. Kiva,
        24, no. 1:1-23.

ROGERS, M.J., and others

1966   Ancient hunters of the far west. Union-Tribune
        Publishing Co., San Diego, 207 pp.
        Reviewed AA 70:164 (Leonhardy).

ROGERS, Rose Mary

1972   Ceramics, Pecos River drainage, Pecos and Crockett
        Counties, Texas. Transactions of the 7th Regional

Archaeological Symposium on Southeastern New Mexico
and Western Texas, pp. 47-70.

ROGERS, Spencer L.

1954   The physical type of the Paa-ko population. School
       of American Research, Monograph no. 19, pt. VI, 48
       pp.

ROGGE, A.E., and FULLER, Steven L.

1977   Probabilistic survey sampling: making parameter
       estimates. *In* Schiffer and Gumerman 1977.

ROHN, Arthur H. (See also under Breternitz, David A.; Luebben,
Ralph A.)

1963a An ecological approach to the Great Pueblo occupa-
       tion of the Mesa Verde, Colorado. Plateau, 36, no.
       1:1-17.

1963b Prehistoric soil and water conservation on Chapin
       Mesa, southwestern Colorado. American Antiquity,
       28:441-455.

1965   Postulation of socio-economic groups from archae-
       ological evidence. *In* Osborne 1965a, pp. 65-69.

1971   Mug House, Mesa Verde National Park, Colorado.
       National Park Service, Archaeological Research
       Series, 7-D, 280 pp.
       Reviewed AAq 38:370 (Euler).

1972   Social implications of Pueblo water management in
       the northern San Juan. Zeitschrift für Ethnologie,
       97, no. 2:212-219.

1973   The Southwest and Intermontane West. *In* The De-
       velopment of North American Archaeology, ed. James
       E. Fitting, Anchor Press & Doubleday, New York, pp.
       185-211.

1974   Payne site investigations. Southwestern Lore, 40,
       nos. 3-4:50-52.

1975   A stockaded Basketmaker III village at Yellow Jack-
       et, Colorado. Kiva, 40, no. 3:113-119.

1977   Cultural change and continuity on Chapin Mesa.
       Regents Press of Kansas, 327 pp.

1978   American Southwest. *In* Chronologies in New World
       Archaeology, ed. R.E. Taylor and C.W. Meighan, Aca-
       demic Press.

ROHN, A.H, and SWANNACK, Jervis D., Jr.

1965   Mummy Lake Gray: a new pottery type. *In* Osborne
        1965a, pp. 14-18.

ROLLINS, W.E.

1933   Pueblo Bonito; a New Mexico mystery in stone. New
        Mexico Magazine, 11, no. 4:15-16, 50-52.

ROMNEY, A. Kimball

1957   The genetic model and Uto-Aztecan time perspective.
        Davidson Journal of Anthropology, 3:35-41.

RONEY, John (See under Quinn, Kathleen.)

ROOSA, William B.

1952   Sandals of Feather Cave. Bulletin of the Texas
        Archaeological and Paleontological Society, 23:
        133-146.

1954   Discoveries near Lucy, New Mexico. Oklahoma Anthro-
        pological Society, Newsletter, 3, no. 4:3.

1956a   The Lucy Site in central New Mexico. American
        Antiquity, 21, no. 3:310.

1956b   Preliminary report on the Lucy Site. El Palacio,
        63:36-49.

1968   Data on early sites in central New Mexico and Michi-
        gan. University of Michigan, dissertation, 433 pp.;
        University Microfilms International.

ROSE, Martin

1970   Deming Ranchette site survey. The Artifact, 8,
        no. 4:9-28.

ROSE, R.H.

1933   Casa Grande's new canopy. Masterkey, 7:51-54.

ROSENTHAL, Eleanor J.

1973   Archaeological investigation at Cottonwood Wash
        site. Arizona State Museum, Archaeological Series,
        20, 16 pp.

ROSENVALL, Lynn A.

1973   Mormon fortifications in western North America.

Calgary University, Archaeological Association, Annual Conference, Proceedings, 4:195-212.

ROSS, Jack A.

1963   Petroglyphs of the Three Rivers area. Central
        States Archaeological Journal, 10, no. 1:33-38.

1964   Preliminary survey and excavation of "Three Caves"
        (Guadalupe Mountains: a training program). El Paso
        Archaeological Society, Special Report no. 1, 8 pp.

1969   Bloom Mound. Transactions of the 5th Regional Ar-
        chaeological Symposium on Southeastern New Mexico
        and Western Texas, pp. 65-74.

1973   Macho Draw chert quarry excavation, Chaves County,
        New Mexico. Awanyu, 1, no. 4:26-31.

ROSS, James L. (See under Fitting, James E.; Lekson, Stephen.)

ROSS, Richard E.

1965   The archaeology of Eagle Cave. Texas Archaeological
        Salvage Project, Papers, no. 7, 163 pp.
        Reviewed AA 69:253 (Baerreis).

ROSS, S.H.

1968   Metallurgical beginnings: the case for copper in
        the prehistoric American Southwest. Annals of the
        Association of American Geographers, 58:360-370.

ROUBICEK, Dennis, CUMMINGS, Ellen, and HARTMAN, Gayle

1973   Preliminary evaluation, archaeology of Rancho Ro-
        mero. Arizona State Museum, Archaeological Series,
        24, 25 pp.

ROUSE, Irving (See also under Kidder, Alfred V.)

1948   Classification of culture in the Southwest. Central
        States Bulletin, 2, no. 3:18.

1954   On the use of the concept of area co-tradition.
        American Antiquity, 19:221-225.

ROVNER, Irwin (See also under Agogino, George A.)

ROVNER, I., and AGOGINO, George A.

1967   An analysis of fluted and unfluted Folsom points
        from Blackwater Draw. Masterkey, 41, no. 4:131-137.

ROYS, Lawrence (See under Martin, Paul Sidney.)

RUBY, Jay W. (See also under Alexander, Wayne.)

1966   Southwestern pottery in Los Angeles County, California: a correction. American Antiquity, 31:440.

1970   Culture contact between aboriginal southern California and the Southwest. University of California (Los Angeles), dissertation, 438 pp.; University Microfilms International.

RUBY, J.W., and BLACKBURN, Thomas

1964   Occurrence of Southwestern pottery in Los Angeles County, California. American Antiquity,. 30:209-210.

RUDY, Jack R.

1953   Archaeological survey of western Utah. University of Utah, Anthropological Papers, 12, 202 pp.
        Reviewed AA 57:1330 (Fenenga), AAq 21:88 (Steward).

1954a   Pine Park Shelter, Washington County, Utah. University of Utah, Anthropological Papers, 18, 46 pp.
        Reviewed AAq 21:198 (Osborne).

1954b   University of Utah archaeological field work, 1952-1953. Southwestern Lore, 19, no. 4:13-15.

1955   Archaeological excavations in Beef Basin, Utah. University of Utah, Anthropological Papers, 20, 99 pp.
        Reviewed AA 58:941 (Smith), AAq 22:316 (Schroeder).

RUDY, J.R., and STIRLAND, Robert D.

1950   An archaeological reconniassance in Washington County, Utah, 1949. University of Utah, Anthropological Papers, 9, 92 pp.
        Reviewed AAq 17:162 (Baldwin).

RUDY, J.R., and STODDARD, Earl

1954   Site on Fremont Island in Great Salt Lake. American Antiquity, 19:285-290.

RUL, Francisco Gonzalez (See under Taylor, Walter W.)

RULE, Pamela

1977   An analysis of the debitage recovered from the upper

floor surface of Unit C, AZ U;12:2 (ASU). Miscellaneous Paper no. 12, U.S. Forest Service, Southwestern Region, Archaeological Report no. 15:137-
140.

RUNYON, John (See also under Smith, Calvin B.)

1972   The Laguna Plata site: L.C.A.S. C-10-C LA-5148.
        Transactions of the 7th Regional Archaeological
        Symposium on Southeastern New Mexico and Western
        Texas, pp. 101-114.

RUPPÉ, Reynold J. (See also under Dittert, Alfred E., Jr.;
  Galinat, Walton C.)

1966a   The archaeological survey: a defense. American
        Antiquity, 31:313-333.

1966b   A survey of the Hohokam remains in the Salt River
        drainage. Report submitted to the National Science
        Foundation by Dept. of Anthropology, Arizona State
        University.

RUPPÉ, R.J., and DITTERT, A.E., Jr.

1952   The archaeology of Cebolleta Mesa and Acoma Pueblo:
        a preliminary report based on further investigation.
        El Palacio, 59:191-217.

1953   Acoma archaeology: a preliminary report of the final
        season in the Cebolleta Mesa region, New Mexico.
        El Palacio, 60:259-273.

RUSCO, Mary Kiehl

1970   A petroglyph site in Humboldt National Forest, White
        Pine County, Nevada. Nevada Archaeological Survey
        Reporter, 4, no. 6:3-8.

1973   Anthropomorphic figures in the Great Basin. Nevada
        Archaeological Survey Reporter, 7, no. 2:4-17.

RUSSELL, Paul

1968   Folsom complex near Orogrande, New Mexico. The
        Artifact, 6, no. 2:11-16.

RYAN, Dennis J. (See under El-Najjar, Mahmoud Yosef.)

SAILE, David G.

1977   'Architecture' in Prehispanic Pueblo archaeology;

examples from Chaco Canyon, New Mexico. World Archaeology, 9, no. 2:157-173.

SALWEN, Bert

1960   The introduction of leather footgear in the Pueblo
        area. Ethnohistory, 7, no. 3:206-238.

SAMPLE, L.L. (See also under Mohr, Albert.)

SAMPLE, L.L., and MOHR, Albert

1960   Some pre-ceramic sites near Farmington, New Mexico.
        Masterkey, 34, no. 4:128-146.

SAMUELSON, Val

1953   Nature and Man, architects of Canyon de Chelly.
        Pacific Discovery, 6 (September):14-17.

SANBORN, Joan L. (See under Sanborn, William B.)

SANBORN, William B.

1952   The Gila cliff dwellings. Natural History, 61, no.
        9:420-423.

1953   Mystery of Scaffold House. Natural History, 62,
        no. 5:224-226.

1955   Crack-in-the-rock. Natural History, 64, no. 1:25-
        27.

1957   Wukoki. Natural History, 66:210-211.

SANBORN, W.B., and SANBORN, Joan L.

1957   Navajo National Monument. Natural History, 66:
        376-381, 390-391.

SANBURG, Monte (See under Lister, Robert H.)

SANDS, G.H.

1957   The U.S. Cavalry at the Gila River cliff dwellings,
        1885. El Palacio, 64:340-346.

SARG, Members of

1974   SARG: a co-operative approach toward understanding
        the locations of human settlements. World Archae-
        ology, 6, no. 1:107-116.

SAUER, Carl

    1944   A geographic sketch of Early Man in America. Geo-
            graphical Review, 34, no. 4:529-573.

SAUER, C., and BRAND, Donald

    1930   Pueblo sites in southeastern Arizona. University
            of California Publications in Geography, 3, no. 7,
            pp. 415-458.

    1931   Prehistoric settlements of Sonora, with special ref-
            erence to cerros de trincheras. University of Cal-
            ifornia Publications in Geography, 5, no. 3, pp.
            67-148.

SAUER, Jonathan D. (See under Bohrer, Vorsila L.)

SAVILLE, Marshall H.

    1924   Pottery figurine of Archaic type from Seriland.
            Museum of the American Indian, Indian Notes, 1,
            no. 4:223-225.

SAYLES, E.B. (See also under Gladwin, Harold S.; Haury, Emil W.)

    1935   An archaeological survey of Texas. Gila Pueblo,
            Medallion Papers, no. 17, 164 pp.

    1936a   Some Southwestern pottery types, series V. Gila
            Pueblo, Medallion Papers, no. 21, 66 pp.

    1936b   An archaeological survey of Chihuahua, Mexico. Gila
            Pueblo, Medallion Papers, no. 22, 119 pp.

    1941a   Infant burial in carrying basket. Bulletin of the
            Texas Archaeological and Paleontological Society,
            13:77-87.

    1941b   Some Texas cave dweller artifacts. Bulletin of the
            Texas Archaeological and Paleontological Society,
            13:163-168.

    1945   The San Simon Branch: excavations at Cave Creek
            and in the San Simon Valley, I. Material culture.
            Gila Pueblo, Medallion Papers, no. 34, 78 pp.

    1965   Late Quaternary climate recorded by Cochise culture.
            American Antiquity, 30:476-480.

SAYLES, E.B., and ANTEVS, Ernst

    1941   The Cochise culture. Gila Pueblo, Medallion Papers,
            no. 29, 81 pp.

SCANTLING, Frederick H.

1939   Jackrabbit Ruin. Kiva, 5, no. 3:9-12.

SCHAAFSMA, Curtis F. (See also under Schaafsma, Polly.)

1964   Archaeological salvage excavation of the Hatch
        Site, LA 3135. Museum of New Mexico, Laboratory
        of Anthropology Notes, 30.

1968a   Archaeological salvage investigations along New
        Mexico Highway 44 near Bernalillo, New Mexico.
        Laboratory of Anthropology Notes, 49.

1968b   Funeral bowls from a Spanish-contact camposanto.
        El Palacio, 75, no. 2:40-43.

1974   The Hatch Site: archaeological salvage excavations
        on Interstate highway 25, Dona Ana County, New Mex-
        ico. Museum of New Mexico, Laboratory of Anthro-
        pology Notes, 96.

1975a   An archaeological clearance survey report on Abiquiu
        Reservoir: the Cerrito Recreation Site. School of
        American Research, contract #1.

1975b   Archaeological clearance survey of four gathering
        lines near Carlsbad, New Mexico. School of American
        Research, contract #8.

1975c   An archaeological survey of Arroyo de los Pinos
        humate mine. School of American Research, contract
        #15.

1975d   Archaeological report to Duval Potash Company.
        School of American Research, contract #20.

1975e   Clearance survey report conducted by the School of
        American Research for Questa Molybdenum Company,
        Taos County, New Mexico. School of American Re-
        search, contract #27.

1976a   Archaeological survey of maximum pool and Navajo
        excavations at Abiquiu Reservoir, Rio Arriba County,
        New Mexico. National Technical Information Service,
        PB-263 996, 285 pp.

1976b   An archaeological survey for the Soil Conservation
        Service near Costilla, New Mexico. School of Amer-
        ican Research, contract #34.

1977a   Evaluation of Abiquiu Reservoir archaeological ma-
        terials for inclusion in the National Park Service
        Inundation Study. School of American Research,
        contract #46.

1977b   An archaeological survey adjacent to San Mateo Mesa.
        School of American Research, contract #50.

1977c   An archaeological clearance survey near Questa, New
        Mexico. School of American Research, contract #53.

1977d   A road and drill pad survey for the Questa Molyb-
        denum Company, Carson National Forest, New Mexico.
        Miscellaneous Paper no. 8, U.S. Forest Service,
        Southwestern Region, Archaeological Report no. 15:
        60-66.

SCHAAFSMA, C.F., and GOODING, John D.

1974a   Archaeological survey between Mancos and Dolores,
        U.S. Highway 184. Colorado Department of Highways,
        Highway Salvage Report no. 4.

1974b   Archaeological survey of U.S. Highway 160-550,
        Durango south. Colorado Department of Highways,
        Highway Salvage Report no. 8.

SCHAAFSMA, Polly

1961   Looking with perspective at "The American Southwest:
        a problem in cultural isolation." Southwestern
        Lore, 27:25-31.

1962   Rock art of the Navajo Reservoir. El Palacio, 69:
        193-212.

1963   Rock art in the Navajo Reservoir district. Museum
        of New Mexico, Papers in Anthropology, 7, 74 pp.
        Reviewed AA 65:1396 (Ellis), AAq 30:113 (Swauger).

1965a   Kiva murals from Pueblo del Encierro (LA70). El
        Palacio, 72, no. 3:7-16.

1965b   Southwest Indian pictographs and petroglyphs. Mu-
        seum of New Mexico Press, 12 pp.

1966a   The destruction and preservation of rock paintings
        and petroglyphs. El Palacio, 73, no. 1:27-31.

1966b   Early Navaho rock paintings and carvings. Museum
        of Navaho Ceremonial Art, Santa Fe.

1966c   Rio Grande petroglyphs in the Cochiti reservoir.
        Laboratory of Anthropology Notes, 77.

1968a   Archaeological salvage investigations along Inter-
        state 25 near Los Lunas, New Mexico. Laboratory
        of Anthropology Notes, 50.

1968b   The Los Lunas petroglyphs. El Palacio, 75, no.

2:13-24.

1971   The rock art of Utah: a study from the Donald Scott
        collection. Papers of the Peabody Museum of Archae-
        ology and Ethnology, 65, 169 pp.

1972   Rock art in New Mexico. University of New Mexico
        Press, 209 pp.

1975a   Rock art of the Cochiti Reservoir district. Museum
        of New Mexico, Papers in Anthropology, 16, 95 pp.

1975b   Rock art and ideology of the Mimbres and Jornada
        Mogollon. The Artifact, 13, no. 3:1-14.

1975c   The horse in rock art. El Palacio, 81, no. 3:4-5.

1976   Preliminary archaeological investigations at Conchas
        Lake, San Miguel County, New Mexico. School of
        American Research, contract #42.

SCHAAFSMA, P., and SCHAAFSMA, Curtis F.

1974   Evidence for the origins of the Pueblo katchina
        cult as suggested by Southwestern rock art. Amer-
        ican Antiquity, 39:535-545.

SCHAAFSMA, P., and VIVIAN, Pat

1975   Malpais Hill pictograph site - AZ BB:2:16 (ASM).
        Arizona State Museum, Archaeological Series, 74,
        9 pp.

SCHABER, Gerald G. (See also under Berlin, G. Lennis.)

SCHABER, G.G., and GUMERMAN, George J.

1969   Infrared scanning images - an archaeological ap-
        plication. Science, 164:712-713.

SCHAEFER, Paul D.

1969   Prehistoric trade in the Southwest and the distri-
        bution of Pueblo IV Hopi Jeddito Black-on-yellow.
        Kroeber Anthropological Papers, no. 41, pp. 54-77.

SCHALK, Randall (See also under Caraveo, Carlos; Lent, Stephen
C.; Wase, Cheryl.)

SCHALK, R., and LENT, Stephen C.

1977   Archaeological survey of 10 proposed drill sites
        in the Blanco Trading Post area, northwest New

Mexico. University of New Mexico, contract report
185-2M (BLM, NPS).

SCHEANS, Daniel J.

1957   An addition to the Anasazi ceremonial bifurcate
        basket complex. Kiva, 22, no. 4:10-12.

SCHEANS, D.J., and REED, Erik K.

1956   Human skeletal material from pipeline excavations.
        In Wendorf, Fox, and Lewis 1956, pp. 392-401.

SCHEICK, Cherie

1976   The River Road Recreational Bikeway survey. Ari-
        zona State Museum, Archaeological Series, 109, 20
        pp.

SCHELLBACH, Louis, III (See also under Harrington, Mark Ray-
    mond.)

1930   An unusual burial in Mesa House ruin. *In* Harring-
        ton, Hayden, and Schellbach 1930, pp. 93-105.

SCHENCK, W. Egbert, and GIFFORD, E.W.

1952   Archaeological sites on opposite shores of the Gulf
        of California. American Antiquity, 17:265.

SCHICK, Asher P. (See under Malde, Harold E.)

SCHIFFER, Michael B. (See also under Hanson, John A.; Reid,
    J. Jefferson; Sullivan, Alan P., III.)

1971   Potsherds and population: a rejoinder to Heinemann.
        The Artifact, 9, no. 2:19-20.

1972a   Archaeological context and systemic context. Amer-
        ican Antiquity, 37:156-165.

1972b   Cultural laws and the reconstruction of past life-
        ways. Kiva, 37:148-157.

1973   Cultural formation processes of the archaeological
        record: applications at the Joint site, east-central
        Arizona. University of Arizona, dissertation, 356
        pp.; University Microfilms International.

1975a   Behavioral chain analysis: activities, organization,
        and the use of space. *In* Martin and others 1975,
        pp. 103-119.

1975b   Comments on environment and behavior at Antelope
        House. *In* Rock and Morris 1975, pp. 123-126.

1976   Behavioral archaeology. Academic Press, 222 pp.
        Reviewed AA 79:492 (Plog), AAq 42:668 (Goodyear).

1978   Chipped stone and human behavior at the Joint Site.
        In Grebinger 1978a, pp. 141-163.

SCHIFFER, M.B., and GUMERMAN, George J.

1977   (ed.) Conservation Archaeology: a guide for cul-
        tural resource management studies. Academic Press,
        512 pp.

SCHLEY, Robert A. (See also under Breternitz, David A.)

1960   Excavation at the Ash Creek site, NA 6657, upper
        Agua Fria drainage. Plateau, 33:1-9.

1961   Diurnal air flow through an earth crevice, Wupatki
        National Monument. Plateau, 33, no. 4:105-111.

1962   Excavation of the Wupatki blowhole site, NA 7824.
        Rand Corporation, Memorandum RM-32-36-RC.

1964   Paho Cave. Plateau, 36, no. 3:89-90.

SCHMIDT, Erich F.

1927a   The Mrs. William Boyce Thompson Expedition. Natural
        History, 26:635-644.

1927b   A stratigraphic study in the Gila-Salt region, Ari-
        zona. Proceedings of the National Academy of Sci-
        ence, 13, no. 5:291-298.

1928   Time-relations of prehistoric pottery types in south-
        ern Arizona. American Museum of Natural History,
        Anthropological Papers, 30, pt. 5, pp. 247-302.

SCHNEIDER, Fred

1966   The Harrell point: a discussion. University of
        Oklahoma, Papers in Anthropology, 7:31-44.

SCHOENWETTER, James (See also under Harris, Arthur H.; Martin,
    Paul Schultz; Wilson, John P.)

1961   The archaeology of environmental change. Chicago
        Natural History Museum Bulletin, 32, no. 5:10-11.

1962   The pollen analysis of eighteen archaeological
        sites in Arizona and New Mexico. *In* Martin, Rinaldo,
        and others 1962, pp. 168-209.

1965   How old is it? The story of dating in archaeology.
        Museum of New Mexico, Popular Series Pamphlet no.
        2, 16 pp.

1966   A re-evaluation of the Navajo Reservoir pollen
        chronology. El Palacio, 73, no. 1:19-26.

1970   Archaeological pollen studies of the Colorado Pla-
        teau. American Antiquity, 35:35-48.

1976   A test of the Colorado Plateau pollen chronology.
        Journal of the Arizona Academy of Sciences, 11, no.
        3:89-96.

SCHOENWETTER, J., and DITTERT, A.E., Jr.

1968   An ecological interpretation of Anasazi settlement
        patterns. *In* Anthropological Archaeology in the
        Americas, ed. B.J. Meggers, Anthropological Society
        of Washington, pp. 41-66.

SCHOENWETTER, J., and EDDY, Frank W.

1964   Alluvial and palynological reconstruction of en-
        vironments, Navajo Reservoir district. Museum of
        New Mexico, Papers in Anthropology, 13, 155 pp.
        Reviewed AA 67:1067 (Rohn), AAq 31:287 (Butzer).

SCHOENWETTER, J., and OLDFIELD, F.

1964   Late Quaternary environments and Early Man on the
        southern high plains. Antiquity, 38, no. 151:226-
        229.

SCHOENWETTER, J., GAINES, S.W., and WEAVER, D.

1973   Definition and preliminary study of the Midvale
        site. Arizona State University, Anthropological
        Research Papers, 6, 173 pp.

SCHOLES, France V.

1937   Notes on Sandia and Puaray. El Palacio, 42:57-59.

SCHOLES, F.V., and MERA, Harry P.

1940   Some aspects of the Jumano problem. Carnegie Insti-
        tution of Washington, Contributions to American
        Anthropology and History, 6, no. 34, pp. 265-299.

SCHOOL OF AMERICAN RESEARCH

1974a   An archaeological survey of five well locations

and access roads. School of American Research, contract #3.

1974b   An archaeological survey of eight well locations and access roads. School of American Research, contracts #4 and #7.

SCHORSCH, Russell L.

1962   A Basket Maker III pit house near Albuquerque. El Palacio, 69:114-118.

SCHREIBER, John P., and BREED, William J.

1971   Obsidian localities in the San Francisco volcanic field, Arizona. Plateau, 43, no. 3:115-119.

SCHROEDER, Albert H. (See also under Colton, Harold S.; Ford, Richard I.)

1943   Prehistoric canals in the Salt River Valley, Arizona. American Antiquity, 8:380-386.

1944   A prehistoric method of collecting water. American Antiquity, 9:329-330.

1947   Did the Sinagua of the Verde Valley settle in the Salt River Valley? Southwestern Journal of Anthropology, 3, no. 3:230-246.

1948   Montezuma Well. Plateau, 20, no. 3:37-40.

1949a   Cultural implications of the ball courts in Arizona. Southwestern Journal of Anthropology, 5:28-36.

1949b   A preliminary examination of the Sacred Mountain ball court. Plateau, 21, no. 4:55-57.

1951a   A new ball court site in the Verde Valley. Plateau, 23, no. 4:61-63.

1951b   Snaketown IV vs. the facts. American Antiquity, 16:263-265.

1952a   The bearing of ceramics on developments in the Hohokam Classic period. Southwestern Journal of Anthropology, 8:320-335.

1952b   The significance of Willow Beach. Plateau, 25, no. 2:27-29.

1953a   The bearing of architecture on developments in the Hohokam Classic period. Southwestern Journal of Anthropology, 9:174-194.

1953b A brief survey of the lower Colorado River from
       Davis Dam to the international border. National
       Park Service, Region 3, 77 pp. (Bureau of Reclama-
       tion, Boulder City.)
       Reviewed AAq 20:88 (Colton).

1953c A few sites in Moapa Valley, Nevada. Masterkey,
       27, nos. 1-2:18-24, 62-68.

1953d Notched stones in Southwestern sites. American
       Antiquity, 19:158-160.

1953e The problem of Hohokam, Sinagua and Salado relations
       in southern Arizona. Plateau, 26, no. 2:75-83.

1953f Statement on the early history and archaeology of
       the Gunnison River Basin. Southwestern Lore, 19,
       no. 3:3-11.

1953- Man and environment in the Verde Valley. Landscape,
54   3, no. 2:16-19.

1954   Four prehistoric sites near Mayer, Arizona, which
       suggest a new focus. Plateau, 26, no. 3:103-107.

1955a Archaeology of Zion Park. University of Utah,
       Anthropological Papers, 22, 210 pp.
       Reviewed AA 59:181 (Meighan), AAq 22:428 (Shutler).

1955b Ball courts and ball games of Middle America and
       Arizona. Archaeology, 8, no. 3:156-161.

1956   Comments on "A trial survey of Mexican-Southwestern
       architectural parallels." El Palacio, 63, nos.
       9-10:299-309.

1957a Comments on Gila Polychrome. American Antiquity,
       23:169-170.

1957b The Hakataya cultural tradition. American Antiquity,
       23, no. 2:176-178.

1960   The Hohokam, Sinagua, and the Hakataya. Archives
       of Archaeology, 5, 214 pp. (4 microcards) (also
       printed as Imperial Valley College Museum Society,
       Occasional Paper no. 3, 143 pp., 1975).
       Reviewed AAq 27:127 (Euler).

1961a The archaeological excavations at Willow Beach,
       Arizona, 1950. University of Utah, Anthropological
       Papers, 50, 174 pp.
       Reviewed AAq 28:114 (Euler).

1961b An archaeological survey of the Painted Rocks Reser-
       voir, western Arizona. Kiva, 27, no. 1:1-28.

1961c Puerco Ruin excavations, Petrified Forest National Monument, Arizona. Plateau, 33:93-104.

1961d The pre-eruptive and post-eruptive Sinagua patterns. Plateau, 34, no. 2:60-66.

1963a Diffusion north out of south-central Arizona. El Palacio, 70, nos. 1-2:13-24.

1963b Hakataya, Patayan, and Hohokam. National Park Service, Region 3, Research Abstract no. 308, 3 pp.

1963c The Sinagua Branch. National Park Service, Region 3, Research Abstract no. 309, 2 pp.

1963d Comment on Gunnerson's "Plateau Shoshonean prehistory." American Antiquity, 28:559-560.

1964a Comments on Johnson's "The Trincheras culture of northern Sonora." American Antiquity, 30:104-106.

1964b The cultural position of Hurst's Tabeguache Caves and Pueblo sites. Southwestern Lore, 29, no. 4:77-79.

1965a Salvage excavations at Natural Bridges National Monument. University of Utah, Miscellaneous Collected Papers, no. 10, Anthropological Papers, 75, pp. 85-110.

1965b Unregulated diffusion from Mexico into the Southwest prior to A.D. 700. American Antiquity, 30:297-309.

1966 Pattern diffusion from Mexico into the Southwest after A.D. 600. American Antiquity, 31:683-704.

1967a Comments on "Salvage archaeology in the Painted Rocks Reservoir, western Arizona." Arizona Archaeologist, 1:1-10.

1967b Themes of environmental adaptation and response in southwestern National Park System areas. Southwestern Lore, 33, no. 2:37-46.

1967- An archaeological survey adjacent to Hovenweep
68   National Monument. Southwestern Lore, 33, nos. 3-4:61-94.

1968a (ed.) Collected papers in honor of Lyndon Lane Hargrave. Archaeological Society of New Mexico, Papers, vol. 1, 170 pp.

1968b Tentative ecological and cultural factors and their effects on Southwestern farmers. In Irwin-Williams

1968a, pp. 17-20.

1969   Spanish entradas, the big houses, and the Indian groups of northern Mexico. The Artifact, 7, no. 4:15-23.

1972   Rio Grande ethnohistory. *In* New Perspectives on the Pueblos, ed. A. Ortiz, University of New Mexico Press, pp. 41-70.

1976   (ed.) Collected Papers in honor of Marjorie Ferguson Lambert. Papers of the Archaeological Society of New Mexico, 3, 264 pp.

SCHROEDER, A.H., and HASTINGS, Homer F.

1958   Montezuma Castle National Monument, Arizona. National Park Service, Historical Handbook Series, no. 27, 40 pp.

SCHROEDER, A.H., and WENDORF, Fred

1954   Excavations near Aragon, New Mexico. *In* Wendorf 1954a, pp. 53-105.

SCHROEDL, Alan R.

1976   The Archaic of the northern Colorado Plateau. University of Utah, dissertation, 131 pp.; University Microfilms International.

1977   The Grand Canyon figurine complex. American Antiquity, 42:254-265.

SCHUETZ, Mardith K.

1956   An analysis of Val Verde County cave material. Bulletin of the Texas Archaeological Society, 27: 129-160.

1957   A carbon-14 date from trans-Pecos Texas. Bulletin of the Texas Archaeological Society, 28:288-289.

1961a   An analysis of Archaic material from three areas of North America. Bulletin of the Texas Archaeological Society, 30:163-182.

1961b   An analysis of Val Verde County cave material; part II. Bulletin of the Texas Archaeological Society, 31:167-205.

1962   An analysis of Val Verde County cave material; part III. Bulletin of the Texas Archaeological Society, 33:131-165.

SCHULMAN, Albert

1949   A Gallina cliff-house. El Palacio, 56:230-234.

1950   Pre-Columbian towers in the Southwest. American Antiquity, 15:288-297.

SCHULMAN, Edmund

1942a   Centuries-long tree indices of precipitation in the Southwest. Bulletin of the American Meteorological Society, 23:148-161, 204-217.

1942b   Variations between ring chronologies in and near the Colorado River drainage area. Tree-Ring Bulletin, 8, no. 4:26-32.

1945   Tree-ring hydrology of the Colorado River Basin. University of Arizona Bulletin, 16, no. 4, 51 pp. (Laboratory of Tree-Ring Research, Bulletin no. 2)

1946   Dendrochronology at Mesa Verde National Park. Tree-Ring Bulletin, 12, no. 3:18-24.

1948a   Dendrochronology at Navajo National Monument. Tree-Ring Bulletin, 14, no. 3:18-24.

1948b   Dendrochronology in northeastern Utah. Tree-Ring Bulletin, 15, nos. 1-2:1-14.

1949a   Chronology at ruins in the Gila Basin. Tree-Ring Bulletin, 15, no. 3:21-22.

1949b   Early chronologies in the San Juan Basin. Tree-Ring Bulletin, 15:24-32.

1949c   An extension of the Durango chronology. Tree-Ring Bulletin, 16, no. 2:12-16.

1950a   A dated beam from Dinosaur National Monument. Tree-Ring Bulletin, 16, no. 3:18-19.

1950b   Miscellaneous ring records, I. Tree-Ring Bulletin, 16, no. 3:21.

1951   Miscellaneous ring records, III. Tree-Ring Bulletin, 17, no. 4:28-30.

1952a   Definitive dendrochronologies: a progress report. Tree-Ring Bulletin, 18, nos. 2-3:10-18.

1952b   Dendrochronology in Big Bend National Park, Texas. Tree-Ring Bulletin, 18, nos. 2-3:18-27.

1952c   Extension of the San Juan chronology to B.C. times. Tree-Ring Bulletin, 18, no. 4:30-35.

1953   Rio Grande chronologies. Tree-Ring Bulletin, 19, nos. 3-4:20-33.

1954   Dendroclimatic changes in semiarid regions. Tree-Ring Bulletin, 20:26-30.

1956a   Dendroclimatic changes in semiarid America. Laboratory of Tree-Ring Research, University of Arizona.

1956b   Tree rings and history in western United States. Economic Botany, 8, no. 3:234-250 (also in Annual Report of the Smithsonian Institution for 1955, pp. 459-473).

SCHULTZ, C. Bertrand

1943   Some artifact sites of Early Man in the Great Plains and adjacent areas. American Antiquity, 8:242-249.

SCHULTZ, Robert E.

1967   Excavation of a single room at Hot Well in the spring of 1966. The Artifact, 5, no. 4:15-29.

SCHUMACHER, P.

1881   Ancient fortification in Sonora. American Antiquarian, 4:227-229.

SCHUSTER, C.

1968   Incised stones from Nevada and elsewhere. Nevada Archaeological Survey Reporter, 2, no. 5:4-23.

SCHWARTZ, Douglas W.

1955a   Havasupai prehistory: thirteen centuries of cultural development. Yale University, dissertation, 313 pp.; University Microfilms International.

1955b   Prehistoric twig figurines from the Grand Canyon. Oklahoma Anthropological Society, Newsletter, 4, no. 4:6-7.

1956a   Demographic changes in the early periods of Cohonina prehistory. *In* Willey 1956, pp. 26-31.

1956b   The Havasupai, 600 A.D.-1955 A.D.: a short culture history. Plateau, 28, no. 4:77-85.

1957   Climate change and culture history in the Grand Canyon region. American Antiquity, 22, no. 4:372-377.

1958   Prehistoric man in the Grand Canyon. Scientific
        American, 198, no. 2:97-102.

1959   Culture area and time depth: the four worlds of the
        Havasupai. American Anthropologist, 61:1060-1070.

1960   Archaeological investigations in the Shinumo area
        of Grand Canyon, Arizona. Plateau, 32:61-67.

1963a   An archaeological survey of Nankoweap Canyon, Grand
        Canyon National Park. American Antiquity, 28:289-
        302.

1963b   The Southwest. *In* Early Indian farmers and villages
        and communities, ed. W.G. Haag, Washington, pp. 112-
        119.

1965   Nankoweap to Unkar: an archaeological survey of the
        upper Grand Canyon. American Antiquity, 30:278-296.

1966   A historical analysis and synthesis of Grand Canyon
        archaeology. American Antiquity, 31:469-484.

1970a   The postmigration culture: a base for archaeological
        inference. *In* Longacre 1970b, pp. 175-193.

1970b   Popovi Da: Indian pottery and Indian values. School
        of American Research, Exploration 1970, pp. 2-7.

1970c   Exploration: the Grand Canyon. School of American
        Research, Exploration 1970, pp. 12-21.

1971   Background report on the archaeology of the site at
        Arroyo Hondo: First Arroyo Hondo Field Report, 1971.
        School of American Research, 16 pp.

1972   Archaeological investigations at the Arroyo Hondo
        Site: Second field report, 1971. School of Ameri-
        can Research, 26 pp.

SCHWARTZ, D.W., and LANG, R.W.

1973   Archaeological investigations at the Arroyo Hondo
        site: third field report. School of American Re-
        search, 47 pp.
        Reviewed AA 77:155 (Gumerman).

SCHWARTZ, D.W., and WETHERILL, Milton A.

1957   A Cohonina cremation. Plateau, 29, no. 3:63-65.

SCHWARTZ, D.W., LANGE, Arthur L., and De SAUSSURE, Raymond

1958   Split-twig figurines in the Grand Canyon. American
        Antiquity, 23:264-274.

SCHWATKA, Frederick

1899   In the Land of Cave and Cliff Dwellers. New ed.,
         Educational Publishing Co., Boston, 385 pp.

SCISCENTI, James V.

1962a   The Cañon de San Diego ruin: salvage excavations
         at LA 5688. Laboratory of Anthropology Notes, 12.

1962b   Laguna-Paguate highway salvage: archaeological sal-
         vage excavations on U.P. 50. Laboratory of Anthro-
         pology Notes, 13.

1962c   The Manuelito project: archaeological salvage ex-
         cavations on Interstate 40. Laboratory of Anthro-
         pology Notes, 14.

1962d   Fragmentary storage rooms in the Largo-Gallina
         district. Laboratory of Anthropology Notes, 64.

SCISCENTI, J.V., and GREMINGER, Henry C.

1962   Archaeology of the Four Corners power projects.
         Museum of New Mexico, Papers in Anthropology, 5,
         128 pp.
         Reviewed AA 66:708 (Sharrock), AAq 29:527 (Breter-
         nitz).

SCOGGIN, Charles (See under Burgh, Robert F.)

SCOTT, Douglas D. (See also under Hull, Deborah A.)

1972   The Nordenskiöld campsite: a test in historic ar-
         chaeology. Kiva, 37, no. 3:128-140.

1977   Two vandalized Pueblo III burials: some key factors
         affecting vandalism of sites. Southwestern Lore,
         43, no. 3:10-14.

SCOTT, Earl W.

1959   Writing on rocks. New Mexico Magazine, 37, no. 6:
         22-23, 57, 62.

SCOTT, Hunter D.

1928   Pueblo-Mission architecture. Masterkey, 2, no. 2:
         15-24.

SCOTT, Stuart D. (See also under Bannister, Bryant.)

1960   Pottery figurines from central Arizona. Kiva, 26,

no. 2:11-26.

1966   Dendrochronology in Mexico. University of Arizona,
        Laboratory of Tree-Ring Research, Papers, 2.

SEAMAN, Timothy

1976   Archaeological investigations on the San Juan-to-
        Ojo 345 KV transmission line for the Public Service
        Company of New Mexico: excavation of LA 11843, an
        early stockaded settlement of the Gallina phase.
        Laboratory of Anthropology Notes, 111G.

SELLARDS, E.H.

1936   Recent studies of Early Man in the southwestern
        part of the United States. American Naturalist,
        70:361-369.

1940   Early Man in America: index to localities and se-
        lected bibliography. Bulletin of the Geological
        Society of America, 51:373-432.
        Reviewed AAq 7:84 (Eiseley).

1952   Early Man in America: a study in prehistory. Uni-
        versity of Texas Press, 211 pp.
        Reviewed AAq 19:190 (Roberts).

1955   Fossil bison and associated artifacts from Milnesand,
        New Mexico. American Antiquity, 20:336-344.

1960   Some early stone artifact developments in North
        America. Southwestern Journal of Anthropology, 16,
        no. 2:160-173.

SELLARDS, E.H., and EVANS, Glen L.

1960   The Paleo-Indian culture succession in the central
        high plains of Texas and New Mexico. *In* Selected
        Papers of the Fifth International Congress of An-
        thropological and Ethnological Sciences, ed. A.F.C.
        Wallace, pp. 639-647.

SELLERS, William

1886   Mounds and relics in Utah. American Antiquarian,
        8:297.

SELTZER, Carl C.

1936   New light on the racial history of the Southwest.
        American Journal of Physical Anthropology, 21, no.
        2, Supplement, p. 17 (abstract).

1944   Racial prehistory in the Southwest and the Hawikuh
        Zunis. Papers of the Peabody Museum of American
        Archaeology and Ethnology, 23, no. 1, 38 pp.

SENSE, Richard

1967   A prehistoric quarry near Ray, Arizona. Kiva, 32,
        no. 4:170-174.

SENTER, Donovan

1934   The work on the old Quarai Mission, 1934. El
        Palacio, 37:169-174.

1937   Tree rings, valley floor deposition, and erosion
        in Chaco Canyon, New Mexico. American Antiquity,
        3:68-75.

SENTER, Florence Hawley (Also listed as Ellis, Florence H.,
and Hawley, Florence M.)

1938   Southwestern dated ruins, IV. Tree-Ring Bulletin,
        5, no. 1:6-7.

SESSIONS, Steven E. (See under Swedlund, Alan C.)

SETZLER, Frank M.

1932   A prehistoric cave in Texas. Explorations and
        Field Work of the Smithsonian Institution in 1931,
        pp. 133-140.

1933   Prehistoric cave dwellers of Texas. Explorations
        and Field Work of the Smithsonian Institution in
        1932, pp. 53-56.

1934   Cave burials in southwestern Texas. Explorations
        and Field Work of the Smithsonian Institution in
        1933, pp. 35-37.

1935   A prehistoric cave culture in southwestern Texas.
        American Anthropologist, 37:104-110.

1939   Exploring a cave in southwestern Texas. Explora-
        tions and Field Work of the Smithsonian Institu-
        tion in 1938, pp. 75-78.

1943   Riding the Yampa. National Parks Magazine, 17, no.
        72:21-26.

1952   Seeking the secret of the giants. National Geo-
        graphic Magazine, 102, no. 3:390-404.

SHACKELFORD, William J.

1955   Excavations at the Polvo site in western Texas.
        American Antiquity, 20:256-262.

SHAEFFER, James B.

1954   The Mogollon complex: its cultural role and histor-
        ical development in the American Southwest. Co-
        lumbia University, dissertation, 234 pp.; University
        Microfilms International.

1956   Kinishba: a Classic site of the western Pueblos.
        Bureau of Indian Affairs, Chilocco Indian School,
        Chilocco, Oklahoma.

SHAFER, Harry J. (See also under Dering, J. Phil.)

1970a   An archaeological reconnaissance of the Sanderson
        Canyon watershed, Texas. Texas Archaeological
        Salvage Project, Survey Reports, no. 7.

1970b   A preliminary report of an archaeological survey
        in the Guadalupe Mountain National Park by the
        Texas Archaeological Society in June, 1970. Mu-
        seum News, 14, no. 3:10-17.

1975   Clay figurines from the lower Pecos region, Texas.
        American Antiquity, 40:148-158.

1977   Art and territoriality in the Lower Pecos Archaic.
        Plains Anthropologist, 22, no. 75:13-21.

SHAFER, H.J., and BRYANT, Vaughn M., Jr.

1977   Archaeological and botanical studies at Hinds Cave,
        Val Verde County, Texas. Texas A&M University,
        Anthropology Laboratory, Special Series, 1, 137 pp.

SHAFER, H.J., and SPECK, Fred, Jr.

1974   A clay figurine cache from the lower Pecos region,
        Texas. Plains Anthropologist, 19:228-230.

SHAFER, H.J., and others

1975   A preliminary report of Hinds Cave, Val Verde
        County, Texas. Texas A&M University, Anthropology
        Laboratory, Report no. 8, 56 pp.

SHARROCK, Floyd W. (See also under Jennings, Jesse D.; Martin,
    Paul Schultz.)

1961a   A preliminary report of 1960 archaeological

            excavations in Glen Canyon. Utah Archaeology, 7,
            no. 1:7-15.

1961b   A preliminary report of 1961 archaeological excava-
            tions in Moqui Canyon and Castle Wash. Utah Archae-
            ology, 7, no. 4:6-11.

1963a   The Hazzard Collection. Archives of Archaeology,
            23, 292 pp. (5 microcards).
            Reviewed AA 67:583 (Ascher).

1963b   A preliminary report of 1962 archaeological excava-
            tions in Glen Canyon. Utah Archaeology, 8, no. 4:
            1-3.

1966a   An archaeological survey of Canyonlands National
            Park. University of Utah, Miscellaneous Collected
            Papers, no. 12, Anthropological Papers, 83, pp.
            49-84.

1966b   Preliminary report on excavations at the Nephi site,
            Nephi, Utah. Utah Archaeology, 12, no. 1:3-11.

SHARROCK, F.W., and KEANE, Edward G.

1962   Carnegie Museum Collection from southeastern Utah.
            University of Utah, Anthropological Papers, 57, 71
            pp.

SHARROCK, F.W., and MARWITT, John P.

1967   Excavations at Nephi, Utah, 1965-1966. University
            of Utah, Anthropological Papers, 88, 60 pp.
            Reviewed AA 72:1550 (Dittert), AAq 35:233 (Rudy).

SHARROCK, F.W., DAY, Kent C., and DIBBLE, David S.

1963   1961 excavations, Glen Canyon area. University of
            Utah, Anthropological Papers, 63, 390 pp.

SHARROCK, F.W., DIBBLE, David S., and ANDERSON, Keith M.

1961   The Creeping Dune irrigation site in Glen Canyon,
            Utah. American Antiquity, 27:188-202.

SHARROCK, F.W., and others

1961   1960 excavations, Glen Canyon area. University of
            Utah, Anthropological Papers, 52, 392 pp.
            Reviewed AA 65:416 (R.B. Woodbury), AAq 29:248
            (Peckham).

1964   1962 excavations, Glen Canyon area. University of
            Utah, Anthropological Papers, 73, 208 pp.

Reviewed AA 69:403 (Longacre); AAq 34:192 (Wheat), 36:219 (Wheat).

SHAWN, Ronnie A.

1971 Morgan creek mortar camp. Transactions of the 6th Regional Archaeological Symposium on Southeastern New Mexico and Western Texas, pp. 49-62.

1972 King Mountain Shelter. Transactions of the 7th Regional Archaeological Symposium on Southeastern New Mexico and Western Texas, pp. 71-88.

SHEETS, John

1977 Facial asymmetry and artificial cranial deformation in a set of American Indian skulls. Southwestern Lore, 43, no. 3:15-21.

SHEETS, Payson D.

1969 The archaeology of the Ely Caves, Dinosaur National Monument. Clearinghouse for Federal Scientific and Technical Information, Dept. of Commerce.

SHELSE, R.C.

1922 Mesa Verde cliff dwellers. Mentor, 10, no. 5:3-12.

SHENK, Lynette O. (See also under Wilcox, David R.)

1976 San Jose de Tumacacori: archaeological synthesis and research design. Arizona State Museum, Archaeological Series, 94, 120 pp.

SHENK, L.O., and TEAGUE, George A.

1975 Excavations at Tubac presidio. Arizona State Museum, Archaeological Series, 85, 234 pp.

SHEPARD, Anna O. (See also under Kidder, Alfred V.)

1939 Technology of La Plata pottery. *In* Morris, E.H., 1939, pp. 249-287.

1942 Rio Grande glaze paint ware: a study illustrating the place of ceramic technological analysis in archaeological research. Carnegie Institution of Washington, Contributions to American Anthropology and History, 39, pp. 129-260.

1948 The symmetry of abstract design with special reference to ceramic decoration. Carnegie Institution

of Washington, Contributions to American Anthropology
and History, no. 47, pp. 217-292.

1953   Notes on color and paste composition. *In* Wendorf
        1953a, pp. 177-193.

1956   Ceramics for the archaeologist. Carnegie Institu-
        tion of Washington, Publication no. 609, 414 pp.
        Reviewed AAq 23:87 (Collier).

1965   Rio Grande glaze-paint pottery: a test of petro-
        graphic analysis. *In* Ceramics and Man, ed. F.R.
        Matson, Viking Fund Publications in Anthropology,
        41, pp. 62-87.

SHERMAN, Peter (See under Gilman, Patricia A.)

SHETRONE, Henry Clyde

1946   A unique prehistoric irrigation project. Annual
        Report of the Smithsonian Institution for 1945, pp.
        379-386.

SHIELDS, Wayne F.

1967   1966 excavations: Uintah Basin. University of Utah,
        Miscellaneous Collected Papers, no. 15, Anthropologi-
        cal Papers, 89, pp. 1-32.
        Reviewed AAq 36:227 (Ambler).

SHIMER, F.H. (See under Shimer, H.W.)

SHIMER, H.W., and SHIMER, F.H.

1910   The lithological section of Walnut Canyon, Arizona,
        with relation to the cliff-dwellings of this and
        other regions of northwestern Arizona. American
        Anthropologist, 12:237-249.

SHINER, Joel L. (See also under Hester, James J.)

1961   A room at Gila Pueblo. Kiva, 27, no. 2:3-11.

1963   Excavation of a pithouse near Zuni pueblo, New Mex-
        ico. Laboratory of Anthropology Notes, 19.

1964   Dating the occupation of site Bc-50 in Chaco Canyon
        National Monument. El Palacio, 71, no. 3:15-17.

1970   Activity analysis of a prehistoric site. Bulletin
        of the Texas Archaeological Society, 41:25-35.

SHINER, J.L., and LARK, W.B.

1954 The archaeological survey of the Standard Pipe Line Company's products line between El Paso, Texas, and Albuquerque, New Mexico. Laboratory of Anthropology Notes, 1.

SHUTLER, Mary Elizabeth (See under Shutler, Richard, Jr.)

SHUTLER, Richard, Jr.

1950 The Dry Creek site: a pre-pottery lithic horizon in the Verde Valley, Arizona. Plateau, 23, no. 1: 6-10.

1951 Two Pueblo ruins in the Verde Valley, Arizona. Plateau, 24, no. 1:1-9.

1952 Excavation of a pithouse in Williamson Valley, Arizona. Plateau, 24, no. 4:130-133.

1956 A notched stone artifact from Black Dog Cave, southern Nevada. Masterkey, 30, no. 3:95-96.

1961a Lost City, Pueblo Grande de Nevada. Nevada State Museum, Anthropological Papers, 5, 85 pp.

1961b The Pueblo Indian occupation of the southern Great Basin. Unversity of Arizona, dissertation, 535 pp.; University Microfilms International.

1965 Tule Springs expedition. Current Anthropology, 6: 110-111.

1967a Archaeology of Tule Springs. *In* Wormington and Ellis 1967, pp. 298-303.

1967b Cultural chronology in southern Nevada. *In* Wormington and Ellis 1967, pp. 305-308.

1968 Tule Springs: its implications to Early Man studies in North America. *In* Irwin-Williams 1968d, pp. 19-26.

SHUTLER, R., and SHUTLER, Mary Elizabeth

1962 Archaeological survey in southern Nevada. Nevada State Museum, Anthropological Papers, 7, 38 pp.

SHUTLER, R., SHUTLER, M.E., and GRIFFITH, James S.

1960 Stuart Rock Shelter, a stratified site in southern Nevada. Nevada State Museum, Anthropological Papers, 3, 36 pp.

SHUTLER R., and others

    1967   Pleistocene studies in southern Nevada. Nevada State
            Museum, Anthropological Papers, 13, 411 pp.

SIEGRIST, Roland

    1972   (ed.) Prehistoric petroglyphs and pictographs in
            Utah. Utah Museum of Fine Arts, 70 pp.

SIGNORI, Aldo (See under Sprague, Roderick.)

SIMMONS, Alan H. (See under Brook, Richard A.)

SIMON, Norman (See under Jarcho, Saul.)

SIMONIS, Don E. (See under Rice, Glen Eugene.)

SIMPSON, James H.

    1850   Journal of a military reconnaissance from Santa Fe,
            New Mexico, to the Navajo country. Reports of the
            Secretary of War, 31st Congress, first session,
            Senate, Executive document 64, pp. 56-139.

    1874   The ruins to be found in New Mexico, and the explor-
            ations of Francisco Vasquez de Coronado. Journal
            of the American Geographical Society, 5:194-216.

SIMPSON, Ruth DeEtte (See also under Harrington, Mark Raymond;
    Ripley, Don.)

    1946a   Those who have gone still live: the Hohokam since
            1400 A.D. Masterkey, 20, no. 3:73-80.

    1946b   The seal was broken. Masterkey, 20:154-156.

    1947   Angled enigmas: a preliminary statement. Masterkey,
            21, no. 1:28-29.

    1950   Tracking the Hohokam. Masterkey, 24, no. 4:126-128.

    1955   Hunting elephants in Nevada. Masterkey, 29:114-116.

    1956a   A hafted side scraper. Masterkey, 30, no. 2:56-57.

    1956b   Finding the scraper at Tule Springs. Masterkey, 30,
            no. 4:110.

    1956c   An introduction to early western American prehistory.
            Southern California Academy of Sciences, Bulletin,
            55:61-71.

    1960   An older date for Tule Springs. Masterkey, 34, no.
            2:82.

SIMS, Agnes C.

1948   An artist analyzes New Mexico's petroglyphs. El
        Palacio, 55, no. 10:302-309.

1949a   Migration story in stone. El Palacio, 56:67-76.

1949b   San Cristobal Petroglyphs. Santa Fe, 26 pp.

1963   Rock carvings, a record of folk history. *In* Dutton
        1963, pp. 214-220.

SIMS, Jack R., Jr., and DANIEL, D. Scott

1967   A lithic assemblage near Winslow, Arizona. Plateau,
        39, no. 4:175-188.

SINCLAIR, John L.

1947   Coronado's headquarters. New Mexico Magazine, 25,
        no. 3:11-13, 49-52.

1951   The pueblo of Kuaua. El Palacio, 58, no. 7:206-214
        (also as Papers of the School of American Research,
        45, 11 pp.).

SKINNER, Elizabeth

1974   Similarity of lithic industries in the Burro Moun-
        tains and Cliff Valley of southwestern New Mexico.
        The Artifact, 12, no. 3:26-44.

SKINNER, E., STEED, Paul P., Jr., and BEARDEN, Susan E.

1974   Prehistory at Milehigh. The Artifact, 12, no. 1:
        1-84.

SKINNER, S. Alan (See also under Gumerman, George J.)

1964   Lizard Cave: a rock shelter in northeastern New
        Mexico. El Palacio, 71, no. 3:22-29.

1965a   The Sedillo site: a pit house village in Albuquerque.
        El Palacio, 72, no. 1:5-24.

1965b   A survey of field houses at Sapawe, north central
        New Mexico. Southwestern Lore, 31, no. 1:18-24.

1966   A ceremonial room at Pottery Mound. Southwestern
        Lore, 32, no. 1:19-23.

1967   Four historic sites near Flagstaff, Arizona. Plateau,
        39, no. 3:105-123.

1968a   Camp Willow Grove, Arizona Territory. Plateau, 41,
        no. 1:1-13.

1968b   Further excavations at the Sedillo site, Albuquerque,
         New Mexico. Southwestern Lore, 34, no. 3:69-81.

1968c   Two historic period sites in the El Rito Valley, New
         Mexico. Plains Anthropologist, 13:63-70.

SLEIGHT, Frederick W.

1946   Comments on Basketmaker-like pictographs in northern
         Utah. Masterkey, 20, no. 3:88-92.

SMILEY, Terah L. (See also under Stokes, M.A.)

1947   Dates from a surface pueblo at Mesa Verde. Tree-
         Ring Bulletin, 13, no. 4:30-32.

1949a   Pithouse number 1, Mesa Verde National Park. Amer-
         ican Antiquity, 14:167-171.

1949b   Tree-ring dates from Point of Pines. Tree-Ring Bul-
         letin, 15, no. 3:20-21.

1950   Miscellaneous ring records, II. Tree-Ring Bulletin,
         16, no. 3:22-23.

1951   A summary of tree-ring dates from some Southwestern
         archaeological sites. University of Arizona, Labor-
         atory of Tree-Ring Research, Bulletin 5, 31 pp.
         Reviewed AAq 18:282 (Giddings).

1952   Four late prehistoric kivas at Point of Pines, Ari-
         zona. University of Arizona, Social Science Bulletin
         21, 72 pp.
         Reviewed AAq 18:401 (Wheat).

1955   (ed.) Geochronology, with special reference to
         southwestern United States. University of Arizona,
         Physical Science Bulletin 2, 200 pp.

1958   (ed.) Climate and man in the Southwest. University
         of Arizona, Program in Geochronology, Contribution
         no. 6.

1961   Evidence of climatic fluctuations in Southwestern
         prehistory. Annals of the New York Academy of Sci-
         ences, 9, no. 1:697-704.

SMILEY, T.L., STUBBS, Stanley A., and BANNISTER, Bryant

1953   A foundation for the dating of some late archae-
         ological sites in the Rio Grande area, New Mexico.
         University of Arizona, Laboratory of Tree-Ring Re-
         search, Bulletin 6, 66 pp.
         Reviewed AA 57:376 (Rowe), AAq 20:292 (Ellis).

SMITH, Allen

1966   A Lake Mohave point from the Uncompahgre Plateau.
        Southwestern Lore, 32, no. 1:23-24.

SMITH, Andrew T. (See under Enloe, James G.)

SMITH, C. Earle, Jr. (See also under Mangelsdorf, Paul C.)

1950   Prehistoric plant remains from Bat Cave. Harvard
        University Botanical Museum, Leaflets, 14, no. 7:
        157-180.

SMITH, Calvin B.

1966   The Paleo-Indian in southeastern New Mexico. Trans-
        actions of the Regional Archaeological Symposium on
        Southeastern New Mexico and Western Texas, 1966,
        Special Bulletin no. 1, pp. 3-8.

1970   Evidence of a distinctive Midland Complex in south-
        eastern New Mexico. Student Anthropologist (Uni-
        versity of Colorado), 2, no. 2:77-81.

1974   Description of a distinctive projectile point from
        southeastern New Mexico. Awanyu, 2, no. 2:20-25.

SMITH, C.B., RUNYON, John, and AGOGINO, George

1966   A progress report on a pre-ceramic site at Rattle-
        snake Draw, eastern New Mexico. Plains Anthropolo-
        gist, 11:302-313.

SMITH, David Beardsley

1962   The identification of incipient agriculture. Bul-
        letin of the Philadelphia Anthropological Society,
        15, nos. 2-3:28-38.

SMITH, David G. (See under Nichols, Robert F.)

SMITH, Elmer R. (See also under Malouf, Carling.)

1936   Utah type metates. Museum of Central Utah, Bul-
        letin, 1, no. 1, 6 pp.

1940a   Areas of prehistoric and historical settlements in
        Utah. Proceedings of the Utah Academy of Science,
        Arts and Letters, 17:18-19 (abstract).

1940b   A brief description of an Indian ruin near Shones-
        burg, Utah. University of Utah, Anthropological
        Papers, 4, 5 pp.

1941   Archaeology of Deadman Cave, Utah. University of
        Utah Bulletin, 32, no. 4, 43 pp.

1942   Early Man in the Great Salt Lake area. Mineralogical
        Society of Utah, News Bulletin, 3, no. 2:27-32.

1950   Utah anthropology: an outline of its history. South-
        western Lore, 16, no. 2:22-33.

1952   The archaeology of Deadman Cave, Utah: a revision.
        University of Utah, Anthropological Papers, 10, 46
        pp.

SMITH, Gerald A., and TURNER, Wilson G.

1976   Indian Rock Art of Southern California. San Ber-
        nardino County Museum, Redlands.

SMITH, G.A., and others

1961   Indian picture writing of San Bernardino and River-
        side Counties. San Bernardino County Museum Associa-
        tion Quarterly, 8, no. 3:1-36.

SMITH, Harvey P. (See under Kelly, Thomas C.)

SMITH, Jack E.

1962   The Wingate site (LA 2714). Laboratory of Anthro-
        pology Notes, 15.

1963a   The Bluewater highway salvage project. Laboratory
        of Anthropology Notes, 20.

1963b   Excavation of the Salcido site, LA 6761. Labora-
        tory of Anthropology Notes, 21.

1965   The archaeology of the upper San Jose valley, north-
        western New Mexico, and its relation to the develop-
        mental stage of the Chaco branch of the Anasazi tra-
        dition. University of California (Los Angeles),
        dissertation, 316 pp.; University Microfilms Inter-
        national.

SMITH, Landon D.

1977a   Archaeological and paleoenvironmental investiga-
        tions in the Cave Buttes area north of Phoenix,
        Arizona. Arizona Archaeologist, 11, 106 pp.

1977b   An archaeological report on the materials recovered
        from site 01-113, Coconino National Forest, Arizona.
        Miscellaneous Paper no. 2, U.S. Forest Service,

Southwestern Region, Archaeological Report no. 15:
18-26.

SMITH, L.D., and DICK, Herbert W.

1977   A preliminary analysis of three sample surveys in
        the Golondrino Mesa area, Santa Fe National Forest,
        New Mexico. Miscellaneous Paper no. 9, U.S. Forest
        Service, Southwestern Region, Archaeological Report
        no. 15:67-91.

SMITH, Shirley (Also listed as East-Smith, Shirley.)

SMITH, S., and AGOGINO, George

1966   A comparison of whole and fragmentary Paleo-Indian
        points from Blackwater Draw. Plains Anthropologist,
        11:201-203.

SMITH, Thomas Edwin

1950   Villages of the past. New Mexico Magazine, 28, no.
        8:17, 47-50.

SMITH, Victor J.

1923   Indian pictographs in the Big Bend in Texas. Publi-
        cations of the Texas Folklore Society, 2:18-30.

1927   Some notes on dry rock shelters in western Texas.
        American Anthropologist, 29:286-290.

1931   Archaeological notes of the Big Bend region. Bul-
        letin of the Texas Archaeological and Paleontological
        Society, 3:60-69.

1932a   Muller Rock Shelter, a report on dry rock shelter
        excavation in the Big Bend region of Texas. West
        Texas Historical and Scientific Society, Circular
        no. 1.

1932b   The relation of the Southwestern Basket Maker to the
        dry shelter culture of the Big Bend. Bulletin of
        the Texas Archaeological and Paleontological Society,
        4:55-62.

1933   Sandals of the Big Bend culture with additional notes
        concerning Basket-Maker evidence. Bulletin of the
        Texas Archaeological and Paleontological Society, 5:
        57-65.

1934   Hord rock shelter. Bulletin of the Texas Archaeo-
        logical and Paleontological Society, 6:97-106.

1935   The split stitch basket, a distinguishing culture
        trait of the Big Bend in Texas. Bulletin of the
        Texas Archaeological and Paleontological Society,
        7:100-104.

1936   The pottery horizons of Texas. Bulletin of the
        Texas Archaeological and Paleontological Society,
        8:94-112.

1938   Carved Rock shelter. Bulletin of the Texas Archae-
        ological and Paleontological Society, 10:222-233.

1940   Cordage of the caves in the greater Big Bend. Bul-
        letin of the Texas Archaeological and Paleontological
        Society, 12:175-194.

1941   Some unusual basketry and bags from the Big Bend
        caves. Bulletin of the Texas Archaeological and
        Paleontological Society, 13:133-151.

1942   Evidence of European influence in the pictographs
        of west Texas. Bulletin of the Texas Archaeological
        and Paleontological Society, 14:38-47.

1943   The use of stone walls for fortification in the Big
        Bend of Texas. Clearing-house for Southwestern Mu-
        seums, News Letter, 55:233-234.

1946   Evidence of European influence in the pictographs
        of west Texas. Bulletin of the Texas Archaeological
        and Paleontological Society, 17:48-62.

1951   The use of rock wall construction by the Indians of
        the Big Bend in Texas. Texas Journal of Science, 3,
        no. 3:343-349.

SMITH, V.J., and KELLEY, J. Charles

1933   The Meriweather rock shelter, a report on rock
        shelter excavation in the Big Bend of Texas. West
        Texas Historical and Scientific Society, Circular
        no. 3.

SMITH, Watson (See also under Beals, Ralph L.; Gifford, James
    C.; Hargrave, Lyndon L.; Montgomery, Ross Gordon.)

1935   Report of some sites tested near Marsh Pass. Rain-
        bow Bridge-Monument Valley Expedition, Preliminary
        Bulletin no. 8, 5 pp.

1949   Excavations in Big Hawk Valley. Plateau, 21, no.
        3:42-48.

1950   Preliminary report of the Peabody Museum Upper Gila

Expedition, Pueblo Division, 1949. El Palacio, 57: 392-399.

1952a   Excavations in Big Hawk Valley, Wupatki National Monument, Arizona. Museum of Northern Arizona, Bulletin 24, 203 pp.
Reviewed AAq 18:399 (Taylor).

1952b   Kiva mural decorations at Awatovi and Kawaika-a; with a survey of other wall paintings in the Pueblo Southwest. Papers of the Peabody Museum of American Archaeology and Ethnology, 37, 363 pp.
Reviewed AA 56:141 (Dozier), AAq 20:89 (Chapman).

1952c   Mural decorations in seventeenth-century Southwestern missions. El Palacio, 59, no. 4:123-125.

1962   Schools, pots, and potters. American Anthropologist, 64:1165-1178.

1970a   Pots of gold. Kiva, 36, no. 1:39-43.

1970b   Seventeenth-century Spanish missions of the Western Pueblo area. Tucson Corral of the Westerners, Smoke Signal no. 21, 24 pp.

1971   Painted ceramics of the western mound at Awatovi. Papers of the Peabody Museum of Archaeology and Ethnology, 38, 630 pp.
Reviewed AA 74:132 (Longacre), AAq 38:248 (Gumerman).

1972   Prehistoric kivas of Antelope Mesa, northeastern Arizona. Papers of the Peabody Museum of Archaeology and Ethnology, 39, no. 1, 162 pp.
Reviewed AA 77:154 (Euler).

1973   The Williams site: a frontier Mogollon village in west-central New Mexico. Papers of the Peabody Museum of Archaeology and Ethnology, 39, no. 2, 46 pp.

SMITH, W., and FONTANA, Bernard L.

1970   Religious sacramentals from Awatovi. Kiva, 36, no. 2:13-16.

SMITH, W., and LIPE, William D.

1973   (ed.) Guidelines: Museum of Northern Arizona Ceramic Series. Museum of Northern Arizona.

SMITH, W., WOODBURY, Richard B., and WOODBURY, Nathalie F.S.

1966   The excavation of Hawikuh by Frederick Webb Hodge:
        report of the Hendricks-Hodge Expedition, 1917-1923.
        Museum of the American Indian, Contributions, 20,
        336 pp.
        Reviewed AA 70:818 (Martin), AAq 34:92 (Reed).

SNODGRASS, O.T.

1973a   A major Mimbres collection, by camera: life among
        the Mimbreños, as depicted by designs on their pot-
        tery. The Artifact, 11, no. 4:9-63.

1973b   A Mimbres ornament. The Artifact, 11, no. 4:64-65.

1975   Realistic art and times of the Mimbres Indians. El
        Paso.

SNOW, Cordelia Thomas

1974   A brief history of the Palace of the Governors and
        a preliminary report on the 1974 excavation. El
        Palacio, 80, no. 3:1-21.

SNOW, David H.

1965   The chronological position of Mexican majolica in
        the Southwest. El Palacio, 72:25-35.

1970a   An inventory of archaeological sites on lands leased
        by the Great Western United Corporation, 1970 season.
        Laboratory of Anthropology Notes, 80B.

1970b   An inventory of archaeological sites on lands leased
        by the California City Development Company, Cochiti
        Pueblo Grant, Sandoval County, New Mexico. Labora-
        tory of Anthropology Notes, 80C.

1971   (ed.) Excavations at Cochiti Dam, New Mexico, 1964-
        1966 seasons. Volume I: LA 272, LA 9154, LA 34.
        Laboratory of Anthropology Notes, 79.

1972a   A preliminary report of archaeological survey: the
        Tetilla Park recreation areas access road, 1972-73,
        Cochiti Dam, New Mexico. Laboratory of Anthropology
        Notes, 80A.

1972b   Survey results LA 5127 - LA 5138, Cochiti Dam and
        reservoir, New Mexico. Laboratory of Anthropology
        Notes, 80G.

1973a   Cochiti Dam salvage project: archaeological excava-
        tion of the Las Majadas site, LA 591, Cochiti Dam,

New Mexico. Laboratory of Anthropology Notes, 75.

1973b   Cochiti Dam salvage project: archaeological excavation at the Torreon site, LA 6178, Cochiti Dam, New Mexico. Laboratory of Anthropology Notes, 76.

1973c   Cochiti Dam salvage project: archaeological investigations at LA 8720, Cochiti Dam, New Mexico, 1971. Laboratory of Anthropology Notes, 87.

1973d   Prehistoric Southwestern turquoise industry. El Palacio, 79, no. 1:33-51.

1974   The excavation of Saltbush Pueblo, Bandelier National Monument, New Mexico, 1971. Laboratory of Anthropology Notes, 97.

1975a   Archaeological survey and assessment, Sebastian Martin-Black Mesa watershed, Rio Arriba County, New Mexico. Laboratory of Anthropology Notes, 114.

1975b   Archaeological survey and assessment: Española-Rio Chama watershed, Santa Fe and Rio Arriba Counties, New Mexico. Laboratory of Anthropology Notes, 115.

1975c   The identification of Puaray Pueblo. *In* Frisbie 1975a, pp. 463-480.

1976   Santiago to Guache: notes for a tale of two (or more) Bernalillos. *In* Schroeder 1976, pp. 161-181.

SNOW, D.H., and FULLBRIGHT, H.J.

1977   Samac analytical notes II: preliminary results of x-ray fluorescence analysis of archaeological materials from southeastern Utah. National Technical Information Service, LA-6701-MS, 15 pp.

SNOW, Harold L.

1926   Ancient pictographs of southern Utah. Improvement Era, 30, no. 2:163-165.

SNOW, William J.

1941   Ancient mound grains. Utah Historical Quarterly, 9, nos. 3-4:133-136.

SNYDER, Ernest E.

1966   Petroglyphs of the South Mountains of Arizona. American Antiquity, 31:705-709.

SNYDER, John Francis

1897   The cliff-dweller's "sandal last." Antiquarian, 1:
        128-130.

1899   The "sandal last" of the cliff-dwellers. American
        Archaeologist, 3, pt. 1:5-9.

SOMER, Arnold E.

1971   Big Spring site. Transactions of the 6th Regional
        Archaeological Symposium on Southeastern New Mexico
        and Western Texas, pp. 111-122.

1972   The Windmill site: 41CX57. Transactions of the 7th
        Regional Archaeological Symposium on Southeastern
        New Mexico and Western Texas, pp. 115-121.

SORROW, William M.

1968a   The Devil's Mouth site: the third season, 1967.
        Papers of the Texas Archaeological Salvage Project,
        14, 70 pp.
        Reviewed AA 71:1210 (Hammatt), AAq 35:118 (Tunnel).

1968b   Test excavations at the Nopal Terrace site, Val
        Verde County, Texas. Papers of the Texas Archaeo-
        logical Salvage Project, 15, 39 pp.
        Reviewed AA 71:1210 (Hammatt), AAq 35:118 (Tunnel).

SOULÉ, Edwin C.

1975   Lost City revisited. Masterkey, 49, no. 1:4-19.

1976   Lost City II. Masterkey, 50, no. 1.

1977   A desert mystery. Masterkey, 51, no. 3.

SOULEN, Harvey

1940   Intricate carved bone dagger from Mimbres Valley,
        New Mexico. Minnesota Archaeologist, 6:88-89.

SOUTHWESTERN CERAMIC CONFERENCE

1958   Cibola White Ware Conference - concordances and
        proceedings. Museum of Northern Arizona, 14 pp.

1959   Concordance of opinion reached at the Second South-
        western Ceramic Conference. Museum of Northern
        Arizona, 16 pp.

1961   Third Southwestern Ceramic Seminar, Museum of North-
        ern Arizona, 5 pp.

1962   Fourth Southwestern Ceramic Seminar. Museum of
        Northern Arizona, 12 pp.

1965   Acoma-Zuni pottery types. Seventh Southwestern
        Ceramic Seminar, Museum of Northern Arizona, 14 pp.

SOWERS, Theodore Carl (See also under Evans, Cecelia.)

1942   Petroglyphs of the Chaco Canyon area. Southwestern
        Lore, 8:24-26.

SPAIN, James N.

1975   Lithic analysis: AZ T:11:31 (ASM) and AZ AA:10:3
        (ASM). Arizona State Museum, Archaeological Series,
        86, 37 pp.

SPAULDING, Peggy (See under Vivian, R. Gwinn.)

SPEARS, C. Duane

1973   Tests in Compound B, Casa Grande National Monument.
        Arizona State Museum, Archaeological Series, 30,
        37 pp.

SPECK, Fred, Jr. (See under Shafer, Harry J.)

SPENCER, Frank C.

1947   Prehistoric fortress. New Mexico Magazine, 25:22,
        45-49.

SPENCER, J.E.

1934   Pueblo sites of southwestern Utah. American Anthro-
        pologist, 36, no. 1:70-80.

SPENCER, L.W.

1928   Cliff-dweller lands. Art and Archaeology, 25:285-
        291.

SPICER, Edward H. (See also under Caywood, Louis R.)

1934   Some Pueblo I structures of the San Francisco Moun-
        tains, Arizona. Museum of Northern Arizona, Museum
        Notes, 7, no. 5:17-20.

SPICER, E.H., and CAYWOOD, Louis R.

1934   Tuzigoot, a prehistoric pueblo of the upper Verde.
        Museum of Northern Arizona, Museum Notes, 6, no.
        9:43-46.

1936   Two Pueblo ruins in west central Arizona. University of Arizona, Social Science Bulletin 10, 115 pp.

SPIER, Leslie

1917a   An outline for a chronology of Zuni ruins. American Museum of Natural History, Anthropological Papers, 18, pt. 3, pp. 207-331. Reviewed AA 21:296 (Kidder).

1917b   Zuni chronology. Proceedings of the National Academy of Sciences, 3:280-283.

1918   Notes on some Little Colorado ruins. American Museum of Natural History, Anthropological Papers, 18, pt. 4, pp. 333-362. Reviewed AA 21:296 (Kidder).

1919   Ruins in the White Mountains, Arizona. American Museum of Natural History, Anthropological Papers, 18, pt. 5, pp. 363-387. Reviewed AA 21:296 (Kidder).

1931   N.C. Nelson's stratigraphic technique in the reconstruction of prehistoric sequences in southwestern America. *In* Methods in Social Science, ed. S.A. Rice, Chicago, pp. 275-283.

SPOEHR, Alexander (See also under Martin, Paul Sidney.)

1949   Southwestern pithouses. American Antiquity, 15:55.

SPRAGUE, Roderick (See also under Robinson, William J.)

1964   Inventory of prehistoric Southwestern copper bells: additions and corrections I. Kiva, 30, no. 1:18-24.

SPRAGUE, R., and SIGNORI, Aldo

1963   Inventory of prehistoric Southwestern copper bells. Kiva, 28, no. 4:1-20.

SPUHLER, James N.

1954   Some problems in the physical anthropology of the American Southwest. American Anthropologist, 56: 604-625.

SQUIER, Ephraim George

1848   New Mexico and California: the ancient monuments and the aboriginal semi-civilized nations. American Review, November, 26 pp.

STACY, V.K. Pheriba

1974   "Cerros de trincheras" in the Arizona Papagueria.
        University of Arizona, dissertation, 235 pp.; Uni-
        versity Microfilms International.

1975   Archaeological survey in the Arizona Papagueria.
        Kiva, 40, no. 3:181-187.

STACY, V.K.P., and HAYDEN, Julian D.

1975   Saguaro National Monument; an archaeological over-
        view. National Park Service, Western Archaeological
        Center, Publications in Anthropology, 1, 54 pp.

STAFFORD, C. Russell

1977   Archaeological investigations at the proposed Seneca
        Lake Recreation Complex, San Carlos Indian Reserva-
        tion, Gila County, Arizona. Arizona State University,
        Office of Cultural Resource Management, report no.
        30, 95 pp.

STALEY, S. McClain

1976   The Westgate site: salvage excavation in Bernalillo
        County, New Mexico. Awanyu, 4, no. 4:6-15.

STALLINGS, William S., Jr. (See also under Mera, Harry P.;
Stubbs, Stanley A.)

1931   El Paso Polychrome. Laboratory of Anthropology,
        Technical Series Bulletin 3, 13 pp.

1932   Notes on the Pueblo culture in south-central New
        Mexico and in the vicinity of El Paso, Texas. Amer-
        ican Anthropologist, 34, no. 1:67-78.

1933   A tree-ring chronology for the Rio Grande drainage
        in northern New Mexico. Proceedings of the National
        Academy of Sciences, 19, no. 9:803-806.

1936a   Dates from Gallo Canyon, east-central New Mexico.
        Tree-Ring Bulletin, 3, no. 1:6-8.

1936b   Dates from Five Kiva House, Utah. Tree-Ring Bul-
        letin, 3, no. 2:13-14.

1937   Some Southwestern dated ruins, I. Tree-Ring Bul-
        letin, 4, no. 2:3-5.

1939a   Dating prehistoric ruins by tree-rings. Laboratory
        of Anthropology, General Series Bulletin 8, 20 pp.
        Reviewed AAq 10:106 (Haury).

1939b   Puaray date erroneous. El Palacio, 46:219.

1941   A Basket Maker II date from Cave du Pont, Utah.
        Tree-Ring Bulletin, 8, no. 1:3-6.

1960   Dating prehistoric ruins by tree-rings. Revised
        edition, Tree-Ring Society, Tucson, 18 pp.

STANFIELD, Scott

1961   A chronology of pre-contact subsistence crops in
        the Southwest. University of Oklahoma, Papers in
        Anthropology, 2, no. 1.

STANFORD, Dennis (See under Dawson, Jerry.)

STANISLAWSKI, Michael B.

1961   Two prehistoric shell caches from southern Arizona.
        Kiva, 27, no. 2:22-27.

1963a   Extended burials in the prehistoric Southwest.
        American Antiquity, 28:308-319.

1963b   Wupatki Pueblo: a study in cultural fusion and
        change in Sinagua and Hopi prehistory. University
        of Arizona, dissertation, 690 pp.; University Micro-
        films International.

1966   Mesoamerican influences in northeastern Arizona.
        Proceedings of the 36th International Congress of
        Americanists, 1:309-319.

1969a   The ethno-archaeology of Hopi pottery making. Pla-
        teau, 42, no. 1:27-33.

1969b   What good is a broken pot? An experiment in Hopi-
        Tewa ethno-archaeology. Southwestern Lore, 35:11-
        18.

STANLEY, F.

1948   The Folsom story. El Palacio, 55:141-150.

STARR, Frederick

1894   The Hemenway southwestern archaeological expedition.
        Internationales Archiv für Ethnographie, 8:270-272.

1900   Shrines near Cochiti, New Mexico. American Anti-
        quarian, 22, no. 4:219-223.

STEED, Paul P., Jr. (See also under Skinner, Elizabeth; Sutherland, Kay.)

1976   Rock art on Alamo Mountain, Otero County, New Mexico:
        a preliminary report. The Artifact, 14, no. 4:1-116.

STEELE, David J.

1969   The determination of prehistoric dietary patterns
        by means of coprolite analysis: a Glen Canyon ex-
        ample. Utah Archaeology, 15, no. 2:3-10.

STEEN, Charlie R. (See also under Steen, Mary; Tanner, Clara
Lee.)

1935a   Ceremonial cigarettes. Southwest Monuments Monthly
        Report, Supplement, October, pp. 287-291.

1935b   Slit tapestry from the upper Salt River Valley,
        Arizona. American Anthropologist, 37:458-459.

1936   Prehistoric village at Saguaro National Monument.
        Southwest Monuments Monthly Report, August, pp.
        150-151.

1937   Archaeological investigations at Natural Bridges
        National Monument. Southwestern Monuments Monthly
        Report, May (Special Report no. 17), pp. 329-337.

1941   The Upper Tonto ruins. Kiva, 6, no. 5:17-20.

1955a   Campers at Pigeon Cliffs, 10,000 B.C. New Mexico
        Magazine, 33:24-25, 53.

1955b   The Pigeon Cliffs site: a preliminary report. El
        Palacio, 62, nos. 5-6:174-180.

1958   A pit oven in Union County, New Mexico. El Palacio,
        65, no. 3:112-113.

1962   Excavations at the Upper Ruin, Tonto National Monu-
        ment, 1940. In Caywood 1962, pp. 1-32.

1965   Excavations in Compound A, Casa Grande National
        Monument, 1963. Kiva, 31, no. 2:59-82.

1966   Excavations at Tse-Ta'a, Canyon de Chelly National
        Monument, Arizona. National Park Service, Archae-
        ological Research Series, 9, 160 pp.
        Reviewed AA 70:421 (Hill).

1976   Excavations at Pigeon Cliff. In Schroeder 1976,
        pp. 19-36.

STEEN, C.R., and JONES, Volney H.

    1941   Prehistoric lima beans in the Southwest. El Palacio,
            48, no. 9:197-203.

STEEN, Frank

    1940   Folsom flints. New Mexico Magazine, 18, no. 2:20,
            37-38.

STEEN, Mary, and STEEN, Charlie R.

    1946   Casa Grande. Arizona Highways, 22, no. 7:8-9.

STEENBERG, F.G.

    1937   Montezuma Castle in 1894. Southwestern Monuments
            Monthly Report, Supplement, November, pp. 397-405.

STEIN, John R. (See also under Gauthier, Rory; Grigg, Paul.)

    1974   Archaeological survey of Anaconda Company drill
            sites on Ojo del Espiritu Santo Grant, Sandoval
            County. University of New Mexico, contract report
            101-99 (BLM).

    1975   Archaeological clearance survey: Ya-Ta-Hey to Pitts-
            burg Mine Public Service Company powerline right-
            of-way. University of New Mexico, contract report
            101-103E (NPS).

STEIN, J.R., and FRIZELL, John

    1977   Archaeological survey of two proposed powerlines
            near the San Juan Generating Station. University
            of New Mexico, contract report 185-2F (BLM).

STEIN, J.R., and PECKHAM, Stewart L.

    1974   An inventory of archaeological and historical re-
            mains in the Cottonwood-Walnut drainage, Chavez
            and Eddy Counties, New Mexico. Laboratory of Anthro-
            pology Notes, 104.

STEIN, J.R., and STUART, David

    1976   Archaeological clearance survey: Star Lake to Gallup
            for 8" pipeline (GASCO). University of New Mexico,
            contract report 101-146 (BLM, NPS, BIA).

STEIN, Mary Anne (See under Ambler, J. Richard; Lindsay, Alex-
    ander J., Jr.)

STEIN, Pat H. (See under Brook, Richard A.)

STEIN, Walter T.

1964   Mammal remains from archaeological sites in the
       Point of Pines region, Arizona. American Antiquity,
       29:213-220.

1967   Locality 1 (C1-244), Tule Springs, Nevada. *In*
       Wormington and Ellis 1967, pp. 309-329.

STEPHENSON, Robert L. (See under Toulouse, Joseph H., Jr.)

STERUD, Gene (See under Davis, Emma Lou.)

STEVENS, Dominique E., and AGOGINO, George A.

1975   Sandia Cave: a study in controversy. Eastern New
       Mexico University, Contributions in Anthropology,
       7, no. 1, 52 pp.

STEVENSON, James

1883a Illustrated catalogue of the collections obtained
       from the Indians of New Mexico and Arizona in 1879.
       Second Annual Report of the Bureau of American
       Ethnology, pp. 307-422.

1883b Illustrated catalogue of the collections obtained
       from the Indians of New Mexico in 1880. Second
       Annual Report of the Bureau of American Ethnology,
       pp. 423-465.

1883c Pueblo of Tallyhogan - burial places of former in-
       habitants. Science, 2, no. 38:580.

1884   Illustrated catalogue of the collections obtained
       from the pueblos of Zuni, New Mexico, and Wolpi,
       Arizona, in 1881. Third Annual Report of the Bureau
       of American Ethnology, pp. 511-594.

1886   Ancient habitations of the Southwest. Bulletin of
       the American Geographical Society, 4:329-342.

STEVENSON, Matilda Coxe

1883   The cliff-dwellers of the New Mexican canyons.
       Kansas City Review, 6, no. 11:636-639.

STEWARD, Julian H.

1929   Petroglyphs of California and adjoining states.
       University of California Publications in American

Archaeology and Ethnology, 24, no. 2, pp. 47-238.
Reviewed AA 33:427 (Strong).

1931 Archaeological discoveries at Kanosh in Utah. El
Palacio, 30, no. 8:121-130.

1933a Archaeological problems of the northern periphery
of the Southwest. Museum of Northern Arizona, Bulletin 5, 24 pp.

1933b Early inhabitants of western Utah: Part I; mounds
and house types. University of Utah Bulletin, 23,
no. 7, 34 pp.

1936 Pueblo material culture in western Utah. University
of New Mexico Bulletin, Anthropological Series, 1,
no. 3, 64 pp.

1937a Ancient caves of the Great Salt Lake region. Bureau
of American Ethnology, Bulletin 116, 131 pp.

1937b Ecological aspects of Southwestern society. Anthro-
pos, 32:87-104.

1937c Petroglyphs of the United States. Annual Report of
the Smithsonian Institution for 1936, pp. 405-425.

1940 Native cultures of the intermontane (Great Basin)
area. Smithsonian Miscellaneous Collections, 100:
445-502.
Reviewed AAq 7:335 (Hibben).

1941 Archaeological reconnaissance of southern Utah.
Bureau of American Ethnology, Bulletin 128, pp.
275-356.

STEWART, Guy R.

1940a Conservation in Pueblo agriculture: I, primitive
practices. Scientific Monthly, 51, no. 3:201-220.

1940b Conservation in Pueblo agriculture: II, presentday
flood water irrigation. Scientific Monthly, 51,
no. 4:329-340.

STEWART, G.R., and DONNELLY, Maurice

1943a Soil and water economy in the Pueblo Southwest: I,
field studies at Mesa Verde and northern Arizona.
Scientific Monthly, 56, no. 1:31-44.

1943b Soil and water economy in the Pueblo Southwest: II,
evaluation of primitive methods of conservation.
Scientific Monthly, 56, no. 2:134-144.

STEWART, Kenneth M.

1967   Excavations at Mesa Grande, a Classic period Hohokam
        site in Arizona. Masterkey, 41, no. 1:14-25.

STEWART, Omer C.

1947a   Archaeological mapping in Colorado. Southwestern
        Lore, 13, no. 2.

1947b   Archaeology, ethnology and history in Colorado.
        Southwestern Lore, 13:24-28.

STEWART, T. Dale

1935   Skeletal remains from southwestern Texas. American
        Journal of Physical Anthropology, 20, no. 2:213-231.

1937   Different types of cranial deformity in the Pueblo
        area. American Anthropologist, 39:169-171.

STEWART, Yvonne G., TEAGUE, Lynn S., and CANOUTS, Valetta

1974   An ethnoarchaeological study of the Vekol copper
        mining project. Arizona State Museum, Archaeo-
        logical Series, 49, 110 pp.

STIGER, Mark A.

1975   The coprolites of Hoy House: a preliminary analysis.
        Journal of the Colorado-Wyoming Academy of Science,
        7.

STIRLAND, Robert D. (See under Rudy, Jack R.)

STIRLING, Matthew W.

1931   Archaeological reconnaissance in Texas and Nevada.
        Explorations and Field-work of the Smithsonian
        Institution in 1930, pp. 173-176.

1940   Indian tribes of pueblo land. National Geographic
        Magazine, 78:549-596.

STOCK, Chester

1931   Problems of antiquity presented in Gypsum Cave.
        Scientific Monthly, 32, no. 1:22-32.

STODDARD, Earl (See under Rudy, Jack R.)

STOKES, M.A., and SMILEY, T.L.

    1963   Tree-ring dates from the Navajo land claim. I. The
            northern sector. Tree-Ring Bulletin, 25, nos. 3-4:
            8-18.

    1964   Tree-ring dates from the Navajo land claim. II.
            The western sector. Tree-Ring Bulletin, 26, nos.
            1-4:13-27.

    1966   Tree-ring dates from the Navajo land claim. III.
            The southern sector. Tree-Ring Bulletin, 27, nos.
            3-4:2-11.

    1969   Tree-ring dates from the Navajo land claim. IV.
            The eastern sector. Tree-Ring Bulletin, 29, nos.
            1-2:2-15.

STOKES, M.A., and others

    1976   Dendrocronología en el norte de México. *In* Braniff
            and Felger 1976, pp. 77-78.

STOKES, William Lee (See also under Hansen, George H.)

    1973   Cliff-wall seepage figures: rock art prototypes?
            Plateau, 45, no. 4:143-148.

STONE, Connie L.

    1977a   An archaeological sample survey of the Alamo Reser-
            voir, Mohave and Yuma Counties, Arizona. Arizona
            State University, Office of Cultural Resource Manage-
            ment, report no. 24, 53 pp.

    1977b   An archaeological sample survey of the Whitlow Ranch
            Reservoir, Pinal County, Arizona. Arizona State
            University, Office of Cultural Resource Management,
            report no. 25, 34 pp.

STONE, Lyle M. (See under Fitting, James E.)

STONER, Victor A.

    1936   A reconnaissance of the Tonto cliff dwellings.
            Southwestern Monuments Monthly Report, April, pp.
            304-310.

STORY, Dee Ann (Also listed as Suhm, Dee Ann.)

STORY, D.A., and BRYANT, Vaughn M., Jr.

    1966   A preliminary study of the paleoecology of the

Amistad Reservoir area. National Science Foundation, Report of Research, GS-667, Austin, 255 pp.

STOWELL, H.W.

1934a   Pictograph hunting. New Mexico Magazine, 12, no. 2: 21-22, 42-44.

1934b   Lost pueblo. New Mexico Magazine, 12, no. 6:10-11, 47-48.

1934c   Canyon de Chelly; the wonder spot near New Mexico's western border. New Mexico Magazine, 12, no. 9:10-11, 42-43.

STUART, David E. (See also under Allan, William C.; Carroll, Charles; Cattle, Dorothy; Gauthier, Rory; Grigg, Paul; Stein, John R.)

STUART, D.E., ALLAN, William C., and ESCHMAN, Peter

1975   An archaeological clearance survey: Chala Cryogenics pipeline, Chaves County, New Mexico. Awanyu, 3, no. 4:36-53.

STUART, Frank C.

1962   Coronado Monument; pueblo of the painted kiva. New Mexico Magazine, 40, no. 3:5-9, 34.

STUBBS, Stanley A. (See also under Smiley, Terah L.)

1930a   Preliminary report of excavations near La Luz and Alamogordo, New Mexico. El Palacio, 29, no. 1:3-14.

1930b   Survey of Governador region. El Palacio, 29:75-79.

1954a   Museum of New Mexico archaeological fieldwork, 1952-1953. Southwestern Lore, 19, no. 4:8-9.

1954b   Summary report on an early Pueblo site in the Tesuque Valley, New Mexico. El Palacio, 61:43-45.

1959a   Prehistoric woven asbestos belt fragment. El Palacio, 66, no. 2:inside back cover.

1959b   "New" old churches found at Quarai and Tabirá. El Palacio, 66, no. 5:162-169.

STUBBS, S.A., and ELLIS, Bruce T.

1955   Archaeological excavations at the chapel of San Miguel and the site of La Castrense, Santa Fe, New Mexico. School of American Research, Monograph no. 20, 21 pp.

STUBBS, S.A., and STALLINGS, W.S., Jr.

1953   The excavation of Pindi Pueblo, New Mexico. School
       of American Research, Monograph no. 18, 165 pp.
          Reviewed AA 57:1092 (Woodbury), AAq 20:399 (Mc-
       Gregor).

STUBBS, S.A., ELLIS, B.T., and DITTERT, Alfred E., Jr.

1957   "Lost" Pecos church. El Palacio, 64:67-92.

STURDEVANT, G.E.

1928   A reconnaissance of the northeastern part of Grand
       Canyon National Park. Grand Canyon Nature Notes,
       3, no. 5:1-6.

STURGIS, Henry F. (See under Jelks, Edward B.)

SUHM, Dee Ann (Also listed as Story, Dee Ann.)

1959   Extended survey of the right bank of the Glen Can-
       yon. *In* Jennings and others 1959, pt. I, pp. 163-
       284.

SUHM, D.A., and JELKS, Edward B.

1962   Handbook of Texas Archaeology: type descriptions.
       Texas Archaeological Society, Special Publication
       no. 1, 299 pp. (also as Texas Memorial Museum,
       Bulletin 4).

SUHM, D.A., KRIEGER, Alex D., and JELKS, Edward B.

1954   An introductory handbook of Texas archaeology.
       Bulletin of the Texas Archaeological and Paleonto-
       logical Society, 25, 582 pp.
          Reviewed AA 59:742 (Wheat), AAq 22:310 (Stephen-
       son and Kelley).

SULLIVAN, Alan P., III

1974   Problems in the estimation of original room func-
       tion: a tentative solution from the Grasshopper
       Ruin. Kiva, 40, nos. 1-2:93-100.

SULLIVAN, A.P., and SCHIFFER, Michael B.

1978   A critical examination of SARG. *In* Euler and
       Gumerman 1978, pp. 168-176.

SULLIVAN, D.S.

1917   Chiricahua petroglyphs. El Palacio, 4, no. 3:90-91.

SUNDT, William M. (See also under Bice, Richard A.)

1971   Locating pueblo sites. Albuquerque Archaeological Society, Newsletter, 6, no. 3:4-7.

1973   Progress report on AS-5: the excavation of a primitive Indian lead mine. Awanyu, 1, no. 4:22-26.

SUSIA, Margaret L.

1964   Tule Springs archaeological surface survey. Nevada State Museum, Anthropological Papers, 12, 34 pp.

SUTHERLAND, Kay

1976   Survey of Picture Cave in Hueco Mountains. The Artifact, 14, no. 2:1-32.

SUTHERLAND, K., and BILBO, Michael

1975   Pine Springs Canyon pictograph site in Guadalupe Mountains National Park. The Artifact, 13, no. 3: 50-66.

SUTHERLAND, K., and STEED, Paul P., Jr.

1974   Fort Hancock rock art: site no. 1. The Artifact, 12, no. 4:3-64.

SUTTON, Myron

1954   Montezuma Well. Arizona Highways, 30, no. 7:30-35.

SUTTON, V.

1937   The sutures of the Mesa Verde cliff dwellers. Mesa Verde Notes, 7:1-2.

SWAN, A.M.

1899   Stone circles and upright stones in New Mexico. American Antiquarian, 21, no. 4:206-207.

SWANCARA, Frank, Jr.

1955   The archaeology of the Great Sand Dunes National Monument, a preliminary survey. Southwestern Lore, 20, no. 4:53-58.

SWANNACK, Jervis D., Jr. (See also under Rohn, Arthur H.)

1969   Big Juniper House, Mesa Verde National Park, Colo-
        rado. National Park Service, Archaeological Re-
        search Series, 7-C, 188 pp.
        Reviewed AAq 36:482 (Zubrow).

SWANSON, Earl H., Jr.

1966   The geographic foundations of the Desert Culture.
        Desert Research Institute, Social Sciences and
        Humanities Publications, 1:137-146.

1968   (ed.) Utaztekan prehistory. Idaho State Univer-
        sity Museum, Occasional Papers, 22, 149 pp.
        Reviewed AA 71:158 (Wallace), AAq 34:336 (Ezell).

SWEDLUND, Alan C.

1975   (ed.) Population studies in archaeology and bio-
        logical anthropology: a symposium. Society for
        American Archaeology, Memoirs, 30, 133 pp.

SWEDLUND, A.C., and SESSIONS, Steven E.

1976   A developmental model of prehistoric population
        growth on Black Mesa, northeastern Arizona. *In*
        Gumerman and Euler 1976, pp. 136-148.

SWEENEY, Catherine L.

1963   Ethnohistoric study in the Glen Canyon. Utah Ar-
        chaeology, 9, no. 3:9-13.

SWEENEY, C.L., and EULER, Robert C.

1963   Southern Paiute archaeology in the Glen Canyon
        drainage: a preliminary report. Nevada State Mu-
        seum, Anthropological Papers, 9:5-9.

SWEET, S.L.

1924   A conservation lesson from the Cliff-Dwellers.
        American Forests and Forest Life, 30:654-657, 690

SWITZER, Ronald R. (See also under Lyons, Thomas R.)

1969a   San Gabriel del Yunque, the first capital of New
        Mexico. University of New Mexico Press.

1969b   Tobacco, pipes, and cigarettes of the prehistoric
        Southwest. El Paso Archaeological Society, Special
        Report no. 8, 63 pp.
        Reviewed AAq 35:504 (Cain).

1969c   An unusual late Red Mesa Phase effigy pitcher.
         Plateau, 42, no. 2:39-45.

1970   A Late Red Mesa, early Wingate Phase effigy neck-
         lace. The Artifact, 8, no. 1:17-32.

1971   The origin and significance of snake-lightning
         cults in the Pueblo Southwest. El Paso Archaeo-
         logical Society, Special Report no. 11, 48 pp.

1974   Effects of forest fire on archaeological sites in
         Mesa Verde National Park, Colorado. The Artifact,
         12, no. 3:1-8.

SWOPE, W.D.

1924   Analysis of the prehistoric art of the Southwest.
         El Palacio, 16:159-162.

TADLOCK, W. LOUIS

1966   Certain crescentic stone objects as a time marker
         in the western United States. American Antiquity,
         31:662-675.

TAFT, Grace Ellis

1913   An Arizona pictograph. American Antiquarian, 35,
         no. 3:140-145.

TAMARIN, Alfred, and GLUBOCK, Shirley

1975   Ancient Indians of the Southwest. Doubleday, 96
         pp.

TANNER, Bill

1947   Cave man of the Sandias. New Mexico Magazine, 25,
         no. 1:14-15, 33.

TANNER, Clara Lee (also listed as Fraps, Clara Lee.)

1936   Blackstone Ruin. Kiva, 2, no. 3:9-12.

1943   Life forms in prehistoric pottery of the Southwest.
         Kiva, 8, no. 4:26-32.

1948   Ancient pottery. Arizona Highways, 24, no. 2:36-39.

1968   Southwest Indian craft arts. University of Arizona
         Press, 206 pp.

1976   Prehistoric Southwestern craft arts. University of
         Arizona Press, 226 pp.

TANNER, C.L., and CONNOLLY, Florence

    1938   Petroglyphs in the Southwest. Kiva, 3, no. 4:13-16.

TANNER, C.L., and STEEN, Charlie R.

    1955   A Navajo burial of about 1850. Panhandle Plains
            Historical Review, 28.

TANNER, Dallas (See under Hunt, Alice P.)

TATUM, Robert M. (See also under Dondelinger, Norman W.)

    1942   Petroglyphs of southern Colorado. Trinidad State
            Junior College, Science Series, no. 2.

    1944a   Southern Colorado collections. Southwestern Lore,
            10:24-26.

    1944b   The petroglyphs of southeastern Colorado. South-
            western Lore, 10, no. 3:38-43.

    1947   Excavation of a stone enclosure in southeastern
            Colorado. Southwestern Lore, 13, no. 2:33-36.

TATUM, R.M., and DONDELINGER, N.W.

    1945   Final report of the archaeological survey of Las
            Animas County, Colorado. Southwestern Lore, 11,
            no. 1:12-14.

TAYLOR, Dee Calderwood

    1954   The Garrison site: a report of archaeological ex-
            cavations in Snake Valley, Nevada-Utah. University
            of Utah, Anthropological Papers, 16, 64 pp.
              Reviewed AA 57:1330 (Fenenga), AAq 21:328 (Malouf).

    1955   Archaeological excavations near Salina, Utah. Utah
            Archaeology, 1, no. 4:3-8.

    1957   Two Fremont sites and their position in Southwest-
            ern prehistory. University of Utah, Anthropological
            Papers, 29, 198 pp.
              Reviewed AA 60:980 (Meighan), AAq 24:327 (Burgh).

TAYLOR, Francisco Manzo (See under Robles Ortiz, Manuel.)

TAYLOR, Herbert C., Jr.

    1948   An archaeological reconnaissance in northern
            Coahuila. Bulletin of the Texas Archaeological
            and Paleontological Society, 19:74-87.

1949   A tentative cultural sequence for the area about
        the mouth of the Pecos. Bulletin of the Texas Ar-
        chaeological and Paleontological Society, 20:73-88.

1951   Comments on west Texas pictographs. Journal of the
        Illinois State Archaeological Society, 1, no. 3:67-
        74.

TAYLOR, Walter W. (See also under Euler, Robert C.)

1948   A study of archaeology. Memoirs of the American
        Anthropological Association, 69, 256 pp.
        Reviewed AAq 19:292 (Woodbury).

1954a   An early slabhouse near Kayenta, Arizona. Plateau,
        26, no. 4:109-116.

1954b   An analysis of some salt samples from the South-
        west. Plateau, 27, no. 2:1-7.

1954c   Southwestern archaeology, its history and theory.
        American Anthropologist, 56, no. 4:561-570.

1958a   Two archaeological studies in northern Arizona.
        Museum of Northern Arizona, Bulletin 30, 30 pp.
        Reviewed AAq 25:429 (Schwartz).

1958b   The Pueblo ecology study: hail and farewell. *In*
        Taylor, W.W., 1958a, pp. 1-17.

1958c   A brief survey through the Grand Canyon of the
        Colorado River. *In* Taylor, W.W., 1958a, pp. 18-30.

1961   Archaeology and language in western North America.
        American Antiquity, 27:71-81.

1964   Tethered nomadism and water territoriality: an
        hypothesis. Proceedings of the 35th International
        Congress of Americanists, pp. 197-203.

1967   A study of archaeology. 2nd ed., University of
        Illinois Press.

1972   The hunter-gatherer nomads of northern Mexico: a
        comparison of the archival and archaeological
        records. World Archaeology, 4, no. 2:167-178.

TAYLOR, W.W., and RUL, Francisco Gonzalez

1960   An archaeological reconnaissance behind the Diablo
        Dam, Coahuila, Mexico. Bulletin of the Texas Ar-
        chaeological Society, 31:154-165.

TAYLOR, William

    1898   The pueblos and ancient mines near Allison, New
            Mexico. American Antiquarian, 20, no. 5:258-261.

TEAGUE, George A. (See under Shenk, Lynette O.)

TEAGUE, Lynn S. (See also under Stewart, Yvonne G.)

    1974   Winkelman and Black Hills Unit - BLM. Arizona
            State Museum, Archaeological Series, 47, 36 pp.

TEAGUE, L.S., and BREMER, Michael

    1976   Archaeological test excavations at AZ EE:5:11 (ASM).
            Arizona State Museum, Archaeological Series, 101,
            10 pp.

TERRAZAS, Silvestre

    1942   Esta surgiendo una enorme zona arqueológica al
            noroeste de Chihuahua? Sociedad chihuahuense de
            estudios historicos, Boletín, 4:146-148.

TERREL, James, and KLEINER, Sally

    1977   Archaeological salvage at ENM 10636, Carson Na-
            tional Forest, New Mexico. Miscellaneous Paper
            no. 1, U.S. Forest Service, Southwestern Region,
            Archaeological Report no. 15:1-17.

THALLON, Robert (See under Morris, Richard.)

THEIL, Al Paul

    1956   Burial ground - 20,000 years old. New Mexico
            Magazine, 34:22-23, 47.

THOMAS, Cyrus

    1898   Introduction to the study of North American archae-
            ology. Robert Clarke Co., Cincinnati, 391 pp.
            Reviewed AA n.s. 1:176 (Holmes).

THOMAS, M.T.

    1883   The cave-dwellers of the San Francisco Mountains.
            Kansas City Review, 7:273-276.

THOMAS, Tully H. (See also under Wendorf, Fred.)

    1952a   The Concho complex: a popular report. Plateau,

25:1-9.

1952b Tanged knives from the vicinity of Concho, Arizona. El Palacio, 59:374-385.

THOMLINSON, M.H.

1965a Reconnaissance report - Bonito Canyon site - 30 April 1950. The Artifact, 3, no. 4:9-11.

1965b Texas Park ruin. The Artifact, 3, no. 4:12-14.

THOMPSON, A.H.

1905 Ruins of the Mesa Verde: ancient cities of the Cliff-dwellers explored. American Antiquarian, 27: 6-8.

THOMPSON, Caroline

1932 Exterior ornamentation on Mesa Verde bowls. Mesa Verde Notes, 3, no. 3:40-43.

THOMPSON, Raymond H. (See also under Johnson, Alfred E.)

THOMPSON, R.H., and LONGACRE, William A.

1966 The University of Arizona archaeological field school at Grasshopper, east central Arizona. Kiva, 31, no. 4:255-275.

THOMPSON, Richard A.

1970a The Grand Canyon National Monument 1970 archaeological survey, preliminary report. Southern Utah State College, Cedar City.

1970b Prehistoric settlement in the Grand Canyon National Monument. Southern Utah State College, Faculty Research Series, 1, 42 pp.

1971 Prehistoric settlement in the Grand Canyon National Monument. Plateau, 44, no. 2:67-71.

THOMS, Alston

1976 Review of northeastern New Mexico archaeology. Awanyu, 4, no. 1:8-36.

THURMAN, Ray

1960 Our trip to Mesa Verde. Central States Archaeological Journal, 7:10-16.

THURSTON, Bertha Parker

1933   Scorpion Hill. Masterkey, 7, no. 6:171-177.

TICHY, Marjorie Ferguson (Also listed as Ferguson, Marjorie,
    and Lambert, Marjorie F.)

1935   The material from Kuaua. El Palacio, 38, nos. 21-
        23:119-122.

1936   Observations on the mission uncovered at Puaray.
        El Palacio, 41:63-66.

1937a   The excavation of Paa-ko ruin, a preliminary report.
        El Palacio, 42, nos. 19-21:109-116.

1937b   A preliminary account of the excavation of Paako,
        San Antonio, New Mexico. New Mexico Anthropologist,
        1, no. 5:73-77.

1938   The kivas of Paako and Kuaua. New Mexico Anthro-
        pologist, 2, nos. 4-5:71-80.

1939   The archaeology of Puaray. El Palacio, 46, no. 7:
        145-163.

1940   New pots for old. New Mexico Magazine, 18, no. 3:
        16-17, 39-40.

1941a   Six game pieces from Otowi. El Palacio, 48, no. 1:
        1-6.

1941b   An unusual specimen from Paa-ko. El Palacio, 48,
        no. 7:155-157.

1944   Exploratory work at Yuque Yunque. El Palacio, 51,
        no. 11:222-224.

1945   The distribution of early elbow pipes. El Palacio,
        52, no. 4:70-73.

1946a   New Mexico's first capital. New Mexico Historical
        Review, 21:140-144.

1946b   Pun-ku, kiva ringing stones. El Palacio, 53, no.
        2:42-43.

1947a   A painted ceremonial room at Otowi. El Palacio, 54:
        59-69.

1947b   A ceremonial deposit from the Pajarito Plateau. El
        Palacio, 54:227-237.

1948   Notes on the possible occurrence of graving tools
        in a New Mexico Pueblo site. El Palacio, 55:257-
        261.

1949a Ancient burial near Santa Fe's Public Welfare Building. El Palacio, 56, no. 3:80-81.

1949b A comparison of Paa-ko clay artifacts other than pottery with similar material from Pecos. El Palacio, 56:202-207.

TIERNEY, Gail D.

1971   Some observations on three prehistoric ruins in the Apache Creek region. Laboratory of Anthropology Notes, 53.

1972   Some notes and observations on the Sitio Creston site. Laboratory of Anthropology Notes, 62.

TINKER, Frank A.

1956   Fortified hills in Baboquivari Valley. Desert Magazine, 19, no. 12:4-7.

TINNEY, Jettie Avant

1949   On the trail of the pit-house people. New Mexico Magazine, 27, no. 2:18-19, 47-49.

TITUS, William A.

1913   Prehistoric pipes from the land of cliff dwellers. Archaeological Bulletin, 4:104-105.

1924   The cliff ruins of the Southwest. Wisconsin Archaeologist, n.s., 3:82-86.

TOBIN, Samuel J.

1947   Archaeology in the San Juan. University of Utah, Anthropological Papers, 8, 13 pp.

1948a Culture sequences in the Southwest. Southwestern Lore, 13, no. 4:55-70.

1948b Problem in Southwestern archaeology. Southwestern Lore, 14, no. 2:41-43.

1950   Notes on Site no. 1, Cahone Ruin, southwestern Colorado. Southwestern Lore, 15, no. 4:46-50.

TOLL, Henry Wolcott, III

1977   Dolores River archaeology: canyon adaptations as seen through survey. Bureau of Land Management (Colorado), Cultural Resources Series, 4, 270 pp.

TOMPKINS, S. (See under Irwin-Williams, Cynthia.)

TONESS, Kay S. (See also under Davis, John V.)

TONESS, K., and HILL, Mack

    1972   An unrecorded rock art cave at Hueco Tanks State Park. The Artifact, 10, no. 4:1-14.

TOULOUSE, Joseph H., Jr. (See also under Bryan, Kirk.)

    1937a   Early Man in New Mexico. El Palacio, 42, nos. 19-21:117-120.

    1937b   Two artifacts from Jemez. El Palacio, 43:107-108.

    1937c   Early Man in the Southwest. El Palacio, 43:130-136.

    1937d   Excavations at San Diego Mission, New Mexico. New Mexico Anthropologist, 2, no. 1:16-18.

    1938   The Mission of San Gregorio de Abo. El Palacio, 45:103-107.

    1940   San Gregorio de Abo Mission. El Palacio, 47, no. 3:49-58.

    1941   Some notes on hand choppers in New Mexico. American Antiquity, 6:263.

    1944   Cremation among the Indians of New Mexico. American Antiquity, 10:65-74.

    1945   Early water systems at Gran Quivira National Monument. American Antiquity, 10:362-372.

    1947   Some observations on "Spanish-American pottery from New Mexico." El Palacio, 54:99-102.

    1949   The mission of San Gregorio de Abo: a report on the excavation and repair of a seventeenth century New Mexico mission. School of American Research, Monograph no. 13, 42 pp.

    1976   A Spanish-colonial rancho in New Mexico. *In* Schroeder 1976, pp. 155-159.

TOULOUSE, J.H., and STEPHENSON, Robert L.

    1960   Excavations at Pueblo Pardo. Museum of New Mexico, Papers in Anthropology, 2, 44 pp.

TOURNEY, J.W.

    1892   Cliff and cave-dwellers of central Arizona. Science, o.s. 20:269-270.

TOVREA, J.H., and PINKLEY, Frank

1936   Tumacacori alcoves or transepts. Southwestern
        Monuments Monthly Report, August, pp. 121-125.

TOWER, Donald B.

1945   The use of marine mollusca and their value in re-
        constructing prehistoric trade routes in the Amer-
        ican Southwest. Excavators' Club, Papers, 2, no.
        3, 56 pp.
        Reviewed AA 49:466 (Richards).

TOWNSEND, Irving D.

1950   Ancient apartment house. New Mexico Magazine, 28,
        no. 1:20-21, 37, 39.

TOZZER, Alfred M.

1927   Time and American archaeology; chronological aspects
        of archaeology in the Southwest and Middle America.
        Natural History, 27:210-221.

TRAPP, Dan

1959   Ancient Man on Highway 95. Nevada Highways and
        Parks, 19, no. 1:20-25.

TRAYLOR, Idris R. (See under King, Mary Elizabeth.)

TREGANZA, Adan E.

1942   An archaeological reconnaissance of northeastern
        Baja California and southeastern California. Amer-
        ican Antiquity, 8, no. 2:152-163.

TREXLER, David W. (See under Walker, Keith F.)

TRIPP, George W.

1963a   Unusual historical Indian burial reported. Utah
        Archaeology, 9, no. 3:1-2.

1963b   Manti mystery. Utah Archaeology, 9, no. 4:1-2.

1966   A Clovis point from central Utah. American Antiq-
        uity, 31:435-436.

1967a   An unusual split willow figurine found near Green
        River, Utah. Utah Archaeology, 13, no. 1:15.

1967b   A mountain sheep skull exhibiting unusual modifica-
        tions. Utah Archaeology, 13, no. 2:4-7.

TRISCHKA, Carl

    1933   Hohokam: a chapter in the history of the Red-on-
            buff culture of southern Arizona. Scientific Month-
            ly, 37:417-433.

TROST, Willy

    1970   An El Paso Polychrome bowl used as a mortuary ves-
            sel. The Artifact, 8, no. 3:1-19.

TROWBRIDGE, L.J.

    1927   Queen of mesas. El Palacio, 22:98-106.

TRUE, Clara D.

    1938   Shrines of a thousand years. New Mexico Magazine,
            16, no. 7:12-13, 42.

TRUE, Delbert (See under Davis, Emma Lou.)

TRUE, D.L., and REINMAN, Fred M.

    1970   An intrusive cremation from a northern Arizona site.
            University of California at Davis, Center for Ar-
            chaeological Research, Publication no. 2:209-229.

TRUMBO, Theron Marcos

    1948   Mystery of the pottery disks. New Mexico Magazine,
            26, no. 10:20-21, 43-46.

    1949   Ancient artists lived on Rattlesnake peak. Desert
            Magazine, 12, no. 8:13-16.

TUGGLE, Harold David

    1970   Prehistoric community relationships in east central
            Arizona. University of Arizona, dissertation, 181
            pp.; University Microfilms International.

TUOHY, Donald R.

    1960   Two more wickiups on the San Carlos Indian Reserva-
            tion. Kiva, 26, no. 2:27-30.

    1965   Nevada's prehistoric heritage. Nevada State Mu-
            seum, Popular Series, 1.

    1966   A silver bracelet from Sandy, Nevada. American
            Antiquity, 31:566-567.

    1967   Locality 5 (Cl-248), Tule Springs, Nevada. *In*

Wormington and Ellis 1967, pp. 373-393.

TURNER, Christy G., II (See also under Adams, William Y.; El-Najjar, Mahmoud Y.; Flinn, Lynn; Jones, W. Paul.)

1958   A human skeleton from the Cohonina culture area. Plateau, 31, no. 1:16-19.

1960a   The location of human skeletons excavated from prehistoric sites in the southwestern United States and northern Mexico. Museum of Northern Arizona, Technical Series, 3, 25 pp.

1960b   Mystery Canyon survey: San Juan County, Utah, 1959. Plateau, 32:73-80.

1960c   II. Physical anthropology of Curtain Cliff site. Plateau, 33:19-23.

1962a   Further Baldrock Crescent explorations: San Juan County, Utah, 1960. Plateau, 34:101-112.

1962b   A summary of the archaeological explorations of Dr. Byron Cummings in the Anasazi culture area. Museum of Northern Arizona, Technical Series, 5, 8 pp.

1963   Petrographs of the Glen Canyon region. Museum of Northern Arizona, Bulletin 38, 74 pp.
        Reviewed AA 66:1441 (Gebhard), AAq 30:356 (Newcomb).

1969   Cranial and dental features of a southeastern Arizona Cochise culture burial. Kiva, 34, no. 4:246-250.

1971   Revised dating for early rock art of the Glen Canyon region. American Antiquity, 36:469-471.

TURNER, C.G., and COOLEY, Maurice E.

1960   Prehistoric use of stone from the Glen Canyon region. Plateau, 33:46-53.

TURNER, C.G., and LOFGREN, Laurel

1966   Household size of prehistoric western Pueblo Indians. Southwestern Journal of Anthropology, 22:117-132.

TURNER, C.G., and MILLER, William C.

1961   1960 northeast Navajo Mountain survey. Plateau, 33:57-68.

TURNER, C.G., and MORRIS, Nancy T.

1970   A massacre at Hopi. American Antiquity, 35:320-331.

TURNER, Edith (See under Turner, Sam.)

TURNER, Sam, and TURNER, Edith

1967   Some archaeological discoveries. Arizona Archae-
       ologist, 1, pp. 35-40.

TURNER, Wilson G. (See under Smith, Gerald A.)

TURNEY, Omar A.

1924   The Land of the Stone Hoe. Arizona Republican
       Print Shop, Phoenix, 11 pp.

1928a Why pictured rocks? Arizona Old and New, 1, no.
       1:8-9, 24-27.

1928b Antiquity of man in America. Arizona, Old and New,
       1, no. 3:7-8, 29-31.

1929   Prehistoric irrigation in Arizona. Arizona State
       Historian, Phoenix, 163 pp.

1929- Prehistoric irrigation (pts. 1-4). Arizona Histor-
   30 ical Review, 2, no. 1:12-52; no. 2:11-52; no. 3:
       9-45; no. 4:33-73.

TUTHILL, Carr (See also under Fulton, William Shirley.)

1940   Excavations at Gleeson, Arizona. Kiva, 5, no. 8:
       29-32.

1947   The Tres Alamos site on the San Pedro River, south-
       eastern Arizona. Amerind Foundation, 4, 88 pp.

1950   Notes on the Dragoon complex. *In* Reed and King
       1950, pp. 51-61.

UNDERHILL, Ruth M.

1944   Pueblo crafts. United States Indian Service, Edu-
       cation Division, Indian Handcraft Pamphlet no. 7,
       147 pp.
          Reviewed AA 49:97 (Smith).

1946a First penthouse dwellers of America. 2nd ed.,
       Laboratory of Anthropology, Santa Fe, 161 pp.

1946b Work-a-day life of the Pueblos. United States
       Indian Service, Indian Life and Customs Pamphlet

no. 4, 174 pp.
Reviewed AA 49:97 (Smith).

UNGNADE, Herbert E.

1963   Archaeological finds in the Sangre de Cristo Moun-
        tains of New Mexico. El Palacio, 70, no. 4:15-20.

VAILLANT, George C.

1932   Some resemblances in the ceramics of Central and
        North America. Gila Pueblo, Medallion Papers, 12,
        50 pp.

VALCARCE, Joseph P., and KAYSER, D.W.

1969   Recently discovered compounds at Casa Grande Ruins
        National Monument. Kiva, 35, no. 1:55-56.

VALEHRACH, Bruce S. (See under Valehrach, Emil M.)

VALEHRACH, Emil M.

1967   A site on the Verde. Arizona Archaeologist, 1,
        pp. 25-34.

VALEHRACH, E.M., and VALEHRACH, Bruce S.

1971   Excavations at Brazaletes Pueblo, 1971. Arizona
        Archaeologist, 6, 45 pp.

VAN CLEAVE, Philip F. (See under Lancaster, James A.)

VAN DEVANTER, D.W.

1940   The proposed national monument at Manuelito, New
        Mexico. American Antiquity, 5:223-225.

VANDIVER, Vincent W.

1937   Pipe Springs National Monument. Southwestern Monu-
        ments Monthly Report, February, pp. 111-122.

VAN DYKE, John C.

1934   The American desert. The Mentor, 12, no. 6:1-22.

VAN VALKENBURGH, Richard F.

1938a   A striking Navaho petroglyph. Masterkey, 12, no.
        4:153-157.

1938b   We found the "Three Turkey" cliff dwellings. Desert
        Magazine, 2, no. 1:10-13, 37.

1940   We found the ancient tower of Haskhek'izh. Desert

Magazine, 3, no. 8:22-24.

1946a   We found the glyphs in the Guijus. Desert Magazine,
         9, no. 3:17-20.

1946b   We found the hidden shrine of old Makai. Desert
         Magazine, 9, no. 11:20-22.

1947   Trail to the Tower of the Standing God. Desert
         Magazine, 11, no. 1:16-18.

1952   We found the lost Indian cave of the San Martins.
         Desert Magazine, 15, no. 1:5-8.

VAN VALKENBURGH, Sallie P. (See also under Abel, Leland J.;
Jackson, Earl.)

1954   Gaming stones in the Southwest. Masterkey, 28,
         no. 3:104-108.

1961   Archaeological site survey at Walnut Canyon National
         Monument. Plateau, 34:1-17.

1962   The Casa Grande of Arizona as a landmark on the
         desert, a government reservation, and a National
         Monument. Kiva, 27, no. 3:1-31.

VERNON, Frank

1971   The Cat Mesa diamond point. Albuquerque Archaeo-
         logical Society Newsletter, 6, no. 2:3-5.

VICKREY, Irene S.

1939   Besh-ba-gowah. Kiva, 4, no. 5:19-22.

1945   Inspiration I. Kiva, 10, no. 3:22-28.

VILLANOVA FUENTES, Antonio

1969   Paquime: un ensayo sobre prehistoria chihuahuense.
         Litográfica Voz, Chihuahua.

VIRGIN, John W.

1898   The ruins of Gran Quivira. American Archaeolo-
         gist, 2, pt. 1:1-6.

VIVIAN, Pat (See under Schaafsma, Polly.)

VIVIAN, R. Gordon (See also under Green, Roger C.; Richert,
Roland Von S.)

1931   Excavation of a room in the Puerco ruin. El Pa-
         lacio, 31, no. 26:416-419.

1934   The excavation of Bandelier's Puaray. El Palacio,
        37, nos. 19-20:153-161.

1935   The murals at Kuaua. El Palacio, 38, nos. 21-23:
        113-119.

1936a   The archaeologists build. New Mexico Magazine, 14,
        no. 11:12-13, 36.

1936b   Restoring Rinconada. El Palacio, 41, nos. 17-19:
        89-97.

1940   New rooms and kiva found in Pueblo Bonito. South-
        western Monuments Monthly Report, February, pp.
        127-130.

1941   Some costs of ruins stabilization. Southwestern
        Monuments Monthly Report, March, pp. 173-176.

1952   History from the trash dump. New Mexico Magazine,
        30, no. 11:14-15, 43, 45.

1956   Alcove house at NA 5700. Plateau, 29, no. 1:6-11.

1959   The Hubbard Site and other tri-wall structures in
        New Mexico and Colorado. National Park Service,
        Archaeological Research Series, 5, 92 pp.
        Reviewed AA 63:872 (Jennings), AAq 26:447 (Smith).

1964   Excavations in a 17th-century Jumano pueblo, Gran
        Quivira. National Park Service, Archaeological
        Research Series, 8, 168 pp.
        Reviewed AAq 31:753 (Danson).

1965   The Three-C site, an early Pueblo II ruin in Chaco
        Canyon, New Mexico. University of New Mexico,
        Publications in Anthropology, 13, 48 pp.
        Reviewed AA 67:1591 (Dittert), AAq 31:281 (Wilson).

VIVIAN, R. Gordon, and MATHEWS, Tom W.

1964   Kin Kletso, a Pueblo III community in Chaco Canyon,
        New Mexico. Southwest Monuments Association, Tech-
        nical Series, 6, pt. 1, pp. 1-115.
        Reviewed AA 69:100 (Ellis).

VIVIAN, R. Gordon, and REITER, Paul

1960   The great kivas of Chaco Canyon and their relation-
        ships. School of American Research, Monograph no.
        22, 112 pp.
        Reviewed AAq 27:128 (Wasley).

VIVIAN, R. Gwinn (See also under Brooks, Danny; Edmonds, Kermit M.; Greenleaf, J. Cameron.)

1965   An archaeological survey of the lower Gila River, Arizona. Kiva, 30, no. 4:95-146.

1967   Highway salvage archaeology near Hunt, Arizona. Plateau, 40, no. 2:51-58.

1969   Arizona highway salvage archaeology 1969. Kiva, 34, nos. 2-3:53-57.

1970a   An Apache site on Ranch Creek, southeast Arizona. Kiva, 35, no. 3:125-130.

1970b   Aspects of prehistoric society in Chaco Canyon, New Mexico. University of Arizona, dissertation, 334 pp.; University Microfilms International.

1970c   An inquiry into prehistoric social organization in Chaco Canyon, New Mexico. *In* Longacre 1970b, pp. 59-83.

1970d   Archaeological investigation of the Corps of Engineers' Phoenix vicinity flood control project area. Arizona State Museum, Archaeological Series, 1, 24 pp.

1970e   Archaeological resources of the Corps of Engineers' channel improvement project area in the Upper Gila. Arizona State Museum, Archaeological Series, 2, 6 pp.

1974   Conservation and diversion: water control systems in the Anasazi Southwest. University of Arizona, Anthropological Papers, 25, pp. 95-112.

VIVIAN, R. Gwinn, and CLENDENEN, Nancy W.

1965   The Denison Site: four pit houses near Isleta, New Mexico. El Palacio, 72:5-26.

VIVIAN, R. Gwinn, and REINHARD, Karl

1975   Archaeological records check - Santa Cruz River Project. Arizona State Museum, Archaeological Series, 78, 11 pp.

VIVIAN, R. Gwinn, and SPAULDING, Peggy

1974   Test excavations at AZ U:13:27 (the Sacaton-Turnkey Project). Arizona State Museum, Archaeological Series, 44, 33 pp.

VIVIAN, R. Gwinn, DODGEN, Dulce N., and HARTMANN, Gayle H.

1978 Wooden ritual artifacts from Chaco Canyon, New Mexico: the Chetro Ketl collection. University of Arizona, Anthropological Papers, 32, 176 pp.

VIVIAN, R. Gwinn, and others

1973 Archaeological resources, Cholla-Saguaro transmission line: Phase II. Arizona State Museum, Archaeological Series, 21, 46 pp.

VOGLER, Lawrence E. (See also under Ferg, Alan; McClellan, Carole.)

1976 Cultural resources of Painted Rock Dam and Reservoir. Arizona State Museum, Archaeological Series, 99, 54 pp.

1977 The SELGEM Azsite computerization project. Arizona State Museum, Archaeological Series, 112, 88 pp.

VOGT, Evon C.

1922 El Morro national monument. El Palacio, 12:161-168.

VOLL, Charles B. (See under Rixey, Raymond.)

VON BONIN, Gerhardt (See under Martin, Paul Sidney.)

VOSY-BOURBON, H.

1929 L'archéologie au Nouveau-Mexique. Journal de la Société des Américanistes de Paris, 20:408-409.

VYTLACIL, Natalie, and BRODY, J.J.

1958 Two pithouses near Zia Pueblo. El Palacio, 65, no. 5:174-184.

WADE, William D.

1970 Skeletal remains of a prehistoric population from the Puerco Valley, eastern Arizona. University of Colorado, dissertation, 217 pp.; University Microfilms International.

WADE, W.D., and KENT, Kate Peck

1968 An infant burial from the Verde Valley, central Arizona. Plateau, 40, no. 4:148-156.

WADSWORTH, Beula M.

   1955   A home for ten thousand years. Arizona Highways,
           31, no. 5:30-33.

WAITMAN, Leonard

   1968   Horse soldier forts of the Mojave Desert. San
           Bernardino County Museum Association Quarterly,
           15, no. 3:1-56.

WALKER, James B.

   1975   Archaeology at Abiquiu reservoir. School of Amer-
           ican Research, Exploration 1975, pp. 20-21.

WALKER, Keith F., and TREXLER, David W.

   1941   An Indian camp site in the northern Finlay Moun-
           tains, Hudspeth County, Texas. Field and Labora-
           tory: Contributions from the Science Departments
           (Dallas), 9:60-69.

WALKER, Noel P., Jr., and POLK, Ann S.

   1973   Archaeological survey of the Apache-Twin Buttes
           and Pantano-Whetstone transmission lines. Arizona
           State Museum, Archaeological Series, 27, 116 pp.

WALLACE, G.H.

   1900   A day in the Cliff Dwellings. Land of Sunshine,
           13, no. 1:23-26.

WALLACE, Roberts M. (See under Danson, Edward Bridge.)

WALLACE, William J.

   1962   Prehistoric cultural development in the southern
           California deserts. American Antiquity, 28:172-
           180.

WALLIS, George A.

   1936   Exploring antiquity. New Mexico Magazine, 14, no.
           10:18-19, 44.

WALTER, Nancy Peterson

   1961   A child of Scorpion Hill. Masterkey, 35, no. 2:
           70-74.

WALTER, Paul A.F.

1916   The cities that died of fear. El Palacio, 3, no.
        4:12-73.

1920   The story of our National Monuments: New Mexico.
        Art and Archaeology, 10, nos. 1-2:7-26.

WALTER, Paul, Jr.

1930   Notes on a trip to Jemez. El Palacio, 29:206-213.

WALTERS, Evelyn

1968   Preliminary report on handprints and pictographs
        in eastern Pecos County. Transactions of the 4th
        Regional Archaeological Symposium on Southeastern
        New Mexico and Western Texas, pp. 65-72.

1971   Further studies of rock art sites in Pecos and
        Crockett Counties. Transactions of the 6th Regional
        Archaeological Symposium on Southeastern New Mexico
        and Western Texas, pp. 9-38.

WARBURTON, Austen D. (See under Flaim, Francis R.)

WARD, Albert E. (See also under Kelly, Roger E.; Weed, Carol
   S.)

1968   Investigation of two hogans at Toonerville, Arizona.
        Plateau, 40, no. 4:136-142.

1969   Tse Tlani: a 12th century Sinagua village. Plateau,
        41, no. 3:77-104.

1970   A Navajo anthropomorphic figurine. Plateau, 42,
        no. 4:146-149.

1971   A multicomponent site with a Desert Culture affinity,
        near Window Rock, Arizona. Plateau, 43, no. 3:120-
        131.

1975a   Archaeological investigations at San Miguel de Car-
        nue: the first field season. Awanyu, 3, no. 2:8-25.

1975b   The PC Ruin: archaeological investigations in the
        Prescott tradition. Kiva, 40, no. 3:131-164.

1975c   Gravestones for Ganado Mucho: a contribution to
        Navajo ethnohistory. Masterkey, 49, no. 3:95-104.

1975d   Inscription House: two research reports. Museum
        of Northern Arizona, Technical Series, 16, 58 pp.

1976a   Archaeology for Albuquerque: a plea for comparative

studies. El Palacio, 82, no. 2:12-21.

1976b   Black Mesa to the Colorado River: an archaeological
         traverse. *In* Gumerman and Euler 1976, pp. 3-105.

1977   The Arbuckle coffee canister: "unrespectable"
         artifacts as archaeological dating devices. El
         Palacio, 83, no. 3:2-9.

WARNER, Thor

1928a   The prehistoric man of Rio Puerco. Art and Archae-
         ology, 26:44-50.

1928b   Rio Puerco ruins. American Anthropologist, 30:85-
         93.

WARNICA, James M.

1961   The Elida site, evidence of a Folsom occupation
         in Roosevelt County, eastern New Mexico. Bulletin
         of the Texas Archaeological Society, 30:209-215.

1965   Archaic sites in eastern New Mexico. Transactions
         of the 1st Regional Archaeological Symposium on
         Southeastern New Mexico and Western Texas, pp. 3-8.

1966   New discoveries at the Clovis site. American An-
         tiquity, 31:345-357.

WARNICA, J.M., and WILLIAMSON, Ted

1968   The Milnesand site - revisited. American Antiquity,
         33:16-24.

WARREN, A. Helene (See also under Harris, Arthur H.; Wilson,
    John P.)

1966a   Petrographic notes on lithic materials in the
         Cochiti area, Cochiti Dam project. Laboratory of
         Anthropology Notes, 91.

1966b   Lithic materials in the Cochiti area, Cochiti Dam
         project, second report. Laboratory of Anthropology
         Notes, 92.

1967a   Pottery of the Torreon site. Laboratory of Anthro-
         pology Notes, 76A.

1967b   Notes on lithic materials in the Cochiti area,
         Cochiti Dam project, third report. Laboratory of
         Anthropology Notes, 93.

1969a   The pottery of Las Majadas. Laboratory of Anthro-
         pology Notes, 75A.

1969b The Nambé project: archaeological salvage at Nambé
       pueblo, Santa Fe County, New Mexico. Laboratory
       of Anthropology Notes, 100.

1969c Tonque: one pueblo's glaze pottery industry dominated
       middle Rio Grande commerce. El Palacio, 76, no. 2:
       36-42.

1970a Centers of manufacture and trade of Rio Grande
       glazes: a preliminary report. Laboratory of Anthro-
       pology Notes, 54.

1970b Notes on manufacture and trade of Rio Grande glazes.
       The Artifact, 8, no. 4:1-7.

1970c A petrographic study of the pottery of Gran Quivira.
       Laboratory of Anthropology Notes, 94.

1973a Majolica - New World or Old? Laboratory of Anthro-
       pology Notes, 88.

1973b New dimensions in the study of prehistoric pottery.
       (A preliminary report relating to the excavations
       at Cochiti Dam.) Laboratory of Anthropology Notes,
       90.

1974a The ancient mineral industries of Cerro Pedernal,
       Rio Arriba County, New Mexico. New Mexico Geo-
       logical Society, Guidebook, 25th Field Conference,
       Ghost Ranch, N.M.

1974b The Cochiti project: archaeological salvage exca-
       vations at Pueblo del Encierro near Cochiti pueblo,
       New Mexico. Laboratory of Anthropology Notes, 98.

WARREN, Richard L. (See under Bannister, Bryant; Robinson,
   William J.)

WASE, Cheryl, and SCHALK, Randall

1977   Archaeological survey of several areal parcels on
       Kerr-McGee lands and BLM lands. University of New
       Mexico, contract report 185-2K (BLM).

WASHBURN, Dorothy Koster

1972   An analysis of the spatial aspects of the site lo-
       cations of Pueblo I-III sites along the middle
       Rio Puerco, New Mexico. Columbia University, dis-
       sertation, 278 pp.; University Microfilms Interna-
       tional.

1974   Nearest neighbor analysis of Pueblo I-III settlement

patterns along the Rio Puerco of the East, New
Mexico. American Antiquity, 39:315-335.

1975   The American Southwest. *In* North America, ed.
       Shirley Gorenstein, St. Martin's Press, New York,
       pp. 103-132.

1977   A symmetry analysis of Upper Gila Area ceramic
       design. Papers of the Peabody Museum of Archae-
       ology and Ethnology, 68, 208 pp.

1978   A symmetry classification of Pueblo ceramic designs.
       In Grebinger 1978a, pp. 101-121.

WASLEY, William W. (See also under Haury, Emil W.; Johnson,
Alfred E.; Olson, Alan P.; Wheat, Joe Ben.)

1957a The archaeological survey of the Arizona State
       Museum. Arizona State Museum, 11 pp.

1957b Highway salvage archaeology in Arizona. Kiva, 23,
       no. 2:4-9.

1957c Highway salvage archaeology by the Arizona State
       Museum, 1956-1957. Kiva, 23, no. 2:17-19.

1960a Temporal placement of Alma Neck Banded. American
       Antiquity, 25:599-603.

1960b Salvage archaeology on highway 66 in eastern Ari-
       zona. American Antiquity, 26, no. 1:30-42.

1960c A Hohokam platform mound at the Gatlin site, Gila
       Bend, Arizona. American Antiquity, 26, no. 2:244-
       262.

1961   Techniques and tools of salvage. Archaeology, 14,
       no. 4:283-286.

1962   A ceremonial cave on Bonita Creek, Arizona. Amer-
       ican Antiquity, 27:380-394.

WASLEY, W.W., and BENHAM, Blake

1968   Salvage excavation in the Buttes Dam site, south-
       ern Arizona. Kiva, 33, no. 4:244-279.

WASLEY, W.W., and JOHNSON, Alfred E.

1965   Salvage archaeology in Painted Rocks Reservoir,
       western Arizona. University of Arizona, Anthro-
       pological Papers, 9, 123 pp.
       Reviewed AA 68:814 (Neely).

WATERMAN, T.T.

1929   Culture horizons in the Southwest. American Anthro-
       pologist, 31:367-400.

1930   Ornamental designs in Southwestern pottery. Museum
       of the American Indian, Indian Notes, 7:497-521.

WATKINS, F.E.

1929   Prehistoric pottery of the Jemez region. Masterkey,
       3, no. 5:20-21.

1930   My experiences as a field archaeologist. Masterkey,
       4:13-20.

WATSON, Don (See also under Franke, Paul R.; Lancaster, James
A.)

1935   Museum acquisitions for 1935. Mesa Verde Notes, 6,
       no. 1:1-5.

1937a The Cliff Dwellers visit the dentist. Mesa Verde
       Notes, 7, no. 1:7-10.

1937b A thousand year old murder mystery. Mesa Verde
       Notes, 7, no. 2:15-16.

1941   Cliff Palace, the story of an ancient city. Edwards
       Bros., Ann Arbor, 142 pp.

1947   Note on the dating of Pipe Shrine House. Tree-
       Ring Bulletin, 13, no. 4:32.

1948   Ancient cliff dwellers of Mesa Verde. National
       Geographic Magazine, 94:349-376.

1954a Cliff dwellings of the Mesa Verde: a story in pic-
       tures. Mesa Verde Museum Association, 52 pp.

1954b Introduction to Mesa Verde archaeology. *In* Lan-
       caster, Pinkley, Van Cleave, and Watson 1954, pp.
       1-6.

1955   Indians of the Mesa Verde. Mesa Verde Museum As-
       sociation, 188 pp.

WATSON, Editha Latta

1927   Some New Mexico ruins. El Palacio, 23, nos. 7-8:
       174-234.

1929   Caves of the upper Gila River, New Mexico. Amer-
       ican Anthropologist, 31:299-306.

1931   Two Mimbres River ruins. American Anthropologist,

33:51-55.

1932   The laughing artists of the Mimbres Valley. Art
       and Archaeology, 33 (July).

1961   Self-illustrated archeology. Science of Man, 1,
       no. 3:76-80.

1966   Prehistoric picture puzzles. The Artifact, 4, no.
       2:10-19.

1969   The ancients knew their paints. The Artifact, 7,
       no. 2:1-6.

WATSON, Patty Joe

1977   Design analysis of painted pottery. American Antiq-
       uity, 42:381-393.

WAUER, Roland H.

1965   Pictograph site in Cave Valley, Zion National Park,
       Utah. University of Utah, Miscellaneous Collected
       Papers, no. 9, Anthropological Papers, 75, pp. 57-
       84.

WEAVER, Donald E., Jr. (See also under Brown, Patricia Eyring;
   Cartledge, Thomas R.; Schoenwetter, James.)

1972   A cultural-ecological model for the Classic Hohokam
       period in the lower Salt River Valley, Arizona.
       Kiva, 38:43-52.

1973   Excavations at Pueblo del Monte and the Classic
       period Hohokam problem. Kiva, 39, no. 1:75-87.

1974   Archaeological investigations at the Westwing Site,
       AZ T:7:27 (ASU), Agua Fria River Valley, Arizona.
       Arizona State University, Anthropological Research
       Papers, 7, 84 pp.

1976   Salado influences in the lower Salt River Valley.
       In Doyel and Haury 1976, pp. 17-26.

1977   Investigations concerning the Hohokam Classic period
       in the lower Salt River Valley, Arizona. Arizona
       Archaeologist, no. 9, 132 pp.

WEAVER, D.E., and RODGERS, James B.

1974   An archaeological survey of the Cave Buttes Dam
       alternative site and reservoir, Arizona. Arizona
       State University, Anthropological Research Papers,
       8.

WEAVER, D.E., BURTON, Susan S., and LAUGHLIN, Minnabell

1978   (ed.) Proceedings of the 1973 Hohokam Conference.
        Center for Anthropological Studies, Contributions,
        2, 105 pp.

WEAVER, J.R.

1967   An Indian trail near Needles, California. University of California, Archaeological Survey Reports,
        70:151-157.

WEBER, Robert H.

1973   The Tajo 2 pit-house site near Socorro, New Mexico.
        Awanyu, 1, no. 1:14-20.

WEBSTER, C.L.

1912   Some burial customs practiced by the ancient
        people of the Southwest. Archaeological Bulletin,
        3, no. 3:69-78.

1912-   Archaeological and ethnological researches in
  14   southwestern New Mexico. Archaeological Bulletin,
        3, no. 4:101-115; 4, no. 1:14-21; no. 2:43-48; 5,
        no. 2:19-25; no. 3:44-46.

WEDEL, Waldo R.

1950   Notes on Plains-Southwestern contacts in the light
        of archaeology. *In* Reed and King 1950, pp. 99-116.

1961   Prehistoric Man on the Great Plains. University
        of Oklahoma Press.

WEED, Carol S. (See also under Gumerman, George J.)

1970   Two twelfth century burials from the Hopi Reservation. Plateau, 43, no. 1:27-38.

1972   The Beardsley canal site. Kiva, 38, no. 2:57-94.

1978   The Central Arizona Ecotone Project and SARG. *In*
        Euler and Gumerman 1978, pp. 87-94.

WEED, C.S., and WARD, Albert E.

1970   The Henderson site: Colonial Hohokam in north
        central Arizona, a preliminary report. Kiva, 36,
        no. 2:1-12.

WEIDE, David L. (See also under Davis, Emma Lou.)

    1970   The geology and geography of the Parowan and Cedar Valley region, Iron County, Utah. *In* Marwitt, Madsen, Dalley, and Adovasio 1970, pp. 173-193.

WELLER, Ted

    1959   San Juan triangle survey. *In* Jennings and others 1959, pt. II, pp. 543-669.

WELLMANN, Klaus F.

    1976   An astronomical petroglyph in Capitol Reef National Park, Utah. Southwestern Lore, 42, nos. 1-2:4-13.

WELLS, Susan L. (See under Peckham, Stewart L.)

WELTFISH, Gene

    1930   Prehistoric North American basketry techniques and modern distributions. American Anthropologist, 32, no. 3:454-495.

    1932a   Preliminary classification of prehistoric Southwestern basketry. Smithsonian Miscellaneous Collections, 87, no. 7, 47 pp.

    1932b   Problems in the study of ancient and modern basketmakers. American Anthropologist, 34, no. 1:108-117.

    1940   Cave dweller twill-plaited basketry. University of Denver, Contributions, 3, pp. 69-89.

WENDORF, Fred (See also under Dittert, Alfred E., Jr.; Fenenga, Franklin; Miller, John P.; Peckham, Stewart L.; Schroeder, Albert H.)

    1948   Early archaeological sites in the Petrified Forest National Monument. Plateau, 21, no. 2:29-32.

    1950a   The Flattop site in the Petrified Forest National Monument. Plateau, 22, no. 3:43-51.

    1950b   A report on the excavation of a small ruin near Point of Pines, east central Arizona. University of Arizona, Social Science Bulletin 19, 150 pp. Reviewed AAq 17:157 (Baldwin).

    1951   Archaeological investigations in the Petrified Forest: Twin Butte site, a preliminary report. Plateau, 24, no. 2:77-83.

    1952   Excavations at Cuyamungue. El Palacio, 59, no. 8: 265-266.

1953a   Archaeological studies in the Petrified Forest
        National Monument. Museum of Northern Arizona,
        Bulletin 27, 203 pp.
        Reviewed AA 57:1093 (Lister), AAq 21:195 (Rouse).

1953b   (assembler) Salvage archaeology in the Chama Val-
        ley, New Mexico. School of American Research, Mono-
        graph no. 17, 124 pp.
        Reviewed AA 56:918 (Cotter), AAq 20:294 (Rinaldo).

1953c   Excavations at Te'ewi. *In* Wendorf 1953b, pp. 34-93.

1954a   (ed.) Highway salvage archaeology, Volume I. New
        Mexico State Highway Dept. and Museum of New Mexico,
        105 pp.
        Reviewed AA 58:201 (Wedel), AAq 21:327 (Di Peso).

1954b   The excavation of a small Pueblo III site near Gal-
        lup, New Mexico. *In* Wendorf 1954a, pp. 1-12.

1954c   A Pueblo II site near Laguna, New Mexico. *In*
        Wendorf 1954a, pp. 13-27.

1954d   A reconstruction of northern Rio Grande prehistory.
        American Anthropologist, 56, no. 2:200-227.

1956a   (ed.) Highway salvage archaeology, Volume II.
        New Mexico State Highway Dept. and Museum of New
        Mexico, 105 pp.
        Reviewed AA 59:373 (Wheat).

1956b   A fragmentary pueblo near Corona, New Mexico. *In*
        Wendorf 1956a, pp. 87-105.

1956c   Some distributions of settlement patterns in the
        Pueblo Southwest. *In* Willey 1956, pp. 18-25.

1957a   A Mimbres pueblo near Glenwood, New Mexico. *In*
        Peckham 1957a, pp. 71-84.

1957b   The New Mexico program in highway archaeological
        salvage. American Antiquity, 23:74-78.

1958   Pot Creek project: 1958 season. El Palacio, 63, no.
        4:150.

1959a   Folsom points from Deming, New Mexico. El Palacio,
        66, no. 3:109.

1959b   The prehistory of northeastern New Mexico. *In*
        Guidebook of the southern Sangre de Cristo Mountains,
        Panhandle Geological Society, pp. 1-13.

1960   The archaeology of northeastern New Mexico. El
        Palacio, 67, no. 2:55-65.

1961   Highway salvage problems in New Mexico and Arizona.
        In Symposium on Salvage Archaeology, National Park
        Service, pp. 41-47.

WENDORF, F., and LEHMER, Donald J.

1956   Archaeology of the Wingate Products Line. *In*
        Wendorf, Fox, and Lewis 1956, pp. 158-195.

WENDORF, F., and MILLER, John P.

1959   Artifacts from high mountain sites in the Sangre de
        Cristo Range, New Mexico. El Palacio, 66, no. 2:
        37-52.

WENDORF, F., and REED, Erik K.

1955   An alternative reconstruction of northern Rio Grande
        prehistory. El Palacio, 62:131-173.

WENDORF, F., and THOMAS, Tully H.

1951   Early Man sites near Concho, Arizona. American
        Antiquity, 17:107-114.

WENDORF, F., FERDON, Edwin N., Jr., and BRADBURY, John

1963   A Tularosa phase pueblo near Luna, New Mexico.
        In Peckham 1963a, pp. 29-40.

WENDORF, F., FOX, Nancy, and LEWIS, Orian L.

1956   (ed.) Pipeline archaeology; reports of salvage
        operations in the Southwest on El Paso Natural
        Gas Co. projects, 1950-1953. Laboratory of Anthro-
        pology and Museum of Northern Arizona, 410 pp.
          Reviewed AA 60:407 (Wheat), AAq 23:199 (Smith).

WENDORF, F., LEOPOLD, L.B., and LEOPOLD, E.B.

1963   Some climatic indicators in the period A.D. 1200
        to 1400 in New Mexico. *In* Symposium on Changes
        of Climate with Special Reference to Arid Zones,
        UNESCO, pp. 265-270.

WENGER, Gilbert R.

1969   Archaeological research at Mesa Verde National
        Park. Naturalist, 20, no. 2:27-30.

WEST, George A.

    1925   Cliff-dwellings and pueblos in the Grand Canyon,
            Arizona. Public Museum of the City of Milwaukee,
            Yearbook, 3 (for 1923), pp. 74-97.

    1927   Exploration in Navajo Canyon, Arizona. Public
            Museum of the City of Milwaukee, Yearbook, 5 (for
            1925), pp. 7-39.

    1932a   A visit to Mesa Verde. Public Museum of the City
            of Milwaukee, Yearbook, 10 (for 1930), pp. 27-44.

    1932b   The Lost City of Nevada. Public Museum of the City
            of Milwaukee, Yearbook, 10 (for 1930), pp. 44-48.

    1932c   A visit to Gypsum Cave, Nevada. Public Museum of
            the City of Milwaukee, Yearbook, 10 (for 1930), pp.
            48-63.

WESTFALL, Deborah (See under Gumerman, George J.)

WETHERILL, B.A.

    1931   How I found the Mesa Verde ruins. Travel, 23:30-35,
            54.

WETHERILL, Ben W.

    1934   Summary of investigations by the Zion National
            Park archaeological party. Zion and Bryce Nature
            Notes, 6:1-9.

    1935   General report of the archaeological work. Rain-
            bow Bridge-Monument Valley Expedition, Preliminary
            Bulletin no. 7, 8 pp.

WETHERILL, John

    1934   Navajo National Monument. Southwestern Monuments
            Monthly Report, February.

    1955a   Notes on the discovery of Kiet Siel. Plateau, 27,
            no. 3:18-20.

    1955b   Notes on the discovery of Betatakin. Plateau, 27,
            no. 4:23-24.

WETHERILL, Milton (See also under McGregor, John C.; Schwartz,
    Douglas W.)

    1935   Pictographs at Betatakin ruin. Southwestern Monu-
            ments Monthly Report, May, pp. 263-264.

1954   A Paiute trap corral on Skeleton Mesa, Arizona.
        Plateau, 26, no. 4:116.

WETHERILL, Richard

1894   Sniders Well. Archaeologist, 2, no. 9:288-289.

1897   The sandal stones. Antiquarian, 1:2-48.

WETHERINGTON, Ronald K.

1964   Early occupations in the Taos district in the con-
        text of northern Rio Grande culture history. Uni-
        versity of Michigan, dissertation, 227 pp.; Uni-
        versity Microfilms International.

1966   A rare feature of pueblo architecture in Taos, New
        Mexico. El Palacio, 73, no. 3:19-25.

1968   Excavations at Pot Creek Pueblo. Fort Burgwin Re-
        search Center, no. 6, 104 pp.
        Reviewed AA 71:1208 (Leone), AAq 35:232 (Gunner-
        son).

WHALEN, M.E.

1977   Settlement patterns of the Lower Hueco Bolson. El
        Paso Centennial Museum.

WHALEN, Norman M.

1971   Cochise culture sites in the central San Pedro
        drainage, Arizona. University of Arizona, disserta-
        tion, 374 pp.; University Microfilms International.

1973   Agriculture and the Cochise. Kiva, 39:89-96.

1975   Cochise site distribution in the San Pedro Valley.
        Kiva, 40, no. 3:203-211.

1976   Archaeological survey in southeastern Imperial
        County, California. Pacific Coast Archaeological
        Society Quarterly, 12, no. 2:25-50.

WHEAT, Joe Ben (See also under Fenenga, Franklin.)

1948-   A double-walled jar from Chihuahua. Kiva, 14, nos.
49   1-4:8-10.

1950   The 1950 season at Arizona W:10:15. Kiva, 16, no.
        3:16-20.

1952   Prehistoric water sources of the Point of Pines
        area. American Antiquity, 17:185-196.

1954a   Crooked Ridge village (Arizona W:10:15). University
        of Arizona, Social Science Bulletin 24, 183 pp.
        Reviewed AAq 22:204 (Wendorf).

1954b   Kroeber's formulation of the Southwestern culture
        area. University of Colorado Studies, Series in
        Anthropology, 4, pp. 23-44.

1954c   A Pueblo I site at Grand Canyon. American Antiquity,
        19:396-403.

1954d   Southwestern cultural interrelationships and the
        question of area co-tradition. American Anthro-
        pologist, 56, no. 4:576-591.

1955a   Mogollon culture prior to A.D. 1000. Memoirs of
        the Society for American Archaeology, 10, 242 pp.
        Reviewed AAq 22:205 (Taylor).

1955b   MT-1, a Basketmaker III site near Yellow Jacket,
        Colorado (a progress report). Southwestern Lore,
        21, no. 2:18-26.

1955c   Prehistoric people of the northern Southwest. Grand
        Canyon Natural History Association, Bulletin 12, 38
        pp.

1967   A Paleo-Indian bison kill. Scientific American,
        216:44-62.

1976   Spanish-American and Navajo weaving, 1600 to now.
        In Schroeder 1976, pp. 199-226.

WHEAT, J.B., GIFFORD, James C., and WASLEY, William W.

1958   Ceramic variety, type cluster, and ceramic system
        in Southwestern pottery analysis. American Antiq-
        uity, 24, no. 1:34-47.

WHEAT, Mrs. Joe Ben (See under Moore, Mrs. Glen E.)

WHEELER, George M.

1879   Report upon United States geographical surveys west
        of the one hundredth meridian. Vol. VII: Archae-
        ology. Washington, 497 pp.

WHEELER, Richard P.

1965   Edge-abraded flakes, blades, and cores in the
        Puebloan tool assemblage. *In* Osborne 1965a, pp.
        19-29.

WHEELER, S.M.

    1935   A dry cave in southern Nevada. Masterkey, 9, no.
            1:5-12.

    1936   A Pueblo II site in the Great Basin area of Nevada.
            Masterkey, 10, no. 6:207-211.

    1937a   Prehistoric miniatures. Masterkey, 11, no. 5:181.

    1937b   An archaeological expedition to Nevada. Masterkey,
            11, no. 6:194-197.

    1938a   A Fremont moccasin from Nevada. Masterkey, 12,
            no. 1:34-35.

    1938b   Recording cave data. American Antiquity, 4:48-51.

    1939a   The Jean L'Empereur expedition in Nevada. Master-
            key, 12:216-220.

    1939b   Split-twig figurines. Masterkey, 13, no. 1:42-45.

    1942   Archaeology of Etna Cave, Lincoln County, Nevada.
            Nevada State Parks Commission, 92 pp.

    1949   More about split-twig figurines. Masterkey, 23,
            no. 5:153-158.

WHEELER, S.M., and FOWLER, Don D.

    1973   Archaeology of Etna Cave, Lincoln County, Nevada -
            a reprint. Desert Research Institute, Publications
            in the Social Sciences, no. 7, 56 pp.

WHITAKER, Kathleen

    1969   Analytical interpretations of petroglyphs. Master-
            key, 43, no. 4:132-143.

WHITAKER, T.W. (See under Cutler, Hugh C.)

WHITE, Adrian S., and BRETERNITZ, David A.

    1976   Stabilization of the Lowry ruins. Bureau of Land
            Management (Colorado), Cultural Resources Series,
            1, 148 pp.

WHITE, C.W. (See under Greenwood, N.H.)

WHITE, Edmund A.

    1965   Salvage work at the McCombs site. The Artifact,
            3, no. 3:2-3.

1968   Rocks and minerals used by prehistoric man in the
        El Paso area. The Artifact, 6, no. 4:11-16.

WHITE, Leslie A.

    1942   (ed.) Lewis H. Morgan's journal of a trip to south-
            western Colorado and New Mexico, June 21-August 7,
            1878. American Antiquity, 8, no. 1:1-26.

WHITE, Richard S., Jr. (See under Moser, Edward.)

WHITEAKER, Ralph J.

    1976a   Archaeological investigations on the San Juan-to-
            Ojo 345 KV transmission line for the Public Service
            Company of New Mexico: the excavation of LA 11828,
            the Arroyo del Palacio site, Rio Arriba County, New
            Mexico. Laboratory of Anthropology Notes, 111B.

    1976b   Archaeological investigations on the San Juan-to-
            Ojo 345 KV transmission line for the Public Service
            Company of New Mexico: excavation of portions of LA
            11841, a Gallina phase pithouse site, Rio Arriba
            County, New Mexico. Laboratory of Anthropology
            Notes, 111D.

    1976c   The Little Deer Tail site: excavation of LA 10705.
            Laboratory of Anthropology Notes, 120.

WHITING, Alfred F.

    1958   Havasupai characteristics in the Cohonina. Plateau,
            39, no. 3:55-60.

WHITMORE, Jane (See also under Beal, John D.; Causey, Christo-
    pher S.)

    1976   An archaeological survey of three right-of-ways
            near Lobo Springs and Mirabel Spring, McKinley
            County, New Mexico. School of American Research,
            contract #44.

    1977a   An archaeological survey for the Duval Corporation,
            Carlsbad, New Mexico. School of American Research,
            contract #47.

    1977b   An archaeological survey of four areas of land near
            Lobo Springs, McKinley County, New Mexico. School
            of American Research, contract #57.

    1977c   An archaeological survey of a portion of Mesa
            Cocina, Sandoval County, New Mexico. School of
            American Research, contract #65.

1977d Archaeological survey in the vicinity of San Mateo
       Mesa and Cañada Las Vacas, McKinley County, New
       Mexico. School of American Research, contract #67.

WHITTLESEY, Stephanie M. (See also under Mayro, Linda L.)

1974   Identification of imported ceramics through func-
       tional analysis of attributes. Kiva, 40, nos. 1-2:
       101-112.

WIDDISON, Jerry

1959   Painted cave. New Mexico Magazine, 37, no. 7:30-33.

WILCOX, David R.

1975a A strategy for perceiving social groups in puebloan
       sites. *In* Martin and others 1975, pp. 120-159.

1975b The relationship of Casa Grande ruin to Compound A.
       Arizona State Museum, Archaeological Series, 83,
       70 pp.

WILCOX, D.R., and SHENK, Lynette O.

1977   The architecture of the Casa Grande and its inter-
       pretation. Arizona State Museum, Archaeological
       Series, 115, 240 pp.

WILCOX, U. Vincent, II, and WILCOX, U. Vincent, III

1972   Ancient disease in the Southwest. Museum of the
       American Indian, Indian Notes, 8, no. 1:4-10.

WILCOX, U. Vincent, III (See under Wilcox, U. Vincent, II.)

WILDER, Carleton S.

1944   Archaeological survey of the Great Thumb area,
       Grand Canyon National Park. Plateau, 17, no. 2:
       17-26.

WILDER, H.H.

1917   Restoration of a cliff-dweller. American Anthro-
       pologist, 19:388-391.

WILKE, Philip J.

1977   A classified introductory bibliography for students
       of inland southern California archaeology. Archae-
       ological Research Unit, University of California
       (Riverside), 43 pp.

WILKINSON, N.M.

1958   Arts and crafts of the Gallina culture. El Palacio,
        65:189-196.

WILLEY, Gordon R. (See also under Ekholm, Gordon F.)

1956   (ed.) Prehistoric settlement patterns in the New
        World. Viking Fund Publications in Anthropology,
        23, 202 pp.
        Reviewed AA 59:923 (Oberg), AAq 23:313 (Haag).

1960   New World prehistory. Science, 131, no. 3393:73-86.

1966   An introduction to American archaeology. Vol. I,
        North and Middle America. Prentice-Hall, 530 pp.
        Reviewed AA 69:522 (MacNeish), AAq 33:106 (Griffin).

WILLEY, G.R., and PHILLIPS, Philip

1955   Method and theory in American archaeology II: His-
        torical-developmental interpretation. American
        Anthropologist, 57, no. 4:723-819.
        Reviewed AAq 23:85 (Spaulding).

1958   Method and theory in American archaeology. Uni-
        versity of Chicago Press, 270 pp.
        Reviewed AAq 24:195 (Meggers and Evans).

WILLIAMS, Jack R.

1951   The San Luis Valley blade. Southwestern Lore, 17,
        no. 1:8-12.

1954   Further notes on the San Luis Valley blade. South-
        western Lore, 20, no. 1:7-9.

1956   The Indians of Carlsbad Caverns National Park.
        Carlsbad, 40 pp.

WILLIAMS, Pete A., and ORLINS, Robert I.

1963   The Corn Creek Dunes site. Nevada State Museum,
        Anthropological Papers, 10, 65 pp.

WILLIAMS-DEAN, Glenna, and BRYANT, Vaughn M., Jr.

1975   Pollen analysis of human coprolites from Antelope
        House. *In* Rock and Morris 1975, pp. 97-111.

WILLIAMSON, Abigail F. (See under Williamson, Ray A.)

WILLIAMSON, Ray A., FISHER, Howard J., WILLIAMSON, Abigail F., and COCHRAN, Clarion

1975   The astronomical record in Chaco Canyon, New Mexico. *In* Aveni 1975, pp. 33-43.

WILLIAMSON, Ted (See under Warnica, James M.)

WILLIS, Elizabeth S. (See under Martin, Paul Sidney.)

WILLISTON, S.W.

1899   Some prehistoric ruins in Scott County, Kansas. Kansas University Quarterly, 7, no. 4:109-114.

WILLISTON, S.W., and MARTIN, H.T.

1900   Some pueblo ruins in Scott County, Kansas. Kansas Historical Collections, 6:124-130.

WILMSEN, Edwin N.

1965   An outline of Early Man studies in the United States. American Antiquity, 31, no. 2:172-192.

1968   Lithic analysis in paleoanthropology. Science, 161: 982-987.

1970   Lithic analysis and cultural inference: a paleo-Indian case. University of Arizona, Anthropological Papers, 16, 88 pp. Reviewed AA 73:1400 (Clay).

WILSON, Eddie W.

1950   The gourd in the Southwest. Masterkey, 24:84-88.

WILSON, Ernest W.

1930   Burned rock mounds of southwest Texas. Bulletin of the Texas Archaeological and Paleontological Society, 2:59-63.

WILSON, John P. (See also under Olsen, Stanley J.)

1962a   The excavation of LA 6380, the Horseshoe site. Laboratory of Anthropology Notes, 117A.

1962b   The excavation of LA 6386, Burro Valley Pueblo. Laboratory of Anthropology Notes, 117B.

1962c   The excavation of LA 6483, the Sowers site. Laboratory of Anthropology Notes, 117C.

1966a   Fort Fillmore, New Mexico, 1966. Laboratory of Anthropology Notes, 43.

1966b   Prisoners without walls. El Palacio, 74, no. 1: 10-28.

1967a   Another archaeological survey in east-central Arizona: preliminary report. Plateau, 39, no. 4:157-168.

1967b   One hundred years later: excavations at Fort Fillmore. El Palacio, 74, no. 2:26-41.

1971   An archaeological survey of the Reserve Oil and Minerals Corporation uranium lease area on the Laguna Indian Reservation, Valencia County, New Mexico. Laboratory of Anthropology Notes, 61.

1972a   An archaeological survey on Pueblo of Laguna lands. Archaeological Society of New Mexico, Supplement no. 2, 26 pp.

1972b   Awatovi - more light on a legend. Plateau, 44, no. 3:125-130.

1973   Quarai. El Palacio, 78, no. 4:14-28.

1975   An archaeological reconnaissance of the lower Chaco River Basin and adjacent San Juan River valley, San Juan County, New Mexico. New Mexico State University, Department of Sociology and Anthropology, Cultural Resources Management Division, Report no. 23, 25 pp.

1976   An early Pueblo II design style. Awanyu, 4, no. 2:8-22.

WILSON, J.P., and KELLY, Roger E.

1966   A working bibliography of Sinagua and Cohonina archaeology. Museum of Northern Arizona, 23 pp.

WILSON, J.P., and OLSEN, Stanley J.

1976   Faunal remains from Fort Sumner, New Mexico. Awanyu, 4, no. 3:16-32.

WILSON, J.P., and SCHOENWETTER, James

1972   The archaeology of the Salcido site, LA 6761. Archaeological Society of New Mexico, Supplement no. 3, 17 pp.

WILSON, J.P., and WARREN, Helene

1973   New pottery type described: Seco Corrugated. Awanyu,
        1, no. 1:12-13.

1974   LA 2298, the earliest pueblito? Awanyu, 2, no. 1:
        8-26.

WILSON, J.P., WINSTON, Jon H., and BERGER, Alan J.

1961   Burials at Kinnikinnick Pueblo. Plateau, 34, no.
        1:28-32.

WILSON, Lucy L.W.

1916a   Excavations at Otowi. El Palacio, 3, no. 2:29-36.

1916b   A prehistoric anthropomorphic figure from the Rio
        Grande Basin. American Anthropologist, 18, no. 4:
        548-551.

1917a   Excavations at Otowi, New Mexico. Art and Archae-
        ology, 6, no. 5:259-260.

1917b   This year's work at Otowi. El Palacio, 4, no. 4:
        87.

1918a   Hand sign or avanyu, a note on a Pajaritan biscuit-
        ware motif. American Anthropologist, 20, no. 3:
        310-317.

1918b   Three years at Otowi. El Palacio, 5, no. 18:290-
        294.

WILSON, Rex L.

1959   Evidence in empty bottles. El Palacio, 66, no. 4:
        120-130.

1965   Archeology and everyday life at Fort Union. New
        Mexico Historical Review, 40 (January):55-64.

1966   Tobacco pipes from Fort Union, New Mexico. El
        Palacio, 73, no. 1:32-40.

WILSON, Suzanne M. (See under Keller, Donald R.)

WIMBERLY, Mark, and others

1975   Environmental parameters, Report I: archaeological
        survey of Three Rivers drainage in Tularosa Basin.
        The Artifact, 13, no. 2:1-39.

1977   Three Rivers drainage system of Tularosa Basin, New
        Mexico. The Artifact, 15.

WINDES, Thomas C. (See under Hayes, Alden C.)

WINDMILLER, Ric

1970   Archaeological salvage excavations of mammoth re-
         mains and a Cochise culture site near Double Adobe,
         southeastern Arizona: a preliminary report. Ari-
         zona State Museum.

1971a   Archaeological survey of part of the Castle Dome-
         Pinto Creek project area. Arizona State Museum,
         Archaeological Series, 5, 30 pp.

1971b   Early hunters and gatherers in southeastern Arizona.
         Cochise Quarterly, 1, no. 2:3-15.

1972a   Ta-e-wun: a Colonial period Hohokam campsite in
         east-central Arizona. Kiva, 38, no. 1:1-26.

1972b   Salvage excavations at two sites in Conoco's Flor
         project. Arizona State Museum, Archaeological Series,
         8, 6 pp.

1972c   TA-E-WUN: a Colonial Hohokam campsite in east-central
         Arizona. Arizona State Museum, Archaeological Series,
         11, 54 pp.

1973a   The late Cochise culture in the Sulphur Spring Val-
         ley, southeastern Arizona: archaeology of the Fair-
         child site. Kiva, 39, no. 2:131-169.

1973b   Archaeological survey of the Castle Dome-Pinto Creek
         project area: final report. Arizona State Museum,
         Archaeological Series, 22, 36 pp.

1973c   Impact of the Oak Wash Dam on archaeological sites.
         Arizona State Museum, Archaeological Series, 25, 19
         pp.

WINDMILLER, R., and BIRKBY, Walter H.

1974   Archaeological excavations at Scorpion Ridge ruin,
         east-central Arizona. Arizona State Museum, Archae-
         ological Series, 48, 40 pp.

WINDMILLER, R., and HUCKELL, Bruce B.

1973   Desert Culture sites near Mormon Lake, northern
         Arizona. Kiva, 39, no. 2:199-211.

WINDMILLER, R., and others

1974   Contributions to Pinto Valley archaeology. Arizona
         State Museum, Archaeological Series, 51, 44 pp.

WING, Kittridge A.

1955   Bandelier National Monument, New Mexico. National
       Park Service, Historical Handbook Series, 23, 44 pp.

WINKLER, James H. (See under Davis, Emma Lou.)

WINNING, Hasso von

1974   The tumpline in Prehispanic figures. Masterkey,
       48, no. 3:108-114.

WINSLOW, Sylvia (See under Davis, Emma Lou.)

WINSTON, Jon H. (See under Wilson, John P.)

WINTCH, Leona F.

1963   Extension of Black's Fork culture materials. Utah
       Archaeology, 9, no. 3:2-9.

WINTER, Joseph C.

1973   The distribution and development of Fremont maize
       agriculture: some preliminary interpretations.
       American Antiquity, 38:439-452.

1974a Aboriginal agriculture in the Southwest and Great
       Basin. University of Utah, dissertation, 199 pp.;
       University Microfilms International.

1974b The Hovenweep archaeological project: a study of
       aboriginal agricultural patterns. Southwestern
       Lore, 40, nos. 3-4:23-28.

1975   Hovenweep 1974. San Jose State University, Archae-
       ological Report, no. 1.

1976a Hovenweep 1975. San Jose State University, Archae-
       ological Report, no. 2 (2 vols.).

1976b The processes of farming diffusion in the Southwest
       and Great Basin. American Antiquity, 41:421-429.

1977   Hovenweep 1976. San Jose State University, Archae-
       ological Report, no. 3.

WINTER, J.C., and WYLIE, Henry G.

1974   Paleoecology and diet at Clyde's Cavern. American
       Antiquity, 39:303-315.

WINTERS, Wayne

1952   The walled city. New Mexico Magazine, 30, no. 7:
        18-19.

WINTHROP, Kathryn, and WINTHROP, Robert

1975   Spindle whorls and textile production in early
        New Mexico. Awanyu, 3, no. 3:28-46.

WINTHROP, Robert (See under Winthrop, Kathryn.)

WIRT, Julia J.

1877   Exploration of a mound near Utah Lake, Utah. Pro-
        ceedings of the Davenport Academy of Natural Sci-
        ences, 2, pt. 1:26, 29, 82.

WISEMAN, Regge N.

1970a   Hypotheses for variation observed in late Pueblo
        manos and metates. Southwestern Lore, 36, no. 3:
        46-50.

1970b   Artifacts of interest from the Bloom Mound, south-
        eastern New Mexico. The Artifact, 8, no. 2:1-10.

1970c   Basketmaker III? Pueblo II? The Artifact, 8, no.
        3:21-28.

1971a   The Neff Site, a ceramic period lithic manufactur-
        ing site on the Rio Felix, southeastern New Mexico.
        The Artifact, 9, no. 1:1-30.

1971b   A mountain lion effigy pipe from southern New Mex-
        ico. The Artifact, 9, no. 3:19-21.

1972   The Puerto del Sur project: archaeological salvage
        excavations along Interstate Highway 25 near Las
        Vegas, New Mexico. Laboratory of Anthropology
        Notes, 70.

1973a   The Bent highway salvage project, Otero County,
        New Mexico. Laboratory of Anthropology Notes, 74.

1973b   Archaeological clearance investigation for the
        Tucson Gas and Electric Company 345 KV San Juan-
        Vail transmission line, New Mexico-Arizona. Labora-
        tory of Anthropology Notes, 112.

1974a   The Malpais reconnaissance: an archaeological in-
        ventory and evaluation of some prehistoric sites
        in the El Malpais Planning Unit, Socorro District,
        Bureau of Land Management. Laboratory of Anthro-
        pology Notes, 103.

1974b An archaeological clearance investigation and impact statement for the World Humates Ltd. mine near San Ysidro. Laboratory of Anthropology Notes, 106.

1974c An archaeological clearance investigation and impact statement conducted for Dames & Moore in the vicinity of Smith Lake, New Mexico. Laboratory of Anthropology Notes, 107.

1974d An archaeological clearance investigation and impact statement for Kerr-McGee's Church Rock II mine and access road near Gallup, New Mexico. Laboratory of Anthropology Notes, 108.

1974e An archaeological clearance investigation and impact statement for the San Ysidro-Southern Union Gas Company storage facility distribution line near San Ysidro, New Mexico. Laboratory of Anthropology Notes, 109.

1975a Sitio Creston (LA4939), a stone enclosure site near Las Vegas, New Mexico. Plains Anthropologist, 20: 81-104.

1975b Test excavations at three Lincoln Phase pueblos in the Capitan Mountains region, southeastern New Mexico. Awanyu, 3, no. 1:6-36.

1975c An archaeological clearance investigation and impact statement for the New Mexico State Highway Department project I-040-6(16)351 near San Jon, New Mexico. Laboratory of Anthropology Notes, 116.

1975d A cultural resource overview of eleven potential locations for a recreational lake in Catron County, New Mexico. Laboratory of Anthropology Notes, 121.

WISEMAN, R.N., COBEAN, Robert H., and PFINGSTEN, Clark C.

1971 Preliminary report of salvage excavations at site LA-2112, Lincoln County, New Mexico. The Artifact, 9, no. 3:1-18.

WISEMAN, R.N., and others

1976 Multi-disciplinary investigations at the Smokey Bear Ruin (LA2112), Lincoln County, New Mexico. COAS Publishing and Research Monographs, 4, 108 pp.

WISSLER, Clark

1915   Explorations in the Southwest by the American Museum. American Museum Journal, 15, no. 8:395-398.

1918   Report on the work at Aztec. Journal of the American Museum of Natural History, 18, no. 8:725.

1919   The Archer M. Huntington survey of the Southwest. Zuni district. General introduction. American Museum of Natural History, Anthropological Papers, 18, pp. i-ix.

1921   Dating our prehistoric ruins. Natural History, 21, no. 1:13-26.

1922   Pueblo Bonito as made known by the Hyde Expedition. Natural History, 22, no. 4:343-354.

1927   The Aztec ruin national monument. Natural History, 27:195-201.

WITHERS, Arnold M.

1944   Excavations at Valshni village, a site on the Papago Indian Reservation. American Antiquity, 10: 33-47.

1973   Excavations at Valshni village, Arizona. Arizona Archaeologist, no. 7, 90 pp.

1976   Some pictographs from northern Chihuahua. *In* Schroeder 1976, pp. 109-112.

WITTER, Dan C.

1970   The Piedra del Diablo site, Val Verde County, Texas. Texas Historical Survey Committee, Archaeological Report, no. 18:1-31.

1974   Clearance survey report conducted by the School of American Research for Southern Union Gas Company. School of American Research, contract #5.

1975a   Archaeological clearance survey report conducted by the School of American Research. School of American Research, contract #6.

1975b   Archaeological clearance survey report for Southern Union Gas Company: SUG pipeline #532-77. School of American Research, contract #17.

WOLF, Arthur H. (See under Hartman, Dana.)

WOLFE, W.L.

    1931   Archaeological report on the Hondo sites. El Pa-
            lacio, 31:108-112.

WOLFMAN, Daniel, WOLFMAN, Marianne L., and DICK, Herbert W.

    1965   A Taos Phase pithouse on Arroyo Seco, New Mexico.
            Adams State College, Series in Anthropology, 1, 22
            pp.

WOLFMAN, Marianne L. (See under Wolfman, Daniel.)

WOOD, Donald

    1971a   Recorded archaeological sites on the Gila River
            Indian Reservation: Phase I. Arizona State Museum,
            Archaeological Series, 3, 17 pp.

    1971b   Archaeological reconnaissance of the Gila River
            Indian Reservation: Phase II. Arizona State Museum,
            Archaeological Series, 7, 26 pp.

    1972   Archaeological reconnasisance of the Gila River
            Indian Reservation: Phase III. Arizona State Museum,
            Archaeological Series, 16, 59 pp.

WOOD, Gerald L.

    1963   Archaeological salvage excavations near Rowe, New
            Mexico. Laboratory of Anthropology Notes, 22.

    1973   Archaeological salvage excavations near Rowe, New
            Mexico. Awanyu, 1, no. 3:19-35.

WOOD, H.B.

    1938   Types of stone used for tools by the Mesa Verde
            Indians. Mesa Verde Notes, 8, no. 1:13-17.

WOOD, John J.

    1971   Fitting discrete probability distributions to pre-
            historic settlement patterns. *In* Gumerman 1971,
            pp. 63-82.

WOOD, John Scott (See under Plog, Fred T.)

WOODALL, J. Ned

    1968   Growth arrest lines in long bones of the Casas
            Grandes population. Plains Anthropologist, 13:152-
            160.

WOODBURY, Angus M.

  1965   Notes on the human ecology of Glen Canyon. University of Utah, Anthropological Papers, 74, 70 pp.
         Reviewed AA 69:403 (Longacre), AAq 32:415 (Martin).

WOODBURY, Edna (See under Woodbury, George.)

WOODBURY, George

  1930   The cliff dwellers of Colorado. Discovery, 12:278-282.

  1931   A preliminary note on the investigation of human hair. Colorado Magazine, 8, no. 2:47-48.

WOODBURY, G., and WOODBURY, Edna

  1932   The archaeological survey of Paradox Valley and adjacent country in western Montrose County, Colorado, 1931. Colorado Magazine, 9:1-21.

WOODBURY, Nathalie F.S. (See under Smith, Watson; Woodbury, Richard B.)

WOODBURY, Richard B. (See also under Smith, Watson.)

  1954   Prehistoric stone implements of northeastern Arizona. Papers of the Peabody Museum of American Archaeology and Ethnology, 34, 240 pp.
         Reviewed AA 57:896 (Colton), 58:583 (Taylor); AAq 21:197 (Wheat).

  1956   The antecedents of Zuni culture. Transactions of the New York Academy of Sciences, ser. 2, 18, no. 6:557-563.

  1959   A reconsideration of Pueblo warfare in the southwestern United States. Proceedings of the 33rd International Congress of Americanists, 2:124-133.

  1960a Nels C. Nelson and chronological archaeology. American Antiquity, 25, no. 3:400-402.

  1960b Nelson's stratigraphy. American Antiquity, 26:98-99.

  1960c The Hohokam canals at Pueblo Grande, Arizona. American Antiquity, 26:267-270.

  1960d Pre-Spanish human ecology in the southwestern deserts. University of Arizona Arid Lands Colloquia, 1958-1959, pp. 82-92.

1960e   Report on aboriginal water control systems. *In*
         Utilization of Arid Lands, an Interdisciplinary
         Study, Second Annual Report, Pt. 4, University of
         Arizona, pp. 1-12.

1961a   Climatic changes and prehistoric agriculture in
         the southwestern United States. Annals of the New
         York Academy of Sciences, 95, art. 1, pp. 705-709.

1961b   Prehistoric agriculture at Point of Pines, Arizona.
         Memoirs of the Society for American Archaeology, 17,
         48 pp.
         Reviewed AA 64:440 (Di Peso), AAq 27:433 (Daifuku).

1961c   A reappraisal of Hohokam irrigation. American
         Anthropologist, 63:550-560.

1961d   Prehistoric agriculture in east-central Arizona.
         University of Arizona Arid Lands Colloquia, 1959-
         1960, 1960-1961, pp. 16-22.

1962   Systems of irrigation and water control in arid
         North America. Proceedings of the 34th Internation-
         al Congress of Americanists, pp. 301-305.

1963a   Indian adaptations to arid environments. *In* Aridity
         and Man: the challenge of the arid lands in the
         United States, ed. Carle Hodge, American Association
         for the Advancement of Science, Publication no. 74,
         pp. 55-85.

1963b   Social implications of prehistoric Arizona irriga-
         tion. Actes du VIe Congrès International des Sci-
         ences Anthropologiques et Ethnologiques, Tome II,
         pp. 491-493.

1966   Village agriculture toward the peripheries - the
         North American Southwest. Proceedings of the 36th
         International Congress of Americanists, 1:219-228.

WOODBURY, R.B., and RESSLER, John Q.

1962   Effects of environmental and cultural limitations
         upon Hohokam agriculture, southern Arizona. *In*
         Civilizations in desert lands, ed. R.B. Woodbury,
         University of Utah, Anthropological Papers, 62:41-
         55.

WOODBURY, R.B., and WOODBURY, Nathalie F.S.

1956   Zuni prehistory and El Morro National Monument.
         Southwestern Lore, 21, no. 4:56-60.

WOODS, Betty

1946   Coronado's stronghold. New Mexico Magazine, 24, no. 5:6.

1952   We explored the Valley of Thundering Water. Desert Magazine, 15, no. 4:4-9.

WOODS, Clee

1941   Pots and Pans. New Mexico Magazine, 19, no. 9:18-19, 41, 43.

1945a   Picture gallery, 900 A.D. New Mexico Magazine, 23, no. 3:18-19, 39-40.

1945b   House of a lost god. New Mexico Magazine, 23, no. 4:12-13, 37.

1945c   I found the cave of a Pima god. Desert Magazine, 8, no. 9:8-10.

1946   Lost city of the sky. Desert Magazine, 9, no. 3: 13-16.

WOODS, Margaret S.

1934   Burial no. 4, Talus Unit no. 1, Chetro Ketl. Southwestern Monuments Monthly Report, August, pp. 61-62.

1935   Talus Unit no. 1, Chetro Ketl. Southwestern Monuments Monthly Report, August, pp. 144-146.

1937   Talus Unit no. 1 at Chaco. Southwestern Monuments Monthly Report, October, pp. 321-323.

WOODWARD, Arthur

1930   Cremation-pit "shrine area" and other "rubbish-heap history." Illustrated London News, July 26, pp. 156-159, 181.

1931   The Grewe site, Gila Valley, Arizona. Los Angeles Museum of History, Science and Art, Occasional Papers, 1, 21 pp.

1932   Gigantic intaglio pictographs in the Californian desert. Illustrated London News, Sept. 10, pp. 378-379.

1936   A shell bracelet manufactory. American Antiquity, 2:117-125.

1941a   Shell and bone carvings of the Hohokam. Los Angeles County Museum, Museum Patrons' Association Quarterly, 1, no. 1:16-19.

1941b   Hohokam mosaic mirrors. Los Angeles County Museum,
        Museum Patrons' Association Quarterly, 1, no. 4:6-11.

1947a   Ancient artists of the Southwest. Los Angeles
        County Museum Quarterly, 6, no. 1:3-6.

1947b   Notes on coral in the Southwest. Masterkey, 21,
        no. 1:25-26.

1953   Spanish metals. *In* Di Peso 1953b, pp. 182-216.

WOODWARD, John A.

1967   A two-headed Seri figurine. Masterkey, 41, no. 4:
        154-156.

WOOLFORD, Samuel (See under Martin, George Castor.)

WOOLLEY, Jack

1975   An archaeological survey of proposed humate strip
        mining areas. School of American Research, con-
        tract #14.

WORD, James H.

1968   A preliminary report on the Baker shelter in Val
        Verde County (41VV213). Transactions of the 4th
        Regional Archaeological Symposium on Southeastern
        New Mexico and Western Texas, pp. 40-59.

1971   The Dunlap Complex in western central Crockett
        County, Texas. Bulletin of the Texas Archaeological
        Society, 42:271-318.

WORD, J.H., and DOUGLAS, C.L.

1970   Excavations at Baker Cave, Val Verde County, Texas.
        Texas Memorial Museum, Bulletin 16, 151 pp.

WORMAN, Frederick C.V.

1953   A report on a cache of obsidian artifacts from the
        Pajarito Plateau. El Palacio, 60:12-15.

1959   1957 archaeological salvage excavations at Los
        Alamos, New Mexico: a preliminary report. El Pa-
        lacio, 66, no. 1:10-15.

1964   Anatomy of the Nevada Test Site. University of
        California, Los Alamos Scientific Laboratory, 32
        pp.

1966   The current status of archaeology at the Nevada

Test Site and the Nuclear Rocket Development Station. University of California, Los Alamos Scientific Laboratory, Report LA-3520, 33 pp.

1967a   Archaeological salvage excavations on the Mesita del Buey, Los Alamos County, New Mexico. University of California, Los Alamos Scientific Laboratory, Report no. LA 3636, 39 pp.

1967b   Nevada Test Site archaeology. Nevada Archaeological Survey, Reporter, 1, no. 2:5-6.

1969   Archaeological investigations at the United States Atomic Energy Commission's Nevada Test Site and Nuclear Rocket Development Station. University of California, Los Alamos Scientific Laboratory, Report LA-4125, 201 pp.

WORMAN, J.L. (See under Matthews, Washington.)

WORMINGTON, H. Marie

1947   Prehistoric Indians of the Southwest. Colorado Museum of Natural History, Popular Series, 7, 191 pp.
       Reviewed AAq 14:69 (Colton).

1948   Preliminary report on excavation at the Turner site in eastern Utah. Southwestern Lore, 14, no. 2:23-24 (abstract).

1949   Ancient Man in North America. Denver Museum of Natural History, Popular Series, 4, 3rd ed., 198 pp.
       Reviewed AA 53:117 (Cotter), AAq 16:79 (Dick).

1955a   A reappraisal of the archaeology of the northern periphery of the Southwestern United States. Proceedings of the 31st International Congress of Americanists, pp. 649-656.

1955b   A reappraisal of the Fremont culture, with a summary of the archaeology of the northern periphery. Proceedings of the Denver Museum of Natural History, 1, 200 pp.
       Reviewed AA 58:1155 (Malouf), AAq 21:429 (Jennings).

1957   Ancient Man in North America. Denver Museum of Natural History, Popular Series, 4, 4th ed., 322 pp.
       Reviewed AA 60:972 (Krieger), AAq 24:204 (Wendorf).

1962   A survey of early American prehistory. American
        Scientist, 50:230-242.

1964   Supplementary comments on Tule Springs. Minnesota
        Archaeologist, 26, no. 4:145.

WORMINGTON, H.M., and ELLIS, D.

1967   (ed.) Pleistocene studies in southern Nevada.
        Nevada State Museum, Anthropological Papers, 13,
        407 pp.

WORMINGTON, H.M., and LISTER, Robert H.

1956   Archaeological investigations on the Uncompahgre
        Plateau in west central Colorado. Proceedings of
        the Denver Museum of Natural History, 2, 129 pp.
        Reviewed AA 59:372 (Jennings), AAq 22:315 (Rinaldo).

WORMINGTON, H.M., and NEAL, Arminta

1951   The Story of Pueblo Pottery. Denver Museum of Na-
        tural History, Museum Pictorial no. 2, 64 pp.

WRIGHT, Barton A., and GERALD, Rex E.

1950   The Zanardelli site: Arizona BB:13:12. Kiva, 16,
        no. 3:8-15

WRIGHT, Gary A.

1965   A desiccated infant burial from the Verde Valley,
        Arizona. Plateau, 37, no. 4:109-120.

WRIGHT, Welty

1940   The type, distribution, and occurrence of flint
        gravers in Texas. Bulletin of the Texas Archae-
        ological and Paleontological Society, 12:31-48.

WYLIE, Henry G. (See also under Green, Dee F.; Winter, Joseph
   C.)

1974   An analysis of lithic artifacts from the Gila Na-
        tional Forest near Reserve, New Mexico, and an ar-
        chaeological survey of the Reserve land exchange,
        Gila National Forest, New Mexico. United States
        Forest Service, Southwestern Region, Archaeological
        Report no. 2, 33 pp.

1975a   Pot scrapers and drills from southern Utah. Kiva,
        40, no. 3:121-130.

1975b   Tool microwear and functional types from Hogup Cave, Utah. Tebiwa, 17, no. 2:1-32.

WYMAN, Leland C.

1952   A prehistoric naturalist. Plateau, 24, no. 4:128-129.

WYMAN, L.C., and AMSDEN, Charles

1934   A patchwork cloak. Masterkey, 8, no. 5:133-137.

WYMAN, L.C., and BOYD, William C.

1937   Blood group determinations of prehistoric American Indians. American Anthropologist, 39:583-592.

YABLON, Ronald K.

1977   An archaeological survey of additional areas associated with the proposed Vaiva Vo-Kohatk Road, Papago Indian Reservation, Pinal County, Arizona. Arizona State University, Office of Cultural Resource Management, report no. 18, 17 pp.

YARNELL, Richard A.

1959   Prehistoric Pueblo use of *Datura*. El Palacio, 66, no. 5:176-178.

1965   Implications of distinctive flora on Pueblo ruins. American Anthropologist, 67:662-674.

YELM, Betty

1935a   Skull deformities of the Cliff Dweller. Mesa Verde Notes, 6, no. 1:14-16.

1935b   Faces of the Mesa Verde people. Mesa Verde Notes, 6, no. 2:17-19.

YOUNG, Dwight S.

1954   Pictographs at an ancient shrine. New Mexico Magazine, 32, no. 11:12-13, 41.

YOUNG, Jon Nathan

1967   The Salado culture in Southwestern prehistory. University of Arizona, dissertation, 131 pp.; University Microfilms International.

1972   The Garden Canyon Site. The Artifact, 10, no. 3:3-20.

458   *The Bibliography*

1973   Prehistoric arrow nock files from Canyon de Chelly.
        Plateau, 45, no. 3:114-116.

YOUNG, L.E.

    1929   The ancient inhabitants of Utah. Art and Archae-
            ology, 27, no. 3:125-135.

ZAHNISER, Jack L.

    1966   Late prehistoric villages southeast of Tucson,
            Arizona, and the archaeology of the Tanque Verde
            Phase. Kiva, 31, no. 3:103-204.

    1970   The archaeological resources of Saguaro National
            Monument. Kiva, 35, no. 3:105-120.

ZASLOW, Bert, and DITTERT, Alfred E., Jr.
    1977   Pattern theory used an an archaeological tool: a
            preliminary statement. Southwestern Lore, 43, no.
            1:18-24.

ZIER, Christian J.

    1977   Prehistoric utilization of the House Creek drainage,
            San Juan National Forest, Colorado. Southwestern
            Lore, 43, no. 2:1-10.

ZIER, C.J., and McPHERSON, Gale

    1976   Excavations near Zuni, New Mexico: 1973. Museum of
            Northern Arizona, Research Papers, 2, 78 pp.

ZINGG, Robert M.

    1939   A reconstruction of Uto-Aztekan history. Univer-
            sity of Denver, Contributions to Ethnography, 2,
            274 pp.
            Reviewed AA 42:325 (Opler), AAq 8:307 (Taylor).

    1940   Report on archaeology of southern Chihuahua. Uni-
            versity of Denver, Contributions, 3, pp. 1-69.
            Reviewed AAq 8:307 (Taylor).

ZUBROW, Ezra B.W.

    1971   Carrying capacity and dynamic equilibrium in the
            prehistoric Southwest. American Antiquity, 36:
            127-138.

    1975a   Ecological perspectives in the Hay Hollow Valley.
            In Martin and others 1975, pp. 17-39.

1975b   Prehistoric carrying capacity: a model.   Cummings
        Archaeology Series, 143 pp.
        Reviewed AA 78:710 (Dumond).

1976   (ed.) Demographic anthropology: quantitative ap-
        proaches. University of New Mexico Press.

Part II
Classified Subject Index

INTRODUCTION

In the following pages, the titles listed in Part I are classified by subarea and topic, but since not all are classified in both ways, an explanation of the categories employed is in order.

DEFINITION OF AREAS (SECTION A)

The areas recognized here have been defined on the basis of both geographical and cultural factors, which results, at times, in a tendency to blur the boundaries. I think that this is unavoidable, because, as every archaeologist knows, cultural boundaries shift with time due to various complex causes, and for the purposes of a work such as this shifting must be ignored.

As has been recognized for many years, river drainage basins seem to have been important foci for cultural differentiation in the Southwest, and they are therefore the principal geographical consideration in defining the areas used in this classification. The cultural aspects rest primarily on the recognition of the five regional developments widely regarded as the main divisions, now clearly definable, of the prehistoric agricultural level in the Southwest as a whole. It has been found logical in some cases to use these cultural categories for items on the list that cover subareas in whole or in part, as follows:

Fremont: essentially areas 1 and 2
Anasazi: essentially areas 3 through 10
Patayan: essentially areas 11 through 13
Hohokam: essentially area 14
Mogollon: essentially areas 15 through 20

In defining some of the areas, useful practicality has played an important part, particularly where modern political boundaries have been followed. In two cases (Utah and New Mexico), this was done because the portions of those states outside the cultural Southwest are small and it seemed to me reasonable to increase the usefulness of the work by covering

their total areas. In two other cases (Sonora and Chihuahua),
our knowledge--and the literature--is so scanty that an attempt
to subdivide them on scientific grounds seems premature, particularly if done by a non-specialist.
As further explained below, Historic, Paleo-Indian, and
most Archaic cultures are *not* included here, but rather in Section B (Topical Classification). The time period here, then,
is roughly the 2000 years between 300 B.C. and A.D. 1700. The
definitions follow:

Area 1   Western Utah (essentially the "Sevier Fremont"
          region, including neighboring Nevada)
Area 2   Eastern Utah-Western Colorado (approximately the
          region of the upper Colorado River drainage)
Area 3   Virgin-Moapa (southwestern Utah, southeastern
          Nevada, and the "Arizona Strip")
Area 4   Kayenta (northeastern Arizona, east to the Chinlee
          valley, Utah south of the San Juan, and a portion
          of south central Utah north of the Colorado)
Area 4a   Canyon de Chelly-Chinlee region
Area 5   Hopi-Little Colorado (Black Mesa south to the
          Little Colorado, lower Little Colorado east to
          the New Mexico line)
Area 6   Cibola (Zuni and Acoma region of west central
          New Mexico)
Area 7   Chaco (northwestern New Mexico south of the San
          Juan)
Area 8   Mesa Verde (northern drainage of the San Juan in
          Utah, Colorado, and New Mexico)
Area 8a   Upper San Juan-Piedra region
Area 9   Gallina (the Largo-Gallina-Governador area of
          north central New Mexico)
Area 10   Rio Grande (the so-called upper and middle parts
          of the Rio Grande drainage in north central New
          Mexico, plus the upper Pecos valley and the [now
          dry] lake basins east of the mountains)
Area 11   Cohonina (the Grand Canyon and the plateau region
          to the south)
Area 12   Prescott (region of west central Arizona center-
          ing on the city of Prescott)
Area 13   Lower Colorado (Colorado River valley and lower
          parts of eastern tributaries from Hoover Dam
          south to the Gulf of California, including the
          adjacent portions of Nevada and California)
Area 14   Hohokam (south central Arizona from the Salt and
          Gila Rivers, with the lower courses of their
          northern tributaries, south to the international
          border, from the Papago Reservation east to the

San Pedro valley)

Area 15   Sinagua (central Arizona from the Flagstaff region
           south through the Verde valley)

Area 16   East Central Arizona (upper Little Colorado south
           to the Gila-Salt region, west to the Tonto Basin
           and east nearly to the New Mexico line)

Area 17   West Central New Mexico (Gila-Salt drainage in
           New Mexico, east to the Rio Grande, west to in-
           clude a portion of Arizona)

Area 18   Southeast Arizona (east of the San Pedro valley
           to the New Mexico line, south of the Gila River
           to the Mexican border)

Area 19   Southwest New Mexico (centers around the Mimbres
           drainage, east to the Rio Grande, west to the Ari-
           zona line, south to the Mexican border)

Area 20   Southeast New Mexico (middle Pecos valley in New
           Mexico, west to the Rio Grande, south to the Texas
           line)

Area 21   Plains Border (south central and southeastern
           Colorado, and New Mexico east of the Sangre de
           Cristo Range and the Pecos valley)

Area 22   Trans-Pecos Texas (including also the counties
           bordering the Pecos valley on the east, and the
           Mexican side of the Rio Grande in Coahuila)

Area 23   Chihuahua (as politically delimited)

Area 24   Sonora (as politically delimited)

NOTES ON TOPICAL CATEGORIES (SECTION B)

The topical headings (listed in the Table of Contents) are for
the most part self-explanatory, but the following need some
comment:

Environment: includes accounts relating to items of flora
    and fauna, as well as climatic and geographical factors.

Historic Indian: includes some items which refer to re-
    mains which are strictly speaking prehistoric, but which
    certainly pertain to the immediate ancestors of identi-
    fiable historic groups (Shoshonean, Athapascan, Yuman,
    Pima-Papago, etc.)

Limited Activity Sites: includes accounts of sites such as
    shrines, rock outlines, burnt rock mounds, and isolated
    features.

Paleo-Indian and Archaic: since some essentially Archaic-
    type cultural groups survived well after most of the
    Southwest had become agricultural, studies of the Archaic
    horizon are sometimes included in the subarea lists, rath-
    er than here.

Physical Anthropology: includes studies of paleopathology
and human coprolites; not classified by subarea.

It will be seen that some possible categories are thus
distributed among several headings in this system. As an example, *diet* would be found under Environment, Agriculture,
Cultivated plants, Domesticated animals, and Physical anthropology. There seems to be no way of avoiding this sort of dif-
ficulty, other than by making the classification impossibly
detailed. In all categories, the aim has been in the general
direction of reasonable consistency, and I hope that for the
most part this has been realized; however, I should point out
that a fair number of the items listed have not been seen by
me or my assistants, and in these cases classification may be
inaccurate or incomplete, unless the titles include clear indications.

In using the topical lists, it must be remembered that the
great majority of excavation reports will not be found therein,
since such works usually contain at least some information
pertaining to a large number of the topical categories. To
have listed them here in a consistent fashion would have en-
tailed a great deal of repetition. They are included, of course,
in their proper places in the regional/cultural classification
(Section A).

SECTION A
REGIONAL/CULTURAL CLASSIFICATION

GENERAL WORKS

Amsden, C.A.   1927b, 1933c
Amsden, M.   1928b
Baldwin, G.C.   1941, 1963
Bancroft   1875
Bandelier   1890a, 1892a
Barber   1877b
Barnett   1973a
Bartlett, J.R.   1854
Baum   1902
Blessing   1935
Bourke   1890
Brewer, J.P.   1936
Brown, F.M.   1937a
Butcher   1955
Carlson, R.   1951
Colton, H.S.   1948
Cummings, B.   1935a, 1953
Duff   1902a
Ellis, F.H.   1975c
Getty   1936
Gladwin, H.S.   1930, 1933, 1957
Halseth   1947b
Haury   1949, 1960b, 1962a
Hewett   1905a, 1905b, 1908, 1926a, 1930
Hodge   1907-10
Holmes   1919
Holmquist   1923
Hyman   1962
Irwin-Williams   1972a
Jeançon and Douglas   1930a
Jennings, J.D.   1956a, 1968, 1974
Judd   1940

Kaemlein   1967
Kidder, A.V.   1924, 1927b, 1928b, 1936b
Kidder, A.V., and Rouse   1962
Kirchhoff   1954
Krieger   1953
Lindig   1964b
Longacre   1973
Magoffin   1930
Manning   1875
Martin, Paul Sidney   1927, 1933
Martin, Paul Sidney, and Plog   1973
Martin, Paul Sidney, Quimby, and Collier   1947
McGregor   1941a, 1965
Mera   1942
Moorehead   1910
Nelson, N.C.   1919a, 1919b
Osborne   1958
Palmer, F.M.   1906
Reed, E.K.   1947a, 1955b, 1964
Renaud   1928a
Rinaldo   1947
Roberts   1935, 1936, 1937b
Schaafsma, P.   1961
Squier   1848
Stirling   1940
Tamarin and Glubock   1975
Tanner, C.L.   1976
Thomas, C.   1898
Tobin   1948a, 1948b
Underhill   1946a
Washburn   1975
Waterman   1929

Tripp 1963b
Weide 1970
Wheeler, S.M. 1935, 1936,
   1937a, 1937b, 1938a, 1939a,
   1942
Wheeler, S.M., and Fowler
   1973
Wirt 1877

               AREA 2
EASTERN UTAH-WESTERN COLORADO

Ambler 1966b
Anderson, K. 1964
Annand 1967
Baldwin, G.C. 1947
Beauvais 1955
Beckwith, F. 1927d
Breternitz 1970
Brown, F.M. 1937b
Buckles 1971
Burgh 1950
Burgh and Scoggin 1948
Day 1962, 1964, 1965
Day and Dibble 1963
Dick 1949
Ferguson, C.W. 1949
Fewkes 1917e
Flaim and Warburton 1961
Gaumer 1937, 1939
Gillin 1938a, 1941
Green, D.F. 1975
Grosscup 1962
Gunnerson, J.H. 1957b, 1957c,
   1957d, 1962a, 1962d, 1962e
Hunt, A.P. 1953, 1956
Hurlbett 1977
Hurst, B.H. 1957
Hurst, C.T. 1940b, 1941a,
   1942a, 1943b, 1944a, 1945a,
   1945b, 1946b, 1946c, 1947a,
   1947b, 1947c, 1948a, 1948b
Hurst, C.T., and Anderson
   1949
Huscher, B.H., and Huscher
   1942a, 1942b, 1943
Huscher, H.A. 1939

Ives 1941a, 1942
Jeançon 1923c, 1927
Judd 1918, 1919b
Kasper 1977
Leach 1966, 1967, 1970
Leh 1936
Lister, R.H. 1951a, 1951b,
   1962
Lister, R.H., and Dick 1952
Lister, R.H., and Sanburg
   1963
Lohr 1948
Madsen, D.B. 1975b
Malde and Schick 1964
Malouf 1941
Moomaw 1957
Morris, R., Glazier, and Thal-
   lon 1937
Morss 1931b
Mulroy and Kowta 1964
Newberry 1876
Pendergast 1961b
Pierson 1958, 1962a
Pierson and Anderson 1975
Reagan 1931a, 1931b, 1931d,
   1931e, 1931f, 1931g, 1931h,
   1931i, 1932a, 1932b, 1932c,
   1933a, 1933b, 1933c, 1933e,
   1933f, 1934a, 1934b, 1935a
Schroeder 1953f, 1964b
Schulman, E. 1948b, 1950a
Setzler 1943
Sheets 1969
Shields 1967
Toll 1977
Tripp 1967a, 1967b
Wintch 1963
Winter and Wylie 1974
Woodbury, A.M., and Woodbury
   1932
Wormington 1948
Wormington and Lister 1956

               ANASAZI
            (Areas 3-10)

Abel 1955

1943, 1944b, 1945, 1946,
1950a, 1967
Bannister, Dean, and Robinson
1969
Barre 1970
Boothly 1888
Carr 1929
Cassell 1945
Cody 1942
Colton, H.S. 1945a, 1952b
Connolly, C., and Eckert 1969
Day 1966a, 1966b
Duffield 1904
Euler 1954b, 1963
Ferguson, C.W., and Black
1952
Fowler, C.S. 1970
Fowler, D.D. 1972, 1973
Fowler, D.D., Madsen, and
Hattori 1973
Gunnerson, J.H. 1962c, 1962e
Hall, E.T. 1942
Hanna 1926
Harrington, E.L. 1930
Harrington, M.R. 1925a, 1925b,
1925c, 1925d, 1926b, 1926c,
1926d, 1926e, 1927a, 1927b,
1927c, 1927d, 1928b, 1929b,
1929c, 1930b, 1930d, 1933b,
1934d, 1937a, 1937b, 1937c,
1937d, 1937e, 1937f, 1942c,
1945b, 1952, 1953a, 1953b
Harrington, M.R., Hayden, and
Schellbach 1930
Haskell 1970
Hayden, I. 1929a, 1929b,
1930a, 1930b
Heizer 1970
Henley 1929
Hester, T.R. 1973
Hester, T.R., and Heizer 1973
Hilton, J.W. 1940
Judd 1917b, 1918, 1919a,
1920, 1921, 1926b
Madsen, D.B. 1975a
Malouf 1940
McGregor 1945b
Meighan 1959b

Miller, K.K. 1967
Mueller 1974
Murbarger 1951
Nusbaum, J.L., Kidder, and
Guernsey 1922
Palmer, E. 1876
Pendergast 1962b
Rudy 1954a
Rudy and Stirland 1950
Schellbach 1930
Schroeder 1953c, 1955a
Shutler, R. 1956, 1961a,
1961b, 1967b
Shutler, R., and Shutler 1962
Shutler, R., Shutler, and Grif-
fith 1960
Smith, E.R. 1940b
Soulé 1975, 1976, 1977
Spencer, J.E. 1934
Stallings 1941
Steward 1940, 1941
Susia 1964
Thurston 1933
Trapp 1959
Tuohy 1965
West 1932b
Wetherill, B.W. 1934
Williams, P.A., and Orlins
1963
Worman 1964, 1966, 1967b,
1969
Wylie 1975a

AREA 4
KAYENTA

Adams, W.Y. 1957, 1960,
1966
Adams, W.Y., and Adams 1959
Adams, W.Y., Lindsay, and
Turner 1961
Aikens 1966a
Ambler 1959
Ambler and Olson 1977
Ambler, Lindsay, and Stein
1964
Anderson, K.M. 1966, 1969a,
1969c, 1971

Turner, C.G., and Lofgren
1966
Turner, C.G., and Miller 1961
Ward 1975d
West 1927
Wetherill, B.W. 1935
Wetherill, J. 1934, 1955a,
1955b
Woodbury, A.M. 1965

AREA 4a
CANYON DE CHELLY-CHINLEE

Adovasio and Gunn 1975
Anderson, E., and Blanchard
1942
Bakkegard and Morris 1961
Bannister, Dean, and Gell
1966
Baum 1903
Bickford 1890
Bradley, Z.A. 1973
Britt 1971c, 1973a
Byers and Morss 1957
Colton, H.S. 1939b, 1939e
Coon 1948
De Harport 1951, 1953
El-Najjar 1974
El-Najjar, Morris, Turner,
and Ryan 1975
Fewkes 1906b
Fry and Hall 1975
Gardner, W.A. 1940
Grant 1978
Guernsey 1931
Hargrave 1934a
Harlan and Manire 1975
Haury 1936e, 1945e
Hurt, W.R. 1947
Jackson, W.H. 1876b, 1878
Jones, V.H., and Morris 1960
Kelley, J.E. 1975
Kidder, A.V. 1926c, 1927c,
1951b
Long 1960
Magers 1975

McDonald 1976
Mindeleff, C. 1895, 1897b
Morris, D.P. 1975
Morris, E.A. 1959a, 1959b
Morris, E.H. 1925a, 1925b,
1928c, 1938, 1941, 1948,
1951
Morss 1927
Newhall 1952
Olson, A.P., and Lee 1964
Reed, E.K. 1946a
Reid 1975
Rock 1975
Rock and Morris 1975
Samuelson 1953
Schiffer 1975b
Simpson, J.H. 1850
Steen, C.R. 1966
Stevenson, J. 1886
Stowell 1934c
Van Valkenburgh, R. 1938b
Young, J.N. 1973

AREA 5
HOPI-LITTLE COLORADO

Adams, W.Y. 1966
Bannister, Dean, and Robinson
1968
Bannister, Hannah, and Robin-
son 1966
Bannister, Robinson, and War-
ren 1967
Bartlett, K. 1977
Beaty 1964, 1966
Beeson 1957b
Bliss and Ezell 1956
Bradley, Z.A. 1959
Breternitz 1957d
Breternitz and Schley 1962
Brew, J.O. 1937, 1939a, 1939b,
1941
Brew, J.O., and Hack 1939
Brewer, J.W. 1936
Brugge 1976a
Bryan, B. 1961b
Buehler 1927

Wilson, J.P.   1972b
Woodbury, R.B.   1954

AREA 6
CIBOLA

Bandelier   1892b
Bannister, Robinson, and
   Warren   1970
Barnes, R.A.   1947
Barnett   1974b
Barth   1933
Beal   1977a, 1977b
Bushnell   1955
Carter, O.C.S.   1906
Cushing   1886
Dittert   1959, 1968a
Dittert and Ruppé   1951, 1952
Fewkes   1891, 1909a
Frisbie   1973
Galinat and Ruppé   1961
Gratz   1977
Harrington, M.R.   1929a
Hodge   1895b, 1897a, 1918a,
   1918b, 1918c, 1920a, 1920b,
   1921, 1922, 1923, 1924a,
   1924b, 1924c, 1926, 1937a,
   1939, 1942, 1952
Isham   1973
Keller, M.   1976
Kroeber   1916a, 1916b
LeBlanc   1976a, 1978
Lummis and Vogt   1926
MacClary   1929
Marquardt   1974
Mera   1939
Mindeleff, V.   1891
Reed, E.K.   1955a
Riley, C.L.   1975
Rinaldo   1964
Roberts   1932b
Ruppé   1966a
Ruppé and Dittert   1952, 1953
Shiner   1963
Simpson, J.H.   1850
Smith, W., Woodbury, and
   Woodbury   1966
Southwestern Ceramic Confer-
   ence   1958, 1959, 1965

Spier   1917a, 1917b, 1918
Stevenson, J.   1883a, 1884
Vogt   1922
Windmiller   1973c
Wiseman   1974a, 1974d
Wissler   1919
Woodbury, R.B.   1956
Woodbury, R.B., and Woodbury
   1956
Zier and McPherson   1976

AREA 7
CHACO

Adams, R.N.   1951
Alexander, R.K.   1963, 1966b
Allan   1972
Allan and others   1976
Allen, J.W.   1972
Allen, J.W., and Kayser   1971
Anderson, D., and Anderson
   1976
Bannister   1964
Bannister, Robinson, and War-
   ren   1970
Barber   1878
Beal   1975a, 1975e, 1976a,
   1976b, 1977c, 1977e
Beal and Whitmore   1976a
Benham   1966
Bickford   1890
Bloom   1921
Bohrer and Adams   1977
Bradfield   1921
Bradley, Z.A.   1971
Brand   1935b
Brand, Hawley, and Hibben
   1937
Brew, A.P.   1962a, 1962b
Broilo and Allan   1973, 1975
Bryan, K.   1926, 1954
Carlson, R.L.   1966
Cassidy and Bullard   1956
Cattanach   1956
Chapman, R.C.   1967
Davis, G.   1975
Dittert   1962a

1962c, 1975
Wilson, J.P., and Schoenwetter
  1972
Wissler 1922
Woods, M.S. 1934, 1935, 1937

AREA 8
MESA VERDE

Adams, W.Y. 1960
Adams, W.Y., and Adams 1959
Agenbroad 1975
Baldwin, G.C. 1949
Baldwin, S.J. 1976
Bannister, Dean, and Robinson
  1969
Bannister, Robinson, and War-
  ren 1970
Barber 1878
Beckwith, F. 1934a
Birdsall 1892
Birkedal 1976
Bradley, B. 1974
Breternitz, D.A. 1973, 1975
Breternitz, D.A., and Breter-
  nitz 1973
Breternitz, D.A., and Nordby
  1972
Breternitz, D.A., Nordby, and
  Nickens 1974
Breternitz, D.A., Rohn, and
  Morris 1974
Brew, J.O. 1935, 1946
Broilo 1973, 1974a, 1974b
Brown, J. 1975
Burgh 1932b, 1933, 1934,
  1937
Burroughs 1959
Bussey 1965a
Carlson, R.L. 1963
Cassidy and Bullard 1956
Cattanach 1972
Caywood 1934
Chapin 1890, 1892
Chapman, A. 1916
Corbett 1962
Cordell 1975a

Cornelius 1938
Cutler 1966
Cutler and Meyer 1965
Daniels, H.S. 1940
Daniels, M. 1916a, 1916b
Danson 1958
Davis, E.L. 1964
Day 1961
Dean 1975
DeBloois 1975
DeBloois and Green 1978
Dennison 1933
Douglass, A.E. 1949
Elisha 1968
Emslie 1975
Erdman, Douglas, and Marr
  1969
Ferguson, C.W. 1959
Fewkes 1908a, 1908b, 1909b,
  1910a, 1910d, 1911b, 1916b,
  1916c, 1916d, 1916e, 1916f,
  1916g, 1916h, 1917a, 1917b,
  1917c, 1917g, 1918a, 1918b,
  1919a, 1919c, 1920a, 1920b,
  1920c, 1920d, 1921a, 1921b,
  1921d, 1921e, 1922a, 1922b,
  1923a, 1923d, 1926c
Flinn, Turner, and Brew 1976
Flora, Daniels, and Cornelius
  1940-41
Foster, G. 1952
Fowler, D.D. 1958, 1959, 1961
Fowler, D.D., and Lister 1959
Franke 1931, 1932, 1933, 1934a,
  1934b, 1935a, 1935b
Franke and Watson 1936
Gannett 1880
Getty 1933, 1935a, 1935b
Gilbert, E.X. 1961
Green, D.F. 1969, 1971, 1974
Gunckel 1897
Gunnerson, J.H. 1959a, 1959e,
  1960a, 1962b
Guthe, A.K. 1949
Hammack, L.C. 1964b
Hargrave 1936a, 1965a, 1965b
Harrill and Breternitz 1976
Haury and Flora 1937

Bice 1967, 1968, 1970
Bice and Davis 1972
Bice and Sundt 1968, 1972
Biella and Chapman 1977
Bierbower 1905
Bliss 1936b, 1948b
Bloom 1922, 1923
Blumenschein 1956, 1958, 1964
Bohrer 1975
Bowen, W.M. 1950
Bradfield 1928a
Branham 1961 '
Brody 1969
Bronitsky 1975, 1977
Brugge 1955
Bullen, A.K., and Bullen 1942
Bussey 1966
Cady and Reiter 1937
Caraveo and Schalk 1977
Carleton 1855
Carroll, Hooton, and Stuart
   1976, 1977
Caywood 1966
Chapman, K.M. 1930
Collins, S.M. 1975
Cope 1875
Cordell 1975b
Davis, E.L., and Winkler
   1959, 1975
Davis, I. 1959
Dechert 1971
Dick 1965b, 1976
Dickson 1972, 1973, 1975
Dittert 1962b
Doty 1977
Douglass, W.B. 1917a, 1917b,
   1917c
Dozier 1958
Dutton 1938a, 1952a, 1953,
   1963, 1964a, 1964c, 1966b
Ellis, F.H. 1964a, 1966a,
   1974b, 1974c, 1974d, 1975d,
   1976
Ellis, F.H., and Brody 1964
Ely 1939
Evans, C., and Sowers 1939
Fenenga and Cummings 1956
Ferdon 1952

Ferdon and Reed 1950
Ferguson, M. 1933
Fisher 1931
Ford 1975
Fox 1975
Frisbie 1975d
Galinat, Reinhart, and Frisbie
   1970
Gauthier 1977
Gauthier and Acklen 1977a
Gauthier and Mashburn 1977
Gilbert, H. 1942
Goddard, S. 1933
Green, Earl 1955
Green, Ernestene L. 1976
Greer 1965a
Grigg and Carroll 1976
Grigg, Fosberg, and Gauthier
   1977
Grigg, Stein, and Stuart 1976
Gunnerson, J.H. 1959d
Guthe, C.E. 1917
Halseth 1926
Halseth and Huddelson 1926
Hammack, L.C. 1962a, 1966b
Harlow 1965a, 1965b
Harrington, J.P. 1916a
Harris, H.H. 1906, 1907
Hattan 1893
Hendron 1937, 1938a, 1938b,
   1940, 1946a, 1946b, 1947
Herold, L.C. 1968
Hewett 1904a, 1904b, 1906,
   1909a, 1909b, 1909c, 1909d,
   1909e, 1928, 1938a, 1938b,
   1938c, 1940
Hewett and Dutton 1953
Hewett, Henderson, and Robbins
   1913
Hibben 1936, 1937b, 1955a,
   1960, 1966, 1967, 1975
Hilton, G. 1918
Holden, J. 1955a
Holmes 1905
Holschlag 1975
Honea 1966, 1967
Howard, R.M. 1959, 1960
Irwin-Williams 1973b

McClellan and Vogler 1977
Michels 1964
Moodie 1930
Moriarty 1968
Olson, B.L. 1973
Peck, S.L. 1953
Pepper, C. 1966
Perkins 1967a
Quinn and Roney 1973
Renk 1972
Rogers, M.J. 1936, 1945
Schroeder 1952b, 1953b, 1961a
Setzler 1952
Stone 1977a
Treganza 1942
Turner, S., and Turner 1967
Van Valkenburgh, R. 1952
Vivian, R. Gordon 1965
Wallace, W.J. 1962
Ward 1976b
Weaver, J.R. 1967
Whalen, N.M. 1976
Wilke 1977
Woodward, A. 1932

AREA 14
HOHOKAM

Ackerly and Rieger 1976
Addis 1893
Ahlo 1975
Allen, N. 1953
Ambler 1962
Amsden, C.A. 1936a, 1936b
Anderson, B.C. 1970
Antieau 1976, 1977a, 1977b,
    1977c
Ayres 1967, 1971
Bahr 1971
Bahti, M. 1970
Bannister and Robinson 1971
Baxter 1888
Boekelman 1936
Bohrer 1970, 1971
Bohrer, Cutler, and Sauer
    1969
Brandes 1957

Breternitz 1964
Brew, S.A. 1975, 1976
Brook, R.A., Davidson, Sim-
    mons, and Stein 1977
Brooks, D., and Vivian 1975
Brown, J.L. 1967
Brown, J.L., and Grebinger
    1969
Brown, P.E. 1976a, 1976b,
    1976c, 1976d, 1976e, 1976f,
    1976g, 1977a, 1977b
Bruder 1975a
Bryan, B. 1963
Burt 1961
Burton 1975a, 1975b, 1976
Busch, Raab, and Busch 1976
Canouts 1977
Canouts and Phillips 1974
Canouts, Fritz, and Hard 1975
Canouts, Germeshausen, and
    Larkin 1972
Canouts and others 1975
Cartledge and Weaver 1974
Caywood 1937
Chenhall 1967b
Ciolek-Torrello and Brew 1976
Clark, R.B. 1972
Cleveland and Masse 1973
Clonts 1974a, 1974b
Colberg-Sigleo 1975
Cosgrove, C.B., Jr., and Felts
    1927a
Crabtree 1973
Cummings, B. 1927a
Cushing 1888
Daniels, M. 1916a
Danson and Wallace 1956
Debowski and Fritz 1974
Debowski and others 1976
Di Peso 1949, 1951a, 1951b,
    1953b, 1956, 1958a, 1958b
Dittert 1972, 1976
Dittert, Fish, and Simonis
    1969
Dixon 1956a
Doelle 1975a, 1975c, 1976a,
    1976c, 1978
Doelle and Brew 1976

McClellan and Vogler 1977
McDonald and others 1974
Midvale 1965, 1968, 1970, 1974
Mindeleff, C. 1896b, 1897a
Moorehead 1898, 1906
Morris, D.H. 1969b
Morris, D.H., and El-Najjar 1971
Niehuis 1946
Olsen 1974
Parks 1927
Patrick 1903
Pinkley, E.T. 1926, 1928
Pinkley, F.H. 1930, 1935, 1936a, 1936b, 1936c
Pinkley, F.H., and Pinkley 1931
Pomeroy 1959
Raab 1973a, 1973b, 1975, 1976, 1977
Raab and others 1974
Reaves 1969, 1975
Reed, E.K. 1963d
Rensch 1934
Reynolds 1974a, 1974b
Reynolds and others 1974a, 1974b
Rice and Simonis 1977
Rippeteau 1972
Robinson 1963
Rodgers 1974, 1975a, 1975b, 1976, 1977
Rose, R.H. 1933
Roubicek, Cummings, and Hartman 1973
Rule 1977
Ruppé 1966b
Scantling 1939
Scheick 1976
Schmidt 1927a, 1927b, 1928
Schoenwetter, Gaines, and Weaver 1973
Schroeder 1943, 1947, 1949a, 1951b, 1952a, 1953a, 1960, 1961b, 1964a, 1967a
Sense 1967
Shenk 1976
Shetrone 1946
Simpson, R.D. 1946a, 1947, 1950

Smith, L.D. 1977a
Spain 1975
Spears 1973
Stacy 1974, 1975
Stacy and Hayden 1975
Stanislawski 1961
Starr 1894
Steen, C.R. 1936, 1965
Steen, M., and Steen 1946
Stewart, K.M. 1967
Stewart, Y.G., Teague, and Canouts 1974
Stone 1977b
Tanner 1936
Teague 1974
Teague and Bremer 1976
Tinker 1956
Turner, S., and Turner 1967
Turney 1924, 1929, 1929-30
Tuthill 1947
Valcarce and Kayser 1969
Van Valkenburgh, R.F. 1946b
Van Valkenburgh, S. 1962
Vickrey 1945
Vivian, R. Gwinn 1965, 1970d
Vivian, R. Gwinn, and Reinhard 1975
Vivian, R. Gwinn, and Spaulding 1974
Vivian, R. Gwinn, and others 1973
Vogler 1976
Wadsworth 1955
Walker, N.P., and Polk 1973
Wasley 1960c
Wasley and Benham 1968
Wasley and Johnson 1965
Weaver, D.E. 1972, 1973, 1974, 1976, 1977
Weaver, D.E., and Rodgers 1974
Weaver, D.E., Burton, and Laughlin 1978
Weed 1972
Wilcox, D.R. 1975b
Wilcox, D.R., and Shenk 1977
Windmiller 1972a, 1972b, 1972c
Withers 1944, 1973
Wood, D. 1971a, 1971b, 1972
Woodbury, R.B. 1960c, 1961c, 1963b

Jackson, B. 1935
Jackson, E. 1939a, 1939b, 1941
Jackson, E., and Van Valkenburgh 1954
Jennings, C.H. 1968a
Jett 1965c
Kayser, D.W. 1969
Kelly, R.E. 1966, 1969a, 1970a, 1970b, 1971
Kent, K.P. 1954
Laguna 1942
Lee, T.A. 1962
Lobo 1965
Lummis 1897
Lundquist 1963
McGregor 1932, 1935, 1936b, 1936c, 1936e, 1937a, 1937b, 1937c, 1941b, 1942b, 1943, 1945a, 1955, 1956, 1958, 1961
McGregor and Wetherill 1939
McGuire 1977
McKee, E.D. 1945
Mearns 1890
Miller, J.D. 1897
Minckley and Alger 1968
Mindeleff, C. 1896a
Morris, E.H. 1928b
Murbarger 1948, 1949, 1950
Noble, C. 1946
Olson, A.P. 1963, 1964a, 1966b
Palmer, S.L. 1940
Peck, F.R. 1956
Pierson 1956, 1959
Pilles 1969, 1976
Pinkley, F.H. 1927, 1928
Powers 1975a
Rigby 1960
Rixey and Voll 1962
Robinson, Harrill, and Warren 1975
Schley 1964
Schreiber and Breed 1971
Schroeder 1947, 1948, 1949a, 1949b, 1951a, 1953-54, 1960, 1961d, 1963c

Schroeder and Hastings 1958
Shimer, H.W., and Shimer 1910
Shutler 1951
Smith, L.D. 1977b
Spicer 1934
Spicer and Caywood 1934
Steenburg 1937
Sutton, M. 1954
Thomas, M.T. 1883
Tourney 1892
Valehrach, E.M. 1967
Valehrach, E.M., and Valehrach 1971
Van Valkenburgh, S. 1961
Vivian, R. Gordon 1956
Wade and Kent 1968
Ward 1969, 1976b
Wasley 1957c
Wilson, J.P. 1967a
Wilson, J.P., and Kelly 1966
Wilson, J.P., Winston, and Berger 1961
Wright, G.A. 1965

AREA 16
EAST CENTRAL ARIZONA

Anderson, H. 1958
Asch 1960
Baldwin, G.C. 1935a, 1937, 1938c, 1938d, 1939d
Bannister and Robinson 1971
Bannister, Gell, and Hannah 1966
Beeson 1966
Bohrer 1962, 1972, 1973
Brancato and Dodge 1973
Breternitz, D.A. 1959b
Breternitz, D.A., Gifford, and Olson 1957
Bron 1884
Brown, J.A., and Freeman 1964
Brown, J.L. 1969, 1973, 1974
Burr 1880
Canouts and Phillips 1974
Carlson, R.L. 1970
Cartledge 1976, 1977

AREA 17
WEST CENTRAL NEW MEXICO

Kunz 1969
Kunz, Gamache, and Agogino
  1973
Lutes 1959
Martin, H.T. 1909
McCabe, H.E. 1973
Mera 1944
Moorehead 1931
Pearsall 1939
Renaud 1929c, 1930b, 1930c,
  1937a, 1942a, 1942b, 1942c,
  1943a, 1943b, 1944a, 1944b,
  1946, 1947
Renaud and Chatin 1943
Robinson, Harrill, and War-
  ren 1973
Schaafsma, P. 1976
Skinner, S.A. 1964
Steen, C.R. 1958
Swancara 1955
Tatum 1944a, 1947
Tatum and Dondelinger 1945
Thoms 1976
Wedel 1961
Wendorf 1959b, 1960
Williams, J.R. 1951, 1954
Williston 1899
Williston and Martin 1900
Wiseman 1975c

AREA 22
TRANS-PECOS TEXAS

Adovasio and Fry 1976
Alexander, R.K. 1970, 1974
Alves 1930, 1931, 1932a,
  1934
Aten 1972
Ayer 1936
Bassham 1971
Bilbo 1969, 1972, 1976
Brice and Phillips 1967
Brook, V.R. 1964, 1965a,
  1965b, 1966a, 1966b, 1967a,
  1967b, 1970, 1971, 1975a
Brook, V.R., and others n.d.
Brunner 1891

Bryant 1974
Calamia 1965
Chelf 1945
Coffin 1929, 1932
Collins, M.B. 1969a
Collins, M.B., and Hester
  1968
Cosgrove, C.B. 1948
Cosgrove, C.B., and Cosgrove
  1965
Crimmins 1929
Davenport 1938a, 1938b
Davenport and Chelf 1941
Davis, J. 1968
Davis, L.B. 1968
Dering and Shafer 1976
Dibble, D.S. 1965, 1970, 1975
Dibble, D.S., and Lorrain 1968
Dibble, D.S., and Prewitt 1967
Epstein 1960, 1963a, 1963b
Fenenga and Wheat 1940
Fletcher 1930, 1931
Fritz, G.L. 1966
Gardner, F., and Martin 1933
Gerald 1976
Gilmore 1937
Gould, L. 1929
Graham, J.A., and Davis 1958
Green, J.W. 1969a, 1969b,
  1971
Green, L.M., and Green 1974
Greer 1966a, 1967b, 1968a,
  1968b, 1975, 1976a, 1976b,
  1976d
Greer and Renfer 1964
Hammersen 1972
Harrington, M.R. 1928c, 1945c
Harris, R.N., and Gowin 1941
Hedrick, J.A. 1968, 1975
Hedrick, Mrs. J.A. 1967
Hill, M. 1971
Hill, T.C., House, and Hester
  n.d.
Holden, W.C. 1937, 1938, 1941
Howard, E.B. 1930a, 1930b
Hutton 1976
Jackson, A.T. 1936, 1937,
  1940

Ascher and Clune 1960
Bandelier 1884b, 1885, 1890c
Blackiston 1905a, 1905b,
   1906a, 1906b, 1906c, 1908,
   1909
Brand 1935a, 1943
Britt 1970c, 1971a
Brooks, P. 1973
Brooks, R.H. 1971
Carey, H.A. 1931, 1955, 1956
Chapman, K.M. 1923
Clark, D.F. 1967
Clune 1960
Contreras 1970
Cutler 1960
Davis, L.B. 1967
Di Peso 1960, 1963, 1966,
   1968a, 1968b, 1969, 1971a,
   1976b, 1977
Di Peso, Rinaldo, and Fenner
   1974
Ekholm 1940
Fritz, G.L. 1968, 1969
Gerald 1954
Green, J.S. 1971
Green, J.W. 1968a
Harcum 1923
Harrington, M.R. 1939
Hasse 1936
Herold, L.C. 1965
Hewett 1923
Hough 1923a
Howard, W.A., and Griffiths
   1966
Kelley, J.C. 1951, 1952,
   1953, 1956
Kelley, J.C., and Abbott
   1966
Kidder, A.V. 1916b, 1939
LeViness 1960a, 1960b
Lister, F.C., and Lister
   1966
Lister, R.H. 1939, 1946,
   1953b, 1958a, 1960b
Lister, R.H., and Lister 1969
Lumholtz 1891a, 1891b, 1902,
   1912
Mangelsdorf 1958

Mangelsdorf and Lister 1956
McCabe, R.A. 1955
Mera 1945
Naylor 1969
Noguera 1926, 1930, 1938
Novelli 1968
O'Neale 1948
Parsons, F.B. 1960
Pastron and Clewlow 1975
Phelps 1964, 1966b, 1968a
Sayles 1936a, 1936b
Schroeder 1969
Schwatka 1899
Taylor, W.W. 1972
Terrazas 1942
Vilanova Fuentes 1969
Wheat 1948-49
Zingg 1940

AREA 24
SONORA

Amsden, M. 1928a
Ascher 1962
Beals 1942
Bowen, T.G. 1965, 1976a,
   1976b
Brand 1935a
Braniff, B. 1978
Brooks, R.H. 1971
Brugge 1963b
Crumrine 1974
Di Peso 1957, 1963, 1966
Dockstader 1961
Drake 1954a
Ekholm 1939, 1940, 1947, 1953
Ezell 1954, 1955
Fay 1953, 1955a, 1956a, 1956c,
   1958a, 1958c, 1961, 1963,
   1968
Felger 1976
Foster, J.W. 1975
Gifford, E.W. 1946
Hayden, J.D. 1956, 1967, 1969,
   1970, 1976b, 1976c
Henrickson and Felger 1973
Hinton 1955

SECTION B
TOPICAL CLASSIFICATION

AGRICULTURE - CULTIVATED PLANTS

Anderson, E. 1944
Anderson, E., and Blanchard
  1942
Brugge 1965
Carter, G.F., and Anderson
  1945
Cutler 1951, 1960, 1966
Cutler and Blake 1970
Cutler and Kaplan 1956
Cutler and Meyer 1965
Cutler and Whitaker 1961
Galinat and Gunnerson 1963,
  1969
Galinat and Ruppé 1961
Galinat, Mangelsdorf, and
  Pierson 1956
Galinat, Reinhart, and Fris-
  bie 1970
Harrington, M.R. 1937a
Haury and Conrad 1938
Hurst, C.T., and Anderson
  1949
Jones, V.H. 1936, 1952
Kaplan 1956, 1963, 1965
Mangelsdorf 1958
Mangelsdorf and Lister 1956
Mangelsdorf and Smith 1949
Reagan 1927a
Steen, C.R., and Jones 1941
Wilson, E.W. 1950

AGRICULTURE - TECHNIQUES

Ayres 1967
Bartlett, K. 1931, 1936
Beckwith, M. 1959
Berlin, Ambler, Hevly, and
  Schaber 1975, 1977
Bohrer 1962, 1967, 1970, 1973
Bohrer and Adams 1977
Bohrer, Cutler, and Sauer 1969
Boothly 1888
Bradley, Z.A. 1959
Bryan, K. 1941
Busch, Raab, and Busch 1976
Carter, G.F. 1945
Colton, H.S. 1965a
Cordell 1977
Cowgill 1957
Cummings, B. 1927a
Davis, J.T. 1960
Dick 1954a
Di Peso 1971a, 1971b
Euler 1959b
Euler and Jones 1956
Fish 1974
Franke and Watson 1936
Galinat and Gunnerson 1963
Gasser 1976
Glassow 1972b
Grady 1976
Halseth 1932b, 1936, 1947a
Haury 1936b, 1945b
Hayes 1976

ARCHITECTURE

Ellis, F.H. 1952
Euler 1954a, 1961
Farmer 1957b
Ferdon 1954, 1955, 1967
Ferdon and Reed 1950
Fewkes 1906a, 1908b, 1910b, 1910c, 1915a, 1916e, 1917a, 1917b, 1917f, 1918b, 1919c, 1921c, 1922b
Fitzpatrick 1946
Fletcher 1931
Fontana, Greenleaf, and Cassidy 1959
Franke 1932
Gaillard 1896
Goodard, P.E. 1928a
Green, R.C. 1956b
Green, R.C., Danfelser, and Vivian 1958
Greenleaf, J.C. 1975b
Gumerman 1966b
Hargrave 1930, 1933a
Harrington, M.R. 1937e, 1953a, 1953b
Haury 1931a, 1950a
Hawley, F.H. 1938b, 1950a
Hayden, J.D. 1942
Hayes and Lancaster 1962
Henderson, P. 1893
Hibben 1948b, 1966
Hobler 1974
Hodge 1895a, 1923, 1924c, 1939
Hoebel 1953
Hoover 1935
Hough 1918, 1923b
Hudson 1972a
Hughes, T.B. 1954
Hurt, W.R. 1947
Jackson, B. 1935
Jackson, E. 1935
Jeançon 1926c
Johnson, A.E. 1961
Judd 1916b, 1917b, 1917c, 1924c, 1924e, 1927b, 1930d, 1964
Keech 1934
Kelley, J.C. 1939, 1949

Kidder, A.V. 1958
Kirk 1941
Lambert 1953-54
Lister, R.H. 1967
Love 1975
Luebben, Herold, and Rohn 1960
Luebben, Rohn, and Givens 1962
Martin, Paul Sidney 1929b, 1930b, 1941, 1942
Martin, Paul Sidney, and Barter 1954
Maxon 1961
McGregor 1936b, 1955
McLellan 1969
McNutt 1975
Mindeleff, C. 1898a, 1898b
Mindeleff, V. 1891
Morgan, J.R. 1977
Morgan, L.H. 1880b, 1881
Morgan, W.F. 1879
Morris, D.H. 1969a
Morris, D.P. 1975
Morris, E.H. 1921b, 1925b, 1934, 1944a, 1949
Ottaway 1975
Page 1970
Patterson, J.L. 1937
Peckham 1958a, 1963c, 1967b
Peet 1896a, 1897b, 1898f, 1899e
Pilles 1969
Pinkley, F. 1936b
Pond 1966
Prudden 1914
Reaves 1969
Reed, E.K. 1956
Reed, E.K., and Ferdon 1950
Renaud 1929a
Reyman 1976
Riley, C.L. 1950
Roberts 1938, 1939a, 1939b
Rohn 1975
Saile 1977
Samuelson 1953
Schorsch 1962
Schroeder 1949b, 1951a, 1953a, 1953d

Capitan 1928
Carlson, R.L. 1970
Carter, D.B. 1932
Chapman, K.M. 1921, 1922,
  1923, 1927c, 1938b, 1961
Chapman, K.M., and Ellis
  1951
Clark, G.A. 1967
Clarke, E.P. 1935
Coale 1963
Collins, M.B. 1969b
Colton, H.S. 1928b, 1939a,
  1939d, 1939f, 1940a, 1941a,
  1941c, 1943a, 1945a, 1952b,
  1953b, 1955a, 1955b, 1956,
  1965c
Colton, H.S., and Hargrave
  1935, 1937
Colton, H.S., Hargrave, and
  Hubert 1940
Colton, H.S., Euler, Dobyns,
  and Schroeder 1958
Compton 1956
Connolly, F.M. 1940
Cooley 1938
Cummings, B. 1935b
Cushing 1886
Danson and Wallace 1956
Dickey 1957
Dietz 1936
Di Peso 1969, 1976a, 1976b,
  1977
Dixon 1959, 1963, 1964a,
  1964b, 1976
Dobyns 1959
Douglas, F.H., and Raynolds
  1941
Dutton 1966a
Ellis, B.T. 1953
Ellis, F.H. 1966c
Euler 1959a, 1971
Euler and Jones 1956
Evans, C., and Sowers 1939
Everitt 1973
Fast and Caywood 1936
Fewkes 1898b, 1898c, 1909a,
  1916a, 1918c, 1919b, 1923b,
  1923c, 1923e

Fontana and others 1962
Fox 1975
Franke 1934b
Freeman 1962
Frisbie 1975c, 1975d, 1977a
Fritz, G.L. 1968
Germann 1926
Gifford, E.W. 1928
Gifford, J.C. 1953
Gifford, J.C., and Smith
  1978
Gillin 1938b
Gladwin, W., and Gladwin 1928b,
  1930d, 1930e, 1931, 1933
Goddard, P.E. 1928b
Gunnerson, J.H. 1956b, 1958a
Guthe, C.E. 1927
Hales 1893
Hall, E.T. 1950
Halseth 1941
Hammack, L.C. 1974
Harcum 1923
Hargrave 1932a, 1935b, 1936a,
  1962, 1974
Hargrave and Colton 1935
Hargrave and Smith 1936
Harlow 1965a, 1965b, 1967,
  1973
Harlow and Frank 1974
Harris, A.H., Schoenwetter,
  and Warren 1967
Hassel 1967
Haury 1930, 1932a, 1936c,
  1938a
Hawley, F.G. 1938
Hawley, F.M. 1929, 1930a,
  1930b, 1931, 1932c, 1936a,
  1938a, 1940, 1950b
Hedrick, J.A. 1971
Hester, T.R., and Hill 1969
Hibben 1949
Hill, J.N. 1977b
Hodge 1904, 1924a, 1924d,
  1950
Holien 1975
Holmes 1886
Honea 1966, 1967, 1973
Horne 1937, 1942

Kidder, A.V. 1938
Krone 1976a
Lavine-Lischka 1975, 1976
Lischka 1969
Lister, R.H. 1951b, 1953a
Lotrich 1939
McAllister, S.L. 1977
Montgomery, A. 1963
Osborne 1965b
Patterson, J.T. 1936, 1937
Peckham 1965
Phelps 1968a
Poteet 1938
Reed, E.K. 1951c
Renaud 1931b, 1935, 1939a,
  1940, 1942c
Rovner and Agogino 1967
Rule 1977
Schiffer 1978
Schneider 1966
Sellards 1960
Shutler 1956
Simpson, R.D. 1956a
Skinner, E. 1974
Smith, C.B. 1974
Smith, E.R. 1936
Smith, S., and Agogino
  1966
Snyder, J.F. 1897, 1899
Spain 1975
Tadlock 1966
Tichy 1948
Toulouse 1941
Turner, C.G., and Cooley
  1960
Vernon 1971
Warren 1966a, 1966b, 1967b
Wetherill, R. 1897
Wheeler, R.P. 1965
Williams, J.R. 1951, 1954
Wilmsen 1968, 1970
Wiseman 1970a, 1971a
Wood, H.B. 1938
Woodbury, R.B. 1954
Worman 1953
Wright, W. 1940
Wylie 1974, 1975a, 1975b
Young, J.N. 1973

ARTIFACTS -
TEXTILES AND CORDAGE

Adams, W.Y. 1957
Adovasio 1970
Baldwin, G.C. 1938a, 1938b,
  1939c, 1939e
Beckwith, F. 1934a
Breazeale 1925
Caywood 1934
Clark, D.F. 1967
Clune 1960
Cornelius 1938
Cosner 1960
Cummings, B. 1915b
Dixon 1958
Douglas, F.H. 1940a
Green, J.S. 1971
Hall, S.M. 1898
Harris, R.N., and Gowin 1941
Heston 1961
Holmes 1884
Hughes, J.T. 1955
Kaemlein 1963, 1971
Kent, K.P. 1941, 1944, 1945,
  1954, 1957, 1962, 1966
Kidder, A.V. 1926c
Koerner 1966
Magers 1975
Mason, O.T. 1897
McGregor 1931, 1948
Morris, E.H. 1928a, 1944b
Mott 1935, 1940
O'Neale 1948
Reagan 1927a
Roosa 1952
Salwen 1960
Smith, V.J. 1933, 1940, 1941
Steen, C.R. 1935b
Stubbs 1959a
Wade and Kent 1968
Wheeler, S.M. 1938a
Winthrop, K., and Winthrop
  1975
Wyman and Amsden 1934

ARTIFACTS - WOOD

Adams, W.Y. 1957
Carlson, R.L., and Armelagos
    1965
Collins, M.B., and Hester
    1968
Farmer 1955a
Fenenga and Wheat 1940
Fewkes 1906b
Gardner, F., and Martin 1933
Gaumer 1939
Gell 1967
Gould, L. 1929
Gunnerson, J.H. 1962a
Harrington, M.R. 1944b
Heizer 1942
Hester, T.R. 1971
Hibben 1938a
Judd 1952
Kellar 1955
Kelley, J.C. 1950
Lister, R.H. 1940a
Martin, Paul Sidney 1934
Mason, J.A. 1928
Metcalf 1970
Mohr 1951
Morris, E.A. 1959b
Morris, E.H. 1941
Nichols 1965
O'Laughlin 1966
Pavesic 1966
Peckham 1965
Pepper, G.H. 1905b
Reed, A.C. 1952
Renaud 1925c
Vivian, R. Gwinn, Dodgen,
    and Hartmann 1978

BIBLIOGRAPHIES

Dick 1953b
Everitt 1973
Fowler, C.S. 1970
Hull, D.A., and Scott 1978
Jelks, Davis, and Sturgis
    1960

Kidder, A.V. 1924
Kidder, A.V., and Rouse 1962
Mead 1968
Oppelt 1976
Reinhart 1971b
Wilke 1977
Wilson, J.P., and Kelly 1966

BURIALS

Afton 1971
Anderson, B.A. 1970
Annis 1959
Ayres 1970b
Brown, J.L. 1969
Brugge 1976a
Buehler 1927
Burgh 1933
Clark, G.A. 1969
Clarke, J.C. 1928
Colton, H.S. 1939g
Cosgrove, C.B., Jr., and Felts
    1927a
Ellis, F.H. 1968a
El-Najjar, Morris, Turner, and
    Ryan 1975
Euler 1957
Fewkes 1910a
Fish, Kitchen, and McWilliams
    1971
Frisbie 1978
Griffin 1967
Greer 1976c
Hall, G. 1973
Hargrave 1934c
Harrill 1967
Harrington, M.R. 1929b, 1945c
Harris, R.K., and Gowin 1941
Hartman 1975
Hawley, F.G. 1947
Heister 1894
Hendry 1943
Hewett 1920b
Hibben 1951a
Horne 1937
Hunter 1955
Hurst, C.T., and Lotrich 1935

Heizer and Berger 1970
Hewett 1932b
Hodge 1920a
Jennings, J.D. 1956c, 1969
Johnson, F. 1957
Knipe 1942
Marwitt and Fry 1973
McGregor 1932, 1934, 1936a,
    1936d, 1936e, 1938b, 1942a,
    1942b
Miller, C.F. 1934, 1935
Miller, J.L. 1942
Moorehead 1934
Morris, E.H. 1936, 1952
Nelson, N.C. 1916a
Nelson, P.R. 1964
Nichols 1962
Nichols and Harlan 1967
Peterson, A. 1935b, 1937,
    1939
Pinkley, F.H. 1927
Pinkley, N.M. 1931
Reed, E.K. 1948c, 1963e
Rensch 1934
Robinson, W.J., and Harrill
    1974
Robinson, W.J., and Warren
    1971
Robinson, W.J., Hannah, and
    Harrill 1972
Robinson, W.J., Harrill, and
    Warren 1973, 1974, 1975
Rohn 1978
Schuetz 1957
Schulman, E. 1946, 1948a,
    1948b, 1949b, 1950a, 1950b,
    1951, 1952b, 1953, 1956b
Senter, F.H. 1938
Shiner 1964
Simpson, R.D. 1960
Smiley 1947, 1949b, 1950,
    1951
Smiley, Stubbs, and Bannis-
    ter 1953
Stallings 1933, 1936a, 1936b,
    1937, 1939b, 1941
Stokes, M.A., and Smiley
    1963, 1964, 1966, 1969

Watson, D. 1947

CHRONOLOGY - TECHNIQUES

Antevs 1936, 1955
Bannister 1962, 1966, 1969,
    1973
Bannister and Robinson 1975
Bannister and Scott 1964
Breternitz 1963a
Cook, H.J. 1927
Cressman 1951
Dean 1969a
Di Peso 1976a
Douglass, A.E. 1921, 1929,
    1930, 1931, 1934-35, 1935,
    1935-40, 1937a, 1942, 1947a,
    1947b
Drake 1954b
Epstein 1968
Ferguson 1959
Findlow and others 1975
Franke 1931
Getty 1933
Gibson 1947
Gladwin, H.S. 1940a, 1940b,
    1944, 1946, 1947
Glock 1934, 1937
Hargrave 1936b
Harrington, M.R. 1951
Haury 1935b, 1945c
Hawley, F.M. 1936b, 1939b
Jelinek 1966a
Judd 1930a
LeBlanc 1975a
Lister, R.H. 1953a, 1960a
Lytle-Webb 1978
Marquardt 1974
McGregor 1930, 1936f, 1938a
Mehringer 1967
Miller, J.P., and Wendorf
    1958
Nelson, N.C. 1916a
O'Bryan 1948, 1949, 1967
Osborne and Nichols 1967
Robinson, W.J. 1976a
Rohn 1978

Schenck and Gifford 1952
Schroeder 1949a, 1955b, 1956,
   1963d, 1965b, 1966
Schuetz 1961a
Stanislawski 1966
Steward 1933a
Swanson 1968
Tower 1945
Vaillant 1932
Weaver, D.E., Burton, and
   Laughlin 1978
Wedel 1950, 1961
Woodward, A. 1947b
Zingg 1939

CULTURAL RELATIONS AND
TRADE - INTERNAL

Alder 1952
Amsden, C.A. 1935
Baldwin, S.J. 1976
Brand 1935c
Bronitsky 1977
Colton, H.S. 1941b
Di Peso 1968a, 1968b
Ellis, B.T. 1953
Euler 1963
Fewkes 1912c, 1917h
Frisbie 1975b
Gerald 1976
Gladwin, H.S. 1937a, 1948
Grater 1954
Grebinger 1976
Gumerman 1978
Gunnerson, J.H. 1960b
Hall, E.T. 1950
Harrington, M.R. 1926b
Hawley, F.M. 1930b, 1932c
Hayden, J.D. 1970, 1972
Husted and Mallory 1967
Ives 1946a
Irwin-Williams 1977
Jack 1971
Johnson, A.E. 1965
Johnston, F.J., and Johnston
   1957
Kidder, A.V. 1936a
Lathrap 1956

Malouf 1939, 1940
Martin, Paul Sidney 1958
Martin, Paul Sidney, and Ri-
   naldo 1951
Pailes 1976, 1978
Peckham and Brugge 1976
Peet 1899f
Reed, E.K. 1950a
Riley, C.L. 1952, 1975, 1978
Rinaldo 1964
Schaefer 1969
Schroeder 1952b, 1953e, 1960,
   1963a
Shaeffer 1954
Smith, V.J. 1932b
Stanislawski 1963b
Steward 1933a
Swanson 1968
Taylor, D.C. 1957
Warren, A.H. 1969c, 1970a,
   1970b
Weaver, D.E. 1976
Weaver, D.E., Burton, and
   Laughlin 1978
Weaver, J.R. 1967
Wetherington 1964
Wheat 1954d
Whittlesey 1974
Winter 1976b
Woodbury, R.B. 1959
Zingg 1939

DOMESTICATED ANIMALS

Colton, H.S. 1970
Hargrave 1965b, 1970b
Hodge 1952
Lange 1950
Olsen 1968a, 1972
Pinkley, J.M. 1965
Reed, E.K. 1951b

DRUGS

Adovasio and Fry 1976
Ariss 1939
Campbell, T.N. 1958

Hayden, J.D. 1945
Haynes and Agenbroad 1975
Haynes and Agogino 1966
Haynes and Irwin-Williams
  1970
Herold, J.L. 1961
Herold, L.C. 1965, 1968
Hester, J.J. 1970
Hevly 1964, 1970
Hewett, Henderson, and Rob-
  bins 1913
Hibben 1937a, 1948a
Hill, J.P., and Hevly 1968
Holbrook and Mackey 1976
Hoover 1935
Hough 1898, 1906, 1930a
Howard, E.B. 1933a, 1936a
Howard, H., and Miller 1933
Howard, R.B. 1959
Hudgens 1975
Huntington, E. 1912, 1914
Hurlbett 1977
Huscher, H.A. 1939
Irwin-Williams 1973b
Irwin-Williams and Haynes
  1970
Ives 1941b
Johnson, L. 1963
Jones, V.H. 1938, 1965
Jones, V.H., and Fonner
  1954
Jorde 1977
Kaplan 1963
Karlstrom, Gumerman, and
  Euler 1974, 1976
Kasper 1977
Kelley, J.E. 1974, 1975
Kelley, R.E. 1971
Kelso 1976
King, M.E., and Traylor 1974
Knox 1953
Lance 1959
Lincoln 1962
Lipe 1967
Lipe and Matson 1971, 1975
Lister, R.H. 1969a
Lyon 1906
Madsen, D.B., and Berry 1975

Madsen, D.B., Currey, and Mad-
  sen 1976
Malde 1964
Martin, Paul Schultz 1963a,
  1963b, 1967
Martin, Paul Schultz, and
  Byers 1965
Martin, Paul Schultz, and
  Mehringer 1965
Martin, Paul Schultz, and
  Sharrock 1964
Martin, Paul Schultz, Schoen-
  wetter, and Arms 1961
Martin, Paul Sidney 1946
Matson 1971
Mehringer and Haynes 1965
Mehringer, Martin, and Haynes
  1967
Miller, A.H. 1932
Miller, R.R. 1955
Minckley and Alger 1968
Mindeleff, C. 1898a
Minnis and Plog 1976
Moriarty 1968
Nickens 1975c
Oldfield 1964
Olsen, S.J. 1964, 1967, 1968b,
  1974
Olsen, S.J., and Olsen 1970
Peet 1900
Phelps 1968b
Plog, F., and Garrett 1972
Price 1944
Raun and Eck 1967
Reed, E.K. 1955c, 1962b, 1963b
Reher 1977
Reid 1975
Richards 1936
Robinson and Dean 1969
Rock and Morris 1975
Rohn 1963a
Samuelson 1953
Sauer 1944
Sayles 1965
Schiffer 1975b
Schley 1961, 1962
Schoenwetter 1961, 1962, 1970
Schoenwetter and Dittert 1968

HISTORIC CULTURES - INDIAN

Harrington, M.R. 1942a
Haskell 1975
Hedrick, J.A. 1971
Hester, J.J. 1962a
Hester, J.J., and Shiner
  1963
Hobler, P., and Hobler 1967
Hodge 1895b, 1897a, 1926,
  1928, 1937b
Houser 1969
Hurst, C.T. 1939
Hurt, W.R. 1942b
Huscher, B.H., and Huscher
  1942a
James, C.D. 1977a
James, C.D., and Bradford
  1974
James, C.D., and Lindsay
  1973
Kayser, J. 1965
Kemrer, M. 1974, 1978
Kent, K.P. 1966
Keur 1941, 1944
Kidder, A.V. 1913, 1920
Kirkland 1942
Longacre and Ayres 1968
Luhrs 1937a
Madsen, D.B. 1975a
Magers 1976
Malcolm 1939
Marmon and Pearl 1958
McCluney 1973
Mera 1939
Moser and White 1968
Naylor 1969
Oldendorph 1964
Opler, M.E. 1971
Opler, M.K. 1939
Peterson, H.M. 1963
Pierson 1960
Reagan 1917b
Reed, E.K. 1943b, 1954b,
  1962c
Riley, C.L. 1954b
Rogers, M.J. 1936
Schaafsma, C. 1968b, 1976a
Schroeder 1953f, 1968b,
  1969, 1972

Schwartz 1955a, 1956b, 1959
Simpson, R.D. 1946a, 1956a
Snow, D.H. 1975c
Stevenson, J. 1883a, 1883b,
  1884
Stewart, G.R. 1940b
Stewart, O.C. 1947b
Stewart, Y.G., Teague, and
  Canouts 1974
Sweeney 1963
Sweeney and Euler 1963
Tanner, C.L. 1968
Tanner, C.L., and Steen 1955
Taylor, W.W. 1972
Tripp 1963a
Tuohy 1960
Underhill 1944, 1946b
Vivian, R. Gwinn 1970a
Walter, P.A.F. 1916
Ward 1968, 1975c
Wetherill, M.A. 1954
Wheat 1976
Wilson, J.P. 1972b
Wilson, J.P., and Olsen 1976
Wilson, J.P., and Warren 1974
Woodward, J.A. 1967
Wyman and Amsden 1934

HISTORIC CULTURES - WHITE

Adams, W.Y. 1959
Alexander, R.K. 1966a
Ashton 1958
Bandelier 1890b
Barnes, M.R. 1971, 1972
Beaubien 1937
Berge 1968a, 1968b
Bloom 1923
Boyd, E. 1970
Bradley, Z.A. 1960, 1961
Brody and Colberg 1966
Caywood 1942, 1950, 1972
Cheek 1974
Colton, H.S. 1940b, 1958
Crampton 1960, 1962, 1964a,
  1964b
Davis, N.Y., and Goss 1977

Cummings, B. 1936, 1939
Duff 1904
Harrington, M.R. 1962-65
Haury 1960c, 1962b
Hewett 1916
Howard, R.M. 1968
Howe 1947
Huntington, W.D. 1953
Jackson, W.H. 1924
James, G.W. 1900
Judd 1924f, 1950b, 1960,
  1962, 1968
Kelley, J.C. 1937
Kidder, A.V. 1960
Lange and Riley 1966, 1970
Lange, Riley, and Lange 1975
LeViness 1961
Lindsay 1961b
Linton 1941
Lister, F.C., and Lister 1968
Lister, R.H. 1960b, 1961
Longacre 1973
Longacre and Reid 1974
Martin, Paul Sidney 1974
McKee, T.M. 1935
McNitt 1957
Mindeleff, C. 1901
Morris, A.A. 1933
Morris, E.H. 1947
Moseley 1966
Nelson, E.G. 1917
Parsons, E.C. 1906
Peet 1896b, 1898c
Pinkley, F.M. 1935
Reed, E.K. 1947b
Richert and Vivian 1974
Riley, C.L. 1951, 1963
Rohn 1973
Sands 1957
Schwartz 1966
Scott, D.D. 1977
Smith, E.R. 1950
Spier 1931
Steenberg 1937
Stevens and Agogino 1975
Switzer 1974
Taylor, W.W. 1954c
Van Devanter 1940

Van Valkenburgh, S. 1962
Walter, P.A.F. 1920
Ward 1975d
Watkins 1930
Wetherill, B.A. 1931
Wetherill, J. 1955a, 1955b
White, L.A. 1942
Woodbury, R.B. 1960a, 1960b

LIMITED ACTIVITY SITES

Ayres 1967
Beeson 1957b
Boyd, H.H. 1940
Brown, H. 1899
Brunner 1891
Carter, G.F. 1964
Colton, H.S. 1952a
Davis, E.L., and Winslow 1965
Douglass, W.B. 1917b, 1917c
Evans, G.L. 1951
Fletcher 1931
Greer 1965b, 1967a, 1975
Hammack, L.C. 1962a
Harner 1953
Hayes and Windes 1975
Henderson, R. 1957b
Hoover 1941
Jackson, A.T. 1936
Judd 1959a
Kelley, J.C., and Campbell
  1942
Kelly, C. 1943b
MacHarg 1926
McCluney 1968
Mera 1933a
Pepper, C. 1966
Pierson 1958
Prince 1904
Raab 1973a
Reagan 1934b
Renaud 1942a, 1943b, 1944a
Sciscenti 1962d
Setzler 1952
Shawn 1971
Stacy 1974
Starr 1900

Mohr and Sample 1959
Moore, J.G., Fry, and Englert 1969
Morris, E.A. 1958
Myers, R.D. 1967
Myers, T.P. 1976
Nance 1972
Nunley 1971
Oldfield 1964
Olson, A.P. 1964b
Peck, S.L. 1957
Peckham 1967b, 1968
Perkins 1967b, 1968
Price 1944
Quimby and Brook 1967
Reinhart 1968
Renaud 1930a, 1932, 1934a
Richards 1936
Rinaldo 1948
Roberts 1927b, 1937a, 1940b, 1940c, 1942, 1943, 1945
Robles Ortiz and Taylor 1972
Rogers, M.J. 1939, 1958
Rogers, M.J., and others 1966
Roosa 1954, 1956a, 1956b, 1968
Rovner and Agogino 1967
Russell 1968
Sample and Mohr 1960
Sauer 1944
Sayles 1965
Sayles and Antevs 1941
Schoenwetter and Oldfield 1964
Schroedl 1976
Schuetz 1961a
Schultz, C.B. 1943
Sellards 1936, 1940, 1952, 1955, 1960
Sellards and Evans 1960
Shutler, R. 1950, 1965, 1967a, 1968
Shutler, R., and others 1967
Simpson, R.D. 1946b, 1955, 1956b, 1956c
Sims, J.R., and Daniel 1967
Smith, A. 1966
Smith, C.B. 1966, 1970

Smith, C.B., Runyon, and Agogino 1966
Smith, C.E. 1950
Smith, E.R. 1942
Smith, S., and Agogino 1966
Staley 1976
Stanley 1948
Steen, C.R. 1955a, 1955b, 1976
Steen, F. 1940
Stein, W.T. 1967
Stevens and Agogino 1975
Stock 1931
Swanson 1966
Tanner, B. 1947
Theil 1956
Thomas, T.H. 1952a, 1952b
Toulouse 1937a, 1937c
Tripp 1966
Tuohy 1967
Turney 1928b
Wadsworth 1955
Wallace, W.J. 1962
Ward 1971
Warnica 1961, 1965, 1966
Warnica and Williamson 1968
Wendorf 1959a, 1960
Wendorf and Thomas 1951
West 1932c
Whalen, N.M. 1971, 1973, 1975
Wheat 1967
Wilmsen 1965, 1968, 1970
Windmiller 1970, 1971b, 1973a
Windmiller and Huckell 1973
Wintch 1963
Wormington 1949, 1957, 1962, 1964
Wormington and Ellis 1967
Wormington and Lister 1956
Wylie 1975b

PHYSICAL ANTHROPOLOGY

Agogino 1961b
Armelagos 1968
Armelagos, Dewey, and Carlquist 1968
Bartlett, K. 1930b

Vogler 1977
Washburn 1972, 1974
Wasley 1961
Weed 1978
Wendorf 1957b, 1961
Wheat, Gifford, and Wasley
  1958
Wheeler, S.M. 1938b
White, A.S., and Breternitz
  1976
Whittlesey 1974
Wilcox 1975a
Willey and Phillips 1955,
  1958
Wilmsen 1970
Winthrop, K., and Winthrop
  1975
Wiseman 1970a
Wood, J.J. 1971
Woodbury, R.B. 1963b
Woodward, A. 1930
Wylie 1975b
Zaslow and Dittert 1977
Zubrow 1971, 1975b, 1976